OCCUPIED AMERICA

OCCUPIED AMERICA

A History of Chicanos

THIRD EDITION

Rodolfo Acuña

California State University at Northridge

HarperCollins*Publishers*, **New York**
Cambridge, Philadelphia, San Francisco, Washington,
London, Mexico City, São Paulo, Singapore, Sydney

Sponsoring Editor: Robert Miller
Project Editor: Lauren G. Shafer
Cover Design: Gabriel Molano
Cover Illustration: Malaquias Montoya
Text Art: Vantage Art, Inc.
Production: Willie Lane
Compositor: ComCom Division of Haddon Craftsmen, Inc.
Printer and Binder: R. R. Donnelley & Sons Company

OCCUPIED AMERICA: A History of Chicanos, Third Edition

Library of Congress Cataloging in Publication Data

Acuña, Rodolfo.
    Occupied America.

    Includes bibliographies and index.
    1. Mexican Americans—History. I. Title.
E184.M5A63 1988   973'.046872   87-8457
ISBN 0-06-040163-X

92 93 10 9

CONTENTS

Preface   ix

part one
THE CONQUEST AND COLONIZATION OF
THE SOUTHWEST   **1**

1   Legacy of Hate: The Conquest of Mexico's
Northwest   **5**
An Overview   5
Background to the Invasion of Texas   6
The Invasion of Texas   9
The Invasion of Mexico   12
The Rationale for Conquest   13
The Myth of a Nonviolent Nation   15
The Treaty of Guadalupe Hidalgo   18
Summary   20
Notes   21

2   Remember the Alamo: The Colonization of
Texas   **25**
An Overview   25
Background   26
The Creation of a Dominant Class   27
Politics of Gender   31
Controlling Mexicans   33
Divide and Conquer   37
The Historian as an Agent of Social Control   39
The Revolt of "Cheno" Cortina   43
The People's Revolt   47
Summary   49
Notes   50

3   Freedom in a Cage: The Colonization of
New Mexico   **54**
An Overview   54
The Distortion of History   55

The Myth of the Bloodless Conquest   56
The Land Grab   60
The Santa Fe Ring   62
The Lincoln County War   65
The Americanization of the Catholic Church   68
The Resistance   70
The End of the Frontier   74
Summary   77
Notes   78

4   Sonora Invaded: The Occupation of Arizona   82
An Overview   82
Building a Myth   84
Euroamerican Colonialism   85
The Polarization of Society   88
Ending the Frontier   91
The Industrializing of Arizona   96
Nativism and *La Liga Protectora Latina*   101
Summary   102
Notes   103

5   California Lost: America for
    Anglo-Americans   107
An Overview   107
The Conquest   108
The Occupation   111
The Changing of Elites   112
The Legitimation of Violence   118
Currents of Resistance   121
The Underclass   126
Summary   129
Notes   130

part two
THE CEMENTING OF AN UNDERCLASS:
THE MEXICAN IN THE UNITED STATES   135

6   The Building of the Southwest: Mexican
    Labor, 1900–1930   141
An Overview   141
Background to the Migration North from Mexico, to 1910   144
Nativist Reactions to Mexican Migration, 1910–1920   158
Mexican Workers, 1910–1920   163
Mexicans Move to the City: The 1920s   168
Mexican Labor in the 1920s   178

Greasers Go Home: Mexican Immigration, the 1920s   185
Summary   188
Notes   190

**7   Mexican American Communities in the
Making: The Depression Years**   **198**
An Overview   198
The Nativist Deportations of the 1930s   200
Mexican American Rural Labor   207
Mexican American Farm Workers' Revolt   209
Mexican American Urban Labor   220
The Mexican American Miners' Revolt   231
Survival in a Failed Utopia: Chicanos in the City   235
Summary   243
Notes   244

**8   World War II and the "Happy Days":
Chicano Communities Under Siege**   **251**
An Overview   251
World War II and the Chicano   253
The Spy Game   259
Mexican American Workers: The War Years   260
Managing the Flow of Labor   261
Keeping America Pure   269
Against All Odds: Continued Labor Struggles   272
Politics of the G.I. Generation   279
Post–World War II Human Rights Struggles   289
Bulldozers in the *Barrios*   295
Summary   298
Notes   299

**9   Goodbye America: The Chicano in the
1960s**   **307**
An Overview   307
A Profile: San Antonio Chicanos, 1960–1965   311
North from Texas   314
The Mexican Connection: Un Pueblo, Una Lucha   320
The Road to Delano: Creating a Movement   324
Echoes of Delano   328
The Legitimation of Protest   330
The Day of the Heroes   338
On the Eve of the Storm   342
Chicanos Under Siege   345
The Provocateurs   350
After the Smoke Cleared   352
Summary   354
Notes   356

10 The Age of the Brokers: The New Hispanics   363

An Overview: The Archie Bunker Generation   363
In Search of *Aztlán*   366
Sin Fronteras (Without Borders)   371
The Celebration of Success: The Legitimation of a Broker Class   377
Education: Inventing an American Tradition   386
A Challenge to Male Domination   394
The Dialectics of Space: Communities Under Siege   396
Justice USA   398
Summary   402
Notes   403

11 The Age of the Brokers: The Rambo Years   413

An Overview   413
The Celebration of Success, Hispanic Style   415
Sal Si Puedes ("Get Out If You Can")   425
The Urban Nightmare   428
The Catholic Church: A Counterhegemonic Force?   430
Final Portrait: The Rambo Years   437
Defending the American Way   438
Central America: Another Vietnam   444
The Decline of the Blue-Collar Sector and Its Impact on Chicanos   446
Trends   448
Notes   451

Index   455

PREFACE

The political consciousness of North Americans has changed since *Occupied America* was first published in 1972. The first edition, influenced by the times and Third World writers such as Frantz Fanon, was angry, filled with moral outrage. Eight years later, the second edition, a calmer work, attempted to persuade the reader by heavily documenting the injustices that relegated most Chicanos to an underclass. *Occupied America II* was less polemical, organized into teaching units: the conquest, the U.S. occupation, immigration, labor, and community. The unit approach, however, confused some readers.

The third edition, while returning to the task of naming and describing past events (a process necessary for laying the groundwork for a strong theoretical base in the future), takes into account that most first-year college students were less than 5 years old during the massive Chicano Moratorium of 1970. This edition has abandoned the unit approach, adopting again an easier-to-follow chronological framework. Its purpose is to dispel the myths that are manufactured by scholars who take refuge in patriotism.

Before attacking the myths, prefatory remarks are in order, so that confusion can be minimized. North Americans and Chicanos themselves are often uncertain about what Chicanos want to be called.* This is not surprising, since for the past 60 years what Chicanos called themselves depended on where they lived, what economic class they occupied, and what Euroamerican society let them call themselves. In the late 1960s, activists, taking their cue from Blacks, attempted to identify as Chicanos. Although the term had been pejorative, activists felt that through their dedication to social change the name would be perceived as positive by the Mexican community in the United States. However, in the early 1970s, the national government intruded in the labeling process and began calling Chicanos "Hispanics" (literally meaning Spanish). This phenomenon coincided with the proliferation of Chicano middle-class business and professional organizations. By the end of the decade, the label "Hispanic" approached hegemony among public and private institutions, as well as among Latinos who had achieved some material success. The poor, nevertheless, still called themselves Mexican, while a small number of activists continued to use "Chicano."

*The word "Chicano" for many years was a pejorative term whose origin is unknown. It was popularly used by the working class to refer to themselves. Often, however, middle-class Mexicans used it disparagingly—meaning low-class Mexicans. In the late 1960s, youth movements and political activists gave "Chicano" a political connotation (similar to the way "Black" became a more political term for "Negro").

The term "Hispanic" begins in contradiction, since Mexicans on either side of the border are not Spanish. Moreover, Chicanos who are proud of their Mexican heritage do not desire to deny their *mestizo* and Indian backgrounds. It is also a mistake to lump all Latin Americans together, since they have separate histories that must be respected. Further, many Central Americans resent the erasure of their identity, and what seems an absorption by Chicanos. They have no wish to become our little brothers and sisters.

What the term "Hispanic" represents is a convenience for middle-class professional "Hispanics" who want acceptance by the majority society. Moreover, the use of the label "Hispanic" marks a return to the philosophy of the Mexican positivists, who, during the dictatorship of Don Porfirio Díaz (in power 1876–1911), wanted to purge the indigenous Mexican and convert Mexico into a European nation. In the modern-day sense, the term is the packaging of Latinos to make them a more attractive commodity. The printed and electronic media have, knowingly or unknowingly, supported the government's effort to divide Mexicans in the United States from those in Mexico. Most of the media have, in fact, set policies requiring the use of "Hispanic."

The choice of the designation "Hispanic" represents a 180-degree about-face from use of the term "Chicano." It almost seems as if we learned nothing from the late 1960s and early 1970s. Because of this, I continue to use the term "Chicano." I have, however, made concessions to the fact that the Central American and Puerto Rican communities have grown in the Southwest and Midwest. More often they are neighbors of Chicanos, whom they marry and with whom they carry on the struggle against oppression. In the process, the Chicanos are themselves changing. It is evident in the speech patterns of many of the youth, in their music, which has more than a dash of *salsa,* and in the arts. Chicanos should be encouraged to read the history of struggle by their sisters and brothers rather than distort history to fit an Hispanic image. For that reason, when referring to all Spanish-speaking peoples in the United States, I use the artificial term "Latino" because at this juncture it has less political baggage than "Hispanic." Another popular term that is sometimes used is *Raza.*

I also employ the terms "Mexican" and "Mexican American" (without a hyphen) when referring to Mexicans in the United States. I realize that purists will have difficulty in accepting "Mexican American," even without a hyphen. From my point of view, the Chicano movement made a mistake in dropping the name "Mexican" from its self-identity. For years, progressive Chicanos had fought to call themselves "Mexican American" against the more conservative members of the community, who did not want to offend Anglo-Americans. Today, "Mexican" is still offensive to many who feel perfectly comfortable with "Hispanic."

I realize that it is easy to criticize in retrospect. But it must be admitted that the term "Chicano" had currency primarily among those on the left who believed that every Mexican American was a potential Chicano. History has proven us wrong, for the lesson of the 1980s is that every Mexican American is also a potential Hispanic. We learned the lesson that the German socialist did after World War I, that a structural crisis in capitalism did not necessarily mean that workers would turn to socialism. In the case of Germany, that nation turned to fascism. In the case of middle-class Chicanos, identifying with progressive causes is not as profitable as accepting manufactured symbols, such as "Hispanic," that facilitate their individual assimilation into Euroamerican society. In fact, the use of the term "Hispanic" provides the rationale for Latinos to ignore the truth and thus the duty to end inequality.

Another controversy that may be ignited by the text is my sometimes harsh criticism of the Chicano middle class vis-à-vis twentieth-century urbanization and the ever increasing division of labor. It is appropriate to point out that middle-class self-interest is not a product of the 1980s but has been an issue since the North American invasion and conquest of Texas and the Southwest. What I am trying to convey is a sense of urgency: Poor Chicanos are not progressing collectively. U.S. census data suggest that 40 percent of all Latinos under the age of 18 are living in poverty and that, by 1990, Latinos will replace Black Americans as the poorest minority in the United States. At the same time this is happening, Latino business leaders and professionals are celebrating the 1980s as "The Decade of the Hispanic." In this context, and in an effort to redirect priorities, I describe when and how this alienation of the middle class from the poor has occurred.

My hypothesis is that because of our changing labor market, college-educated Chicanos will make gains, while the poor will get poorer. With the accelerated division of labor, distance between the two classes will increase. The basic difference between now and the 1930s, for example, is that while organizations such as the League of United Latin American Citizens (LULAC) sometimes opposed working-class interests, the majority of the members, because of nationalism reinforced by extreme racism among Euroamericans, promoted the improvement of the lower classes. They had no problem distinguishing who they were. No matter how slowly they moved, LULAC and other Chicano organizations were often at the vanguard of social change—which is not true of most Chicano organizations now.

Today, however, facilitated by suburbanization of the Chicano middle class, a government policy that promotes the interests of the Chicano middle class at the expense of the poor has emerged. Other factors, such as a decline in nationalism outside the *barrio,* have also widened the gap between the middle class and the poor. And nationalism with all its limitations has historically linked the various social classes. Increasingly, Chicanos raised in the more affluent, integrated communities take on the identification of the majority society. Thus physical separation and lack of knowledge of history and Mexican culture complete an alienation from the lower classes.

Lastly, this edition more so than the previous editions realizes that most North Americans have developed a defined mind-set. This mind-set is forged by the educational system as well as the nation's institutions. The vast majority of North Americans of all colors are believers; they do not search for truth or facts but rely on their convictions. Consequently, when they read a counterhegemonic work such as *Occupied America,* they rebel. It goes against their beliefs and their common sense; and when pushed too far, they question not their beliefs but the facts.

Students and North Americans in general increasingly have become intellectual fundamentalists in the 1980s. Symbols such as the Statue of Liberty or the Alamo have become holy shrines. What they learn in high school or in the media becomes scripture, and they do not want to hear facts that contradict what they believe. This mind-set prevents an understanding of the flaws in society and of why some have been blessed and others condemned to a life of poverty. "America is the land of opportunity and anyone can make it!" is a common assertion. *Occupied America* seeks to dispel the myths. In other words, it strives to make this edition less imperfect than the first and second editions.

I am indebted to many friends and colleagues in the preparation of this text. It would be impossible to list them all. My special thanks to the reviewers: James D. Cockcroft; Richard Griswold del Castillo, San Diego State University; Mauricio Mazón, University of Southern California; Ricardo Romo, University of Texas at Austin; and Dennis Nodín Valdés, University of Minnesota. I also appreciate the comments of Andrés Jiménez, Bill de la Torre, Howard Shorr, and Marta López. I am sincerely honored by Malaquias Montoya's permission to use his mural on this edition's cover; Montoya has never abandoned the struggle. I acknowledge the support of Gilbert Cardenas and his *Galería Sin Fronteras* in Austin, Texas, in finding just the right artwork. I also extend my gratitude to Harper & Row editors Robert Miller and Lauren Shafer. Gratitude goes to my sons Frank and Walter, and to my parents, Francisco and Alicía, who are deceased but who are always in my heart. I dedicate this edition to the Chicano community, but most of all to my wife, Guadalupe Compean, and our daughter, Angela. They started a new life for me.

Rodolfo Acuña

OCCUPIED
AMERICA

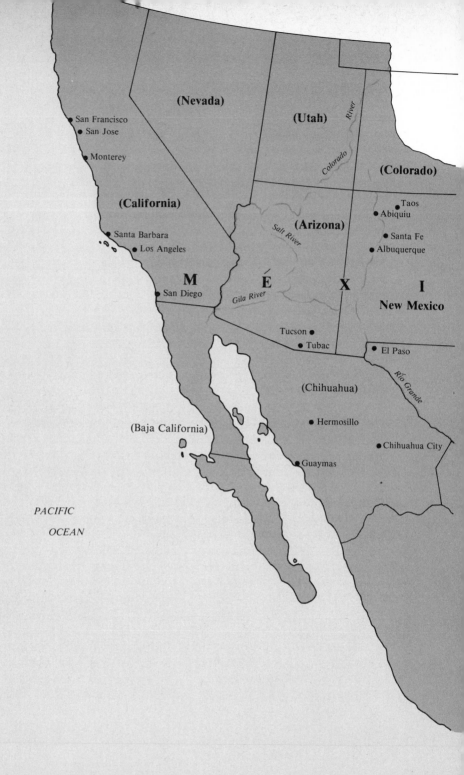

The Mexican Republic, 1822

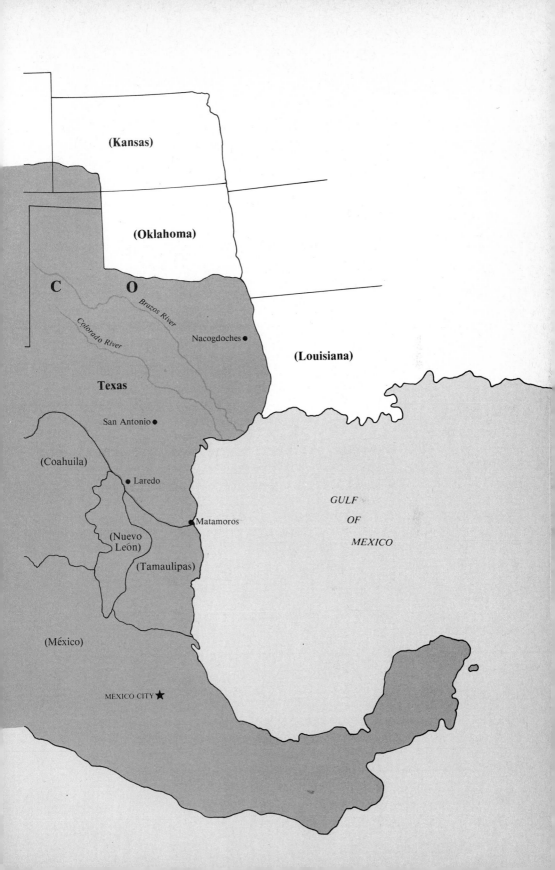

Present-day United States of America

A   D   A

Minnesota

Lake Superior

Michigan

Wisconsin

MI

Lake Michigan

Lake Huron

Lake Ontario

Maine

Hudson R.

VT NH

New
York

MA
RI
CT

Iowa

Illinois River

Pennsylvania

NJ

Ohio

River

Delaware

Missouri

Illinois

Indiana

Ohio

West
Virginia

Virginia

MD

WASHINGTON D.C.

Mississippi River

Kentucky

North Carolina

Arkansas

Tennessee

South Carolina

NORTH

ATLANTIC

OCEAN

Mississippi

Alabama

Georgia

Louisiana

Florida

GULF OF MEXICO

Straits of Florida

one

THE CONQUEST AND COLONIZATION OF THE SOUTHWEST

The modern nations of Mexico and the United States of America are both products of European expansion. Spain exploited New World resources and native labor to extend its empire throughout the world. In 1521 Spain conquered Mexico, and, for the next 300 years, it exploited Indian and Black labor to accumulate tremendous wealth. It based its control of Mexico on a division of labor that reflected race, class, and gender. Cohabitation between Spaniards and indigenous peoples and between both of those groups and Black slaves was common. During the colonial period, the mixture of races produced a *mestizo* (Indian and Hispanic) people who became the majority in modern Mexico.

Spanish conquest and colonialism retarded Mexico's economic development. The pre-Columbian societies had evolved to a high state and had a population approaching 30 million. The largest contemporary European nation, France, numbered 20 million—Spain had about 8 million people. Mexican cities, larger than London and Madrid, thrived. As the result of a holocaust of warfare, disease, poverty, and overwork, Mexico's indigenous population fell, by 1605, to 1.075 million; and by 1650, 90 percent of the native population had been wiped out.

By 1810, New Spain extended from Utah in the north to Central America in the south. Traces of a common language, laws, religion, and economic and political institutions linked the people in the various regions. Local agriculture supplied miners, and merchants over the years had accumulated surpluses from trade. World conditions and internal dissatisfaction with class privileges given to *peninsulares* (Spaniards born in Spain) agitated class struggle. Finally, in 1810 Father Miguel Hidalgo gave his famous *Grito de Dolores,* beginning the Mexican Revolution, and within 11 years New Spain became modern Mexico.

1

Mexico became a nation in 1821; without the protection of nationhood it would have been the victim of international plunder. The nation needed time to consolidate its population of some 6 million people. Internationally, the United States and England circled above her, like vultures, waiting for the stillness. Mexico's most vulnerable region lay in its northwest; distance from Mexico City and proximity to the United States were a handicap.

Conditions for Mexicans had deteriorated considerably since 1519. Spanish colonialism modified and integrated pre-Hispanic agriculture, trade, and distribution systems into a colonial, externally oriented system that produced for profit, rather than for feeding people. The *hacienda* and the colonial plunder also altered land use patterns. Mexico in 1821 was bankrupt, and it needed time to build an infrastructure to unify the new country. Moreover, unlike its North American neighbor, Mexico did not have a racially homogeneous society.

Comparisons between Mexico and the United States are unfair. First, North Americans were not indigenous to the continent; North Americans as British subjects colonized North America much the same as Europeans colonized Australia and South Africa. Second, British colonialism did not produce a mixed people. The official policy was to exterminate the native populations. The founding fathers had no intention of incorporating Blacks or Native Americans as equals. Third, the colonies dominated one-third of the British trade. The substitution of a North American elite for a British ruling class immediately created a powerful North American merchant class that influenced, if not dominated, national politics. In the case of the Mexican merchants, independence did not prove as lucrative, and a 50-year struggle for control of the national government followed independence.

Geography also favored the North American states. They occupied coastal lands with good harbors, encouraging the development of commerce. The new nation sat on the best farmland in the world, with plenty of water. Most of it became part of the national domain, and the sale of millions of acres to land companies and land-hungry Europeans allowed the new government to pay off debts and to consolidate politically. Speculators also accumulated large surpluses, as did cotton and tobacco growers, whose exploitation of slave labor made production highly profitable. Mexico's resources, in contrast, had been plundered and its land monopolized by a few *latifundistas* and the Catholic Church. The lack of political stability and poor transportation retarded the modernization of agriculture and the development of national markets.

By stealing British technology, in the 1790s, the United States got an early start in mechanizing production. Thus North Americans had an advantage over other New World and European countries, facilitating rapid accumulation of capital and the domination of New World markets.

By 1820, only 4.9 percent of North Americans lived in cities. The United States had a population of 9.6 million persons, over a million and a half of whom were slaves. (Native Americans did not count in this census.) Northern merchants had invested their profits in industry, and the first two decades of the century saw the formation of an industrial class. Along with western farm and southern plantation interests, industrialists encouraged the search for resources, markets, and land. Land remained an important source of profit. Expansion into Mexico, although not motivated by the need for *lebensraum,* or living space—since the United States had millions of acres of undeveloped and unused land—proved profitable.

Part One of the text deals with U.S. expansion through conquest and its effect on the Mexican peoples. Chapter 1, "The Legacy of Hate," describes the U.S. invasions of Mexico in the mid-1830s and 1840s. The thesis is that the United States, a colonial power long before the Spanish American War of 1898, forged its present borders through expansionist wars, and, except in the movies, no such thing as the "Winning of the West" ever happened. North Americans took the land through violence, and the corruption of Mexican officials cannot be used as justification for conquest. North American troops committed atrocities that indeed left a legacy of hate. The Treaty of Guadalupe Hidalgo ended the Mexican-American War; however, a pattern for Mexican–North American relations had been established.

Chapter 2, "Remember the Alamo," deals with the relationship between Euroamericans and Mexicans after the War of 1836. Mexicans did not welcome North Americans with open arms, and they had no cause to consider themselves U.S. citizens. On the other hand, Anglo-Americans viewed Mexicans as aliens whom they had beaten in a "just" war. Throughout the nineteenth century, Mexicans, although most had been born in Texas, occupied an underclass. The chapter describes how Euroamericans pushed Mexicans to the south and established privileges for themselves through the manipulation of the political process. Legalized violence in the form of the Texas Rangers suppressed the Mexican population. The Civil War brought further changes: the demand for Mexican labor as a result of the emancipation of Black slaves and the expansion of cotton. The post–Civil War period is also noted for the establishment of political machines. Throughout the period, Mexicans resisted by armed conflict. The 1880s brought the railroad and the beginning of Texas's industrialization.

Chapter 3, "Freedom in a Cage," continues the themes of conquest for economic goals—the establishment of economic privileges by newcomers through the use of political and social control. The case of New Mexico differs from that of Texas because some 60,000 Mexicans lived in the territory. Also, while the vanguard of the Texas invasion was composed of slaveowners and land speculators, at the forefront of the New Mexican infiltration were North American merchants. Cooptation of Mexican elites and institutions such as the church became important elements in controlling the masses. Resistance was predictable, and, throughout the nineteenth century, conflicts, verging on class and race warfare, raged in New Mexico. The railroad integrated the territory and set the stage for the territory's modernization.

Arizona, historically linked to Sonora, Mexico, is the focus of Chapter 4, "Sonora Invaded." Sonora continued to supply the bulk of the territory's labor to the 1880s. Isolated from the United States until the 1880s, Arizona had access to the rest of the world principally through the Sonoran port of Guaymas. After the coming of the railroad, large-scale exploitation of the territory's resources was possible. Absentee investors controlled Arizona's copper industry which, by the turn of the century, had become a capital- and labor-intensive enterprise. Militancy and trade union organization by Mexican miners opened a new chapter in Mexican–North American relations.

Chapter 5, "California Lost," explains how the political process, supported by the state's social institutions, brought about the changing of elites. California and Texas became states, not territories, precisely because North Americans made up the majority. The flood of North Americans arrived shortly after the conquest in response to the discovery of large gold deposits in northern California. Soon large capitalist interests monopolized the state. The political process encouraged encroachment on the land of the Mexican *rancheros.* Still, the *rico,* or the rich, in California were reluctant to side with the masses and often supported the state in the oppression of the poor. The Catholic Church also upheld the state's hegemony. Resistance raged until the 1880s, taking the form of social banditry and repatriation movements. Life began to change in the 1880s as the railroads linked the southern half of California to the rest of the state and nation.

chapter *1*

Legacy of Hate: The Conquest of Mexico's Northwest

AN OVERVIEW

The United States invaded Mexico in the mid-nineteenth century during a period of dramatic change. Rapid technological breakthroughs transformed the North American nation, from a farm society into an industrial competitor. The process converted North America into a principal in the world marketplace. The wars with Mexico, symptoms of this transformation, stemmed from the need to accumulate more land, to celebrate heroes, and to prove the nation's power by military superiority.

This chapter examines the link between the Texas (1836) and the Mexican (1845–1848) Wars. It analyzes North American aggression, showing how European peoples known as "Americans" acquired what is today the Southwest. The words "expansion" and "invasion" are used interchangeably. The North American invasions of Mexico are equated with the forging of European empires in Asia, Africa, and Latin America. The urge to expand, in the case of the United States, was not based on the need for land—the Louisiana Purchase, central Illinois, southern Georgia, and West Virginia lay vacant. Rather, the motive was profit—and the wars proved profitable, with the Euroamerican nation seizing over half of Mexico.[1]

North Americans fought the Texas War—that is, U.S. dollars financed it, U.S. arms were used on Mexican soil, and Euroamericans almost exclusively profited from it. President Andrew Jackson approved of the war and ignored North American neutrality laws. The so-called Republic held Texas in trusteeship until 1844, when the United States annexed it. This act amounted to a declaration

5

of war on Mexico. When Mexico responded by breaking diplomatic relations, the North Americans used this excuse to manufacture the war. Many North Americans questioned the morality of the war but supported their government because it was their country, right or wrong.

This chapter does not focus on the wars' battles or heroes, but on how North Americans rationalized these invasions and have developed historical amnesia about its causes and results. War is neither romantic nor just, and the United States did not act benevolently toward Mexico. North Americans committed atrocities, and, when they could, Mexicans responded. Eventually, the Treaty of Guadalupe Hidalgo ended the Mexican-American War, and northern Mexico became part of the North American empire. The treaty, however, did not stop the bitterness or the violence between the two peoples. In fact, it gave birth to a legacy of hate.

BACKGROUND TO THE INVASION OF TEXAS

Anglo justifications for the conquest have ignored or distorted events that led up to the initial clash in 1836. To Anglo-Americans, the Texas War was caused by a tyrannical or, at best, an incompetent Mexican government that was antithetical to the ideals of democracy and justice. The roots of the conflict actually extended back to as early as 1767, when Benjamin Franklin marked Mexico and Cuba for future expansion. Anglo-American filibusters* planned expeditions into Texas in the 1790s. The Louisiana Purchase, in 1803, stimulated U.S. ambitions in the Southwest, and six years later Thomas Jefferson predicted that the Spanish borderlands "are ours the first moment war is forced upon us."[2] The war with Great Britain in 1812 intensified Anglo-American designs on the Spanish territory.

Florida set the pattern for expansionist activities in Texas. In 1818 several posts in east Florida were seized in unauthorized, but never officially condemned, U.S. military expeditions. Negotiations then in progress with Spain finally terminated in the Adams-Onis, or Transcontinental, Treaty (1819), in which Spain ceded Florida to the United States and the United States, in turn, renounced its claim to Texas. Texas itself was part of Coahuila. Many North Americans still claimed that Texas belonged to the United States, repeating Jefferson's claim that Texas's boundary extended to the Río Grande and that it was part of the Louisiana Purchase. They condemned the Adams-Onis Treaty.

Anglo-Americans continued pretensions to Texas and made forays into Texas similar to those they had made into Florida. In 1819 James Long led an abortive invasion to establish the "Republic of Texas." Long, like many Anglos, believed that Texas belonged to the United States and that "Congress had no right or power to sell, exchange, or relinquish an 'American possession.' "[3]

In spite of the hostility, the Mexican government opened Texas, provided that settlers agreed to certain conditions. Moses Austin was given permission to settle in Texas, but he died shortly afterwards, and his son continued his venture.

---

*A *filibuster* is an adventurer who engages in insurrectionist or revolutionary activity in a foreign country.

In December 1821 Stephen Austin founded the settlement of San Félipe de Austin. Large numbers of Anglo-Americans entered Texas in the 1820s as refugees from the depression of 1819. In the 1830s entrepreneurs sought to profit from the availability of cheap land. By 1830 there were about 20,000 settlers, along with some 2,000 slaves.

Settlers agreed to obey the conditions set by the Mexican government—that all immigrants be Catholics and that they take an oath of allegiance to Mexico. However, Anglo-Americans became resentful when Mexico tried to enforce the agreements. Mexico, in turn, became increasingly alarmed at the flood of immigrants from the U.S.[4]

Many settlers considered the native Mexicans to be the intruders. In a dispute with Mexicans and Indians, as well as with Anglo-American settlers, Hayden Edwards arbitrarily attempted to evict settlers from the land before the conflicting claims could be sorted out by the Mexican authorities. As a result Mexican authorities nullified his settlement contract and ordered him to leave the territory. Edwards and his followers seized the town of Nacogdoches and on December 21, 1826, proclaimed the Republic of Fredonia. Mexican officials, supported by some Anglo-Americans (such as Stephen Austin), suffocated the Edwards revolt. However, many U.S. newspapers played up the rebellion as "200 Men Against a Nation!" and described Edwards and his followers as "apostles of democracy crushed by an alien civilization."[5]

In 1824 President John Quincy Adams "began putting pressure on Mexico in the hope of persuading her to rectify the frontier. Any of the Texan rivers west of the Sabine—the Brazos, the Colorado, the Nueces—was preferable to the Sabine, though the Río Grande was the one desired."[6] In 1826 Adams offered to buy Texas for the sum of $1 million. When Mexican authorities refused the offer, the United States launched an aggressive foreign policy, attempting to coerce Mexico into selling Texas.

Mexico could not consolidate its control over Texas: the number of Anglo-American settlers and the vastness of the territory made it an almost impossible task. Anglo-Americans had already created a privileged caste, which depended in great part on the economic advantage given to them by their slaves. When Mexico abolished slavery, on September 15, 1829, Euroamericans circumvented the law by "freeing" their slaves and then signing them to lifelong contracts as indentured servants. Anglos resented the Mexican order and considered it an infringement on their personal liberties. In 1830 Mexico prohibited further Anglo-American immigration. Meanwhile, Andrew Jackson increased tensions by attempting to purchase Texas for as much as $5 million.

Mexican authorities resented the Anglo-Americans' refusal to submit to Mexican laws. Mexico moved reinforcements into Coahuila, and readied them in case of trouble. Anglos viewed this move as an act of hostility.

Anglo colonists refused to pay customs and actively supported smuggling activities. When the "war party" rioted at Anahuac in December 1831, it had the popular support of Anglos. One of its leaders was Sam Houston, who "was a known protégé of Andrew Jackson, now president of the United States. . . . Houston's motivation was to bring Texas into the United States."[7]

In the summer of 1832 a group of Anglos attacked a Mexican garrison and were routed. A state of insurrection existed, and Mexican authorities defended Texas. Matters worsened when the Anglo settlers met at San Félipe in October 1832. This convention drafted resolutions which they sent to the Mexican government and to the state of Coahuila, calling for more autonomy for Texas. A second convention was held in January 1833. Significantly, not one Mexican pueblo in Texas participated in either convention, many clearly branding the act sedition. Increasingly it became evident that the war party under Sam Houston was winning out.[8] Houston was elected to direct the course of events and Austin was appointed to take the grievances and resolutions to Mexico City.

Austin left for Mexico City to press for lifting of restrictions on Anglo-American immigration and for separate statehood. The slave issue also burned in his mind. Austin, anything but conciliatory, wrote to a friend, "If our application is refused . . . I shall be in favor of organizing *without it.* I see no other way of saving the country from total anarchy and ruin. I am totally done with conciliatory measures and, for the future, shall be uncompromising as to Texas."[9]

On October 2, 1833, Austin wrote the San Antonio *ayuntamiento* encouraging it to declare Texas a separate state. He later explained that he had done so "in a moment of irritation and impatience"; nevertheless, his actions were not those of a moderate. Contents of the note fell into the hands of Mexican authorities, who questioned Austin's good faith. Subsequently, they imprisoned him, and much of what Austin had accomplished in the way of compromise was undone.

Meanwhile, the U.S. minister to Mexico, Anthony Butler, crudely attempted to bribe Mexican officials into selling Texas. He offered one official $200,000 to "play ball."[10]

In the autumn of 1834 Henry Smith published a pamphlet entitled *Security for Texas* in which he advocated open defiance of Mexican authority. Anglo land companies added to the polarization by lobbying in Washington, D.C., and within Texas for a change in governments. The Galveston Bay and Texas Land Company of New York, acting to protect its investments, worked through its agent Anthony Butler, the U.S. minister to Mexico, to bring about U.S. cooperation.[11]

According to Dr. Carlos Castañeda:

> The activities of the "Land Companies" after 1834 cannot be ignored. Their widespread advertisement and indiscriminate sale of "landscrip" sent hundreds, perhaps thousands, to Texas under the impression that they had legitimate title to lands equal to the amount of scrip bought. The Galveston Bay and Texas Land Company, which bought the contracts of David S. Burnet, Joseph Vahlein, and Lorenzo de Zavala, and the Nashville Company, which acquired the contract of Robert Leftwitch, are the two best known. They first sold scrip at from one to ten cents an acre, calling for a total of seven and one-half million acres. The company was selling only its permit to acquire a given amount of land in Texas, but since an empresario contract was nontransferable, the scrip was, in fact, worthless.[12]

The scrip was worthless as long as Texas belonged to Mexico.

On July 13, 1835, a general amnesty released Austin from prison. While en route to Texas, he wrote a cousin from New Orleans that Texas should be Americanized, speculating that it should one day come under the American flag. Austin called for a massive immigration of Anglo-Americans, *"each man with his rifle,"* who he hoped would come "passports or no passports, *anyhow."* He continued: "For fourteen years I have had a hard time of it, but nothing shall daunt my courage or abate my . . . object . . . to *Americanize* Texas."[13]

Anglos saw separation from Mexico and eventual union with the United States as the most profitable political arrangement. Texas-Mexican historian Castañeda notes:

> Trade with New Orleans and other American ports had increased steadily. This development was naturally distasteful to Mexico, for the colonists fostered strong economic ties with . . . the United States rather than with Mexico. Juan H. Almonte in his 1834 report, estimated the total foreign trade of Texas— chiefly with the United States—at more than 1,000,000 pesos, of which imports constituted 630,000 and exports, 500,000. He calculated the exportation of cotton by the settlers in 1833, as approximately 2,000 bales.[14]

Colonel Almonte recognized the fundamental economic conflict, and his report recommended concessions to the *Tejanos,* but also urged that "the province be well stocked with Mexican troops."[15]

THE INVASION OF TEXAS

Not all the Anglo-Americans favored the conflict. Austin, at first, belonged to the peace party. Ultimately, this faction joined the "hawks." Eugene C. Barker states that the immediate cause of the war was "the overthrow of the nominal republic [by Santa Anna] and the substitution of centralized oligarchy," which allegedly would have centralized Mexican control. Barker admits that "earnest patriots like Benjamin Lundy, William Ellery Channing, and John Quincy Adams saw in the Texas revolution a disgraceful affair promoted by the sordid slaveholders and land speculators."

Barker parallels the Texas filibuster and the American Revolution, stating: "In each, the general cause of revolt was the same—a sudden effort to extend imperial authority at the expense of local privilege." According to Barker, in both instances the central governments attempted to enforce existing laws that conflicted with the illegal activities of some very articulate people. Barker further justified the Anglo-Americans' actions by observing: "At the close of summer in 1835 the Texans saw themselves in danger of becoming the alien subjects of a people to whom they deliberately believed themselves morally, intellectually, and politically superior. The racial feeling, indeed, underlay and colored Texan-Mexican relations from the establishment of the first Anglo-American colony in 1821." The conflict, according to Barker, was inevitable and, consequently, justified.

Texas history is a mixture of selected fact and generalized myth. Many historians admit that smugglers were upset with Mexico's enforcement of her import laws, that Euroamericans were angry about emancipation laws, and that an increasing number of the new arrivals from the United States actively agitated for independence. But despite these admissions, many historians like Barker refuse to blame the United States.[16]

Austin gave the call to arms on September 19, 1835, stating, "War is our only recourse. There is no other remedy."[17] Anglo-Americans enjoyed very real advantages in 1835. They were "defending" terrain with which they were familiar. The 5,000 Mexicans living in the territory did not join them, but the Anglo population had swelled to almost 30,000. The Mexican nation was divided, and the centers of power were thousands of miles from Texas. From the interior of Mexico, Santa Anna led an army of about 6,000 conscripts, many of whom had been forced into the army and then marched hundreds of miles over hot, arid desert land. Many were Mayan and did not speak Spanish. In February 1836 the majority arrived in Texas, sick and ill-prepared to fight.

In San Antonio the dissidents took refuge in a former mission, the Alamo. The siege began in the first week of March. In the days that followed, the defenders inflicted heavy casualties on the Mexican forces, but eventually the Mexicans won out. A score of popular books have been written about Mexican cruelty in relation to the Alamo and about the heroics of the doomed men. The result was the creation of the Alamo myth. Within the broad framework of what actually happened—187 filibusters barricading themselves in the Alamo in defiance of Santa Anna's force, which, according to Mexican sources, numbered 1,400, and the eventual triumph of the Mexicans—there has been major distortion.

Walter Lord, in an article entitled "Myths and Realities of the Alamo," sets the record straight. Texas mythology portrays the Alamo heroes as freedom-loving defenders of their homes; supposedly they were all good Texans. Actually, two-thirds of the defenders had recently arrived from the United States, and only a half dozen had been in Texas for more than six years. The men in the Alamo were adventurers. William Barret Travis had fled to Texas after killing a man, abandoning his wife and two children. James Bowie, an infamous brawler, made a fortune running slaves and had wandered into Texas searching for lost mines and more money. The fading Davey Crockett, a legend in his own time, fought for the sake of fighting. Many in the Alamo had come to Texas for riches and glory. These defenders were hardly the sort of men who could be classified as peaceful settlers fighting for their homes.

The folklore of the Alamo goes beyond the legendary names of the defenders. According to Lord, it is riddled with dramatic half-truths that have been accepted as history. Defenders are portrayed as selfless heroes who sacrificed their lives to buy more time for their comrades-in-arms. As the story goes, William Barret Travis told his men that they were doomed; he drew a line in the sand with his sword, saying that all who crossed it would elect to remain and fight to the last. Supposedly all the men there valiantly stepped across the line, with a man in a cot begging to be carried across it. Countless Hollywood movies have dramatized the bravery of the defenders.

In reality the Alamo had little strategic value, it was the best protected fort west of the Mississippi, and the men fully expected help. The defenders had 21 cannons to the Mexicans' 8 or 10. They were expert shooters equipped with rifles with a range of 200 yards, while the Mexicans were inadequately trained and armed with smooth-bore muskets with a range of only 70 yards. The Anglos were protected by the walls and had clear shots, while the Mexicans advanced in the open and fired at concealed targets. In short, ill-prepared, ill-equipped, and ill-fed Mexicans attacked well-armed and professional soldiers. In addition, from all reliable sources, it is doubtful whether Travis ever drew a line in the sand. San Antonio survivors, females and noncombatants, did not tell the story until many years later, when the tale had gained currency and the myth was legend. Probably the most widely circulated story was that of the last stand of the aging Davey Crockett, who fell "fighting like a tiger," killing Mexicans with his bare hands. This is a myth; seven of the defenders surrendered, and Crockett was among them. They were executed. And, finally, one man, Louis Rose, did escape.[18]

Travis's stand delayed Santa Anna's timetable by only four days, as the Mexicans took San Antonio on March 6, 1836. At first, the stand at the Alamo did not even have propaganda value. Afterwards, Houston's army dwindled, with many volunteers rushing home to help their families flee from the advancing Mexican army. Most Anglo-Americans realized that they had been badly beaten. It did, nevertheless, result in massive aid from the United States in the form of volunteers, weapons and money. The cry of "Remember the Alamo" became a call to arms for Anglo-Americans in both Texas and the United States.[19]

After the Alamo and the defeat of another garrison at Goliad, southeast of San Antonio, Santa Anna was in full control. He ran Sam Houston out of the territory northwest of the San Jacinto River and then camped an army of about 1,100 men near San Jacinto. There, he skirmished with Houston on April 20, 1836, but did not follow up his advantage. Predicting that Houston would attack on April 22, Santa Anna and his troops settled down and rested for the anticipated battle. The filibusters, however, attacked during the *siesta* hour on April 21. Santa Anna knew that Houston had an army of 1,000, yet he was lax in his precautionary defenses. The surprise attack caught him totally off guard. Shouts of "Remember the Alamo! Remember Goliad!" filled the air. Houston's successful surprise attack ended the war. He captured Santa Anna, who signed the territory away. Although the Mexican Congress repudiated the treaty, Houston was elected president of the Republic of Texas.

Few Mexican prisoners were taken at the battle of San Jacinto. Those who surrendered "were clubbed and stabbed, some on their knees. The slaughter . . . became methodical: the Texan riflemen knelt and poured a steady fire into the packed, jostling ranks." They shot the "Meskins" down as they fled. The final count showed 630 Mexicans dead versus 2 Texans.

Even Santa Anna was not let off lightly; according to Dr. Castañeda, Santa Anna "was mercilessly dragged from the ship he had boarded, subjected to more than six months' mental torture and indignities in Texas prison camps."[20]

The Euroamerican victory paved the way for the Mexican-American War. Officially the United States had not taken sides, but men, money, and supplies poured in to aid fellow Anglo-Americans. U.S. citizens participated in the invasion of Texas with the open support of their government. Mexico's minister to the United States, Manuel Eduardo Gorostiza, protested the "arming and shipment of troops and supplies to territory which was part of Mexico, and the dispatch of United States troops into territory clearly defined by treaty as Mexican territory."[21] General Edmund P. Gaines, Southwest commander, was sent into western Louisiana on January 23, 1836; shortly thereafter, he crossed into Texas in an action that was interpreted to be in support of the Anglo-American filibusters in Texas: "The Jackson Administration made it plain to the Mexican minister that it mattered little whether Mexico approved, that the important thing was to protect the border against Indians and Mexicans."[22] U.S. citizens in and out of Texas loudly applauded Jackson's actions. The Mexican minister resigned his post in protest. "The success of the Texas Revolution thrust the Anglo-American frontier up against the Far Southwest, and the region came at once into the scope of Anglo ambition."[23]

THE INVASION OF MEXICO

In the mid-1840s, Mexico was again the target. Expansion and capitalist development moved together. The two Mexican wars gave U.S. commerce, industry, mining, agriculture, and stockraising a tremendous stimulus. "The truth is that [by the 1840s] the Pacific Coast belonged to the commercial empire that the United States was already building in that ocean."[24]

The U.S. population of 17 million people of European extraction and 3 million slaves was considerably larger than Mexico's 7 million, of which 4 million were Indian and 3 million *mestizo* and European. The United States acted arrogantly in foreign affairs, partly because its citizens believed in their own cultural and racial superiority. Mexico was plagued with financial problems, internal ethnic conflicts, and poor leadership. General anarchy within the nation conspired against its cohesive development.[25]

By 1844 war with Mexico over Texas and the Southwest was only a matter of time. James K. Polk, who strongly advocated the annexation of Texas and expansionism in general, won the presidency by only a small margin, but his election was interpreted as a mandate for national expansion. Outgoing President Tyler acted by calling upon Congress to annex Texas by joint resolution; the measure was passed a few days before the inauguration of Polk, who accepted the arrangement. In December 1845, Texas became a state.[26]

Mexico promptly broke off diplomatic relations with the United States, and Polk ordered General Zachary Taylor into Texas to "protect" the border. The location of the border was in doubt. The North Americans claimed it was at the Río Grande, but based on historical precedent, Mexico insisted it was 150 miles farther north, at the Nueces River.[27] Taylor marched his forces across the Nueces into the disputed territory, wanting to provoke an attack.

In November 1845, Polk sent John Slidell on a secret mission to Mexico to negotiate for the disputed area. The presence of Anglo-American troops between the Nueces and the Río Grande and the annexation of Texas made negotiations an absurdity. They refused to accept Polk's minister's credentials, although they did offer to give him an ad hoc status.[28] Slidell declined anything less than full recognition and returned to Washington in March 1846, convinced that Mexico would have to be "chastised" before it would negotiate. By March 28, Taylor had advanced to the Río Grande with an army of 4,000.

Polk, incensed at Mexico's refusal to meet with Slidell on his terms and at General Mairano Paredes's reaffirmation of his country's claims to all of Texas, began to draft his declaration of war when he learned of the Mexican attack on U.S. troops in the disputed territory. Polk immediately declared that the United States had been provoked into war, that Mexico had "shed American blood upon the American soil." On May 13, 1846, Congress declared war and authorized the recruitment and supplying of 50,000 troops.[29]

Years later, Ulysses S. Grant wrote that he believed that Polk provoked the war and that the annexation of Texas was, in fact, an act of aggression. He added: "I had a horror of the Mexican War . . . only I had not moral courage enough to resign. . . . I considered my supreme duty was to my flag."[30]

The poorly equipped and poorly led Mexican army stood little chance against the expansion-minded Anglos. Even before the war Polk planned the campaign in stages: (1) Mexicans would be cleared out of Texas; (2) Anglos would occupy California and New Mexico; and (3) U.S. forces would march to Mexico City to force the beaten government to make peace on Polk's terms. And that was the way the campaign basically went. In the end, at a relatively small cost in men and money, the war netted the United States huge territorial gains. In all, the United States took over 1 million square miles from Mexico.[31]

THE RATIONALE FOR CONQUEST

In his *Origins of the War with Mexico: The Polk-Stockton Intrigue,* Glenn W. Price states: "Americans have found it rather more difficult than other peoples to deal rationally with their wars. We have thought of ourselves as unique, and of this society as specially planned and created to avoid the errors of all other nations."[32] Many Anglo-American historians have attempted to dismiss it simply as a "bad war," which took place during the era of Manifest Destiny.

Manifest Destiny had its roots in Puritan ideas, which continue to influence Anglo-American thought to this day. According to the Puritan ethic, salvation is determined by God. The establishment of the City of God on earth is not only the duty of those chosen people predestined for salvation but is also the proof of their state of grace. Anglo-Americans believed that God had made them custodians of democracy and that they had a mission—that is, that they were predestined to spread its principles. As the young nation survived its infancy, established its power in the defeat of the British in the War of 1812, expanded westward, and enjoyed both commercial and industrial success, its sense of mission heightened. Many citizens believed that God had destined them to own and occupy all of the land from ocean to ocean and pole to pole. Their mission, their destiny made manifest, was to spread the principles of democracy and Christianity to the unfortunates of the hemisphere. By dismissing the war simply as part of the era of Manifest Destiny the apologists for the war ignore the consequences of the doctrine.

The Monroe Doctrine of the 1820s told the world that the Americas were no longer open for colonization or conquest; however, it did not say anything about that limitation applying to the United States. Uppermost in the minds of the U.S. government, the military, and much of the public was the acquisition of territory. No one ever intended to leave Mexico without extracting territory. Land was the main motive for the war.

This aggression was justified by a rhetoric of peace. Consider, for example, Polk's war message of May 11, 1846, in which he gave his reasons for going to war:

> The strong desire to establish peace with Mexico on liberal and honorable terms, and the readiness of this Government to regulate and adjust our boundary and other causes of difference with that power on such fair and equitable principles as would lead to permanent relations of the most friendly nature, induced me in September last to seek reopening of diplomatic relations between the two countries.[33]

The United States, he continued, had made every effort not to provoke Mexico, but the Mexican government had refused to receive an Anglo-American minister. Polk reviewed the events leading to the war and concluded:

> As war exists, and notwithstanding all our efforts to avoid it, exists by the act of Mexico herself, we are called upon by every consideration of duty and patriotism to vindicate with decision the honor, the rights, and the interests of our country.[34]

Historical distance from the war has not lessened the need to justify U.S. aggression. In 1920 Justin H. Smith received a Pulitzer prize in history for a work that blamed the war on Mexico. What is amazing is that Smith allegedly examined over 100,000 manuscripts, 120,000 books and pamphlets, and 200 or more periodicals to come to this conclusion. He was rewarded for relieving the Anglo-American conscience. His two-volume "study," entitled *The War with Mexico,* used analyses such as the following to support its thesis that the Mexicans were at fault for the war:

> At the beginning of her independent existence, our people felt earnestly and enthusiastically anxious to maintain cordial relations with our sister republic, and many crossed the line of absurd sentimentality in the cause. Friction was inevitable, however. The Americans were direct, positive, brusque, angular and pushing; and they would not understand their neighbors in the south. The Mexicans were equally unable to fathom our goodwill, sincerity, patriotism, resoluteness and courage; and certain features of their character and national condition made it far from easy to get on with them.[35]

This attitude of self-righteousness on the part of government officials and historians toward U.S. aggressions spills over to the relationships between the majority society and minority groups. Anglo-Americans believe that the war was advantageous to the Southwest and to the Mexicans who remained or later migrated there. They now had the benefits of democracy and were liberated from their tyrannical past. In other words, Mexicans should be grateful to the Anglo-Americans. If Mexicans and the Anglo-Americans clash, the rationale runs, naturally it is because Mexicans cannot understand or appreciate the merits of a free society, which must be defended against ingrates. Therefore, domestic war, or repression, is justified by the same kind of rhetoric that justifies international aggression.[36]

Professor Gene M. Brack questions historians who base their research on Justin Smith's outdated work: "American historians have consistently praised Justin Smith's influential and outrageously ethnocentric account."[37]

THE MYTH OF A NONVIOLENT NATION

Most studies on the Mexican-American War dwell on the causes and results of the war, sometimes dealing with war strategy.[38] One must go beyond this point, since the war left bitterness, and since Anglo-American actions in Mexico are vividly remembered. Mexicans' attitude toward Anglo-Americans has been influenced by the war just as the easy victory of the United States conditioned Anglo-American behavior toward Mexicans. Fortunately, some Anglo-Americans condemned this aggression and flatly accused their leaders of being insolent and land-hungry, and of having manufactured the war. Abiel Abbott Livermore, in *The War with Mexico Reviewed,* accused his country, writing:

> Again, the pride of race has swollen to still greater insolence the pride of country, always quite active enough for the due observance of the claims of universal brotherhood. The Anglo-Saxons have been apparently persuaded to think themselves the chosen people, annointed race of the Lord, commissioned to drive out the heathen, and plant their religion and institutions in every Canaan they could subjugate. . . . Our treatment both of the red man and the black man has habituated us to feel our power and forget right. . . . The passion for land, also, is a leading characteristic of the American people. . . . The god Terminus is an unknown deity in America. Like the hunger of the pauper boy of fiction, the cry had been, 'more, more, give us more.'[39]

Livermore's work, published in 1850, was awarded the American Peace Society prize for "the best review of the Mexican War and the principles of Christianity, and an enlightened statesmanship."

In truth, the United States conducted a violent and brutal war. Zachary Taylor's artillery leveled the Mexican city of Matamoros, killing hundreds of innocent civilians with *la bomba* (the bomb). Many Mexicans jumped into the Río Grande, relieved of their pain by a watery grave.[40] The occupation that followed was even more terrorizing. Taylor was unable to control his volunteers:

> The regulars regarded the volunteers, of whom about two thousand had reached Matamoros by the end of May, with impatience and contempt. . . . They

robbed Mexicans of their cattle and corn, stole their fences for firewood, got drunk, and killed several inoffensive inhabitants of the town in the streets.[41]

Numerous eyewitness accounts to these incidents exist. For example, on July 25, 1846, Grant wrote to Julia Dent:

> Since we have been in Matamoros a great many murders have been committed, and what is strange there seems [sic] to be very week [sic] means made use of to prevent frequent repetitions. Some of the volunteers and about all the Texans seem to think it perfectly right to impose on the people of a conquered City to any extent, and even to murder them where the act can be covered by dark. And how much they seem to enjoy acts of violence too! I would not pretend to guess the number of murders that have been committed upon the persons of poor Mexicans and our soldiers, since we have been here, but the number would startle you.[42]

On July 9, 1846, George Gordon Meade, who, like Grant, later became a general during the U.S. Civil War, wrote:

> They [the volunteers] have killed five or six innocent people walking in the street, for no other object than their own amusement. . . . They rob and steal the cattle and corn of the poor farmers, and in fact act more like a body of hostile Indians than civilized Whites. Their officers have no command or control over them.[43]

Taylor knew about the atrocities, but Grant observed that Taylor did not restrain his men. In a letter to his superiors, Taylor admitted that "there is scarcely a form of crime that has not been reported to me as committed by them."[44] Taylor requested that they send no further troops from the state of Texas to him. These violent acts were not limited to Taylor's men. The cannons from U.S. naval ships destroyed much of the civilian sector of Vera Cruz, leveling a hospital, churches, and homes. The bomb did not discriminate as to age or sex. Anglo-American troops destroyed almost every city they invaded; first the locality was put to the test of fire and then plundered. *Gringo* volunteers had little respect for anything, desecrating churches and abusing priests and nuns.

Military executions were common. Captured soldiers and civilians were hanged for cooperating with the guerrillas. Many Irish immigrants, as well as some other Anglos, deserted to the Mexican side, forming the San Patricio Corps.[45] Many of the Irish were Catholics, and they resented treatment of Catholic priests and nuns by the invading Protestants. As many as 260 Anglo-Americans fought with the Mexicans at Churubusco in 1847:

> Some eighty appear to have been captured. . . . A number were found not guilty of deserting and were released. About fifteen, who had deserted before the declaration of war, were merely branded with a "D," and fifty of those taken at Churubusco were executed.[46]

Others received 200 lashes and were forced to dig graves for their executed comrades.[47]

These acts were similar to those in Monterey, as George Meade wrote on December 2, 1846:

> They plunder the poor inhabitants of everything they can lay their hands on, and shoot them when they remonstrate; and if one of their number happens to get into a drunken brawl and is killed, they run over the country, killing all the poor innocent people they find in their way to avenge, as they say, the murder of their brother.[48]

As General Winfield Scott's army left Monterey, they shot Mexican prisoners of war.[49]

Memoirs, diaries, and news articles written by Anglo-Americans document the reign of terror. Samuel E. Chamberlain's *My Confessions* is a record of Anglo racism and destruction. He was only 17 when he enlisted in the army to fight the "greasers." At the Mexican city of Parras, he wrote:

> We found the patrol had been guilty of many outrages. . . . They had ridden into the church of San José during Mass, the place crowded with kneeling women and children, and with oaths and ribald jest had arrested soldiers who had permission to be present.[50]

On another occasion, he described a massacre by volunteers, mostly from Yell's Cavalry, at a cave:

> On reaching the place we found a "greaser" shot and *scalped,* but still breathing; the poor fellow held in his hands a Rosary and a medal of the "Virgin of Guadalupe," only his feeble motions kept the fierce harpies from falling on him while yet alive. A Sabre thrust was given him in mercy, and on we went at a run. Soon shouts and curses, cries of women and children reached our ears, coming apparently from a cave at the end of the ravine. Climbing over the rocks we reached the entrance, and as soon as we could see in the comparative darkness a horrid sight was before us. The cave was full of our volunteers yelling like fiends, while on the rocky floor lay over twenty Mexicans, dead and dying in pools of blood. Women and children were clinging to the knees of the murderers shrieking for mercy. . . . Most of the butchered Mexicans had been scalped; only three men were found unharmed. A rough crucifix was fastened to a rock, and some irreverent wretch had crowned the image with a bloody scalp. A sickening smell filled the place. The surviving women and children sent up loud screams on seeing us, thinking we had returned to finish the work! . . . No one was punished for this outrage.[51]

Near Satillo, Chamberlain reported the actions of Texas Rangers. His descriptions were graphic:

> [A drunken Anglo] entered the church and tore down a large wooden figure of our Saviour, and making his lariat fast around its neck, he mounted his horse and galloped up and down the *plazuela,* dragging the statue behind. The venerable white-haired Priest, in attempting to rescue it, was thrown down and trampled under the feet of the Ranger's horse.[52]

Mexicans were enraged and attacked the Texan. Meanwhile, the Rangers returned:

> As they charged into the square, they saw their miserable comrade hanging to the cross, his skin hanging in strips, surrounded by crowds of Mexicans. With yells of horror, the Rangers charged on the mass with Bowie Knife and revolver, sparing neither age or sex in their terrible fury.[53]

Chamberlain blamed General Taylor not only for collecting over $1 million (from the Mexican people) by force of arms, but also for letting "loose on the country packs of human bloodhounds called Texas Rangers." He goes on to describe the Rangers's brutality at the Rancho de San Francisco on the Camargo road near Agua Fria:

> The place was surrounded, the doors forced in, and all the males capable of bearing arms were dragged out, tied to a post and shot! . . . Thirty-six Mexicans were shot at this place, a half hour given for the horrified survivors, women and children, to remove their little household goods, then the torch was applied to the houses, and by the light of the conflagration the ferocious *Tejanos* rode off to fresh scenes of blood.[54]

These wanton acts of cruelty, witnessed by one man and augmented by the reports of other chroniclers, add to the evidence that the United States, through the violence of its soldiers, left a legacy of hate in Mexico.[55]

THE TREATY OF GUADALUPE HIDALGO

By late August 1847 the war was almost at an end. Scott's defeat of Santa Anna in a hard-fought battle at Churubusco put Anglo-Americans at the gates of Mexico City. Santa Anna made overtures for an armistice that broke down after two weeks, and the war resumed. On September 13, 1847, Scott drove into the city. Although Mexicans fought valiantly, the battle left 4,000 dead, with another 3,000 prisoners. On September 13, before the occupation of Mexico City began, *Los Niños Héroes* (The Boy Heroes) leapt to their deaths rather than surrender. These teenage cadets were Francisco Márquez, Agustín Melgar, Juan Escutia, Fernando Montes de Oca, Vicente Suárez, and Juan de la Barrera. They became "a symbol and image of this unrighteous war."[56]

The Mexicans continued fighting. The presiding justice of the Supreme Court, Manuel de la Peña, assumed the presidency. He knew that Mexico had lost and that he had to salvage as much as possible. Pressure increased, with U.S. troops in control of much of Mexico.

Nicholas Trist, sent to Mexico to act as peace commissioner, had arrived in Vera Cruz on May 6, 1847, but controversy with Scott over Trist's authority and illness delayed an armistice, and hostilities continued. After the fall of Mexico City, Secretary of State James Buchanan wanted to revise Trist's instructions. He ordered Trist to break off negotiations and return home.[57] Polk wanted more land from Mexico. Trist, however, with the support of Winfield Scott, decided to ignore Polk's order, and began negotiations on January 2, 1848, on the original terms. Mexico, badly beaten, her government in a state of turmoil, had no choice but to agree to the Anglo-Americans' proposals.

On February 2, 1848, the Mexicans ratified the Treaty of Guadalupe Hidalgo, with Mexico accepting the Río Grande as the Texas border and ceding the Southwest (which incorporated the present-day states of California, New Mexico, Nevada, and parts of Colorado, Arizona, and Utah) to the United States in return for $15 million.

Polk, furious about the treaty, considered Trist "contemptibly base" for having ignored his orders. Yet he had no choice but to submit the treaty to the Senate. With the exception of Article X, which concerned the rights of Mexicans in the ceded territory, the Senate ratified the treaty on March 10, 1848, by a vote of 28 to 14. To insist on more territory would have meant more fighting, and both Polk and the Senate realized that the war was already unpopular in many circles. The treaty was sent to the Mexican Congress for ratification; although the Congress had difficulty forming a quorum, the treaty was ratified on May 19 by a 52 to 35 vote.[58] Hostilities between the two nations officially ended. Trist, however, was branded as a "scoundrel," because Polk was disappointed in the settlement. There was considerable support in the United States for acquisition of all Mexico.[59]

During the treaty talks Mexican negotiators, concerned about Mexicans left behind, expressed great reservations about these people being forced to "merge or blend" into Anglo-American culture. They protested the exclusion of provisions that protected Mexican citizens' rights, land titles, and religion.[60] They wanted to protect their rights by treaty.

Articles VIII, IX, and X specifically referred to the rights of Mexicans. Under the treaty, Mexicans left behind had one year to choose whether to return to Mexico or remain in "occupied Mexico." About 2,000 elected to leave; most remained in what they considered *their* land.

Article IX of the treaty guaranteed Mexicans "the enjoyment of all the rights of citizens of the United States according to the principles of the Constitution; and in the meantime shall be maintained and protected in the free enjoyment of their liberty and property, and secured in the free exercise of their religion without restriction."[61] Lynn I. Perrigo, in *The American Southwest,* summarizes the guarantees of Articles VIII and IX: "In other words, besides the rights and duties of American citizenship, they [the Mexicans] would have some special privileges derived from their previous customs in language, law, and religion."[62]

The omitted Article X had comprehensive guarantees protecting "all prior and pending titles to property of every description."[63] When article X was deleted by the U.S. Senate, Mexican officials protested. Anglo-American emissaries reassured them by drafting a Statement of Protocol on May 26, 1848:

> The American government by suppressing the Xth article of the Treaty of Guadalupe Hidalgo did not in any way intend to annul the grants of lands made by Mexico in the ceded territories. These grants . . . preserve the legal value

which they may possess, and the grantees may cause their legitimate (titles) to be acknowledged before the American tribunals.

Conformable to the law of the United States, legitimate titles to every description of property, personal and real, existing in the ceded territories, are those which were legitimate titles under the Mexican law of California and New Mexico up to the 13th of May, 1846, and in Texas up to the 2nd of March, 1836.[64]

Considering the Mexican opposition to the treaty, it is doubtful whether the Mexican Congress would have ratified the treaty without this clarification. The vote was close.

The Statement of Protocol was strengthened by Articles VIII and IX, which guaranteed Mexicans rights of property and protection under the law. In addition, court decisions have generally interpreted the treaty as protecting land titles and water rights. In practice, however, the treaty was ignored and during the nineteenth century most Mexicans in the United States were considered as a class apart from the dominant race.[65] Nearly every one of the obligations discussed above was violated, confirming the prophecy of Mexican diplomat Manuel Crescion Rejón, who, at the time the treaty was signed, commented:

Our race, our unfortunate people will have to wander in search of hospitality in a strange land, only to be ejected later. Descendants of the Indians that we are, the North Americans hate us, their spokesmen depreciate us, even if they recognize the justice of our cause, and they consider us unworthy to form with them one nation and one society, they clearly manifest that their future expansion begins with the territory that they take from us and pushing [sic] aside our citizens who inhabit the land.[66]

As a result of the Texas War and the Anglo-American aggressions of 1845–1848, the occupation of conquered territory began. In material terms, in exchange for 12,000 lives and more than $100 million, the United States acquired a colony two and a half times as large as France, containing rich farmlands and natural resources such as gold, silver, zinc, copper, oil, and uranium, which would make possible its unprecedented industrial boom.[67] It acquired ports on the Pacific that generated further economic expansion across that ocean. Mexico was left with its shrunken resources to face the continued advances of the United States.

SUMMARY

The colonial experience of the United States differs from that of Third World nations. Its history resembles that of Australia and/or South Africa, where colonizers relegated indigenous populations to fourth-class citizenship or noncitizenship. North American independence came at the right time, slightly predating the industrialization of nineteenth-century Europe. Its merchants took over a lucrative trade network from the British; the new Republic established a government that supported trade, industry, and commercial agriculture. A North American ideology which presumed that Latin Americans had stolen the name

"America" and that God, the realtor, had given them the land, encouraged colonial expansion.

Mexico, like most Third World nations after independence, needed a period of stability. North American penetration into Texas in the 1820s and 1830s threatened Mexico. The U.S. economic system encouraged expansion, and many of the first wave of migrants to Texas had lost their farms due to the depression of 1819. Land in Texas, generously cheap, provided room for the spread of slavery. Although many North Americans in all probability intended to obey Mexican laws and meet conditions for obtaining land grants, North American ethnocentricism and self-interest soon eroded those intentions. Clearly land values would zoom if Texas were part of the United States.

North American historians have frequently portrayed the Texas invasion as a second encounter in the "American War of Independence." Myths such as that of a tyrannical Mexican government have justified the war. In truth, the cause of the war was profit. Mexico did not invade Texas; it belonged to Mexico. Few if any of the North Americans in Texas had been born there or had lived in Texas for more than five years. Most had just recently arrived. Some rich Mexicans supported the North Americans for obvious reasons—it was in their economic self-interest. A stalemate resulted, with Euroamericans establishing the Texas Republic. In 1844, the United States broke the standoff and annexed Texas.

President James K. Polk manufactured the war with Mexico. Some North Americans opposed the war—not on grounds that it violated Mexico's territorial integrity, but because of the probability of the extension of slavery. Many North American military leaders admitted that the war was unjust, and that the United States had committed an act of aggression. However, patriotism and support for the war overwhelmed reason in the march "To the Halls of the Montezumas [sic]." North Americans, buoyant in their prosperity, wanted to prove that the United States was a world-class power.

The war became a Protestant Crusade. Texans made emotional pleas to avenge the Alamo. Both appeals were instrumental in arousing North Americans to the call to arms, to prove their valor and power of the young "American" democracy. North American soldiers committed atrocities against Mexican civilians; few were punished.

The Treaty of Guadalupe Hidalgo ended the war, and the United States grabbed over half of Mexico's soil. The war proved costly to Mexico and to Mexicans left behind. According to the treaty, Mexicans who elected to stay in the conquered territory would become U.S. citizens with all the rights of citizenship. However, the Treaty of Guadalupe Hidalgo, like those signed with the indigenous people of North American, depended on the good faith of the United States and its ability to keep its word.

NOTES

1. Robert W. Johannsen, *To the Halls of the Montezumas: The Mexican War in the American Imagination* (New York: Oxford University Press, 1985). An excellent account of North Ameri-

can popular support for the war. Also see Norman E. Tutorow, *Texas Annexation and the Mexican War* (Palo Alto, Calif.: Chadwick House, 1978).

2. Manual Medina Castro, *El Gran Despojo: Texas, Nuevo México, California* (México, D.F.: Editorial Diogenes, 1971), p. 9; Carlos E. Castañeda, *Our Catholic Heritage in Texas, 1519–1933,* vol. 6, *Transition Period: The Fight for Freedom, 1810–1836* (New York: Arno Press, 1976), p. 86.

3. Richard W. Van Alstyne, *The Rising American Empire* (New York: Norton, 1974), p. 101; T. R. Fehrenbach, *Lone Star: A History of Texas and the Texans* (New York: Macmillan, 1968), p. 128; Castañeda, vol. 6, pp. 160–162.

4. Walter Prescott Webb, *The Texas Rangers: A Century of Frontier Defense* (Austin: University of Texas Press, 1965), pp. 21–22.

5. Fehrenbach, pp. 163–164.

6. Van Alstyne, p. 101.

7. Eugene C. Barker, *Mexico and Texas, 1821–1835* (New York: Russell & Russell, 1965), pp. 52, 74–80, 80–82; David J. Weber, ed., *Foreigners in Their Native Land* (Albuquerque: University of New Mexico Press, 1973), p. 89, quoted in Fehrenbach, p. 182.

8. Castañeda, vol. 6, pp. 252–253; Fehrenbach, p. 181.

9. Nathaniel W. Stephenson, *Texas and the Mexican War: A Chronicle of the Winning of the Southwest* (New York: United States Publishing, 1921), p. 51.

10. Stephenson, p. 52; Barker, p. 128. Castañeda, in vol. 6, p. 234, refers to Col. Anthony Butler, Jackson's minister to Mexico, as "an unscrupulous, passionate and scheming character." The new proposal provided final confirmation of the United States's intentions. Gene M. Brack, *Mexico Views Manifest Destiny, 1821–1846: An Essay on the Origins of the Mexican War* (Albuquerque: University of New Mexico Press, 1975), pp. 67–68, states that Jackson told the minister to do anything to get Texas.

11. Stephenson, p. 52.

12. Castañeda, vol. 6, pp. 217–218.

13. Fehrenbach, p. 188. Hutchinson, p. 6, quotes a letter from Austin to Mrs. Mary Austin Holly: "The fact is, we must and ought to become a part of the United States. Money should be no consideration. . . . The more the American population is increased the more readily will the Mexican government give it up. . . . For fourteen years I have had a hard time of it, but nothing shall daunt my courage or abate my exertions to complete the main object of my labors, to *Americanize* Texas."

14. Castañeda, vol. 6, pp. 240–241.

15. Fehrenbach, p. 180.

16. Barker, pp. 146, 147, 148–149, 162.

17. Fehrenbach, p. 189.

18. Walter Lord, "Myths and Realities of the Alamo," *The American West* 5, no. 3 (May 1968): 18, 22, 24; Ramón Martínez Caro, "A True Account of the First Texas Campaign," in Carlos E. Castañeda, *The Mexican Side of the Texas Revolution* (Dallas: P. L. Turner Co., 1928), p. 103.

19. Lord, p. 25.

20. Carlos Castañeda, *Our Catholic Heritage in Texas, 1519–1933,* vol. 7, *The Church in Texas Since Independence, 1836–1950,* p. 5.

21. Lota M. Spell, "Gorostiza and Texas," *Hispanic American Historical Review,* no. 4 (November 1957): 446.

22. Brack, pp. 74–75.

23. Burl Noggle, "Anglo Observers of the Southwest Borderlands, 1825–1890: The Rise of a Concept," *Arizona and the West* (Summer 1959): 122.

24. Van Alstyne, p. 106.

25. Medina Castro, p. 74, Charles A. Hale, *Mexican Liberalism in the Age of Mora, 1821–1853* (New Haven, Conn.: Yale University Press, 1968), pp. 11–12, 16.

26. On March 1, 1845, Congress passed the joint resolution, but it was not until July 1845 that a convention in Texas voted to accept annexation to the United States. The political maneuverings behind annexation in the U.S. Congress document the economic motive underlying it. Van Alstyne, p. 104, writes: "The pro-annexationists, some of whom like Senator Robert J. Walker

of Mississippi had speculated heavily in Texas real estate, managed to influence public opinion in both North and South to the point where, on March 1, 1845, sufficient votes were mustered in Congress to authorize admission to the Union. There was a small margin of votes in each house in favor of annexation: in the House of Representatives, 22; in the Senate, only two."

27. José María Roa Barcena, *Recuerdos de la Invasión Norte Americana (1846–1848),* ed. I. Antonio Castro Leal (México, D.F.: Editorial Porrua, 1947), pp. 25–27.

28. Albert C. Ramsey, ed. and trans., *The Old Side or Notes for the History of the War Between Mexico and the United States* (reprint ed., New York: Burt Franklin, 1970), pp. 28–29; Ramón Alcaraz et al., *Apuntes para la Historia de la Guerra Entre México y los Estados Unidos* (México, D.F.: Tipografía de Manuel Payno, Hiho, 1848), pp. 27–28. For an excellent account of Slidell's mission, see Dennis Eugene Berge, "Mexican Response to United States Expansion, 1841–1848" (Ph.D. dissertation, University of California, 1965). Berge fully documents Slidell's arrogance, stating that at one point he even threatened war.

29. J. D. Richardson, *A Compilation of the Messages and Papers of the Presidents,* 10 vols. (Washington, D.C., 1905), 4:428–442, quoted in Arvin Rappaport, ed., *The War with Mexico: Why Did It Happen?* (Skokie, Ill: Rand McNally, 1964), p. 16. Mexican authorities had been requested by Taylor to leave the area; most impartial sources consider his refusal a hostile act, especially since he accompanied it by a naval blockade of Mexican supply ships servicing Matamoros. Troops clashed initially on April 26, 1846; but the first major confrontation did not take place until May 8, 1846, 12 miles north of Matamoros (Berge, pp. 196–297). In short, the movement of U.S. troops forced the war on Mexico (Brack, p. 146).

30. Grady McWhiney and Sue McWhiney, eds., *To Mexico with Taylor and Scott, 1845–1847* (Waltham, Mass.: Praisell, 1969), p. 3.

31. Brack, p. 2.

32. Glenn W. Price, *Origins of the War with Mexico: The Polk-Stockton Intrigue* (Austin: University of Texas Press, 1967), p. 7.

33. Rappaport, p. 16.

34. Rappaport, p. 16.

35. Justin H. Smith, *The War with Mexico,* vol. 2 (Gloucester, Mass.: Peter Smith, 1963), p. 310.

36. More recently it has become fashionable for political theorists to oversimplify the war by reducing it to the victory of one system of production and land tenure over a less progressive one. This kind of extreme economic determinism results in the same conclusions that Justin Smith arrived at. See Raúl A. Fernández, *The United States–Mexico Border: A Politico-Economic Profile* (Notre Dame, Ind.: University of Notre Dame Press, 1977), p. 7; Seymour V. Connor and Odie B. Faulk, *North America Divided: The Mexican War, 1846–1848* (New York: Oxford University Press, 1971).

37. Brack, p. 185.

38. Brack, p. 10, states that the general view has been that Mexico erred because it chose to fight rather than "negotiate."

39. Abiel Abbott Livermore, *The War with Mexico Reviewed* (Boston: American Peace Society, 1850), pp. 8, 11, 12.

40. T. B. Thorpe, *Our Army on the Rio Grande,* quoted in Livermore, p. 126.

41. Alfred Hoyt Bill, *Rehearsal for Conflict* (New York: Knopf, 1947), p. 122.

42. John Y. Simon, *The Papers of Ulysses S. Grant,* vol. 1 (London, England, and Amsterdam: Feffer & Simons, 1967), p. 102.

43. William Starr Meyers, ed., *The Mexican War Diary of General B. Clellan,* vol. 1 (Princeton: Princeton University Press, 1917), pp. 109–110.

44. Quoted in Livermore, pp. 148–149.

45. Smith, vol. 1, p. 550, n. 6.

46. Smith, vol. 2, p. 385, n. 18.

47. Livermore, p. 160.

48. Meyers, vol. 1, pp. 161–162.

49. Winfield Scott, *Memoirs of Lieut.-General Scott,* vol. 2 (New York: Sheldon, 1864), p. 392.

50. Samuel E. Chamberlain, *My Confessions* (New York: Harper & Row, 1956), p. 75.

51. Chamberlain, pp. 87, 88.

52. Chamberlain, p. 174.

53. Chamberlain, p. 174.

54. Chamberlain, pp. 176–177.

55. Stephen B. Oates, *"Los Diablos Tejanos:* The Texas Rangers," in Odie B. Faulk and Joseph A. Stout, Jr., eds., *The Mexican War: Changing Interpretations* (Chicago: Sage, 1973), p. 121.

56. Alonso Zabre, *Guide to the History of Mexico: A Modern Interpretation* (Austin, Tex.: Pemberton Press, 1969), p. 300.

57. Dexter Perkins and Glyndon G. Van Deusen, *The American Democracy: Its Rise to Power* (New York: Macmillan, 1964), p. 273.

58. Robert Self Henry, *The Story of the Mexican War* (New York: Ungar, 1950), p. 390.

59. See John D. P. Fuller, *The Movement for the Acquisition of All Mexico* (New York: DaCapo Press, 1969).

60. Letter from Commissioner Trist to Secretary Buchanan, Mexico, January 25, 1848, *Senate Executive Documents,* no. 52, p. 283.

61. Wayne Moquin et al., eds., *A Documentary History of the Mexican American* (New York: Praeger, 1971), p. 185.

62. Lynn I. Perrigo, *The American Southwest* (New York: Holt, Rinehart and Winston, 1971), p. 176.

63. Perrigo, p. 176.

64. *Compilation of Treaties in Force* (Washington, D.C.: Government Printing Office, 1899), p. 402, quoted in Perrigo, p. 176.

65. Weber, p. 14, states that the Supreme Court in *McKinney v. Saviego,* 1855, found that the treaty did not apply to Texas.

66. Antonio de la Peña y Reyes, *Algunos Documentos Sobre el Tratado de Guadalupe-Hidalgo* (México, D.F.: Sec de Rel. Ext., 1930), p. 159, quoted in Richard Gonzales, "Commentary on the Treaty of Guadalupe Hidalgo," in Feliciano Rivera, *A Mexican American Source Book* (Menlo Park, Calif.: Educational Consulting Associates, 1970), p. 185.

67. Leroy B. Hafen and Carl Coke Rister, *Western America,* 2nd ed. (Englewood Cliffs, N.J.: Prentice-Hall, 1950), p. 312.

chapter 2

Remember the Alamo: The Colonization of Texas

AN OVERVIEW

The Texas War was profitable. The Lone Star state had rich soil and an abundance of natural resources that helped the North American nation develop into a world industrial power. Texas's resources and easy access to Mexican labor accelerated capital accumulation throughout the nineteenth century. White Texans pushed Mexicans into South Texas, concentrating them and holding them in colonial bondage.

Blacks throughout most of the nineteenth century comprised Texas's largest nonwhite minority, generally living in slavery in the northeast and center of the state until the Civil War. Meanwhile, North Americans waged continual war against Native Americans. Violence spilled over into everyday relations among whites, and shootings became an everyday occurrence. The acceptance of violence encouraged depredations toward Mexicans and other minorities.

This chapter, on Texas, as well as the three that follow, on New Mexico, Arizona, and California, describes the process of colonial domination and Mexican resistance to colonialism. The conquest, as mentioned, set a pattern for racial antagonism and violence, justified by slogans such as "Remember the Alamo!" and myths about the Mexicans' treachery. North Americans had not fought their so-called war of independence to give Mexicans political or economic equality. From the beginning, laws and traditions limited Mexican access. The political system favored the rights of North Americans, and even Texas Mexicans who had fought for so-called independence like Juan Seguín were driven off their lands. The system favored the merchants and land speculators, and supported them with special police such as the Texas Rangers.

Colonial domination in Texas did not rely solely on the use of violence; the support of the majority was essential. The state maintained social control through the formation of an ideology that upheld the values and goals of the new society. It rationalized the privilege of commercial, agrarian, and other special interests. The state institutionalized racism and justified discrimination toward Mexicans. Institutions such as the schools and churches and myth makers such as historians reinforced and legitimated a multitiered society based on class and race.[1]

During the nineteenth century, in all probability, only a minority of the Texas Mexicans accepted North American hegemony. And many Mexicans resisted their underclass status. Their rebellion took the form of social banditry, mob revolts, and, often, as in the case of Juan Cortina, revolutionary action. Mexican nationalism, which flourished well into the twentieth century, was nurtured by their almost total exclusion from North American cultural and social institutions.

In the decades of the nineteenth century, Texas passed through its precapitalist stage. The frontier areas where Mexicans were concentrated had limited access to state or national markets. The role of Mexicans changed after the Civil War, when the freeing of Black labor and the spread of cotton increased demand for Mexican labor. The coming of the railroad in the late 1870s and 1880s accelerated the commercialization of agriculture and again increased the demand for Mexican labor.

BACKGROUND

Anglo-Mexican hostilities did not end after 1836. Mexico refused to recognize the Republic of Texas. The issue of the prisoners of war continued. Anglo-Texans kept Mexican soldiers in cages, where many died of starvation and where they suffered untold indignities.[2]

The boundary question also remained unanswered, with all the territory between the Río Grande and the Nueces River in dispute. Anglo-American immigration into the Republic of Texas increased, reaching 100,000 by the 1840s.

To escape violence, Mexicans moved farther South. Substantial numbers settled in the disputed territory. When hostilities erupted into war, South Texas became the gateway for Zachary Taylor's invasion of northern Mexico, and the Mexicans there suffered greatly from Anglo-American violence.

In the years before annexation to the United States, the neo-Texans actively warred on the Indians and stepped up their diplomatic front against Mexico. President Mirabeau B. Lamar dreamed of expanding the republic and, in 1839 and 1840, taking advantage of Mexico's problems with France, pressed for a settlement of the boundary question, offering Mexico $5 million if it would accept the Río Grande as the territorial border. In 1841 Lamar signed a treaty with Yucatán, a southeastern Mexican state, which was attempting to secede from Mexico. That same year Lamar sent the ill-fated Santa Fe Expedition into New Mexico in a scheme to add that area to the republic (see Chapter 3).

During the late 1830s tension increased along the border. Black Texan slaves crossed into Mexico to freedom, aggravating the situation. By 1855 some

4,000 fugitive slaves had run away to northern Mexico. Texas authorities valued the loss at $3.2 million and blamed Mexican authorities for encouraging slaves to escape. When owners demanded their return, the Mexican authorities refused. Anglo-Texans led several expeditions to recover runaways, greatly adding to border tensions. Their anger at authorities soon was generalized to include all Mexicans; they were all suspected of aiding the Blacks.[3] Tensions grew so strong in 1853 that the federal government stationed 2,176 soldiers in the state of Texas out of a standing national army of 10,417. Moreover, the Texas Constitution excluded from citizenship or ownership of property anyone who had refused to participate in the so-called revolution.[4] Naturally all Mexicans were presumed guilty of supporting the Mexican government which the North Americans had overthrown. In this environment, North Americans drove Mexicans out of eastern and central Texas, concentrating them in San Antonio and south Texas.

THE CREATION OF A DOMINANT CLASS

Before 1848, the valley of the Río Grande supported many thousands of cattle. Towns, such as Laredo, Guerrero, Mier, Camargo, and Reynosa, had been founded before 1755. Self-reliant communities raised corn, beans, melons, and vegetables and also tended sheep and goats. Commerce between the people on both sides of the river bound them together. Life for Mexicans in the other sections of Texas, while not exactly the same, closely resembled the life style of the Río Grande people. It was not the highly organized and profit-yielding structure Anglos were accustomed to and considered productive. Compared to the technological standards of the United States, the economy of the valley was underdeveloped.

As technological changes took place in the region's economy, class divisions became more marked within the Mexican community; the upper class more often aligned themselves with the new elite, either to maintain their privilege or to move vertically within the new system. In many cases rich Mexicans became brokers for the ruling elite and helped control the Mexican masses. In Brownsville men like Francisco Ytúrria, Jeremiah Galván, and the Spaniard José San Román amassed fortunes by allying themselves with Charles Stillman.[5]

Charles Stillman arrived in the valley in 1846, establishing a trading center in a cotton field across the river from Matamoros. Within four years trade with Mexico developed the town of Brownsville. This boom drove land prices up and attracted more Anglo-Americans.

Many newcomers were war veterans who still looked upon Mexicans as the losers. They felt that Mexicans benefited from the Anglo-American occupation. These men felt few qualms about taking property from them. Racial and nativist arguments justified their chicanery. At first, Stillman and others feared that the state of Texas would protect Mexican land claims, so they attempted to create their own state. They played on the Mexicans' regional feelings and many Mexicans supported the separatist movement.[6] The group enlisted powerful congressional allies such as Henry Clay and William Seward. Separatists were led by Richard King, James O'Donnell, Stillman, Captain Mifflin Kenedy, and Sam

Belden—all prominent members of the privileged elite. Their plans for secession proved unnecessary because it was soon evident that the state of Texas supported the Anglos' encroachments.

Stillman employed unscrupulous means to build up his annual earnings to $50,000. His trading post stood on land that did not belong to him; the land around Brownsville belonged to the descendants of Francisco Cavazos. After 1848 the Cavazos's title to the land was known as the *Espíritu Santo* Grant. Stillman wanted the land, so he devised a scheme to create confusion about ownership. Squatters moved onto the Cavazos's land and claimed veterans' as well as squatters' rights. Ignoring the fact that these actions violated the Treaty of Guadalupe Hidalgo and its Statement of Protocol, Stillman purchased the squatters' claims, as well as other questionable titles, refusing to deal with the Cavazos family and knowing he had the support of the troops at Fort Brown.

The Cavazos family fought Stillman in the courts. Judge Waltrous, the presiding magistrate, was a friend of Stillman. Moreover, many Anglos believed that the "whole *Espíritu Santo* Grant should be thrown out on the grounds that the owners were Mexicans." Stillman, however, had made many enemies who pressured the judge to decide against Stillman. On January 15, 1852, Judge Waltrous ruled in favor of the Cavazos family, validating their title to the land. Stillman had his lawyers, the firm of Basse and Horde, offer $33,000 for the grant, which in 1850 was evaluated at $214,000.[7] Stillman also made it known that he would appeal the decision, so the Cavazos family accepted the offer; the legal costs to defend the grant would have been prohibitive. Moreover, the Cavazos family knew that Stillman had influence in the political and judicial hierarchy of the state. After the sale the law firm transferred title to Stillman, yet he did not pay the $33,000; neither did the law firm, since it went bankrupt.

In the 1850s, the border became a battleground, with U.S. merchants waging an economic war against Mexico. Ranger "Rip" Ford estimates that as much as $10 to $14 million passed by way of the Río Grande annually.[8] Fierce competition existed between U.S. and Mexican merchants; violence increased. In 1855, along the Nueces River, 11 Mexicans were lynched. In 1857, in San Antonio, Mexican cartmen were literally run out of business by Anglo freighters who were angry because Mexicans carried goods more cheaply and quickly between Indianola and San Antonio; the freighters attacked the Mexican cartmen, murdering an estimated 75.[9] In the same year residents of Uvalde County passed a resolution prohibiting Mexicans from traveling through the county unless they had a passport. At Goliad the townspeople killed several Mexicans because they drove carts on public roads.[10]

In spite of the violence, border towns grew. Matamoros increased from 18,000 to 50,000 by the end of 1862 and became an international marketplace, with an estimated weekly volume of $2 million in trade during the 1850s.[11] The potential in profits from this growth attracted North American merchants, who formed associations to control trade and who openly engaged in smuggling, cattle rustling, and other crimes. In 1858 Governor Ramón Guerra of Tamaulipas created *La Zona Libre,* the Free Zone, within which Mexican merchants were exempt from federal tariffs (paying only small municipal taxes and an administrative fee). The purpose of *La Zona* was to combat rampant smuggling from which Anglo-American merchants made vast fortunes. The act exempted Matamoros, Reynosa, Camargo, Mier, Guerrero, and Nuevo León. In 1861 Mexican federal law extended the zone from the Gulf of Mexico to the Pacific within 12.5 miles of the border with the United States.[12]

U.S. merchants vehemently objected to trade advantages gained by Mexican merchants in Mexico. Brownsville business leaders applied political pressure on the U.S. government to intervene and to invade Mexico if necessary. They claimed that they lost from $2 to $6 million annually. They made numerous charges against Mexicans, claiming that they sponsored frequent raids into the United States.

U.S. merchants exploited the controversy; the claim of the "Mexican threat" justified maintenance of large contingents of U.S. troops along the border. The presence of forts contributed greatly to the economy of the region, for forts meant soldiers, horses, and government contracts. The additional revenues were a bonanza for the traders and cattle dealers along the border. A withdrawal of troops would have caused an economic depression for the valley merchants and ranchers. Increasingly, they relied on the forts and soldiers as a source of revenue which they protected at any cost.[13] Their presence also kept the Mexican majority in its place.

San Antonio, the Texas city with the largest Mexican population, remained a frontier outpost, limited in its potential capital growth by its remoteness from markets and lack of access to good transportation.[14] Tensions between North Americans and Mexicans stymied San Antonio's economic development. Houston and Galveston, more strategically located than the Alamo city, had better access to Texas, U.S., and world markets. What prosperity San Antonio experienced depended on Mexico. After 1844, the smuggling trade with Mexico grew, and San Antonio merchants profited handsomely. These traders also furnished the ranches and smaller towns around it with goods and supplies. During the Civil War, merchants amassed large fortunes running cotton through Mexico, making possible the expansion of the cotton industry as well as the city's commercial houses.

In the period between 1836 and the Civil War, Mexicans made up the majority of San Antonio's population. After the Civil War, Anglos, Germans, and French outnumbered the *Tejano*. The Mexican elite's prestige eroded and the newcomers monopolized the banks and commercial houses. Racial and social segregation increased as Mexicans became a minority. The process was completed in 1877, when the railroad linked San Antonio to U.S. markets, ending San Antonio's precapitalist stage.

Throughout Texas, the Mexicans' land and wealth quickly passed into the hands of an oligarchy. By 1860, Anglo-Americans completely dominated the Texas economy. A census taken in that year showed that 263 Texans owned over $100,000 in real property; 57 of these wealthy men lived in southeast Texas; only 2 were of Mexican extraction, and their holdings were in Cameron County. Bexar County had 7 wealthy Texans, not one of whom was a Mexican. Of significance is that the real property value and the personal worth of the 261 Texans was roughly in balance, while the 2 Mexicans' personal worth was far below their real wealth.[15] In spite of this, however, some affluent Mexicans continued to own medium-sized ranches and commercial houses.

The new political order promoted capital accumulation. Stillman's associate, Richard King, was the arch-robber baron of South Texas. His career is difficult to assess since his descendants control his records and have carefully censored them. Richard King amassed over 600,000 acres of land during his lifetime, and his widow increased the family holdings to over 1,000,000 acres.

The King Ranch Corporation commissioned a professional author and artist, Tom Lea, to eulogize Richard King in a two-volume work entitled *The King Ranch.* Lea portrays King as a tough-minded, two-fisted Horatio Alger who brought prosperity to South Texas. In the process Richard King, according to Lea, never harmed anyone, except in self-defense. Lea denies charges against King and ignores the allegations that he unscrupulously drove out small Mexican ranchers to steal their land and was brutal to those who opposed him. When referring to Mexican resentment toward Anglos like King, Lea writes it off as jealousy.[16]

Richard King was born in 1824 in New York City of poor Irish immigrant parents. As a youth he ran away to sea, eventually becoming a pilot on a steamboat, mastered by Mifflin Kenedy. The two men became fast friends. The Mexican-American War took them to the Río Grande, and after the war they stayed and cashed in on the boom. King ran a flophouse at Boca del Río and later bought a vessel from the U.S. government and went into the freighting business. Much of his work consisted of smuggling goods to the Mexican ranchers and miners in northern Mexico.

Although Charles Stillman was at first the principal competitor of King and Kenedy, in 1850 they joined him. The association prospered, soon monopolizing the waterborne trade into northern Mexico. In 1852 King purchased the *Santa Gertrudis* Grant. Title to 15,500 acres cost him less than 2¢ an acre. King also entered into a land-purchasing partnership with Gideon K. Lewis, later buying Lewis's shares.

During the Civil War King was pro-South and profited from the war trade by selling cattle, horses, and mules to the troops. He continued his freighting operations, running Union blockades by flying the Mexican flag. In 1866 Stillman left the border area, and King and Kenedy took over many of his operations.

In the 1870s, the Mexican Border Commission reported that much of the border friction was caused by Texas thieves. The report claimed that Mexicans raided the Nueces area to retrieve their stolen cattle and that Richard King branded calves "that belonged to his neighbors' cows."[17] The report indicted King, charging that he did not respect the law and that he employed known cattle rustlers such as Tomás Vásquez and Fernando López to steal cattle and horses from Mexicans. Other prominent Texans such as Thadeus Rhodes, a justice of the peace in Hidalgo County, were also accused of making huge profits from cattle rustling.[18]

During this period King became president of the Stock Raisers Association of Western Texas, formed by Texas ranchers to protect their "interests." They organized a private militia, called minute companies, to fight so-called Mexican bandits. When the minute companies disbanded, Ranger Captain Leander McNeely took over the fight for them. In 1875, McNeely violated a federal injunction prohibiting him to enter Mexican territory, and, with his Rangers, he crossed the border, torturing and murdering four innocent Mexicans. King rewarded McNeely's men, paying them $500 in appreciation for their services.

King made his money as a smuggler; he associated with a band of cutthroats and, in fact, played a leading role in their operations. He was accused of cattle rustling and of murdering small landowners to get their property. Lastly, King paid bonuses to the Rangers in appreciation for their services.

During the 1860s the size of the Mexican population declined in relation to Anglos. In 1860 about 12,000 Mexicans versus just over 600,000 Anglos and 182,000 Blacks lived in Texas. Slave labor lessened dependence on Mexican workers. After the Civil War, a number of economic developments took place. The emancipation of the slave changed the economy of Texas and destabilized its captive labor force. Cattle raising boomed during the 1860s and 1870s, spurred by transportation improvements and demand for beef on the domestic and world markets. Demand for sheep increased and by the 1880s cotton production reached an all-time high.

The lack of a stable workforce caused a restructuring of Texas agriculture and, by 1870, sharecropping became common (in sharecropping, an owner lends land to tenants, who usually gave the landlord back one-half to two-thirds of the crop). The expansion of the railroads facilitated the rush of Anglos to Texas; soon even some border counties had equal Mexican and Anglo populations.[19] Finally, by 1890 the open range for cattle declined as mechanization and irrigation expanded agriculture. The changed production methods increased the demand for Mexican labor, and Mexicans returned to Texas in large numbers.

The abolition of slavery changed the attitude of many planters toward Mexicans. Mexican workers, now more valuable, were used as surplus labor to depress wages of the Black pickers, who were now wage earners. Planters on the Colorado River, near Bastrop in San Marcos and Navidad, Lavaca County, where Mexican labor had been threatened and expelled before the Civil War, were now desperate for Mexican labor.[20] By the 1880s Mexican migration to Texas from Mexico accelerated and internally it began to fan out.

POLITICS OF GENDER

Social relations between Mexicans and the dominant society became more rigid with the passage of time. Contact often depended upon class or gender. Intermarriage between the native aristocracy and the white ruling elite was not uncommon, both because of the lack of white women and for control of the native population. The colonial situation also led to sexual subjugation through prostitution.

Intermarriage between Anglos and Mexicans offers an interesting paradox. Although Mexicans were considered a mongrel and inferior race, the whites were not above marrying them. Captain Mifflin Kenedy, for instance, married the wealthy widow Petra Vela de Vidal, who reportedly helped him gain the support of a large number of Mexicans whose vote was essential to establish his power.

During the nineteenth century, it became popular to speak about the "dark-eyed *señoritas.*" Dr. Arnoldo De León, in his superb work "White Racial Attitudes Toward Mexicanos in Texas, 1821–1920," writes: "There existed at least some indication that Mexican women could have been accepted by whites in Texas under certain circumstances without reservation." In some instances Mexican women were compared favorably to the ideal southern belle, and especially *Las Güeras* (the blonds) were praised. These light-skinned Mexicans were described as of pure Spanish descent from northern Spain with "faultlessly white" flesh and blue eyes.[21] As more Anglos moved into the area, intermarriage declined and racially mixed couples became subject to social disapproval and eventually persecution.[22]

As in the case of the Black in the South, the dominant society fabricated sexual myths about Mexicans. According to De León, "Texas history is replete with accounts (by white men) suggesting that, if Mexican women easily lapsed from propriety, they especially coveted company (and intimacy) of white men."[23] This attitude is natural to privileged classes, who may use the sexual act not only to assert dominance but also to seek reassurance of their self-concept of superiority.

Only a few serious studies have been made of the role of the Mexican woman on the frontier. Jane Dysart, in "Mexican Women in San Antonio, 1830–1860: The Assimilation Process," deals with the question of intermarriage, and her conclusions reinforce De León's. She describes the woman as active participants in society. For instance, she states that during the colonial period Mexican women played a much greater role in government than generally portrayed by historians. On the frontier, women had much more freedom than in established areas, where traditions and social constraints demanded a less visible profile. According to Professor Dysart, Josefa Becerra Seguín "drilled the troops stationed in San Antonio during her husband's frequent absences." In spite of the "liberating influences of the frontier, the role of the Mexican woman," was largely that of a pawn.[24]

Distinctions were made between the light-skinned Mexican women and those of the poorer classes, and skin color often determined social status. In a letter to his cousin John Donelson Coffee, Jr., dated January 20, 1855, R. W. Brahan, Jr., referred to contacts with women of Castilian blood whose "parents avowed their determination to have them wed to genuine Americans."[25] Brahan dwelt on Mexican women's color. Of some he said, "Their complexion is very fair," but he described poorer Mexican women as "styled greasers." His conditional racism was evident: "many of these 'greasers,' of fine figures & good features, the color of a mulatto, are kept by votaries of sensuality."

Dysart underscores the class nature of intermarriage in Texas and more specifically San Antonio. For instance, between 1837 and 1860,

906 Mexican women wed Mexican men, while only 88 chose to marry Anglos. But of those Anglo-Mexican unions almost half, or 42, involved women from high status families. The significance of those interracial marriages goes far beyond their numbers, since at least one daughter from every *rico* family in San Antonio married an Anglo.[26]

Only five unions between Mexican males and Anglo females were verified.

Intermarriage with Anglos was based on "economic necessity" more than on any other single factor. The Mexican family received some legal protection and freedom from the stigma of disloyalty, while the Anglo got a wife and property, since, under the law, daughters inherited property on an equal basis with their brothers. Intermarriage accelerated "Americanization," and although youngsters maintained strong Mexican influences "during their early childhood," they strongly identified with the father's ethnic group. For instance, the daughters of Antonio Navarro became Methodists, which is in itself an indication of assimilation, and affiliation with English-speaking Roman Catholic parishes by the mixed couples was common.[27]

This is not to say that the *ricos* escaped racial discrimination through intermarriage and assimilation, for even rich *Tejanos* were victims of racism. The majority of San Antonio Mexicans, even if Americanized, were not treated as equals. "Only the women and children with Anglo surnames, light skins, and wealth had a reasonable chance to escape the stigma attached to their Mexican ancestry."[28] The chance offered by intermarriage was perhaps the only one available to Mexican women, but even that decision was made by the male head of the family based on class interests and material factors that operated in an Anglo-dominant society.

The average Mexican woman, however, did not take part in the debate as to her value as a commodity. The darker she appeared, the stronger the racism. The case of Chepita or, as sometimes called, Chipita Rodríguez of San Patricio, Texas, is an example of frontier justice. She arrived in San Patricio with her father in 1836. Shortly afterward the father was murdered and Chipita began a relationship with a cowboy who abandoned her and took their son. In 1863, an errant cowboy accompanied by a younger man arrived in San Patricio. While at Chipita's, the two men argued. Chipita found the older man dead. Thinking that her son had murdered him, she attempted to hide the body by dumping it in the river.[29] An all-white jury found Chipita guilty of murder, recommending leniency because of her advanced age and a doubt as to whether she had murdered the cowboy. Chipita was hanged.

CONTROLLING MEXICANS

As elsewhere in the Southwest, the railroad played a key role in the economic development of San Antonio after the Civil War. In the 1870s, San Antonio merchants and business leaders financed a line between their city and Galveston. By 1885, two more lines passed through the city, connecting north Texas and Mexico. The railroad encouraged the development of a cattle trade and brought tourists to the city. Between 1865 and 1885, San Antonio grew to 37,000, a 208 percent increase. Unfortunately for Mexicans, the majority of the newcomers were Anglos, who, in turn, ostracized them.

San Antonio, a mercantile outpost for the U.S. commercial empire, based its prosperity on beef packing, brewing, tourism, and a military installation. By the mid-1880s Bryan Callagan II organized a political machine in San Antonio.

Callagan, whose mother was from an elite Mexican family, spoke fluent Spanish, and built his power base on the Mexican wards. Mexicans supported the machine because it insured *some* protection, patronage, and indirect political participation.

In South Texas, machine politics also became popular after the Civil War. The machine handed out patronage—for example, city jobs, contracts, franchises, and public utilities and, in the case of poor Mexicans, gave them a primitive form of welfare. The machine won elections by turning out the Mexican vote. In the border towns, the machine also controlled the custom houses. The indiscriminate use of the Texas Rangers bolstered the machine's political hegemony.

Characteristically, the poor had few alternatives. In San Antonio the *ricos* rarely sided with the masses of Mexicans. They displayed attitudes and interests based on their class and even emphasized racial differences between themselves and the lower classes, stating that the poor did not belong to the white race. Many old families openly sympathized with the Ku Klux Klan. The stronghold of the Mexican elite centered in San Antonio where Alejo Ruiz, Vicente Martínez, John Barrera, Rafael Ytúrris, and José Antonio Navarro allied themselves with ultraconservative elements. After the Civil War they even campaigned on behalf of northern Democrats, advocating the supremacy of the white race. They seemed oblivious to persecution of their fellow Mexicans[30] and actively supported the Anglo ruling class by brokering the Mexican vote.

The violence which had characterized earlier relations between the two groups increased in the 1870s and 1880s with the arrival of larger numbers of Anglos in Texas. During the 1880s and 1890s, lynchings continued to be commonplace. Mexicans resisted. In August 1883 Captain Juan Cardenas in San Antonio headed a protest march on San Pedro Park because Mexicans could not use the dance floor. Protestors attacked Fred Kerble, the lessee, because he had yielded to town demands excluding Mexicans. The next year Mexicans fled the Fort Davis area to escape daily lynchings; the townsfolk encouraged the exodus, hoping that it would continue until the last Mexican left the district.[31] Many Mexicans were forced to seek the protection of some of the local Anglo powers, who treated them as serfs. For instance, in Cameron County in South Texas, Colonel Stephen Powers built a powerful political machine which later his partner Jim Wells inherited.[32] They controlled several counties from 1882 to 1920. They always helped their Mexicans to vote, transporting them to the polls and marking their ballots for them. Professor De León states that in the border areas whites employed Mexicans to cross into Mexico to recruit people whom the bosses paid to vote for selected candidates. Hundreds would be imported, marched to the county clerk's office, and naturalized for the modest sum of 25¢.[33]

Wells based his political power on his ability to deliver the Mexican vote. Wells went to baptisms, marriages, and funerals and played godfather to the Mexican people. By the early 1920s he lost control, but the machine stayed intact, with power divided among his lieutenants. He died in 1922. Wells had shared his power with the Klebergs, who owned the King Ranch. Ed Vela from Hidalgo and the Guerra family, which controlled Starr County, were among his Chicano lieutenants.[34]

The Guerras had one of the best organizations in the valley and with the Yzaguirre and Ramírez families owned most of Starr County. The founder of the line was José Alejandro Guerra, a surveyor for the Spanish crown in 1767. He had received *porciones* in the valley which his heir Manuel Guerra inherited. Manuel started a mercantile house in Roma, Texas, in 1856. He married Virginia Cox, daughter of a Kentuckian father and a Mexican mother. Guerra, a banker and rancher, became Jim Wells's right arm. For political favors he exchanged credit and teacher certificates. Guerra became the Democratic party of Starr County. The Republican party, which was nationally the more progressive of the two parties, opposed him.

The machine was ruthless in its pursuits. In 1888 W. W. Shelby, leader of the Blues (the Democrats) and boss of Duval County, lost an election to Lino Hinojosa, leader of the Reds (the Republicans), by a two to one margin; however, Hinojosa was not allowed to take office because he did not speak English. Domingo Garza ran against Shelby in 1900, but just before the election Garza was thrown into jail on suspicion of murder; charges were later dropped, but he lost the election. In 1906 Shelby resigned and the machine appointed Deodora Guerra.[35]

The Guerras controlled the two counties into the 1940s. Politics in the valley were untouched by state authorities. It was common knowledge that, up to the 1940s, if someone raised the ire of the bosses, an assassin was employed from the interior of Mexico.[36]

Even Judge J. T. Canales of Brownsville, a maverick, often cooperated with the machine. He served in the state legislature from 1909 to 1911, in 1917, and in 1919 and served as a county judge in 1914. Along with Alonso Perales, Manuel González, Ben Garza, Andrés de Luna, and Dr. George I. Sánchez, he represented the progressive Chicano movement of the times.

At one point Canales quarrelled with the Guerras in Starr County. In 1933 he organized a new party to oppose them. While he addressed a crowd in Río Grande City, a shooting broke up the rally. Two of Guerra's men were arrested, tried in Corpus Christi, and sentenced to 25 years. They were returned to Starr pending an appeal. The Guerras allowed them to escape. Five members of Canales's new party were deputized, tracked them down, and killed the escapees. The Guerras had them arrested. They were tried in Austin, where the Guerras aided the prosecution and Canales the defense. "After an eloquent plea of self-defense, in which Canales wept in the court room, the five men were acquitted."[37] This political opposition was, however, rare.

A recent work by Evan Anders attributes machine politics, in part, to the history of the Spanish *patron–peon* relationship. Anders, however, oversimplifies the phenomenon, since "boss rule" in South Texas resembled political machines in eastern U.S. cities. An important difference between bossism in South Texas and the East was that the machine had fewer constitutional restraints. Moreover, Texas-Mexicans had limited access to organizational alternatives such as trade unions.[38]

Machine politics often involved the more affluent Mexicans, giving them a stake in the system and a measure of upward mobility and protection. Frequently, affluent Mexicans acquired power because of their influence over the Mexican vote, while, at the same time, the brokers gained prestige with the Mexicans themselves because they had access to patronage and the ability to intervene occasionally on behalf of poor Mexicans. In a few cases, the Mexican brokers prevented North American extremes.

North American reformers, blaming Mexicans for corrupt machines, attempted to end bossism by disenfranchising them. In 1890 a constitutional amendment was passed requiring foreigners "to file for citizenship six months before the election." In 1902, reformers passed a poll tax. Both these measures failed to limit the power of the bosses. The Jim Wells machine remained intact to the 1920s and its demise can in part be attributed to Wells's failure to check the extreme violence of the Texas Rangers in South Texas in 1915 and 1917.[39]

The political situation in Mexico added to borderland tensions. The border served as a haven for revolutionaries who actively campaigned against Mexican dictator Porfirio Díaz. One such revolutionary, Catarino Garza, a journalist, traveling salesman, and former Mexican consul at St. Louis, Missouri, in 1885 organized *mutualistas* (mutual aid societies) in the valley. Garza exhorted Mexicans to unite and fight racism.[40] In Corpus Christi Garza accused a U.S. customs inspector, Victor Sebree, of assassinating Mexican prisoners who actively opposed Díaz. The two met during an election at Río Grande City in 1888, and Sebree shot and wounded Garza. Mexicans, incensed because nothing happened to Sebree, threatened to lynch him, but the local U.S. army post commander intervened. Garza recovered and continued his activities. Four years later he was ready to launch an invasion of Mexico.

Anglo-American authorities supported the dictatorship of Díaz and cooperated with his regime to suppress any Mexican revolutionary movement originating on the U.S. side of the border. The Garza Movement was centered in Starr and Duvall counties, 100 miles from the Río Grande and Fort Ringgold. On three different occasions in 1891 Garza crossed into Mexico and attempted to liberate it from Díaz. Twice his small bands reached Nuevo León, where Mexican troops turned them back. Garza, who had about 1,000 followers and was reported to have widespread support, was pursued by the U.S. cavalry, sheriffs, and marshals.[41]

Mexican authorities denounced Garza in the spring of 1891 and they called Mexican inhabitants of the valley "ignorant" and unscrupulous." Military authorities spread hysteria by asking for an additional 10,000 troops. U. S. authorities claimed that Garza had cost them $2 million.[42]

Newspaper accounts inflamed residents, spreading rumors that Mexicans had armed themselves. They rekindled old fears of a Mexican revolt, and wrote that General Juan Cortina, the scourge of the valley during the 1860s and 1870s, was going to return to Texas from Mexico City to lead the revolution.[43] (See pages 43–47.) The *New York Times* reported:

> A great sensation has been created by the telegraphic announcement from the City of Mexico that General Juan Cortina, one of the greatest revolutionary leaders of Mexico, has been arrested and imprisoned in the San Juan Ulúa Prison by order of President Diaz for attempting to incite another revolutionary

uprising against the Government. The City of Matamoras [sic] is General Cortina's old home. He was, twenty-five years ago, a desperate and greatly-feared man in Mexico. He ruled the Rio Grande border country from Laredo to the mouth of the river. . . . His influence was so great that he could inaugurate a powerful revolutionary movement against the Mexican Government by a single pronunciamiento with his signature attached. His exploits at the time of the Civil War caused the United States Government to lose many thousands of dollars. When President Diaz's revolution ended in success, General Cortina was summoned to the City of Mexico . . . [Cortina] has been kept in constant surveillance by President Diaz ever since to prevent him from inciting further revolutions.[44]

The Garza revolution ended, but opposition to Díaz kept the border unsettled. Federal authorities stationed large numbers of armed troops at the border, ensuring that Mexicans would stay in their place.

DIVIDE AND CONQUER

In August 1894, Blacks attacked Mexicans at Beeville, Texas. Growers encouraged antagonism between different ethnic groups. They brought Mexicans into Beeville to drive down wages of Blacks and to create a labor surplus. Blacks blamed the Mexicans, rather than the growers, for their depressed state and raided the Mexican quarter. Throughout this period considerable tension developed between Mexicans and Blacks. The federal government encouraged this antagonism by stationing Black soldiers in Mexican areas, using them to control the Mexican population. At Fort McIntosh in Laredo, the 10th Cavalry, a Black unit, participated in suppressing Mexicans.[45]

By the late 1880s both Populists and Republicans campaigned for the disenfranchisement of all Mexicans. The Populist, or People's, party, while fighting the growth of agribusiness and demanding reforms in government, led attacks on Mexicans, blaming them for the decline of small farms and the demise of rural America. In San Antonio A. L. Montalvo vowed to fight for civil rights and condemned the Populists for attempting to reduce the Texas-Mexicans "to the category of pack animals, who may be good enough to work, but not good enough to exercise their civil rights."[46]

Many of the interests of the People's party were identical to the Mexicans', but the party regarded them as its enemy. In Texas Populists had made an effort to forge an alliance with Blacks, while attacking Mexicans and threatening to deport them. They viewed Mexicans as a threat because the Democratic party had manipulated their vote. Local Anglo leaders through their political machine corralled Mexicans and through fraud, corruption, and force kept this vote in line. Instead of organizing progressive elements within the Mexican community and attempting to destroy the machines, the Populists made Mexicans their scapegoats, using crass racist arguments.[47]

The 1880 census counted about 43,000 Mexicans in Texas. Most lived in the southern part, where they remained the overwhelming majority until large numbers of North Americans arrived in the 1890s. The Euroamerican newcomers formed their own neighborhoods, strictly segregating Mexicans in the older parts of town.[48] The arrival of more North Americans strengthened that race's control of the political, social and economic institutions. Generally, because Mexicans were too poor to mount independent political movements, they had to rely on their Mexican bosses for whatever influence they could achieve. An exception was in Laredo, where Mexicans, known as *guaraches* (sandals), opposed the Anglos, known as *botas* (boots).

The Anglo still considered the Mexicans as aliens and made attempts through the courts to exclude them from citizenship. In 1896 Ricardo Rodríguez was denied his final naturalization papers. The authorities argued in court that Rodríguez was not white or African and "therefore not capable of becoming an American citizen." They wanted to keep "Aztecs or aboriginal Mexicans" from naturalization. Rodríguez won his case based on the Treaty of Guadalupe Hidalgo.[49]

In January 1896, authorities found the mutilated body of Aureliano Castellón. Castellón made the mistake of courting Emma Stanfield, a white girl, over the objections of her brothers. He had been shot eight times and his body burned. On June 30, 1896, the *San Antonio Express* published a note entitled "Slaughter the *Gringo*" signed by 25 Mexicans. Allegedly, the signers threatened to kill only *gringos* and Germans, exempting Blacks, Italians, and Cubans.

Two years later, the Spanish-American War caused general panic spread among Anglos, who believed that Mexicans would ally themselves with Spain and begin border raids. In places such as San Diego, Texas, Anglos formed minutemen companies to "protect" themselves. The uprisings never took place and Anglos soon learned that Mexicans had little empathy for Spain, but the situation gave racists an excuse to persecute all Mexicans.

The White Cap movement of South Texas in the late 1890s aggravated conditions. (Texas white caps should not be confused with the Mexican white caps of New Mexico; see Chapter 3.) Texas white caps were an Anglo-American vigilante group. They demanded that white planters refuse to rent to Blacks and Mexicans and fire Mexican field hands. White cap activity centered in Wilson, Gonzales, and DeWitt counties, where they terrorized Mexicans.[50]

According to Dr. De León, violence without guilt raged during this period: "Astonishing numbers of Mexicans in the nineteenth century fell victim to lynch law and cold-blooded deaths at the hands of whites who thought nothing of killing Mexicans."[51] Social attitudes reinforced by violence froze Mexicans into a caste system which facilitated exploitation of their labor in the twentieth century.

The state population increased from a million in the early 1870s to just over 3 million at the turn of the century. By 1900, Texas-Mexicans still largely concentrated in rural areas, counted about 70,000; unofficially the number was closer to 165,000.[52] Mexicans numbered less than 5 percent of Texas. Blacks were the state's largest minority; however, Mexicans would soon challenge Blacks for that position. The railroad and the fencing of the range had "domesticated [southern Texas] into a uniform pattern in town, farm, and ranch of Anglo rule over an Hispano population."[53] Changes in the last two decades of the nineteenth century, along with the spread of cotton and commercial agriculture, set the stage for the next century and the modernization of the Texas economy. Organized land companies and irrigation projects put enormous tracts of land into production, increasing the demand for Mexican labor.

THE HISTORIAN AS AN AGENT OF SOCIAL CONTROL

Throughout the nineteenth century, Texas had a history of violence. The system, however, condoned more extreme forms of terror toward Mexicans, since it considered them foreigners and not entitled to equal protection under the law. Authorities favored the North American and, in an altercation between the two races, the Mexican was presumed at fault. A mindset developed that Mexicans did not count. In South Texas, while the Mexican population outnumbered the North American, the latter controlled politics and the land. This situation alarmed the Anglo minority, who often feared a Mexican rebellion much the same as the Southern plantation owner feared a slave revolt. Therefore, Mexicans knew that any form of confrontation would be harshly punished.

The state did not rely solely on violence to control Mexicans. Class divisions in the *Tejano* community often led to the elites' cooperation with North American power brokers. The state's ability to manipulate information and popular forms of "common sense" spread confusion among Mexicans. From the beginning, the historian played a key role in blaming the victim and distorting the reasons for the violence. Instead of portraying them as brutal men who used Gestapo-like tactics, historians made heroes out of the Texas Rangers.

Walter Prescott Webb, until his death in March 1963, was the most respected professor on the history faculty of the University of Texas at Austin. Past president of the American Historical Association, he wielded tremendous influence among scholars and graduate students. His most important works were *The Texas Rangers, The Great Plains, Divided We Stand,* and *The Great Frontier;* in addition, he wrote countless articles.

Webb's writings impacted on the historiography of the West. Recently, however, some scholars have begun to question many of his conclusions, implying that they are racist. Among these scholars are Américo Paredes, Llerena B. Friend, and Larry McMurtry.

McMurtry writes of Webb's *The Texas Rangers:* "The flaw in the book is a flaw of attitude. Webb admired the Rangers inordinately, and as a consequence the book mixes homage with history in a manner one can only think sloppy. His own facts about the Rangers contradict again and again his characterization of them as 'quiet, deliberate, gentle' men."[54] McMurtry then underscores some of the inconsistencies. He faults Webb's description of the Rangers's role in the siege of Mexico City: "A sneak thief stole a handkerchief from them. They shot him." One Texas Ranger was shot, and the Rangers retaliated by killing 80 Mexicans. McMurtry concludes: "[These] are hardly the actions of men who can accurately be called gentle." McMurtry also questions Webb's description of Ranger Captain L. H. McNeely as a "flame of courage."[55] McMurtry states of McNeely, "He did a brilliant, brave job, and his methods were absolutely ruthless." McNeely tortured Mexicans and shot them down in cold blood. On November 19, 1875, he crossed the border with 31 men and attacked a ranch that he thought housed Mexican troops. He was mistaken, and he murdered a number of innocent Mexican workers. When he discovered his error, he merely rode off. Webb's apology for the Rangers is that "affairs on the border cannot be judged by standards that hold elsewhere." McMurtry responds: "Why they can't is a question apologists for the Rangers have yet to answer. Torture is torture, whether inflicted in Germany, Algiers, or along the Nueces Strip. The Rangers, of course, claimed that their end justified their means, but people who practice torture always claim that."[56]

Webb had become a Ranger by proxy. And, while he must have recognized the brutality of these violent men, he closed his eyes to it. McMurtry writes:

> The important point to be made about *The Texas Rangers* is that Webb was writing not as an historian of the frontier, but as a symbolic frontiersman. The tendency to practice symbolic frontiersmanship might almost be said to characterize the twentieth century Texan, whether he be an intellectual, a cowboy, a businessman, or a politician.[57]

McMurtry's work explores the effect of this frontiersmanship. Although it would be unfair to suggest that Webb intentionally distorted history, his works were, nevertheless, racist.

By the end of Webb's long career, his viewpoint of the Chicano had changed. When he published an article, in *True West* in October 1962, "The Bandits of Las Cuevas," he received a letter from Enrique Mendiola of Alice, Texas, whose grandfather owned the ranch that the Rangers, under McNeely, mistakenly attacked. Mendiola stated:

> Most historians have classified these men as cattle thieves, bandits, etc. This might be true of some of the crowd, but most of them, including General Juan Flores, were trying to recover their own cattle that had been taken away from them when they were driven out of their little ranches in South Texas. They were driven out by such men as Mifflin Kenedy, Richard King and [the] Armstrongs.[58]

Webb's reply to Mendiola was revealing:

> To get a balanced account, one would need the records from the south side of the river, and these are simply not available. . . . The unfortunate fact is that the Mexicans were not as good at keeping records as were the people on this side. . . . I have often wished that the Mexicans, or some one who had their confidence, would have gone among them and got their stories of the raids and counter raids. I am sure that these stories would take on a different color and tone.[59]

Mexicans did, in fact, record their story in *corridos* (ballads). The *Corridos* glorified the deeds of men who stood up to the oppressors and are still sung in the Río Grande Valley and in other places in the Southwest. *Corridos* to Juan

Cortina were composed when he resisted the *gringo* in the 1850s.[60] From those early times to the present, *corridos* have recorded the Mexicans' struggle against racism and injustice. They present a uniform view of the Rangers; to the Mexican, on the other hand, they were assassins, who were viewed in much the same way as Jews see the Gestapo.

The Anglo-American view of the Texas Ranger was expressed by Rip Ford, a Ranger himself, who wrote: "A Texas Ranger can ride like a Mexican, trail like an Indian, shoot like a Tennesseean, and fight like the very devil!"[61] T. R. Fehrenbach, in 1968, wrote in his *Lone Star: A History of Texas and the Texans:*

> To fight Indians and Mexicans, Ranger leaders had to learn to think like both, or at least, to understand what Mexicans and Indians feared. The collision between the Anglo-American and the Mexican on the southern frontier was inevitable, but some aspects of this were unfortunate. Contact did not improve either race; it seemed to strengthen and enhance the vices of both. The Ranger arrived with instinctive Teutonic directness, preferring the honest smash of the bullet to the subtlety of the knife. But against the Mexican, bluntness turned into brutality, because it was almost impossible for the Protestant Anglo-Celt to understand the Hispanic mind. Impatient with Mexican deviousness, the Ranger reacted with straight force. But the Mexican, to keep the records straight, slipped from deviousness to outright treachery; history records that Mexicans killed more Texans by the result of parleys than on all the battlefields. Each side felt themselves justified because of the incomprehensible and despised cultural attributes of the foe. The Rangers seemed barbaric Nordics, void of all gentlemanly intrigue or guile; they saw the Mexicans as treacherous, lying people, who never wanted to do the obvious, which was to call their play and fight.[62]

Webb, who was even less objective in his analysis of racial differences between the Rangers and the Mexicans, wrote of the Ranger:

> When we see him at his daily task of maintaining law, restoring order, and promoting peace—even though his methods be vigorous—we see him in the proper setting, a man standing alone between a society and its enemies.[63]

Conversely, he wrote of Mexicans:

> Without disparagement it may be said that there is a cruel streak in the Mexican nature, or so the history of Texas would lead one to believe. This cruelty may be a heritage from the Spanish of the Inquisition; it may, and doubtless should, be attributed partly to the Indian blood.[64]

This type of reasoning justified the Rangers's violence to many Anglo-Americans; the "vigorous methods" were necessary in dealing with "savage adversaries."

Américo Paredes gives another perspective of the Rangers. He described them as representatives of Anglo ranchers and merchants who controlled the valley of the Río Grande. Their commitment was to keep order for an Anglo oligarchy. Violence served the interests of Texas capitalists as a means of maintaining a closed social structure that excluded Mexicans from all but the lowest levels. They recruited gunslingers who burned with a hatred of Mexicans, shooting first and asking questions afterward. Paredes writes: "That the Rangers stirred up more trouble than they put down is an opinion that has been expressed by less partisan sources."[65]

Paredes expressed how Mexicans felt. His research was based on oral traditions and documents, and his findings refuted Webb's distortion of reality. For example, concerning the murder of the Cerdas, a prominent family near Brownsville in 1902, Paredes wrote:

> The Cerdas were prosperous ranchers near Brownsville, but it was their misfortune to live next to one of the "cattle barons" who was not through expanding yet. One day three Texas Rangers came down from Austin and "executed" the elder Cerda and one of his sons as cattle rustlers. The youngest son fled across the river, and thus the Cerda ranch was vacated. Five months later the remaining son, Alfredo Cerda, crossed over to Brownsville. He died the same day, shot down by a Ranger's gun.[66]

Paredes's report was based not only on official sources but on eyewitness accounts. Marcelo Garza, Sr., of Brownsville, a respected businessman, told Paredes that a Ranger shot unarmed Alfredo, stalking him "like a wild animal."

Webb's version was based on Ranger sources. According to Webb, Baker, a Ranger, surprised Ramón De La Cerda branding a calf that belonged to the King Ranch. De La Cerda shot at Baker and the Ranger shot back, killing Ramón in self-defense. The Ranger was cleared at an inquest, but Mexicans did not accept this verdict and disinterred De La Cerda's body and conducted their own inquest. They found

> "evidence" [quotes are Webb's] . . . to the effect that De La Cerda had been dragged and otherwise maltreated. Public sentiment was sharply divided. . . . The findings of the secret inquest, together with wild rumors growing out of it, only served to inflame the minds of De La Cerda's supporters.[67]

Again, Webb's sources were compromised, since he based his conclusion that the people were being agitated on Ranger reports. Late in his career, Webb admitted that a double standard of justice operated for Mexicans and Anglos. Therefore, it was natural that they should question findings of the inquest, especially the facts behind this particular shooting. The Cerdas were a well-known and respected family whose land the Kings coveted.

More telling is Webb's quote as to who posted bail for Baker: "Captain Brooks reported that Baker made bail in the sum of ten thousand dollars, and that he was supported by such people as the Kings, Major John Armstrong— McNeely's lieutenant—and the Lyman Brothers."[68]

Further, Webb did not question the financial support of the Kings for the Rangers. Shortly afterward Baker shot Alfredo. The Cerda affair exposed the use of violence to take over land and then legalize murder through the court system.

It was not an isolated incident; it represented the activity of Rangers throughout the century.

During the uprising led by Juan Cortina, hundreds, if not thousands, of Mexicans were victimized because they were relatives of partisans or because they were suspected of being associated with revolutionaries. Rangers, operating independently of the traditional law enforcement agencies, were proud of their efficiency in dealing with Mexicans.

THE REVOLT OF "CHENO" CORTINA

Mexicans did not accept North American rule and they hardly felt like a liberated people. *Tejanos,* while taking regional pride in their state, continued to feel more affinity racially and culturally with Mexicanos south of the Río Bravo than with the aggressive North Americans who called them "greasers." Denied the opportunity to acquire property, to exercise political control over their own lives, and to maintain their rights within the society, many resisted and took to the highway. Added to this were conditions of lawlessness that prevailed among all groups on the frontier, the disruptions of the Mexican and Civil wars, and the often corrupt nature of the administration of justice. These circumstances made attempts to survive outside the law inevitable.[69]

E. J. Hobsbawm, in his *Primitive Rebels: Studies in Archaic Forms of Social Movement in the 19th and 20th Centuries,* sheds light on the *bandidos'* motives. Taking Mexican banditry in the context of history and the conquered status of Mexicans in the Southwest, it represented "in one sense . . . a primitive form of organized social protest, perhaps the most primitive we know."[70] Often Mexicans reacted to discrimination by committing antisocial acts against the society that victimized them. Society called these Mexicans bandits, while the poor Mexican vicariously rode with them.

According to Robert J. Rosenbaum, "Mexicano social bandits ran the gamut from men like Gregorio Cortez . . . to hard-bitten killers and robbers who gained renown and community approval because they usually attacked Anglos."[71] The South Texas political environment created social banditry. Cortez became a border hero in the early 1900s when he killed a lawman who attempted to arrest him unjustly. For the next ten days, an army chased Cortez over 500 miles, capturing him only after a fellow *Tejano* informed on him. A series of trials, lasting four years, followed during which the Texas-Mexican masses made Cortez a folk hero. An all-white jury convicted Cortez, who was pardoned in 1913. Countless *corridos* immortalized Cortez and his war with the *gringos.*

The social bandits directed their activities against Anglo-Americans, and only in time of dire need did they steal from their own people. In this way they retained the support of the Mexican people, who considered them heroes, Robin Hoods of a sort (even though they rarely gave to the poor). The bandit was described as "the tough man . . . unwilling to bear traditional burdens of the common man in a class society, poverty and meekness."[72] The bandits revolted against the *gringo* and the people admired them for doing what they themselves were unwilling to do.

While Cortez and other Mexican rebels easily fit the Hobsbawm model of the primitive rebel, Juan N. Cortina, who has been called the "Red Robber of the Río Grande," goes beyond the *bandido* model. Unlike the social bandit, he had an organization with a definite ideology that led guerrilla warfare against the *gringo* establishment. As with so much of the Chicano's history, Mexican records must be examined, especially those of Tamaulipas, to understand the rise of Juan Cortina.[73]

As in the case of the social rebels, an attempt has been made to discredit Cortina's motives. Many Anglo-American historians have labeled him an outlaw, portraying him as an illiterate rogue who came from a good family but "turned bad." Lyman Woodman, a retired military officer, wrote a biography of Cortina, describing him as a "soldier, bandit, murderer, cattle thief, mail robber, civil and military governor of the State of Tamaulipas, and general in the Mexican army" who was, in short, a *gringo* hater.[74]

An analysis of Cortina is difficult. He is important because he proves that strong ties existed between *Tejanos* and Mexicans south of the Río Bravo. A change of flag did not lessen these bonds.

Juan "Cheno" Cortina, a product of Mexico's northern frontier, was born on May 16, 1822, in Camargo, located on the Mexican side of the river. His parents were from the upper class, and his mother owned a land grant in the vicinity of Brownsville where the family moved to during the War of 1846.[75] Cortina, a regionalist, identified with northern Mexico and had fought to defend it from the Anglo-Americans.

In the period after the war, however, Cortina gave little indication that he was a champion of Mexican rights. He backed the filibustering expeditions led by José María Cabajal in 1851 which were financed by local Anglo merchants who wanted to separate the Río Grande Valley from Texas to form the Republic of the Sierra Madre. The separatists, led by people like King and Kenedy, were hardly friends of Mexicans. He also rustled Mexican cattle in partnership with the nefarious German Adolphus Glavecke. Glavecke testified against Cortina in the spring of 1859, and Cortina was indicted for cattle rustling. Glavecke continued a personal vendetta against Cortina. He had political clout, serving at various times as alderman for the city of Brownsville, and played a major role in building the legend of Cortina as a notorious bandit.[76]

The betrayal, indictment, and prosecution embittered Cortina and changed his life. Cortina's revolutionary career began accidentally on a hot July morning in 1859. While returning to his mother's ranch, he saw Marshal Bob Spears pistol-whipping a Mexican who had had too much to drink. The victim had worked for Cheno's mother. Cheno offered to take responsibility for the offender, but Spears replied, "What is it to you, you damned Mexican?" Cortina fired a warning shot, and then shot the marshal in the shoulder. He then rode off with the victim.

With no possibility of a fair trail, Cheno prepared to leave for Tampico, Mexico. Before his departure with 50 to 60 followers, he rode into Brownsville and raised the Mexican flag. Cortina's detractors claim that he plundered the city; however, his partisans point out that, when he had the city at his mercy, he did not rob and steal, as he certainly would have done had he been a bandit. He and his men attacked only those who had blatantly persecuted Mexicans, killing the jailer and four other men, including William P. Neal and George Morris, both of whom had murdered innocent Mexicans but continued to walk the streets.[77]

Cortina did not plan to lead a revolution when, from his mother's *Rancho del Carmén,* he published a circular justifying his actions. His "declaration of grievances" reviewed the injustice that Mexicans suffered at the hands of the occupiers. According to Cortina, he had gone to Brownsville solely to punish those guilty of terrorizing Mexicans, and he appealed to the Anglo-American government to bring the "oppressors of the Mexicans" to justice and not to protect them. Cortina, after issuing his statement, again prepared to emigrate to Mexico.

Seeking revenge, Brownsville citizens took Tomás Cabrera prisoner. Cabrera, a man of advanced age, was Cortina's friend. When Cortina learned that his friend had been arrested, he recruited an army of about 1,200 men, demanding the old man's release and threatening to burn Brownsville if the townspeople did not comply. The Brownsville Tigers (the local militia) and the Mexican army at Matamoros attacked him, but Cortina defeated them in battle, whereupon the *gringos* lynched Cabrera. Rangers were called, but he defeated them as well. The merchants protested to Mexican authorities, but the Mexicans disclaimed responsibility, since Cortina was a U.S. citizen.[78]

Flushed by his victories, he "envisioned raising an army powerful enough to force the Texas authorities to grant the Mexicans those rights . . . guaranteed them by the Treaty of Guadalupe Hidalgo."[79] He issued a proclamation that "reviewed the crimes against Mexicans" and suggested that the colonized form a secret society to achieve justice. He called for the liberation of Mexicans and the extermination of the "tyrants." He charged that the Mexicans' land had been stolen from them by "flocks of vampires, in guise of men." Cortina continued:

> It would appear that justice had fled from this world, leaving you to the caprice of your oppressors. . . . The race has never humbled itself before the conqueror. . . . Mexicans! My part is taken; the voice of revelation whispers to me that to me is entrusted the work of breaking the chains of your slavery, and that the Lord will enable me, with powerful arm to fight against our enemies.[80]

Not all Mexicans supported Cortina; the upper class often allied itself with the ruling class.[81] Cortina's support was among the poor, a fact that is admitted by Ranger "Rip" Ford:

> Sometimes Cortina would make a speech in the market place and the poor would listen intently to what he had to say. He would not harm the innocent, but would fight for the emancipation of the hungry *peons* along the border. . . . They must love the land for the land was all they had.[82]

State authorities reacted violently. Many innocent people became victims. Federal troops poured into the valley, forcing Cortina across the border. A state commissioner wrote Governor Sam Houston: "The Mexicans are arming every-thing that can carry a gun, and I anticipate much trouble here. I believe that a general war is inevitable. . . . New arms have been distributed to all the *rancheros,* so I apprehend trouble."[83] Houston appealed to the federal government for assistance and wrote to the secretary of war for help.[84]

The *San Antonio Light* played up the Cortina threat, headlining, "Browns-ville Captured: 100 Americans Slain." New Orleans merchants demanded more U.S. troops to fight Cortina. Rumors circulated in the national press that Cortina had captured Corpus Christi. Coincidentally, this came at a time when the U.S. government was removing troops from Brownsville, Laredo, and Eagle Pass.[85]

In February 1860 Washington sent Robert E. Lee to Texas to lead the expeditions against Cortina. Mexican authorities cooperated with Lee. However, throughout March Lee could not catch the elusive Cortina and began referring to "that myth Cortina."

Rumors circulated that Cortina threatened all strategic points, but by May Lee believed that Cortina had left Texas. Cortina had not abandoned his war with the *gringo;* he had merely shifted his base of operations. He went to Tamaulipas, where from 1861 to 1867 he defended the state against the French. He became for a time its military governor as well as a general in the Mexican army. After the war with France, he allegedly controlled the politics of Tamaulipas, making and unmaking governors. He cleaned up banditry in Tamaulipas. Anglo-Americans claimed that he "told thieves in Mexico that he would hang them for stealing in that country, but that there was plenty for them to take in Texas." From his Mexican base he supposedly led rustling operations against the Anglo-Americans and had a flourishing trade with Cuba, thus hitting at the heart of Anglo-American concerns—its economy.[86]

On the U.S. side, a network of supporters, who acted as spies, aided Cortina. It was reported that King and Kenedy lost 200,000 head of cattle and 5,300 horses from 1869 to 1872. Rip Ford wrote: "Cortina hates Americans, particularly Texans. . . . He has an old and deep-seated grudge against Brownsville."[87]

A reign of terror followed that is difficult to assess because of the sensationalism and outright lies of the press. Cortina was used as a pretext for violence. Robert Taylor, a commissioner sent by Houston to investigate conditions on the border, filed a confidential report: "I am sorry to say a good many of the latter [Anglos] . . . who have been Burning and Hanging and shooting Mexicans without authority by law are more dreaded than Cortina."[88]

The 1870s saw an intensification of hostilities between North Americans and Mexicans. Vigilantes took the law into their hands spreading more terror. They effectively used Cortina as an excuse, stating in October 1871 that Cortina had formed a cavalry corps. Rangers had 14 companies in 1870; when they were disbanded two years later, 27 state militia minutemen companies took their places. Merchants, claiming that they were losing 5,000 cows a month, increased the tensions as they called for more federal troops and demanded that the United States take over northern Mexico to the Sierra Madres.[89]

The Frontier Protection Act of 1874 reestablished the Rangers, and six mounted batallions of 75 men each roamed the region. During the spring and summer of that year a virtual race war raged. Anglo ranchers had more than adequate support in these wars: "After a group attacked Woakes' Store some fifteen miles from Corpus Christi in 1875, Anglos began general warfare against Mexicans in the region, killing wantonly many peaceful Mexican residents who had no connection with any bandit activity."[90] Naturally, they blamed Cortina for the invasion.[91]

The Anglo forces had no success against Cortina, but during the 1870s, as U.S. political influence with the Mexican government increased, pressure was brought to eliminate him. In 1875 he was taken to Mexico City and jailed on charges of cattle rustling. When Porfirio Díaz seized power, Cortina was exiled to Mexico City. He did not return to the border until the spring of 1890, when he visited the area for a brief time, receiving a hero's welcome.

THE PEOPLE'S REVOLT

The El Paso Salt War of 1877 is an example of a people's revolt. Mexicans in the country banded together along lines of race and class, taking direct action in response to the political chicanery of foreigners. The mob's action was not based on an abstract political ideology, but was an emotional response to the oppression. It was a class struggle against the rich, powerful *gringo* establishment. It became a people's revolt against the foreign occupier's domination.

Mexicans settled in the El Paso area in the early 1600s, and until the 1840s most of the population lived south of the Río Grande. After the Mexican-American War, settlements sprang up north of the river, capitalizing on the Chihuahua–Texas–New Mexico trade. Soon a handful of Anglo-Americans joined the overwhelmingly Mexican population in El Paso County. The Anglos took immediate control of the county's politics, managing the Mexican vote through agents whom the bosses rewarded by patronage. The Mexican population, dispersed in small hamlets around the present-day city of El Paso, was not familiar with the way Anglo politics worked. By 1870 El Paso, like Brownsville and San Antonio, was "dominated by a handful of leading merchants or financial men." Anglo-Americans held the majority of elected offices as well as the wealth of the county.[92]

In 1862, Mexicans lived marginally. Their existence was lightened by the discovery of salt at a location about 100 miles from El Paso. People rode to the salt beds to collect salt for their personal use as well as for sale to Mexicans south of the river. It did not occur to them to claim the salt beds, for the pits were community property. Sam Maverick, from San Antonio, staked out a large portion of the beds. Still Mexicans used the remaining portion, content to extract what they could use.

A group of North American politicians, who became known as the Salt Ring, conspired to gain control of the beds used by the Mexicans. In the election of 1870 A. J. Fountain, leader of the anti-Ring forces, ran against Salt Ring leader, W. W. Mills, for state senator. Fr. Antonio Borajo, a local parish priest of Italian descent, supported Fountain, who promised to make the pits public.

When Fountain attempted to keep his campaign promise, Borajo demanded that he stake out the beds and share the profits with him. The state senator refused, ending his political career. Borajo then struck an alliance with Louis Cardis, another Italian; they supported Charles Howard in 1875 for county judge. Cardis, it was agreed, would run for state senator. Both candidates were elected. Borajo and Cardis both spoke Spanish and were able to manipulate the Mexican majority. Once elected, however, Howard backed out of the alliance and staked out the beds in his father-in-law's name.[93] In 1877, Howard lost his bid for reelection, having earned the enmity of the Italians, but he kept control of the beds.

Howard attempted to charge Mexicans for the salt they removed, and in June 1877 he warned them not to remove any salt.[94] When Borajo incited the people from the pulpit, the bishop ousted him for meddling in politics. The friction continued, and two Mexicans were arrested when local authorities learned that they intended to remove salt. Several hundred *paisanos* (countrymen) of one of the arrested men forcibly freed him and called mass meetings to demand their rights to the salt.

Soon afterward, they captured Howard and held him prisoner until he promised to leave El Paso and to post a bond to guarantee that he would not return. Although Howard left El Paso, he intended to return, knowing that the authorities would support him. Upon his return he shot Cardis down in cold blood; local officials refused to prosecute him or forfeit his bond.[95]

Texas governor Richard B. Hubbard had ordered Major John B. Jones of the Texas Rangers into the area. When he arrived, the Mexican people approached him. They produced the U.S. Constitution and showed him the amendments which gave them the right to assemble and bear arms. Jones guaranteed them that Howard would be arrested and charged with murder.[96] Howard was arrested, but Jones had a change of mind, and he actively cooperated with Howard. Howard wrote a friend that he "did not wish to see general punishment visited on the rioters, who were ignorant as mules and misled, but thought that the leaders should be punished and made to respect the law," concluding that, "if the governor don't [sic] help us, I am going to bushwhacking."[97]

Local authorities released Howard and supported his claim. Rangers set out with him to see to it that Mexicans did not take the salt. Francisco "Chico" Barela, an Ysleta farmer, organized a group of 18 Chicanos to oppose the Rangers. At first they hesitated to take direct action, but when word arrived from Borajo, "Shoot the *gringo* and I will absolve you," they shot Howard on December 17, 1877.[98]

The Salt War had begun. Moves to punish the Mexicans touched off several days of rioting, which were finally suppressed by Rangers, posses, and other *gringos.* Governor Hubbard sent to Silver City for 30 hired gunmen, who were put under the command of Sheriff Charles Kerner. Among them was John Kinney, the self-styled King of Cattle Rustlers. The revolt was put down brutally "with rapes, homicides, and other crimes."[99] Many Mexicans fled in terror to Mexico, where during the winter they perished from exposure and starvation. The gang from New Mexico was finally dispersed. Since it was claimed that they were acting to suppress a revolt, no one was ever punished. In fact, the Texas Rangers even demanded that Mexico pay $31,000 in reparations.[100]

According to Professor Seymour Connor, "The denouement of the affair included a congressional investigation, a diplomatic exchange between the United States and Mexico, and reestablishment of Fort Bliss in El Paso. Thereafter, no open attempt was made to subvert private ownership of the salt deposits."[101] Denial of community ownership of the salt pits represented the removal of a remnant of rights to which Mexicans were entitled before the conquest. The fact that Mexicans were in the majority might have afforded them some protection had they had access to the political power of the new system imposed on them. However, even the potential advantage of their numbers was soon lost as the commercial and industrial boom of the 1880s brought a flood of Anglos to the area.

SUMMARY

The Texas War set the pattern for North American–Mexican relations. "Remember the Alamo!" justified the Anglo-American invasion and fanned racial hatred and violence toward Mexicans. The 1830s and 1840s saw a period of Anglo-American nationalism and patriotism; North Americans seemed intent on driving every Mexican out of Texas. The political system legitimated police repression and gave the Texas Rangers a license to murder Mexicans. By the 1850s, Mexicans had virtually abandoned central and eastern Texas.

The 1850s saw the makings of vast ranching empires. These operations required Mexican labor. Newcomers made fortunes along the border by smuggling and cattle rustling. Mexicans themselves became pawns. Poor Mexicans generally retained their Mexican nationalism and culture. Their isolation and Anglo racism prevented the assimilation into Euroamerican society. In southern Texas, North American merchants and ranchers, with the support of local government officials and the Texas Rangers, expanded at the expense of the small Mexican rancher. Finally, clashes between the races frequently led to lynchings and other forms of terror. Mexicans resisted these outrages. In the case of Juan Cortina, rebellion reached revolutionary proportions.

The structure of the labor market changed after the Civil War. Black emancipation led to labor shortages, creating a demand for more Mexican workers. The expansion of cotton, an end to the plantation, and the shortage of labor made sharecropping common by the 1870s. After the arrival of the railroads, large numbers of North Americans migrated into the Lone Star state as a result of heavy real estate promotion by land companies.

This second North American invasion further stratified *Tejanos,* and their proportional decrease made them more vulnerable. The railroad ended the frontier and accelerated the fencing of the open range. Commercial outposts such as San Antonio became transportation centers, encouraging a thriving cattle industry. In the 1880s, South Texas underwent a transition from a ranch to a farm economy. This change required more capital and more Mexican labor.

The poor Mexicans had limited options. Machine politics became popular in San Antonio and South Texas after the Civil War, following the pattern of eastern bossism. Patronage and an informal relief system made machines palatable to some Mexicans, who had no other alternative. In fact, the only way many could vote was by accepting machine protection. The lack of free suffrage for Mexicans would have flourished whether the machines existed or not. Political bosses such as Jim Wells built their power on their ability to deliver the Mexican vote, while upper- and middle-class Mexicans often acted as political brokers. By the turn of the century, however, reformers attempted to end the power of the bosses by denying Mexicans suffrage. Bossism then merely took other forms.

NOTES

1. See Carl Boggs, *Gramsci's Marxism* (London: Pluto Press, 1976); Quintin Hoare, ed., *Antonio Gramsci: Selections from Political Writings, 1910–1920* (New York: International Publishers, 1977); Hoare, ed. *Antonio Gramsci: Selections from Political Writings, 1921–1926* (1978).

2. T. R. Fehrenbach, *Lone Star: A History of Texas and the Texans* (New York: Macmillan, 1968), p. 245.

3. Ronnie G. Tyler, "The Callahan Expedition of 1855: Indians or Negroes?" *Southwest Historical Quarterly* 70, no. 4 (April 1967): 575, 582; Arnoldo De León, "White Racial Attitudes Toward Mexicanos in Texas, 1821–1920" (Ph.D. dissertation, Texas Christian University, 1974), p. 141.

4. Jack C. Vowell, "Politics at El Paso: 1850–1920" (Master's thesis, Texas Western College, 1952), p. 145.

5. John Salmon Ford, *Rip Ford's Texas,* Stephen B. Oates, ed. (Austin: University of Texas Press, 1963), p. 467.

6. Clarence C. Clendenen, *Blood on the Border: The United States Army and the Mexican Irregulars* (New York: Macmillan, 1969), p. 18.

7. Charles W. Goldfinch, *Juan Cortina, 1824–1892: A Re-Appraisal* (Brownsville, Tex.: Bishop's Print Shop, 1950), pp. 21, 31.

8. Ford, p. 467; Frank H. Dugan, "The 1850 Affair of the Brownsville Separatists," *Southwestern Historical Quarterly* 61, no. 2 (October 1957): 270–273; Edward H. Moseley, "The Texas Threat, 1855–1860," *Journal of Mexican American History* 3, (1973): 89–90.

9. De León, pp. 7, 147; David J. Weber, ed., *Foreigners in Their Native Land* (Albuquerque: University of New Mexico Press, 1973), pp. 155–156.

10. *Report of the Mexican Commission on the Northern Frontier Question* (New York, 1875), in Carlos E. Cortes, ed., *The Mexican Experience in Texas* (New York: Arno Press, 1976), p. 129.

11. Michael Gordon Webster, "Texan Manifest Destiny and Mexican Border Conflict, 1865–1880" (Ph.D. dissertation, Indiana University, 1972), pp. 30, 75.

12. *Report of the Mexican Commission,* p. 208; Raúl Fernández, *The United States–Mexico Border: A Politico-Economic Profile* (Notre Dame, Ind.: University of Notre Dame Press, 1977), p. 79; Webster, pp. 74–76.

13. Webster, p. 76; James LeRoy Evans, "The Indian Savage, the Mexican Bandit, the Chinese Heathen: Three Popular Stereotypes" (Ph.D. dissertation, University of Texas, 1967), p. vii.

14. David R. Johnson, John A. Booth, and Richard J. Harris, eds., *The Politics of San Antonio* (Lincoln: University of Nebraska Press, 1983), p. 5.

15. Ralph Wooster, "Wealthy Texans," *Southwestern Historical Quarterly* (October 1967): 163, 173.

16. Tom Lea, *The King Ranch,* 2 vols. (Boston: Little, Brown, 1957). The facts of King's life presented in the following discussion are based on Lea's work. (See vol. 1, p. 457.)

17. Lea, vol. 1, p. 275.

18. *Report of the Mexican Commission,* pp. 29–30, 62, 105.

19. Fehrenbach, pp. 678–679. Weber, p. 146, states that 11,212 Mexicans lived in Texas in 1850, constituting only 5 percent of the population. See also John R. Scotford, *Within These Borders* (New York: Friendship Press, 1953), p. 35.

20. De León, p. 140.

21. De León, pp. 112–113, 115, 116, 122.
22. E. Larry Dickens, "Mestizaje in 19th Century Texas," *Journal of Mexican American History* 2, no. 2 (Spring 1972): 63.
23. De León, p. 126.
24. Jane Dysart, "Mexican Women in San Antonio, 1830–1860: The Assimilation Process," *Western Historical Quarterly* (October 1976): 366.
25. Quoted in Aaron M. Boom, ed., "Texas in the 1850's as Viewed by a Recent Arrival," *Southwestern Historical Quarterly* (October 1966): 282–285.
26. Dysart, p. 370.
27. Dysart, pp. 370–374.
28. Dysart, p. 375.
29. Arnoldo De León, *They Called Them Greasers* (Austin: University of Texas Press, 1983), pp. 80–81.
30. De León, "White Racial Attitudes," pp. 161, 159–160.
31. De León, "White Racial Attitudes," pp. 172, 239.
32. O. Douglas Weeks, "The Texas-Mexican and the Politics of South Texas," *American Political and Social Science Review* (August 1930): 611–613.
33. De León, "White Racial Attitudes," p. 164.
34. Edgar Greer Shelton, Jr., "Political Conditions Among Texas Mexicans Along the Rio Grande," (Master's thesis, University of Texas, 1946), pp. 26–28, 32–36.
35. Shelton, pp. 39, 76–79.
36. Shelton, pp. 36–37.
37. Shelton, pp. 98, 123, 90.
38. Evan Anders, *Boss Rule in South Texas* (Austin: University of Texas Press, 1982).
39. Anders, p. 283.
40. De León, "White Racial Attitudes," pp. 234–235, 263–264; Emilio Zamora, "Mexican Labor Activity in South Texas, 1900–1920 (Ph.D. dissertation, The University of Texas, Austin, 1983), pp. 86–87.
41. "Another Fight in Texas," *New York Times,* January 4, 1892; M. Romero, "The Garza Raid and Its Lessons," *North American Review* (Spring 1892): 327.
42. Romero, p. 324; "Mexico Wants Benavides Very Much," *New York Times,* February 23, 1893; "Benavides Said to Be an American," *New York Times,* February 28, 1893.
43. "Excitement in Juarez, Mexico," *New York Times,* November 13, 1893.
44. *New York Times,* November 18, 1893.
45. De León, "White Racial Attitudes," pp. 238, 239.
46. De León, "White Racial Attitudes," pp. 166, 168.
47. Fehrenbach, p. 627; Rupert N. Richardson, *Texas: The Lone Star State,* 2nd ed. (Englewood Cliffs, N.J.: Prentice-Hall, 1958), pp. 271, 274.
48. Arnoldo de León, *The Tejano Community,* 1836–1900 (Albuquerque: University of New Mexico Press, 1982), p.20.
49. De León "White Racial Attitudes," pp. 232, 226–227, 186–187.
50. De León, "White Racial Attitudes," pp. 267–268.
51. De León, "White Racial Attitudes," pp. 192–193.
52. De León, *The Tejano Community,* p.22.
53. D. W. Meinig, *Imperial Texas* (Austin: University of Texas Press, 1969), p. 65.
54. Larry McMurtry, *In a Narrow Grave* (Austin, Tex.: Encino Press, 1968), p. 40.
55. McMurtry, p. 40. Anglo-Americans in Texas generally applauded McNeely. According to Webster, pp. 149, 152, rancher Richard King gave the Rangers a $500 bonus in appreciation for services rendered. In Las Cuevas, however, McNeely encountered a superior force of Mexicans, and it took U.S. troops to bail him out.
56. McMurtry, p. 41.
57. McMurtry, p. 43. The renowned historian W. E. Hollon, in a letter to the author in October 1972, wrote that a few weeks before Webb was killed, he said "that he did not feel like writing any more, but that he regretted that he probably would not have time to re-write his *Texas Rangers* and

correct his comments and prejudices about the Mexicans as reflected in that book. All of us who grew up in Texas on Texas history two generations ago, did not know any better in our attitudes toward the Negroes and Mexicans. It takes a long time to grow out of one's environment. So, don't be too harsh on Webb. He grew into the most tolerant, intellectual giant that Texas ever produced."

58. Llerena B. Friend, "W. P. Webb's Texas Rangers," *Southwestern Historical Quarterly* (January 1971): 321.
59. Friend, p. 321.
60. Américo Paredes, *With a Pistol in His Hand* (Austin: University of Texas Press, 1958).
61. Editorial by John Salmon Ford in the *Texas Democrat,* September 9, 1846, quoted in Fehrenbach, p. 465.
62. Fehrenbach, pp. 473–474.
63. Walter Prescott Webb, *The Texas Rangers: A Century of Frontier Defense* (Austin: University of Texas Press, 1965), p. xv.
64. Webb, p. xv.
65. Paredes, p. 31.
66. Paredes, p. 29.
67. Webb, p. 463.
68. Webb, p. 464.
69. Paul S. Taylor, *An American-Mexican Frontier* (New York: Russell & Russell, 1971), p. 49.
70. E. J. Hobsbawm, *Primitive Rebels: Studies in Archaic Forms of Social Movement in the 19th and 20th Centuries* (New York: Norton, 1965), p. 13.
71. Robert J. Rosenbaum, *Mexicano Resistance in the Southwest* (Austin: University of Texas Press, 1981), p. 55.
72. Hobsbawm, p. 13.
73. The best work on the Cortina years is Webster. See also Pedro Castillo and Albert Camarillo, eds., *Furia y Muerte: Los Bandidos Chicanos* (Los Angeles: Aztlán, 1973).
74. Webb, p. 176; Lyman Woodman, *Cortina: Rogue of the Rio Grande* (San Antonio, Tex.: Naylor, 1950), p. 8.
75. Goldfinch, p. 17; José T. Canales, *Juan N. Cortina Presents His Motion for a New Trial* (San Antonio, Tex.: Artes Gráficas, 1951), p. 6.
76. Evans, pp. 107, 118; *Report of the Mexican Commission,* pp. 28–29.
77. Webb, p. 178; Goldfinch, p. 44; Webster, p. 18; Evans, pp. 107, 121.
78. Goldfinch, p. 45; *Report of the Mexican Commission,* pp. 137–139.
79. Goldfinch, p. 48.
80. Wayne Moquin et al., eds., *A Documentary History of the Mexican American* (New York: Praeger, 1971), pp. 207–209. For the complete text of the speech, delivered on November 23, 1859, see *Report of the Mexican Commission,* p. 133, n. 62.
81. Evans, p. 111.
82. Ford, *Rip Ford's Texas* pp. 308–309.
83. Woodman, p. 53.
84. Woodman, p. 55.
85. Evans, pp. 105, 113.
86. Woodman, pp. 59, 98–99.
87. Ford, *Rip Ford's Texas,* p. 371.
88. Evans, p. 127.
89. *Report of the Mexican Commission,* pp. 154–155, Webster, pp. 79–80.
90. Evans, p. 132.
91. Leonard Morris, "The Mexican Raid of 1875 on Corpus Christi," *Texas Historical Association Quarterly* 55, no. 2 (October 1900): 128.
92. Vowell, pp. 72–73; Fehrenbach, p. 289; Carey McWilliams, *North from Mexico* (New York: Greenwood Press, 1968), p. 110.
93. Webster, p. 234; Webb, p. 350; Vowell, pp. 65–66.
94. Vowell, p. 66. Leo Metz, "The Posse Stuns New Mexican Wagon Train. Opening Round of Magoffin's Salt War," *El Paso Times,* February 17, 1974. There had been a previous encounter

over salt in December 1853, when James Wiley Magoffin, who had claimed salt pits in the San Andrés Mountains, sought to prevent salt gatherers from New Mexico from taking salt from them. An armed conflict almost broke out between Texans supporting Magoffin and New Mexicans, but a New Mexican court found in favor of the salt gatherers.

95. Vowell, p. 69.
96. Leon Metz, "San Elizario Salt Gatherers Pursue Justice by the Gun," *El Paso Times,* March 10, 1974.
97. Webb, p. 356.
98. Webb, pp. 360–361; Vowell, pp. 69–70.
99. Leon Metz, "Atrocities, Plunder Mark End of El Paso Salt War," *El Paso Times,* March 17, 1974; Webster, p. 238.
100. Joe B. Frantz, "The Borderlands: Ideas on a Leafless Landscape," in Stanley R. Ross, ed., *Views Across the Border: The United States and Mexico* (Albuquerque: University of New Mexico, 1978), p. 89.
101. Seymour V. Connor, *Texas: A History* (New York: Crowell, 1971), p. 235.

chapter 3

Freedom in a Cage: The Colonization of New Mexico

AN OVERVIEW

North American merchants moved into New Mexico in the 1820s to expand trade between the United States and Santa Fe. For the next 25 years, merchants formed a fifth column, becoming the vanguard for the invasion of New Mexico in the mid-1840s. A minority of the New Mexican *ricos* supported the North American conquest; however, northern New Mexican villages and Pueblo Indians resisted the occupation.[1]

New Mexico had a population of some 60,000, but, partly because of racism, it remained a territory until 1912. The situation facilitated the control of the New Mexican government by a minority of North Americans.

New Mexico's most abundant resource was its land, much of it owned either by the Mexican elites or the villages. North American colonizers violated the Treaty of Guadalupe Hidalgo and destroyed communal holdings. Through the political process, they also gained control of private land grants. The New Mexicans struggled against this destruction of the old way and engaged in armed resistance to the expansion of the Maxwell Land Grant; in the Lincoln County War; and in the northern New Mexican villages.

Since the 1820s, North American merchants made fortunes from the Santa Fe and Chihuahua trade. After the Civil War, a political machine, the Santa Fe Ring, coordinated the plunder of the territory. Members profited handsomely, supplying military forts and Indian reservations with food and goods. Fortunes were also made by control of the open range. Cattle raisers monopolized grazing lands and pushed out the Mexican subsistence farmers and sheep herders. Bloody range wars followed as encroachments on Mexican land increased and racial antagonisms intensified as Anglos from Texas and other parts of the United States poured into the territory.

The railroad arrived in New Mexico in the late 1870s, allowing the exploration and exploitation of the territory's mineral resources. Industrialization accelerated the destruction of the subsistence farmer and the communal villages as large U.S. government reclamation programs encouraged the commercialization of agriculture. By the turn of the century, dramatic changes resulted in the demise of the New Mexican way of life. Politically, socially, and economically, New Mexicans were isolated, participating in governance only through the rich *caciques,* or bosses, who brokered them through the Democratic and Republican parties.

THE DISTORTION OF HISTORY

"We are white too!"

As mentioned, the state monopolizes the production of ideas. In a colonial society, social control is facilitated by erasing the historical memory of the colonized. Many New Mexicans have historically found security in believing that they assimilated into Anglo-American culture and that they effectively participate in the democratic process. This historical distortion has been articulated so often that many New Mexicans believe it. The reality is that a small oligarchy of Anglo-Americans, aided by a small group of *ricos,* established their privilege at the expense of the Mexican masses.

In order to survive economically, many descendants of the original New Mexican settlers found it convenient to separate themselves from Mexicans who arrived at the turn of the twentieth century. Many New Mexicans called themselves *Hispanos,* or Spanish-Americans, as distinguished from other Mexicans. They rationalized that they were the descendants of the original settlers, who were Spanish *conquistadores.* According to them, New Mexico was isolated from the rest of the Southwest and Mexico during the colonial era; thus, they remained racially pure and were Europeans, in contrast to the *mestizo* (half-breed) Mexicans.

Through this process, they distanced themselves from intense racism toward Mexicans, allowing them to better their economic and, in some cases, their social status. George Sánchez, Arthur L. Campa, Carey McWilliams, and others have exploded this "fantasy heritage." Indeed, the *Hispanos* were Mexicans, for the majority of the original settlers from Mexico in 1598 were males who, over the years, mixed with the Pueblo Indians as well as with Mexican Indians who settled in the area. During the nineteenth century, although the label Spanish-American was used throughout the Southwest and Latin America, New Mexicans were commonly referred to by Anglo-Americans as Mexicans. Nancie González wrote that it was not until the twentieth century that New Mexicans denied their Mexican identity. During the 1910s and 1920s a large number of Mexican laborers entered New Mexico, and, at the same time, many Texans, Oklahomans, and other southerners settled in the eastern plains, intensifying discrimination against Mexicans. More affluent New Mexicans, thinking of themselves as Caucasians, rationalized to the Anglos: "You don't like Mexicans, and we don't like them either, but we are Spanish-Americans, not Mexicans."[2] By this simple denial of their heritage, New Mexicans thought they could escape discrimination and become eligible for higher-paying jobs.

THE MYTH OF THE BLOODLESS CONQUEST

Another myth is that New Mexicans peacefully joined the Anglo nation and "became a willing enclave of the United States." The myth of the "bloodless conquest of New Mexico" has been repeated by a majority of historians and is believed by most people. By this sleight of hand New Mexicans are not seen as the victims and, consequently, the enemies of the Anglo-Americans, but rather as their willing friends. In fact, the majority of the 50,000 to 60,000 people who lived in New Mexico were not enthusiastic about the United States invasion of their land.[3] Considerable anti-American feeling existed before the U.S. occupation, and only a handful of merchants saw it as an advantage.[4]

North Americans began regular contacts with New Mexico in the 1820s when they initiated the Santa Fe Trade. North Americans had secretly traded with New Mexicans since the Louisiana Purchase, in 1803. Eighteen years later, when Mexico won its independence, it liberalized its trade policies. The following year St. Louis merchants began their annual caravan from Missouri to Santa Fe. Meanwhile, North American commercial interests headquartered their operations at Taos. Charles Bent, the leader of the North Americans, built Bent's Fort near there. Bent married a prominent Mexican woman, establishing excellent ties with New Mexican merchants and elites.

Prior to the Santa Fe Trail, New Mexicans traded almost exclusively with Chihuahua, whose merchants controlled this commerce while New Mexicans accumulated small profits. After 1826, however, New Mexicans organized their own caravans to Chihuahua, generating internal economic activity. These changes brought about the exchange of money and allowed for the amassing of greater amounts of capital.

Meanwhile, Bent monopolized the trade with the indigenous peoples. This commerce had been almost exclusively in the hands of Mexican merchants. Mutual interests brought North American and Mexican traders closer. By the 1840s, Mexican merchants sent their children to parochial schools in St. Louis as well as to business houses (as apprentices). The Santa Fe trade flourished— commerce increased from $15,000 worth of goods in 1822, to $90,000 four years later, to a quarter of a million annually by the early 1830s. In 1846 the Santa Fe trade carried a million dollars' worth of merchandise. And, although North Americans made most of the profits, a handful of New Mexicans also profited handsomely.

As a result of increased trade, the New Mexican elites bettered their standard of living. Such benefits, however, did not trickle down to the poor farmers, shepherds, or Pueblo Indians, who, in fact, were threatened by the progress. As trade increased, so did the Euroamericans' political influence. Anglos received large land grants from the Mexican government. On the eve of the U.S. invasion, moreover, North Americans in New Mexico regularly interfered in the government's affairs.

New Mexico's economy had undergone dramatic changes during the Mexican period. The presence of North American merchants accelerated mercantile capitalism, which lasted until the late 1870s. This process encouraged encroachment on village lands and widened the gap between rich and poor. According to Professor Roxanne Dunbar Ortiz, class solidarity between the poor Mexican and Pueblo Indians tightened, challenging the political hegemony of the rich.

The Revolt of 1837 resulted from the growing antagonism between rich and poor. The Mexican national government had restructured and centralized control, appointing a non–New Mexican to the governorship. It also put a tax on various commodities. Most New Mexicans complained about this infringement upon their rights. However, the elite families only complained, while the pueblo and poor Mexican villagers in the Tewa Basin revolted. The rebels captured Santa Fe, executing the newly appointed governor. For the next six months the rebels ran an orderly government, making several democratic innovations. The national government, in league with the rich ranchers from Río Abajo, suffocated the movement.

Throughout the Mexican period, New Mexicans harbored anti–North American feelings. The experience in Texas and the racism of the Anglo did not go unnoticed. The monopolist tendencies of the North Americans in New Mexico threatened many locals. The claims by the Texas Republic that its western boundary was the Río Grande also irritated New Mexicans, since its eastern half was endangered.

In 1841 General Hugh McLeod led an expedition of about 300 Texans, divided into six military companies, into New Mexico. Governor Manuel Armijo sounded a general alarm. His militia was badly equipped, but he succeeded in tricking the Texans into believing he had a large army and the Texans *surrendered.* Although McLeod claimed he was simply leading a trading expedition, New Mexicans believed that they were being attacked. They blamed Bent and his party for the invasion and imprisoned him in Santa Fe. A mob attacked the house of United States counsel, Manuel Alvárez, with the intention of killing him. New Mexicans accused the United States government of complicity;[5] Anglos arrogantly denied the charge.

The fate of the expedition caused considerable controversy. One source charged: "Many of the prisoners were shot down in cold blood, others cruelly tortured, and most of them forced into a death march southward apparently as dreadful as the march of Bataan."[6] However, historian Hubert Howe Bancroft's account gave little credence to stories of atrocities, writing that, to the New Mexicans, "they [the Texans] were simply armed invaders, who might expect to be attacked, and if defeated, to be treated by the Mexicans as rebels, or at best —since Texan belligerency and independence had been recognized by several nations—as prisoners of war. . . . There can be no doubt that Governor Armijo was fully justified in seizing the Texan invaders, disarming them, confiscating their property, and sending them to Mexico as prisoners of war."[7]

Texans retaliated, and a nasty guerrilla war with racial overtones followed. During 1842 and 1843, clashes between the two sides increased. For example, in 1843 the Texans under Colonel A. Warfield attacked the small town of Mora and plundered innocent Mexicans. Bent was accused of contraband and theft, collusion with the Texans, harboring thieves, and selling firearms to Indians. He fled to the Arkansas River in Colorado (he later moved in and out of New Mexico and eventually became its governor). Bent's associate, Carlos Beaubien, wisely left the area temporarily. Colonel Jacob Snively raided a New Mexican caravan, shooting 23 Mexicans.[8] In 1843 Padre Antonio José Martínez, a leader of the opposition to the so-called American party, wrote to Antonio López de Santa Anna, warning him of Anglo encroachments and the construction of forts on the Arkansas and Platte rivers. He told Santa Anna that Anglos were depleting buffalo herds and criticized Armijo's policy of allowing foreigners to colonize empty lands.[9]

By the time Zachary Taylor attacked northern Mexico, no love was lost between Anglo-Americans and the New Mexicans. Colonel Stephen Watts Kearny, in June 1846, prepared approximately 3,000 members of the Army of the West to occupy the Mexican lands from New Mexico to California. His instructions were to use peaceful persuasion whenever possible, force when necessary. Kearny, in contact with the North Americans at Taos, planned his invasion. By late June he was ready to march west from Fort Leavenworth along the Santa Fe Trail. As Kearny approached New Mexico, he sent James W. Magoffin, a well-known merchant in New Mexico, with an ultimatum to Governor Armijo, stating that if the New Mexicans surrendered, they would not be disturbed; otherwise, they would suffer the consequences.[10]

Armijo, despite the fact that he had a shortage of arms and trained troops, had been prepared and could have defended the province. By August 1846, Kearny captured Las Vegas, New Mexico, and prepared to attack Santa Fe. He had to pass through Apache Canyon, a narrow passage southeast of Santa Fe, where Armijo could easily have ambushed him. Surprisingly, Kearny met no resistance at the canyon. Armijo had fled south without firing a shot, allowing the Army of the West to enter the capital. Some sources claim that negotiators bribed Armijo to sell out the province. In fact, Magoffin later submitted a $50,000 bill to Washington, D.C., for "expenses," of which he received $30,000. There is no proof that Armijo took the bribe, but there can be little doubt that his actions were highly suspicious, especially since Magoffin later boasted that he bribed Armijo.[11] The myth of a bloodless conquest stems largely from Armijo's inaction; however, resistance had gone underground, and by the fall of 1846 a movement to expel the hated *gringo* was afoot.

On August 22, Kearny issued a proclamation to the people of New Mexico, announcing the intention of occupying the province as a permanent possession of the United States. This was the first statement revealing the real purpose of the war—the acquisition of territory. Pretensions of defense of Texan boundaries, avenging Mexican insults, and indemnity were abandoned. Kearny's action clearly violated international law.[12] Kearny, lulled into thinking that there would be no further resistance, on September 25 left for California. In mid-December Colonel Alexander W. Doniphan, sent south to conquer Chihuahua, observed before leaving: "A people conquered but yesterday could have no friendly feeling for their conquerors, who have taken possession of their country, changed its laws and appointed new officers, principally foreigners."[13]

Influential New Mexicans conspired to drive their oppressors out of the province. Patriots included Tomás Ortiz; Colonel Diego Archuleta, a military commander; the controversial Padre Martínez; and the Reverend Juan Félipe Ortiz, vicar general of the diocese and brother of Tomás. They planned to attack the Anglo authorities during the Christmas season, when many of them would be in Santa Fe and when Anglo-American soldiers could be expected to be drinking heavily. However, the plans were uncovered by Governor Bent, who, "beginning to feel uneasy over the sullen reaction of the 'mongrels' to Anglo-American rule," had organized an elaborate spy system.[14]

After this initial discovery, the original leadership did not take part in other plots, and Anglo-Americans believed that the resistance of New Mexicans had been broken. Resentment, however, smoldered among the masses. Pablo Montoya, a Mexican peasant, and Tomasito Romero, a Pueblo Indian, led the opposition. On January 19, 1847, they attacked, killing Governor Bent and five other important members of the American bloc. Rebels destroyed documents and deeds which exposed "the land schemes of the American party."[15] There were also widespread acts of resistance in Arroyo Hondo and other villages.

The role of Padre Martínez is uncertain. He is accused of being the instigator, and his brother Pascual allegedly took part in the revolt.[16] However, Padre Martínez also apparently tried to restrain the rebels. He was a realist, and he knew that an unorganized revolt would be disastrous; he also knew the consequences of failure.

Under Colonel Sterling Price, well-armed soldiers retaliated by attacking some 4,500 Mexican and Pueblo Indians armed with bows, arrows, and lances. The army slaughtered rebels on the snow-covered ground outside the insurgent capital of Taos. Offenders retreated into the pueblo's church, fighting bravely in face of intense artillery fire:

> About 150 Mexicans were killed; some twenty-five or thirty prisoners were shot down by firing squads; and many of those who surrendered were publicly flogged. Colonel Price's troops are said to have been so drunk at the time that the Taos engagement was more of a massacre than a battle.[17]

The trial of surviving rebels resembled those in other occupation situations: "One of the judges was a close friend of the slain governor and the other's son had been murdered by the rebels. The foreman of the grand jury was the slain governor's brother and one of the jurors a relative of the slain sheriff." The town was so emotionally charged that it was surprising that the defendants received any kind of trial at all. Fifteen rebels were sentenced to death—one for high treason. Most historians have condemned the charges against rebels as illegal, since a state of war existed and the defendants were still Mexican citizens.[18]

Resistance continued, inflamed by the rule of Colonel Price, which was so despotic that even the Anglos objected. Guerrilla warfare was led by Manuel Cortés, a fugitive of the Taos rebellion. Significantly, military occupations of New Mexico lasted until 1851. That year James S. Calhoun, who was soon to become governor, stated that "treason is rife."[19]

THE LAND GRAB

Land, New Mexico's basic resource, was at the heart of the Pueblo Indians' grievances against the Spaniards. When Spanish elites attempted to "build large hereditary estates using Pueblo lands and labor," the Indians revolted.[20] Indigenous hostility forced the colonial administration to make modifications in the Spanish land tenure system in the eighteenth century; community and private land grants were distributed in order to accelerate the development of agriculture and pastoral societies. During the eighteenth and nineteenth centuries, the communal grants were especially useful in populating the frontier.

The Spanish elites formed large sheep- and cattle-ranching operations while the poor survived through subsistence farming, supplemented by sheep grazing. Many of the poor relied on *partido* contracts (raising sheep for a large owner, taking half the increase). Over the years many northern New Mexican villagers grew close to the Pueblo Indians through trade and intermarriage. Both suffered the fate that "life outside their communities was necessarily one of illegal or criminal activity since nearly everything was forbidden."[21] Independence promised changes in the political structure; however, hope soon dimmed with the North American penetration, infiltration, and conquest.

After independence, local elites dominated political and economic institutions. The arrival of trade launched the province out of the feudal period, and the surplus capital from trade made possible the expansion of the elites' holdings, encouraging the encroachment on communal lands. This process accelerated with the North American conquest.

After the Taos Rebellion, a military dictatorship ruled New Mexico for four years. The military government used violence to crush revolutionary movements. Not until March 1851 did New Mexico's first civilian governor take office. When military rule ended, the people were supposedly free. The Mexican ranchers of Río Abajo, land speculators (prominent in the North American clique and mostly lawyers), and the Catholic Church remained influential. From 1851 to 1861, the territorial governors established local government based on North American law, and, in the process, destroyed familiar Mexican forms of government. In order to maintain control, authorities kept a large number of forts in the territory.

The small number of North American elites who arrived formed alliances with the *ricos* as well as with the church. Through these surrogates, a clique manipulated local politics, allowing large families and their extended networks to control municipalities while they ruled the territory. As in the case of Texas, political machines formalized these arrangements after the Civil War. In the case of New Mexico, the Santa Fe Ring controlled territorial politics, while a number of smaller, satellite rings operated at the county levels. In the two decades that followed the Civil War, ring members grabbed an estimated 80 percent of the New Mexico land grants.

The Santa Fe Ring's power rested in its control of the territorial bureaucracy. Through its Washington connections, it influenced the appointment of the governor, who, in turn, influenced the appointment of judges, surveyors, and other officials. From this point, they centralized control of the territory: "Colonialism has not only involved the conquest of foreign land and people, but a conquest of agricultural and subsistence producers, with accompanying appropriation of their lands, resources and labor."[22] The new policies ignored the Treaty of Guadalupe Hidalgo, invalidating Spanish and Mexican land titles. Colonial bureaucrats intentionally confused land laws and titles in order to create an environment that legitimized the ring's plunder. Lawyers and speculators "had a field day using fees, intimidation, bribery, and fraud to realize great profit and enormous power."[23]

The Anglo-American land grab in New Mexico resembled the one that took place in Texas. The difference was that in New Mexico the Mexican settlements were more extensive. The province had many villages and some cities. Santa Fe had grown into a trade center. Some mining occurred, and both Mexicans and Anglos realized the future mining potential of the territory. Extensive agriculture existed. Sheep raising gave the people their principal contact with the outside world.

After 1848, Anglo-Americans moved into New Mexico to enjoy the spoils of conquest. Victory meant the right to exploit the territory's resources. These opportunists formed an alliance with the rich Mexican class and established their privilege, controlling the territorial government and administering its laws to further their political, economic, and social dominance. They maintained their power through political influence in Washington, D.C., access to capital, and command of technological innovations. Systematically, these people used these advantages to gain total control.[24] The following is a summary of the methods used to plunder the territory.

First, New Mexico was a territory and the United States president appointed executive and judicial posts. These and other state offices went to Anglo-Americans who had influence in Washington.

Second, the ruling elite controlled the police—local, state, and federal. Through violence the ruling class could enforce its schemes.

Third, control of the legislature by the political oligarchy was maintained through the influence of the *ricos.*

Fourth, the new economic order made access to capital imperative. Anglos owned banks, prime sources from which Mexicans could obtain capital. Merchants and later bankers charged excessive interest rates, the New Mexicans used their land as collateral, and foreclosures followed the Mexicans' inability to meet payments.

Fifth, government allowed speculators to initiate exploitive land and timber policies which eroded the land, hastening the demise of the small farmer.

Sixth, reclamation projects in general did not help small farmers. After the Civil War the corporate agriculturalists, those who raised crops in large quantities, were subsidized by water supplied at government expense. Reclamation projects further changed the balance of nature, greatly affecting the Río Grande; they reduced the supply of water in many areas and provided too much water in other places. The people had no say as to where the government would build dams. New Mexican farmers had to pay for "improvements" through taxes whether they wanted them or not, and when they could not pay the increased taxes, their land was forfeited.[25] Large farm corporations were granted extensive land tracts. Using mechanization, they led in the production of cash crops, such as cotton. Small farmers could not compete, because they did not have the capital to mechanize.

Seventh, the federal government granted large concessions of land to railroad corporations and to some institutions of higher learning.

Eighth, conservationists, concerned over industry's rape of timber and recreation land, moved, at the turn of the century, to create national forests. Shepherds were not allowed to graze their flocks on national forest lands without permits, which over the years went increasingly to the large operators.[26] In the process Mexicans in New Mexico lost 2 million acres of private lands and 1.7 million acres of communal lands.

Today, the federal government owns 34.9 percent of the land in New Mexico, the state government owns 12 percent, while federal Indian reservations own 6.8 percent. The state and federal governments together, therefore, own 53.7 percent of New Mexico, with the forestry service controlling one-third of the state's land.[27] Government control of public lands did not ensure public use or the public good. Special interests that had access to government and its resources were, consequently, able to monopolize New Mexico's wealth.

THE SANTA FE RING

After the Civil War political control became more concentrated. An influx of newcomers and capital formalized and extended the range of the North American elite and the *ricos,* with the creation of a network of speculators.

The advantage of the Anglo merchants in the years after the conquest broadened to include the influx of many lawyers, who used government to make a killing in real estate ventures. To facilitate these thefts, they formed small political cliques, which resembled the political machines of the eastern United States. Most cliques were associated with, and subservient to, the Santa Fe Ring, which Carey McWilliams described as "a small compact group of Anglo-American bankers, lawyers, merchants, and politicians who dominated the territory through their ties with the *ricos* who in turn controlled the votes of the Spanish-speaking."[28] The network woven by the ring paled its eastern counterparts.

The leaders, Thomas B. Catron, Stephen B. Elkins, and Le Baron Bradford Prince, were prominent Republicans. A number of Democrats as well as rich Mexicans also belonged. The ring controlled the governor and most of the officeholders in the territory and was supported by Max Frost, editor of the *New*

Mexican, the territory's most influential newspaper. "Frost, who was at one time during his active career indicted in a land fraud prosecution, acted as the journalistic spokesman for the Ring, effectively using the press to discredit critics of the Ring and to place its activities in the best possible light."[29]

Thomas B. Catron, the ring's official leader, arrived in New Mexico in the late 1860s, eventually becoming United States attorney general for the territory. "Throughout his life in New Mexico, Catron wielded more power than any other single individual in the territory. Through land grant litigation and by purchases he acquired more than one million acres of land."[30]

Stephen Elkins, a lawyer and close friend of Catron, arrived in New Mexico in 1863. Eight years later he was president of the First National Bank of Santa Fe. He represented the ring's interests in Washington, becoming a delegate to the United States Congress and later serving as secretary of war under President Benjamin Harrison.[31] In 1884 he became chairman of the executive committee of the National Republican Committee.

Le Baron Bradford Prince came from New York, where he had had experience in machine politics. Through the influence of powerful friends in Washington, he was offered the governorship of New Mexico, but he turned it down to become chief justice of New Mexico in 1879. Later, in the 1890s, he became governor.

Governor Edmund Ross, appointed by President Grover Cleveland, described the ring's network and influence:

> From the Land Grant Ring grew others, as the opportunities for speculation and plunder were developed. Cattle Rings, Public Land Stealing Rings, Mining Rings, Treasury Rings, and rings of almost every description grew up, till the affairs of the Territory came to be run almost exclusively in the interest and for the benefit of combinations organized and headed by a few longheaded, ambitious, and unscrupulous Americans.[32]

This maze of rings was further complicated by a proliferation of joint stock companies, private investment pools, and individual speculators, all active in the promotion of land, railroads, milling, farming, small-scale manufacturing, and shipping.[33]

One of the ring's most infamous capers was its takeover of the Maxwell Land Grant. The land was originally granted to Charles Beaubien and Guadalupe Miranda in 1841. When the grantees requested execution two years later, Fray Martínez objected on grounds that part of the land belonged to the people of Taos and because it was going to members of the North American clique. Over the next years, various other groups claimed parts of the Beaubien–Miranda Grant: Indians, Mexican tenant farmers, Mexican villages, and Anglo squatters.

Lucien Maxwell, the son-in-law of Beaubien, bought Miranda's share of the grant in 1858, as well as a tract from his father-in-law's share. Some years later, after the death of his father-in-law, Maxwell began to buy up other shares. His total outlay was not more than $50,000.

In 1869 Maxwell sold his grant to a British combine, which also included members of the Santa Fe Ring for $1.5 million. Miguel A. Otero was among the speculators. After it took control of the Maxwell Land Grant, the combine had problems because tenant farmers lived on the property. Another complication was that the discovery of gold on the property in 1866 brought in many prospectors. The combine also learned that the federal government laid claim to a portion of the grant for reservation and park land. When it became common knowledge, Mexican and Anglo squatters moved onto the land, believing it would become public domain and under United States law they would be entitled to it. The squatters each cultivated between 20 to 50 acres of irrigated land.[34] Lastly, the grant had not been surveyed and its boundaries were unknown. Therefore, in order to clear title to the grant, the combine had to eliminate each of these obstacles.

While Lucien Maxwell estimated the size of the grant at between 32,000 and 97,424 acres. Once the ring gained control of the grant, it was expanded to 1,714,765 acres. The Mexican Colonization Act limited this type of grant to 22 leagues (97,000 acres). The expansion of the Maxwell grant threatened the land titles of the residents of Colfax County and they prepared to defend their property. On September 14, 1875, T.J. Tolby, a Methodist minister and a leading opponent of the ring, was killed. Cruz Vega, a Mexican and constable of the Cimarron precinct, was accused of the murder; although he denied any involvement, he was lynched. Vigilantes alleged Vega was employed by the ring; however, the hanging itself seems to have been racially motivated. The Tolby murder set the stage for a bloody war between the company and the squatters. *Mexicanos* generally remained aloof during the 1870s. Anglos resented Mexicans, not only on racial grounds, but because they believed Mexicans were the source of the ring's power.[35]

During the 1880s, more Mexican *paisanos* moved onto the land; slowly they became more involved. When the squatters formed the Squatters Club to raise money for defense, in 1881, only one Mexican was in the club; by 1887 the two groups rode together. In that year the combine brought legal proceedings against the squatters. M. P. Pels, the company agent, attempted to divide squatters by promising cash settlements if they would leave. On July 23, 1888, 75 armed Mexicans and Anglos turned back the sheriff. Masked riders patrolled the area, frustrating company efforts to evict them. Jacinto Santistevan and his son Julian were among the leaders of the resistance. Like the other squatters, Santistevan was a small farmer, with 160 acres of fenced land, of which he farmed 80. The total value of Santistevan's holding was estimated at $300.[36]

The period of unity was short-lived, however. In 1888, the same year in which the riders faced the sheriff successfully, a division arose. When Anglos refused to help Mexicans run company agent Charles Hunt out of Vermejo Park, the Mexicans were so angered that "many vowed never to aid Americans again."[37]

On February 21, 1891, a company business agent was killed and the company retaliated, mounting a 23-man posse to track down the killers. Violence remained at a pitched level after this incident: Mexicans burned crops, cut fences, and destroyed buildings. They killed cattle, and, as the spring wore on, armed skirmishes became more frequent. Cowhands were reluctant to risk their lives for the company; Mexican violence increased. Unexpectedly, the company changed its tactics and began to single out *paisanos* for preferential treatment. During 1893 it continued its court battle and just plain wore Santistevan down. That year Jacinto left, marking the beginning of the end;[38] many farmers came to terms with the company. Under Dutch leadership, the reorganized Maxwell Land and Railway Company was more formally brought into the Santa Fe network, and when the case finally went to the higher courts, the ring's agent protected its interest.

Throughout the violence, the Santa Fe group continued its relentless drive to gain control of the land by manipulating the law. It influenced the territorial legislature to pass statutes that "authorized the courts to partition grants or put them up on the sale block, even when the smallest owner petitioned such action. Another territorial law, enacted in January 1876, annexed Colfax County to Taos County for political purposes for at least two court terms."[39] Thus, where the ring owned even a small portion of land, it could force a sale; and since the ring also controlled Taos judges, the annexation was assured. During this period the ring received the cooperation of the appointed governors, who refused to intervene even though there was considerable bloodshed. Moreover, the government commissioned John T. Elkins, a brother of Stephen B. Elkins, to survey the Maxwell Grant. Finally, on April 18, 1887, a decision was reached by the United States Supreme Court, which completely disregarded the rights of the Indians, Mexicans, and squatters. It found in favor of the Maxwell Company (which the ring now owned), dispossessing the Indian and the Mexican tenant farmers and marking the end of an era.[40]

THE LINCOLN COUNTY WAR

After the Civil War cattle raisers made immense profits from the open range where they used the land and water free of charge. The causes of the Lincoln County War were similar to those in Colfax County. This controversy indirectly involved the Santa Fe Ring, centering on one of its smaller satellites and its challengers. The power poles in this rivalry were led by Anglo-Americans—one a Republican and the other a Democrat. In Lincoln, small Anglo farmers were not involved as they had been in Colfax County. Losers, as always, were the poor —principally Mexican sheepherders and farmers.

Lincoln County is located in the plains area of New Mexico. Mexicans established small villages and farms there prior to the 1870s, when Anglos began arriving in large numbers. In the 1870s demand for beef and mutton in the United Kingdom and in the eastern United States created a boom. New markets had opened in February 1875, when a refrigerated ship with dressed beef left for Liverpool, England. With an opportunity to profit in cattle, the adventurers moved into Lincoln County, clashing with the Mexicans, who herded sheep on the open range.[41]

The Lincoln County War (1876–1878) often has been portrayed as a personal feud or as a cattle or range war, with the conflict growing out of cattle rustling and range rights. Robert N. Mullin, editor of Maurice Garland Fulton's *History of the Lincoln County War,* has clarified this situation:

The Lincoln County War was essentially a struggle for economic power. In a land where hard cash was scarce, federal contracts for the supply provisions, principally beef, for the military posts and for the Indian reservations, were the grand prize. Since the early 1870's Laurance Gustave Murphy had been the Lincoln County sub-contractor for William Rosenthal and the political clique at Sante Fe which enjoyed a near-monopoly in supplying the government with beef, even though neither Rosenthal nor Murphy himself then raised or owned any significant number of cattle. They were challenged by John H. Chisum, owner of the largest herds in the territory, who declined to do business through Rosenthal but instead bid direct on the beef contracts. Thus began Chisum's struggle with Murphy and his successors along with their backers at Santa Fe —a struggle out of which grew the Lincoln County War.[42]

By the 1870s, Lincoln County had become a haven for outlaws. The group led by Murphy hired Anglo-American gangs as rustlers for their beef-supply business, thus bringing into the territory people who had little concern for law or life. The largest group migrating into Lincoln consisted of Texans, who brought with them "a tradition of violence nurtured by the Civil War," blood feuds, and hatred for Mexicans. Relations between cattle raisers and sheep herders were not good elsewhere in the nation, but they were especially bad in New Mexico.[43]

One outlaw band, the Harrell clan, rode into the town of Lincoln, formerly the Mexican pueblo La Placita, in 1873 and began abusing townspeople. When Constable Juan Martínez attempted to restrain them, a gun fight followed in which three of the bandits and Constable Martínez were killed. The outlaws retaliated by attacking the town and shooting indiscriminately into a crowd of people attending a dance, killing four Mexicans. Troops finally chased the Harrells out of the county, but en route they killed José Haskell because he had a Mexican wife. As they rode toward Texas, Ben Turner, a member of the gang, was shot from ambush, whereupon they began another rampage, killing five Mexican freighters.

By January 27, 1874, the *New Mexican* in Sante Fe announced that Lincoln County had exploded into an "unfortunate war between the Texans and the Mexicans."[44] There is ample proof, however, that the Santa Fe Ring wanted to focus the public's attention on racial conflicts in order to conceal the economic struggle which caused the hostilities. Essentially, the war involved the power play between the Murphy group, who controlled Republican party politics in Lincoln, and John H. Chisum, who represented the Democrats.

Juan Patrón emerged as the Mexican leader in Lincoln. Born in 1855 in La Placita, he attended parochial schools in New Mexico, eventually graduating from the University of Notre Dame in Indiana. Friends described him as "honest, studious, and industrious."[45] His father was killed by the Harrell clan. In 1878 he was a delegate to the territorial House of Representatives, where deputies elected him speaker. He functioned, without pay, as the town's only schoolteacher.

In 1875, Patrón worked as a clerk of the probate court. John Copeland, an Anglo rancher, and his neighbor John Riley, a member of the Murphy clan, accused two Mexican workers of stealing property from their ranches. The workers fled because of threats by Copeland; Copeland and Riley chased them, killing one and capturing the other. Copeland and Riley decided to take their prisoner to Fort Stanton, seven miles away, and although these "cowboys" were accustomed to riding, they set out on foot with the prisoner in front of them. When the unarmed Mexican allegedly attempted to escape, they shot him. They reported their version of the incident to Probate Judge Laurence Murphy, an associate of Riley and leader of the Murphy ring, who acquitted them.

Patrón investigated the incident and concluded that the men were shot at the ranch and not, as alleged, on the road. His demand for a grand jury investigation was denied. Determined not to allow this injustice to go unpunished, Patrón, as probate clerk, signed a warrant for the arrest of Copeland and Riley, enlisted a posse, and rode to the Copeland ranch. The group eventually found both men, took them prisoner, and interrogated them. Concluding that the two Mexicans had been shot in cold blood, many in the posse wanted to shoot the accused murderers, but Patrón calmed them. When troops arrived from Fort Stanton (called by one of Riley's friends), the posse released the two *gringos.* Riley went into his house, got a gun and shot Patrón in the back. The army arrested the Mexicans, including Patrón, who was taken prisoner and held in the post hospital, where he remained in critical condition for some time. Although Patrón was indicted on the demand of John Riley, he did not go to trial. He recovered to lead the Mexicans during the Lincoln County War.

Juan Patrón and most Mexicans sided with Chisum against Murphy, probably because they considered the Murphy ring to be the enemy. The Murphy group's involvement with the Harrell gang and the Riley–Copeland affair undoubtedly influenced the Mexicans to support Chisum.[46]

The Lincoln County War began in the spring of 1877 when an Englishman, John H. Tunstall, opened a mercantile store that competed with the Murphy establishment. Alexander McSween, a lawyer, and Chisum were Tunstall's principal associates. In addition, the Chisum–Tunstall group opened a bank that competed with the First National Bank, controlled by Stephen Elkins and Catron.

When Dolan threatened Tunstall, two armed camps formed. Most Mexicans joined Juan Patrón in backing the Tunstall group. Tensions mounted and bloodshed followed. Dolan employed the Jesse Evans gang to do the dirty work. Even though the gang had a few Mexican members, it viciously murdered and persecuted the Mexican community. Finally, Tunstall was murdered by Dolan's men, whereupon the Englishman's supporters, among whom was the notorious William Bonnie, alias Billy the Kid, immediately sought revenge. Dolan attacked Patrón in the *New Mexican,* charging that he was leader of the county's lawless Mexican element.

Both groups recruited sharpshooters. Among the newcomers to the territory were John Selman and his so-called scouts. Selman, a well-known cattle rustler, was hired by Dolan. According to Maurice Fulton, "During the latter part of September, Selman's group moved to the vicinity of Lincoln and inaugurated a worse type of terrorism than heretofore known." With Dolan forces, they committed "apparently motiveless deeds of violence." Sam Corbet, in a letter to

Tunstall's father, wrote: "They killed two men and two boys (Mexicans) only about 14 years old, unarmed and in the hay field at work. Rode right up to them and shot them down." These actions "roused the Lincoln County Mexicans, some even determined to visit retaliation on the first *Americanos,* in particular *Tejanos,* that came their way."[47]

Governor Samuel B. Axtell sided with the Dolan faction and refused to intervene. However, the murders of Reverend Tolby in Colfax and of Tunstall, a British subject, attracted national and international attention, contributing to Axtell's political demise. On September 4, 1878, over the protests of Catron, Elkins, and other prominent ring members, General Lew Wallace was appointed governor by President Rutherford B. Hayes. Wallace was a Republican, so New Mexicans waited nervously to see if he would follow in Axtell's footsteps. President Hayes had given him a mandate to clean up the trouble in Lincoln County, and he took vigorous action to do so. He formed a local militia, led by Juan Patrón, and peace was restored in 1879.

Because of harassment, Patrón moved to Puerto de Luna, several hundred miles away. Misfortune hounded him. While in a saloon having a drink with a friend, a cowboy named Mitch Maney shot him. Many believed Dolan had hired Maney as an assassin, and certainly the subsequent trial raises some questions. Although Maney was a penniless cowboy, one of the most expensive legal firms in the territory defended him. Moreover, his prosecutor was Thomas Catron. A hung jury resulted and Maney was never retried.[48] However, the fact that the ring was both defense and prosecution proved to many that a conspiracy existed. Juan Patrón, an effective and honest leader, was a threat to the establishment. One can speculate that if his challenge to the ring had gone unpunished, other dissidents might have been encouraged to rebel. His violent death, therefore—whether there was evidence of design or not—served to intimidate incipient rebels.

Mexican shepherds and Texas cowboys continued to fight for land and water. But, by the 1880s, the cattle raisers eliminated the Mexican as a competitor. During the decade the conflict degenerated into a race war. Time favored the Anglos, with railroads linking Lincoln County to markets. During the same period railroads spurred wool shipments, and soon nearly 3 million head of sheep roamed the territory, but now the sheep belonged to the Anglo-Americans. A thousand ewes brought $15,000 a year, whereas a Mexican herder could be employed for less than $200 annually.[49] Thus, in the end, economics brought about a victory of sheep—without Mexicans.

THE AMERICANIZATION OF THE CATHOLIC CHURCH

The Roman Catholic Church, the most important institution to New Mexicans, directly touched their lives from cradle to grave. However, unlike the Irish clergy, who supported their congregations when Irish-Americans faced repression in the eastern United States, the New Mexican clergy became an active ally of the state, accelerating the assimilation process.

Soon after the occupation, the church limited its functions to strictly spiritual matters. With few exceptions it did not champion the rights of the poor;

instead, it worked to Americanize New Mexicans. It became an alien clergy that related more to the power establishment and a few rich Anglo-American parishioners than to the masses. It became a pacifying agent, encouraging Mexicans to accept the occupation.

The undisputed leader of the Mexican clergy was Antonio José Martínez. His devotion to the Catholic Church was deep and abiding, but he saw it as an institution for benefit, not enslavement, of humanity. Padre Martínez was one of the most important figures in New Mexican history, as well as one of the most beloved.

The "priest of Taos," as he was known, was born in Abiquir in Río Arriba County, on January 7, 1793. Martínez had been married, but his wife and daughter died. He then became a priest, and, in 1824, Martínez took charge of a parish in Taos, where after two years he established a seminary. Graduates of the school were greatly influenced by him, spreading his ideas throughout New Mexico. He taught grammar, rhetoric, and theology, as well as law. From 1830 to 1836 he was a member of the departmental assembly of the state under the Mexican government, and in 1835 he published a newspaper called *El Crepúsculo (The Dawn)*. He also wrote and printed books and pamphlets. Martínez took progressive religious stands, refusing to collect tithes from the poor and opposing large land grants, insisting that the land should go to the people. Even before the Anglo occupation Martínez had opposed Anglo encroachments, and was involved in the first liberation movement. He served in the legislature from 1851 to 1853. Martínez frequently criticized the church for "its policy of allowing the clergy to exact excessive and oppressive tithes and fees for marriages, funerals, and like services."[50] He also advocated separation of church and state.

In 1851, however, Padre Martínez's liberal, people-oriented philosophy of the role of the church was challenged with the arrival in New Mexico of a new vicar general, Fray J. B. Lamy. French by birth, Lamy had worked in the Baltimore diocese and in the mid-1850s became a bishop. His partisans claimed that he revitalized religion in New Mexico by founding schools, building churches, and increasing the number of priests in his diocese from 10 to 37. They also claimed that through his alliance with the government he was able to maintain control of education, which might otherwise have been lost to the Protestant churches. His critics allege that he did this at a tremendous cost, and they condemn him for his failure to speak out against the injustices suffered by the people.[51]

Even his admirers concede that Lamy was a "cultured" Frenchman who never fully understood the traditions of Mexicans and had little respect for their clergy. Lamy was the product of postrevolutionary France and came into fullness of mind "after reign of libertarian principles, and during the restoration of the Church," when liberalism was looked upon as anti-Catholic.[52] "His [Lamy's] idea was to create a little France [prerevolutionary] in a 'wilderness of neglect.' Lamy began to replace local church architecture with that patterned after the French."[53] In order to realize his dream, Lamy needed money, and he raised it by taxing the poor—that is, by tithing and by collecting church fees for baptism, marriage, and other rites.

Lamy persecuted the Holy Brotherhood of Penitents. The brotherhood was most popular among the poor of northern New Mexico. Descended from the Third Order of St. Francis of Assisi, it practiced public flagellation and, during Holy Week, imitated the ordeals of Christ. A secret society, it was a strong force in local politics; prominent leaders like Antonio José Martínez belonged to it. Establishment Mexicans like Miguel A. Otero looked down on the Penitents, stating, "At present they are found among those classes of natives where ignorance predominates."[54] Lamy and his successors fought to abolish the brotherhood, slandering and libeling them, persecuting them, and even denying them the sacraments.[55]

Soon after Lamy's arrival, a power struggle erupted between him and the Mexican clergy, many of whom were Martínez's former students. Critics attacked Martínez and his followers on the grounds of not being celibate (charges that were not proved), but the real reason was the involvement of the Mexican clergy in temporal matters, especially their functioning as advocates for the people. The people wanted a native clergyman who knew their language, traditions, and problems. In contrast, Anglo-American priests came from an alien culture.[56] They did not concern themselves with the material welfare of Mexicans, and attempted to Americanize them.

At first, Martínez avoided an open rift with Lamy, keeping quiet even when he excommunicated close friends. Gradually, however, Lamy's edicts became more obtrusive. Finally, when Lamy sent a letter to all the parishes insisting that priests collect tithes and first fruits and telling them to withhold the sacraments from those who did not comply, Martínez rebelled. When Lamy finally excommunicated Martínez, the padre defied the bishop by continuing his ministry until his death, on July 28, 1868.

Lamy set the pattern for church–state cooperation and the church's almost unconditional state support. The bishop himself never had a high estimation of New Mexicans, writing in his later years: "Our Mexican population has quite a sad future. Very few of them will be able to follow modern progress. They cannot be compared to the Americans in the way of intellectual liveliness, ordinary skills, and industry; they will thus be scorned and considered an inferior race."[57] In return for the unconditional support of the church, the state granted it a monopoly over education.

THE RESISTANCE

The 1880s saw increased opposition to land encroachments. Mexicans suffered from the impact of the railroad; private contractors stripped the timber from the land; competition with Anglo workers strained an already bad economic situation; and inequalities in the pay scale for Anglo and Mexican workers heightened. By the middle of the decade, Mexicans organized the Association of the Brotherhood for the Protection of the Rights and Privileges of the People of New Mexico, whose stated purpose was to free New Mexico from corrupt politicians and monopolies.

A leading figure in the struggle against the encroachers, Juan José Herrera formed *Las Gorras Blancas* (the White Caps) around 1887.[58] Herrera, at the time, served as a district organizer for the Knights of Labor, a national trade union, founded in 1869 by garment workers.[59] By the 1880s, the railroads spread throughout the Southwest, blatantly exploiting the people and their resources. In response workers organized the Knights in San Miguel County in 1884, and, in three years, it had three assemblies in the city of Las Vegas, New Mexico. Most of its members worked for the Atchison, Topeka & Santa Fe Railway.

In 1887 the union formed the Las Vegas Grant Association to give legal aid to the townspeople in their struggle against land speculators. This was part of the Knights' national debate that condemned land speculators and the railroads for their theft of public lands. The Knights believed that those who worked the land should own it.

Herrera, a native of New Mexico, had lived in Santa Fe and San Miguel counties until 1866, when he left the territory. Coming in contact with the Knights in Colorado, he reputedly became acquainted in 1883 with the philosophy of Joseph P. Buchanan, founder of the anarchist Red International. Four years later Herrera returned to Las Vegas.[60] Meanwhile, a rift occurred within the Knights, between its president, Terence Powderly, and union militants. Juan José, joined by his two brothers Pablo and Nicanor, formed part of the left faction.

San Miguel County is located in northern New Mexico, a mountainous land. Its principal town is Las Vegas. "The tract of land that came to be known as the Las Vegas Grant contained 500,000 acres of fine timber, agricultural and grazing lands, the meadows in the area of the future town of Las Vegas being especially rich." As early as 1821, grants to portions of this region had been awarded to individuals; however, because of Indian attacks, most of the grantees failed to settle on their lands. Nevertheless, by 1841, 131 families lived around Las Vegas. "On June 21, 1860, Congress confirmed 496,446 acres as belonging to the town of Las Vegas."[61] A large sector of the population of Las Vegas subsisted by grazing sheep and farming. The land, in accordance with Mexican law and traditions, was held in common by the people and could not be sold. After the Civil War this way of life was challenged by the arrival of Anglo-Americans, who were accustomed to squatting on public domain land and had little knowledge or respect for village lands or the open range. In the 1880s they began to buy tracts from New Mexicans even though, according to Mexican law, the settlers, as users of the land, did not have the right to sell it if such a sale conflicted with communal interests.

Land grabbers claimed an absolute right to lands and fenced their claims, enclosing as many as 10,000 acres. The fencing denied Mexicans access to timber, water, and grazing lands. Naturally Mexicans resented the enclosure, and they became paranoid when Anglos brought a suit, *Milhiser v. Padilla,* in 1887 to test ownership. The court found that "the Las Vegas Grant was a community grant and that the plaintiffs had no case. . . . However, the plaintiffs muted the finding by dropping their case on November 25, 1889, thus not allowing the judgement to be finalized."[62] The favorable court decision did nothing to deter fencing and other encroachments. The attitude of territorial authorities was one of apathy and indifference. The rapid increase in the county's population intensified the struggle for its resources.[63]

On November 1, 1889, Mexicans defended themselves. "Armed with rifles and pistols, draped in long black coats and slickers, their faces hidden behind white masks," 66 horsemen rode into Las Vegas. They converged on the jail, asking for Sheriff Lorenzo López, and then on the home of Miguel Salazar, the prosecuting attorney. No property was damaged at this time, but the action climaxed a year of fence cutting by night riders. Illegal acts were blamed on *Las Gorras Blancas,* and indictments of Mexicans were issued. The secrecy of the organization was an advantage, making it difficult to identify and bring charges against the participants in the raids. The White Caps had public support, and claimed a membership of 1,500. On November 25, county officials brought 26 indictments against 47 suspects, among whom were Juan José and Pablo Herrara.

On December 16, the townspeople marched through the city to demand the release of suspected White Caps. On March 11, 1890, *Las Gorras* toured East Las Vegas, leaving copies of their platform, which in part read:

Nuestra Plataforma

Our purpose is to protect the rights and interests of the people in general and especially those of the helpless classes.

We want the Las Vegas Grant settled to the benefit of all concerned, and this we hold is the entire community within the Grant.

We want no "land grabbers" or obstructionists of any sort to interfere. We will watch them.

We are not down on lawyers as a class, but the usual knavery and unfair treatment of the people must be stopped.

Our judiciary hereafter must understand that we will sustain it only when "justice" *is* its watchword.[64]

Many Anglos and establishment Mexicans condemned the platform as anti-American and revolutionary. Miguel A. Otero described the White Caps as "a criminal organization."[65] *The Optic,* the town newspaper, portrayed them as a destructive influence in the community. However, by 1890, the White Cap raids spread to Santa Fe County.

Las Gorras continued cutting fences and destroying property. They attacked the railroad, since it appropriated land for rights-of-way and brought people and commerce that destroyed the old way of life. The government stepped up activities against them. Governor Le Baron Prince threatened to send troops into the area if local authorities did not stop *Las Gorras.* He proposed that one or two companies of federal troops be stationed in San Miguel to demonstrate power and protect railroad property and that detectives be employed to infiltrate *Las Gorras.* He was not able to carry out his plans because the secretary of the interior did not cooperate.[66] When Prince, finally, visited Las Vegas, he learned, to his dismay, that four-fifths of those he met sympathized with *Las Gorras.*

Meanwhile, Terence Powderly, president of the Knights of Labor, became concerned about *Las Gorras*'s militancy and the group's link to the union through the Herreras. Even local Euroamerican members worried about *Las Gorras* infiltration and "the large number of 'Mexican people' of the lower classes who were being admitted to their union."[67] Many moderate members grew nervous about the alleged violence of Las Gorras. They also resented these night riders' intrusion into labor politics—on April 3, 1890, for instance, Las Gorras posted wage rates in which they told the workers what to demand for cutting and hauling railroad ties. The previous month 300 armed men had destroyed approximately 9,000 ties belonging to the Santa Fe Railway. Las Gorras harassed workers who did not support the rate standard. Ultimately, however, the railroad undercut Las Gorras by announcing that it would no longer purchase ties in San Miguel County. This reprisal cost the county $100,000 annually and caused high unemployment. Hungry workers blamed Las Gorras instead of the railroad. During this period, Powderly and the Knights' leadership disavowed any connection with Juan José.

The involvement of the Herreras and Las Gorras in the People's party (partido) also irked the national Knights' leadership. The party had been formed in San Miguel in 1888. Juan José did not join until two years later. The People's party challenged the boss-ridden Republicans and attracted many disillusioned members of both parties. By 1890, many party loyalists boasted that a majority of San Miguel voters supported their organization.[68] Within the rank and file, various factions vied for leadership. Of course, the Herreras represented the militants. Félix Martínez and Nestor Montoya, representing a sizable faction, led the moderates. When the party nominated Pablo Herrera for the territorial House of Representatives, immediate opposition developed within the party, with moderates charging that the Herreras were extremists.[69]

La Voz del Pueblo, a Spanish-language newspaper founded by Nestor Montoya, vehemently opposed the ring. In 1890 Montoya, joined by Félix Martínez, moved the newspaper from Santa Fe to Las Vegas "to champion the cause of the people against the agents of corruption." In Las Vegas La Voz, while not condoning fence cutting, did explain the reasons for it.[70]

In 1890, the People's party swept the county elections, winning four seats in the Assembly. It was one thing to win elections, however; passing reform legislation to regulate railroad rates or, for that matter, to protect the Las Vegas grant represented a different challenge. Soon after his election, Assemblyman Pablo Herrera announced his disillusionment. Speaking before the legislature in February 1891, he said:

> Gentlemen . . . I have served several years' time in the penitentiary but only sixty days in the legislature. . . . I have watched the proceedings here carefully. I would like to say that the time I spent in the penitentiary was more enjoyable than the time I spent here. There is more honesty in . . . prison than . . . [in] the legislature. I would prefer another term in prison than another election in the house.[71]

Pablo Herrera returned to San Miguel and attempted to revive Las Gorras Blancas; he was expelled from the Knights of Labor and was isolated. He became a fugitive after killing a man in Las Vegas. Herrera was eventually fatally shot by Félipe López, a deputy sheriff.[72]

Reforms at the county level were frustrated, and attacks on the White Caps continued. Beset by factionalism, *el partido* faded away. The party had not developed a clear platform and its members often did not share its class interests. Félix Martínez, an influential journalist and businessman, looked at the People's party as a vehicle for reform and as a means of acquiring personal power. Martínez did not want to radicalize society—merely to increase Mexican representation and stop Anglo-American land encroachments. Throughout his tenure in the *partido,* Martínez continued to negotiate with Democratic party leaders.

Sheriff Lorenzo López represented conservatives within the *partido.* Already a *jefé político* (political boss), he joined because of a rift with his brother-in-law Eugenio Romero, the boss of San Miguel's Republican party. Again Juan José, who had been elected probate judge, led the radicals. He had the support of the poor, who distrusted the first two factions, viewing them as *políticos.* The poor liked Juan José's direct methods, and they knew that he voiced their interests.

During 1889 and 1890, under the leadership of Juan José, the White Caps effectively stemmed land speculation; however, after this effort he put his energies into the *partido,* struggling to keep it from ripping itself apart. Cutting fences gave way to long-drawn-out litigation that often diluted the people's initial enthusiasm and hope.

Government infiltration and provocateuring also took its toll. For example, Pinkerton agent Charles A. Stiringo, the infamous Spanish-speaking spy, infiltrated the *partido* and became good friends with Nicanor Herrera. Stiringo regularly reported on the activities of the Herreras. For these and other reasons, by 1896, the *partido* faded.

In 1894 the United States Court of Private Land Claims ruled the San Miguel claim a community grant, but the court limited its decision to house lots and garden plots, excluding common pasturage.[73] And while *los hombres pobres* continued to cut fences as late as 1926, they failed to stop the influx of Anglos and capital that symbolized the changes that were taking place.

THE END OF THE FRONTIER

The Santa Fe Ring's heyday lasted from 1865 to 1885. Government corruption, warfare, and political favoritism all marred these years. Excesses that drew national attention to the lawlessness in New Mexico forced changes. After 1885, machine politics took another form. Many merchant capitalists became bankers, and they invested their profits in mining, cattle, and land. By the 1890s, the railroad had spread throughout the territory, attracting a massive influx of capital and labor. The railroad made possible the marketing of the territory's resources.

In 1879 the arrival of the Atchison, Topeka & Santa Fe Railway ended New Mexico's isolation. Two years later the railroad joined the Southern Pacific at Deming, New Mexico, giving the territory its first transcontinental link. Towns such as Las Cruces, Silver City, and Gallup emerged and/or grew as the result of railroad links. Meanwhile, the territory's population jumped from 119,000 in

1880 to 195,000 20 years later. Property values increased from $41 million in the 1880s to $231 million by the start of the 1890s. The number of cattle expanded from 347,000 to 1.63 million.

It is ironic that, although the Santa Fe Ring had promoted the introduction of the railroad in New Mexico in hopes of making greater profits, its arrival contributed to the ring's demise. Young merchants and lawyers resented the monopoly and privileges enjoyed by the ring and challenged its power. The first threat to its domination came in the guise of a reform movement. Reformers wanted to limit the machine's control of the Mexican vote and the manipulation of elections. This encouraged some ring members to branch out and build their own independent power bases.[74]

The ring's decline did not end violence, that remained at a high level into the 1890s. Although the number of Euroamericans increased, Mexicans still had a substantial majority. Unfortunately, Mexican politicians did not join the People's party to bring about reform. Instead, political brokers manipulated the system to their own advantage.

The issue of statehood is an example of the blatant opportunism of "Spanish American" brokers. Many *politicos* opposed statehood because, according to them, it "meant Anglo-American rule, taxes, public schools, anti-Church policies, and the acquisition of their remaining lands."[75] The territorial system assured their power as local bosses. Moreover, the rich Mexicans vehemently opposed public education. They rationalized this opposition on religious grounds, but stated more candidly: *"Educar un muchacho es perder un buen pastor"* ("To educate a boy is to lose a good shepherd"). Further, they resented the prospect of paying taxes to educate the poor. In New Mexico, out of 109,505 inhabitants, 57,156 did not know how to read or write. The overwhelming majority of the illiterate were Mexican. Of 44,000 children, only 12,000 Mexican youngsters attended schools. The church supported the rich in the matter of public education, since reform would have ended its monopoly.

The 1890s were turbulent with the furor over the Maxwell Land Grant coincided with the San Miguel County wars, and its conclusion came at about the same time. By 1896 only Stonewall County remained in open rebellion, with violence taking the form of burning 130 tons of hay in December 1898 north of Stonewall. Improved transportation ended isolation, facilitating the influx of more federal troops and company posses. By the turn of the century, no longer was New Mexico's development in the hands of local entrepreneurs. Large amounts of capital entered the territory from the eastern United States and Europe to exploit its resources. An indication of this change was that, by 1900, the Rocky Mountain Timber Company had acquired the Maxwell Land Grand Company.[76]

Modernization turned large numbers of *paisanos* into wage earners. Many worked on the railroads, in the mines, and on commercial farms. Industrialization promoted "urbanism, capital-intensive production, and a mass labor force of individual wage earners that rapidly overwhelmed local society, no matter how collectivized."[77] The transformations forced New Mexicans to defend themselves.

Some joined unions such as the Knights of Labor; others organized mutual aid societies *(mutualistas)*—self-help groups—in Las Vegas, Santa Fe, Española, Albuquerque, Rosewell, and Las Cruces.

Mining exploration in eastern Arizona was initiated from southwestern New Mexico and the first rail links were between the Arizona mines and Lordsbury, New Mexico. Miners from Chihuahua and points south passed through southern New Mexico en route to the mines of Arizona and the sugar beet fields and mines of Colorado. The governor's control of the militia, however, helped to frustrate the development of a militant trade union movement in the territory. Unlike the case of Arizona, the Western Federation of Miners did not gain a foothold in New Mexico. Instead, the more moderate United Mine Workers formed locals.

After the turn of the century, the federal government encouraged large farming operations by the construction of dams. Small farmers could not compete with large commercial farmers. Although the agribusinesses represented a small portion of the population, they controlled more than half of the grazing land. These large-scale enterprises worsened the status of many New Mexicans.[78]

Commercial farming was propelled in the Mesilla Valley around Deming and Lordsburg, as elsewhere in New Mexico. It attracted a large army of migrant workers from Mexico. Anglo-American stock raisers had encroached on New Mexican grazing land since the 1880s.

The 1900s brought another wave of encroachers. The U.S. Congress, concerned that Mexicans owned a majority of small independent farms, refused to admit New Mexico to statehood in 1903. Monopolists used this occasion to further their interests. In order to encourage the sale of the public domain and attract more North Americans, they withdrew their opposition to homesteading. Monopolists wanted access to the public domain; however, they knew that the conservationist mood of Congress would not tolerate its sale to large owners. They, therefore, encouraged the sale of the public lands to homesteaders, knowing that it would be impossible for them to succeed. These lands lacked water, with the monopolists themselves owning most of the land irrigated by federal water projects. When the homesteaders failed, the monopolists purchased their land.

In all, the federal government distributed 30 million acres to homesteaders —7 million in 1909 alone. The system had a devastating effect on the New Mexican subsistence farmers, who had, aside from farming, grazed small flocks of sheep on the land in order to supplement their farming. Additionally, the small New Mexican farmer could not compete with commercial farmers. In order to survive, New Mexicans had to run sheep on shares for larger concerns. And others had to look for day work. These changes modified the gender division of labor. Women assumed additional responsibilities, irrigating their holdings and caring for the animals while their husbands looked for work, traveling to the mines, railroads, and the cities.[79]

As land resources also became scarcer, the migration from the small villages to the cities accelerated. In the cities New Mexicans sold their labor. Occupational and social segmentation was common, and Mexicans suffered increasingly from racial and cultural discrimination.

Machine politics until the 1930s mediated conflicts between Anglos and Mexicans; the Catholic Church served the same function. Appointments like that of Miguel Otero as territorial governor in 1897 proved meaningless to the power of Mexicanos, since he strengthened his own machine politics in New Mexico to the degree that even an appointment as a notary public became a political favor. During the administration of Otero, the first native New Mexican to serve as territorial governor under U.S. rule, the spoils system sank to lower depths. Otero came from an old New Mexican family. His father had been prominent in politics, participating in bringing the railroad to the territory. His mother was from South Carolina.[80]

Statehood in 1912 brought the issue of New Mexican civil rights into focus. Octaviano A. Larrazolo, a Mexican-born leader, raised the issue of equality of Mexicans at the constitutional convention. Some Anglo-Americans protested against raising the race issue, but a coalition of Mexicans and Anglo sympathizers put a measure through assuring that the Chicanos' rights to vote, to hold office, and to sit on juries could not be denied on account of "religion, race, language or Spanish languages" and assuring the use of Spanish in public documents.[81] On paper it was a victory for the New Mexicans.

Larrazolo, a separatist, represented a break with the politics of accommodation. He made full use of the race issue. The first governor of the state was an Anglo, William C. MacDonald, who served from 1912 to 1917. Larrazolo organized a "native-son" movement, and although he was a Republican, in 1916 he backed Ezequiel Cabeza de Baca against the Anglo-Republican candidate. Cabeza de Baca won, but he died after a month in office and his Anglo lieutenant governor succeeded him. In 1918 both parties nominated New Mexicans to office; Larrazolo won and served from 1919 to 1921; he proved a capable and liberal executive, but the party never nominated him again. After 1921 the politics of accommodation resumed, with Mexicans occupying token positions in selected numbers and the political machines "neatly arranging the rival tickets of major parties in such a manner that Anglo runs against Anglo, and native competes with one of his group."[82]

SUMMARY

New Mexico, with some 60,000 inhabitants, had a much larger population than many western territories that Congress admitted to statehood during the nineteenth century. Members of Congress were reluctant to admit a territory with a majority of Mexicans. In return, many Mexican villagers and Pueblo Indians resented the North American conquest and resultant encroachment on their land. Armed rebellion was common, with active resistance to the North American military occupation. In fact, the history of New Mexico explodes the myth that New Mexicans willingly became incorporated into the North American union.

Resistance was the most intense among the poor; many of the *ricos,* to be sure, cooperated with North American elites. The territorial government lasted for 60 years, during which time the new bureaucracy created a climate of political favoritism and plunder. Official corruption made a mockery of the Treaty of

Guadalupe Hidalgo, which had guaranteed both individual and community grants. It resulted in the destruction of subsistence farming and the New Mexican traditional life style.

New Mexico's invasion began with the penetration of North American merchants in the 1820s, opening an era of mercantile capitalism that lasted to the late 1870s. It ended with the arrival of the railroad. The railways ushered in the industrial period, accelerating the decline of ruralism and the expansion of capital-intensive industries. Local merchants furnished the initial capital for this development. Large investments from eastern U.S. and European capitalists followed.

After the Civil War, merchants, lawyers, and rich ranchers formed the Santa Fe Ring. As in the case of the rest of the United States, machine politics flourished during the next two decades. Poor Mexicans, Indians, and poor whites rebelled against land monopolization which increased their dependence. The Maxwell Land Grant and the Lincoln County War are examples of this resistance to the Santa Fe Ring's economic and political stranglehold.

Industrialization encouraged the centralization and concentration of capital. Substantial industrial expansion occurred in the mines, railroads, and commercial farms. This period saw the further decline of the subsistence farmer and the end of communal property. Land fell into the hands either of the monopolists or the government, which served as a caretaker for the rich.

Mexicans resisted these changes by joining trade unions and/or forming *mutualistas.* Some allied themselves with groups like *Las Gorras Blancas,* whose supporters cut fences in order to stop land enclosures. During the 1890s, the poor joined the People's party to seek political solutions. As in the case of other third-party movements, the People's party failed. In the twentieth century, an attempt to use nationalist strategies also failed because of the Mexicans' extreme poverty.

Mexicans were concentrated in the north of the territory. By the twentieth century more Mexicans from Mexico itself arrived to work in the mines and on commercial farms. More Anglo-Americans also came; many of them were Texans who settled in the eastern portion of New Mexico. Some New Mexicans, calling themselves "Spanish Americans," believed that they could avoid racism by claiming that they were descended from the brutal *conquistadores.*

NOTES

1. Roxanne Dunbar Ortiz, *Roots of Resistance: Land Tenure in New Mexico, 1680–1980* (Los Angeles: Chicano Studies Research Center Publications, U.C.L.A., 1980), p. 66.
2. Nancie González, *The Spanish-Americans of New Mexico: A Heritage of Pride* (Albuquerque: University of New Mexico Press, 1967), p. 205.
3. The population statistics are not exact. According to Hubert Howe Bancroft, *History of Arizona and New Mexico, 1530–1888* (Albuquerque: Horn & Wallace, 1962), p. 642, the U.S. Census of 1850 listed a population of 61,547, exclusive of the Indian population; in 1860 the figure was 80,853, of whom 73,859 were native to New Mexico. D. W. Meinig, *Southwest: Three Peoples in Geographical Change, 1600–1970* (New York: Oxford University Press, 1971), p. 31, writes that by the late 1840s there were about 70,000 *Hispanos* and about 10,000 Pueblo Indians.

4. Howard R. Lamar, *The Far Southwest, 1846–1912: A Territorial History* (New York: Norton, 1970), p. 30.
5. Ward Alan Minge, *Frontier Problems in New Mexico Preceding the Mexican War, 1840–1846* (Albuquerque: University of New Mexico Press, 1965), pp. 41, 44; Lamar. p. 53.
6. Warren A. Beck, *New Mexico: A History of Four Centuries* (Norman: University of Oklahoma Press, 1962), pp. 126–127.
7. Bancroft, pp. 324, 327.
8. Lamar, p. 53.
9. Benjamin M. Read, *Illustrated History of New Mexico* (New York: Arno Press, 1976), pp. 407–408; Minge, pp. 304–306.
10. Magoffin had come to the region in 1828 and was married to María Gertrudes Váldez. He met with President Polk before the march, giving him a considerable amount of information about New Mexico. Stella M. Drumm, ed., *Down the Santa Fe Trail and into New Mexico* (New Haven, Conn.: Yale University Press, 1962), p. xxiv.
11. Lynn I. Perrigo, *The American Southwest* (New York: Holt, Rinehart and Winston, 1971), p. 164; Ralph Emerson Twitchell, *The Conquest of Santa Fe 1846* (Española, N.M.: Tate Gallery Publications, 1967), p. 52.
12. Carolyn Zeleny, "Relations Between the Spanish Americans and Anglo-Americans in New Mexico: A Study of Conflict and Accommodation in Dual Ethnic Situation" (Ph.D. dissertation, Yale University, 1944), p. 137.
13. Quoted in Beck, p. 134.
14. Alvin R. Sunseri, "New Mexico in the Aftermath of the Anglo-American Conquest" (Ph.D. dissertation, Louisiana State University and Agricultural and Mechanical College, 1973), p. 131.
15. Ralph Emerson Twitchell, *The History of the Military Occupation of the Territory of New Mexico* (New York: Arno Press, 1976), p. 125; Lamar, p. 70.
16. Twitchell, *Conquest of Santa Fe,* p. 133.
17. Carey McWilliams, *North from Mexico* (New York: Greenwood Press, 1968), p. 118.
18. Bancroft, p. 436; Zeleny, p. 118; (Sister Mary) Loyola, *The American Occupation of New Mexico, 1821–1852* (New York: Arno Press, 1976), p. 71.
19. Sunseri, p. 143; Larry Dagwood Ball, "The Office of the United States Marshall in Arizona and the New Mexico Territory, 1851–1912" (Ph.D. dissertation, University of Colorado, 1970), p. 23.
20. Dunbar Ortiz, p. 41.
21. Dunbar Ortiz, p. 62.
22. Dunbar Ortiz, p. 94.
23. Robert J. Rosenbaum, *Mexicano Resistance in the Southwest* (Austin: University of Texas Press, 1981), p. 23.
24. Robert Johnson Rosenbaum, "Mexicano Versus Americano: A Study of Hispanic-American Resistance to Anglo-American Control in New Mexico Territory, 1870–1900" (Ph.D. dissertation, University of Texas, 1972), p. 5. Meinig, pp. 63–64.
25. González, p. 52.
26. González, p. 53.
27. Stan Steiner, *La Raza: The Mexican Americans* (New York: Harper & Row, 1969), p. 8.
28. McWilliams, p. 122.
29. Robert W. Larson, *New Mexico's Quest for Statehood, 1846–1912* (Albuquerque: University of New Mexico Press, 1968), p. 143.
30. William A. Keleher, *The Maxwell Grant* (Santa Fe: Rydal Press, 1942), p. 152.
31. Larson, p. 143.
32. Quoted in Howard R. Lamar, *The Far Southwest, 1846–1919* (New Haven, Conn.: Yale University Press, 1966), p. 150.
33. Herbert O. Brayer, *William Blackmore: The Spanish-Mexican Land Grants of New Mexico and Colorado, 1863–1878* (1949), reprinted in Carlos E. Cortés, ed., *Spanish and Mexican Land Grants* (New York: Arno Press, 1974), p. 173.
34. Keleher, *The Maxwell Grant,* p. 150; Rosenbaum, "Mexicano Versus Americano," p. 42; Lamar, *The Far Southwest, 1846–1919,* p. 142; Rosenbaum, "Mexicano versus Americano," pp. 71, 75–79.

35. Keleher, p. 29; F. Stanley, *The Grant That Maxwell Bought* (Denver: World Press, 1953), p. i; Rosenbaum, "Mexicano Versus Americano," pp. 61, 64.
36. Rosenbaum, "Mexicano Versus Americano," pp. 80, 86–91, 98.
37. Rosenbaum, "Mexicano Versus Americano," pp. 92–93.
38. Rosenbaum, "Mexicano Versus Americano," pp. 95–96, 99.
39. Larson, p. 138.
40. Keleher, pp. 109–110.
41. Charles L. Kenner, *A History of New Mexican-Plains Indian Relations* (Norman: University of Oklahoma Press, 1969), p. 41; Brayer, pp. 244–245; Beck, pp. 255, 260.
42. Maurice G. Fulton, *History of the Lincoln County War,* Robert N. Mullen, ed. (Tucson: University of Arizona Press, 1968), p. 8.
43. Rosenbaum, "Mexicano Versus Americano," p. 115; Meinig, p. 34.
44. Rosenbaum, "Mexicano Versus Americano," p. 116.
45. Fulton, pp. 406–407.
46. Rosenbaum, "Mexicano Versus Americano," p. 119; Fulton, pp. 45–47.
47. Fulton, pp. 291–292.
48. Fulton, pp. 405–409.
49. Rosenbaum, "Mexicano Versus Americano," p. 340; Perrigo, p. 279.
50. Pedro Sánchez, *Memorias Sobre la Vida del Presbitero Don Antonio José Antonio Martínez* (Santa Fe: Compania Impresora del Nuevo Mexicano, 1903), reprinted in David Weber, ed., *Northern Mexico on the Eve of the North American Invasion* (New York: Arno Press, 1976), p. 11; William A. Keleher, *Turmoil in New Mexico, 1846–1868* (Santa Fe: Rydal Press, 1952), p. 132, n. 71; Keleher, *The Maxwell Grant,* pp. 15, 133.
51. Zeleny, p. 257–258; Larson, p. 82; Perrigo, pp. 219–220. On April 7, 1974, the Santa Fe *New Mexican* published an article called "Was He Racist? Carson Debate Set," by Don Ross. It reported that the G.I. Forum opposed naming a national forest after Kit Carson because he was anti-Mexican; Loyola, p. 35.
52. Paul Horgan, *Lamy of Santa Fe: His Life and Times* (New York: Farrar, Straus & Giroux, 1975).
53. Ray John De Aragón, *Padre Martínez and Bishop Lamy* (Las Vegas: Pan-American Publishing, 1978), p. 98.
54. Alex M. Darley, *The Passionist of the Southwest or the Holy Brotherhood* (1893), reprinted in Carlos E. Cortés, ed., *The Penitentes of New Mexico* (New York: Arno Press, 1974), p. 5; Francis Leon Swadesh, *Los Primeros Pobladores* (Notre Dame: University of Notre Dame Press, 1974), p. 78; Miguel Antonio Otero, *Otero: An Autobiographical Trilogy,* vol. 2 (New York: Arno Press, 1974), p. 46.
55. Alice Corbin Henderson, *Brothers of Light: The Penitentes of the Southwest* (1937), reprinted in Cortes, *Penitentes of New Mexico,* p. 77; Swadesh, p. 75.
56. Horgan, p. 229; on p. 353 Horgan makes the point that Martínez died one of the richest men in New Mexico.
57. Quoted in De Aragón, p. 105.
58. Robert W. Larson, "The Knights of Labor and Native Protest in New Mexico," in Robert Kern, ed., *Labor in New Mexico: Union, Strikes and Social History Since 1881* (Albuquerque: University of New Mexico Press, 1983), p. 4.
59. Rosenbaum, "Mexicano Versus Americano," pp. 132–133, 139–140; Andrew Bancroft Schlesinger, "Las Gorras Blancas, 1889–1891," *Journal of Mexican American History* (Spring 1971): 87–143.
60. Larson, "The Knights of Labor," p. 36.
61. Schlesinger, pp. 93, 44.
62. Rosenbaum, "Mexicano Versus Americano," p. 148.
63. Rosenbaum, "Mexicano Versus Americano," p. 198.
64. *The Optic,* March 12, 1890, quoted in Schlesinger, pp. 107–108.
65. Otero, vol. 2, p. 166.
66. Rosenbaum, "Mexicano Versus Americano," pp. 171, 200. Ironically, Judge James O'Brien, on July 30, 1890, wrote to Prince: "The so-called outrages are the protests of a simple pastoral people against the establishment of large landed estates, or baronial feudalism, in their native territory."

67. Rosenbaum, "Mexicano Versus Americano," p. 156; Larson, "The Knights of Labor," p. 39.

68. Schlesinger, pp. 121, 122.

69. Rosenbaum, "Mexicano Versus Americano," pp. 225, 229, 235.

70. Rosenbaum, "Mexicano Versus Americano," p. 201.

71. Schlesinger, p. 123.

72. Rosenbaum, "Mexicano Versus Americano," p. 247.

73. Rosenbaum, "Mexicano Versus Americano," pp. 324, 261. Between 1891 and 1904 the Court of Private Land Claims heard cases involving 235,491,020 acres, allowing 2,051,526 acres to remain intact. Weber, p. 157, writes, "In New Mexico, for example, more than 80 percent of the grant builders lost their land. There, since community grants and communal holdings were more common than individual grants, the slowness of litigation had its greatest impact on small farmers and herders."

74. Lamar, pp. 172–201.

75. Lamar, p. 190.

76. William Taylor and Elliot West, "Patron Leadership at the Crossroads: Southern Colorado in the Late Nineteenth Century," in Norris Hundley, Jr., ed., *The Chicano* (Santa Barbara: Clio, 1975), p. 79.

77. Kern, p. 4.

78. Carolyn Zeleny, *Relations Between the Spanish-Americans and Anglo-Americans in New Mexico* (New York: Arno Press, 1974), pp. 176–177.

79. Joan Jensen, "New Mexico Farm Women, 1900–1940," in Kern, p. 63.

80. Zeleny, *Relations Between the Spanish-Americans and Anglo-Americans in New Mexico,* 179, 187, 190, 192–193, 200–201, 216, 217.

81. Zeleny, *Relations Between the Spanish-Americans and Anglo-Americans in New Mexico,* 218–219.

82. Zeleny, *Relations Between the Spanish-Americans and Anglo-Americans in New Mexico,* 222–224, 229–230.

chapter *4*

Sonora Invaded: The Occupation of Arizona

AN OVERVIEW

> Many people believe that the American West was conquered by rugged in-
> dividuals with little more than a good horse and fast gun. Small ranchers,
> farmers, miners and businessmen did try to make a go of it, but they were
> quickly displaced by investors with access to national and international sources
> of capital. Few Mexicans enjoyed such access, so Hispanic [sic] [Mexican]
> communities across the Southwest were soon overwhelmed by mining, railroad
> and land and cattle companies who monopolized the richest mineral deposits,
> the best grazing lands and the choicest stretches of river flood plain.[1]

In 1848, maps showed southern Arizona as part of the Mexican state of Sonora.
Spanish colonialism had disrupted the evolution of various indigenous societies,
from the Yaqui and Mayo in southern Sonora to the Papago, Pima, and Hopi in
the north. Spain, in order to retain and to exploit Sonora's resources, moved their
subjects into the area. Over the years, the newcomers mixed with the indigenous
populations. By the time Spanish colonial rule ended, a world political restructuring had created the Mexican nation. This phenomenon produced Sonora, which
was part of Mexico. Sonora was far from a perfect society, with class and racial
conflict common. Sonora had an estimated population of over 100,000, most of
whom were indigenous peoples and *mestizos*. The elite families, as elsewhere,
enjoyed economic, social, and political privileges. The 1848 land grab took Sonoran land north of the Gila River. Five years later the Mesilla Treaty (Gadsden
Purchase) seized the land south of the Gila to the present-day border.

82

According to North American myth, the land and its resources held little attraction for the United States; the main motive, according to U.S. historians, was that the Anglos wanted Arizona so that they could build a direct railroad route from El Paso to the Pacific ocean. In reality, however, many Euroamerican investors sought Arizona's mineral resources. A railroad was not built for over two and a half decades. In contrast, North American entrepreneurs moved almost immediately into what is now southern Arizona to exploit its minerals. These newcomers arrived before the army, bringing with them eastern capital. In the usual scheme of things, Mexicans, Pimas, and Papago Indians provided the labor. Transportation facilities mostly served Sonora and its excellent port of Guaymas, which North Americans also coveted.

Early forms of mercantile capitalism evolved from mining. The army forts and the miners needed supplies, and traders and freighters made fortunes from this enterprise. The Pima and Papago farms furnished most food needs of the territory. Other supplies entered Arizona through Guaymas and from New Mexico.

The military played an important role in maintaining social control over this society. As in the case of Texas and New Mexico, the people were stratified according to race and class. During the early period, the few North Americans occupied a privileged position. They maintained good relations with Mexican elites in Arizona and Sonora, often intermarrying. This social contact between the *ricos* and the North Americans dimmed in the 1880, as the frontier ended and the railroad brought in more Anglo women, and as the need for Mexican, Pima, and Papago Indians for defense against the Apache ceased. After this point, any democracy brought about by the "foxhole" faded away.

During the early decades tension existed between the Anglo and Mexican. Border incidents frequently occurred. North American racism fostered the belief that Mexicans were inferior and, consequently, they were paid less than North Americans for the same job. Anglo-Americans also had the attitude that Mexicans encroached upon their land and that even Sonora belonged to them. During the 1850s, Anglos attempted to provoke Mexico into war in order to retake what was "theirs" and to unify the nation in the face of the inevitable sectional conflict.

In 1863 Arizona separated from New Mexico and became the Arizona territory. As in the case of Texas and New Mexico, a political machine controlled government patronage. During the decades that followed, the North American population increased, with Anglo farmers settling along the rivers in the center of the territory. Political power shifted to the north.

Arizona, like the rest of the Southwest, underwent a dramatic transformation during the 1880s as the so-called Indian problem ended and the railroad made possible the large-scale exploitation of the territory's resources. Improved transportation brought industrialization and more Anglo-Americans and, along with them, eastern and foreign capital. The industrialization of mining and then the commercialization of agriculture greatly affected Mexicans in Arizona. After the 1890s, Mexicans turned to various forms of organizations, including *mutualistas* and trade unions, to defend themselves against increased exploitation and racism.

BUILDING A MYTH

Two overused rationalizations for North American conquest are that the United States invaded a tyrannical government and that the land was nearly uninhabited and nonproductive until the industrious Yankee liberated it. (Note: North Americans in the nineteenth century talked in terms of liberation of land, not of people.) The major portion of the Mesilla Valley was in northern Sonora, aka Arizona. The United States did not want it solely for the purpose of a southern railway route. The main attraction was the Mesilla's mineral wealth.

Many of the agronauts who passed through the area after 1848 on their way to California became interested in the mineral wealth of Mesilla. Historian Hubert Howe Bancroft wrote that although many U.S. citizens criticized the government's purchase of worthless land for a railroad route, "the northern republic could afford to pay for a railroad route through a country said to be rich in mines."[2] Bancroft wrote: "Still the fame of hidden wealth remained and multiplied; and on the consummation of the Gadsden purchase in 1854, we have seen, Americans like [Charles] Poston and [Sylvester] Mowry began to open the mines. Eastern capital was enlisted."[3] Further, it was no coincidence that Poston and Herman Ehrenberg, both successful miners, were surveying for gold and silver in the Santa Cruz Valley in 1854, the year that the treaty was ratified.[4]

Historian Howard Lamar underscored the point that those dubious about the value of the purchase were consoled by both public and private promoters who soon countered criticism with the rumor that rich mineral deposits existed in the Gadsden area.[5] Moreover, in spite of the fact that the U.S. military did not take possession until 1856, the Ajo copper mine in the Sonoita region, which had been discovered by Mexicans, was worked by a San Francisco company from 1855.[6]

Sonora was, in fact, a land renowned for its mineral wealth. Mexicans as well as foreigners in Sonora knew of the mineral potential of southern Arizona. For example, Juan A. Robinson, a merchant and at times the U.S. consul in Guaymas and a long-time Sonora resident, knew Sonora well, since he had lived in the state long before the signing of the Gadsden Treaty. Anglo-Americans in Sonora were well aware of southern Arizona's mineral wealth. Before Mexican independence, extensive ranching and farming existed there. In 1736 *bolas de plata* (nuggets of silver) were found 10 miles southwest of Nogales, Arizona. The mine, which yielded large amounts of silver, significantly was called *Arizonac* or *La Mina Real de Arizona.*[7] As early as 1760 Mexicans found ore in Cananea, just across today's U.S. border. In 1830 Don Francisco de Gamboa's work, which listed the mines in New Spain, was translated into English. It included mines in Upper Pimeria in Sonora, where "some large masses of virgin silver were found in the year 1736."[8] Southern Arizona's topography resembled that of the rest of Sonora, and citizens from that state never doubted its potential.

The French also showed interest in Sonora. In January 1852, Jecker-Torre y Cia, a company with French connections, signed a contract with the local government to exploit northern Sonora. The exploring company was called *La Mineral de la Arizona.* An ill-fated French expedition was launched from San

Francisco, California. The French, however, did not abandon their interest in Sonora, and it is said that this interest encouraged the intervention of Napoleon III in Mexican affairs in the 1860s.[9]

Most works have ignored the economic motives for the seizure of southern Arizona. James Neff Garber's definitive work on the *Gadsden Treaty* deals with the political history of the negotiations but almost totally ignores the motivational factor.[10] It is true that the United States wanted a southern railroad route, but it was not San Diego that was the ideal terminal. The Sonoran port of Guaymas was coveted.

James Gadsden, the U.S. minister to Mexico, attempted to purchase Sonora, but when Mexico proved unwilling to sell this area, Gadsden settled for the mineral potential of southern Arizona and New Mexico. He used heavy-handed methods in the negotiations, threatening Mexican ministers that, if they did not sell southern Arizona and parts of New Mexico, "we shall take it."[11] Mexico ceded over 45,000 square miles, of which some 35,000 were in southern Arizona, for $10 million.[12] It was too much money to pay for land through which a railroad route was no longer feasible, for without the port of Guaymas, the Mesilla was considered worthless and uninhabitable. Therefore, it is logical to conclude that a prime motive was the exploitation of the potential mineral wealth of "Occupied Sonora."

EUROAMERICAN COLONIALISM

Until 1863, Arizona was a frontier of New Mexico, isolated from Santa Fe by hundreds of miles of deserts, mountains, and Apache land. According to Professor Howard Lamar: "Most of the first comers were often motivated by passions more akin to the desire to filibuster and to gain riches by quick exploitation than to satisfy land hunger."[13] The possibility of another California bonanza brought many North Americans to the area. These adventurers set up mining operations with capital from Ohio, New York, Philadelphia, and Washington backers. A high percentage were southerners and Texans who had an antipathy toward Mexicans.

Arizona's geographical isolation presented a barrier to its economic development. Capitalists needed cheap labor and inexpensive transportation. Vast deserts separated the Arizona mines from California ports, and eastern routes were even more hazardous. Climate, lack of transportation, and frontier conditions made it impossible to attract white labor in sufficient quantities. Anglo-American capitalists who came to the territory knew of these liabilities and realized that Sonora, Mexico, was the key to their economic survival. Sonora had a good supply of experienced miners and manual laborers. Essential to making the mines and other industries of the territory pay was the Sonoran seaport of Guaymas, one of the finest on the Pacific Coast.

The stakes were high; the mines were rich in bullion and Mexican labor made their exploitation possible. This economic dependence led to conspiracies to annex Sonora, and thus Guaymas, in order to control the mineral development of all Sonora and ensure a ready flow of labor.

Mexican authorities charged that Anglos in Arizona encouraged Apaches to raid Sonora in order to weaken it and make it vulnerable for annexation. The Sonoran historian Laureano Calvo Berber wrote: "The North American government permitted unscrupulous traders to trade with the Apaches at various crossings on the Colorado River, buying property that they stole [in Sonora] and supplying them with equipment, arms, and munitions."[14] On January 25, 1856, Joaquín Corella, head of Arizpe's *ayuntamiento,* wrote a letter to the Sonoran governor:

> The Gadsden Treaty, we repeat, has again brought misfortune to Sonora; it has deprived the state of its most valuable land, as well as resulting in the protection of the Apache who launch their raids from these lands [Arizona] and to North Americans [bandits] who live among them, because in less than twenty-four hours they can cross the boundary; there the robbers and assassins remain beyond punishment; in our opinion it is vital as well as indispensable to garrison the border with sufficient troops that are always alert, since only in this way can their operation be successful and [only in this way] can they defend the integrity of a state threatened by filibusters.[15]

Private treaties were negotiated by Anglo-Americans with Apache bands. Arizona miners and ranchers struck bargains with the Apaches, ensuring them sanctuary in Arizona in return for immunity from Apache raids, "providing economic ends [the Apaches'] could be served by raiding elsewhere."[16] Charles D. Poston, owner of the Sonora Exploring and Mining Company and later called the "Father of Arizona," made such a treaty with the Apaches. He negotiated the treaty through Dr. Michael Steck, superintendent of Indian Affairs in New Mexico.[17]

Poston admitted that Steck instructed the Apaches "that they must not steal any of my stock nor kill any of my men. The chiefs said they wanted to be friends with the Americans, and would not molest us if we did not interfere with 'their trade with Mexico.' "[18] Steck made other treaties for Anglo-Americans during this period. Moreover, the U.S. army ignored the Apache raids into Mexico. In fact, Captain R. S. Ewell, the commanding officer at Fort Buchanan, was more interested in exploiting the Patagonia mine, of which he was part owner, than administering military and civil affairs.[19]

Cynical disregard for Mexican life was evident in the private treaty provisions of noninterference with the Apaches' "trade with Mexico." A side effect of the Apache raids was that they forced many Sonoran citizens to seek refuge in Arizona, making cheaper labor more available. Annexationists knew that the Apache was depopulating Sonora. Thus, many Anglo-Americans publicly stated that they hoped Apaches and Mexicans would club one another to death. Sylvester Mowry, a prominent miner, in an address to the Geographical Society in New York on February 3, 1859, stated:

> The Apache Indian is preparing Sonora for the rule of a higher civilization than the Mexican. In the past half century the Mexican element has disappeared

from that which is now called Arizona, before the devastating career of the Apache. It is every day retreating further south, leaving to us (when the time is ripe for our own possession) the territory without the population.[20]

Not every North American approved of Anglo perfidy. The *Weekly Arizonian,* on April 28, 1859, strongly condemned the use of the Apache to annihilate Sonorans: "It is, in fact, nothing more nor less than legalized piracy upon a weak and defenseless state, encouraged and abetted by the United States government." Prominent miner and soldier Herman Ehrenberg echoed the *Arizonian:* "If we hate Mexicans, or if we want to take their country, we want no blood-thirsty savages to do the work for us, or to injure them."[21] Ehrenberg knew that Mexican labor as well as trade with Sonora was essential to the growth of Arizona, and condemned the policy of making separate treaties with the Apache.

Annexationists wanted title to all Sonoran mines without having to worry about the former owners. They were racists, who looked upon Sonorans as half-breeds who were not assimilable into the superior Anglo-Saxon population. Anglo-Americans did not want Mexicans as citizens; they needed them as laborers. Illustrative at this point was the Henry Crabb filibuster of 1857. Crabb led about a hundred Californians into Sonora on what was described as a peaceful colonizing expedition. The party marched into the state in military formation, disregarding an order to leave. The Sonorans ambushed the Californians, executed Crabb, and cut off his head and preserved it in alcohol. Anglo-Americans retaliated against Mexicans in Arizona, and a small-scale war broke out. President James Buchanan condemned the Mexican "brutality" and attempted to use it as an excuse to invade Mexico. Many Mexicans fled across the border, abandoning Arizona, and paralyzing the mines and Arizona's economy. Owners and supervisors of mines used their influence to cool emotions on both sides. "Crabb's ill fortune prevented later attempts of a similar nature, but the spirit of filibusterism was potent in Arizona, and the Sonoran authorities were always fearful and suspicious."[22]

Expansionist forces were active in Washington, where Senator Sam Houston sponsored a resolution to make Mexico a protectorate. Twenty-two years later Poston confirmed expansionist intentions:

Among other secrets, it may now be told that President Buchanan and his cabinet, at the instigation of powerful capitalists in New York and New England, had agreed to occupy northern Sonora by the regular army and submit the matter to Congress afterwards. Ben McCullough was sent out as agent to select the military line, and Robert Rose was sent as consul to Guaymas with an American flag prepared expressly to hoist over that interesting seaport upon receiving proper orders.[23]

In 1859 Buchanan sent the *St. Mary's* to Guaymas to precipitate a fight. The incident resembled Commodore Stockton's provocation in Texas. His pretext was the refusal of Governor Ignacio Pesqueira to allow Charles P. Stone to survey public lands of Sonora. The Mexican government had signed a contract with the

Jecker-Torre Company and a group of Anglo-American capitalists, in which the foreigners would get one-third of the public lands and an option to buy another third in return for surveying public lands. Pesqueira, resenting Stone's arrogance, as well as the prospect of foreigners—especially Anglo-Americans—owning two-thirds of Sonora's northern frontier, challenged the contract. When Stone's party resembled a military operation more than a survey team, Pesqueira, remembering the Texas and Southwest experience, ordered Stone out of the state.

Stone encouraged Washington, D.C., to take action:

> I have carefully studied the country and people for eight months past, in which time I have had an excellent opportunity of gaining information from my position in the Survey of the Public Lands, and I feel confident that the only means of saving this state from a return to almost barbarism will be found to be its annexation to the United States. In this opinion I only agree with the most intelligent inhabitants of the State, both native and foreign.[24]

Captain William Porter of the *St. Mary's* demanded that Pesqueira allow Stone to continue his survey and in May protested Stone's expulsion. Anglo-American partners pressured Buchanan to intervene. Captain Ewell of Fort Buchanan entered Sonora, and his insolent manner increased tensions. Finally, in November Captain Porter threatened to bombard Guaymas. Pesqueira replied that if one bomb fell on Guaymas, he would not be responsible for Anglo-American property or lives in Sonora. While the *St. Mary's* left, the incident did not end. On December 19, 1859, Buchanan complained that Mexicans expelled peaceful Anglo-Americans, violating their personal and real property rights. He requested the U.S. Congress to approve occupation of Sonora as well as Chihuahua.[25] However, sectional differences and the pending Civil War prevented Buchanan from waging yet another unjust war.

THE POLARIZATION OF SOCIETY

Relations between the Apache and North Americans gradually deteriorated. Although Euroamericans initially bought peace with the Apaches, in 1854–1857, the alliance gave way to bitter warfare during the Civil War and its aftermath.

In the New Mexican period, Santa Fe appointees ran the frontier government headquartered at Tucson. Self-government did not reach Arizona until the 1860s, when it became a separate territory. During the Civil War, most North Americans in Arizona had pro-Southern sympathies. In order to defend Arizona from possible sedition and from the Apache, the U.S. government dispatched more federal troops to Arizona. According to the 1864 census, Arizona had 4,187 residents, mostly Mexicans, along with some 30,000 indigenous peoples. The Arizona population was concentrated in the Santa Cruz Valley (location of Tucson and Tubac), the lower reaches of the Gila and Colorado rivers, and central Arizona.

From the beginning, Anglo-Americans in Arizona formed a privileged class. Mining, the territory's leading industry, required large capital investments.

Access to large amounts of capital eluded most Mexicans. Two societies developed: the Mexicans performed the manual labor and the Anglos served as entrepreneurs. There were, of course, poor Euroamericans, but even they discriminated against Mexicans. Racism kept the two groups divided. And, of course, some rich Sonorans retained their privileged status. The situation resembled that in Texas and New Mexico, differing mainly in that border conflict in this area generated even more anti–Anglo-American sentiments.

Sonoran elites were well aware that the *gringos* coveted their land and that their privileged position would end if the United States absorbed territory. Still, considerable cooperation existed between the two groups of elites, in some cases it was consummated by marriage. Southern Arizona in the 1850s was the epitome of the wild frontier and few white women lived there. Prominent Anglo-Americans, such as Governor Anson Stafford, married into Sonoran families. Between 1872 and 1899, intermarriage remained high, with 148 of 784, or 14 percent of all marriages, being between Anglo men and Mexican females; during the same period only 6 involved Mexican men and Anglo women. This situation changed drastically in the twentieth century; by 1946 only 3 percent of the marriages were between Anglo men and Mexican women, and only 1 percent between Mexican men and Anglo females.[26] Historian Kay Briegel indicates that the sparseness of the Anglo population of both women and men made intermarriage desirable for the Anglos in Arizona: First, because there were few women who were not of Mexican descent. Second, the Anglos needed harmonious relationships with the Mexicans, which were encouraged by intermarriage, so that the Mexicans would help them defend themselves against the Apache threat. Third, marriage enabled them to do business with their wives' brothers and fathers. Once the railroad ended Arizona's isolation, bringing both Anglo women and men, and once the Indian threat was reduced, this special relation ended and intermarriage was taboo.[27]

Throughout the century, Mexicans did not necessarily, however, view contact with North Americans as a culturally uplifting experience. Many Mexicans saw Anglos as rude and pushy, devoid of tradition and manners. In 1869, Mexican mothers, afraid to allow their daughters to associate with North American children, allegedly because they had bad manners, formed their own school.[28]

Women's activities varied. Although they worked as housewives, domestics, and even in *cantinas* (bars), women also operated businesses and subsistence farms. Eulalia Elías (1788–1860) ran the first major cattle ranch in Arizona. She belonged to a wealthy and powerful founding family. (She was admitted to the Arizona Women's Hall of Fame in the 1980s.) Such opportunities were not open to poor Mexicans of either gender and, consequently, class conditioned the kind of work or opportunities of Mexican women. The highest job a woman could aspire to was that of a school teacher. For instance, in the 1870s, Rosa Ortiz ran a Mexican private school where students learned in Spanish.

During the New Mexican years, a division of labor was rationalized based on race. Myths like that of the "Murderous Apache and the Mexican Outlaw, [who] rivalled each other in their deeds of pillage, robbery, and slaughter"[29] justified both the genocidal war against the Apache and the reduction of Mexican labor to peon status. Euroamericans viewed both the Apache and Mexican as inferior and warranting domination by a superior and orderly race.[30] The Mexican Heritage Project has concluded that "as early as 1860, just six years after the Gadsden Purchase, Tucson's Hispanic [sic] [Mexican] work force was clustered in blue collar occupations—carpenters, blacksmiths, freighters, cooks, laborers and washer women. That same year, Anglos controlled nearly 88 percent of the town's wealth as recorded in property values, even though they represented less than 30 percent of Tucson's population. It did not take long for the Anglo newcomers to seize Tucson's economic and political reins."[31]

At the extreme, peonage, the practice of legally binding debtors or members of their families to a creditor until they paid the debt, was inherited from the Mexican period and practiced by Anglo-Americans in Arizona. For a number of reasons, it did not become a permanent institution: First, proximity of the border made it easy for a runaway to cross into Sonora. Second, it was cheaper to pay a man wages and cut him loose when there was no work. Third, soon after slavery was abolished, peonage was also made illegal. Nevertheless, the practice did continue de facto for many years in Arizona as well as in other places in the United States. During the 1850s and 1860s, many mines, ranches, and businesses practiced peonage. In 1864 Sylvester Mowry praised the institution stating:

> The lower class of Mexican, with the Opata and Yaqui Indians, are docile, faithful, good servants, capable of strong attachment when firmly and kindly treated. They have been "peons" (servants) for generations. They will always remain so, as it is their natural condition.[32]

Peonage, protected by law, was abolished by the Fourteenth Amendment to the Constitution. Peons who ran away were hunted down, tried, and punished. The punishment, in many instances, was inhumane. Witness, for example, the following cases. N. B. Appel owned a mercantile store in Tubac. His servant, indebted to him for $82.68, ran away and allegedly stole a rifle and other articles of worth. Authorities returned the peon to Appel and prosecuted him. Found guilty, he publicly received fifteen lashes.[33] A similar episode occurred on the Riverton Ranch, where seven peons escaped but were returned and charged with debt and theft. The overseers, George Mercer, whipped them and cut off their hair as punishment. Mercer's shears got out of control and he took some skin with the hair. Stories of the "scalping" spread as far as San Francisco. Mercer publicly denied the charge, but readily admitted the whippings.[34]

A double wage standard existed for Mexicans and Anglos. In the mines Mexicans' wages were 30¢ a day for wood choppers or ore sorters (this was called peon's wages); $12.50 to $15.00 a month for pick and crowbar men *(barrateros)* and ore carriers *(tantateros);* and $25.00 to $30.00 a month for skilled workers such as furnace tenders or smelters. In addition, they received 16 pounds of flour a week. They worked for 12 hours a day, 6 days a week. These wages, which prevailed through most of the 1800s, were slightly above those paid in Sonora. The mine operators' actual outlay for wages was even lower, because they recovered most of their capital from their company stores. Operators extended liberal credit to miners and charged them outrageous prices—stores made as much as 300 percent profit on their goods. Aside from making outlandish profits, the stores assured a stable workforce; indebted miners had to remain in order to pay off their debts.[35]

Anglo-American workers demanded wages double those received by Mexicans and were paid from $30.00 to $70.00 a month.[36] Mexicans, assigned the dirtiest jobs—"Mexican work"—were the first fired. When Anglo-Americans did not receive preferential treatment, they spread the word that "the managers . . . employed foreigners and greasers, and would not give a white man a chance."[37] Preferential treatment reinforced the ethnic division within what might have become a unified working class and thus enhanced the operators' goal of maintaining depressed wages.

It is true that, as in the case of New Mexico, a selected number of Mexicans prospered under colonialism. Some Mexicans, returning from the California diggings, realized that the wealth was not in the mines but in services. Some started small mercantile businesses, while others freighted ores and other goods. Félipe Amabisca and Antonio Contreras, for instance, arrived in Arizona City in 1858, and Amabisca opened a mercantile store. In partnership with Contreras, he also established a freighting business, making hauls from Tucson to Los Angeles. Esteván Ochoa, originally from Chihuahua, educated in Independence, Missouri, and formerly from New Mexico's Mesilla, relocated to Tucson and started a freighting business, shipping goods from Santa Fe to Tucson. In 1860, Ochoa entered into a partnership with Pinckney Randolph Tully, with whom he often made shipments valued at between $25,000 and $50,000. Ochoa, well liked and respected in Tucson, donated the property for the new public school built in the mid-1870s. M. G. Samaniego, another prosperous merchant, was also influential.

However, the Ochoas and the Samaniegos were the exceptions, and often, in the early years, they identified more with the Anglos than with their own people. The overwhelming number of Mexicans worked at a subsistence level. In Arizona, North Americans monopolized government and the access to it. By the 1870s, fewer Mexicans were "making it"; upward mobility, in fact, lessened as capital-intensive operations increased and as Mexican access to available capital became an impossible dream.

ENDING THE FRONTIER

After the Civil War, machine politics became popular in Arizona. The Federal Ring, centered in Tucson, was not limited to partisan politics per se. Federal appointees along with business leaders and voters lobbied Congress for appropriations to subsidize military operations, highways, Indian reservations, and the railroad. Freighters like Tully and Ochoa profited handsomely from contacts with the ring. The ring brought limited prosperity, and, by the 1870s, Tucson as well as the rest of Arizona culturally became Anglo.

By 1878, the territory grew to 40,000. In 1853, Tucson had 350 residents; seven years later the figure increased to 623, and in 1864 to 1,526, the majority of whom were Mexicans. In 1870, Tucson had 8,007 residents, with a larger number of Anglos. The bulk of the new Euroamerican immigrants settled in the north. In 1877, territorial authorities moved Arizona's capital from Tucson to Prescott. The number of elected Mexican officials declined after this point. And, by the 1880s, fewer Spanish surnames appeared even in the social columns of Tucson newspapers.

By the 1870s, the military partially controlled the Apache, encouraging the migration of white Americans. A decade later the railroad opened the way for more North American newcomers. The almost complete pacification of the Apache allowed white miners to penetrate the mountains next to the Apache reservation, beginning large-scale mining explorations. Arizona was no longer an isolated frontier. In turn, mining stimulated cattle and farming enterprises, attracting large numbers of Texas cowboys, who, according to Professor Raquel Rubio Goldsmith, imposed "on the region their English language and dislike of Mexicans."[38]

Tucson, by the 1870s, was an important center for trade and transportation. Travelers on the way to California stopped there, and Tucson merchants supplied the military posts, the mines, and the farms in its area.[39] The city's growth was stunted, however, when the government decided to "abandon the Guaymas route for its army supplies."[40] The decision affected Tucson and the majority of Mexicans in the territory. California–Yuma became a popular route for supplying Arizona. This road took a more northern route, following the Gila River, almost completely bypassing Tucson.

The impact of the military's decision is best understood in the context of Arizona's dependence on military contracts. The new military contractors, Hooper, Whiting and Company, paid large sums of money to re-elect Federal Ring congressman Richard McCormick to counter Tucson's lobbying against a northern route.[41] Freighting was a big business, with California and New York investors supporting certain companies for federal contracts.

The last decades of the nineteenth century were a time of rapid agricultural and commercial expansion. Before the 1870s, Arizona's only true agriculturalists were the Pimas and the Papagos. "It [Arizona] had no banks, few roads, fewer cities, no industrial or agricultural base; it only had a scattering of miners, troops and Indians." The first bank of Arizona evolved in Prescott in 1877 to serve 3,000 miners in the nearby Bradshaw Mountains. Before this, "mercantile capitalists acted as bankers."[42] The Bank of Arizona did not challenge the monopoly of San Francisco and New York bankers.

The Homestead Act of 1862 also brought about changes. Farmers trickled into Arizona. By the 1870s, irrigation was introduced to the Salt River Valley, and, in 1871, Pumpkinville, population 300, became Phoenix. By the middle of the decade, North American farmers cultivated hay and cotton. The development of commercial agriculture had a radical effect on Mexican–North American relations.

The entry of large numbers of North Americans intensified discrimination and segregation based on race. Mexican newcomers moved into *barrios* (neighborhoods) and *colonias* (colonies) isolated from whites. Tucson housed the largest

Mexican population, which lived close to the old plaza and to the south. Even after the railroad integrated Arizona into the U.S. market system, Mexicans continued to trade with Mexico. Culturally Mexicans and Anglos grew further apart as the twentieth century approached. Mexicans celebrated *las fiestas patrias* and San Juan's Day (St. John the Baptist) on June 24—dancing, picnicking, and swimming in the Santa Cruz River. Many traveled to Magdalena, Sonora, for the feast of San Francisco in early October. Tucson's Mexican population also patronized traveling Sonoran troupes. Spanish-language newspapers regularly accentuated the separate literary and social life of Mexicans.[43]

The mining boom came in the 1880s, spurred by railroads as well as by new technology and engineering. Telegraph and electrical wires required copper, and the copper mines of southern Arizona attracted San Francisco, eastern U.S., and foreign capital. In 1880 the Copper Queen Mining Company, financed by California capitalists and Louis Zeckendorf, was founded in Bisbee. Phelps Dodge Company, the largest copper producer in the territory, was owned by eastern capitalists.[44]

The mining boom stimulated activity throughout the territory. More miners created a demand for food, cattle, and services. New industries received increased federal protection, which meant more army forts, which in turn meant more government contracts. Indians were herded into reservations, and again more government contracts followed. The demand for large quantities of wood for the mine shafts spread the boom to northern Arizona.

The growing activity attracted more white settlers, and the territory's population increased from 40,000 in 1880 to 90,000 seven years later.[45] Anglos outnumbered Mexicans, with the market value of property increasing to $26 million.

As the territory's population multiplied, polarization between the two societies increased. In agriculture Mexicans formed the workforce. Discrimination intensified as new colonials, mostly farmers, arrived from Utah, Colorado, and points east. They were "peace-loving and God-fearing" settlers who, at the time, were also racist, considering Mexicans the intruders.

In the late 1850s Mexicans began to move out of the Santa Cruz–Sonoita region, pioneering new areas around the junction of the Gila and Colorado rivers. They panned for gold, they travelled into western Arizona and pioneered many new strikes, followed by an avalanche of Anglo adventurers. Even after the boom, Mexicans lingered on to rework abandoned Anglo diggings. Mining treasures of the Black Canyon mines, Bradshaw District, and Walnut Grove yielded to the Mexican's *batea* (a cone-shaped placering pan). In spite of harassments in mining areas during the 1860s, Mexicans continued to push the frontier back.

Relations between Anglos and Mexicans at the mining sites were often strained. The Walker diggings at Lynx Creek are representative of Anglo-Mexican clashes.[46] A Mexican by the name of Bernardo Freyes discovered gold at the diggings near Prescott, Arizona. He was paid $3,000 and exiled to Sonora by Anglo-American miners. As they began to work the diggings, they feared that word of the strike might attract Mexican miners. During 1863–1864 the town of Walker passed a law that "no Mexicans shall have the right to buy, take up, or preempt a claim on this river [the Hassayampa] or in this district for the term of six months." The only Mexican exempted was Lorenzo Parra, who had been among those who bought Freyes out. The town did not allow Mexicans to own claims, but it did permit them to work for wages. Walker was nicknamed "Greaserville."

The 1870s brought more changes affecting Mexicans. Machines replaced Mexicans in mining and agriculture. By the turn of the century, fewer farm hands were needed, and farm labor became increasingly seasonal:

> Coincident with large scale mining, raching and farming the economic position of the Mexican declined. Mexicans had been involved in small scale mining and raching in Sonora and Arizona. The use of barbed wire by Anglos to fence huge Anglo farms and ranches brought about economic subordination of Mexicans.[47]

They lost what land they had and were forced into wage labor in cotton, cattle, and copper.

In the mines the *arrastra* and the *patio* processes* were phased out. For a brief period, hardrock miners drove Mexicans out of the mines, or into exclusively pick and shovel jobs. Less manual labor and more skilled labor was required. Mexican miners did not enjoy the benefits of the new well-paying jobs (hardrock miners, smelters, blacksmiths, carpenters, millwrights, and so on); the mine owners imported Anglo-Americans and Europeans to reap the harvest of the Mexicans' pioneering labors. Adding to the Mexicans' plight during the 1870s and 1880s were the frequent shutdown of mines because of mechanization, change of owners, the declining value of metals, and the fluctuation of the economic cycle. For a time placering (ore prospecting) offered a safety valve, with many Mexicans turning to prospecting when no other work was available. They would work exhausted ground, literally wringing ore from the soil.

Throughout Arizona, mining towns such as Clifton stood as tributes to the Mexicans' abilities. Although Mexicans had known about copper in the mountains north of the Gila, this area had not been worked. In 1864 Henry Clifton rediscovered the body of ore, but many Anglos believed that area was too isolated to develop, and Clifton himself left the site. A group of North Americans from southeastern New Mexico explored the area in the early 1870s and registered claims. At the same time, mining explorations increased. These entrepreneurs employed exclusively Mexican labor. One of the developers was Henry Lesinsky, who incorporated the Longfellow Copper Company. He recognized the Mexicans' skill in smelting and hired an experienced Mexican crew. The settlement of Clifton was "built entirely by Mexican labor." Within a few years the mines at Clifton produced thousands of tons of ore.[48]

In Arizona, as in other places elsewhere in the Southwest, "acts of lawless violence, including murders, robberies, and lynching" were all too common and "too often . . . [there was] a clamor for the expulsion of all Mexicans."[49] During the Crabb filibuster of 1857, "there were public meetings held to urge the expul-

---

Arrastra refers to a burro- or horse-drawn mill where ore was pulverized; *patio* refers to a court or leveled yard where ore was spread out and then pulverized.

sion of the hated 'greasers' from the mines and from the country. A war of races at times seemed impending."[50] Mexicans were blamed for every crime imaginable.

The double standard of justice in Arizona was notorious. Mexican authorities, partly because they were aware of the biased administration of justice in border areas, often refused to extradite alleged criminals who had fled into Sonora. The Mission camp affair was typical. According to Arizona officials, on December 24, 1870, some Mexicans killed Charles Reed, James Little, and Thomas Oliver and wounded Reed's wife in a dispute over the Mexican's alleged theft of some furniture and five horses. The culprits fled into Sonora, and Arizona authorities wanted them back. According to the Mexicans' account, the employer abused them and when he severely beat one of them, they armed and protected themselves.[51] A group of Anglos did not wait to learn what had really happened and rode to the ranch of Francisco Gándara, brother of the former governor of Sonora, to get revenge. They accused Gándara of stealing a mule, which he denied. A shoot-out between the Anglos and Gándara's men followed. Gándara and one of the assailants, James Bodel, were killed. The Anglo gang then left the ranch and hunted down and killed a Mexican who had vowed to avenge Gándara.

The press on both sides of the border hurled accusations at the other. Naturally, the Sonoran press wrote about the issue of discrimination in Arizona.[52] Governor Pesqueira refused to extradite the accused Mexicans, although he carried on lengthy negotiations with the Arizona governor, A. P. K. Safford. Similar incidents occurred throughout the 1870s. Anglo-Americans used the affairs to justify attacks on Mexicans, and Mexicans reacted to the violence by fighting back.

Antipathy toward Mexicans reached its highest level in places where there were "cowboys." In Tombstone, Arizona, famous for harboring the most corrosive outlaws of Texas, owners of businesses and mines would not hire Mexicans because they did not want to incur the wrath of cowboys who controlled the town. Cowboys formed gangs to raid defenseless Mexican villages. The shooting of Mexicans became commonplace, with cowboys showing little respect for women or children.[53]

As in other territories and states in the Southwest, Mexicans in Arizona had to fight the land-grant battle, although on a smaller scale. Grants in the Arizona territory were guaranteed by the Gadsden Purchase treaty, but in controversies characterized by fraud and delay, Mexicans lost their land. Congress in 1870 authorized the surveyor-general of Arizona "to ascertain and report" upon claims.[54] According to Bancroft:

Most of the claims are doubtless equitably valid and will eventually be confirmed, though since 1879 the surveyor-general has investigated fourteen of them or more, and recommended them for approval or rejection. This delay on the part of the government has been entirely inexcusable, as the matter might have been easily settled fifteen years ago. Since that time lands have increased in value; conflicting interests have come into existence; probably fraudulent schemes have been concocted; and even a hope has been developed that all the Mexican titles might be defeated. Owners have no real protection against squatters, cannot sell or make improvements, and in fact have no other right than that of paying taxes; while on the other hand the rights of settlers are jeopardized by possibly invalid claims, and a generally unsettled and unsatisfactory system of land tenure is produced.[55]

By 1880 the Southern Pacific reached Tucson and by 1890 the territory had 1,000 miles of line. The rail lines, added to the 700 miles of canals, made a fairly complete transportation network.[56] Arizona's population increased rapidly. The number of those engaging in commerce jumped from 591 in 1870 to 3,252 in 1880.[57] Until the 1870s pesos were used as the dominant currency and trade was mainly through Sonora. Shipping was more convenient through Guaymas than hauling ores to the California coast. As mentioned, government policy changed this dependence on Sonoran markets in 1870. Moreover, the influence of the Yuma and Gila river farmers increased. The railroad completely changed Arizona's contact from north and south, to east and west.[58] Capital investment in large-scale mining, ranching, and agriculture increased with the arrival of the railroad.[59]

THE INDUSTRIALIZING OF ARIZONA

In the 1890s Sonoran workers continued to furnish a large proportion of Arizona's labor needs. However, increasingly large numbers of Mexican workers arrived from Chihuahua and points south via El Paso. Much of this labor found employment in the Arizona mines. With the arrival of the railroad, opportunity for upward mobility became more restricted, and, as Arizona became more industrialized, many small Mexican businesses could not compete. For example, the railroad wiped out Estebán Ochoa and Pinckney Randolph Tully's freighting business, making its $100,000 worth of equipment obsolete overnight.

Racism toward Mexicans increased with the end of the Apache threat. Mexicans more frequently became scapegoats for societal problems. During the depression of 1893, nativism rose, and even the more prosperous Mexicans felt the sting of Euroamerican racism. In 1894 nativists formed the American Protective Association in Tucson.[60]

A group of Mexican elites founded *La Alianza Hispano-Americana* on January 14, 1894, in response to this new tension. "Through this organization they sought to maintain political representation as well as continue the contribution of Mexican-Americans to the development of Arizona and the greater Southwest."[61] Ignacio Calvillo, one of the founders of the organization, stated, "In those days the English and Spanish-speaking had a hard time getting along. The element opposed to the Spanish-American people in the Southwest had organized itself into the American Protective Association."[62] *La Alianza,* at first a local organization, expanded, and in 1897 it held its first national convention. By 1910 it had over 3,000 members in Arizona, Texas, New Mexico, California, and Mexico. In 1913, influenced by the women's suffrage movement, it voted to admit women to full membership.[63]

Mexican workers were anything but docile in the face of these changes.

Organizations such as *La Alianza* motivated resistance. In 1897 Mexican railroad workers struck at Mammoth Tank, 40 miles west of Yuma. When the 200 strikers saw the undersheriff and a posse ride up, they mistakenly thought that he had come to interfere with the strike. Because he could not communicate in Spanish, the undersheriff did not make it clear that he was in fact chasing a man unconnected with the strike. Threatened by the workers, he fired his pistol in the air. The infuriated Mexicans took the sheriff's gun away from him. A deputy with a shotgun dispersed the crowd. Reinforcements were sent to Mammoth Tank and the strike leaders were shipped to prison in San Diego, California.[64] Most strikes during this early period were spontaneous. The more militant union organization took place in the mines, where a year-round workforce grouped laborers in an intense industrial environment.

The 1880s saw dramatic changes in Arizona. The population jumped from 40,000 to 90,000 during the decade. The 1890 census showed that North Americans outnumbered Mexicans. The influx of miners created a demand for food, clothing, building materials, cattle and so on. By the mid-1880s Tombstone had 15,000 residents, and Mormon farmers moved into the Salt River Valley in ever greater numbers.

Copper became the mainstay of the territory's economy. Demand for the metal grew as its uses increased. Technology and engineering altered the methods in mine production. Mexican labor had been used during the exploration phase, but once transportation made it possible to ship greater quantities of copper, skilled hardrock miners, many of whom were Cornish, worked the rich veins. However, as this supply was exhausted and demands grew, the industry was forced to restructure. Refining and concentration methods made possible the mining of lower-grade ores, for which less skilled labor could be used. Larger corporations bought out the smaller companies that did not have sufficient investment for this capital- and labor-intensive production. In the process, the hardrock miner was phased out, replaced by pick and shovel workers. Frustrated by this loss in status, the hardrock miner pecked down, blaming the Mexican instead of the mine owners for the changes. This division of labor ultimately played into the hands of the owners, who agitated the white miners against the Mexicans.

The hardrock miners formed the first trade unions. Driven by the deskilling of the mining industry caused by its modernization, the miners desperately sought to protect their status through collective bargaining. The process of mass production led to the importation of large numbers of Mexicans whom hardrock miners scapegoated as the cause of their calamity. The new unions often prioritized the ban of Mexicans from their camps and restriction of Mexican immigration. Union leaders, instead of educating the rank and file, more often reflected these base prejudices and, in fact, fanned them as a means of gaining worker support. They branded "cheap labor" as Mexican work. This lack of working class unity allowed employers to continue using a double wage standard that paid Mexicans less than Anglos; in fact, the Euroamerican workers jealously guarded this privilege. Mexicans, in turn, resented getting paid less for the same work and what went with it—segregated housing, facilities and so on.

Even the Western Federation of Miners (WFM), a union led by radicals, did not recruit Mexicans in Arizona because of the hostility of Euroamerican miners toward them. Mexican miners themselves organized *mutualistas* and became more conscious of their new status. Arizona legislators, aware of the new militancy among miners of all colors, passed a special law in 1901 that created the Arizona Rangers, who closely resembled the Texas Ranges. Supposedly formed to stop cattle rustling, this unit were more often used as strikebreakers.[65]

In 1903, labor relations deteriorated when the Arizona legislature passed an eight-hour day law. Mine owners reacted by cutting the workers' wages by 10 percent. On the morning of June 3, three days after the law went into effect, miners walked off the job, shutting down the smelters and mills, beginning what Jeanne Parks Ringgold, granddaughter of then-sheriff Jim Parks of Clifton, called the "bloodiest battle in the history of mining in Arizona."[66]

The walkout of the Clifton miners was 80 to 90 percent effective. Between 1,200 and 1,500 strikers participated, of whom 80 to 90 percent were Mexican. Clifton was the center of the largest producing district in Arizona. During the strike armed miners took control of the mines and shut them down. Strike activity engulfed neighboring mining camps at Morenci and Metcalf. Mining companies refused to negotiate.[67]

Mexicans controlled the strike; many leaders came from the ranks of Mexican *mutualistas*. The *Bisbee Daily Review* of June 3, 1903, wrote: "The Mexicans belong to numerous societies and through these they can exert some sort of organization stand together."[68] At first there was cooperation among the ethnic groups. The leaders were Abraham Salcido, the president of a Mexican society; Frank Colombo, an Italian; and W.H. Laustanau, a Rumanian; and A.C. Cruz, a Mexican.[69] Two days later the *Bisbee Daily Review* observed that "the strike is now composed almost entirely of Mexicans. Quite a number of Americans have left."[70] During the *huelga* (strike), tempers rose and racial animosities heightened. Among the demands were free hospitalization, paid life insurance for miners, locker rooms, fair prices at the company store, hiring of only men who were members of the society, and protection against being fired without cause.

The governor ordered the Arizona Rangers into Clifton–Morenci to intimidate Mexican workers, and on June 9, 1903, workers staged a demonstration of solidarity. In direct defiance of the Rangers, 2,000 Mexicans marched through the streets of Morenci in torrential rains. A clash seemed inevitable, but the storm dispersed the strikers. A flood panicked the townspeople, drowning almost 50 people and causing some $100,000 worth of damage.[71]

The local sheriff reported that Mexicans had armed themselves and requested assistance from the governor. The Mexican consul in Arizona, a tool of Porfirio Díaz, was sent "to talk some sense to the Mexicans." Federal troops, along with six companies of national guards, were sent to the trouble area, and martial law was declared.[72] However, this overwhelming show of force did not end the strike; rather the flood did.

The strike leaders—Salcido, Colombo, Laustanau, and Cruz—were convicted for inciting a riot. (Laustanau died in the Yuma State Penitentiary as the result of prolonged solitary confinement.) The Clifton–Morenci strike is important because it predated the Cananea, Sonora, strike (precursor of the Mexican Revolution) by three years, with many of the strikers in Morenci–Clifton taking part in the Cananea struggle. Salcido, who was released in 1906, organized anti-Díaz forces and engaged in pro-labor activities on both sides of the border. U.S. authorities, at the urging of Mexican officials, deported him to Mexico, where the government put him in infamous San Juan de Ulúa prison. While the Clifton–Morenci strike failed, it contributed to politicizing Mexican miners in Arizona and Mexico.

Clifton–Morenci continued as the center of militancy. It became the home of Mexican political exiles such as Teresa de Urrea, popularly known as *la Santa de Cabora*. The Yaqui Indians of Sonora venerated her, invoking her name when they rebelled against the government in the 1890s. At Tomochic, Chihuahua, the Mexican army slaughtered an entire village when the townspeople protested past and present injustices. Tomochicans had made a pilgrimage to Sonora to visit Teresa. Meanwhile, Teresa fled to the United States, where she was a close friend of Lauro Aguirre, a revolutionary journalist. Via Nogales and El Paso, Teresa finally settled in Clifton.

Although evidence does not directly link Teresa to revolutionary activity, her father and stepmother were involved. The home of her stepmother was used as a headquarters for the *Partido Liberal Mexicano* (PLM). Revolutionaries such as Praxedis Guerrero lived and organized in Clifton–Morenci–Metcalf camps.

Labor difficulties intensified in the Clifton–Morenci district, which, for a time, was the major copper producer in Arizona.[73] Breakthroughs in technology made possible mass production, increasing demand for pick and shovel labor.[74] World War I also boosted the demand for copper. Production increased from 23,274,965 pounds in 1883 to 719,035,514 pounds in 1917.[75] The size and importance of the Arizona industry added significantly to labor unrest.

The WFM began to organize all workers in the area after the 1903 strike. The Arizona Federation of Labor also organized miners. Trade unionists formed alliances with small business owners and farmers to counter the power and special privileges of the copper barons. The small people resented the fact that the copper companies did not pay their share of taxes. Prior to and just after Arizona statehood (1912), this popular coalition controlled state politics. However, by 1914, the copper barons successfully divided the coalition through a campaign of intimidation, subversion, libel, and slander. The copper barons directly or indirectly owned many of the state's newspapers and waged an active propaganda war against all trade unions.

By 1915, conditions again forced workers to strike when the owners lowered wages. Because the mining interests owned all the land, their company stores had a monopoly. Through the stores the miners were constantly kept in debt.[76]

The workers' indebtedness to the company was further increased by the company's monopoly of the water supply. The owners deducted water fees from the workers' wages. Abuse of Mexicans was not limited to the owners: "Petty foremen and minor officials . . . [forced them] to buy chances on worthless, or nearly worthless, items . . . to get or keep a job. Shift bosses collected from $5 to $15 a month for such services."[77] Foremen made a profit by renting shacks to the workers for $10 a month. This was a high rate, considering that Mexican workers earned only $2.39 for a 7½-hour shift.

In August 1915, conditions unified workers to the point that they welcomed

WFM leadership. They demanded a $3.50 per day minimum for all underground miners, regardless of their race. Once again, Mexican leadership was highly visible. Many were veterans of Sonoran copper mines and had experience in strikes in the Mexican state. In September, when the owners rejected the WFM's demands, miners went on strike. The strike lasted five months and involved no major violence because Arizona governor George W. P. Hunt and local sheriff James Cash were determined not to permit another Ludlow massacre (the year before at Ludlow, Colorado, soldiers shot down miners and their families who were striking Rockefeller mining interests).

The miners won a raise of $2.50 per day for surface workers and $3.00 for men working underground. Workers were forced to abandon the WFM for the Arizona State Federation of Labor, an affiliate of the American Federation of Labor (AFL). The mine owners conceded because labor stopped production. The war in Europe also drove copper prices up, making it unprofitable for the copper barons to continue the strike. This strike, however, ultimately stiffened the mine managers' resolve to smash labor in Arizona.

The 1915 victory did not end miners' grievances and throughout the next three years spontaneous strike activity continued in Miami, Globe, Ray, Ajo, Jerome, and Warren, as well as Clifton–Morenci. After this point, led by Phelps Dodge's Walter Douglas, mine owners took the offensive and purchased control of local newspapers. They then divided labor from its small-business and farmer allies. Tensions increased as the mine owners became more rigid and arbitrary. Capitalists effectively stirred nativist sentiments among Anglo-Americans. Unfounded fears of Pancho Villa justified the firing of some 1,200 Mexican miners at Ajo in 1916, when they requested a raise and a grievance committee.[78] In that year owners attempted to discipline workers by locking out Clifton miners, forcing them to subsist on $1.25 a month; the owners ended the lockout only when the price of copper was too high to keep the mines closed.

Union organization was frustrated by ideological and personal differences. The WFM had become the International Union of Mine, Mill, and Smelter Workers. Its president, Charles Moyer, a former militant, had moved to the right, and different factions within the international challenged his leadership. The members divided into pro- and anti-Moyer forces. The national AFL leadership supported Moyer, but the Arizona State Federation of Labor, controlled by radicals, ignored Moyer and actively worked with disgruntled miners. Finally, the Industrial Workers of the World (IWW), representing the syndicalist position, were considered the most militant branch of labor.[79]

By 1917, the price of copper skyrocketed. Instead of sharing their windfall profits with miners, the copper barons sought to increase their surpluses by depressing wages. They refused to negotiate on any terms, intentionally provoking miners, daring them to strike. Their strategy was simple: they branded all unions radical and extremist, equating them with the IWW. The owners infiltrated the unions, employing labor spies who goaded miners into isolated cases of violence. These agents provocateurs also began spreading rumors about rival unions and factions, agitating the IWW, state federation, and WFM miners against each other.

Throughout this period, the "copper" press libeled the mine workers. Moreover, the copper barons controlled local, state, and federal authorities, who turned the other way or cooperated with them in their war to destroy the unions. Vigilantes rounded up miners in Jerome and shipped them out of town. In Bisbee, vigilantes herded about 1,200 strikers into bull pens, loaded them into cattle cars, shipped them into the New Mexican desert, and dumped them. President Woodrow Wilson responded to this gross violation of the U.S. Constitution by appointing a presidential mediation commission. No one was punished for the crime, although evidence proved that the copper barons, especially Walter Douglas of Phelps Dodge, had planned the deportation. Contemporaries speculated that the federal government, and President Wilson in particular, did not take any action because Wilson's intimate friend Cleveland Dodge was vice president of the company. Dodge, who had been on the board of trustees of Princeton University when Wilson was appointed president of Princeton, took an active role in Wilson's election for New Jersey governor and then the U.S. presidency. Moreover, their families vacationed together.

The 1917 strikes broke the stereotype of docile Mexicans. Mine owners increasingly looked at them as agitators and subversives. Consequently, during the recession of 1921, mine owners seized the opportunity to repatriate large numbers as well as to rid the camps of Mexicans and the unions. At this time, many Mexican miners migrated to the cotton fields of Arizona and California, furnishing the leadership in later agricultural strikes.

NATIVISM AND *LA LIGA PROTECTORA LATINA*

At the state constitutional convention in Phoenix on October 10, 1910, labor organizers demanded the limitation of aliens because, according to them, alien labor offered unfavorable competition, drove wages down, and stifled union organization. At the convention labor leaders introduced resolutions to exclude non–English-speaking persons from hazardous occupations in the mines, forcing the mines to employ 80 percent U.S. citizens. These resolutions, if they had been passed, would have driven Mexicans from the mines and caused hardships among the Mexican population. As one mine owner pointed out, 50 percent of Mexican miners he employed would have to be fired, even though they had been with the company for as long as 25 years. Union leaders replied that workers should have learned English or declared their intention to become citizens. Owners' representatives prevented these resolutions from becoming law— because they knew the importance of Mexican labor to continued growth of Arizona.

The labor-sponsored Claypool-Kinney bill was introduced in November 1914. "The provisions of the bill were that no firm could hire more than twenty percent aliens" and it prohibited anyone who was deaf, dumb, or did not speak English to be employed in a hazardous occupation. The intent was evident: to exclude Mexicans from the mines.

In 1914 at Phoenix, Mexicans formed *La Liga Protectora Latina,* to oppose Claypool-Kinney. Ignacio Espinosa, Pedro G. de la Loma, and Jesús Meléndez led the society.[80] By May 1915 the Tempe lodge had 80 members and had established a bureau to provide employment referral and financial assistance. *La*

Liga supported striking miners at Ray and began to involve itself with the education and protection of Mexicans. By 1917 it had 30 lodges, focusing on political and legal action to protect the rights of Mexicans, increased mutual aid for *Liga* members, and greater emphasis on education. *La Liga*'s leadership was predominantly middle class and it resented labor's militancy, often opposing the union leadership during some strikes. The group preferred to represent the Mexican miners itself. *La Liga* was also nationalist, and resented the anti-Mexican biases within the labor movement in Arizona.

La Liga had strong ties to the Republican party. For instance, it held a series of meetings with Republican Governor Tom Campbell, calling for night classes, especially in mining areas.[81] And although Campbell was anti-labor, *La Liga* supported his candidacy because Democrats were attempting to revive the 80 percent bill. At its third annual convention, members established a commission headed by Amado Cota Robles to lobby the state legislature for bilingual education at the primary level. Under Cota Robles's leadership, *La Liga* began night classes in Spanish, arithmetic, geometry, geography, and Mexican history. Emphasis was on learning English and on reading. By 1919, lodges had been established in Arizona, California, New Mexico, and Philadelphia with 3,752 members, and the group began publication of a journal, *La Justicia.* [82] However, by 1920 the organization started to decline. When the dues were raised to a $3.00 initiation fee and $1.25 a month, poor members protested, and a division took place along class lines.

Basically, *La Liga* was a middle-class organization with nationalist goals. Many of its members were conservative and some had fled Mexico because of the revolution. The leadership was, however, concerned with the rights of Mexicans, and dealt with Republicans because the Democrats and union leadership wanted to exclude them. Again, the lack of consciousness on the part of labor alienated rather than unified the working class.

SUMMARY

North Americans purchased the Mesilla Valley because they wanted access to its mineral resources. They needed outside capital and Mexican labor to exploit these riches. An immediate barrier to the development of the area was the Apache. Anglo-Americans temporarily solved the problem by making private treaties with the Apache that allowed them sanctuary in Arizona after their raids on Sonora. These treaties bought peace for the Euroamericans, while weakening their southern neighbor, preparing it for what Anglos believed their eventual takeover. Once the Apache raids turned on Arizona settlements, Anglos used poor Mexicans, Pimas, and Papagos to defend the territory. This dependence on the Mexican brought about an alliance with the Mexican elite, with whom the Anglos intermarried and entered into business partnerships. Once the Apache threat was removed, the arrival of the railroad lessened the reliance on the Mexican for defense purposes, and the immigration of larger numbers of white women decreased the number of intermarriages, contact between the two races became more strained.

During the first decade of North American rule, Arizona was part of the New Mexican Territory, and Santa Fe administered it. The Civil War changed Arizona's status, and it became an independent territory. After the war, a political machine, centered in Tucson, controlled the territory's patronage and lobbied the federal government for liberal contracts to supply the numerous military forts and Indian reservations in Arizona. Merchants accummulated surpluses in this trade. In the 1860s, mining finds contributed to the economy of Arizona; the 1870s saw increased activity in mining, and medium-size operations began in the Clifton–Morenci area. Other mining camps sprang up; most notable was the silver strike at Tombstone. By the 1870s, Anglo-Americans migrated into central Arizona, establishing farms there.

The 1880s saw dramatic changes. The Apache was confined to the reservation, the railroad linked Arizona to the rest of the nation, and eastern and foreign capital entered Arizona to buy out pioneering mining ventures, converting them into labor- and capital-intensive operations. These large corporations also moved into northern Mexico—in particular, Chihuahua and Sonora. In the twentieth century, copper became king in Arizona. New methods of production required larger numbers of unskilled workers, drawing thousands of Mexicans into the territory.

Racism at first divided the working class. Many North American miners refused to join strikes involving Mexicans and, in fact, struck to exclude Mexicans from the mining camps. Mexicans lived in segregated housing; their *colonias* were often called *Chihuahuita.* By the turn of the century, Mexican miners grew restless and participated in a series of strikes. The first dramatic encounter was the 1903 Clifton–Morenci strike, in which 2,000 Mexicans took part. Militant strike leaders were imprisoned after a flood ended a possible confrontation between the miners and the National Guard. The mining camps were the centers of Mexican exiles working for the overthrow of dictator Porfirio Díaz. Radical anarchists such as Práxedis Guerrero worked in the mines and agitated workers after 1904. In all probability, many of the Clifton-Morenci miners participated in the Cananea, Sonora, strike of 1906. Mexicans were also active in the 1915 and 1917 strikes as well as other smaller industrial protests. By 1921, many of these miners filtered into cotton production, as a further restructuring of the industry occurred.

NOTES

1. Mexican Heritage Project, *Del Rancho al Barrio: The Mexican Legacy of Tucson* (Tucson: Arizona Historical Society, 1983), p. 15.
2. Hubert Howe Bancroft, *History of Arizona and New Mexico 1530–1880* (Albuquerque: Horn & Wallace, 1962), p. 493.
3. Bancroft, p. 579.
4. Howard R. Lamar, *The Far Southwest, 1846–1912: A Territorial History* (New York: Norton, 1970), p. 418.
5. Lamar, p. 417.
6. Bancroft, pp. 496, 498.
7. John B. Brebner, *Explorers of North America, 1492–1806* (Cleveland: World Publishing, 1966),

p. 407; Francisco R. Almada, *Diccionario de historia geografía y biografía sonorenses* (Chihuahua: n.p., 1952), pp. 140–144.

8. Don Francisco Xavier de Gamboa, *Commentaries on the Mining Ordinances of Spain,* vol. 2, trans. Richard Heathfield (London: Longman, Reese, Orme, Brown and Green, 1830), p. 333.

9. Jack A. Dabbs, *The French Army in Mexico, 1861–1867* (The Hague: Mouton, 1963), pp. 14, 65, 241, 283.

10. James Neff Garber, *The Gadsden Treaty* (Gloucester, Mass.: Peter Smith, 1959).

11. J. Fred Rippy, "A Ray of Light on the Gadsden Treaty," *Southwestern Historical Quarterly* 24 (January 1921): 241.

12. Bancroft, p. 491; Edwin Corle, *The Gila: River of the Southwest* (Lincoln: University of Nebraska Press, 1967), p. 181. Michael C. Meyer and William L. Sherman, in *The Course of Mexican History* (New York: Oxford University Press, 1979), p. 353, list the area as 30,000 square miles.

13. Lamar, 418.

14. Laureano Calvo Berber, *Nociones de Historia de Sonora* (México, D.F.: Libería de Manuel Porrua, 1958), p. 50.

15. Fernando Pesqueira, "Documentos Para la Historia de Sonora," 2nd series, vol. 3 (Manuscript in the University of Sonora Library, Hermosillo, Sonora).

16. Joseph F. Park, *The History of Mexican Labor in Arizona During the Territorial Period* (Tucson: University of Arizona Press, 1961), pp. 15–16. Park's work is the best account of this subject.

17. Lamar, p. 419.

18. Charles D. Poston, "Building a State in Apache Land," *Overland Monthly* 24 (August 1894): 204.

19. See P. G. Hamlin, ed., *The Making of a Soldier: Letters of General B. S. Ewell* (Richmond, Va.: Whittel & Shepperson, 1935); and Clement W. Eaton, "Frontier Life in Southern Arizona, 1858–1861," *Southwestern Historical Quarterly* 36 (January 1933).

20. Sylvester Mowry, *Arizona and Sonora* (New York: Harper & Row, 1864), p. 35.

21. Quoted in Park, p. 20.

22. Bancroft, p. 503.

23. *Arizona Weekly Star,* quoted in Park, p. 29.

24. Stone to Lewis Cass, Guaymas, December 23, 1858, dispatches from United States consuls in Guaymas.

25. Edward Conner to Cass, Mazatlán, Mexico, May 26, 1859, dispatches from United States consuls in Mazatlán, Mexico, GRDS, RG 59; *La Estrella de Occidente,* November 18, 1859; Alden to Cass, Guaymas, November 18, 21, 1859; Thomas Robinson to Alden, Guaymas, November 20, 1859, dispatches from U.S. consuls in Guaymas; Rudolph F. Acuña, "Ignacio Pesqueira: Sonoran Caudillo," *Arizona and the West* 12, no. 2 (Summer 1970): 152–154; Rodolfo F. Acuña, *Sonoran Strongman: Ignacio Pesqueira and His Times* (Tucson: University of Arizona Press, 1974), pp. 52–64.

26. Harry T. Getty, "Interethnic Relationships in the Community of Tucson" (Ph.D. dissertation, University of Chicago, 1950), pp. 208–209.

27. Kay Lysen Briegel, "Alianza Hispano-Americana, 1894–1965: A Mexican American Fraternal Insurance Society" (Ph.D. dissertation, University of Southern California, 1974) p. 27; see Marcy Gail Goldstein, "Americanization and Mexicanization: The Mexican Elite and Anglo-Americans in the Gadsden Purchase Lands, 1853–1880," Ph.D. dissertation, Case Western Reserve University, 1977, for good treatment on elites.

28. Jay J. Wagoner, *Arizona Territory 1863–1912: A Political History* (Tucson: University of Arizona Press, 1970), p. 70.

29. Thomas Farish, *History of Arizona* (San Francisco: Filmer Brothers, 1915), p. 346, quoted in Park, p. 40.

30. Rufus Wyllys, *Arizona: The History of a Frontier State* (Phoenix: Hobison & Herr, 1950), p. 81.

31. Mexican Heritage Project, p. 15.

32. Mowry, p. 94.

33. *Weekly Arizonian,* June 30, 1859.

34. *Weekly Alta Californian,* May 28, 1859.

35. *Report of Frederick Brucknow to the Sonoran Exploring and Mining Company upon the History, Prospects and Resources of the Company in Arizona* (Cincinnati: Railroad Record, 1859), pp.

17–18; *Fourth Annual Report of the Sonora Exploring and Mining Company, March 1860* (New York: Minns, 1860), pp. 12–14.

36. Raphael Pumpelly, *Across America and Asia,* 4th ed., rev. (New York: Leypodt & Holt, 1870), p. 32.
37. Park, p. 78.
38. Raquel Rubio Goldsmith, "Hispanics in Arizona and Their Experiences with the Humanities," in F. Arturo Francisco Rosales and David William Foster, *Hispanics and the Humanities in the Southwest: A Directory of Resources* (Tempe: Center for Latin American Sudies, Arizona State University, 1983), p. 14.
39. C. L. Sonnichsen, *Tucson: The Life and Times of an American City* (Norman: University of Oklahoma Press, 1982), p. 91.
40. Lamar, p. 453.
41. Lamar, pp. 453–454.
42. Lamar, Larry Schweikart, 454; *History of Banking in Arizona* (Tucson: University of Arizona Press, 1982), p. 1.
43. Patricia Preciado Martin, *Images and Conversations: Mexican Americans Recall a Southwestern Past* (Tucson: University of Arizona Press, 1983).
44. Lamar, p. 475.
45. Ibid.
46. The events at Lynx Creek are described by Robert L. Sprude in "The Walker-Weaver Diggings and the Mexican Placero, 1863–1864," *Journal of the West* (October 1975): 64–74.
47. Jacqueline Jo Ann Taylor, "Ethnic Identity and Upward Mobility of Mexican Americans in Tucson" (Ph.D. dissertation, University of Arizona, 1973), p. 16.
48. James Colquhoun, "The Early History of the Clifton–Morenci District," reprinted in Carlos E. Cortés, ed., *The Mexican Experience in Arizona* (New York: Arno Press, 1976).
49. Hubert Howe Bancroft, *History of Arizona and New Mexico* (San Francisco: History Company, 1889), p. 575.
50. Bancroft, *History of Arizona and New Mexico* (1889), pp. 503, 575.
51. Editorial, *La Estrella de Occidente,* April 12, 1872.
52. "La Prensa de Arizona y los Horrores Perpetados en el Río Gila," *La Estrella de Occidente,* March 22, 1872; "Asesinator en el Gila," *La Estrella de Occidente,* March 22, 1872; "Trouble Ahead," *Arizona Citizen,* June 24, 1871.
53. Douglas D. Martin, *Tombstone's Epitaph* (Albuquerque: University of New Mexico Press, 1951), pp. 139–165.
54. Wagoner, p. 164.
55. Bancroft, *History of Arizona and New Mexico* (1889), pp. 599–600.
56. Lamar, p. 475.
57. Bancroft, *History of Arizona and New Mexico* (1889), p. 602.
58. David J. Weber, ed., *Foreigners in Their Native Land* (Albuquerque: University of New Mexico Press, 1973), p. 211.
59. By the 1880s Mexicans, even in Sonora, began to change their attitude toward Anglos. The capitalist class there, which owned the resources but did not have sufficient capital to develop them, began to cooperate with Anglo-American and foreign investors. See Acuña, *Sonoran Strongman* for background material.
60. Briegel, pp. 34–38.
61. Manuel P. Servín, "The Role of Mexican-Americans in the Development of Early Arizona," in Manuel P. Servín, ed., *An Awakening Minority: The Mexican-American,* 2nd ed. (Beverly Hills, Calif.: Glencoe Press, 1974), p. 28.
62. José A. Hernández, *Mutual Aid for Survival: The Case of the Mexican American* (Melbourne, Fla.: Krieger, 1983).
63. Briegel, pp. 51, 64.
64. Frank Love, *Mining Camps and Ghost Towns* (Los Angeles: Westernlore Press, 1974), pp. 141, 143.
65. Carl M. Rathbun, "Keeping the Peace Along the Mexican Border," *Harper's Weekly* 50 (November 17, 1906): 1632.

66. Park, p. 257.

67. Hernández ms.

68. Quoted in Park, p. 257.

69. Wagoner, p. 386.

70. *Bisbee Daily Review* June 5, 1903, quoted in Park, p. 257.

71. James H. McClintock, *Arizona: The Youngest State,* vol. 2 (Chicago: Clarke, 1916), p. 424.

72. Park, p. 258.

73. James R. Kluger, *The Clifton-Morenci Strike: Labor Difficulty in Arizona, 1915–1916* (Tucson: University of Arizona Press, 1970), p. 9.

74. Michael E. Parrish, "Labor, Progressives, and Copper: The Failure of Industrial Democracy in Arizona During World War 2" (Unpublished paper, History Department, University of California at San Diego), p. 6.

75. Mario T. García, "Obreros: The Mexican Workers of El Paso, 1900–1920" (Ph.D. dissertation, University of California at San Diego, 1975), p. 24.

76. Kluger, p. 20.

77. Kluger, p. 23.

78. Parrish, p. 32.

79. See James W. Byrit, *Forging the Copper Collar: Arizona's Labor Management War, 1901–1921* (Tucson: University of Arizona Press, 1982); Parrish, p. 22.

80. James D. McBride, "The *Liga Protectora Latina:* A Mexican-American Benevolent Society in Arizona," *Journal of the West* (October 1975): 83.

81. McBride, p. 83.

82. McBride, pp. 85, 86, 87.

chapter 5

California Lost: America for Anglo-Americans

AN OVERVIEW

California, fronting the Pacific Ocean, was the most isolated province in New Spain. Travel by land or sea was slow, dangerous, and costly. The Spaniards did not colonize California until 1769, when Spain sent a majority of mixed-blood subjects—Spanish, Indian, and Black—to plant the Spanish flag and colonize the half-million indigenous peoples there. During most of the Spanish period, the mission system served as the backbone of colonialism. Gradually, civilian pueblos evolved from the *presidios* (forts) that supported the missions and chartered Indian communities. Spanish authorities allocated some land grants, and the *rancho* culture spread during this period. Labor, whether in the missions or on the *ranchos,* was performed mostly by the indigenous peoples. Because of California's location and Spanish policy forbidding trade outside the Spanish empire, trade did not regularly occur until after Mexican independence.

Mexico liberalized trade policies. In the case of California, technical breakthroughs in sailing allowed more frequent contact with the region. Otter hunters, hide and tallow traders, whalers, and beaver trappers arrived by land and sea. Many of these newcomers stayed in California. The 1820s saw the beginning of a prosperous hide and tallow trade involving missions and the growth of small *ranchos.* Civilians stepped up pressure to privatize more lands; in the mid-1830s the mission properties were secularized.

California increasingly became integrated into the U.S. market economy. Close ties developed between the North American and British merchants who remained and married in California. These merchants played a role similar to that of the traders arriving in New Mexico about the same time. The North American presence grew in the 1840s, when farm families traveled overland from the United States. They settled in the inner valleys, which they said were not populated— Indians did not count.

In the 1840s John C. Frémont arrived in California, claiming he was on a mapping expedition. Soon afterward Frémont raised the Bear Flag, repeating the Texas soap opera. Although some *rancheros* supported the North Americans, the majority of the poor and Mexican elites did not accept liberation. Anglo-American racism toward Mexicans was rampant. The military occupation ended sooner than in New Mexico and Arizona because the gold rush brought an avalanche of North Americans who overnight outnumbered the Mexican population 10 to 1. Shortly California became a state (1850). Euroamericans shoved Mexicans into the southern part of the state, where they remained the majority for the first two decades after the conquest.

The gold rush encouraged the accumulation of large amounts of capital. California gold helped develop other sections of the Southwest and the growth of industry. Entrepreneurs who could afford capital-intensive mining operations monopolized local government. State-sanctioned violence kept Mexicans in their place. Moreover, they had limited access to the courts—they could not sit on juries and testify in court; many lacked the necessary capital to sue. Measures such as the Land Act of 1851 and the foreign miner's tax encouraged mass violence against Mexicans. And they were also driven off the land by gross violations of the Treaty of Guadalupe Hidalgo. As Mexicans were alienated from their land, equality under the law became a sham.

Social control was maintained through an acceptance of the inferiority of the Mexican. When squatters, vigilantes, and posses indiscriminately lynched and terrorized Mexicans, the state did little to control those outrages. Within two decades Mexicans lost the majority of their ranches, and the little political representation they had had in the south vanished. They remained segregated in the old *plaza* areas. No institutions served as their advocates; even the Catholic Church supported the state's legitimacy. The resulting resistance by Mexicans on an individual level produced widespread social banditry.

By the 1880s, the railroads linked southern and northern California. The Mexican became a minority throughout the state and even in Los Angeles. A real estate boom followed as elites in that city advertised land. The growth of California agriculture and of Los Angeles set the groundwork for another wave of Mexicans who arrived after 1900.

THE CONQUEST

When Spanish colonialism ended, in 1821, California became part of the Mexican republic. Mexico liberalized trade and immigration policies, and thereafter the number of foreigners entering the province increased. The early penetration of mercantile capitalism produced changes, converting missions into thriving enterprises as well as contributing to the growth of the *rancho* system. Hundreds of newcomers stayed, becoming the vanguard for the later invasion of California.

During the first years, the missions principally benefited from the new trade. The *rancho* class remained small until the secularization of the missions in 1834. After this point, *ranchos* were carved out of mission holdings (and legally belonging to the native Californians) along the coast. During the Mexican period, the Euroamericans had formed strong ties with the Mexican *rancheros,* often intermarrying with them.

Prior to 1841, foreigners consisted of ex-sailors, commercial agents, and businessmen who assimilated with Mexicans; after this date, newcomers brought their wives and families. North American farmers arrived overland from the Midwest. They settled in the inland areas—uninhabited, according to them, since only Indians lived there. Some went bankrupt and lost their lands as the result of the panic of 1837 (note the parallel between Texas, when Anglo-Americans migrated there after the depression of 1819).

About 1,500 Anglos reached California between 1843 and 1846. They mixed less readily and there was less intermarriage. Not surprisingly, the Texas adventure affected Mexican attitudes toward immigrating Anglos. Anglo-American trade with Asia increased, and the ports of California became even more valuable. Moreover, the discovery of gold by Francisco López in 1842 at San Feliciano Canyon in southern California attested to the mineral wealth of the territory.

In 1835 President Andrew Jackson authorized his diplomatic agent to Mexico to offer $500,000 for San Francisco Bay and the northern part of Alta California; the minister added to the insult of the offer by attempting to bribe Mexican authorities. Two years later Jackson urged Texas to claim California so that Anglo-Americans could bypass negotiations. In 1842 the U.S. minister to Mexico praised California's potential, proposing that efforts to acquire California be renewed.[1]

That same year Commodore Thomas Jones raised the Stars and Stripes over Monterey. He believed that the United States had already started the war with Mexico. The excuse made by many Anglo historians is that "the United States did not intend to be caught unprepared in any ruse between the great powers to acquire California."[2] John C. Frémont led three expeditions into the Southwest for the U.S. army's topographical engineers. Although these expeditions were supposedly scientific, they were heavily armed. On his second expedition, in 1843–1844, Frémont "mapped, surveyed, and charted the trails" to and in California. Thomas Oliver Larkin, the U.S. consul at Monterey, served as an agent, reporting on conditions and fomenting discontent among *Californios* while President James K. Polk conspired to pull off another Texas adventure in California.[3]

The last link in the United States's Bismarckian conspiracy was the third expedition of Frémont, who left St. Louis for California in May 1845. Part of the peaceful scientific expedition reached California by the end of May, whereupon Frémont marched to Monterey to purchase supplies. There he met with Larkin. José Castro, the commander of the Monterey garrison, was highly suspicious and watched Frémont closely. Frémont asked to be allowed to quarter in California for the winter, and permission was granted, with the stipulation that the expedition stay away from coastal settlements. By March 1846 the main body of

Frémont's expedition entered California. Emboldened by additional soldiers, Frémont raised the U.S. flag at Hawk's Peak, about 25 miles from Monterey. His actions give credence to Leonard Pitt's conclusion: "The United States connived rather cynically to acquire California, provoked the native Californians into a dirty fight, and bungled a simple job of conquest."[4] Castro, understandably, ordered Frémont to leave California. Just as the expedition was about to depart, Lieutenant Archibald H. Gillespie, a marine, reached Frémont and delivered to him personal letters in addition to verbal instructions from Polk.[5] Frémont was told that the war with Mexico was near and to hold in readiness. He returned to the Sacramento Valley.

Anglo-American immigrants in California joined Frémont and, adopting the symbol of the Bear Flag, declared war on Mexico.[6] Many Mexican ranch owners were convinced that joining the invaders represented their self-interest; the poor, on the other hand, were patrotic and harbored anti-*gringo* sentiments.[7] Meanwhile, the behavior of the Bear Flaggers antagonized their few friends.

In June 1846, Frémont's soldiers took Mexican General Mariano Vallejo prisoner at his ranch in Sonoma. Vallejo, who had been sympathetic to Anglo-Americans, and his brother were sent to Sutter's Fort and subjected to indignities and harassments. Frémont further alienated rich merchants and landowners by initiating a policy of forced loans, confiscating land and property.[8]

Bear Flaggers terrorized the Mexicans and Indians, stealing cattle and horses, looting homes, and wounding and murdering innocent people. On one occasion a scouting party under Kit Carson came upon José de los Reyes Berreyesa and his twin nephews, Francisco and Ramón de Haro. The men were unarmed, but the Anglos shot at them anyway. They killed Ramón, whereupon Francisco "threw himself upon his brother's body." One of the assassins then shouted, "Kill the other son of a bitch!" Seeing his two nephews killed, the old man said to the Anglos: "Is it possible that you kill these young men for no reason at all? It is better that you kill me who am old too!" Bear Flaggers obliged by killing him.[9] It is of significance that the Berreyesa killings had no military value.

Mexicans resisted, but they had limited arms. Commodore John Drake Sloat arrived in July, landed 250 marines at Monterey, and raised the U.S. flag on the 10th.[10] He was replaced by Commodore Robert F. Stockton, a well-known expansionist (see Chapter 1). Frémont was promoted to the rank of major and placed in command of the California Battalion of Volunteers. Naval forces entered Los Angeles harbor, and Captain Archibald Gillespie was put in charge of occupying the area.

At Los Angeles a resistance movement was led by José María Flores. His guerrillas chased the *gringos* into the hills. Although the patriots were poorly armed, they defeated Gillespie and forced him to surrender. Thousands of Angelenos viewed and cheered Flores's men.

Colonel Stephen Walts Kearny, leader of the Army of the West, arrived from New Mexico. He brought only 125 men with him, because Kit Carson had advised him that Mexicans were "cowardly" and could be easily subdued. On December 5, 1846, the invaders were met by a force of 65 Mexicans at San Pasqual Pass, northeast of San Diego. Led by Andrés Pico, the Mexicans, armed with lances, attacked the army. Although outnumbered, they won the battle, killing 18 Anglos and suffering no losses. Kearny and many of his men were wounded.[11] The conquerors, however, had warships, marines, and a well-armed cavalry.

Kearny's reinforcements soon arrived. The regrouped Anglos, led by Kearny, marched north to Los Angeles in late December. Frémont approached Los Angeles from the north. Flores led the Mexicans, but this time they were overwhelmed. Kearny's army entered Los Angeles on January 10, 1847. At the Cahuenga Pass, Andrés Pico surrendered to him and signed the Treaty of Cahuenga. After the conquest, U.S. troops poured into California, securing their occupation.

THE OCCUPATION

The newcomers relied almost totally on the marketplace and the transaction of capital. Continued economic development required the relentless exploitation of resources to spur growth of industry in the Northeast. Before the conquest the California economy had just begun to enter the international marketplace. The province had been an underdeveloped region much like the western states. The *rancho* system, which provided California's principal commodity, had depended on Indian labor. Other Indians practiced subsistence agriculture on municipal lands.

The army of occupation ensured Americanization of California. At first the process moved slowly because Mexicans significantly outnumbered the encroachers. But on January 24, 1848, before the signing of the Treaty of Guadalupe Hidalgo, James Wilson Marshall found gold on John Sutter's property, and almost overnight thousands of outsiders flooded into California, overwhelming Mexicans and ending any hope they might have had of participating in the new government.

By 1849 almost 100,000 people lived in California, 13,000 of whom were Mexicans. This large white population qualified the territory for statehood. A constitutional convention was held in August of that year at Monterey. Eight of 48 delegates to the convention were *Californios* who had the opportunity, if they had voted as a bloc, to champion the rights of the masses. However, like elites in other colonial situations, they attempted to ally themselves with colonizers to promote their own class interest. At this point their relations with the colonizers were cordial. The possibility of prestigious positions within the new order and the belief that they were different from the *cholo* masses (pejorative term for low-caste Mexicans) separated them from their base. Instead of voting as a bloc, *Californios* voted for what appeared to be their own immediate self-interests. Of the eight Spanish-speaking delegates, only José A. Carrillo voted for the admission of free Negroes into California, and he did this out of political opportunism, since he felt that it would better California's chances for early statehood. *Californios* could also have voted as a bloc to split the territory into north and south, a move that would have given Mexicans control of the southern half. Again, they voted for their self-interest; many of the delegates belonged to the propertied class and believed that taxes would be placed on northern commerce rather than on land.

Generally, the state constitution was favorable to Anglo-Americans. Mexicans won only token victories: suffrage was not limited to white males (the Mexicans were half-breeds), laws would be printed in Spanish and English, and so on. On the other hand, they accepted even the California Bear, the symbol of the conquest, as the state symbol. Tragically, "the constitution was the only document of importance in whose drafting the Mexican Californians shared."[12]

THE CHANGING OF ELITES

Capitulation at Monterey exposed Mexican workers to higher levels of exploitation. California had experienced changes during the 1830s, with secularization of the missions that controlled agriculture and the hide and tallow trade. In 1827 the missions had 210,000 branded cattle, with an estimated 100,000 unbranded cows. They slaughtered 60,000 cows and sold 30,000 to 40,000 hides annually; each brought two pesos. After secularization the land passed to private owners and the *rancho* system. Although under law Indians legally owned half of the secularized property, they never received the benefits. Secularization in fact reduced them to working for wages as *vaqueros* (cowboys) in the expanding *rancho* system or as laborers in pueblos. The lower-class *mestizos* and mulattoes joined the Indians in this labor pool.[13]

Conditions for Mexicans in California varied with location. In the northern part of the state, the gold rush made them an instant minority, while in the southern part they remained the majority for the next 20 years. Los Angeles became the center for Mexicans, mirroring life in other pueblos. Population in Los Angeles had declined, with many of its citizens rushing north from 1849 to 1851 to find their fortune. The Mexicans were joined on the northern river banks by Chileans, Peruvians, and other Latin Americans but remained the majority of these so-called Latinos. Many Latinos were experienced placerers, and their early successes infuriated Anglo-American miners. In 1848 about 1,300 Mexicans and 4,000 Yankees worked in the fields and not much friction existed, but by mid-1849 nearly 100,000 miners panned for gold. Food and other resources were scarce and competition increased. In short, there was not enough gold for the "80,000 Yankees, 8,000 Mexicans, 5,000 South Americans, and several thousand Europeans" seeking gold by the end of 1849.[14]

The gold rush established a pattern of North American–Mexican relations. The 1850 census indicated that 50 percent of Californians worked in gold mining; in 1852, a peak year, gold mines produced $80 million. According to the 1860 census, 38 percent of Californians still worked in gold mining. By 1865, Californians had mined three-quarters of a billion dollars in gold. Large amounts of capital derived from gold mining further concentrated wealth in the hands of a few, engraining the monopolization of California politics by elites. Gold belonged to those who could afford the stamp mills, smelters, and foundries.

An important result of the mining of gold was the introduction of a banking system. Saloon keepers, express and stage operators, and mercantile capitalists— especially those who owned wholesale and retail warehouses—were the first bankers. They bought and sold gold, transporting it to the East or holding it for safekeeping, charging 5 percent per month for their services. In 1854, investors founded the Bank of California; by the following year 19 banks and 9 insurance companies operated in California. Capitalists made fortunes that later financed larger enterprises. For example, Collis P. Huntington, later of Big Four (the Southern Pacific) fame, started in warehousing.

The accumulation of capital enabled bankers to expand their operations. In California they invested heavily in the Comstock Strike of 1859. San Francisco capitalists underwrote ventures throughout the Southwest. They also bankrolled iron works, flour mills, and sugar beet refineries. By 1862, they founded the San Francisco Stock Exchange Board, facilitating even more rapid growth.

Gold created a get-rich-quick mentality. Most argonauts wanted to strike it rich and go home; few planned to remain in California. For many speculators, however, hopes for instant fortune did not materialize. The frustration of shattered dreams drove men to invent rationalizations and find scapegoats.

Mexicans became the scapegoats for Anglo-American miners' failures, and Anglo-American merchants resented the success of Mexican peddlers and mule dealers.[15] A movement to exclude foreigners from the mines gained popular support. General Persifor F. Smith expressed the Anglos' feelings in a circular published in 1849:

> The laws of the United States inflict the penalty of fine and imprisonment on trespassers on the public lands. As nothing can be more unreasonable or unjust than the conduct pursued by persons, not citizens of the United States, who are flocking from all parts to search for and carry off gold from lands belonging to the United States in California, and as such in direct violation of law, it will become my duty, immediately upon my arrival there, to put those laws in force, and to prevent their infraction in future, by punishing by the penalties provided by law, all those who offend.
>
> As these laws are probably not known to many about to start to California, it would be well to make it publicly known that there are such laws in existence, and that they will in future be enforced against all persons, not citizens of the United States, who shall commit any trespass over the land of the United States in California.[16]

Anglo miners applauded the Smith "doctrine" because they believed if foreigners were allowed to mine, they would take all the gold out of the United States of America and strengthen some other nation at the expense of Anglo-America. They pressed politicians to exclude "foreigners" and persecuted them. Conditions got so bad by the autumn of 1849 that the Mexican minister in Washington, citing the Treaty of Guadalupe Hidalgo, sent an official protest condemning violent treatment of Mexicans in California.[17]

Considerable sentiment for exclusion existed in the California legislature. G. B. Tingley of Sacramento warned of a foreign invasion and described Mexicans and Latins in the following terms:

> Devoid of intelligence, sufficient to appreciate the true principles of free government; vicious, indolent, and dishonest, to an extent rendering them obnoxious

to our citizens; with habits of life low and degraded; an intellect but one degree above the beast in the field, and not susceptible of elevation; all these things combined render such classes of human beings a curse to any enlightened community.[18]

Many legislators would have voted for total exclusion. However, Thomas Jefferson Green, a Texan, hater of Mexicans, expansionist, and white supremacist, proposed a compromise bill. Green, responsible for seeking new sources of revenue for the state government, sponsored the idea of taxing foreigners $20 per month. Legislators knew that if they placed a direct tax on all Californians for the right to mine, there would be trouble. Foreigners, however, could not vote. Anglo legislators rationalized that the tax would prevent violence, since foreigners with licenses would have the right to mine and would consequently be accepted. On April 13, 1850, the California state legislature passed its first foreign miner's tax.[19] The measure affirmed the right of the Anglos to exclude Mexicans from the public domain and thus deny them access to capital necessary to upward mobility.

Although the courts upheld the constitutionality of the legislation in *People v. Naglee* in 1850, the act failed; neither the foreigners nor the Anglo-Americans reacted as expected. Foreigners, for the most part Mexicans, objected to the arbitrary tax. Rather than pay the exorbitant fee, they abandoned their diggings, and many former boom villages turned into ghost towns as one-half to three-fourths of the "foreigners" left the mines.[20] This crippled commerce in mining-related businesses. White miners did not accept the licensed foreigners, and drove Latinos off the sites (license or no license), beat them, and even lynched them. After a series of such events, so-called Mexican banditry flourished.

The tax itself was repealed less than a year after it had passed, not because the legislators cared about Mexicans or other foreigners, but because the merchants pressured Sacramento for relief. The *Daily Pacific News* wrote: "The Mexican is, so far as the development of the resources of the country is concerned, the most useful inhabitant of California."[21]

Money power had repealed the law, but discrimination continued in the mines. "As early as 1852 the state assembly committee on mines recommended in its report that a resolution be sent to Congress declaring the importation by foreign capitalists of large numbers of Asiatics, South Americans, and Mexicans (referred to as 'peons' and 'serfs')" be made illegal.[22]

A change in the structure of mining was already underway by the early 1850s as placerers played out. Miners turned to quartz mining, which entailed digging 50-foot holes. At first Mexicans enjoyed more success than *gringos,* apparently because they were more patient and skilled, but the arrival of new machinery limited Mexicans to wages and manual work as the Anglo-Americans claimed the privilege of running the operations.[23]

The gold rush almost over, the Yankees turned to the exploitation of farmland. In 1851 a land law set in motion the mechanism through which Mexicans could be legally robbed of their land. Anglo-Americans entered California, as elsewhere in the Southwest, believing that they had special privileges by right of conquest. To them it was "undemocratic" that 200 Mexican families owned 14 million acres of land.[24] Armed squatters forced the Mexicans off their land, the legislature taxed them out of existence, and claimants insidiously bled them by the costs of litigation of the Federal Land Act of 1851. The Treaty of Guadalupe Hidalgo and its Statement of Protocol, which gave Mexicans specific guarantees, was completely ignored. William Gwinn, a notorious anti-Mexican who sponsored the land law, later admitted that his purpose was to force Mexicans off the land by encouraging squatters to invade them.[25]

A popular belief among historians is that the size of Spanish-Mexican land grants in great part determined the size of holdings in the Anglo period. However, considering the game of monopoly that capitalists played in California during the nineteenth and twentieth centuries, results would most likely have been the same whether or not there had been large *ranchos*. Given the fact that California was an undeveloped region that needed large amounts of capital to exploit, it was highly probable that land would become concentrated in the hands of the few Anglo capitalists. The Southern Pacific alone accumulated 11,588,000 acres, an area which is equivalent to one-fifth of privately owned land today in California and is larger than the 8,850,000 acres of the Californios.[26]

The California Land Act gave Anglo-Americans an advantage and encouraged them to homestead Mexican-owned land. Its ostensible purpose was to clear up land titles, but, in fact, it placed the burden of proof on landowners, who had to pay exorbitant legal fees to defend titles to land that was already theirs. Judges, juries, and land commissioners were open to intrigue and were guided by their prejudices. Hearings were held in English, which put Spanish-speaking grantees at an additional disadvantage. The result was that the commission heard over 800 cases, approving 520 claims and rejecting 273.[27]

The Land Act, by implication, challenged the legality of Mexican land titles. It told land-hungry Anglo-Americans that there was a chance that *Californios* did not own the land. The squatters then treated the *ranchos* as public land on which they had a right to homestead. They knew that local authorities would not or could not do anything about it. They swarmed over the land, harassing and intimidating many landowners.

Through their nonfeasance law officers condoned the legal and physical abuse that followed. Examples of suffering and loss among *rancho* owners abound. "José Suñol was killed somewhere on confirmed land, shortly after his family had acquired title."[28] In 1858, 200 squatters and 1,000 "gun-carrying settlers" ambushed surveyors and held Domingo Peralta hostage. Salvador Vallejo, rather than lose everything, sold his Napa ranch for $160,000; he had paid $80,000 in legal fees to secure title.[29] José Joaquín Estudillo paid $200,000 in litigation fees for Rancho San Leandro; squatters burned his crops while they appealed the case.

Speculators like Henry Miller, a former German butcher, used numerous schemes to steal land. One of his favorite devices was to buy into ranches held by several owners. Even though he was a minority owner, he could then graze as many head of cattle as he wished; also, according to California law, if one of the property owners, even one owning the smallest portion, called for a partition of the land, the property would be sold at auction. Miller could then buy cheap.

By 1853, squatters had moved onto every *rancho* around San Francisco:

> In 1856, when the [Land Act] board had concluded its deliberations, most of the great Mexican estates in the northern half of California had been preempted by squatters or sold off by their owners to pay the legal fees incurred in trying to have the titles validated.[30]

Mexicans had been frozen out of northern California, and only in the southern half of the state did the former Mexican elite have any influence. The economy of southern California depended on cattle. The *rancheros* experienced a brief boom in the early 1850s when they were able to drive 55,000 head of cattle to San Francisco annually at $50 to $60 a head, but by 1855 the price of cattle fell and economic conditions of the southern Mexican ranchers began to crumble. In 1850 the state legislature had initiated a tax on land.[31] Although the majority of the state's population and capital were in northern California, the tax burden fell on the southern portion of the state. In 1852 six southern California cattle counties had a population of 6,000 (mostly Mexican) and paid $42,000 in property taxes and $4,000 in poll taxes, whereas northern California, with 120,000 persons, paid only $21,000 in property taxes and $3,500 in poll taxes.[32] At the same time *rancheros* were obligated to pay county, road poll, and other special taxes. Between 1850 and 1856 the tax rate doubled while mines were exempted; landowners felt the brunt of the load.[33] *Rancheros* were unable to cope with the fluctuation in the economy and pay taxes. Inexperienced in the new economic order, they had speculated and mortgaged their property heavily during the early 1850s:

> By 1860 the economic downturn of the "ricos" became evident. The total value of real estate in San Diego that year was $206,400 and of this figure, the total value of the land belonging to Mexicans had fallen to $82,700 while the value of the Anglos lands rose to $128,900. These are impressive figures, since in 1850 the Mexican had held the overwhelming amount of property.[34]

Loan sharks hastened the ruin of the *ricos,* charging them 10 percent interest, compounded monthly[35] The government did nothing to protect people against these usurous practices.

Intermarriage with daughters of the *ricos* was profitable. Horace Bell describes the Anglo males in such marriages as "matrimonial sharks" marrying "unsophisticated pastoral provincials." He wrote, "Marrying a daughter of one of the big landowners was in some respects a quicker way to clean her family of its assets than to lend money to the 'old man.'" Stephen C. Foster married Don Antonio María Lugo's daughter, who was a widow and a wealthy woman in her own right with future interests in her father's holdings. Two granddaughters of Lugo who were also the daughters of Isaac Williams married Anglos. One of them, John Rains, inherited the Chino Ranch. All of the granddaughters of General Mariano Vallejo of Sonoma married Anglos; he had obviously forgotten that "his liberators" had once called him a greaser. According to Bell, "Mostly the native daughters married good looking and outwardly virile but really lazy, worthless, dissolute vagabond Americans whose object of marriage was to get rich without work." Many of them brought the women whom they married to ruin.

As in other southwestern states, there is little indication that any significant number of Mexican men, whether rich or poor, married Anglo women. There was a scarcity of Anglo women, and the old game of supply and demand operated with the conquerors monopolizing the available supply of women, who were reduced to the level of a commodity. Bell explained that the head of a family often "felt that the future was in the hands of the invading race" and that the marriage of the daughter to a *gringo* was a form of protection. Bell also thought that "the girls felt that they acquired prestige by marrying into the dominant race."[36] To marry a *gringo* was to be accepted as white; to marry a *gringo* was to associate oneself with privilege.

Racism cut across class lines and did not exclude *ricos,* whether or not they were married to *gringos.* Section 394 of the Civil Practice Act of 1850 prohibited Chinese and Indians from testifying against whites. In *People v. Hall* (1854), the court reversed the conviction of George Hall because it had been based on the testimony of the Chinese. In April 1857 Manuel Domínguez, one of the signers of the first California constitution and a wealthy landowner, was denied the right to testify. Domínguez, a Los Angeles supervisor, was declared incompetent as a witness because of his Indian blood.[37] Most *ricos* were not pure-blooded Castilians, but descendants of the frontier people, who were a mixture of Indian, Black, and Spanish. Another direct slap at the Spanish-speaking came in 1856 when the California Assembly refused funds to translate laws into Spanish and further passed an antivagrancy act which was commonly referred to as the "greaser act" because section two specified "all persons who are commonly known as 'Greasers' or the issue of Spanish or Indian blood."[38]

Natural disasters of the 1860s accelerated the decline of *Mexicanos.* In 1862 a flood devastated California ranches. Then two years of drought, followed by falling cattle prices, made it necessary for ranch owners to mortgage their property at outlandish interest rates, resulting in foreclosures. In Santa Barbara, by 1865 a herd of 300,000 cattle had been reduced to 6,000 to 7,000 by the drought, with only a third of the sheep remaining.[39] In the 1860s epidemics broke out, and in 1868 entire families in poor *barrios* such as Sonoratown in Los Angeles were decimated.[40]

Prior to 1860, *Californios* owned all the land valued at over $10,000; by the 1870s they owned only one-fourth of this land and most Mexican ranchers had been reduced to farming rented property.[41] Within a decade Mexicans were relatively landless in California.

As Mexicans lost their land, they also lost their political power. Only in southern California, where Mexicans had an absolute majority, did they retain some local representation, but even there Anglos dominated political offices. The gigantic increase of Anglos statewide crowded Mexicans out of public office.

Mexicans were not experienced in competing in the game of Anglo politics, which was especially crooked in California. During these years, Mexican bosses such as Tomás Sánchez and Antonio Coronel delivered the Mexican vote in Los Angeles. By 1851 all native Mexicans had been excluded from the state Senate; by the 1860s only a few Mexicans remained in the Assembly; and by the 1880s people with Spanish surnames could no longer be found in public offices. And although many *ricos* became disenchanted with the Anglo rule, most of them continued to broker for the Anglo-American machine. In places like Los Angeles the Mexican population had grown with migration from outside of California. These were Mexicans for the most part from the laboring classes, and class differences between the *ricos* and *cholos* increased as the number of laborers increased.[42]

THE LEGITIMATION OF VIOLENCE

Vigilante mobs set the tone for a kaleidoscopic series of violent experiences for Mexicans and Latin Americans. Following are some of the tragic incidents that were recorded. On June 15, 1849, a "benevolent, self-protective and relief society" called the Hounds attacked a Chilean *barrio* in San Francisco. The drunken mob killed a woman, raped two, looted, and plundered. In 1851, when the foreign miner's tax was passed, Antonio Coronel, a schoolteacher, came upon a mob that was about to lynch five foreigners accused of stealing 5 pounds of gold. Although Coronel offered to pay them that amount for the release of the prisoners, the Anglo miners refused, and whipped three of the men and hanged two.[43]

The most flagrant act of vigilantism happened at Downieville in 1851,[44] when, after a kangaroo trial, a mob lynched a Mexican woman they called Juanita. She was the first woman hanged in California. Popular lore rationalized that Juanita was a prostitute (implying that the lynching was lamentable but, after all, she was antisocial). In reality, her name was Josefa; she was not a prostitute, and in fact "she was Sonorian [sic] and all agreed her character was good, that is she was above the average of camp women, of those days." (The attribution of bad character is part of the racist justification for abuse, but the nature of her character is irrelevant to the judgment that lynching of anyone is wrong.)

Josefa lived with a gambler, Manuel José. According to J. J. McClosky, an early resident of Downieville, she "was about 26 years old, slight in form, with large dark eyes that flashed at times . . . like a devil." On July 4, 1851, during a drunken rage, Fred Cannon, one of the miners, intentionally broke down Josefa's door. The next morning José approached Cannon and asked him to pay for the door. Cannon became belligerent: "That door of yours would fall down if anyone coughed—show me the damage." As they went to inspect the door, Josefa stepped out of the house and became involved in an argument with Cannon, who shouted, "I'm getting mighty tired of standing out here arguing with a lyin' son of a bitch about nothing." When Cannon threatened José, who did not want to fight, Josefa intervened: "Go on, why don't you hit me?" Cannon called Josefa a whore and the enraged Josefa went to the door of her home and said, "This is no place to call me bad names, come into my house and call me that." As Cannon entered the house, continuing to call Josefa vile names, she avenged her honor by killing him with a knife. Josefa had thus stood up to years of abuse in which Mexicans, especially women, were fair game for arrogant bullies.

Although the miners wanted to lynch Josefa and José on the spot, they held a kangaroo trial. "Cannon was popular along the river and had many friends who were interested in vengeance and not justice. The hard feelings against Mexicans, engendered by the late war, were not likely to be put aside by a frenzied half-drunken mob of frontier miners" who put Cannon's body on display in a tent, dressed in a red flannel shirt, unbuttoned to display the wound. Throughout the trial Cannon was described as a calm and peaceful man. The defense brought out that Josefa was pregnant and that they would be killing two people. Josefa was condemned to hang while José was banished.

Senator John B. Weller was in town but he did nothing to stop the hanging. Weller was an ambitious politician who was later to become governor, and one voteless Mexican made no difference. Over 2,000 men lined the river to watch Josefa hang at the bridge. After this, lynching became commonplace and Mexicans came to know Anglo-American democracy as *"Linchocracia."*[45]

On July 10, 1850, four Sonorans were charged with the murder of four Anglos near Sonora, California. A group of Anglo-Americans had come upon the Mexicans while they were burning two of the Anglo corpses, which were already in a decomposed state. The Mexicans explained that it was their custom to burn the dead (three of the four belonged to the Yaqui tribe). Justice of the Peace R. C. Barry believed the men innocent and attempted to forestall violence, but the mob had its way. The four men were hanged.[46]

Public whippings and brandings were common. To the Anglo-Americans, "whether from California, Chile, Peru, or Mexico, whether residents of 20 years' standing or immigrants of one week, all the Spanish-speaking were lumped together as 'interlopers' and 'greasers.'"[47]

Violence had to be justified. In the case of vigilante action, the stance was that the mob championed the law and was attempting to rectify conditions by demanding "an eye for an eye." Another justification was that Mexicans' criminal nature had to be controlled; to Anglo-Americans every Mexican was a potential outlaw, and Anglos used the outlaw activity as an excuse to rob and murder peaceful Mexicans.

Racial tensions polarized the two communities, especially in Los Angeles, where, although Mexican elites actively cooperated with the new order, they often became victims of mob violence. One such celebrated case involved the Lugo brothers, Francisco, 16, and Menito, 18, accused of killing a white man and his Indian companion.[48] This case is interesting since the men involved were the grandsons of Antonio María Lugo. The Anglo-American populace was pitted against one of the richest and most powerful California families. The Lugos were defended by Joseph Lancaster Brent, a Los Angeles attorney and a native of Maryland, who had strong southern sympathies and who related to the *ricos* exceedingly well (one patriarch to another).

In January 1851 the Lugos, with 15 or 20 ranch hands, rode up the Cajon Pass from their San Bernardino ranch in pursuit of Indians who had raided their stock. On their return they met Patrick McSwiggin and a Creek Indian. Later the Irishman and the Indian were found dead, and Francisco and Menito were charged with murder.[49]

Only about 75 Anglo-Americans lived permanently in Los Angeles, dwelling in perpetual fear of a *Californio* revolt. The McSwiggin murder inflamed the Anglos. The town mayor further polarized the situation: ". . . full of credulity and fright, [he] rushed around calling upon all the Americans to arm themselves and report to him for service."[50] The mayor so overreacted that he became a joke.

At the inquest Ysidro Higuera testified that he had seen the Lugos and another Mexican kill the deceased. The Higuera testimony was questioned because he had been previously convicted of horse stealing and because he had been persuaded to testify by the jailer, George W. Robinson, who hated the Lugos. The *vaqueros* who had ridden with the Lugos swore that the brothers had never left the camp and that they had not killed the deceased.[51]

Meanwhile, a justice of the peace held the prisoners without bail, an abuse applauded by the Anglo population. When the district court judge reversed this order and released the Lugos on a $10,000 bond, he was immediately accused of taking a payoff. Anglo-Americans threatened to take matters into their own hands. *Californios* feared that the brothers would be lynched before the court could release them on bail. Captain John "Red" Irving and about 25 men approached Brent and demanded $10,000 to release the Lugos, threatening to lynch the boys if they were not paid. The Lugos refused the offer and Irving vowed to kill the brothers before they were released on bond. Brent became convinced that the only way to save the brothers was a show of force. Sixty armed *Californios* showed up, followed by U.S. troops, whose presence prevented a confrontation. The Lugo boys were escorted by the *Californios* to the judge, who released them on bail after which they were escorted to their ranch by the armed *Californios*.

A month later, Red Irving and his men set out for the Lugo ranch to kill the brothers, but word of their plan got back to the Lugos. Their Cahuilla Indian friends set a trap for the gang, leading them into a ravine where all except one were killed. After additional turmoil the court finally dismissed the case on October 11, 1852. Brent had done a brilliant job of defending the Lugos; it was rumored that he collected a fee of $20,000, a measure of the price for justice.[52]

The fear of an uprising of *Californios* and racism established a pattern of indiscriminate attacks on Mexicans. Any incident became an excuse for a series of other violent incidents. For example, in 1856 Juan Flores (to be discussed later) escaped from San Quentin Prison and rallied 50 Mexicans to his cause. During the time Flores was chased, a group of *gringos* stopped two Mexicans near San Gabriel because they looked "suspicious" and began mistreating them. The Mexicans attempted to escape. The *gringos* killed one and then pursued the other, and a massive roundup of Mexicans followed.

The El Monte gang (a group of Anglos dominated by Texans from El Monte, California) arrested Diego Navarro, who was seen riding away from the gun battle. Navarro claimed that he was on his way to San Gabriel when he saw the gunfight; he rode away because he knew that all Mexicans were automatically considered guilty. The gang threw hot tar on his family home and broke into the house, and dragged him out and executed him, along with two other Mexicans who were accused of being members of the Flores gang.

Shortly afterward, Encarnación Berreyesa was lynched in San Buenaventura. The justification for the hanging was that Berreyesa was a member of the Flores gang; however, the truth was that the family had been victims of continual persecution. On March 28, 1857, a letter by José S. Berreyesa, reprinted in *El Clamor Público* from the *San Francisco Daily Herald,* reminded Californians of the terrible series of tragedies that had visited his family since the arrival of Anglo-Americans. Troubles started, the letter said, with Bear Flaggers' assassination of the elder Berreyesa and his two nephews. The family's sufferings were compounded when in July 1854 the body of an Anglo-American was found on the San Vicente ranch, which belonged to the Berreyesa family. A band of Anglos from Santa Clara, suspecting that the Berreyesas had murdered the man, invaded the house of Encarnación Berreyesa, dragged him out while his wife and children looked on, and suspended him from a tree. When he did not confess to the killings, vigilantes left him half dead and turned on his brother Nemesio. Nemesio's wife fled to San José to summon friends to help. When friends reached the ranch, they found him dead, dangling from a tree. Encarnación took his family to San Buenaventura to be with relatives and friends. However, at the time of the Flores affair a vigilance committee mobilized. Though Berreyesa was not officially accused of being a follower of Flores, he was charged with the murder of an Anglo in Santa Clara. Under the cover of night Anglos lynched Encarnación. The letter writer then listed members of the Berreyesa family who had been murdered: "Encarnación, José R. Berreyesa, Francisco de Haro, Ramón de Haro, Nemesio Berreyesa, José Suñol, José Galindo, Juan Berreyesa—fathers, brothers, cousins." Similar travesties occurred during the early 1850s when the legendary Joaquín Murietta was hunted down.

A double standard of justice existed for Mexicans and Anglos. On July 26, 1856, Francisco Ramírez wrote in *El Clamor Público* that conditions had never been so bad. Six years of assassinations had created armed camps in California. "The criminals have always escaped. Justice is almost never administered." Ramírez attacked Anglo-Americans' indiscriminate murder of *Mexicanos,* demanding an immediate cessation of violence. Ramírez was temperate, although his patience was strained by the Ruiz incident. William W. Jenkins, a deputy sheriff, alleged that Antonio Ruiz had interfered in an argument between the deputy and Ruiz's landlady. When Ruiz protested the deputy's mistreatment of the landlady, the armed Jenkins shot Ruiz in the chest. The defense, which had the support of the court, based its case on discrediting the witnesses to the Mexican's death. Police officials backed Jenkins. It took the jury only 15 minutes to reach a verdict of not guilty. Soon afterward Jenkins returned to the task of maintaining "law and order" in Los Angeles.

CURRENTS OF RESISTANCE

From 1855 through 1859 *El Clamor Público* was published in Los Angeles by Francisco P. Ramírez, a young Chicano who had been a compositor for the Spanish page of the *Los Angeles Star.*[53] In 1859, because of lack of money, the newspaper went out of business. After this venture Ramírez returned to Sonora, where he continued to work as a newspaper publisher. In the 1860s he appeared again in California, where he had jobs as a printer, postmaster, and the official translator for the state. He tried a comeback in 1872 as editor of *La Crónica* in Los Angeles.

Ramírez's editorials reflected the *Mexicanos'* disappointments with Anglo justice. On June 19, 1855, his newspaper editorials began on a moderate tone by calling for justice within the system and recognizing that California was now part of the United States. He asked the *Californios* for financial support, writing that a free press was their best guarantee of liberty. He pledged his paper to an independent course, promising that the newspaper would "uphold the Constitution of the United States, convinced that only through it will we obtain liberty. . . . We shall combat all those opposed to its magnanimous spirit and grand ideas."[54] Ramírez's editorials soon started to change, and his coverage became more nationalistic. In an article on the filibuster William Walker, Ramírez commented that "World history tells us that the Anglo-Saxons were in the beginning thieves and pirates, the same as other nations in their infancy . . . [but] the pirate instinct of old Anglo-Saxons is still active."[55]

Throughout the paper's publication Walker remained the special target of Ramírez's editorials, as did the other "pirates"—politicians and filibusters—who had designs on Mexico or Latin America. In September 1855 Ramírez reprinted an article that questioned:

> Who is the foreigner in California? He is what he is not in any other place in the world; he is what he is not in the most inhospitable land which can be imagined. . . . The North Americans pretend to give us lessons in humanity and to bring to our people the doctrine of salvation so we can govern ourselves, to respect the laws and conserve order. Are these the ones who treat us worse than slaves?[56]

The article condemned lynchings of Mexicans. By October he encouraged Mexicans and Chileans to join Jesús Isla's *Junta Colonizadora de Sonora* and return to Mexico. He promoted this emigration society even when it was evident that it was not getting the proper support from Mexico. Ramírez's loss of faith in the U.S. government is beyond question.

On May 10, 1856, Ramírez condemned Anglo-American racism, writing:

> California has fallen into the hands of the ambitious sons of North America who will not stop until they have satisfied their passions, by driving the first occupants of the land out of the country, villifying their religion and disfiguring their customs.[57]

Ramírez urged Mexicans to return to Sonora. One reader objected to Ramírez's "return-to-Mexico" stance, saying: "California has always been the asylum of Sonorans, and the place where they have found good wages, hospitality, and happiness." The writer implied that Mexicans never had it so good. Ramírez caustically replied that the letter did not merit comment and asked: "Are the Californios as happy today as when they belonged to the Republic of Mexico, in spite of all of its revolutions and changes in government?"[58]

Pages of *El Clamor Público* also reveal a schism between establishment Mexicans and *cholos*. Oppression and its attendant discrimination were obvious; however, many elites continued to work within the system and cooperated with Anglo-Americans to frustrate not only resistance movements but the Mexicans' justifiable demands.

Resistance often expressed itself in antisocial behavior. The best-known case in California is that of Joaquín Murietta; lesser known is that of Juan Flores. Writers of the time freely labeled Flores's activities as the "Juan Flores Revolution."[59] However, it soon became more popular just to write him off as a bandit.

Flores, 21 years old, escaped from San Quentin Prison, where he served a term for horse stealing. He returned to Los Angeles and formed a group of almost 50 *Mexicanos*, including Pancho Daniel. There was widespread unrest. The murder of Antonio Ruiz had divided Mexicans across class lines, with the lower classes harboring deep-seated grievances against Anglos.[60] The Flores band operated around San Juan Capistrano. When Los Angeles sheriff James Barton and a posse went to investigate, the rebels killed the sheriff. Rumors spread that they intended to kill all whites. A vigilante committee was organized, and Anglos flooded into Los Angeles for protection.

The Flores revolt split Mexicans in two: the *ricos* backed the Anglo-Americans in suppressing the rebels and *los de abajo* (the underdogs) supported Flores. Ramírez condemned the "bandits" in an editorial dated January 31, 1857, and called for *Californios* to join in the protection of their families and enforcement of laws. In doing so, Ramírez represented the class interests of his subscribers. Tomás Sánchez, the Democratic party *cacique* (boss), and Andrés Pico, the hero of the battle against Kearny at San Pasqual Pass, led the posse comprised of Anglos and *Mexicanos*. They joined with the El Monte gang to pursue Flores.

El Monte was the *gringo* stronghold—the only community in the Los Angeles area that was predominately Anglo-American. Many inhabitants were former Texans (some were even ex-Rangers). In almost every altercation between Mexicans and Anglos, the El Monte crowd posed as defenders of white supremacy. Many Mexicans considered them outlaws. The El Monte gang, which operated separately from the Los Angeles posse, captured Flores and Daniel, but the two escaped. Anglos then insured "justice" by hanging their next nine captives.

Meanwhile Andrés Pico with California Native Americans tracked Flores. Pico emulated the *gringos* and hanged two Mexican rebels. Martial law was imposed and the entire section of "Mexican Town" in Los Angeles was surrounded. The search for Flores was relentless, with houses broken into in the middle of the night and suspects herded to jail. During the hunt 52 men were crammed into the jails; many of them were later discharged for lack of evidence. With the exception of Pancho Daniel, the entire gang was captured. Flores was hanged after being convicted by a kangaroo court on February 14, 1857.[61]

El Clamor Público praised Andrés Pico in an editorial published on February 7 and congratulated him for cooperating with the citizens of El Monte. Ramírez celebrated the spirit of unity and even wrote that *Californios* had vindicated their honor. The *ricos* denied a race war existed. Professor Pitt notes, "Sánchez and Pico, who gladly rode with Texans to track down 'their own kind,' thereby won the gringos' everlasting gratitude." They were rewarded; Sánchez became sheriff and Pico was made a brigadier in the California militia and was also elected to the state Assembly.[62] Many *Mexicanos* did not share the enthusiasm of *El Clamor Público* and the *ricos,* and condemned their participation in suppressing the Flores–Daniel rebellion. The poor could not forget the ethnic distinctions between "American" citizens.[63]

Why had Ramírez supported this action? The only explanation is that he believed the cooperation of Mexicans with the Anglos would improve relations between the two peoples—that is, the two peoples of the class that read his newspapers. These hopes were shattered by lynchings of Mexicans throughout the state, and Ramírez had a change of heart. While he had applauded the hanging of Flores, several months later when Daniel was captured and hanged, Ramírez called his execution "barbaric and diabolic" and admonished the *Mexicano* population, writing: "And you, imbecile Californios! You are to blame for the lamentations that we are witnessing. We are tired of saying: open your eyes, and it is time that we demand our rights and interests. It is with shame that we say, and difficult to confess it: you are the sarcasm of humanity!" He scolded readers for not voting and for putting up with indignities, calling them "cowards and stupids." He warned *Californios* that until they cared, they could never cast off the "yoke of slavery."[64] In less than four years, Ramírez changed from an assimilationist to a nationalist. Regrettably, he could not understand the class conflict which divided the Mexican people.

Mexicans were not treated as individuals, and when some Mexicans took to the highway, all were collectively guilty in the eyes of most *gringos* in California. Voices of criticism were gradually silenced as the Mexican population grew too poor to support newspapers. The California of Mexicans and Anglos grew further apart, with *Mexicanos* growing more resentful of *gringos.*

Social Banditry

When people cannot earn a living within the system or when they are degraded, they strike out. Rebellion against the system can take the form of organized resistance, as in the case of Juan Cortina in Texas, or it can express itself in bandit activity.

Tiburcio Vásquez was born in Monterey on August 11, 1835. His parents had a good reputation, and Vásquez had an above-average education for the times. Vásquez never married. In about 1852 he was involved in the shooting of a constable and fled to the hills.[65] At the end of his career Vásquez explained the incident and his reasons for turning *bandido:*

> My career grew out of the circumstances by which I was surrounded. As I grew to manhood I was in the habit of attending balls and parties given by the native Californians, into which the Americans, then beginning to become numerous, would force themselves and shove the native born men aside, monopolizing the dance and the women. This was about 1852. A spirit of hatred and revenge took possession of me. I had numerous fights in defense of my countrymen. The officers were continually in pursuit of me. I believed we were unjustly and wrongfully deprived of the social rights that belonged to us.[66]

By the middle of the 1850s California "was experiencing an economic depression. Money was short, the great flood of gold was nearly played out, land and cattle prices were down, and banditry was rampant."[67] Vásquez attracted a large following and his popularity grew among the poor. The *ricos* were afraid that he wanted to incite an uprising or revolution against the "Yankee invaders" of California, and from all indications the rural poor supported and shielded him.[68] The *Los Angeles Express* (date unknown) quoted Vásquez as claiming, "Given $60,000 I would be able to recruit enough arms and men to revolutionize Southern California."

In the fall of 1871 Vásquez and his men robbed the Visalia stage. His reputation as a *desperado* grew and he was soon blamed for crimes that he did not commit. The magnitude of the manhunts increased. Authorities paid informers in an effort to locate Vásquez. Throughout 1871 Vásquez not only continued his activities but avoided arrest. The Mexican populace aided him, for "to some, Vásquez must have seemed a hero dealing out his own particular brand of justice. Certainly his reputation was growing fast."[69]

On August 16, 1873, he and his men robbed Snyder's store in Tres Pinos of $1,200. This daring raid escalated Vásquez to statewide prominence. Newspapers sensationalized Vásquez's raids, and wanted posters circulated. Vásquez prudently shifted activities to southern California.

During the next year his newspapers played up his exploits, and Sheriff Harry Morse quickened the chase, covering 2,720 miles in 61 days searching for Vásquez. Authorities learned that Vásquez was hiding out at the ranch of George Allen, better known as Greek George, and surrounded the ranch. Vásquez was captured. An all-Anglo jury found him guilty, and he was sentenced to hang.

George A. Beers, a special correspondent for the *San Francisco Chronicle,* offered a partial explanation of why Vásquez captured the imagination of the Mexican populace:

> Vásquez turned to the life of a bandido because of the bitter animosity then existing, and which still exists, between the white settlers and the native or Mexican portion of the population. The native Californians, especially the lower classes, never took kindly to the stars and stripes. Their youth were taught from the very cradle to look upon the American government as that of a foreign nation.
>
> This feeling was greatly intensified by the rough, brutal conduct of the worst class of American settlers, who never missed an opportunity to openly exhibit their contempt for the native Californian or Mexican population—designating them as "d————d Greasers," and treating them like dogs. Add to this the fact that these helpless people were cheated out of their lands and possessions by every subterfuge—in many instances their property being actually wrested from them by force, and their women debauched whenever practicable—and we can understand very clearly some of the causes which have given to Joaquin (Murietta), Vásquez, and others of their stripe, the power to call around them at any time all the followers they required, and which secured to them aid and comfort from the Mexican settlers everywhere.[70]

Vásquez's execution deepened racial tensions. Two weeks after the hanging, a man named Romo killed two Anglo-Americans who had participated in

Vásquez's capture; he was captured and lynched. Groups of *Mexicanos* met secretly and the *ricos* feared a race war which would include them.

The Role of the Church

The Catholic Church played the same role in California as it did in New Mexico —that is, it cooperated with the elites, actively Americanizing and destroying any nationalist base that existed. In 1850 the Right Reverend Francisco Diego y Moreno was replaced by Fr. Joseph Sadoc Alemany, a non-Mexican, as the head of the church in Los Angeles. A Frenchman replaced Fr. Gonzales Rubio. "During this period the Catholic hierarchy was anxious to put into effect a program for Americanizing the foreign born members of the church."[71] In 1852 the Plenary Council of Bishops, meeting at Baltimore, laid out a master plan of stricter enforcement of tithes and increased effort to establish parochial schools. The impoverished state of the masses of Mexicans and Indians was not discussed, but it was decided to renew political pressure on the Mexican government to recover control of the Pious fund (a large fund collected during the Spanish colonial period for the benefit of the missions).[72]

Bishop Taddeus Amat summed up the priority of the church in 1870, stating that the church was "the main support of society and order, which imperatively demands respect for legitimate authority and subjugation to legitimate law."[73] Therefore, European and Spanish priests teamed to control the *plaza* in Los Angeles and to discourage Mexicans from rebelling against what the church considered "legitimate authority."

Meanwhile, the construction of new churches further segregated the Mexican poor. St. Viviana's Cathedral, built in 1876, served a North American parish, as did St. Vincent's (1886), St. Andrews's (1886), and Sacred Heart (1887). St. Joseph's, built a year later, also catered to Euroamericans. The construction of the churches in the 1880s coincided with the arrival of thousands of North Americans who found sanctuary for their racism in these segregated houses of worship. The Mexicans continued to attend the *placita* (the plaza church), Our Lady Queen of the Angels.

THE UNDERCLASS

The railroad substantially changed social relations in California. Mexicans were affected in obvious ways. The isolation they enjoyed during the 1850s and 1860s abruptly ended. Over the next three decades Mexicans played the role of a small and politically insignificant minority.

The dominance of Chinese labor, supplemented by native Californians, lessened the reliance on Mexican labor during the 1850s. The Chinese worked in the mines, on the farms, and then in railroad construction. In 1851, 4,000 Chinese lived in California; nine years later that number grew to 34,933, and in 1870 to 49,277. Chinese outnumbered Mexicans in the state.

During the 1870s, irrigation projects increased demand for farm labor, a need that the Chinese filled. Anglo-Americans reacted to the influx of Chinese

with more frequent race riots. Anglo-American nativists lynched Chinese workers, and a nascent labor movement called for their expulsion from the United
States, leading to the Chinese Exclusion Act of 1882. California Indians could not
fill the state's need for workers because the North American occupation had
reduced their numbers. Ultimately, the Mexican would become the principal
source of cheap labor.

Mexican labor made a transition from pastoral occupations to menial wage
work. They took jobs at the lowest rung of the ladder. Increasingly, they became
wage earners, driven from subsistence farming by the sale of common lands. As
the farming and grazing society faded, unemployment and poverty worsened.

The transcontinental railroad completed its link to California in 1869. Over
the next decade, the octopus spread throughout the state. Meanwhile, the railroad
brought 70,000 newcomers a year to California.

Tiburcio Vásquez's death ended the era of intense Mexican rebellion. Anglo-Americans in southern California, who in the first years had lived in fear of
a Mexican uprising, soon numerically overwhelmed Mexicans. Railroads ended
the dominance of the Mexican population in southern California just as the gold
rush had in northern California. Los Angeles, where the Southern Pacific (which
by the end of the 1870s monopolized 85 percent of the state's rails) arrived in
1876, is typical of this change. The Mexican population increased only slightly
from 1,331 in 1850 to 2,231 in 1880, whereas the Anglo population rose from
under 300 to some 8,000 during this same period. By 1890 the city had grown
to 50,395 (101,454 in the county), with the Mexican population increasing
slightly.[74]

Los Angeles underwent other changes. In 1850 it had one factory employing two men; in 1880 it had 172 factories and 700 workers. Property values in
this same period increased from $2,282,949 to $20,916,835.

The 1880s transformed Los Angeles into a modern city. However, Mexicans
did not participate in the new prosperity. Their status changed little from the
Mexican period, with 65 percent employed as manual laborers, as contrasted to
the 26 percent of Anglo-Americans employed in laboring occupations. The economic order froze Mexicans into a set class and occupational mobility was limited
among all workers; race and a historical tradition of oppression facilitated continued subjugation.

Although their status remained the same as in the Mexican era, subtle shifts
had taken place. For instance, not only were they set off from the upper levels
of society by class, as they had been before, but now they were separated also from
others in the lower levels by race. They became easy scapegoats for failures of the
economic system. After 1848 land became less accessible. In 1850 60 percent of
the Mexican families had property of one kind or another in Los Angeles, whereas
in 1870 less than 24 percent owned property.

While the isolation of Los Angeles ended, segregation of Mexicans became
more complete. In southern California, Anglos became the majority in the 1870s.
By 1873 the participation of Mexicans on juries became rarer, as did their involvement in any other forms of government. Mexican political bosses declined in
power, and, by the 1880s, they had little to broker; they even lost influence in local

politics. City officials ignored problems of health and urbanization in the *barrios* (Sonoratown). Between 1877 and 1888 infant mortality was double that of Anglos; the death rate among Mexicans between ages 5 and 20 was also double, with smallpox a leading killer. Cost of medical care was prohibitive. Doctors charged for house calls according to how far the patient lived, and, since most doctors did not live close to the Mexican *colonia,* the usual fee was $10—a week's salary for most Mexicans.[75]

Segregation was not limited to Los Angeles or southern California. Thirteen miles south of San Jose, the Almaden mercury mines, active since the Mexican period, employed a majority of Mexicans. Fifteen hundred miners worked at the Quicksilver Mine Company; using ancient methods, they carried ore out of the underground mines with 200-pound sacks strapped to their foreheads and resting on their backs. Miners produced 220,000 pounds per month. The company kept tight control of its workers, segregating them not only on the basis of race but on a division of labor based on race. The Cornish miners lived separately from the Mexicans. Mexican Town had a distinctively lower standard of living, and neither Mexican workers nor their families were allowed contact with English adults or children, who attended a separate school and church.[76]

Mexicans attempted to deal with these problems within their own community. They formed self-help associations, such as *La Sociedad Hispanoamericana de Beneficio Mutua,* which was founded in Los Angeles in 1875, to raise money for hospitals and charitable purposes, and the Sisters of Charity established a hospital for indigents in 1887.[77] Organizations in these years reflected the Mexicans' isolation and as a consequence became increasingly nationalistic, celebrating the Mexican patriotic holidays such as the 16th of September and the 5th of May and sponsoring parades, speeches, and other festivities.

Meanwhile, large corporations gained tighter control of California. The Southern Pacific Railroad alone owned more land than all of the *rancheros* combined. By the 1870s, the Southern Pacific was the state's largest employer. Most of its holding were in the southern half of the state. During the land boom of the 1880s the Southern Pacific advertised throughout the East and Europe for buyers. It even established an employment agency for the new settlers.[78]

Industrial growth created a heavy demand for cheap labor. As noted, Chinese workers filled the need in the preliminary stages. After the Exclusion Act, other groups filled the vacuum. The reclamation programs of the early 1900s caused a revolution in agriculture that forced California capitalists to look to the most logical and available source of labor—Mexico. Further changes were brought about by the discovery of oil and the opening of the Panama Canal in the 1900s. The isolation of California and Los Angeles had completely ended. Beginning in the 1880s, Los Angeles was firmly in the hands of a ruling elite, led by the *Los Angeles Times.* In downtown Los Angeles, land speculators, bankers, and developers ran the city and county for personal gain.

Discrimination toward Mexicans in the wage labor market increased; a dual wage system persisted, with Mexicans and Chinese paid less than Anglos. This arbitrary treatment of Mexicans often led to confrontations. For instance, on August 20, 1892, a mob in Santa Ana broke into the jail and hanged Francisco

Torres, a native of Colima, Mexico.[79] Torres worked at the Modjeska Ranch for a wage of $9.00 for a 6-day week. The ranch foreman, William McKelvey, withheld money from Torres's check for a road poll tax, but not from any of the other workers' pay. Torres refused the check, demanding full payment, and in an ensuing argument killed McKelvey. Torres stated that he did not have a gun, that he had taken a club away from the larger man, and that, in fear that the foreman would use his gun, he had killed McKelvey with a knife in self-defense.

A posse captured Torres and he was charged with murder. The press inflamed the populace, calling Torres a "brutal greaser." Before Torres could be tried, a mob broke into the jail and executed him, hanging a sign around his neck which read, "Change of venue." The *Santa Ana Standard* wrote:

> Torres was a low type of Mexican race, and was evidently more Indian than white. True to his savage nature he had no more regard for human life than for the merest trifle. . . . He belongs to a class of outlaws in southern California and old Mexico.[80]

In contrast, *Las Dos Repúblicas,* wrote:

> This time the victim has been a Mexican whose guilt perhaps consisted solely in his nationality. . . . A town which occupies so high a rank in world civilization ought not to let crime such as this go unpunished.[81]

The execution went unpunished. Prominent citizens of Santa Ana were known to have participated in the lynching, but no attempt was made to prosecute them. A year later Jesús Cuen was lynched in San Bernardino.[82] During these incidents, racial tensions remained high, but by this time it did not matter whether the *ricos* were embarrassed or not; California had been lost.

By 1900, the railroad fully integrated California into the nation's marketplace. California had made the complete transition from a Mexican province to a North American state. Its population, overwhelmingly white in color and culture, numbered a million and a half.

SUMMARY

The Bear Flag invasion climaxed 25 years of Anglo-American infiltration. California during this time had begun its transformation from a feudal civilization to one of primitive capital accumulation, intensifying the division of labor and creating a society dominated by ranchers. A number of the ranchers, because of self-interest, supported the idea of annexation to the United States. Other *rancheros* and the masses of the poor defended California.

The discovery of gold ended any real opportunity for Mexicans to develop a political, social, or economic base. North Americans soon overwhelmingly outnumbered Mexicans, and entrepreneurs who amassed large amounts of capital as the result of the gold rush controlled the government. Official policy encouraged the "decline of the *Californios.*" Laws such as the Land Act of 1851 and the California foreign miner's tax led to violence toward Mexicans in the transition from a Mexican pastoral to an Anglo-American capitalist society. By the 1860s most of the *rancheros'* properties fell, by hook or by crook, into the hands of North Americans.

Throughout this process, the California *rancheros* did not as a class offer leadership to the masses. In fact, they often cooperated with Anglos to put down spontaneous rebellions. Moreover, they frequently acted as *patrones* (political bosses) turning out the Mexican vote in exchange for an illusion of power and respect. Some, like Mariano Vallejo, obsequiously catered to the new ruling class. Many *rancheros* believed that they could protect their lands by marrying their daughters to North Americans.

Social banditry was popular in California. Men such as Juan Flores, Joaquín Murrieta, and Tiburcio Vásquez attracted noteriety and the support of the Mexican masses. With time, newspaper publishers such as Francisco Ramírez came to understand the causes for the Mexicans' lack of access to California governing institutions. In particular, Mexicans could not raise the capital that would have allowed them economic or political participation in the system. In southern California, as more Anglo-Americans entered, the Mexican population became proportionately smaller and, by the 1880s, Mexicans constituted a minority in Los Angeles. In the segregated areas near the *plaza* in Old Town, public services were bad and sanitation even worse.

The Catholic Church openly defended the legitimacy of the new order. In places like Los Angeles it followed a policy of segregating the poor and appointing alien clergy to Our Lady Queen of the Angels (the *plaza*) Church.

The railroad took California further into its industrial stage. It made possible a real estate boom that brought a flood of midwesterners to Los Angeles. Tourists also streamed into southern California, and, by the turn of the century, farm work, construction, and menial labor attracted large numbers of Mexicans back to California.

NOTES

1. John W. Caughey, *California: A Remarkable State's Life History,* 3rd ed. (Englewood Cliffs, N.J.: Prentice-Hall, 1970), pp. 142, 144, 156, 157.
2. Andrew F. Rolle, *California: A History* (New York: Crowell, 1963), p. 191.
3. Manuel Castanares, "Collección de documentos relativos al departamento de California" (1845) in David Weber, ed., *Northern Mexico on the Eve of the United States Invasion* (New York: Arno Press, 1976).
4. Leonard Pitt, *The Decline of the Californios* (Berkeley and Los Angeles: University of California Press, 1966), p. 26.
5. Whether Frémont received orders from Polk to incite the war cannot be proven. George Winston Smith and Charles Judah, *Chronicles of the Gringos* (Albuquerque: University of New Mexico Press, 1968), p. 141 and 149, do, however, make a good case for such a conclusion. See also Simeon Ide, *Biographical Sketch of the Life of William B. Ide* (Glorieta, N. Mex.: Rio Grande Press, 1967), p. 133; and *Who Conquered California?* (Glorieta, N. Mex.: Rio Grande Press, 1967).
6. Oscar Lewis, ed., "California in 1846" (San Francisco: Grabhorn Press, 1934), in Carlos E. Cortés, ed., *Mexicans in the U.S. Conquest of California* (New York: Arno Press, 1976), p. 31.

7. Richard Griswold del Castillo, "*La Raza Hispano-Americana:* The Emergence of an Urban Culture Among the Spanish Speaking of Los Angeles, 1850–1880" (Ph.D. dissertation, University of California at Los Angeles, 1974), p. 45.

8. Pitt, p. 27; Griswold del Castillo, p. 49.

9. Pitt, p. 30.

10. Walter Colton, *Three Years in California* (New York: A. S. Barnes, 1850), p. 2.

11. Walton Bean, *California,* 2nd ed. (New York: McGraw-Hill, 1973), p. 104; Caughey, p. 168. Bean places the number of Americans killed at 22, with 16 wounded. Bill Mason of the Los Angeles County Museum stated in an interview that the number of Mexicans present was exaggerated. Mason said that researchers had been able to document the presence of only 65 Mexicans at San Pasqual; popular accounts place the number at approximately 150. Dewitt C. Peters, *Kit Carson's Life and Adventures, from Facts Narrated by Himself* (Hartford, Conn.: Dustin, Gilmain, 1875), pp. 282–283, confirms that word of the Mexican force was received by Kearny in late October.

12. Robert F. Heizer and Allan F. Almquist, *The Other Californians* (Berkeley: University of California Press, 1971), p. 149; Bean, pp. 132–134; Stephen Clark Foster, delegate to the Constitutional Convention of 1849, *El Quachero: How I Want to Help Make the Constitution of California—Stirring Historical Incidents,* in Carlos E. Cortés, ed., *Mexicans in California After the U.S. Conquest* (New York: Arno Press, 1976).

13. José Bandini, *A Description of California in 1828* (Berkeley: Friends of the Bancroft Library, 1951), reprinted in Carlos E. Cortés, ed., *Mexican California* (New York: Arno Press, 1976), pp. vi, 11; Don Thomas Coulter, *Notes on Upper California: A Journey from Monterey to the Colorado River in 1832* (Los Angeles: Glen Dawson, 1951), reprinted in Cortés, *Mexican California,* p. 23; Heizer and Almquist, p. 120.

14. Heizer and Almquist, p. 144.

15. Heizer and Almquist, pp. 143, 144.

16. Quoted in Leonard Pitt, "The Foreign Miner's Tax of 1850: A Study of Nativism and Anti-Nativism in Gold Rush California" (Master's thesis, University of California at Los Angeles, 1955), p. 9.

17. David J. Weber, ed., *Foreigners in Their Native Land* (Albuquerque: University of New Mexico Press, 1973), p. 151.

18. Pitt, "Foreign Miner's Tax," pp. 49–50.

19. Richard Morefield, "Mexicans in the California Mines, 1848–1853," *California Historical Quarterly* 24 (March 1956): 38.

20. Heizer and Almquist, pp. 121, 145.

21. *Daily Pacific News,* October 19, 1850.

22. Heizer and Almquist, p. 155.

23. Morefield, p. 43.

24. Charles Hughes, *The Decline of the Californios: The Case of San Diego, 1846–1856,* reprinted in Cortés, *Mexicans in California,* p. 17.

25. Mario T. García, *Merchants and Dons: San Diego's Attempt at Modernization, 1850–1860,* reprinted in Cortés, *Mexicans in California,* p. 70.

26. Bean, p. 224; Caughey, p. 344.

27. García, p. 70. Pitt, *Decline of the Californios,* p. 118, states that 813 titles were reviewed and 32 rejected. Bean, p. 157, says that more than 800 cases were heard, that 604 were confirmed and 209 rejected. We rely here on the García figures cited.

28. Pitt, *Decline of the Californios,* p. 119.

29. Hughes, p. 17.

30. Heizer and Almquist, p. 150.

31. Griswold del Castillo, p. 76; Albert Michael Camarillo, "The Making of a Chicano Community: A History of the Chicanos in Santa Barbara, California, 1850–1930" (Ph.D. dissertation, University of California at Los Angeles, 1975), p. 43.

32. Caughey, *California,* p. 219.

33. Hughes, p. 18.

34. García, p. 70.

35. Horace Bell, *On the Old West Coast* (New York: Morrow, 1930), pp. 5–6.

36. Bell, pp. 255–257.

37. Heizer and Almquist, pp. 128–129, 131.

38. Heizer and Almquist, p. 151.

39. Camarillo, p. 65.

40. Richard Griswold del Castillo, "Health and the Mexican Americans in Los Angeles, 1850–1867," *Journal of Mexican History* 4 (1974): 21; Richard Romo, "Mexican Workers in the City: Los Angeles, 1915–1930" (Ph.D. dissertation, University of California at Los Angeles, 1975), p. 80.

41. Camarillo, p. 68.

42. Griswold del Castillo, *"La Raza,"* p. 29.

43. Pitt, *Decline of the Californios,* pp. 50–51.

44. William B. Secrest, *Juanita: The Only Woman Lynched in the Gold Rush Days* (Fresno, Calif.: Saga-West, 1967), pp. 8–29.

45. Secrest, p. 23; *El Clámor Público,* April 4 and 16, 1857.

46. Pitt, *Decline of the Californios,* pp. 61–63.

47. Pitt, *Decline of the Californios,* p. 53.

48. W. W. Robinson, *People Versus Lugo: Story of a Famous Los Angeles Murder Case and Its Aftermath* (Los Angeles: Dawson's Book Shop, 1962), reprinted in Cortés, *Mexicans in California After the U.S. Conquest,* p. 6.

49. Joseph Lancaster Brent, *The Lugo Case: A Personal Experience,* reprinted in Cortés, *Mexicans in California,* pp. 12–13; Robinson, pp. 1–5.

50. Robinson, p. 14; Brent, p. 4.

51. Robinson, pp. 10–11, 17–18, 40; Brent, pp. 17–19.

52. Robinson, pp. 21–22, 26–27, 33–37, 40; Brent, pp. 20–33.

53. See Pitt, *Decline of the Californios,* chap. 17, for a biography of Ramírez.

54. *El Clamor Público,* June 19, 1855.

55. *El Clamor Público,* August 20, 1855.

56. *El Clamor Público,* September 18, 1855.

57. *El Clamor Público,* May 10, 1856.

58. *El Clamor Público,* May 17, 1856.

59. Bell, p. 72.

60. Griswold del Castillo, *"La Raza,"* pp. 195–196.

61. Hubert Howe Bancroft, *Popular Tribunals,* vol. 1 (San Francisco: History Company, 1887), pp. 501–503; Griswold del Castillo, *"La Raza,"* pp. 195–196.

62. Pitt, *Decline of the Californios,* p. 174.

63. Griswold del Castillo, *"La Raza,"* p. 197.

64. *El Clamor Público,* December 18, 1858.

65. Ernest May, "Tiburcio Vásquez," *Historical Society of Southern California Quarterly 24* (1947): 123–124, places the time in spring of 1851. May's article is unsympathetic. He writes that Vásquez was in the company of Anastacio García, whom May calls an outlaw, and José Guerra. May admits that Constable Hardimount had been rude to Mexicans. Guerra was caught and hanged. Griswold del Castillo, *"La Raza,"* p. 198, states that Vásquez began his career by escaping from a lynch mob.

66. Robert Greenwood, *The California Outlaw: Tiburcio Vásquez* (Los Gatos, Calif.: Talisman Press, 1960), p. 12.

67. Heizer and Almquist, pp. 150–151.

68. May, p. 124; Greenwood, p. 13; Griswold del Castillo, *"La Raza,"* p. 199.

69. Greenwood, pp. 23–24.

70. Greenwood, p. 75.

71. Griswold del Castillo, *"La Raza,"* pp. 270, 271.

72. Griswold del Castillo, *"La Raza,"* p. 272.

73. Quoted in Griswold del Castillo, *"La Raza,"* p. 271.

74. Griswold del Castillo, *"La Raza,"* p. 66; Caughey, pp. 349–350.

75. Griswold del Castillo, *"La Raza,"* pp. 156, 202; Griswold del Castillo, "Health," p. 22.

76. Albert Camarillo, *Chicanos in California* (San Francisco: Boyd & Foster, 1984), pp. 24–25.

77. Griswold del Castillo, *"La Raza,"* p. 227; Griswold del Castillo, "Health," p. 22.

78. Caughey, pp. 344–345.

79. Jean F. Riss, "The Lynching of Francisco Torres," *Journal of Mexican American History* (Spring 1972): 90–111.

80. Riss, p. 109.

81. Riss, p. 111.

82. Griswold del Castillo, *"La Raza,"* p. 193. Also see Richard Griswold del Castillo, "Myth and Reality: Chicano Economic Mobility in Los Angeles, 1850–1890," *Aztlán* 6, no. 2 (Summer 1975): 151–171.

two

THE MAKING OF AN UNDERCLASS: THE MEXICAN IN THE UNITED STATES

In the nineteenth century, dramatic changes took place in the Southwest, as the region evolved from a precapitalist subsistence economy, in which surpluses were used for consumption, to a mercantile capitalist system, in which merchants, freighters, commercial farmers and ranchers, and others made profits from trade and its monopolization. The coming of the railroad accelerated the area's industrialization. Later on, entrepreneurs invested in the surpluses from production, a development that brought about the continued accumulation of wealth as trade expanded from the *plaza,* to the U.S. and world market system. The evolving economy greatly affected Mexicans, since each stage intensified a division of labor in which Mexicans occupied the less skilled and lowest paid jobs.

Changes in the twentieth century were even more dramatic than those in the nineteenth. In 1900, the United States led the world in industrial output; 80 years later, the nation entered the postindustrial period. Factories shut down in increasing numbers, and, in the process, non- and semi-skilled workers became an endangered species.

Nowhere was this shift more heavily felt than in steel. At the turn of the century, North America was the world's leading steel producer; 13 years later it manufactured more than Great Britain, Germany, and France combined. Few then would have predicted the demise of an industry that had once absorbed uneducated European immigrant masses, along with a few Mexicans and Blacks. After World War II, more minorities entered steel and heavy industry in general; because of union wages, they accumulated sufficient surpluses to buy their homes, educate their children, and enjoy a relatively high standard of living. By the mid-1980s, however, this option was closed.

During the twentieth century, the Southwest was fully integrated into the North American market system—first by the railroad, then by highways, and finally by air. New methods of production, made possible by technological advances, boosted factory output. Industrial expansion was not limited to the cities but extended to the farms. Growth encouraged more complex forms of organization. Farms became factories. Machines displaced year-round farm workers and gave rise to the demand for armies of migrants who formed assembly lines in the fields. Capital flowed into agriculture, monopolizing large tracts of acreage and organizing even small operators into food and fruit exchanges. Agribusiness maintained a competitive edge by keeping wages below the subsistence level. Its strategy was to attract more migrants than were necessary, in order to hold the labor supply at the flood level. Corporate agriculture mimicked the urban industrialists who reduced workers to a pair of arms.

Farm production increased. In 1870, one of every two workers was employed in agriculture. In 1929, one in five worked in farm production. Today, an agricultural workforce of 3 percent of the U.S. population can feed the entire country. Such advances have been made possible not so much by the superiority of Euroamerican farmers as by the availability of the best farmland in the world. Government research and large surpluses accumulated from "working 'em cheap" made technology affordable.

North American nativism disrupted patterns of foreign labor recruitment, limiting or excluding European and Asian immigration. Mexicans escaped being put on immigration quotas. Consequently, Mexican workers replaced their European and Asian counterparts. In the Southwest, and in portions of the Midwest, dependence on Mexican labor grew. Mexicans did not work exclusively in agriculture, however. They moved to the cities, which they used as winter quarters in the migrant trek. The core of Mexicans came to the United States in response to the demand for labor. Others came for political reasons—either because they opposed Mexican dictator Porfirio Díaz or because they opposed the Mexican revolutionaries that overthrew him.

The Mexicans' experience in the United States revolves around changes in North American production during the first three-quarters of the century. Migrancy disorganized the Mexicans, making them vulnerable to severe economic exploitation that Anglo racism justified. Movement to the mining camps and to the cities ended the *peon* status of many Mexicans, converting them into wage laborers. The more sedentary environment of the mining camps, meanwhile, created the conditions that encouraged Mexicans to form or join trade unions. Racism and nativism, however, checked their access to the labor internationals.

Mexicans faced additional problems in North America's unplanned cities, where they competed for space with other ethnics. Possession of land depended on group status, and Mexicans generally occupied space "where only the weeds grew." Because of housing shortages, Mexicans were forced into tenement-like shelters where they had to adopt new ways of life. Ghettoization was the rule in most cities where Mexicans lived.

The story of the Mexicans during the twentieth century is, therefore, the history of adaptation to the U.S.'s labor market needs. It is also the story of their struggle to obtain equal justice—social, political, and economic—and the effect that their lack of access to North American institutions had in depriving them of basic human rights.

The organization of Part Two is as follows. Chapter 6, "The Building of the Southwest: Mexican Labor, 1900–1930," deals with the conditions in Mexico and the United States that led to the mass migration of Mexicans north of the Río Bravo. Nativist reaction to this migration is recorded. Migrancy limited the Mexicans' organizational responses to their new environment. As cities in the Southwest grew, more Mexicans migrated to perform the pick and shovel work. Although urban living made it more possible for Mexicans to organize, it produced, at the same time, problems such as inadequate housing, unequal access to education and a class-biased judicial system, as well as a racist bureaucracy.

San Antonio and Los Angeles emerged as cities with the largest Mexican populations. In San Antonio, Mexicans concentrated in the West Side, while in Los Angeles many lived in the Civic Center and immediately to the east. Los Angeles early established a pattern in which the middle class filtered out of the *barrio.* Middle-class leadership was important in both San Antonio and Los Angeles. In Texas, the middle class was more defined, and, by the 1920s, this class tended to assimilate. During the first two decades, labor strikes were spontaneous and, outside of mining, few Chicanos belonged to trade unions. By the 1920s, labor organization took a more permanent form.

Chapter 7, "The Forging of the Mexican American Community: The Depression Years," focuses on the 1930s. Job shortages and bad times brought nativism to the surface, and, in the guise of cost effectiveness, local authorities throughout the Southwest and Midwest repatriated a half-million Mexicans. The depression had a dramatic effect on this community. In California, for instance, poor whites displaced Mexicans in agriculture as the Dust Bowl created mass migration from other parts of the country.

Texas was more organizationally developed than other Southwest states. There the League of United Latin American Citizens (LULAC), already recognized as the advocate for Mexicans, generally called for assimilation into North American society. Similar organizations were formed in other states. Aside from middle-class groups, the poor joined and organized associations to help them survive.

The Wagner Act of 1935 affected the growth of industrial unions. Although they began to trickle into the unions, Mexicans during the 1930s remained politically isolated. Dennis Chávez's election to the U.S. Senate from New Mexico was an exception. A sense of national unity developed among Mexican Americans in the latter part of the decade.

Chapter 8, "The Mexican American, the War, and 'Happy Days,'" describes the impact of world war on North American society and relates how Mexican Americans adjusted to the changed conditions. World War II underscored the contradictions of a "democratic society" and the role of the Mexican American in it. Mexican Americans served with distinction in the military, while at home racism led to the legitimation of violence toward their youth. During this period, North Americans rented their *braceros,* or laborers, from Mexico, reinforcing the pattern of Mexican subservience. Of particular importance for Mexican Americans were the dramatic social and economic shifts brought about by the war. Government spending made billionaires of select individuals and corporations; it also accelerated the Southwest's industrialization and the urbanization of the Mexican American.

With growing urbanization, there was increased assimilation of the Mexican American into the life of the country. Events after the war greatly affected Mexican Americans. With the Cold War and the rise of a pseudo-nationalism, Euroamericans became increasingly intolerant. The destruction of an independent Congress of Industrial Organizations (CIO) removed a developing link between the community and labor. During the 1950s, interest in reform waned, and the McCarran-Walter Act and Operation Wetback witch hunts became popular. In response, Chicanos joined organizations for the protection of the foreign-born. In general, however, middle-class Mexican American groups, out of fear, bent to the political winds.

In spite of the times, participation in political and civil rights activities became more common among Mexican Americans. During the Happy Days (the 1950s) their political involvement grew. The elections of Henry B. González (San Antonio) and Edward R. Roybal (Los Angeles) were landmarks. By the end of the 1950s, the Mexican American Political Association (MAPA) had been formed in California.

Government policy supported the funding of urban renewal projects and redevelopment of inner cities as well as the building of freeways. This process also encouraged suburbanization. As the inner cities became more vulnerable, the bulldozers destroyed many Mexican American communities, displacing thousands, and making millions for local elites. Urban renewal and other government programs in places like Los Angeles frustrated the forging of Chicano communities.

Chapter 9, "Goodbye America: The Chicano in the 1960s," covers the decade known for student unrest, civil rights struggles, and antiwar protest. It was also a time when Mexican Americans became both more urbanized and more segregated. Underlying changes in the economy affected Mexican Americans, who were becoming less competitive in the labor market. As government spending accelerated a high-tech–military establishment in the Southwest, Anglo-Americans migrated to the region in search of new opportunities. Mexican Americans, for the most part, remained in marginal occupations. Their median education ran four years behind that of the Anglos, who were rapidly moving out of blue-collar jobs and into higher paying white-collar positions. The job-training gap alarmed many Mexican Americans, who increasingly formed ad hoc education committees.

Growth also marked the decade: the Mexican population in cities such as San Antonio, Los Angeles, Houston, and Chicago expanded dramatically. The so-called discovery of "poverty in America" in the early 1960s had an immediate impact. The recognition of an underclass, along with the civil rights struggle, encouraged John Kennedy and Lyndon Johnson to seek programs to calm the waters. Motivated by both idealism and self-interest, the baby-boom generation mobilized in protest against the war in Vietnam. The war on poverty and then the Vietnam War set the tone for the participation of Mexican American youth and the grass roots themselves in the struggle for justice, social and community programs, and the end of the war. Young people dominated the movement for a time, with the 1968 walkouts, protests against the Catholic Church, and demonstrations against the war; they rewrote the agendas of traditional organizations such as LULAC and the G.I. Forum. It was also a time of self-identification, with activists calling themselves Chicanos instead of Latin Americans, Spanish Americans, or even Mexican Americans.

Chapter 10, "The Age of the Brokers: The New Hispanics," covers the years 1971–1979. The late 1960s had been a period in which injustice could no longer be tolerated; there were attempts to define *chicanismo* in strict nationalist terms. The 1970s saw a change of political heart, symbolized by the transition from Archie Bunker to Rambo. The "Age of the Hispanic" brought with it the acceptance of moderate and right-wing leadership and an isolation of the left of center. While the Chicano had often blindly fought injustice, the new Hispanics believed that through their influence the Mexican American community could achieve progress. In this conciliatory environment, most of the 1960s civil rights gains were wiped out by the end of the decade. The 1970s represented a reaffirmation of the Chicano middle class as brokers for the community and their legitimation by the private and public sectors.

Although the support of undocumented workers became a major issue for all sectors of the Mexican American community, a decline in nationalism took place, with individuals turning away from *chicanismo* and incorporating the values of the "me decade." In spite of this, progressive strains remained alive as Chicanos continued to struggle.

Chapter 11, "The Age of the Brokers: The Rambo Years," records the decline of the North American industrial empire. This transition limited the choices of Mexican Americans either to going to college or to selling hamburgers. A grinding away of the Chicano unionized factory worker widened the gap between the educated and the uneducated. The Rambo years saw the rise of politicians such as Henry Cisneros (San Antonio) and Federico Peña (Denver), who represented the aspirations of the new Hispanic. Although Chicanos celebrated these successes, there was little emphasis on where the community was going.

Other signs of a loss of community vitality were evident. Among many in the middle class, trickle-down economics came into fashion. In addition, the Rambo mentality threatened another Vietnam, this time in Central America, with the potential of Chicano Garcias fighting Central American Garcias. Throughout this period of retreat, however, a small sector of the middle class as well as a number of organizations kept faith with progressive ideals. Involvement of the Catholic Church marked a new development in the Chicano community and broadened its organizational alternatives.

chapter **6**

The Building of the Southwest: Mexican Labor, 1900–1930

AN OVERVIEW

Throughout history the role of the working class has been ignored or, at best, hidden in crevices. Only recently have a minority of U.S. historians begun to recognize the role of Blacks in the building of the South and the United States as a whole. Without Black labor the dramatic expansion of cotton could not have taken place; Blacks provided the energy for its production. Reduced to a robot-like status, the Black plowed the soil, planted the seed, cultivated the crops, and picked the cotton. Similarly, many Euroamericans regarded the Southwest as the "Great American Desert," whose marginal lands remained unproductive until the genius of North American engineering brought in irrigation and drainage to make them gardens in the sun. It was Mexican labor, however, that built the Southwest; without Mexican labor, the development of agriculture, mining, construction, and the railroads would have been retarded.

In 1900, New Mexico, Arizona, and Oklahoma had not been admitted into the Union. New Mexico and Arizona had too many Mexicans; Oklahoma had too many Indians. Rapid population change made statehood possible. The automobile, truck, tractor, refrigerated car, and radio unified the region politically, and rapid delivery to the East encouraged expansion of production. In the early twentieth century, the Southwest became a leading producer of oil, cotton, fruits and vegetables, fish, and copper. The federal government built mammoth-size dams to furnish water and hydroelectric power to farms and cities. For all its prosperity, however, the Southwest during the first three decade of the century remained an economic colony of the East. Absentee ownership and management

141

were common. Little manufacturing took place, and easterners exploited its resources by controlling tariffs, interest rates, freight prices, and the cost of farm products. Finally, the region had a lower population density than the East; southwestern towns remained too small to attract economic activities that employed agriculture workers on the off-season or as casual workers during times of depression.

These factors greatly influenced labor–management relations in the Southwest. And as capitalists exploited the region's other resources, they exploited labor. The geographic proximity of Mexico became key to the region's development. A surplus of cheap labor could readily, and inexpensively, be imported into the United States. By hiring Mexicans at lower wages than were prevalent in other parts of the United States, corporate farmers could afford the cost of land, irrigation, and oppressive freight charges.

Perhaps as important, large grower interests had the money and power to lobby government to grant them special advantages—for example, the passage of protective tariffs and the construction of dams to tap water resources at taxpayers' expense. The enactment of the Dingley Tariff in 1897 and the Reclamation Act of 1902 put millions of additional acres into production. California soon entered the Cotton Kingdom, as did Arizona. Growth, however, was not limited to cotton. The increased demand for fresh vegetables and fruits saw an expansion in these farm commodities. For instance, California did not share in the vegetable and fruit market nationally in 1900, but, in 1929, it produced 40 percent of the total share.[1] These changes could not have taken place without government funding and Mexican labor.

The expansion of agriculture coincided with the restructuring of the U.S. reserve labor pool of unskilled workers. The 1880s saw the total exclusion of Chinese labor, and, through the next three decades, Asian immigration was all but brought to a standstill. A succession of immigration laws based on ethnicity, class, and ideology limited the number of Europeans entering the country. The Literacy Act of 1917 shut out the bulk of European cheap labor, eliminating the huddled masses who performed the backbreaking work that only the uneducated would do for poverty wages. In 1921 and 1924, immigration laws put central and southern Europeans on a quota. These regulations forced northern capitalists to recruit Blacks from the South, while southwestern and midwestern growers dipped into Mexico. Deprived of unlimited numbers of poor workers, urban and rural industrialists stepped up mechanization by the late 1920s; a half-century later, technological innovations would make the majority of Mexicans in the United States unable to satisfy Euroamerican cheap labor market needs.

It would be an error to assume that all Mexicans during this period were migrant farm workers. A portion had lived in urban and rural centers of the Southwest since before the Euroamerican invasion. After the Civil War, Mexicans began to trickle into Texas and New Mexico, which already had sizable numbers of Mexicans. They formed patriotic associations and *mutualistas* and sponsored conferences in an attempt to address the problems of segregation, racism, and the lack of economic and political opportunity.

The preponderance of Mexicans worked in agriculture, in the most strenuous jobs, those generally reserved for nonwhites. They were scorned and paid the lowest wages for what employers labeled "Mexican work." The seasonal aspect of their employment contributed to their poverty. Unable to organize, they moved from farm to farm, isolated from friends and in contact only with their immediate families. Moreover, their Indian features made them vulnerable to racist attacks. And because they had no documents, they could be deported at will.

The dramatic growth of southwestern cities during the first three decades of the century generated a significant number of jobs. For instance, during this period Los Angeles City grew from 50,000 to 1.2 million; Los Angeles County expanded from 101,000 to 2.2 million. Mexican migration to Los Angeles was in great part due to the fact that Los Angeles county was one of the most productive agricultural regions in the United States; it was also due to the fact that Los Angeles's size enabled the city to offer Mexicans supplemental employment (as did San Antonio and a northern city, Chicago).[2] Texas's largest city, San Antonio had a population of 96,517 in 1910, a growth of 81 percent since 1900; by 1930, the population numbered 231,542. Growth meant jobs in the construction of a booming city. Menial jobs were plentiful in brickyards, in flour mills, and on streetcar maintenance crews. Mexicans were almost exclusively found in industries paying poverty-level wages.

Mexicans in the city faced the problems of poverty—such as poor housing and inadequate municipal services—which worsened as their numbers increased; racism too was common. Police harassment, a lack of educational opportunity, and the humiliation of "No Mexicans Allowed" signs were the usual experience of the newcomer. The types of employment available were often based on race. Sometimes the Mexicans protested the inequality they suffered; more often, like other immigrants, they accepted it because of their vulnerability.

Because of the long border and the proximity of Mexico, they frequently looked upon their situation as temporary. In other instances, because conditions in their hometowns were even worse, they viewed the city as a place where they could make money. This mentality often immobilized recent arrivals and thus became a factor that aided in their control. Even the Mexican political exiles, although they fought for the rights of Mexican workers, wanted to return. Further, after 1910, the political exiles were largely conservative, with little affinity for the poor. Changes, however, were in the making and, in the 1920s, some 40 percent of Mexican immigrants lived in urban centers.

In the city, Mexicans had to struggle to gain acceptance into trade unions. The craft union leadership dominated the union movement vis-à-vis the American Federation of Labor (AFL), which viewed unskilled workers as inferior and alien. Because Mexicans were shunned by organized labor, most Mexican strikes were spontaneous, led by temporary nationalist associations. Mexican activity in the mines proved an exception. By the 1910s internationals such as the Western Federation of Miners vigorously organized Mexican workers. A decade later many Mexican miners, displaced by technology and union-busting tactics, migrated to the cotton fields. The 1920s saw militancy among farm workers, and, as migrancy slowed, they organized more permanent associations. Mexican merchants and year-round workers who belonged to local *mutualistas* became more conscious of the exploitation of Mexican labor. The temporary nationalism of Mexican consuls added to the trend to form Mexican unions. The 1920s also saw the formation of the League of United Latin American Citizens (LULAC) in Texas. LULAC's rise came about as the result not so much of generational change as of urbanization and increased division of labor, which saw the natural creation of a small professional middle class in Texas.

Frequent depressions and recessions victimized the Mexican worker. Municipal relief in the form of public sector jobs went to U.S. citizens, excluding the great bulk of Mexicans. So-called aliens were at the bottom of the ladder; consequently, in hard times, forced to take charity, they were further stereotyped as burdens on society. The Mexicans' poverty was thus not simply the result of a time lag in the process of adjustment to the expanding economy. Their deprivation was not temporary, but created in major part by the economic and social organization of the Southwest.

BACKGROUND TO THE MIGRATION NORTH
FROM MEXICO, TO 1910

The first U.S. industrial revolution spread to agriculture in the Southwest by the 1850s, with McCormick's machine reaping grain in fields that had once belonged to the Mexicans. Mining bonanzas attracted large numbers of Anglos. Railroad interests laid track linking east and west, greatly accelerating the development of the Southwest. The Southwest supplied raw materials for the East, which in turn provided the "colony" with manufactured goods and capital. Fuel and minerals were needed, as well as food for the European immigrants who worked in the new factories. The refrigerated car went into service one year before transcontinental railroads were completed in 1869. Both railroads and refrigerated cars proved to be revolutionary in the last quarter of the nineteenth century. Eastern and foreign capital gushed into the Southwest, industrializing production.

Prior to 1880 contact between the United States and Mexico had been limited to the settled borderlands of northern Mexico. Except for New Mexico, the Mexican population remained relatively small, outnumbered by the Chinese in California and the Blacks in Texas. When Mexican labor first migrated to the ocuppied territory, it was mostly from northern Mexico. By the 1880s, however, changes in Mexico and the United States took place that altered this pattern, with huge numbers of immigrants arriving from Mexico's interior.

Spanish colonialism had delayed the northward migration by depopulating Mexico. By independence, in 1821, Mexico's population entered an upward spiral. By the end of the colonial period, the Mexican economy began to stabilize, and a nucleus of merchants, mine owners, and professionals wanted to follow the example of the United States and industrialize the country. A power struggle followed between these capitalists and the old elite—large landowners, the military, and the Catholic Church. Capitalists won by the mid-1850s, when Benito Juárez's liberal party finally took what proved to be full control of government. However, Mexico's economic growth was severely destabilized by its extensive land losses to the United States, the Wars of Reform (1858–1861), and French intervention (1861–1867), which prevented the rapid modernization of Mexico. Although recovery was slow, by 1850 mining production regained its 1805 level. The power of commercial and industrial interests grew as, by the middle of the century, these liberal forces took control of Mexico, beginning the capitalist exploitation of the nation's land, resources, and labor.

The mechanization of the textile industry affected the country's social structure: "With the development of the factory system during this period, this new urban-based group slowly increased in both numbers and economic strength."[3] Predictably, industrialization produced an urban middle and professional class as well as an urban working class. Growth of the factory and mining sectors created a demand for farm products, and agriculture expanded. Encouraged by liberal legislation of the 1850s, large landowners encroached on the communal property of the *municipios* and the small subsistence farmers. The objective was to make land more productive, and it resulted in further monopolization.

As early as 1823 Mexico had 44,800 miners and 2,800 textile workers.[4] In that year seven mills operated around Mexico City; by 1845, 74 textile factories functioned in the nation. According to Professor James Cockcroft, "The cotton textile industry doubled its installed capacity between 1854 and 1879. A rough estimate of the economically active population in 1861 showed 61 percent to be *jornaleros* [day laborers] in agriculture and mining and another 2.5 percent to be stably employed in factories or artisanal workshops."[5] In the late 1870s, capitalists intensified "economic developmentalism" under the dictatorship of Porfirio Díaz, with Mexican elites cooperating with foreign investors, laying the basis for an industrial economy.

Early Mexican Worker Movement

Expansion of production made possible rapid capital accumulation. Industrialization freed a sector of the Mexican labor force from the land, making it available to work in the new industries. The state protected the new industrialist class, and, because of inflation, and the relatively small rise in salaries, the workers' labor could be purchased at ever cheaper wages; higher prices for goods also ensured larger profits.

Mechanization resulted in a decline in many handicraft trades such as tobacco processing, silver working, leather goods finishing, and textile weaving. Mexico had an extensive shop system, both in the rural villages and in the cities. The artisans in these shops had reasonable security and enjoyed material benefits. As industrialization and land enclosure brought about the elimination of many crafts, many artisans lost status and were uprooted: "Among those who crowded into the working-class *barrios* of the cities and towns of Mexico was a growing class of dispossessed artisans, whose talents were less needed in an industrial age."[6] Many of these craftworkers, along with urban tradespeople, had historically organized into guilds. Frustrated in the 1850s, they became the vanguard in forming *mutualistas* and in condemning the effects of industrialization. For artisans, mutual aid societies became a means of protecting their economic and social status, whereas for workers they provided some sort of security through burial funds, savings, medical expenses, unemployment compensation, and pensions. Early workers' groups emphasized education, sponsoring night classes and libraries.[7]

The ideological perspective of the members was varied. The anarchist philosophy of Joseph Proudhon and Mikhail Bakunin was popular among early organizers. The Greek immigrant Plotino C. Rhodakanaty, who in the 1860s headed *El Grupo de Estudiantes Socialistas* (The Socialist Student Group), an organization whose ideological orientation could be called anarchist or libertarian socialist was also influential. Francisco Zalacosta, Santiago Villanueva, and Hermengildo Villavicencio, prominent members of the group, soon formed a secret cell (that included women) called *La Social,* dedicated to organizing the proletariat. In 1865 they led the first industrial strike at the San Ildefonso and La Colmena cotton mills. Three years later, still under the leadership of Santiago Villanueva, anarchists led the first successful strike at La Fama Montanesa in Mexico City. Workers at other mills, inspired by this victory, also struck when employers reduced their wages. The Juárez government backed management and abrogated progressive labor laws passed under Maximilian. The Juárez administration attempted to infiltrate the *mutualistas* by granting them annual stipends, but the anarchist faction opposed any government support or sponsorship.

Conditions also grew more desperate among the *campesinos* (farm workers). At Chalco, a peasant revolt broke out in 1869 which the Juárez government suffocated. The 1870s witnessed increased discontent among the artisans and workers. In the Valley of Mexico *El Gran Círculo de Obreros de México* (The Great Center of the Workers of Mexico) was organized, with the purpose of eventually establishing a national labor central. Thirty-two thousand textile workers belonged to the *Gran Círculo* in 1873. Within the *Gran Círculo* the anarchists and the moderates struggled ideologically.

The *Gran Círculo* called the first Mexican workers' congress in 1876. *La Social* participated in this congress, sending women delegates. The next year farm workers formed *El Primer Congreso Campesino de la Ciudad de México* (The First Congress of Farm Workers of Mexico City). At the second workers' congress, held in 1879, Carmen Huerta, a *Mexicana,* was elected president.[8] "These organizations espoused mutual aid, workers' defense, and a wide range of radical ideologies (Christian humanism, liberalism, utopian socialism, workers' internationalism, and anarchism) plus a few conservative ones."[9] The growth of these workers' groups, however, was stunted in the 1880s. At that time the government suppressed them because of their growing militancy and the policy of the Mexican government in promoting an environment of stability for industrial development.

The Decline of Ruralism and the Push to the North

Mexico's population had increased during the century. In the 1840s the population was about 7 million. In 1875, it reached 9.5 million, five years later it was closer to 10.5 million, and by 1895, the population numbered 12.6 million.[10] At the end of the *porfiriato* in 1910 Mexico had a population of over 15 million and, although this number was considerably less than the 25 million of the pre-conquest, this population growth brought changes. Most significantly, the population increased during a period of dramatic economic and social transformations. During the last quarter there was a decline in ruralism. While Mexico in 1910 was still largely rural, it had 22 cities of between 20,000 to 50,000, five of 50,000 to 100,000 and two over 100,000.[11] Moreover, Mexico had a small industrial proletariat with 16.3 percent of its labor force working in industry (68 percent worked in agriculture). Also noticeable was a small but growing middle class.[12]

Modernization had led to the demise of the communal village and commercialization of the *hacienda.* This process had been accelerated with Porfirio Díaz's coup in 1876, when he became president. His policies encouraged the industrialization of agriculture, mining, and transportation, which led to the uprooting of the Mexican peasants, many of whom moved northward. "Economically, railroad building and industrialization were the most important innovative processes generating social change in Mexico during the porfiriato."[13] Foreign capital to a large degree financed this phenomena. Betwen 1880 and 1910, 15,000 miles of railroad were built, most lines running north and south, with spurs providing better access to mineral deposits and making the cultivation of specialized crops such as sugar cane more profitable.[14]

The importance of the railroads cannot be overemphasized. As in the case of the Southwest, they unified the area internally and they linked the country with the United States. Railroads accelerated the nation's industrial and agricultural growth. They stimulated the flow of capital into the economy, increasing the possibility of commerce and exploitation of Mexico's resources. The decline of ruralism and the uprooting of the Mexican peasant would be a prime factor in Mexican migration to the United States.

Industrialization uprooted many *peones* either because mechanization displaced them or because they were attracted to better paying jobs on railroad construction crews, in the mines of northern Mexico, or in the nascent urban industries. Before the twentieth century, Mexican laborers had begun their northward migration to the mines of Coahuila and Chihuahua and to the smelters of Monterrey (Nuevo León). Pay in the north was 75¢ a day versus 25¢ a day in the interior.[15] Aside from the pay differential, inflation drove up the cost of living to the point that workers could not subsist. Between 1876 and 1910, the price of maize increased 108 percent, beans 163 percent, and chile 147 percent. Real income for the masses declined 57 percent.

Land enclosures increased in the *porfiriato.* Private property holders like the Zapata family lost their lands, as did the communal landholders *(ejidatarios),* to big commercial farmers interested in expanding the sugar industry in Morelos by developing large plantations with cheap labor and by constructing sugar mills on the plantations themselves.[16] During that period too, foreign investment, especially Anglo-American, rose sharply. Mexican historian Victor Alba says that U.S. corporations owned three-quarters of mineral holdings in Mexico and that, by 1910, "U.S. investment amounted to more than $2 billion, more than all the capital in the hands of Mexicans."[17] According to Alba the Díaz government gave foreign investors preferential treatment. For example, Edward L. Doheny bought oil-yielding tracts in Tampico for $1 an acre and companies exporting oil did not pay taxes.[18] Furthermore, during labor disputes the Mexican government intervened on the side of management.

The interference of U.S. capitalists kept Mexico's economy destabilized, thus ensuring a constant supply of raw materials and cheap labor for their parent corporations in the Southwest. United States Steel, Guggenheim, Anaconda, Standard Oil, and others were active in Mexico.

U.S. capitalists built Mexican railroads. Well before 1900 over 22,000 railroad cars transporting an estimated 77,000 Mexicans entered the United States,[19] a factor that facilitated the movement of Mexicans to the border. By the mid-1880s, Chihuahuan farmers, after planting their crops, traveled to eastern Arizona and local mines, working for day wages, returning at harvest time.

Worker Opposition to Díaz Crystallizes

Meanwhile, industrialization intensified class struggle, led by artisans, miners, and railway and textile workers. Díaz in the 1880s suffocated the *Gran Círculo* and brutally suppressed strikes. Conditions in the rural areas also worsened for *campesinos* and peasants. Most important, Díaz offended middle-class and old-line *juaristas;* Díaz curtailed bourgeois freedoms that flourished between 1867 and 1880[20]. And journalists and liberals called for a return to the Constitution of 1857. The government forced numerous critics into exile; from the United States many continued their opposition to Díaz. Some, like Catarino Garza and Lauro Aguirre, attempted to organize revolutions to overthrow the dictator.

Internal opposition to Díaz crystallized in 1906. Strikes occurred in mining, railroad, and textile industries. Textile manufacturing had made Orizaba a metropolitan area of nearly 100,000. A group of French capitalists owned the majority of the textile mills. For survival, workers formed *mutualistas,* later organizing *El Gran Círculo de Obreros Libres* (GCOL).[21]

Conditions at Mexican factories were oppressive, with young children often working 16-hour shifts. Driven by the material circumstances, even children took an active part in the struggle against exploitation. For example, María Díaz started working in the mills around Guadalajara at the age of 8 in 1904. After being dismissed at age 12 for union activities, she moved to another factory to organize workers there. During the Mexican Revolution she continued to support progressive elements.[22]

In Orizaba, throughout 1906, union organizers recruited textile workers; by June the Mexican government arrested *Gran Círculo* (GCOL) leaders. During the fall of that year a series of small strikes broke out. Owners responded to worker militancy by cutting wages and forming an employers' association that severely restricted the workers' freedoms by forbidding them to read the newspaper or to have house guests without permission. Mill owners escalated the struggle by locking out 30,000 workers at Orizaba alone. On January 4, 1907, Díaz ordered employees to return to the mills or face the consequences.[23]

At the Río Blanco mill, workers refused to return to the job. On the morning of January 7 they congregated in front of the mill, blocking entrances.

The men marched on the company store, which was foreign-owned and the "most hated symbol of capitalist exploitation and foreign domination."[24] In this instance, the women agitated the men to take action: Margarita Martínez and Isabel Díaz de Pensamiento, who had been insulted that morning by clerks at the store, harangued them into action. When the clerks panicked, fired on the marchers, and killed a number of them, the angry workers looted and burned the store. Authorities arrested many workers and pursued and killed others.

Federal troops arrived on January 8. As the strikers prepared to return to work the next day, federal authorities marched six prisoners to the burned company stores and shot them as their comrades watched. Soldiers shot a seventh worker at Río Blanco when he defiantly cursed the executioners, "unable to contain his rage at what he had seen." In total about 150 workers and 25 soldiers were killed.[25]

In Cananea, Sonora, a group of 30 miners formed *La Unión Liberal Humanidad* in January 1906. Its charter members belonged to the Liberal Club of Cananea, an affiliate of the PLM. Workers had grievances against the Consolidated Copper Company, including the fact that Anglos worked 8 hours while Mexicans labored for 10 to 12 hours at half the Anglo wage. On the evening of May 31, Mexican workers walked off the Oversight mine, demanding 5 pesos for an 8-hour day. Two thousand miners joined the strike. Sonoran governor Rafael Izábal sent state militia to support mine owner Colonel William C. Greene. Mexican miners were unarmed, while Greene's men were heavily armed. Tempers rose and a company employee killed three demonstrators. Mexican workers burned the lumber yard. Arizona Rangers crossed the international line to help Greene. Díaz ordered his henchman General Luis Torres into the area. Torres immediately issued an ultimatum to miners—go back to work or get drafted into the army. The general arrested a hundred men and sent dozens to prison.[26] (See Chapter 4 for the connection between the Clifton–Morenci strike of 1903 and the Cananea strike three years later.)

In July of that year mechanics on the Mexican Central Railroad in Chihuahua struck the line. Workers shut down repair shops from the border to Mexico City, and by mid-August the strike involved 1,500 mechanics and 3,000 other railroad employees. As expected, Díaz ordered workers to return to the job, charging that they had violated the Constitution of 1857.

Injustices at the mills, mines, and railroads were mirrored in other industries and in the countryside. Modernization had improved communication, through an increase in newspapers, easier transportation, and concentration of workers in urban areas and company towns. The improved communication network facilitated the spread of knowledge of these injustices throughout urban centers and rural areas.[27]

By 1910, foreign investors controlled 76 percent of all corporations, 95 percent of mining, 89 percent of industry, 100 percent of oil, and 96 percent of agriculture. The United States owned 38 percent of this investment, Britain 29 percent, and France 27 percent.[28] Trade with the United States had jumped from $7 million in 1860 to $63 million in 1900. Anglo-Americans alone owned over $100 million in the state of Chihuahua. In contrast, 97.1 percent of the families in Guanajuato were without land, 96.2 percent in Jalisco, 99.5 percent in Mexico (state), and 99.3 percent in Puebla.[29]

Given the population boom in Mexico and the flight of capital, Mexicans did what people have always done—they followed the resources. The policy of Díaz toward the large exodus of Mexican citizens was one of indifference, for he placed little value on the *peon* and *campesino.* This was not the case with the Catholic Church or *hacendados* in Jalisco, Guanajuato, and Michoacán, who complained that the country was being depopulated. In 1906 the *Partido Liberal Mexicano* demanded that the Mexican government repatriate Mexicans, pay for their transportation and give them land. Three years later Francisco Madero called the flight of Mexicans to the United States a "serious national disease."[30]

In the first decade of the twentieth century, Mexicans departed from their traditional areas of settlement. In 1908 Victor Clark in a U.S. government study titled, *Report of the Immigration Commission,* stated: "As recently as 1900, immigrant Mexicans were seldom found more than one hundred miles from the border. Now they are working as unskilled laborers and as section hands as far east as Chicago and as far north as Iowa, Wyoming, and San Francisco."[31] Incoming Mexicans settled permanently only in Texas; Clark estimated that prior to 1908 about 60,000 entered the United States annually, with most Mexicans remaining for only a brief period.[32] Officially 103,000 immigrants entered the United States by 1900, but the actual number may have been much higher. Likewise, the official figure of 222,000 for 1910 may in fact be too low; experts estimate that the number may have been as high as 500,000.[33]

Early Radicalism North of the Río Bravo

The first two decades of the 1900s were formative years. In their great majority, Mexicans worked in agriculture and few were educated enough to participate beyond the local struggles. *Mexicanos* developed limited networks within the white radical or labor communities; when interested they were more concerned with the events in Mexico than with the plight of Mexican workers in the United States. Moreover, being concentrated in rural areas, most Mexicans were isolated.

The best known Mexican radical in the United States, without a doubt was Ricardo Flores Magón. He spent over 20 years in the United States, writing about not only tyranny in Mexico, but economic, political, and social discrimination suffered by Mexicans in "Utopia." Flores Magón, born in Oaxaca in 1873, crossed into the United States in 1904, with the intent of agitating for the overthrow of the dictator. He and his group published a newspaper, *Regeneración.* In the course of the struggle, Flores Magón became acquainted with many exiles who had taken to organizing Mexican workers, and as he learned about the fate of these workers in the United States he reported on the injustices. By 1906, *Regeneración* had a circulation of 30,000, and was read aloud to the masses in cities and hamlets where *Mexicanos* congregated.[34] From the United States, Magón planned three abortive invasions.

When not in jail for his political activities, Flores Magón and his colleagues published *Regeneración,* in which they included commentaries about bad working conditions, discrimination, police brutality, and lynchings of Mexicans in the United States. In March 1918 the PLM issued a manifesto calling for a world anarchist revolution. The courts sentenced Magón to 20 years and his comrade Librado Rivera to 15 years for violation of U.S. neutrality acts. "When [Alvaro] Obregon finally gained U.S. approval of their return to Mexico in November 1922, Ricardo Flores Magón mysteriously died in his cell—murdered, according to Rivera."[35]

Aside from their revolutionary activities in overthrowing Diáz, many PLM members organized among Mexican workers in the United States. For instance, Práxedis G. Guerrero, born in León, Guanajuato, in 1882, dedicated his life to organizing the oppressed. Guerrero worked as a miner in Colorado and as a woodcutter in San Francisco. In 1905 he joined the PLM, and in 1906 he set up *Obreros Libres* in Morenci, Arizona. Guerrero contributed articles to *Regeneración*. On December 30, 1910, Guerrero was killed in a clash between federal and PLM troops at Janos, Chihuahua.

True to the PLM's anarchist principles, women took leadership roles within the group. *Regeneración* published countless articles about their participation in the movement. For instance, in Laredo, Texas, Sara Estela Ramírez was a staunch supporter of Flores Magón and participated in union activity. A socialist, she worked for the Federal Labor Union and *La Sociedad de Obreros, Igualdad y Progreso,* a mutual aid society formed in the mid-1880s. In San Marcos, Texas, in 1913 Elisa Alemán of San Antonio gave a speech urging women to participate in the PLM. In the 1911 invasion of Baja California Margarita Ortega acted as a messenger and gun runner and crossed enemy lines to care for the wounded. She and her daughter, Rosaura Gotari, were exiled to the United States, where authorities hounded the two women. Gotari died, and Ortega, with her comrade Natividad Cruz, returned to struggle; both were captured and executed.[36]

Throughout the first two decades of the twentieth century, PLM organizers could be found speaking in the *plazas* of Los Angeles, Tucson, San Antonio, and countless other localities, condemning injustices in the United States and Mexico. Other exiles used these forums to espouse their causes and to recruit followers. They helped raise the consciousness of many workers, pinpointing the causes of their oppression. Anarchists such as the *magonistas* had contact with North American anarchists such as Emma Goldman, while socialists such as Lazaro Gutiérrez de Lara formed alliances with Anglo-American socialists. The two movements popularized the plight of the Mexican worker on both sides of the border.

One of the first national labor figures of Mexican extraction was Lucy Eldine Gonzales from Johnson County, Texas. Most historians list her as Mexican-Indian; a current biographer raises the possibility that she may also have been part Black. Lucy Gonzales married Albert Parsons, who was executed as a conspirator in the Haymarket Riot of 1886. She was an avowed anarchist who published newspapers, pamphlets, and books, traveled and lectured extensively, and led many demonstrations. In the 1870s she was a charter member of the Chicago Working Women's Union, and in 1905 she was a founding member of the Industrial Workers of the World (IWW). Twenty-two years later she was elected to the National Committee of the International Labor Defense. Gonzales believed that "the abolition of capitalism would automatically produce racial and sexual equality." Despite her involvement in national and international issues, she did not directly participate in the organization of Mexican workers.[37]

Mexican Labor in the United States, 1900–1910

The Southwest during the early twentieth century was still relatively un-developed. Southwesterners worked principally at occupations involving the soil and subsoil. Except in California and Texas, Mexicans remained the core of workers involved in manual labor. In Texas, this exception was changing by the last decades of the nineteenth century.

In Arizona, mine owners traveled to El Paso as early as 1872 to recruit Mexican labor (see Chapter 4). Mexicans took jobs in coal and copper mining operations which others refused, chopping timber, doing general clean-up work, and performing pick and shovel work. Mines in northern Mexico attracted work-ers from the interior. These mines, most of which were owned by U.S. capitalists, served as a stepping-stone into the United States and kept mines there supplied with experienced labor.[38]

Mexicans in Texas had been employed as *vaqueros* during the nineteenth century, but the agricultural revolution was underway. The open range disap-peared by the 1870s, and wire fencing during the next decade raised the price of land. In the Río Grande Valley, Mexican workers cleared brush and planted cotton and winter vegetables. In Nueces in 1900, 107,860 head of cattle roamed the land, whereas 25 years later the number of cattle had dwindled to 10,514; in Dimmit County cattle declined from 74,641 to 7,334 during the same period. Migrant farm laborers thus displaced *vaqueros.* Tenant farming became common during the first two decades of the twentieth century in Texas, with one-third of the land worked by sharecroppers.[39]

Cattle ranches had dominated much of the area in the 1880s; this changed with the arrival of railroads (see Chapter 2). At the turn of the century, extensive irrigation projects and commercial farming radically changed south Texas. Com-mercial farming introduced a paternalistic system of open racism, social segrega-tion, and sharecropping. Commercialized farms began around 1904 with the arrival of large land companies that brought in small farmers. Many larger ranches were subdivided and sold to these new settlers. The digging of artesian wells and utilization of Mexicans with flamethrowers to clear the land of mesquite converted the valley into cash-producing farm areas, with fast profits made on cotton and vegetables.[40]

Many farmers owned plots of between 80 and 160 acres; one family could cultivate 40 to 50 acres and rent the remaining land to a tenant or two. Work in agriculture was literally a family affair, with women and child labor common. White tenants got land and contracts superior to those offered to Mexicans. Anglos received two-thirds of the profits from vegetables and three-quarters of the profits from cotton. Mexicans generally received only half the profits, an arrangement which greatly favored the owner. Farmers offered Anglos larger sections than *Mexicanos,* and often the Anglo tenant would sublease to Mexicans or other whites. Many white landlords did little work, with Mexicans performing most of the manual labor. The system had many abuses. Many growers forced Mexican sharecroppers to leave, when it appeared that they had a good crop, by withholding credit, harassing them, or calling immigration officials. White tenants averaged $3,750 compared to $500 a year for Mexicans during the 1920s.

On farms over 500 acres, contractors furnished Mexican crews from border towns. Few Mexicans owned farms during the early 1900s, but some later acquired 40- to 50-acre farms. Up to the late 1920s cotton was the area's main crop, but after this spinach and other vegetables took a greater share of the market. By the mid-1920s Mexicans began to move off *ranchos* to *colonias,* which served as a base for their migrant way of life. Such a life style took Mexicans to California, Colorado, and Michigan.[41]

The Dingley Tariff of 1897 created the sugar beet boom in the United States by placing a high duty on imported sugar. Sugar beet companies in Colorado, Kansas, and California quadrupled between 1900 and 1907. To ensure a large supply of produce, sugar beet refineries made contracts with farmers, promising them an ample supply of cheap labor. Firms such as the Holly Sugar Company and the American Sugar Beet Company recruited and transported large numbers of Mexicans to farms throughout the Southwest, Northwest, and Midwest. The Mexicans increasingly displaced Germans, Russians, and Belgians in sugar beets. The Minnesota Sugar Company (now the American Crystal Sugar Company) provided transportation, housing, and credit and moved Mexican workers to Minnesota. By the winter of 1912, a Mexican *colonia* formed on the west side of St. Paul, where Mexican beet workers found refuge from the harsh winters.[42] In 1909 the Great Western Company in Colorado alone employed 2,600 Mexican beet workers.

The growth of agriculture was spurred by the Newlands Reclamation Act of 1902, which authorized construction of large dams and furnished a reliable and inexpensive supply of water. This act was originally intended to ensure the Jeffersonian dream of a nation of small farmers. It limited the number of acres that could be subsidized; after ten years those possessing land in excess of 160 acres had to sell at pre-dam prices, with no family able to possess more than 480 acres. The owner of the property had to reside on the farm. In practice, however, the law was never properly enforced.

Agriculture grew in other areas; for example, in 1904 Kingsville, Texas, did not exist; ten years later it was a town of 3,000 residents. Life centered around a machine shop and a railroad roundhouse. Nearby in Corpus Christi, sheep and cattle gave way to cotton, vegetables, and pecans. In Nueces County, growers produced 498 bales of cotton in 1899; 11 years later 8,566 bales were grown. Such change and development generated a demand for more Mexicans.[43]

In 1907 the *California Fruit Grower* magazine noted that Mexicans were "plentiful, generally peaceable, and are satisfied with very low social conditions." The next year the first commercial cotton was harvested in the Imperial Valley of California. Improved refrigerated railway cars and more sophisticated canning and food preservation techniques also contributed to the agricultural revolution in the Southwest. From 1907 to 1920, orange and lemon production in California quadrupled; between 1917 and 1922, cantaloupes doubled, grapes tripled, and lettuce quadrupled. Such unprecedented production intensified the need for Mexican labor in California agriculture.[44]

Although agriculture was overtaking sheep raising, the wool industry was also expanding. In 1850 the Southwest harvested 32,000 pounds of wool; 30 years later it increased to 4 million pounds. Again the demand for Mexican shearers and shepherds increased as production zoomed.[45] Mexican labor also worked in the lumber industry.

During this period there was limited mobility for Mexican workers. An Anglo-American mechanic conceded, "They will never pay a Mexican what he's really worth compared with a white man. I know a Mexican that's the best blacksmith I ever knew. He has made some of the best tools I ever used. But they pay him $1.50 a day as a helper, working under an American blacksmith who gets $7 a day." Most Mexicans worked in farming, in mining, and on the railroad, but they began to migrate to the cities, with places like Los Angeles becoming urban centers.[46]

Industrial expansion in the East created a demand for natural resources, while the railroad provided linkage to centers of distribution. As the railroad spread from Mexico City to Chicago, it played a key role in the dispersion of Mexicans, with Los Angeles, San Antonio, El Paso, and Kansas City becoming distribution centers. Colonies set up by railroad crews where they worked later were raided by farmers and ranchers for labor. For example, the first Mexican colony was established in Fort Madison, Iowa, by 1885. In Kansas City in 1907, 30 percent of the laborers had left the railroad for the wheatfields. The same process occurred with desertions to cotton.[47]

Society left Mexicans few avenues by which to improve oppressive work conditions. North American unions often perceived Mexicans as enemies and made little effort to organize them. Generally Mexicans earned lower wages and in addition they were often used as strikebreakers. The American Federation of Labor openly discriminated against Mexicans and many of its affiliates, such as the Texas Federation of Labor, proposed a limitation on Mexican immigration. North American labor took great pains to distance itself from anything that might appear radical. In fact, "often the Texas Federation of Labor belligerently joined management in efforts to defeat Chicano strikes." Most Anglo miners condemned Mexicans as scabs and refused to work with them, much less admit them into their unions. They claimed that Mexicans were careless and exercised bad judgment.[48]

As Mexican workers settled, they protested poor working conditions and low wages. For instance, in 1901, 200 Mexican construction workers struck the El Paso Electric Street Car Company for higher wages. The company hired Juárez residents to replace strikers. After negotiations the company agreed not to employ outsiders, but refused to increase wages. El Paso police helped the company to break the strike by protecting strikebreakers. Workers struck again in 1905.

In 1903, Japanese and Mexican workers in Oxnard, California, protested the practices of the Western Agricultural Contracting Company. The company withheld a percentage of the workers' salaries until the end of the contract. Workers were charged for unnecessary services. They were paid in scrip and thus were forced to buy at the company store at inflated prices. The beet workers formed the Japanese–Mexican Labor Association and after a series of meetings struck on February 28. From the beginning "the growers, the major contractors, major businessmen, the judges, juries, sheriffs, and officials," all of whom were Anglo, united to oppose workers. On March 23 an armed conflict broke out and Luis Vásquez died of shotgun wounds.[49]

Workers won a limited victory with the concession that union members be employed on the majority of the contracting companies' farms. After the strike they formed the Sugar Beet and Farm Laborers Union of Oxnard and petitioned the American Federation of Labor for affiliation. Samuel Gompers, president of the AFL, turned down the request unless the membership guaranteed that Chinese and Japanese would not be admitted, but the Mexican workers refused to abandon their Japanese comrades.[50]

In the same year as the Oxnard conflict, Mexican workers at the Johnston Fruit Company in Santa Barbara, California, struck for higher wages and shorter hours. Lemon pickers and graders demanded the lowering of the 10-hour day to 9 hours. When demands were not met, they walked off the job, paralyzing operations. It was at the height of the season and workers got their 9-hour day and overtime. It was the first time that Mexican workers had stopped production in the area.[51]

Mexican workers in the spring of that year struck Henry E. Huntington's Pacific Electric railway. Mexican track workers had formed *La Unión Federal Mexicana* (the Mexican Federal Union). A. N. Nieto served as executive secretary; it had 900 track workers, a bank account of $600, and headquarters in Sonoratown (as the Mexico *barrio* in Los Angeles was called). They demanded a raise from 17.5¢ an hour to 20¢ an hour, 30¢ an hour for evenings, and 40¢ an hour for Sundays. While company officials at first acceded to demands, Huntington countermanded the agreement, and 700 Mexican workers walked off the job, leaving only 60 "Irishmen, negroes and whites." The Los Angeles Merchants and Manufacturers Association and the Citizens Alliance joined with Huntington to fight trade unions and to keep Los Angeles as an open shop city. They recruited Mexicans from El Paso to replace strikers. Huntington raised salaries of scabs to 22¢ an hour—2¢ more than the union demanded. And even though the union gained the support of Samuel Gompers and Eugene Schmitz, the San Francisco Union Labor party mayor, as well as contributions from the Los Angeles Council of Labor and the local chapter of the Socialist party, it lost. Anglo car men belonging to the Amalgamated Association of Street Car Employees planned a walkout on April 29, but only 12 of 764 walked out. Failure of Anglo-American workers to support the Mexican strike doomed it.

A year later *La Unión Federal* protested a reduction in pay from $1.75 a day to $1.00. Pacific Electric claimed that the cut represented what workers owed the company for housing. The rents were double the going rate and the housing was in a deplorable state. Dr. J. Powers of the Los Angeles County Health Department called it a "menace to public health and a disgrace to civilized communities." Another unsuccessful strike against the railway company was in 1910.[52]

In 1905, in Laredo, Texas, a city of approximately 16,000, of whom three-fourths were Mexican, Chicano workers formed the Federal Labor Union representing various skilled and nonskilled workers in the Mexican Railway Company shops located in that city. It served cooperative and trade union functions and had close ties with local *mutualista* groups. The union published a weekly socialist newspaper, *El Defensor del Obrero,* to educate workers and the public. In November 1906 it called its first general strike, demanding an increase from 75¢ to $1.00 per 10-hour day. When Mexican workers pointed out that Anglo workers had received similar concessions, the railway responded that there was a difference between the two races. After a hard fight, the company finally acceded on February 8, 1907, to a 25¢ a day raise, but reserved the right to retain strikebreakers. Some of the union members refused to return to work.

The Federal Labor Union of Laredo then organized miners, chartering Mine Workers Union Local 12340. A month after settlement of the railway strike, Chicano smelter workers walked off the job. When the Mexican Railway Union threatened to call a general strike in support of the strikers, the mining company settled. Conditions on the railway deteriorated and in March members voted a general strike. The Federal Labor Union failed to organize a wide enough base and the general strike failed. When the Mexican Railway Company moved across the line to Nuevo Laredo, Tamaulipas, the Federal Labor Union died.[53]

In 1907, 150 smelter workers in El Paso walked off the job demanding a raise from $1.20 to $1.50 a day. They won a 20¢ a day pay increase, but the company had hired nonunion workers in the interim and refused to fire them. Disgusted, about half the strikers left for Colorado.

Also in 1907, 1,600 Mexican workers struck the Texas and Pacific Company in Thurber, Texas, for better working conditions including an 8-hour day, "the removal of company fences around the town and the removal of armed guards." The United Mine Workers supported the strikers, who won an increase in wages, an 8-hour day, and bimonthly pay periods.[54]

Strike activity during the first decade of the twentieth century points to worker discontent with labor conditions. The spirit of Mexican labor was indeed rebellious. Strikes alone, however, could not change conditions. Led by temporary associations, the strike lasted for the duration of a specific grievance, and even when workers won their demands, the victories proved short-term. The groups could not maintain wage rates in the face of constant pressure from employers. Mexican workers had no strike funds; most were noncitizens; and they were concentrated in unskilled sectors where a surplus of labor was common. Resentment among the masses of Mexican workers was not enough to change conditions permanently.

Early Currents of Social Resistance

During these years, wherever Mexicans moved, they established *mutualistas,* which had become popular vehicles for organizing. The groups varied greatly in their political direction from apolitical to reformist to radical, but all met needs for "fellowship, security, and recreation" and were basically a form of collective and voluntary self-help and self-defense.[55] Their motto, *Patria, Unión y Beneficencia,* became a common unifying symbol throughout the Southwest and eventually throughout the Midwest as well.

By 1900, Mexicans turned to the arena of education, which, next to labor, has been their most intense battleground. In most places school authorities segregated them into "Mexican" schools. The Chicano community fought segregation, inferior schools and education, the discrimination of IQ exams, poor teaching, the lack of Mexican teachers, and the socialization process that condemned them to failure and then conditioned them to accept it. Education, an important vehicle in the maintenance of class, was in the hands of local business leaders, ranchers, and bankers. They were supported by lower-class white voters who needed to defend their own status by maintaining the myth of Mexican inferiority. The reasons given for excluding Mexicans from Anglo-American schools followed a pattern: Mexicans were ill-clad, unclean, and immoral; interracial contact would lead to other relationships; they were not white and learned more slowly; and so forth.[56]

In West Texas Mexicans were a small minority and generally heavily segregated. San Angelo had a population of about 10,000 inhabitants, with not more than 1,000 to 1,500 Mexicans. About 200 Mexican children attended segregated schools staffed by ill-prepared Anglo teachers. The townspeople generally viewed Mexicans as "foreign." In 1910, when new buildings for the white children were completed, the school board assigned the old buildings to the Mexicans. The Mexican community quietly protested by withholding their children from the school census, thus denying state aid to the school district. They stated that the reason that they would not cooperate was that they did not receive full benefit of state funds. On June 4 they confronted the board, stating that they wanted to share the buildings with the Anglo children or at least have their buildings on the same grounds. They also complained that their furnishings were inferior, the Mexican children were not learning, and they needed a male teacher. The board refused to meet the parents' demands.

Although Mexican parents pressed for integration, their children continued to be assigned to segregated schools. On September 19, 1910, in protest, only two Mexicans appeared at the refurbished school, while seven showed up at the North Ward white school. Their entrance was blocked; the board stated that "to admit the Mexicans into white schools would be to demoralize the entire system and they will not under any pressure consider such a thing."[57]

During the boycott, many parents sent their children to the Immaculate Conception Academy, a Catholic school which segregated Mexican students into a "Mexican room." Reverend B. A. Hodges, a Protestant minister, stated that "the Roman Catholic Church, with the increase of the American membership, more and more discriminated against the Mexicans." The Catholic school refused a request to integrate.

The Presbyterian Church in 1912 set up a mission school, teaching the writing of English and Spanish, mathematics, geography, and physiology. Mrs. Jennie Suter, who was described as having "Spanish" blood (which probably meant she was part Mexican), worked among the Mexicans and was influential in converting many to the church. Mrs. Suter's salary was often unpaid due to a lack of funds. By 1913 the school was "booming," with 34 Mexican children attending. The Catholic Church vehemently opposed the school. "The priests and the sisters have made a house-to-house canvass, using persuasion, offer of rewards, threats, etc. to change the children back to their school." They then tried to buy Mrs. Suter away.[58]

The tension of maintaining the boycott split the Mexican group. The second year, 1911, again only seven Chicano students attended the segregated schools. The boycott continued to some degree for several years, but by 1915 attrition brought it to an end.

NATIVIST REACTIONS TO MEXICAN MIGRATION, 1910–1920

By 1910 the population of Mexico reached 15.16 million. In that year, at least 382,002 persons of Mexican extraction lived in the United States.[59] Victor S. Clark's 1908 study dramatically documented the plight of Mexicans transported thousands of miles to the Southwest: "One is told of locked car doors and armed guards on the platform of trains to prevent desertion on route." The report describes the exploitation of Mexicans in the United States and sets the tone for later stereotypes of Mexicans as physically weak, undependable, and indolent, their only virtues being that they were docile and worked for low wages.[60]

Clearly the dramatic influx of Mexicans resurfaced nativist sentiments toward them.* The 1910 *Report of the Immigration Commission* confirmed that they were the lowest paid of any laborers and that the majority worked as transient and migratory labor, did not settle, and returned to Mexico after only a few months. It warned: "The assimilative qualities of the Mexicans are slight because of the backward educational facilities in their native land and a constitutional prejudice on the part of the peons toward school attendance." The report concluded that Mexicans regarded public relief as a "pension."[61] In 1913, primarily due to an economic depression, the commissioner sounded the alarm, indicating that Mexicans might become a public charge.[62] Newspapers created an anti-Mexican hysteria by making Mexicans scapegoats during times of depression. This is a pattern of repression that would be repeated throughout the twentieth century.

The Mexican Revolution intensified discrimination against immigrants.

---

*Nativism in the historical sense should not be confused with its anthropological use. Historically speaking it refers to anti-immigrant sentiments, whereas in the anthropological sense it refers to a "revival of indigenous culture, especially in opposition to acculturation." "Nativism" in this text refers to an ultranationalist group of Anglo-Americans who considered themselves the true Americans, excluding even the Indian. Moreover, in this text we loosely use the word *Anglo* to refer to white Americans, who include Italians, Jews, and Slavs. As in the case of any rule, it has its exceptions.

From the beginning of the conflict, in 1910, U.S. corporations and persons doing business in Mexico called for military intervention. Many supported Porfirio Díaz because he was friendly to their interests. The North American press from the start whipped up anti-Mexican sentiments. Especially strident were the Hearst newspapers and the Chandlers, who ran the *Los Angeles Times*. Organizations like *el Partido Liberal Mexicano* represented a threat to many Anglo-Americans, who believed that Mexicans in the United States were on the verge of revolt. In Los Angeles the *magonistas* encouraged labor organization among Mexicans and supported the AFL's appointment of Juan Ramírez as an organizer in 1910–1911 as well as the formation of *Jornaleros Unidos* (later chartered by the AFL).[63]

On November 18, 1913, the Los Angeles police assigned several officers to investigate a subversive plot by Mexican "reds" and *cholos*. According to the *Los Angeles Times,* at least 10 percent of the city's 35,000 Mexicans were "known to the police to be rabid sympathizers of the outlaw [Pancho] Villa." This anti-Mexican hysteria coincided with the advent of the First World War, in 1914, and business's demand for more Mexican labor. Once Mexicans arrived, the Anglo-American public reacted with characteristic nativism. The Justice Department suspected German agents in the city of recruiting Mexicans as spies and saboteurs. Police authorities hired a former *porfirista* to spy on this community. The hysteria reached ridiculous levels and Los Angeles officials talked about placing Mexicans in "workhouses" or "isolation" camps.

The intense propaganda which accompanied U.S. intervention in Mexico's internal affairs contributed to widespread fear among Anglo-Americans. The bombardment of Vera Cruz, in March 1914, cost over 300 lives. The authorities justified their actions by alleging that they were stopping a possible shipment of German arms to the *huertistas* (followers of the reactionary Mexican president, Victoriano Huerta).

For the next three years, Los Angeles officials ignored all legitimate complaints of harassment on the pretext that Mexicans were pro-German. When 200 Mexican laborers for the Pacific Sewer Pipe Company went on strike in 1918, authorities labeled the strike German-made. Two days after Villa's raid on Columbus, New Mexico, in March 1916, Los Angeles County supervisors requested federal action in deporting *"cholos* likely to become public charges."[64]

The United States's entry into World War I relaxed efforts to control immigration, counterbalancing Anglo-American antipathies toward Mexicans. In 1916 the commissioner general of immigration commented that "the volume of refugees of a nonpolitical stripe has greatly increased. Fortunately for this, a general revival of industrial activity throughout the Southwest, and even in regions more remote from the border, has created a demand for unskilled labor."[65]

In 1917 a substantial number of Mexicans voluntarily returned to Mexico. The reasons varied. On May 18, 1917, draft laws were passed and Mexicans were reluctant to be conscripted into a foreign army. The cost of living had increased in the United States, while conditions had improved in Mexico. By the end of June nearly 10,000 Mexicans had returned to Mexico. The Mexican government, fearing the effects of the exodus of so many productive workers, campaigned to entice them back.

Meanwhile, the war caused a labor shortage and the U.S. government

enlisted Catholic bishops to assure Mexicans that they would not be drafted.[66]
U.S. officials exempted Mexicans from the literacy provision of the Immigration
Act of 1917. Previous acts had excluded "contract laborers" and "persons likely
to become a public charge." However, the wording was so broad and vague that
employers and contractors who made large profits from importing labor ignored
the laws. After 1917 the $8 head tax was a major obstacle to poor Mexicans, who
had no recourse but to remain in Mexico or enter the United States without
documents. But because a labor shortage threatened to cripple the war effort,
industrialists and growers pressured the federal authorities to waive those sections
of the immigration act that limited the free flow of Mexican labor. The commissioner of immigration affirmed that U.S. employers feared they might have to pay
higher wages if Mexicans were excluded. Soon afterward exemptions allowed
illiterate contract workers from Mexico to enter the United States and the head
tax was waived because of pressure from U.S. farmers, who were in the "habit
of relying to a considerable extent upon seasonal labor from Mexico."[67]

Even though the United States was at war, the military during this period
did not control the border. At the same time, local authorities and the public at
large continued to discriminate against Mexicans. While the Labor Department
assured Congress that the exemptions and the open border were only "stop-gap"
procedures, the measures remained in effect until the end of the 1921 fiscal year,
when a surplus of labor developed in the United States. In the four years the
exemptions were in force (1917 to 1921), 72,862 Mexicans entered the United
States with documents, and hundreds of thousands crossed the border without
documents.[68] The influx of undocumented workers continued as long as jobs in
the United States were plentiful, and as long as the U.S. government looked the
other way. By the 1920s Mexican migration was no longer limited to the Southwest, but began to spread into the Midwest.

During the 1910s the arrival of large numbers of Mexicans triggered what
Dr. Ricardo Romo has labeled a "brown scare." In Los Angeles the rapid
expansion of industry caused social problems which Anglos blamed on the Mexicans. In placing the blame, the Anglos focused on the arrival of 50,000 Mexicans,
while ignoring the flood of 500,000 new Anglos.

Social and racial integration of Mexicans was slow, with discrimination
depending greatly on how dark the Mexican was. Mexicans had few choices as
to where they could live; aside from social discrimination, transportation costs
were high and they were consequently forced to pay inflated rents for inadequate
housing just to be near work. For example, in Los Angeles the largest concentration of Mexicans was in the Central Plaza district. Near the *plaza* 40.1 percent
of the Mexican workers surveyed worked for the Southern Pacific Railroad. In
an area of less than 5,000 square feet of living space, 20 needy families lived in
dilapidated house courts.[69]

World War I intensified industrialization and urbanization in California.
The war industries attracted many Mexicans and Blacks. The large numbers of
Mexicans settling in Los Angeles created new social and economic pressures. An
already overcrowded housing situation worsened. Anglo-Americans blamed the
blight on the Mexicans and charged that these foreigners contributed to a rapid

disintegration of traditional "American values."[70] Mexicans by 1919 comprised 5 percent of Los Angeles's population of over a million. Twenty-eight percent of Mexicans lived in houses with no sinks, 32 percent had no lavatories, and 79 percent had no baths. The infant mortality for Anglos was 54 out of 1,000, while the rate for Mexicans was 152 out of 1,000. In 1914, 11.1 percent of the deaths in Los Angeles were Mexicans.

The brown scare was most intense in Texas, where the number of *Mexicanos* killed by rangers, local authorities, and vigilantes climbed into the thousands. Local groups, individuals, and the *mutualistas* began to express their protests against such outrages more actively. Often oppression of U.S. Mexicans triggered protests in Mexico. In Rock Springs, Texas, in November 1910, a mob lynched Antonio Rodríguez, 20, while he awaited trial. Rodríguez was taken out of his cell, tied to a stake, and burned alive. This barbarous act touched off anti-American riots throughout Mexico. The Rodríguez murder took place just before the Mexican Revolution officially began, on November 20, 1910.

The following June, Antonio Gómez, 14, was asked to leave a place of business in Thorndale, Texas. He refused and had a fight with a Texas-German who died from a wound inflicted by Gómez's knife. Gómez was taken from jail by a mob and beaten and his body dragged around town tied to the back of a buggy. The *Orden Caballeros de Honor,* a Texas association, protested the Thorndale assassination.[71]

León Cardenas Martínez, age 15, was arrested for the murder of Emma Brown in July 1911 in Saragosa, Texas. He signed a confession after a carbine was held to his head. Cardenas was sentenced to death; later the sentence was reduced to 30 years. The townspeople denied Cardenas due process by breaking up support meetings and running his lawyer out of town. Cardenas's family was also literally run out of town by a mob.[72]

Nicasio Idar, publisher of the Texas based *La Cronica,* protested the Cardenas murder. He played an important role in convening *El Primer Congreso Mexicanist* on September 11, 1911, to discuss (1) deteriorating Texas-Mexican economic conditions; (2) loss of Mexican culture and the Spanish language; (3) widespread social discrimination; (4) educational discrimination; and (5) lynchings. Men and women attended workshops and discussed issues still relevant today. Delegates also condemned the insult to state representative J. T. Canales, who had been called "the greaser from Brownsville." The *Congreso* created *La Liga Feménil Mexicanista,* whose first president was Jovita Idar. The women's contingent was comprised in large part of schoolteachers, and was therefore prominent in the discussions on education.

La Agrupación Protectora Mexicana (Mexican Protective Association), founded in 1911 in San Antonio, actively defended human rights for Mexicans. While it engaged in union organizing, it also focused mainly on fighting against police brutality and lynchings. Its members had worked to release Gregorio Cortez (see Chapter 2). The *Agrupación* functioned until 1914, when internecine strife split the organization.

Texas authorities used every opportunity to strengthen their despotic rule in South Texas and along the Río Bravo. Starting in 1915, Texas used the Plan of San Diego as an excuse to step up an unprecedented reign of terror along the border. The plan itself called for a general uprising of Mexicans and other minorities on February 20. The supporters would execute all white males over age 16—Blacks, Asians, and Native Americans would be exempted. The Southwest would become a Chicano nation, and Blacks and Native Americans would also form independent countries. Many Mexicans, at the time, found the plan adventuristic and outright racist. Flores Magón, in *Regeneración,* never acknowledged or supported the plan, stating on one occasion that authorities wanted "to make it appear as if the Mexican uprising in that section of the United States is part of the Plan of San Diego."[73]

Clearly the most controversial section in the plan called for the murder of all white males over 16. The sensationalism surrounding this statement has muddled a discussion of the merits of or need for an uprising. Extremism must be placed in the context of the prevailing conditions. And differences must be drawn between normal circumstances and the violence suffered by Mexicans in Texas. Few, for instance, would have considered it extreme for Europeans occupied by the Germans during World War II to have published a similar plan. However, another standard seems to exist for Third World peoples.

According to the study of Professors Don M. Coerver and Linda B. Hall, North American authorities found the plan on Basilio Ramos, a supporter of Mexican president Victoriano Huerta. Officials did not take the plan seriously. By July 1915 a new plan had been issued and a series of raids took place in the lower Río Grande Valley. "One of the most disturbing features was that the raiders—supposedly *huertistas* in their sympathies—could operate freely in areas of northern Mexico controlled by *carrancistas,* who were concerned about a possible political comeback by Huerta."[74] By this time, Luis de la Rosa, a former deputy sheriff in Cameron County, and Ancieta Pizaña, a *carrancista,* were first and second in command of the revolution. They had a force of 50 men. Federal authorities viewed the raids as banditry and rustling. When the raids increased in intensity, however, they grew alarmed.

Coerver and Hall try to make a connection between *carrancistas* and the plan, suggesting that Mexican president Venustiano Carranza exploited the plan in negotiations for recognition. According to the authors, de la Rosa and Pizaña recruited freely in northern Mexico and *carrancista* general Emiliano P. Nafarrate gave the rebels carte blànche. And although Carranza called publicly for the arrest of the two, he allowed them to operate unimpaired.

Tensions continued into 1916. By this time Nafarrate joined de la Rosa. They had popular support among Valley Mexicans. The FBI labeled the uprisings as German-inspired. As a consequence of negative propaganda, Texas raised the number of Rangers to 50, encouraging an intensification of the carnage. On June 18, President Wilson federalized the National Guards of Texas, New Mexico, and Arizona, a force of 100,000 men, to patrol the border. (The copper barons of Arizona had pressured Wilson to take this action to quell labor agitation, which they also claimed was German-inspired.) Between July 1915 and July of the following year, rebels made a total of 30 raids into Texas. U.S. authorities admitted shooting, hanging, or beating to death 300 "suspected" Mexicans, while the rebels killed 21 Euroamericans during this same period.[75]

In 1917 the atrocities peaked with 35,000 U.S. soldiers on the border. George Marvin wrote in *World's Work* magazine in January 1917:

> The killing of Mexicans . . . along the border in these last four years is almost incredible. . . . Some Rangers have degenerated into common mankillers. There is no penalty for killing, no jury along the border would ever convict a white man for shooting a Mexican. . . . Reading over Secret Service records makes you feel as though there was an open gun season on Mexicans along the border.[76]

Walter Prescott Webb excused the "Reign of Terror" by stating that the Revolution created border incidents. Webb alleged that Germany had agents scattered throughout Mexico, that German officers trained Mexican soldiers, and that Germany supposedly had a powerful wireless station in Mexico City. Moreover, Webb asserted, prohibition also contributed to lawlessness and paranoia. According to Webb, when U.S. citizens heard that Germans supplied Mexicans with guns, that the IWW was passing out incendiary literature, and that the Japanese were supplying Mexicans, all in an effort to take over the Southwest, "their anger was lashed into fury. . . . In the orgy of bloodshed that followed, the Texas Rangers played a prominent part, and one of which many members of the force have been heartily ashamed." Most experts state that German involvement along the Río Grande was unproved and that the involvement of the IWW and the Japanese was just not true.[77]

MEXICAN WORKERS, 1910–1920

Production in the Southwest conditioned the work experience and settlement patterns of Mexican workers. Because the region was undeveloped, it needed large armies of migrants or casual workers—for instance, for ranching, agriculture, railroad work, irrigation construction, and other pick and shovel labor. In 1900, most Mexicans worked in agriculture; they remained the least urbanized immigrant group in the United States. By 1920, however, 47 percent of the Mexicans of foreign stock lived in urban areas.[78]

When the Mexican immigrants migrated to the Southwest, they did not have the advantage of the labor infrastructure that was available to European immigrants to eastern cities, who built on each others' experiences. Europeans could organize more easily in urban settings than Mexicans, who constantly moved. Labor organization, which was rare in rural areas, was an urban phenomenon that followed definite cycles: workers first formed temporary labor associations, graduating to trade unions—more often in the craft sector. The skilled trades were able to accumulate cash surpluses and hire paid organizers and staffs. In contrast, the Mexican experience was one of dispersal, isolation, migrancy, and poverty. Conditions in the Southwest frustrated the transition to temporary associations, let alone to trade unionism. Southwest cities where Mexicans concentrated were also notorious for their antiunion biases. Throughout the 1910s, *multualistas* continued as the most popular form of association for Mexicans.

Another factor affecting Mexican labor was the huge number who arrived in the United States. By World War I, immigration laws began to have an impact on Europeans. Like the Mexicans, most European immigrants could not read or write, and the 1917 literacy requirement drastically reduced European immigration. Numbering about 1.2 million in 1914, it fell to 300,000 three years later. As a consequence, demand for the Mexican increased. During the 1910s Mexicans could be found in the packinghouses and railroad yards of Chicago, Kansas City, Detroit, and St. Louis. At the end of the decade, officially 651,596 Mexican workers and their families lived in the United States. (The count was taken before the harvest season).[79]

Efforts by Mexicans to organize began in the first decade of the century. In August 1910, workers, 90 percent of whom were Mexicans, struck the Los Angeles Gas Works for higher wages. They were influenced by the IWW. After two weeks the company settled for $2.25 a day and agreed to hire union members. *Magonistas* actively participated in Los Angeles Mexican politics and labor circles. For instance, *La Liga Pan-Americana de Trabajo* was led by Julio Mancillas (secretary), Francisco B. Velarde (organizer), and Lazaro Gutiérrez de Lara (treasurer), all members of the PLM. *La Liga* operated a socialist library and center for study and discussed the role of the Mexican proletariat at its meetings.

In 1911 California State Federation of Labor organizer Juan Ramírez helped form *La Unión de Jornaleros Unidos* Local 13097 with *magonista* Amelio B. Velarde as its secretary. It affiliated with the AFL and actively organized migrants and unskilled workers in the Long Beach and San Pedro areas.

Because of state legitimation of violence in Texas, labor agitation proved more difficult than in other sections of the country. Stuart Jamieson writes that "Mexicans [in Texas] on the land had a social and economic status similar to that of Negroes in other sections of the South. They were a large, lowly paid racial minority, and most of them were disenfranchised by the State poll tax. As laborers or tenants their bargaining position was much weaker than that of the landlords or employers."[80] As Mexican tenant farmers fell heavily into debt, their status often resembled that of *peones*, forced to work out their contracts under armed guards. Many Mexican migrants, meanwhile, traveled in family groups by train or horse-drawn vehicles. The Texas Socialist party organized renters into the Renters Union of America and later the Land League of America; the party assigned J. A. Hernández to work with Mexicans. His organizational efforts were compromised by limited funds, the size of Texas, and the harshness of police reprisals. Texas authorities arrested union members on charges of sedition and deported others. They justified repression by falsely linking the Socialist party to the Plan of San Diego and successionist aspirations of many Chicanos. Moreover, Socialist party influence declined because of white chauvinism and racism of some of its members.[81]

When, in 1917, federal authorities allocated funds to build Camp Wilson in San Antonio, Mexican workers attempted to end the old contract system. Over 2,000 met at the hall of *La Sociedad Benevolencia Mexicana*, forming *La Unión Transitoria*. They voted to eliminate the labor contracts, setting up their own committees to negotiate with the construction firm. Farm workers also attended the meeting and vowed to bypass the contractor and deal directly with farmers. Seven hundred came to a follow-up session. On July 11, San Antonio authorities arrested the organizers for undisclosed reasons. Employers set up their own hiring halls and then imported workers directly from Mexico.[82]

Important to Mexican workers was the IWW, whose agitation was primarily among the casual workers. The International grouped trade unionists of all political stripes under its umbrella, but anarchists were by far the most energetic. The most dramatic strike involving the Wobblies was the so-called Wheatland Riot, of August 3, 1913, at the Ralph Durst Ranch in Wheatland, California.

Mexicans comprised a minority of the 1,000 to 1,500 workers involved in the strike. Essentially, Durst attracted more workers than needed, allowing him to depress wages to 78¢ to $1.00 a day. Durst charged workers for water, and cheated and insulted them.

The workers organized and presented demands to Durst: "water twice a day, separate toilets for women and men and a $1.25 a hundred [pounds]." A riot broke out when local authorities and vigilantes attacked a worker rally. During the ensuing riot two workers, the district attorney, and a deputy were killed. Governor Hiram Johnson ordered four National Guard companies into the area to support Durst. Over a hundred workers were arrested. Two union organizers were convicted and sentenced, one to 12 and one to 13 years.[83]

Labor struggles occurred in other states as well. In Colorado mine owners suppressed strikes in 1883, 1893, and 1903 by expelling organizers and importing strikebreakers. In the 1910s northern Colorado was in a state of upheaval with mine operators calling for and receiving aid from the governor. Organizers and workers were arrested. In 1913 agitation shifted to southern Colorado, centering in Huerfano and Las Animas counties, an area of 120 miles. In September a 15-month strike commenced which involved Greeks, Italians, Slavs, and Mexicans. The United Mine Workers represented miners; owners were led by the Colorado Fuel and Iron Company, in which the Rockefellers, John D. Sr. and Jr., owned 40 percent of the stock. As soon as the strike was called, miners were evicted from company housing into tent colonies. As winter approached, conditions worsened.[84]

The governor ordered the National Guard into the area in October 1913. The Baldwin-Feltz Detective Agency hunted down and killed strike leaders. Running gun battles raged. Strikers accused guard members of pressuring strikebreakers to remain on the job, holding them in virtual peonage. A congressional investigation restored calm for a time. In April 1914 the National Guard withdrew, leaving 35 men in the Ludlow area; 1,200 men, women, and children remained in the tent colony. On April 20 the members of the guard occupied a hill overlooking the camp, mounted a machine gun, and exploded two bombs. The miners armed themselves and the guard attacked. "The Chicano tents and dugouts were among the first hit; of the eighteen victims nine were Chicanos, five of them children." Ten days of bitter fighting followed, with at least 50 persons killed. When it was all over, a grand jury indicted 124 strikers, not charging a single deputy. Guardsmen who were court-martialed were acquitted. Mine owners refused to negotiate, forcing the union to call off the strike.[85]

New Mexico, uncharacteristically calm during this period, suffered repressive work conditions. Copper mines in Grant County, adjacent to eastern

Arizona—which was the center of militant strike activity—remained without major incident. A partial explanation is the extent of control by New Mexico business and political elites who, at will, used the military to intimidate workers. There was some unrest in Dawson, Madrid, Gallup, and other mining towns; still workers remained quiet. Six hundred miners in Dawson alone died as a result of mine disasters in 1913, 1920, and 1923.[86]

In 1917 in Arizona mine locals 80, 84, and 86 had a membership of some 5,000 Mexican miners. The AFL resolved at its state convention to organize 14,000 Mexican miners in the state. However, this unity was short-lived, and the AFL leadership soon forgot its commitment. With the advent of the war, organized labor, influenced by Gompers, increasingly looked upon Mexicans as competitors. Gompers feared that Mexicans would not remain in the rural areas, but would filter into the urban factories. He vehemently criticized the federal government for using Mexican labor on a construction project at Fort Bliss, near El Paso, because he wanted these jobs solely for "Americans."[87]

Throughout the 1910s Mexican and other miners united against the copper barons (see Chapter 4). This struggle came to a head in 1917. On June 24, Mexican miners struck at Bisbee and Jerome. The Cochise County sheriff immediately labeled the strike as subversive and announced intentions of deporting any member of the IWW. With the aid of a vigilante committee, he deported 67 Mexicans in Jerome and some 1,200 in Bisbee. In Bisbee every Mexican male who could not prove that he was employed was herded into the local ballpark. The sheriff seized the telegraph and telephone office and did not permit news dispatches. Local authorities and nativists loaded Mexicans into box cars and shipped them outside of Columbus, New Mexico, where they dumped them in the open desert without food or water (see Chapter 4).[88]

Due to the demand for cotton fiber for tires and other products, as well as the expansion of irrigation projects, Arizona's cotton production escalated. By World War I, the family farm was disappearing in the state, with land there even more concentrated than in California. Migrant labor was very important to Arizona's farms, and between 1918 and 1921 the Arizona Cotton Growers Association imported over 30,000 Mexicans. Sporadic collective action by farm workers began about this time. Mexican farm workers were greatly influenced by what had happened in mining.

In the spring of 1917, a number of farm strikes hit the Corona, Riverside, Colton, Redlands, and San Bernardino area of California. Mexicans in these communities lived in desperate economic conditions. The cost of living had zoomed as a result of World War I, but their wages remained the same. On March 5, Mexican workers struck the Corona Lemon Company. Anglos refused to join the protest. Local authorities arrested Juan Peña and other leaders on unspecified charges. On March 27, 300 Mexican and Japanese orange pickers struck Riverside. Authorities violently suppressed these and other work stoppages, in addition to importing large numbers of strikebreakers from El Paso.[89]

In April 1917 in Colton, California, Mexican workers protested the 50 percent reduction in wages by the Portland Cement Company. Management responded that the pay was high for Mexicans. When workers protested, the company fired 50 workers, triggering a walkout by 150 employees. They formed a union called *Trabajadores Unidos* and after two weeks won a 5¢ an hour raise, union recognition, and removal of strikebreakers. After the victory, however, the organization deteriorated into a fraternal lodge.[90] San Diego historian Jeffrey Garcilazo makes an important contribution in linking some of these workers to previous mine unrest in Arizona and Mexico.

Although establishment of *La Confederación Regional Obrera Mexicana* (CROM) in Mexico in 1918 encouraged Mexican labor organization in the United States, on the whole, it proceeded slowly. Growers, aided by a relaxation of immigration law during World War I, stymied organizational efforts by massive importations of labor from Mexico. Anglo-American labor leaders simplistically continued to call for immigration quotas instead of organizing these exploited workers. The only escape for Mexican workers was to leave the fields for the city. In some cases, farmers went to extremes to protect their supply and went so far as to handcuff workers at night so that they would not run away.[91]

The utility of Mexican workers as well as their abundance did not go unnoticed by the steel magnates in the Midwest. During the 1919 steel strike in the Chicago-Calumet area, the steel companies imported large numbers of Mexicans whom they worked under guard. Throughout the history of the U.S. labor movement the role of strikebreaker has always fallen not to any particular ethnic group, but rather to the latest arrival, whether it be Mexican, Polish, Italian, or any other nationality. Mexicans employed in the steel industry before the strike had supported collective bargaining efforts. Although Mexicans were stereotyped as scabs, they were in the minority among the strikebreakers during the steel strike. During the strike, which lasted from September 22, 1919, to January 7, 1920, steel mills employed some 50 different nationalities, about a third of whom were U.S. citizens of northern European extraction. This group controlled the craft trades, were better paid, had shorter hours, and were better treated than the other ethnic groups, who were played off against each other by management for jobs and promotions. A nationality report by Homestead Steel Works, Howard Axle Works, and Carrie Furnaces on October 8, 1919, showed that out of the 14,687 employed by these mills, only 130 were Mexican—that is, Mexicans comprised less than 1 percent of the workforce.[92]

Sugar beet companies continued their relentless search for Mexican labor. By 1919, 98 U.S. factories produced upwards of a million tons of sugar annually. Leading producers of sugar beets were Michigan, Ohio, and Wisconsin in the Midwest, Colorado, Utah, and Idaho in the mountain region, and California in the Far West. Continuing increased production and the heavy reliance on Mexican labor led farm journals in 1920 to refer to the sugar crop as a "Mexican Harvest."[93]

Professor Mario T. García of the University of California at Santa Barbara, in his article "Racial Dualism in the El Paso Labor Market, 1880–1920," notes that Mexicans generally received lower pay than Anglo-Americans, producing an almost static occupational pattern. In 1900, 71.51 percent of the El Paso Mexican workers worked as laborers, service workers, or operatives. Twenty years later the percentage had declined slightly to 67.54 percent, and by 1940 it showed little change, declining to 66.36 percent. The number of professionals remained insignificant (1900, 3.03 percent; 1920, 3.31; 1940, 2.42). Professor García also analyzes the position of Mexican women in the situation of racial dualism. Hearings conducted in El Paso in November 1919 by the Texas Industrial Welfare Commission found that Mexican women were "the lowest-paid and most vulnerable workers in the city." El Paso laundries employed large numbers of *Mexicanas* to work at unskilled jobs, whereas Anglo women received the skilled jobs. *Mexicanas* earned $8.00 a week compared to $16.55 for Anglo women. The hearings revealed that some *Mexicanas* actually earned only $4.00 to $5.00 a week. In the department stores Anglo women generally worked on the main floor, whereas *Mexicanas* worked in the rear or basement. Anglos earned as high as $40.00 a week compared to Mexican clerks who were paid from $10.00 to $20.00. *Mexicana* workers constituted the overwhelming majority of workers in the El Paso garment industry. Workers in a union shop were reported to average between $18.00 and $20.00 a week for piece work, although the owner of one factory conceded that they averaged $9.50. *Mexicanas* who testified before the commission stated that they earned from $6.00 to $9.00. Employers attempted to explain away this difference by claiming that Anglo women outworked *Mexicanas,* that they hired *Mexicanas* only because they could not employ a sufficient number of "white" women, and that, after all, the standard of living among Mexicans was much lower than that of whites and so they required less money.[94]

Mexicans throughout the Southwest suffered from this dual wage system. In Los Angeles, for example, the occupational status of Mexicans declined during the first two decades of the twentieth century. In 1900, 2.8 percent worked as professionals; 20 years later the figure fell to 1.5 percent. In this same period, the percentage of unskilled workers rose from 57.7 percent to 71.5 percent. In 1920, 89.5 percent of the Mexicans worked a blue-collar laborers versus 53 percent of Anglos.

MEXICANS MOVE TO THE CITY: THE 1920s

Professor Irving Bernstein writes that "the symbol of the twenties is gold. This was the age of the gold standard, a time when people with money slept with confidence: their banknotes were redeemable in the precious metal." For the Mexican and other workers, however, gold has always represented oppression. Far from instilling confidence, the metal has cemented their underclass status.

The 1920s saw dramatic changes that would affect all labor: North Americans rapidly shifted to the cities as the immigration from Europe slowed. Between 1920 and 1929, almost 20 million North Americans left the farm for the city. The depression of 1921 further concentrated land in the hands of the few, displacing the small farmer. Mechanization during the 1920s also contributed to the big harvest, which increased demand for temporary labor.[95] The new immigration policy kept unskilled workers out of the country, encouraging the immigration of skilled workers and further mechanization. Consequently, technological developments in the labor market would later have an impact on the Chicano.

San Antonio: The West Side

Like North Americans, Mexicans became increasingly urbanized during the 1920s. San Antonio and Los Angeles were popular destinations. Because of the concentration of the Mexican population there and the stability of the community, organizations multiplied. By 1920, San Antonio had grown to 161,379 residents, of whom about 60,000 were Mexicans. At the end of the decade about 70,000 of the city's 232,542 residents were *Mexicanos.* During the 1910s, San Antonio became a center for Mexican exiles, with 25,000 arriving in 1913 alone. In the 1920s religious refugees joined the exile community. These Mexican refugees were largely middle and upper class, in contrast to the majority of Mexicans who worked as laborers.

The flood of Mexicans into the Alamo City could not be absorbed either by the existing housing or labor market infrastructure. Two-thirds of the Mexicans in the West Side lived in shacks that filled the open spaces between the warehouses and the rails, surrounded by a red light district. Crowded courts— a series of one- and two-room units sharing an outside toilet and a water spigot—met the housing needs of the poor. Mexicans also lived in long one-storey *corrales* extending 100 yards with overcrowded stalls, resembling stables. Workers paid between 90¢ and $1.25 a week for these unsanitary quarters. Blight worsened with the heavy influx of farm workers during the off-season.[96]

Powerless, too poor to pay the poll tax, they voted only when someone else paid the tab. The Commission Ring ran the city for the interest of elites, giving free land to the military in order to attract bases. In the 1920s the $38 million spent annually by military personnel in San Antonio made the merchants prosperous. However, because the installations did not pay taxes, little money was left for civic improvements. One result was that few recreation clubs served the poor, who congregated at Milam Park, waiting to be picked up for work.

Mutualistas thrived throughout the Southwest and Midwest. However, as the organizational alternatives for Mexicans expanded, a transition took place that replaced the *mutualistas* as the dominant form of association for Mexicans. Since the last quarter of the nineteenth century, *mutualistas* such as *La Sociedad Benevolencia Mexicana* (1875) and *La Sociedad de la Unión* (1886) had been established in San Antonio. Comprised almost totally of middle-class and laboring people, a dozen or so regular and labor *mutualistas* functioned in San Antonio in the 1920s. The wealthy Mexicans had their own social clubs and, as a rule, did not join the *mutualistas.* The largest association, *La Unión,* had 1,540 members, mostly skilled workers and some *jornaleros.* They operated as insurance groups, giving funeral benefits to members and a stipend to the widows. They paid 25¢ a month and a dollar when a member died. These *mutualistas* interacted with each other and comprised an informal network that spoke for the community.

Within this network, the Mexican community supported newspapers; the most popular, the Spanish-language daily *La Prensa,* covered a variety of events. For example, the wife of the editor, Beatriz Blanca de Hinojosa, wrote a column. Along with Aurora Herrera de Nobregas of *La Epoca,* Blanca de Hinojosa advocated the end of the double standard for women. Although feminist ideas were expressed, most Mexican women of the time reluctantly identified themselves as feminists. An exception, *Prensa* columnist Arianda wrote that feminism did not have to be destructive since it simply expressed the "realization that women are not inferior to men." She called on women to agitate against alcoholism, militarism, child labor, and the "degredation of women." María Luisa Garza, editor of *La Epoca,* attended the 1922 Pan American Women's Conference in Baltimore. She later resigned to found *Alma Femenina.* The status of women in the *mutualistas* varied, with most groups admitting women and allowing them to hold office. Contrary to popular myth, not all Mexican women remained in the house; 16 percent of Mexican women worked outside the home versus 17 percent of all women in Texas.[97]

Mutualistas often supported their compatriots accused of crimes, raising funds and petitioning authorities on their behalf. When the court sentenced Agustín Sánchez of San Antonio to death for murder, Mexicans formed a committee to seek a stay of execution, believing he had acted in self-defense. In general *mutualistas* did not allow any political discussions at their meetings. Members did not feel, however, that the protection of their civil rights was a political issue. They regularly allowed groups such as *La Liga Pro-Mexicana* (1927), a civil rights organization, to use their facilities for free, and they also loaned the facilities to labor associations. Some even contributed funds to a bilingual school.

San Antonio *mutualistas* stayed away from radicals such as the Industrial Workers of the World. However, they had contact with Clemente Idar, an organizer for the American Federation of Labor. In this vein the Mexican community in San Antonio failed to support a bakers' strike in 1917, led by *La Sociedad Morelos Mutua de Panaderos,* because the Anglo press labeled it an IWW venture. The bakers, on strike for one year, did not receive any support from the AFL or the Mexican press.

The *mutualistas* themselves "avoided radical, violent protest, preferring to be ignored by the Anglo press and work in relative autonomy." Class differences among members of the different groups were apparent and frustrated solidarity. Even so, members closed ranks in the face of discrimination. The labor *mutualistas,* such as *La Sociedad Mutualista de Zapateros, Porfirio Díaz* (1918), were by no means radical. Most Mexicans appeared to have been interested in their own economic survival.

The *mutualistas,* for the most part nationalistic, maintained ties with the Mexican consul, who frequently attended their functions. Federico Allen Hinojosa, editor in chief of *La Prensa* throughout the 1920s, played to these nationalist sentiments and predicted that the flood of Mexicans arriving in the United States would bring in a "reconquest of the lands lost in the dismemberment of 1837 and 1847" and a "repopulation of our *raza* in the lost regions." By 1926, the San Antonio *mutualistas* formed *La Alianza de Sociedades Mutualistas de San Antonio. Mutualistas* mainly attracted the Mexican-born Chicanos. They also appealed more to families than to young single males or females. Their popularity lessened as the organizational alternatives increased.

After World War I many Mexican American veterans returned to San

Antonio. Some of them organized or formed societies that differed from the mutual aid societies. In fact, they became more concerned with their U.S. status and less concerned about their Mexicanism. New leaders such as J. Luz Sáenz, a World War I veteran who in the early 1930s wrote *Los México-Americanos en la Gran Guerra,* emerged. As a rule, the *veteranos* pursued their rights more aggressively than the first generation. At one point, the *mutualistas* petitioned President Wilson to do something about the negative stereotyping of Mexicans in the movies. In 1922–1923, they protested what they called the Ku Klux Klan–Texas Ranger alliance.[98]

By the 1920s, many Mexicans came to the realization that they would not be returning to Mexico. The evolution of the so-called *Hijos* movement is a case in point. The *Hijos de México* (Sons of Mexico), organized in San Antonio in 1897, admitted only Mexican citizens and promoted Mexican culture. The association disbanded in 1914, but organized itself nine years later. In 1921, Professor Sáenz, along with Santiago Tafolla, a lawyer, and other Mexican American World War I veterans and professionals, formed *La Orden de Hijos de América.* This group did not make citizenship a requirement, but it did emphasize the betterment of the Mexican American in the United States. Within two years *Los Hijos de América* had 250 members with three branches in South Texas.

By 1922 a split occurred inside *Los Hijos de América* and a dissident group formed *Los Hijos de Texas.* Led by Feliciano G. Flores, a police officer, and attorney Alonso Perales, the society worked for the interests of Americans of Mexican descent. In 1927, *La Orden de Caballeros* was formed. Many leaders of these groups also held offices in the various *mutualistas,* with *Los Hijos de América* belonging to the San Antonio Alliance of Mutualista Societies. However, leaders such as Perales and Sáenz never belonged to *mutualistas.*

The transition to another form of organization came with the establishment of the League of United Latin American Citizens (LULAC). *Tejanos,* for years, had discussed the need for a statewide organization that would become national. They took the first steps in 1927 when Alonso Perales called together leaders from South Texas to discuss the possibilities of merging into one organization. *Los Caballeros de América* and *Los Hijos de América* led the movement. At least one source claims that it was at this point that they formed the League of United Latin American Citizens.[99] Anyway, within two years, Ben Garza, head of *Los Hijos de América,* called leaders together, finalizing the formation of LULAC. The members represented the educated elite; knowing English well and highly urbanized, they involved themselves in civil rights issues—betterment of schools and voter registration drives. Their goal was to Americanize the Mexican American. They wanted economic, social, and racial equality.

Segregation increased during 1920s, as did the "No Spanish Rule." The number of special Mexican school districts doubled from 20 to 40 in Texas from 1922 to 1932. School authorities required Mexicans to attend their own schools, while not restricting Anglo children by neighborhood or even county. As the heavy influx of Mexican children increased nativism and racism, strategies to isolate the youngsters flourished. By 1928, Mexicans comprised 13 percent of the Texas school population (Blacks made up 16.8 percent). In 1920, 11,000 Mexican students attended San Antonio elementary schools, with only 250 matriculated in high school. Authorities often claimed that Mexican Americans were slow learners; however, in 1925, Mexican students in the Texas city scored 70 percent higher on I.Q. tests administered in Spanish. In 1928, in the entire state of Texas, only 250 Mexicans attended college. To compound the injustice, the districts profited from Mexican schools—that is, when students did not attend school, the districts spent the money on all-white schools.[100]

An important desegregation case was filed in 1928. In *Vela v. Board of Trustees of Charlotte Independent School District,* Félipe Vela claimed that the school district had not allowed his adopted daughter to attend the white school because she was Mexican. According to him, she was not Mexican and therefore could not be excluded. The superintendent of Texas Education found that whether the girl was Mexican or not was irrelevant since the district did not have the legal authority to segregate Mexican children on a racial basis. Since she spoke English, she was entitled to go to the white school. The state board of education affirmed this decision, but Texas Mexicans remained segregated in many places until the 1970s, since the case held that school districts could segregate for educational purposes. While LULAC did not participate in the *Vela* case, it was in the vanguard of later desegregation suits. *Mutualistas* such as *La Alianza Hispano-Americana* also played a part.

Los Angeles: Where Only the Weeds Grow[101]

The 1920s saw Los Angeles pass San Antonio as the Euroamerican city with the largest Mexican population. Unlike San Antonio, Los Angeles did not stand at the crossroads between Mexico and the eastern half of the United States; travel to the California city was more arduous. After the Guadalajara–Nogales–Los Angeles line was completed in 1927, however, movement to the West Coast became easier.

In 1917, 91.5 percent of Mexicans in Los Angeles worked in blue-collar occupations versus 53.0 percent of the white population. Sixty-eight percent of the Mexicans performed manual labor versus 6 percent of the white Angelenos.[102] Los Angeles had an abundance of capital needing only cheap labor to produce rapid economic growth. The Mexican was essential to progress.

In the period 1900–1920, California's population jumped from 1,485,053 to 3,426,861, an increase of approximately 131 percent. The Mexican population in all probability grew to a quarter of a million. (Professor Pedro Castillo estimates the population of Mexicans in Los Angeles in 1900 at between 3,000 and 5,000 and at between 30,000 and 50,000 20 years later.)[103]

The Mexican joined a polyglot of races in Sonoratown (near the present *plaza*). As the population density increased and land values shot up, the city elite began to plan more efficient use of its space—that is, to seek greater profits. City and county buildings competed for room in the Civic Center, encroaching on the Mexican *barrio.* As a result, much of the *plaza* population moved east of the Los Angeles River. Rail transportation, key to industrial development, attracted industry and warehouses.

Many middle-class and most wealthy Mexicans lived either in the outskirts of the *barrios* or among the Anglos. For the poor, however, housing in Los Angeles, as in San Antonio and other urban centers, was atrocious. Los Angeles's downtown elite controlled city and county government and promoted an unregulated land boom, attracting industry and developing the agricultural resources of the region. Mexicans had been segregated in Los Angeles since the arrival of the Anglo-American. Segregation worsened with the second Anglo invasion, beginning in the 1880s, when real estate speculators brought North Americans in by the trainload.

By the 1920s, Mexicans crowded into makeshift housing. The main settlement still hovered around the *plaza.* In 1912, a contemporary described the infamous Sonoratown as shacks and tents and "nondescript barn-tenements of one and two rooms" jammed with one and often two or more families. These residents shared a common toilet and water faucet situated in the rear of the courtyard. Many of the courts were torn down between 1906 and 1913, when the Los Angeles Housing Commission was given the power of eminent domain. It tore down buildings and courts without, as promised, finding residents alternative housing.[104]

By the end of the 1910s, approximately 10 percent of Mexicans still lived in the Civic Center orbit. In those years, Mexicans moved to the Belvedere–Maravilla area in the unincorporated portion of the county, about four miles east of the Civic Center. About 30,000 Mexicans lived there by the end of the 1920s. "Maravilla Park is just west of Coyote Pass. It has always been almost 100 percent Mexican. The first homes were the worst kind of shacks, like hobo jungles, built of old oil cans, old tin, boxes, scrap lumber, etc., that could be found."[105] Conditions for Mexicans in Los Angeles deteriorated during the decade. Elizabeth Fuller in a 1920 study found that 92 percent of the homes she visited did not have gas and 72 percent had no electricity.[106]

Between Sonoratown and Belvedere–Maravilla, Mexicans occupied the crevices of Boyle Heights, once a fashionable Euroamerican community. At the turn of the century, Boyle Heights was changing from a white to a Jewish neighborhood. Its topography was uneven with many ravines, *arroyos,* and bridges connecting the Heights. Mexicans clustered in shanties or courtyards in this unwanted land, which real estate speculators developed to squeeze quick profits. Housing codes were almost nonexistent, with city regulations calling for only one toilet for every ten men and another for every ten women. Relations between Mexicans and their neighbors had changed little since 1914, when William Wilson McEuen wrote: "All races meet the Mexican with an attitude of contempt and scorn and they are generally regarded as the most degraded race in the city."[107] Finally, some poor Mexicans lived along the Pacific Electric routes in the maintenance yards. They occupied small *colonias* in the outskirts of Los Angeles near farms, brickyards, and mills.

Other sections of the city excluded Mexicans. A 1930 report boasted, "Lynwood, being restricted to the white race, can furnish ample labor of the better class." In 1927, El Segundo reported that no Blacks or Mexicans lived in that city. Long Beach had between 10,000 and 14,000 Mexicans, but advertised "Long

Beach has a population of 140,000 people—98 percent of whom are of the Anglo-Saxon race."[108]

The U.S. census in 1920 suggested that some 21,598 Mexican children attended Los Angeles schools. By 1930, that number had jumped to 55,005, 14.2 percent of the total. Infant mortality in Los Angeles among Mexicans ran two and a half times that among Anglo babies. Although Mexicans comprised one-tenth of the population, they made up one-fourth of the tuberculosis cases at city clinics. In 1924–1925, a plague hit Sonoratown; 30 Mexicans died of pneumonic plague and five of bubonic plague. The city exterminated 140,000 rats in the *barrio.*

The organizational life of Mexicans in Los Angeles resembled that of other Mexican *colonias.* Historian Ricardo Romo states that, after 1918, Mexican *mutualistas* had three primary functions: to meet the immigrant families' basic needs; to maintain their culture (raise ethnic consciousness); and to defend the community against injustice and violations of their civil rights. Although Los Angeles *mutualistas* fulfilled these goals to some degree, the Los Angeles Mexican community was not as well defined, and the *mutualistas* did not play as vital a role as in San Antonio, where Mexicans were more isolated and concentrated. In Los Angeles, moreover, the Mexican community did not have the same relationship with the rest of the state that San Antonio had with South Texas. As in the Southwest generally, the Mexican consul in Los Angeles played an influential role. *La Cruz Azul* (for women) and *La Comisión Honorífica* (for men) did charitable work under the auspices of the consul.

In 1927, *mutualistas* formed a federation, which, a year later, evolved into an association of Mexican trade unions. Integration into established organized labor proved impossible at the time. Samuel Gompers, president of the AFL, looked upon Mexicans as a "great evil." In 1924, after visiting Los Angeles, Gompers stated: "It appeared to me that every other person on the streets was a Mexican." Gompers instructed the AFL lobbyist to do everything possible to put Mexicans on a quota.[109]

Because of entrenched discrimination against Mexicans, the *mutualistas,* even when they joined forces and enlisted the aid of important individuals, were sometimes powerless to stop injustice. One of the more sensational cases was that of Aurelio Pompa, a Mexican immigrant, convicted in 1923 for killing an Anglo. Pompa committed the act in self-defense. The defense committee hired Mexican American attorney Frank Domínguez to defend Pompa. Many *mutualistas,* such as *La Sociedad Melchor Ocampo,* and other civic groups supported him. They pressured the Mexican consul for support. Juan de Heras, editor of *El Heraldo,* led the movement to free Pompa. Supporters presented a petition with 12,915 signatures to Governor F. W. Richardson. Even Mexican President Alvaro Obregón petitioned Richardson to save Pompa's life. In spite of the pressure, Pompa was executed.[110]

Chicago: Mexico in the Midwest

The 1920s saw Mexican workers increasingly moving outside the Southwest into places like Alaska and the Midwest. As noted earlier, the quota on European immigration forced farmers and railroads to recruit Mexicans, as well as southern Blacks, as replacements. In the 1920s, Mexicans comprised 40 percent of the total railroad maintenance crews of Chicago. Sugar beet companies also widely dispersed Mexicans throughout the Midwest, Northwest, and Southwest. By 1927 about 15,000 Mexicans labored in the beet fields of Michigan, Ohio, Indiana, Minnesota, Iowa, and the Dakotas. Like the railroads, the sugar beet growers paid low wages for seasonal work. In the off-season, Mexicans often migrated to nearby cities in search of employment or entertainment. This pattern resembled the experience of workers in Mexico, where subsistence-level and even more prosperous small farmers supplemented their limited production by working in the mines. They also frequented the larger towns for trade and recreation.

Another factor attracting Mexicans north was the wage differential between city and farm and between regions. Finally, employment agencies in Texas and Mexico advertised for Mexican workers to go to the Midwest. From March 1 to the end of August 1923, agencies recruited 34,585 Mexicans for nonagricultural jobs in the Midwest and Pennsylvania.

Chicago developed as the Midwest Mexican capital. The 1910 census showed 672 Mexicans in Illinois. By 1920, 1,224 Mexicans lived in Chicago alone and, by the end of the decade, almost 20,000 resided in the Windy City. Eighty-two percent of Mexicans worked at unskilled jobs. An estimated 58,000 Mexicans lived in the Midwest by the late 1920s, comprising 4 percent of the Mexican population in the United States.[111]

As in other cities, Mexicans clustered in *barrios* close to the workplace. They suffered the now-redundant litany of abuses experienced by the poor: overcrowded housing, low-paid jobs, inadequate schooling, police harassment, and little hope for the future. The bitter cold made life in Chicago more severe than in the Southwest. They were, as elsewhere, victims of a criminal justice system that had little sympathy for Mexicans. One response was the formation, as in the Southwest, of *mutualistas.* For instance, Paul S. Taylor reported that on April 11, 1924:

> . . . the mutualistic societies established in Chicago have turned to the Mexican consul of the city, informing him that more than seven Mexicans are being tried for murder in the first degree in various cities, including Chicago, and probably they will be given the death sentence.[112]

A Davenport, Iowa, newspaper, *El Trabajo,* for example, documented the network and unity among Midwestern Mexicans. *El Trabajo* reported support for José Ortiz Esquivel of Illinois, who had been sentenced to death on June 12, 1925, for the murder of his sweetheart. The Mexican community sent donations and successfully moved back the execution date to June 24. Ortiz would be the first man in Illinois in 15 years to be executed. *El Trabajo* implored its readers to fight against this double standard of justice. The newspaper equated the Ortiz case with Mexican deaths throughout the Southwest. Apparently, efforts of the Midwest community were successful, since the Illinois supreme court granted Ortiz a new trial.[113]

In the face of injustice, Midwestern Mexicans remained highly nationalistic.

When Anglo-Americans complained about the rights of U.S. citizens being violated in Mexico, *El Correo Mexicano,* a Chicago newspaper, on September 30, 1926, replied:

> The Chicago Tribune and other North American papers, like the Boston Transcript, should not be scandalized when an American citizen in Mexico is attacked, not by the authorities, as here, but by bandits and highwaymen.[114]

The *Correo* ridiculed North Americans for calling for immediate justice in Mexico when *bandits* killed a U.S. citizen, pointing out that Mexicans in Chicago and other U.S. cities were daily victims of the *police.*

In Chicago police regularly arrested Mexicans for disorderly conduct; in 1928–1929 this charge constituted almost 79 percent of their misdemeanor offenses. Another common booking in Chicago and in the rural Southwest was vagrancy. In Chicago Polish police officers were especially brutal toward Chicanos. They looked upon Mexicans as competitors. A desk sergeant in 1925 readily admitted that he hated Mexicans and that he had told officers at another station not to take chances with Mexicans: "They are quick on the knife and are hot tempered."[115]

Many arrests were made using "dragnet" methods—that is, police would make sweeps of streets and places like pool halls, arresting Mexicans for carrying a jackknife or on the usual charge of disorderly conduct. Once the Mexicans were in custody, Chicago police extracted confessions by (1) not giving the prisoner anything to eat for three days; (2) physical beatings; (3) sticking a revolver in the prisoner's mouth; or (4) beatings with a rubber hose.[116]

Poverty among Mexicans made justice difficult, if not impossible, since over three-quarters "did not have the money to hire a lawyer to defend them when they found themselves in trouble." The quality of the defense attorney was generally poor, and the inability to speak English handicapped the defendant.

As in other regions, the *mutualistas* provided Mexicans with a vehicle for self-amelioration. According to Dr. Louise Kerr, "Like many earlier immigrants, the Mexicans were primarily concerned with daily physical survival and had little time to indulge in the luxury of defining long-term ambitions." Associations such as trade unions represented a higher level of worker consciousness.

Women in this hostile environment relied heavily on their own institutions, such as using midwives to deliver children. They supplemented their husbands' incomes by taking in boarders, ironing, or doing domestic work. Socially, Mexicans were segregated. In East Chicago two theater owners limited Mexicans to the Black section and in Gary a section of the municipal cemetery was reserved for Mexicans.

In spite of distance from Mexico and extreme poverty, Mexicans remained nationalists. "A widow with three small children, told that she would have to apply for citizenship before she could be given a mother's pension, chose rather to relinquish her right to the pension." The rest of the Mexican community helped her. They followed Mexican politics closely and took sides on elections and other issues there.

Settlement houses such as Hull House became popular centers for Mexican families, providing needed educational services, as well as recreation. These houses served as intermediaries between Mexicans and the municipal apparatus, including police and public health and welfare agencies.[117]

Protestant missionary work made heavy inroads among Chicago Mexicans, and by the early 1930s, 23 percent of the active church-going Mexicans in the city were Protestants. Protestants were successful because they offered social services, legal aid, medical assistance, classes in English, and other aid. The Masons also sponsored three lodges among *Mexicanos.*

Finally, as in the case of San Antonio and Los Angeles, some Mexicans used *mutualistas* to improve their work situation. Mexican workers in South Chicago formed *La Sociedad Mutualista de Obreros Libres Mexicanos* (Mutual Aid Society of Independent Mexican Workers), which funded a Mexican band. A major obstacle to working class solidarity, however, was the Catholic Church, which opposed militant unionism. This institution had become more conservative as the result of the *cristero* revolt in Mexico during the 1920s. The *cristeros* were militant Catholics who refused to obey the Mexican government's attempts to end the Catholic Church's special privileges. Bitter conflicts followed.

There was no doubt about the influence of the Catholic Church among Mexicans in Chicago. The center for Mexican Catholics was Our Lady of Guadalupe Chapel built by the Inland Steel Company for Mexican workers in South Chicago. After Mexicans were excluded from Polish and Slavic Catholic parishes, Mexicans took over the Italian parish of St. Francis, in the near West Side, by 1928. The Catholic Church assigned the first Spanish-speaking priest to serve the growing Mexican population. The Back of the Yards Poles and Irish—adamantly anti-Mexican—discouraged them from attending their churches. Active church attendance among Catholic Mexicans was low.[118]

After 1924, migration patterns changed, with greater numbers of Mexicans arriving directly from Mexico. Increasingly, single men left and more married couples rooted themselves in Chicago. In 1924, *Mexicanas* were less than a third of the Mexican population; 11 years later they comprised over 50 percent. Mexicans in the Midwest cities were undercounted by the census. Linna E. Bressette reported that, in 1920, 1,210 Mexicans lived in Chicago, none in Gary, Indiana, and 233 in Toledo, Ohio. Eight years later, according to her, 25,000 resided in Chicago, 10,000 in Gary, and 8,000 in Toledo.[119] Outside of Chicago, the largest number of Mexicans lived in Detroit, where Henry Ford imported them in 1918. During the 1920s, 16,000 Mexicans migrated to that city, attracted by employment opportunities. Many alternated between agriculture and factory jobs, working in the beet fields and orchards of northern Michigan, and in the winter in the factories.[120]

In 1923, 948 Mexicans were imported to Pennsylvania by Bethlehem Steel to work in the mills. In order to help the impoverished and the ill, Mexicans organized three beneficent associations in this small colony. In 1927 they founded *La Unión Protectora,* which was disbanded because Mexicans believed that aliens could not organize a union. They organized *La Sociedad Azteca Mexicana* the next year; by 1930 it had 130 members (that organization still exists today and owns a social hall).

By the 1920s the Mexican population of St. Paul, Minnesota, was settled.

In 1924 Luis Garzán and friends formed the Anahuac Society, to sponsor dances to raise money for the needy. They held parties at the Neighborhood House, a community center. In the fall of 1930 the Mexican women formed the Guild of Catholic Women at the Mission of Our Lady of Guadalupe.[121]

MEXICAN LABOR IN THE 1920s

The 1920s also saw an increase in the Mexican population in Colorado (from both Mexico and New Mexico). Most Mexicans concentrated in the southeastern part of the state, in Las Animas and Huerfano counties, where an estimated 25,000 Mexicans lived, out of 35,000 counted in Colorado. Officially, the 1920 census listed 10,894 Mexicans. Colorado refined one-fourth of all sugar processed in the United States. Since 1905, Russian-Germans had done the manual labor associated with sugar beet production, but World War I cut off this supply. The 1921 and 1924 Immigration Acts further affected the supply of sugar beet workers, and employment agents recruited Mexicans to do this backbreaking work. Railroads also hired Mexicans; an estimated 5,000 worked on the maintenance crews within the state. Mines and industries requiring cheap labor also hired Mexicans. Mexicans often lived isolated in small lonely clusters of two to eight families. Some movement to the cities took place. For instance, 1,390 Mexicans lived in Denver and 2,486 in Pueblo. As increased numbers of Mexicans triggered nativism, Ku Klux Klan activity was recorded at Walensburg.[122]

The Mexican community also grew in Utah, where Chicanos worked in the railroads, in mines, and on farms. At the beginning of the decade 1,200 Mexicans lived in Utah; ten years later the number grew to over 4,000. Juan Ramón Martínez, a native of New Mexico, formed the Provisional Lamanite Branch in 1921. The usual *mutualistas,* Mexican protective associations, and *La Cruz Azul* were formed by the mid-1920s. Mexicans regularly celebrated the *Cinco de Mayo* and other Mexican holidays. By 1930 Our Lady of Guadalupe Church had been established as a mission.[123]

Smaller numbers of Mexicans lived in Idaho, Washington, and Oregon in the 1920s. Individually Mexicans moved there prior to World War I. After the war, sugar beet companies imported Mexicans to Idaho. By the late 1920s, more Mexicans worked on railroad maintenance crews in the region. As agriculture became more labor-intensive, the industry also attracted more Mexicans to Oregon and Washington. The depression, however, slowed migration into the region.[124]

During the 1920s, U.S. agribusiness continued as the leading employer of Mexicans. Expansion of commercial agriculture and the end of cheap labor from Europe resulted in the recruitment of Mexicans and southern Blacks. By this period, Mexicans were the main source of cheap labor in Texas, Arizona, and New Mexico. California, the Midwest, and Colorado increasingly looked to the Mexican as the answer to their labor needs. Agriculture restructured itself: it moved to ensure an oversupply of labor and to concentrate production and distribution.[125]

In 1921, California producers formed the Valley Fruit Growers of San

Joaquin County, the Sun-Maid Raisin Growers Association (which included 75 to 90 percent of the raisin farmers), the Western Growers Protective Association, the California Growers Exchange, to name just a few. The Arizona Cotton Growers Association served as the model for the San Joaquin Valley Agriculture Labor Bureau, founded in 1925. The bureau consisted of six county farm bureaus, six county chambers of commerce, and raisin, fresh fruit, and cotton producers. Its job was to maximize profit by developing a pool of surplus labor that could be hired at the lowest possible rate; "migratory farm labor was as peculiar to California as slavery was to the old South."

Even when farm profits rose, growers were reluctant to increase workers' wages or improve living conditions. California was the ideal location for these "farm factories," for its climate allowed year-round production. In many places, the federal government furnished water at below-cost levels, making the irrigation of vast areas possible. By the 1920s California had 118 distinct types of farms producing 214 different agricultural products.[126]

The Southern Pacific Railroad alone owned 2,598,295 acres in southern California. The Kern County Land Company controlled some million acres in Kern County. Farm monopolization in California reached high levels by the end of the 1920s, with 37 percent of all large-scale farms in the United States operating in that state and 2.1 percent of California farms producing 28.5 percent of all U.S. agricultural products. Technological advances made many workers in preharvest operations unnecessary. At the same time, they required large capital outlays. Mechanization displaced many year-round farm workers and increased dependence on migrant labor since more production meant larger labor pools at harvest time. U.S. farms mechanized at an unprecedented rate. After 1920, the harvest combine displaced many Mexicans in the wheat fields of northern Texas and the Midwest. Even so, from 1920 to 1930, the number of Mexicans in agriculture tripled, increasing from 121,176 to 368,013. The reason was that mechanization made it possible to cultivate more land; also, as animals were displaced by machines, land which had been used for feed could be turned to cash crops.[127]

Increasingly Mexicans organized collective bargaining units. *La Liga Protectora Latina* of Arizona (discussed in Chapter 4) championed farm worker causes. In the late 1910s, it filed charges against Rafael Estrada, a bully and agent for cotton growers. On May 15, 1919, it submitted a long list of complaints to Governor Thomas E. Campbell and among other things charged that Mexican workers were paid less than what they had been promised by the Arizona Cotton Growers Association (ACGA). The Arizona Federation of Labor began an organizational drive among cotton pickers in the Salt River Valley. The ACGA countered by having Mexican leaders deported. Six Mexicans were arrested on a farm near Glendale, Arizona, in June 1920 when they complained of low wages and breach of contract. When one of the deportees, Apolino Cruz, was picked up for deportation, his 8-year-old son was left on a ditch bank. Friends later took the boy to Tempe, and the ACGA shipped him to Mexico unescorted. Deportations were common. The Arizona Federation of Labor hired R. M. Sánchez and E. M. Flores to meet with Mexican President Adolfo de la Huerta, calling his attention to gross violations of human rights in an effort to enlist his support. The

Mexican president attempted to stop Mexican migration to the United States, an action which enraged growers.[128]

A joint Arizona-Sonora commission investigated work conditions. It found 12,000 to 15,000 Mexicans housed in tents in the Salt River Valley, where temperatures reached well over 100 degrees. The investigation uncovered gross violations—poor and inadequate housing, poor transportation, abusive treatment by ACGA foremen, cases of illegal deportations in response to workers' complaints about mistreatment (200 Mexican workers had been cut adrift without pay). The ACGA arrogantly ignored charges and offered pickers 4¢ a pound more (when the market fell later in the year, the pay raise was rescinded). Governor Campbell distorted findings and assured the Sonora governor that grievances had been corrected. The union prepared to fight.

The U.S. Justice Department sided with the ACGA. Its agents raided the AFL Hall in Phoenix, arrested Sánchez without a warrant, and eventually turned him over to military authorities who held him for another two weeks before charging him with desertion on November 19, the day before the ACGA was to meet. The *Arizona Republican* had labeled Sánchez an alien and a radical. Sánchez was released on February 3, 1921—after the harvest season ended. The AFL employed Lester Doane and C. N. Idar, the latter from Texas, for an organizational drive. In 1921 they formed 14 federal unions, averaging 300 to 400 per local, mostly in Maricopa County. Success was short-lived. The 1921 depression slowed the momentum. Within a year the locals dwindled.

Mexicans continued to migrate to cotton fields. Differentials in pay rate often influenced geographic dispersion. For instance, in Texas a cotton picker averaged $1.75 a day, in Arizona $2.75, in California $3.25, and, ironically, in Arkansas, Louisiana, and Mississippi $4.00 a day. Better pay in other regions encouraged migration from Texas into the Midwest; in turn, Texas cotton growers kept their labor reservoir full by recruiting heavily from Mexico. In Texas counties such as Nueces, 97 percent of the cotton workers were Mexicans and 3 percent were Black. Mexicans comprised 65 percent of the Southwest's seasonal labor with 20 percent Blacks and 15 percent whites.[129] In 1921 the Rural Land Owners Association spent $1,000 advertising for cotton pickers. One of the reasons growers kept wages low was that they believed that higher wages would provide labor with the necessary resources to leave.

Railroads paid Mexicans the lowest industrial salaries, ranging from 35¢ to 39¢ an hour. In packinghouses they earned between 45¢ to 47¢ an hour, while in steel they earned 45¢ to 50¢ for 8 hours or 44¢ for 10 hours. Salaries were much higher than those in the Southwest; most important was that they worked year-round. However, even with higher pay, two-thirds of Mexicans in Chicago earned less than $100 a month which was below the poverty line. Competing for limited housing, they paid $27.00 a month compared to $21.00 for an Irish family with the same conveniences. Families relied heavily on the women to supplement their incomes (65 percent of the males were unmarried). The majority of working wives labored outside the home, although a large number kept lodgers. The cold winters added extra burdens; warm clothing and heating were expensive and respiratory diseases were common. *Mexicanos* seldom received adequate medical attention.

In the plants management played Blacks and Mexicans against each other.

Not one of the steel plants employed a single supervisor of Mexican extraction. Rank and file Anglo workers practiced open racism toward Mexican workers. Chicanos were excluded from building trades by unions that generally required citizenship for membership. The American Federation of Railroad Workers did not have a single Mexican tradesman. Organized labor continued to stereotype Mexicans as wage cutters. Other ethnics were antagonistic toward them. Factory tensions carried over into the streets; many neighborhoods would not rent to them. In 1922 a series of small riots broke out.

The Mexican population elsewhere in the Midwest (Ohio, Indiana, Michigan, Wisconsin, and Illinois) grew from 7,583 in 1920 to 58,317 ten years later. By the end of the decade, Midwest Mexicans had become more urbanized (from just under 70 percent to some 88 percent). Nationwide by 1930, 40.5 percent of the Mexican males were in agriculture, 26 percent in manufacturing, and 16.3 percent in transportation.

An important factor in geographical dispersal during the 1920s was the continued impact of reclamation projects on the growth of sugar beet and cotton production. These crops, valued at $28,043,322 in 1928, represented 34.6 percent of all crops produced on the four reclamation projects in the Southwest and Mexicans constituted 65 percent of common labor in these areas. Most of the beet workers came via Texas and from there spread out to the rest of the southwestern fields and then throughout the Midwest. The seasonal nature of the work also encouraged dispersion and urbanization as many workers migrated to cities in search of work or shelter during the winter months.[130]

In 1922, Mexicans comprised 24 percent of the sugar beet contract labor in Michigan, Ohio, Iowa, Kansas, and Minnesota; in 1926 50 percent. In 1922 they comprised 16 percent of the work force in Nebraska, Colorado, Idaho, and Montana; in 1926 42 percent. In 19 states some 800,000 acres produced 7,500,000 tons with an estimated value of $60 to $65 million a year. Of the estimated 58,000 hired hands about 30,000 were Mexicans.

Beet workers formed small societies of the *mutualista* variety. Best known was *La Sociedad de Obreros Libres* (Free Workers Society) of Gilcrest, Colorado. Also, the *Alianza Hispano-Americana* organized in the beet fields around Brighton, Colorado, and Cheyenne, Wyoming. Wages remained low; for instance, in 1924 an entire family, including children as young as 6, would average $782.00 for six months' work. Growers continuously depressed wages; in 1920 workers averaged $33.71 per acre, in 1924, $23.72, and in 1933, $12.37. Labor contractors further pushed down rates by oversupplying growers with workers.

Whites planted, irrigated, and cultivated, while Mexicans did heavier work of weeding, hoeing, thinning, and topping. Growers encouraged workers' indebtedness to company stores. The IWW formed the Agricultural Workers Industrial Union Local 110 but had limited success. Colorado authorities intimidated workers and state troopers went into the fields to discourage strike activity. Beet workers demanded improved housing, clean drinking water, sanitary facilities, and payment of wages at a guaranteed rate. Management responded that demands were reasonable, but did nothing. The local Knights of Columbus subverted workers' efforts by labeling actions a "red socialist menace."

In 1927 the American Federation of Labor again recruited C. N. Idar, this time to organize beet workers. In the next two and a half years Idar traveled Colorado, Nebraska, and Wyoming. He was able in 1929 to put together a labor front comprised of the AFL, IWW, the communists, and the various Mexican unions. The loosely knit group, called the Beet Workers Association, was held together by the force of Idar's leadership. When he took ill and had to leave, the association fell apart. During the 1930s union organizing was frustrated when large numbers of unemployed Anglos broke the Mexican efforts.[131]

Although Texas growers continually renewed their labor supply from Mexico, they became concerned about the constant drain as the Mexicans dispersed across the country. By the 1920s not only was their labor in demand as far away as Pennsylvania and Montana, but Mexicans had acquired a new mechanism of mobility—the automobile. Many Texas growers blamed autos for ruining "their Mexicans" and began to hire those who did not have transportation. Mexicans traveled and worked in family groups; autos and trucks made them more independent, for they were not solely dependent on the contractors. The growers did not counter this labor drain by paying their workers to encourage them to remain, but found ways to restrict travel.

Basically, Texas-Mexicans were landless and depended on wages. They were vulnerable to exploitation. A form of debt peonage existed; local sheriffs arrested Mexicans by enforcing vagrancy laws and contracted workers to local farmers. Law enforcement officials deceived Mexicans into believing that they faced imprisonment if they left without paying commissary debts. Growers also tried to restrain recruitment drives by northern sugar beet companies. Labor contractors from Michigan and northern Ohio alone hired about 10,000 Texas-Mexicans each year. In May 1929 the first session of the 41st Texas Legislature passed the Emigrant Labor Agency law, which levied a $7,500 occupation tax on out-of-state labor contractors; this act was enjoined, but the Texas legislature passed another law which stood (and was in effect to the 1940s). The law gave local authorities a means to harass out-of-state labor contractors. Mexicans had to leave Texas by night.[132]

In 1922, Mexican workers in Fresno, California, formed the Grape Pickers Union of the San Joaquin Valley; that same year Mexican cantaloupe workers organized in Brawley, California. Undoubtedly, many such small unions existed, but large-scale organization efforts were limited by the Mexicans' vulnerability to deportation and the willingness of U.S. capitalists to do anything to disorganize labor. In times of labor tensions, agribusiness used immigration authorities to sweep Mexican *colonias*. Mexicans were vulnerable because some 80 percent had no documents. During World War I, Wobblies were treated as subversives and tried under the Federal Espionage Act. The California Criminal Syndicalism Act of 1919 made it a felony to "teach, advocate, aid or abet acts of violence to effect political change." Judge Busick, on August 23, 1923, extended the law when he issued an injunction against the IWW, its various committees, officers, and members. In short, "anyone who belonged to a group which advocated criminal syndicalism was guilty of a felony punishable by imprisonment from one to fourteen years." In California 504 Wobblies and communists were arrested. Their bail was usually set at $15,000 and 264 were actually tried, 164 convicted, and

128 sentenced to San Quentin. The press stereotyped Mexicans as IWW members and used this pretext to criminalize them.[133]

Farm workers in California faced overwhelming opposition by agribusiness. The most powerful growers' association, the American Farm Bureau Federation (AFBF), united farmers nationally. In the 1970s it was a $4 billion empire as large as Du Pont or General Motors and had organizations in 2,800 out of 3,000 counties in 49 states and Puerto Rico. Government workers at taxpayers' expense organized farmers into county farm bureaus which federated into state bureaus which consolidated into a national farm bureau. The AFBF was the creation of the Agricultural Extension Service at various state colleges of agriculture whose county agents promoted the idea. By the 1920s and 1930s, U.S. and state chambers of commerce and the National Association of Manufacturers supported the AFBF. Over the years it separated from the extension service officially but protected the service from government cuts. Large growers controlled the AFBF and through it lobbied to exclude farm workers from regulatory legislation. It won congressional support for its programs. President Warren G. Harding called in the president of the Farm Bureau for advice, setting a precedent for future presidents.[134]

Many U.S. labor leaders did not believe Mexicans were educated to the level that trade unionism required. *Mutualistas,* brotherhoods, and protective associations, however, had laid the groundwork for the development of the "job conscious labor movement." In November 1927 the Federation of Mexican Societies, mostly *mutualistas,* met in Los Angeles with the express purpose of encouraging members to support trade unionism by financing organizational efforts. Shortly afterward, on March 23, 1928, they formed *La Confederación de Uniónes Obreras Mexicanas* (CUOM) (Federation of Mexican Workers Unions). This organization had communist and IWW sympathizers. In their by-laws members recognized the principle of class struggle and that they belonged to an exploited class.

CUOM held its first convention in May 1928. Many delegates came from the *mutualistas;* eventually it encompassed 21 locals with approximately 2,000 to 3,000 members. CUOM called for the restriction of immigration and solidarity with the AFL, highlighted unemployment and labor exploitation, and emphasized the importance of establishing Mexican schools. In spite of an optimistic start, by 1929 CUOM dwindled to a handful of members.

In 1928 another Mexican union was formed in the Imperial Valley of California. Again local *mutualistas* led the struggle. That year farmers expressed optimism; crops flourished and an abundant supply of Mexican workers was available to harvest them. Indeed, at harvest time Mexicans comprised 90 percent of field workers. In recent years the Mexican population had stabilized. More and more Mexicans lived and worked year-round as field hands, merchants, and non-farm workers.[135]

The valley produced two main crops—lettuce and cantaloupes. Both required highly specialized harvesting methods in picking and packing. Labor contractors managed work crews. Growers paid contractors, who in turn paid workers after subtracting their fee from each man's earnings. Contractors withheld the first week's wages until the end of the harvest. Many workers complained that contractors often absconded with their money.

The steady growth and relative stability of a community of year-round workers contributed to unifying the Mexicans. They formed two *mutualistas–La Sociedad Mutualista Benito Juárez* of El Centro, in 1919, and *La Sociedad Mutualista Hidalgo* of Brawley, in 1921. *La Liga Latina Protectora* had also been active in El Centro, and *La Alianza Hispano-Americana* had lodges in the area.

In conjunction with the Mexican consul, the *mutualista* leaders formed *La Unión de Trabajadores del Valle Imperial.* On May 3, 1928, the union sent letters to cantaloupe growers and the chambers of commerce at Brawley and El Centro. They requested: wages be increased to 15¢ per standard crate of cantaloupes or 75¢ an hour; that growers supply free picking sacks and ice; that growers deposit workers' withheld wages in the bank instead of allowing contractors to hold them; and that growers take over from the contractors the responsibility for paying workmen's compensation, because contractors did not pay it. The growers refused. On May 7 workers at the Sears Brothers Ranch walked out. Sheriff Charles L. Gillett arrested four Mexicans for disturbing the peace. Soon, two to three thousand workers joined the strike.

Newspapers, public opinion, and local authorities openly supported growers. On May 10 Sheriff Gillett shut down the union's offices and outlawed all future strikes. Growers could not believe that "their Mexicans" had caused trouble; they blamed "reds and radicals" instead of working conditions. The district attorney supported the growers because "they had millions invested in crops." Sheriff Gillett stated that if Mexicans did not like it there, they could return to Mexico. He continued mass arrests and the courts set bail from $250 to $1000. Charges were dropped if workers pleaded guilty and promised to return to work. Workers who did not return to work were deported. The tactics broke the strike.

The labor struggles of the 1920s proved that Mexicans were neither tractable nor docile. A marked rise in the consciousness of Mexican workers took place. A sense of community with other Mexican workers developed as the Mexicans' dependency on seasonal work lessened. The migrants' sole contact with their primitive unit, the family, widened.[136] In 1928, the Federation of Mexican Workers Unions formed in response to the Imperial Valley Cantaloupe Strike of that year. The Mexican movement thus evolved from self-help associations to groups attempting to change society. The reasons for this change included their increased numbers, urbanization, the growing realization that they would not return to Mexico, the principles behind the Mexican Revolution, and the growth of trade unionism in Mexico. Not least of all was the Mexicans' own life experiences in the United States. Before the 1920s, many Mexicans had worked in the copper mines of Arizona. In the 1920s, because of the depression of 1921, and policy changes of the copper barons, many Mexican copper miners went to the cotton fields. Many streams converged in agriculture to contribute to increased collective Mexican militancy.

GREASERS GO HOME: MEXICAN IMMIGRATION, THE 1920s

Opposition to Mexican immigration crystallized in the 1920s. Reaction toward Mexicans intensified as their numbers became larger. In Mexico road and rail transportation was no longer disrupted by the intense fighting of the revolution. Moreover, prices in Mexico rose 300 percent faster than wages. They corresponded with a labor shortage in Colorado, Wyoming, Utah, Iowa, and Nebraska in 1920 that resulted in the heavy importation of Mexicans into those states. Industrialists imported Mexicans to work in the mills of Chicago—first as an army of reserve labor and then as strikebreakers. During the 1919–1920 and 1920–1921 seasons the Arizona Growers Association spent $325,000 recruiting and transporting Mexicans to cotton areas.

Suddenly in early 1921 the bottom fell out of the economy and a depression caused heavy unemployment. If in times of prosperity their numbers had generated hostility, in time of crisis Mexicans became the scapegoats for the failure of the U.S. economy. The corporate interests which had recruited Mexicans felt little responsibility to them and these capitalists left thousands of Mexicans throughout the country stranded and destitute. In Arizona, although transportation fees had been deducted from the pay of Mexican workers, growers did not give them return passage. *El Universal* of Mexico City on March 5, 1921, reported: "When they arrived at Phoenix a party of Mexican workers were taken to Tempe and introduced to a concentration camp that looks like a dung-heap." According to this source the men were chained and put into work parties. The situation was repeated in Kansas City, Chicago, and Colorado.

In Fort Worth, Texas, 90 percent of 12,000 Mexicans were unemployed; whites threatened to burn out Mexicans and rid the city of "cheap Mexican labor." Truckloads of Mexicans were escorted to Texas chain gangs. In Ranger, Texas, terrorists dragged a hundred Mexican men, women, and children from their tents and make-shift homes, beat them, and ordered them to clear out of town. In Chicago employment of Mexicans shrank by two-thirds between 1920–1921. Police made frequent raids and strictly enforced vagrancy laws. Conditions grew so bad that Mayor William Hall Thompson allocated funds to ship several hundred families back to the border. The *Denver Post* headlined "Denver Safety Is Menaced by 3,500 Starving Mexicans." Mexican workers from the Denver area were shipped to the border. Although these workers had been recruited to the United States, the U.S. government did little to ameliorate their sufferings. The Mexican government in contrast spent $2.5 million to aid stranded Mexicans.[137] Many workers would have starved if it had not been for Mexican President Alvaro Obregón.

Nativist efforts to restrict the entry of southern and eastern Europeans bore fruit with the passage of the Immigration Act of 1921. Many wanted to include Mexicans in the provisions of the act, but Congress felt that the opposition of agribusiness to their inclusion might block passage of the bill. The 1921 act was generally considered too lenient. Nativists replaced it three years later with a permanent quota act that excluded most Asians and drastically cut the flow from southern and eastern Europe, identified as "racially inferior Europe." The act started a battle between the restrictionists, who wanted to keep the country "Anglo-American" and felt too many foreigners would subvert the "American way of life," and the capitalists, who set aside prejudices for low-cost labor, remembering that the 1917 act had hurt them financially. They opposed any restrictions on the free flow of Mexicans to the United States, especially since the supply of European labor was cut.

In 1923 the commissioner of immigration turned his attention more fully to Mexicans: "It is difficult, in fact impossible, to measure the illegal influx of Mexicans crossing the border." By 1923, the economy had sufficiently recovered to entice Mexican workers to the United States in large numbers again.

This "legal" migration was accompanied by an avalanche of undocumented workers who were encouraged to avoid the head tax as well as visa charges by U.S. employers and government authorities. The new migration differed from that of earlier years, becoming more permanent. Permanency and large numbers of Mexicans alarmed nativists, who deplored the fact that the Johnson bill, which later became the Immigration Act of 1924, did not limit Mexicans. Debate over the issue of Mexican immigration was heated in both houses of Congress. The decision to exclude Mexicans from the quota was a matter of political opportunism. Albert Johnson of Washington, chairman of the House Immigration and Naturalization Committee and sponsor of the bill, bluntly stated that the committee did not restrict the Mexicans because it did not want to hinder the passage of the 1924 Immigration Act. Johnson promised that the committee would sponsor another bill to create a border patrol to enforce existing laws, and he claimed that a quota alone would not be effective. Representative John E. Raker of California seconded Johnson, and he saw no need for further legislation to restrict Mexicans. Raker felt that enforcement of existing laws would cut their numbers to 1,000 annually, by ending the employers' practice of paying the head tax for them and by excluding illiterates (according to Raker, "from 75 to 90 percent of all Mexicans in Mexico are illiterate").

Nativists were not convinced. Secretary of Labor James J. Davis called for a quota for the Western Hemisphere. He was alarmed that Mexican labor had infiltrated into U.S. industries such as iron and steel and arranged meetings with Samuel Gompers to plan a strategy to remove this "menace." Representative Martin Madden of Chicago, chairman of the House Appropriations Committee, stated, "The bill opens the doors for perhaps the worst element that comes into the United States—the Mexican *peon*. . . . [It] opens the door wide and unrestricted to the most undesirable people who come under the flag."[138] Representative John O. Box of Jacksonville, Texas, a former Cherokee county judge and ordained Methodist minister, seconded Madden and demanded a 2 percent quota for Mexicans based on the 1890 population as well as additional funds for its enforcement. Box supported an amendment to put only Mexico on a quota basis, exempting the rest of the nations in the Western Hemisphere. The Johnson bill, however, passed the House without the proposed amendment.

In the U.S. Senate, Frank B. Willis of Ohio echoed restrictionist sentiment:

"Many of [them] . . . now coming in are, unfortunately, practically without education, and largely without experience in self-government, and in most cases not at all qualified for present citizenship or for assimilation into this country."[139] Senator Matthew M. Neeley of West Virginia charged: "On the basis of merit, Mexico is the last country we should grant a special favor or extend a peculiar privilege. . . . The immigrants from many of the countries of Europe have more in common with us than the Mexicanos have."[140]

Antirestrictionists argued that it would be difficult to enforce such a quota, that Mexicans stayed only temporarily anyway, that they did work white men would not, and that an economic burden would result. However, the argument of Pan-Americanism proved to be the most effective. Many senators supported Pan-Americanism as a vehicle for establishing the political and economic dominance of the United States over Latin America. Senator Holm Bursum of New Mexico stated that he did not favor disrupting Pan-Americanism, that Mexico was sparsely populated anyway, and "so far as absorbing the Mexican population . . . that is the merest rot."[141]

In 1924 hostility to Mexican immigration peaked. Although border officials strictly applied the $8 head tax, plus the $10 visa fee, Mexicans still entered with and without documents. Johnson's committee, true to its promise, began hearings on the Mexican problem. Reports of the commissioner of immigration underscored that *peones* benefited from the reduction of European immigrants. In 1926 the commissioner wrote that 855,898 Mexicans entered with documents and predicted, "It is safe to say that over a million Mexicans are in the United States at the present time [including undocumented], and under present laws this number may be added to practically without limit."[142]

An open fight broke out in Congress in 1926. Restrictionists introduced two bills. The bill proposed by John Box simply sought to apply quota provisions to the whole Western Hemisphere; the other bill, sponsored by Robert L. Bacon of New York, sought to apply them only to Mexico. The Box bill emerged as the main one before the House. Western representatives opposed any attempt to restrict Mexicans. S. Parker Frieselle of California stated that he did not want California based upon a Mexican foundation: There is nothing else available to us.[143]

Representative John Nance Garner of Texas emphasized that Mexicans returned home after the picking seasons:

All they want is a month's labor in the United States, and that is enough to support them in Mexico for six months. . . . In our country they do not cause any trouble, unless they stay there a long time and become Americanized; but they are a docile people. They can be imposed on; the sheriff can go out and make them do anything.[144]

In the end, both the restrictionists and the antirestrictionists displayed nativist and racist attitudes. The antirestrictionists wanted an open border because they needed Mexican labor. Box candidly accused opponents of his bill of attempting to attract only the "floating Mexican *peons*" for the purpose of exploiting them, charging that "they are to be imported in trainloads and delivered to farmers who have contracted to grow beets for the sugar companies." Box stated, "They are objectionable as citizens and as residents."[145] During committee hearings, Box questioned a farmer as to whether what the farmer really wanted was a subservient class of Mexican workers "who do not want to own land, who can be directed by men in the upper stratum of society." The farmer answered, "I believe that is about it." Box then asked, "Now, do you believe that is good Americanism?" The farmer replied, "I think it is necessary Americanism to preserve Americanism."[146] The quota act had drastically reduced the available labor pool and agricultural and industrial interests committed themselves to keping the Mexican unrestricted.

In 1928 the commissioner general of immigration recommended "that natives of countries of the Western Hemisphere be brought within the quota provisions of existing law." The commissioner specifically recommended restriction of Mexicans, stating, "The unlimited flow of immigrants from the Western Hemisphere cannot be reconciled with the sharp curtailment of immigration from Europe."[147] A definite split developed between the Department of Labor, which favored putting Mexicans on a quota system, and the Department of State, which opposed it because the State Department knew that such action would seriously weaken its negotiations with Latin America concerning economic trade treaties and privileges for Anglo-American interests. Anglo-American racism was a sensitive area. Placing Mexicans on a quota would be a legal affirmation of discrimination toward all Latin Americans. State Department officials were involved in sensitive negotiations with Mexican officials, who threatened to expropriate Anglo-American oil. The State Department, representing Anglo-American foreign investors and exporters, joined southwestern industrialists to kill restrictionist measures. They attempted to sidetrack debates, and for a time congressional debate centered around enforcement of existing immigration laws. Many members of Congress were not satisfied and pushed for quantitative restrictions. Anglo-American labor supported the restrictionists, and questioned, "Do you want a mongrel population, consisting largely of Mexicans?"[148]

Growers and other industrialists joined forces with the departments of State, Agriculture, and Interior and formed a solid front to overwhelm restrictionists, heading off the passage of a bill placing Mexicans on a quota. By 1929, conditions changed, lessening Mexicans migration to the United States.

SUMMARY

Between the turn of the century and the Great Depression, approximately one-tenth of Mexico's population shifted "north from Mexico," in one of the largest mass migrations of people in the history of the world. This movement occurred during a period of great economic and social development which saw the industrialization of the Southwest, the demise of the small farmers, a world war, recessions, and depression. Mechanization and urbanization in the Southwest required cheap labor, which became less abundant as nativist sentiment completely shut off the flow of workers from Asia and drastically limited European immigration. The reception Mexicans received was mixed. Lower- and middle-class Anglo-Americans blamed them for the disorganization of society which was in fact caused by the restructuring of industry; in contrast, industrialists, rural and urban, saw Mexicans as necessary for building the Southwest.

Mexican workers came to the United States both because of conditions in their homeland and the increased demand for labor in northern Mexico and the United States. For the first decade of the twentieth century, Mexican labor was concentrated in the Southwest. However, World War I and the immigration acts of 1917, 1921, and 1924 drastically limited European immigration, intensifying a demand for Mexicans and Blacks in the Midwest. The flow of Mexicans followed the railroads and the expanding sugar beet industry. Stepped-up production, at the same time, forced labor agents in the Southwest to recruit Mexican labor south of the Río Bravo even more aggressively.

Mexicans were divided into political, economic, and religious refugees. Those who came before the Mexican Revolution were protesting the dictator Porfirio Díaz and his modernization of Mexico at the expense of political liberties. Many of these refugees offered leadership to the masses of Mexicans who began to flood into the United States at the turn of the century in response to economic conditions in the United States. Perceiving the racism and exploitation of these workers, they used their newspapers to document numerous stories of injustice; they became the vanguard of labor militancy. Many refugees coming to the United States after the revolution were from the middle and upper classes. Those arriving in the 1910s were political exiles, while emigrants in the 1920s were religious refugees. Both groups, although concerned about racism, opposed any type of radical solution.

At the turn of the century, Mexicans overwhelmingly worked in rural occupations; by the 1920s, substantial numbers lived in urban centers. During this transition, the Mexicans' responses changed. Those who worked as seasonal migrants found it difficult to organize, since often the workers' community was limited to their immediate families. Uprooted from friends and associates, they were constantly on the move. Once this migration slowed, Mexicans formed temporary associations, usually *mutualistas,* to solve the most pressing problems. Frequently, Mexican merchants and the consul used these mutual aid societies as a natural vehicle for worker organization. Approaches differed according to the economic conditions in each state or region. In Texas, Mexican Americans formed LULAC, a middle-class and professional group that was committed to the Americanization of Mexicans.

On the eve of the Great Depression, the transition from Mexican to Mexican American manifested itself in the changing character of the new organizations. Mexican American *barrios* now had traceable boundaries. Moreover, the shift from temporary one-issue groups to trade unions and middle-class statewide associations was well underway. The depression would have a dramatic impact on the development of Mexican American organizations, as the nation turned away from the gold standard.

NOTES

1. Mark Reisler, *By the Sweat of their Brow: Mexican Immigrant Labor in the United States, 1900–1940* (Westport, Conn.: Greenwood Press, 1976), p. 5.
2. Ernesto Galarza, "Without Benefit of Lobby," *Graphic Survey* 66, no. 3 (May 1931): 81.
3. John Hart, *Anarchism and the Mexican Working Class* (Austin: University of Texas Press, 1978), p. 13.
4. Manuel Díaz Ramírez, *Apuntes sobre el movimiento obrero y campesino de México* (México, D.F.: Ediciones de Cultura Popular, 1974), p. 12; Rodney D. Anderson, *Outcasts in Their Own Land: Mexican Workers, 1906–1911* (De Kalb: Northern Illinois University Press, 1976), pp. 12, 18, 26–27, 37.
5. James Cockcroft, *Mexico* (New York: Monthly Review Press, 1983), p. 81.
6. Anderson, p. 81.
7. Alberto Trueba Urbina, *Evolución de la huelga* (México, D.F.: Ediciones Botas, 1950), pp. 60, 63; Anderson, pp. 79, 86; Díaz Ramírez, p. 52; Hart, pp. 50–51.
8. Díaz Ramírez, pp. 66, 67–68, 70, 83; Hart, pp. 32–41; Anderson, p. 81.
9. Cockcroft, p. 82.
10. Lawrence Anthony Cardoso, "Mexican Emigration to the United States, 1900–1930: An Analysis of Socio-Economic Causes" (Ph.D. dissertation, University of Connecticut, 1974), p. 23.
11. Eric Wolf, *Sons of the Shaking Earth* (Chicago: University of Chicago Press, 1959), p. 247; Anderson, pp. 38, 43.
12. Hudson Stroude, *Timeless Mexico* (New York: Harcourt Brace Jovanovich, 1944) p. 210.
13. James D. Cockcroft, *Intellectual Precursors of the Mexican Revolution, 1900–1913* (Austin: University of Texas Press, 1968), p. 14.
14. Charles C. Cumberland, *Mexico: The Struggle for Modernity* (New York: Oxford University Press, 1968), p. 216.
15. Cardoso, pp. 34–35.
16. Cockcroft, *Intellectual Precursors,* pp. 32, 46.
17. Victor Alba, *The Mexicans* (New York: Praeger, 1967), p. 106.
18. Alba, p. 106.
19. Cardoso, pp. 57, 54; Alba, p. 106.
20. Cockcroft, *Intellectual Precursors,* p. 82.
21. Anderson, pp. 88, 92; Juan Gómez-Quiñones, "The First Steps: Chicano Labor Conflict and Organizing, 1900–1920," *Aztlán* 3, no. 1 (1973): 20; Charles C. Cumberland, *Mexican Revolution: Genesis Under Madero* (Austin: University of Texas Press, 1952), p. 16.
22. Dawn Keremitsis, *La Industria Textil Mexicana en el Siglo XIX* (México, D.F.: SepSetentas, 1973), pp. 208, 209, 210. Fewer women were employed in the interior of Mexico than in northern Mexican mills. It can be assumed that there was a surplus of male workers in the interior, whereas in the north a labor shortage existed at this time. For example, at La Estrella in Coahuila, out of 600 workers, 200 were women and 100 were children. In 1897 La Buena Fe employed 63 men, 74 women, and 33 children. La Aura employed 28 men and 40 women, and at El Labrador there were 19 men, 20 women, and 20 children working. In Coahuila men and women received the same wages, whereas children were paid less. See also Octavio A. Hernández, *Esquena de la economia mexicana hasta antes de la revolución,* quoted in Keremitsis, p. 210.
23. Anderson, pp. 133–134; Hart, pp. 83–103, 139–141; Ward Sloan Albro III, "Richardo Flores Magón and the Liberal Party: An Inquiry into the Origins of the Mexican Revolution of 1910" (Ph.D. dissertation, University of Arizona, 1967), pp. 114–115. Albro places the date as January 22; the mills at Puebla, Vera Cruz, Tlaxcala, Jalisco, Queretaro, and Mexico City were also involved.
24. Anderson, pp. 157, 159.

25. Anderson, pp. 163–164, 167; Albro, p. 115, places the number at between 200 and 800; the bodies were taken to Vera Cruz and dumped into the sea.
26. Laureano Clavo Berber, *Nociones de Historia de Sonora* (México, D.F.: Publicaciones del Gobierno del Estado de Sonora, 1958), p. 277; Antonio G. Rivera, *La Revolución en Sonora* (México, D.F.: n.p., 1969), pp. 139, 159.
27. Anderson, pp. 117–119; Gómez-Quiñones, p. 18.
28. Peter Baird and Ed McCaughan, "Labor and Imperialism in Mexico's Electrical Industry," *NACLA Report on the Americas* 6, no. 6 (September–October 1977): 5.
29. Tomás Almaguer, "Historical Notes on Chicano Oppression: The Dialectics of Racial and Class Domination in North America," *Aztlán* (Spring–Fall, 1974): 40; Cardoso, pp. 18, 57; Ed McCaughan and Peter Baird, "Harvest of Anger: Agro-Imperialism in Mexico's Northwest," *NACLA Latin America and Empire Report* 10, no. 6 (July–August 1976): 5.
30. Cardoso, p. 59.
31. Victor S. Clark, *Mexican Labor in the United States*, U.S. Department of Commerce Bulletin no. 78 (Washington, D.C.: Government Printing Office, 1908); Taylor, *An American-Mexican Frontier: Nueces County, Texas* (New York: Russell and Russell, 1971), p. 173.
32. Gilbert Cardenas, "Public Data on Mexican Immigration into the United States: A Critical Evaluation," in W. Boyd Littrell and Gideon Sjoberg, eds., *Current Issues in Social Policy Research* (New York: Russell Sage, 1976), p. 2. Also see Larry García y Griego, *"Los Primeros Pasos al Norte:* Mexican Migration to the United States" (Bachelor's thesis, Princeton University, 1973).
33. Jorge A. Bustamante, "Mexican Immigration and the Social Relations of Capitalism" (Ph.D. dissertation, University of Notre Dame, 1975), p. 50; Cardoso, p. 60.
34. Juan Gómez-Quiñones, *Sembradores: Ricardo Flores Magón y el Partido Liberal Mexicano: A Eulogy and Critique* (Los Angeles: Aztlán, 1973), p. 23; Cockcroft, *Intellectual Precursors,* p. 124. Also see Robert E. Ireland, "The Radical Community, Mexican and American Radicalism," *Journal of Mexican-American History* (Fall 1971): 22–29.
35. *Regeneración,* September 3, 1910, quoted in Ward Sloan Albro III, "Magonismo: Precursor to Chicanismo?" (Manuscript, Texas Arts and Industries University at Kingsville, n.d.), p. 5; Cockcroft, Intellectual *Precursors,* p. 231.
36. Albro, "Flores Magón," pp. 79–81, 85; Gómez-Quiñones, *Sembradores,* p. 46; *Regeneración,* January 14, 1911; Emilio Zamora, "Chicano Socialist Labor Activity in Texas, 1900–1920," *Aztlán* 6, no. 2 (Summer 1975): 235; *Regeneración,* October 25, 1913. Numerous feminist groups such as *El grupo feminino* "Luz y vida" of Los Angeles, *Regeneración,* April 15, 1916, and *El grupo feminino* "Grupo Práxedis G. Guerrero" of San Antonio, *Regeneración,* March 25, 1916, participated in the struggle.
37. Carolyn Asbaugh, *Lucy Parsons: American Revolutionary* (Chicago: Herr, 1976), pp. 267–268; Richard O. Boyer and Herbert M. Morais, *Labor's Untold Story,* 3rd ed. (New York: United Electrical, Radio and Machine Workers of America, 1974).
38. D. W. Meinig, *Southwest: Three Peoples in Geographical Change, 1600–1970* (New York: Oxford University Press, 1971), pp. 62–63; García y Griego, pp. 39, 50, 65. Cardoso, p. 38, summarizes the new technology—the steam shovel, dynamite, surveying devices, etc.
39. Paul S. Taylor, *Mexican Labor in the United States,* vol. 1 (New York: Arno Press, 1970), p. 320; García y Griego, pp. 19, 20. See also George O. Coalson, *The Development of the Migratory Farm Labor System in Texas: 1900–1954* (San Francisco: R & E Research Associates, 1977), an excellent work on the expansion of the cotton industry in Texas; David Montejano, "Race, Labor Repression and Capitalist Agriculture: Notes from Texas, 1920–1930" (Berkeley, Calif.: Institute for the Study of Social Change, 1977), p. 2; Mark Reisler, "Passing Through Our Egypt: Mexican Labor in the United States, 1900–1940" (Ph.D. dissertation, Cornell University, 1973), p. 10; and Pauline R. Kibbe, *Latin Americans in Texas* (New York: Arno Press, 1974), p. 168.
40. Victor B. Nelson Cisneros, *"La Clase Trabajadora en Tejas, 1920–1940,"Aztlán* 6, no. 2 (1975): 242–243; Taylor, *American-Mexican Frontier,* p. 84; Douglas E. Foley, Clarice Mora, Donald E. Post, and Ignacio Lozano, *From Peones to Politicos: Ethnic Relations in a South Texas Town, 1900–1977* (Austin: University of Texas Press, Center for Mexican American Studies, 1977), pp.

3–4, 12–13, 14; Coalson, p. 47; Edgar Greer Shelton, Jr., "Political Conditions Among Texas Mexicans Along the Rio Grande" (Master's thesis, University of Texas, 1946), p. 9.

41. Taylor, *American-Mexican Frontier,* pp. 85–89, 131; Montejano, pp. 20, 24, 31; Foley et al., pp. 6–7, 70–71, 85.

42. Robert N. McLean and Charles A. Thomson, *Spanish and Mexicans in Colorado: A Survey of the Spanish Americans and Mexicans in the State of Colorado* (New York: 1924), reprinted in Carlos E. Cortés, ed., *Church Views of the Mexican American* (New York: Arno Press, 1974), p. 34; *Gopher Historian* (Fall 1971): 5.

43. Cardoso, pp. 40–44, 49; Manuel Gamio, *Mexican Immigration to the United States* (New York: Dover, 1971), p. 37.

44. Reisler, "Passing Through Our Egypt," pp. 8–9, 13, 15.

45. García y Griego, p. 16; Winifred Kupper, ed., *Texas Sheepman* (Austin: University of Texas Press, 1951), pp. 37, 62, 63, 118; Edward N. Wentworth, *American Sheep Trails* (Ames: Iowa College Press, 1948), p. 522; Cardoso, p. 33.

46. Victor Clark, *Mexican Labor in the United States,* U.S. Department of Commerce Bulletin no. 79 (Washington, D.C.: Government Printing Office, 1908), pp. 494, 507, 511.

47. George C. Kiser, "Mexican American Labor Before World War II," *Journal of Mexican American History* (Spring 1972): 123; Official Report of the Governor's Spanish Speaking Task Force, Submitted to Governor Robert D. Ray and the 66th General Assembly, *Conoceme en Iowa* (Des Moines, 1976), p. 4.

48. Clark, Bulletin no. 79, p. 485; Kiser, p. 125; Zamora, p. 221; Clark, pp. 492–493.

49. Ernesto Galarza, *Farm Workers and Agribusiness in California, 1947–1960* (Notre Dame, Ind.: University of Notre Dame Press, 1977), p. 3; Stuart Jamieson, *Labor Unionism in American Agriculture* (New York: Arno Press, 1976), pp. 53–54; Porter Chaffee, "Organizational Efforts of Mexican Agricultural Workers" (Unpublished ms., Oakland, Calif.: Works Progress Administration Federal Writers Project, 1938), pp. 6–7; Norman Lowenstein, "Strikes and Strike Tactics in California Agriculture: A History" (Master's thesis, University of California at Berkeley, 1940), pp. 22–24; Gómez-Quiñones, "The First Steps," pp. 24–26.

50. Gómez-Quiñones, "The First Steps," p. 26; Sam Kushner, *Long Road to Delano* (New York: International Publishers, 1975), p. 20; Chaffee, pp. 6–7.

51. Alberto M. Camarillo, "Chicano Urban History: A Study of Compton's Barrio, 1936–1970," *Aztlán* (Fall 1971): 25.

52. Charles Wollenberg, "Working on *El Traque,*" in Norris Hundley, Jr., ed., *The Chicano* (Santa Barbara: Clio Books, 1975), pp. 96–98, 102–105; Louis B. Perry and Richard S. Perry, *A History of the Los Angeles Labor Movement, 1911–1941* (Los Angeles: University of California Press, 1963), p. 71.

53. Zamora, pp. 223–226.

54. Mario T. García, "Racial Dualism in the El Paso Labor Market, 1880–1920," *Aztlán* 6, no. 2 (Summer 1975): 213; Gómez-Quiñones, "The First Steps," p. 22.

55. Carl Wittke, *We Built America,* rev. ed. (Cleveland: Case Western Reserve University, 1967), p. 466; Kaye Lyon Briegel, "*Alianza Hispano-Americana,* 1894–1965: A Mexican Fraternal Insurance Society" (Ph.D. Dissertation, University of Southern California, 1974), pp. 12–15; José Amado Hernández, "The Development of Mutual Aid Societies in the Chicano Community," *La Raza* 3, no. 2 (Summer 1977): 15.

56. Meyer Weinberg, *Minority Students: A Research Appraisal* (Washington, D.C.: Department of Health, Education and Welfare, 1977), p. 286; Arnoldo De León, "Blowout 1910 Style: A Chicano School Boycott in West Texas," *Texana* 12, no. 2 (November 1974): 124.

57. B. A. Hodges, *A History of the Mexican Mission Work* (1931), reprinted in Cortes, p. 5; De León, pp. 124, 129.

58. Hodges, pp. 5–7.

59. Elizabeth Broadbent, "The Distribution of Mexican Population in the U.S." (Ph.D. dissertation, University of Chicago, 1941), pp. 3, 33.

60. Clark, p. 496 Clark, Bulletin no. 78, pp. 471, 496. Other recent works of interest have been compiled by Antonio José Ríos-Bustamante, ed., *Immigration and Public Policy: Human Rights for Undocumented Workers and Their Families* (Los Angeles: Chicano Studies Center Publica-

tions, University of California, 1977). Gilbert Cardenas of the University of Texas at Austin has also done solid research in the area of migration. His works include: "A Theoretical Approach to the Sociology of Mexican Labor Migration" (Ph.D. Dissertation, University of Notre Dame, 1977); "Public Data on Mexican Immigration into the United States: A Critical Evaluation," in Littrell and Sjoberg, which deals with the limitations and abuses of data research by the INS; and "United States Immigration Policy Toward Mexico: A Historical Perspective," *Chicano Law Review* 2 (Summer 1975). Also see Gilbert Cardenas and Esteban Flores, "Political Economy of International Migration," prepared for the Joint Annual Meeting of the Latin American Studies Association and African Studies Association, Houston, Texas, November 1977.

61. U.S. Congress, *Report of the Immigration Commission,* 61st Cong., 3rd sess. (1910–1911), I:682–691, quoted in Job West Neal, "The Policy of the United States Toward Immigration from Mexico" (Master's thesis, University of Texas at Austin, 1941), pp. 58–59.

62. U.S. Department of Labor, "Report of the Commissioner General of Immigration," *Report of the Department of Labor* (Washington, D.C.: Government Printing Office, 1913), p. 337.

63. *Regeneración,* February 4, February 18, 1911.

64. Romo, pp. 109, 116, 117–118, 122.

65. U.S. Department of Labor, "Report of the Commissioner General of Immigration," *Report of the Department of Labor* (Washington, D.C., Government Printing Office, 1916), p. 397.

66. Cardoso, pp. 83–87.

67. Quoted in Neal, p. 81.

68. Neal, p. 100. Mark Reisler, *By the Sweat of Their Brow* p. 38, states that 34,922 Mexicans had returned to Mexico, 15,632 were still employed in 1921, 414 had died, and 21,400 had deserted and found other employment.

69. Ricardo Romo, "Mexican Workers in the City: Los Angeles, 1915–1930" (Ph.D. dissertation, University of California at Los Angeles, 1975), pp. 56–57, 81–83, 106–107.

70. Romo, pp. 104, 109–111, 123.

71. Jay S. Stowell, *The Near Side of the Mexican Question* (Garden City, N.Y.: Doubleday, 1921), pp. 41, 44, 48; Leo Grebler, Joan W. Moore, and Ralph C. Guzmán, *The Mexican-American People: The Nation's Second Largest Minority* (New York: Free Press, 1970), p. 109; Américo Paredes, *With a Pistol in His Hand* (Austin: University of Texas Press, 1958); José E. Limón, *"El Primer Congreso Mexicanista de 1911:* A Precursor to Contemporary Chicanismo," *Aztlán* (Spring and Fall 1974): 80, 88, 89.

72. *Regeneración,* August 5, 1911; *"La Víctima de los 'Civilizados,' " Regeneración,* August 26, 1911; Ricardo Flores Magón, *"A Salvar a un Inocente," Regeneración,* September 9, 1911; *"En defensa de los Mexicanos," Regeneración,* August 17, 1912.

73. William M. Hager, "The Plan of San Diego: Unrest on the Texas Border in 1915," *Arizona and the West,* 5, no. 4 (Winter 1963): 330–336; Walter Prescott Webb, *The Texas Rangers,* 2nd ed. (Austin: University of Texas Press, 1965), pp. 484–485, 478–479; Juan Gómez-Quiñones, *"Plan de San Diego* Reviewed," *Aztlán* (Spring 1970): 125–126; Charles C. Cumberland, "Border Raids in the Lower Rio Grande Valley—1915," *Southwestern Historical Quarterly* 57 (January 1954): 290–294; *Regeneración,* October 2, 1915.

74. Don M. Coever and Linda B. Hall, *Texas and the Mexican Revolution: A Study in State and National Border Policy, 1910–1920* (San Antonio: Trinity University Press, 1984), p. 87.

75. Coerver and Hall, pp. 85–108.

76. Edwin Larry Dickens, "The Political Role of Mexican-Americans in San Antonio" (Ph.D. dissertation, Texas Tech University, 1969), p. 38. Also see George Marvin, "The Quick and the Dead on the Border," *The World's Word* (January 1917): 295.

77. Webb, pp. 474, 475, 478.

78. Grebler, Moore, and Guzmán, p. 84.

79. Lawrence A. Cardoso, *Mexican Emigration to the United States, 1897–1931* (Tucson: University of Arizona Press, 1980), pp. 52–53.

80. Jamieson, p. 260.

81. Gómez-Quiñones, "The First Steps," pp. 28–29; *Regeneración,* October 15, 1910; Zamora, pp. 227–230.

82. Julie Leininger Prycior, *"La Raza* Organizes: Mexican American Life in San Antonio, 1915–1930

as Reflected in Mutualista Activities" (Ph.D. dissertation, University of Notre Dame, 1979), pp. 107–108.

83. Jamieson, p. 59; Hyman Weintraub, "The I.W.W. in California, 1905–1931" (Master's thesis, University of California at Los Angeles, 1947), pp. 5, 9, 16, 18, 49, 50, 68–69, 71–72. See James Weinstein, *The Decline of Socialism in America, 1912–1925* (New York: Knopf, 1967).

84. Samuel Yellen, *American Labor Struggles* (New York: Russell, 1936) pp. 205–206; Colorado Adjutant General's Office, *The Military Occupation of the Coal Strike Zone of Colorado by the National Guard, 1913–1914;* Walter Fink, *The Ludlow Massacre, 1914;* George P. West, *Report on the Colorado Strike,* U.S. Commission on Industrial Relations, 1915, reprinted in Leon Stein and Philip Taft, eds., *Massacre at Ludlow. Four Reports* (New York: Arno Press, 1971), esp. pp. 15–16, 31.

85. Fink, p. 75; Colorado Adjutant General's Office, pp. 60–61; West, p. 124, 135; Yellen, pp. 234–235, 240–241; Gómez-Quiñones, "The First Steps," p. 30; McLean and Thomson, p. 7.

86. Robert Kern, ed., *Labor in New Mexico: Unions, Strikes, and Social History Since 1881* (Albuquerque: University of New Mexico Press, 1983), pp. 6–7.

87. Ricardo Romo, "Response to Mexican Immigration, 1910–1930," *Aztlán* 6, no. 2 (Summer 1975) 186–187.

88. Ralph Guzmán, *The Political Socialization of the Mexican American People* (New York: Arno Press, 1976), pp. 65–66, Gómez-Quiñones, "The First Steps," p. 34; Andrés Jiménez Montoya, *Political Domination in the Labor Market: Racial Division in the Arizona Copper Industry,* Working Papers Series, (Berkeley, Calif.: Institute for the Study of Social Change, 1977), p. 12.

89. Jeffrey M. Garcilazo, "Mexican Strike Activity in the Riverside and San Bernardino Areas, 1917," Annual Association for Chicano Studies Conference, 23 March 1985.

90. Gómez-Quiñones, "The First Steps," p. 35; Reisler, "Passing Through Our Egypt," p. 69.

91. Jamieson, p. 63; Kushner, p. 53; Garcilazo, p. 10.

92. Taylor, *Mexican Labor,* vol. 2, pp. 114–117; Romo, "Responses to Mexican Immigration," pp. 187–190; "The Commission of Inquiry, Interchurch World Movement, *Report on the Steel Strike of 1919* (New York: Harcourt Brace Jovanovich, 1920), pp. 3, 132–133.

93. McLean and Thomson, pp. 29–30, 34.

94. García, "Racial Dualism," pp. 197–218; Mario T. García, "Obreros: The Mexican Workers of El Paso, 1900–1920" (Ph.D. dissertation, University of California at San Diego, 1975), pp. 199, 201–205.

95. Irving Bernstein, *History of the American Worker 1920–1933: The Lean Years* (Boston: Houghton-Mifflin, 1960), pp. 47–50.

96. Prycior, pp. 15–17; Frances Jerome Woods, *Mexican Ethnic Leadership in San Antonio* (Washington, D.C.: Catholic University Press, 1949), p. 20; Emilio Zamora, "Mexican Labor Activity in South Texas, 1900–1920" (Ph.D. dissertation, University of Texas, Austin), p. 160; Julia Kirk Blackwelder, *Women of the Depression: Caste and Culture in San Antonio, 1929–1939* (College Station: Texas A&M Press, 1984), p. 18.

97. Kathleen González, "The Mexican Family in San Antonio," (Master's thesis, University of Texas at Austin, 1928), pp. 5–6; Prycior, p. 77.

98. Prycior, pp. 83, 97–98, 105.

99. Adela Sloss Vento, *Alonso S. Perales: His Struggle for the Rights of Mexican-Americans* (San Antonio: Artes Gráficas, 1977), p. vii.

100. Meyer Weinberg, *A Chance to Learn: A History of Race and Education in the United States* (New York: Cambridge University Press, 1977), pp. 145–165.

101. The title is taken from Guadalupe Compean, "Where Only the Weeds Grow: An Ecological Study of Mexican Housing in Boyle Heights, 1910–1940" (Unpublished paper, School of Architecture and Urban Planning, University of California, Los Angeles, December 1984).

102. Ricardo Romo, *East Los Angeles: History of a Barrio* (Austin: University of Texas Press, 1983), p. 102.

103. Pedro Castillo, "The Making of a Mexican Barrio: Los Angeles, 1890–1920" (Doctoral dissertation, University of California, Santa Barbara, 1979), p. 20.

104. John Emmanuel Kienle, "Housing Conditions Among the Mexican Population of Los Angeles" (Master's thesis, University of Southern California, 1912), p. 6; Castillo, p. 104.

105. Cloyd V. Gustavson, "An Ecological Analysis of the Hollenbeck Area of Los Angeles" (Master's thesis, University of Southern California 1940), p. 43.

106. Elizabeth Fuller, "The Mexican Housing Problem in Los Angeles," in Carlos E. Cortés, ed., *Perspectives on Mexican-American Life* (New York: Arno Press, 1974), p. 6; Mark Reisler, "Passing Through Our Egypt," p. 153; Romo, "Mexican Workers," p. 84.

107. Compean, p. 4; William Wilson McEuen, "A Survey of the Mexicans in Los Angeles" (Master's thesis, University of Southern California, 1914), p. 36.

108. Quoted in Romo, "Mexican Workers," p. 95.

109. Romo, *East Los Angeles,* pp. 138, 149; Reisler, *By the Sweat of Their Brow,* pp. 85–86, 169.

110. Romo, "Mexican Workers," pp. 186–188.

111. Reisler, *By the Sweat,* pp. 99–102.

112. Paul S. Taylor, "Crime and the Foreign Born: The Problem of the Mexican," in Carlos E. Cortés, ed., *The Mexican-American and the Law* (New York: Arno Press, 1974), p. 232.

113. *El Trabajo,* April 18, May 16, May 23, June 11, June 14, June 26, July 31, 1925.

114. Quoted in Taylor, "Crime and the Foreign Born," p. 232.

115. Taylor, "Crime and the Foreign Born," pp. 224, 225, 235; Reisler, p. 194; quoted in Taylor, "Crime and the Foreign Born," p. 235.

116. Paul Livingston Warnshuis, *Crime and Criminal Justice Among Mexicans of Illinois,* in Cortés, *The Mexican-American and the Law,* pp. 282–284.

117. Warnshuis, pp. 287, 320. See also Louise Año Nuevo Kerr, "The Chicano Experience in Chicago: 1920–1970" (Ph. D. dissertation, University of Illinois at Chicago Circle, 1976), pp. 36, 39, 47, 49–50, 52, 53; Reisler, *By the Sweat of Their Brow,* pp. 141–142.

118. Kerr, pp. 54–58; Taylor, *Mexican Labor,* vol. 2, p. 135. For good contemporary accounts of Protestant missionary work, see Cortés, *Church Views of the Mexican American,* esp. Vernon M. McCombs' essay "From Over the Border," pp. 91, 92, 135, 151.

119. Linna E. Bressette, *Mexicans in the United States: A Report of a Brief Survey,* in Cortés, *Church Views of the Mexican American,* p. 8.

120. John R. Scotford, *Within These Borders* (New York: Friendship Press, 1953), p. 105.

121. Kerr, pp. 76–77. For a glimpse of life in Chicago, see Robert C. Jones and Louis Wilson, *The Mexican in Chicago,* in Cortés, *Church Views of the Mexican-American.* and Stanley A. West, *The Mexican Aztec Society: A Mexican-American Voluntary Association in Diachronic Perspective* (New York: Arno Press, 1976), pp. 98, 137, 139, 140 deals with Mexicans in Pennsylvania. and Barbara June Macklin, *Structural Stability and Cultural Change in a Mexican-American Community* (New York: Arno Press, 1976), p. 30 focuses on Toledo, Ohio; and, "Minnesotans of Mexican Heritage," *Gopher Historian* 26, no. 1 (Fall 1971): 7 Carl Wittke, *We Built America,* rev. ed. (Cleveland: Case Western Reserve University, 1966, p. 466 states that *La Sociedad Mutualista Mexicana* was established soon afterward in St. Paul.

122. McLean and Thomson, pp. ix, x, 17.

123. Paul Morgan and Vince Mayer, "The Spanish-Speaking Population of Utah: From 1900 to 1935" (Working Papers Toward a History of the Spanish-Speaking People of Utah, American West Center, Mexican-American Documentation Project, University of Utah, 1973), pp. 32–34, 41, 46–47, 50–52.

124. Erasmo Gamboa, "Chicanos in the Northwest: An Historical Perspective," *El Grito* (Summer 1973): 58–59, 60–62; Richard W. Slatta, "Chicanos in the Pacific Northwest: An Historical Overview of Oregon's Chicanos," *Aztlán* (Fall 1975): 328–329; Erasmo Gamboa, "Under the Thumb of Agriculture: Braceros and Mexican American Workers in the Pacific Northwest" (Ph.D dissertation, University of Washington, 1984), pp. 24–26.

125. Reisler, *By the Sweat of Their Brow,* pp. 77–78.

126. Royce D. Delmatier, Clarence F. McIntosh, and Earl G. Waters, eds., *The Rumble of California Politics, 1848–1970* (New York: Wiley, 1970), pp. 212, 216–217; Carey McWilliams, *Factories in Fields: The Story of Migratory Labor in California* (Santa Barbara and Salt Lake City: Peregrine Publishers, 1971) pp. 185, 188; Jamieson, pp. 71–72.

127. Carey McWilliams, *California: The Great Exception* (Westport, Conn.: Greenwood Press, 1949), p. 95; McWilliams, *Factories in Fields,* p. 117; Galarza, *Farm Workers,* p. 98; Reisler, "Passing Through Our Egypt," pp. 138–139; and Jamieson, p. 70 deal with California Farms; John Phillip

Carney, "Postwar Mexican Migration: 1945–1955, with Particular Reference to the Policies and Practices of the United States Concerning Its Control" dissertation, University of Southern California, 1957, p. 19, focus on mechanization.

128. Herbert B. Peterson, "Twentieth-Century Search for Cibola: Post World War I Mexican Labor Exploitation in Arizona," in Manuel Servín, ed., *An Awakening Minority: The Mexican American,* 2nd ed. (Beverly Hills, Calif.: Glencoe Press, 1974) pp. 117, 119–121.

129. Peterson, pp. 122, 123; Jamieson, p. 195; Montejano, p. 18; Taylor, *American-Mexican Frontier,* pp. 101, 103.

130. Reisler, *By the Sweat of Their Brow,* p. 102; Kerr, pp. 25–26, 33–36; George Hinman, *Report of the Commission on International and Interracial Factors in the Problems of Mexicans in the United States,* National Conference concerning Mexican and Spanish Americans in the United States (Austin: University of Texas, 1926), pp. 14, 27, 29; Taylor, *Mexican Labor,* vol. 2, pp. 111–112, 119–120, 222, 229; Immigration Committee, "Mexican Immigration," Chamber of Commerce of the United States, Washington, D.C., July 1930 (draft in the Bancroft Library), pp. 21, 27; Reisler, "Passing Through Our Egypt," pp. 102–103: Selden C. Menefee, *Mexican Migratory Workers of South Texas* (Washington, D.C.: Works Progress Administration, 1941), reprinted in Cortés, *Mexican Labor in the United States,* pp. 17–26, 41.

131. Coalson, p. 36; Reisler, *By the Sweat of Their Brow,* p. 88; Mark Erenberg, "A Study of the Political Relocation of Texas-Mexican Migratory Farm Workers to Wisconsin" (Ph.D. dissertation, University of Wisconsin, 1969), p. 11; Immigration Committee, p. 11; McWilliams, *Factories in Fields,* p. 89; Briegel, p. 94; Taylor, *Mexican Labor,* p. 184; Gamio, p. 86; Jamieson, pp. 236–239.

132. Montejano, pp. 7, 8, 22, 24, 27, 35; Taylor, *American-Mexican Frontier,* p. 150; Coalson, p. 26; Montejano, pp. 35–37; Carey McWilliams, *Ill Fares the Land: Migrants and Migratory Labor in the United States* (New York: Arno Press, 1976), p. 264.

133. Lowenstein, p. 25; Chaffee, p. 7; Jamieson, p. 76; Hinman, p. 80; Joan London and Henry Anderson, *So Shall Ye Reap* (New York: Crowell, 1971), p. 25; Weintraub, p. 164; McWilliams, *California,* p. 148.

134. Orville Merton Kile, *The Farm Bureau Through Three Decades* (Baltimore: Waverly Press, 1948); William J. Block, *The Separation of the Farm Bureau and the Extension Service* (Urbana: University of Illinois Press, 1960); Samuel R. Berger, *Dollar Harvest: The Story of the Farm Bureau* (Lexington, Mass.: Heath, 1971); Clark A. Chambers, *California Farm Organizations* (Berkeley: University of California Press, 1952), p. 22. Grant McConnell, *The Decline of Agrarian Democracy* (Berkeley: University of California Press, 1957), p. 160.

135. Jamieson, p. 75; *Report of Governor C.C. Young's Fact Finding Committee in California,* October 1930 (Reprint, San Francisco: R & E Research Associates, 1970), p. 123, 126; George T. Edson, "Mexicans in the Beet Fields of Northern Colorado," August 27, 1924, in the Bancroft Library, pp. 5–10; Lowenstein, p. 25; Jamieson, p. 76; Robin Fitzgerald Scott, "The Mexican-American in the Los Angeles Area, 1920–1950: From Acquiescence to Activity" (Ph.D. dissertation, University of Southern California, 1971), pp. 25–26; Charles Wollenberg, "Huelga, 1928 Style: The Imperial Valley Cantaloupe Worker's Strike," *Pacific Historical Review* (February 1969): 48.

136. Galarza, "Without Benefit of Lobby," p. 81.

137. Cardoso, "Mexican Emigration," p. 97; Reisler, *By the Sweat of Their Brow,* pp. 39, 50–51, 53; Reisler, "Passing Through Our Egypt," pp. 84–85; Morgan and Mayer, pp. 8, 39; *El Universal* quoted Herbert B. Peterson, "Twentieth-Century Search for Cibola's Post World War I Mexican Labor Exploitation in Arizona," in Manuel Servín, ed., *An Awakening Minority: The Mexican-American,* 2nd ed. (Beverly Hills, Calif.: Glencoe Press, 1974), pp. 127–128.

138. U.S. Department of Labor, *Annual Report of the Commissioner General of Immigration* (Washington, D.C.: Government Printing Office, 1923), p. 16; Reisler, *By the Sweat of Their Brows,* pp. 55, 66–69; Neal, pp. 106, 107–108.

139. Quoted in Neal, p. 112.

140. Quoted in Neal, p. 113.

141. Quoted in Neal, p. 117.

142. U.S. Department of Labor, *Annual Report of the Commissioner General of Immigration* (Washington, D.C.: Government Printing Office, 1926), p. 10.

143. U.S. Congress, House Committee on Immigration and Naturalization, *Seasonal Agricultural Laborers from Mexico: Hearing No. 69.1.7 on H.R. 6741, H.R. 7559, H.R. 9036,* 69th Cong., 1st sess. (1926), p. 24.

144. U.S. Congress, *Seasonal Agricultural Laborers,* p. 190.

145. U.S. Congress, *Seasonal Agricultural Laborers,* p. 325.

146. U.S. Congress, *Seasonal Agricultural Laborers,* p. 112.

147. U.S. Department of Labor, *Annual Report of the Commissioner General of Immigration* (Washington, D.C.: Government Printing Office, 1928), p. 29.

148. Quoted in Robert J. Lipshultz, "American Attitudes Toward Mexican Immigration, 1924–1952" (Master's thesis, University of Chicago, 1962), p. 61.

chapter 7

Mexican American Communities in the Making: The Depression Years

AN OVERVIEW

With the United States at the brink of bankruptcy after the stock market crash, job opportunities dried up, and nativism resurfaced with renewed vigor.[1] Although legal migration slowed to a trickle during the Great Depression, undocumented Mexicans continued to arrive through the revolving door. Mexicans were unwanted, and Euroamerican authorities shipped some 500,000 back to Mexico. A hysterical public treated even Mexican Americans, who were citizens, as aliens. The Mexican American population had changed since the turn of the century; at the start of the 1930s, just under 55 percent lived in urban centers. Migration to the cities quickened during the next ten years, as opportunities in agriculture dried up, with farmers hiring white over brown in California. In Texas, the farmer relied heavily on the undocumented to depress wages even further. Moreover, the gap between the city and rural wages widened.

During the 1930s, driven by desperate conditions, *Mexicanos* permanently broke the stereotype of their docility. A slight majority of the total Mexican population was U.S.-born, making them less vulnerable than in the past.[2] There was no going home for many of them, and they realized that only through organization could they better their situation. Other factors such as the rising nationalism of the 1920s, the example of the Mexican Revolution, and the growing core of proletarianized workers heightened their consciousness. Added to this was the mood of the nation. An ideology of protest legitimized strikes. Leftists, more aware of the divisive nature of racism, encouraged the recruitment of Mexicans and other minorities to progressive causes. New attention was paid to the plight of Chicano farm workers, who had heretofore been ignored by all sectors of organized labor.

The New Deal was a reaction to the restlessness of the 1930s. Intended to reorganize capitalism and head off rebellion, the New Deal also provided the illusion that the workers had a friend in the White House. And although Franklin Roosevelt was immensely popular among Mexicans, most did not benefit from his programs. They were noncitizens and/or agriculture laborers—two sectors generally excluded from New Deal programs. Mexicans who were U.S. citizens also had the burden of proving themselves "Americans."

Other policy changes would, in the long run, help Mexicans, however. The 1930s represented a great leap forward into industrial unionism. Historically, the crafts discriminated against minorities; although by no means pure, the industrial unions were more open to Mexican membership. Encouraged by the National Labor Relations Act (1935)—known as the Wagner Act—industrial unionists challenged the craft-oriented American Federation of Labor by forming the Congress of Industrial Organizations (CIO), which became a rival of the AFL. The CIO sought to organize the nonunionized, including Mexicans. In the restructuring of the labor movement, Chicanos became more actively involved as leaders in newly formed unions.

The picture was not entirely a rosy one. Although the Wagner Act helped organize the industrial sector, it discriminated against Mexicans by excluding farm workers from its protection. This was important, since a substantial portion of the Mexican workforce remained in agriculture. In Texas, some 50 percent of Chicanos were farm laborers. They were left powerless in the face of an agribusiness establishment. If anything, the influence of the American Farm Bureau Federation, the largest association of farmers, increased during the 1930s. At the same time, the farm worker suffered from an expanded labor pool, vigilantes, and the Associated Farmers of America (formed to break farm-worker militancy by any means necessary). The Wagner Act also split the urban and rural proletariats. And, finally, legislation for the benefit of farm labor remained a low priority for organized labor.

The Communist party was an important element in the movement to organize the unorganized. Although its members were idealistic and, to their credit, insisted on organizing on the principle of worker solidarity, a concept that included racial equality, members often played a disruptive role during the first half of the 1930s by party building at the expense of worker solidarity. They sometimes lost sight of the fact that Mexican nationalism was a necessary step in achieving worker unity. During the second half of the decade, the party changed its tactics and joined the organizing efforts of the CIO, adding to worker unity and breaking down some barriers to Mexicans joining unions. In general, however, racism in the trade union movement remained very much alive.

The Communist party also widened the options for the poor to other forms of resistance. In 1925, it had organized the International Labor Defense (ILD) to give workers legal support. The ILD offered invaluable assistance, taking on issues such as immigration and housing. Throughout the 1930s, the ILD also mobilized those who were out of work into Unemployed Councils (by mid-decade, the councils merged with the Workers Alliance). More often than not, although originated by the communists, the ILD and the councils were led by grass-roots workers with no affiliation with the party.[3]

Mexican women worked in industries, such as agriculture, garment, and food processing, in which conditions worsened in the 1930s. Sweatshops were common. Chicanas broke the stereotype that they were docile and unorganizeable. One-fifth of Chicanas in the workforce were employed in agriculture, and they participated in the militant strikes, either in the fields or in worker camps. In the canneries, garment factories, and pecan-shelling industry, Chicanas were in the vanguard of the rank and file. The formation of the CIO and the United Cannery, Agricultural, Packing, and Allied Workers of America (UCAPAWA) gave Chicanas more alternatives; Chicana leaders emerged within the ranks of UCAPAWA and the International Ladies Garment Workers Union (ILGWU).

During the depression years, the hegemony of the Mexican American middle class as the sole advocate for Mexicans was challenged. Still, private and public agencies looked to this sector as the legitimate voice of the community. Often its own class interests conflicted with ethnic and racial pride, since it viewed its mission as uplifting the Chicano poor and facilitating their Americanization. On the other hand, sometimes the class interests of the bourgeoisie clashed with those of the poor, and middle-class Mexican Americans resented attempts to radicalize that community. At the same time, progessive trends existed within the middle class in the protection of Mexican rights. During the 1930s, national Mexican American organizations such as the League of United Latin American Citizens (LULAC) and the Mexican American Movement (MAM) represented currents within the middle class.

This chapter deals with these trends in the context of Mexicans in rural and urban labor, and their response to urbanization, dispersal, and nativist reactions on the part of Anglos. Within this framework, Chicano communities in urban centers took on their own character. By the 1930s, San Antonio's West Side had formed its roots. During this decade, too, migration to Los Angeles accelerated. Mexicans lived throughout Los Angeles County, dispersed in agricultural *colonias,* near brickyards, and in the East Side. During the 1930s Mexicans were in the process of forging communities. Significant events were taking place on a national scale as well. The New Deal, through the massive investment of capital, was helping develop the Southwest. In the 1930s, heavy industry moved into Los Angeles. Other private industries and, later in the decade, defense contractors, encouraged by cheap land, cheap labor, the lack of unions, and low taxes, began settling in the region. Transformations in the labor market, along with the arrival of the bulldozer, altered the way of life for Chicanos.

THE NATIVIST DEPORTATIONS OF THE 1930s

Measures to control immigration had already been initiated during the Calvin Coolidge administration, whose policy Herbert Hoover continued. The consulate in Mexico City restricted visas, and the U.S. formed its first border patrol. However, many Anglo-Americans, feeling that administrative restrictions were not enough, became more vocal. At the House Committee on Immigration and Naturalization hearings in 1930, debates were a replay of previous sessions. Agricultural and industrial interests again defended the Mexicans' "special standing" and again nativists opposed them. The Harris bill, one of the several bills introduced in 1930, advanced three new arguments for restriction: widespread unemployment, racial undesirability, and un-Americanism.[4]

The best example of overt racism can be found in a report prepared for Representative John Box of Texas by Dr. Roy L. Garis of Vanderbilt University. Garis reported to the congressional committee as an authority on eugenics that "the following statement made to the author by an American who lives on the border seems to reflect the general sentiment of those who are deeply concerned with the future welfare of this country:

> 'Their [the Mexicans'] minds run to nothing higher than animal functions—eat, sleep, and sexual debauchery. In every huddle of Mexican shacks one meets the same idleness, hordes of hungry dogs, and filthy children with faces plastered with flies, disease, lice, human filth, stench, promiscuous fornication, bastardy, lounging, apathetic peons and lazy squaws, beans and dried chili, liquor, general squalor, and envy and hatred of the gringo. These people sleep by day and prowl by night like coyotes, stealing anything they can get their hands on, no matter how useless to them it may be. Nothing left outside is safe unless padlocked or chained down. Yet there are Americans clamoring for more of this human swine to be brought over from Mexico.'

Garis's American said that the only difference between Mexican women of the lower and higher classes was that high-class Mexican women were just more "sneaky in adultery."[5]

At the same hearings, a prominent Pasadena, California, medical doctor testified: "The Mexican is a quiet, inoffensive necessity in that he performs the big majority of our rough work, agriculture, building, and street labor. They have no effect on the American standard of living because they are not much more than a group of fairly intelligent collie dogs."[6]

In the Senate the Harris bill was placed on the calendar without scheduled hearings. If applied it would have reduced the number of Mexicans entering the country annually from 58,000 to 1,900. It obviously discriminated against Mexicans, because it singled them out as the only group to be withdrawn from special status. Harris complained that Mexican immigration was especially offensive, since Mexico sent the largest number of undesirables to the United States. He cited unemployment among Anglo-Americans and made unsubstantiated statements to alarm listeners about the number of Mexicans entering the United States. For example, he claimed that "thousands and thousands" of Mexicans were "subject to charity" in the southwestern states, that a third of the children born in California were Mexicans, and that in a few years Mexicans would take over. The Harris bill passed the Senate by voice vote of 51 to 16. On May 15 senators referred the bill to the House, where it was placed on the calendar.

Proponents of the bill maintained that Mexican migration had slowed only temporarily and that, as soon as the economic situation bettered here or there was trouble in Mexico, Mexicans would return. Again, as in the congressional debates of the 1920s, agricultural and industrial interests lobbied against the bill. They argued that, after all, the Mexican was preferable to the "Filipino or Puerto Rican." By August of 1930 the House had still not taken action on the bill, but by that time the depression had reduced the number of Mexicans entering the United States with documents to a few hundred and the House saw no reason to pursue the issue.[7]

The Solution to the "Mexican Problem"

Recent studies estimate that 500,000 to 600,000 "Mexicans and their U.S.-born children departed from 1929–1939."[8] It is speculated that half this number came from Texas. Generalizing from this experience, researchers believe that little difference existed between the deportee and the repatriated Mexicans. Authorities manipulated the process to drive Mexicans out of the country and, in the case of the U.S.-born children, between 60 and 75 percent of the total, they had little choice.

At this point, the repatriation process can be divided into two parts: (1) the urban-based programs, centering in southern California and the Midwest, and (2) the rural-based programs, or more specifically the Texas experience. As mentioned, administrative control of Mexican migration had begun in 1928. When the Great Depression devastated the country, nativist sentiment to exclude Mexicans galvanized. However, because of the interest of the Hoover administration in bettering relations with Mexico, as well as the opposition of agricultural interests seeking a surplus of Mexican labor, a concrete national policy toward repatriation did not develop. "It is important to note [that] sentiment against Mexican immigration did not spring exclusively from conditions of the Great Depression but had been growing since the mid-1920s."[9] Every year since the passage of the 1924 Immigration Act, a national debate to exclude Mexicans resurfaced. The depression merely spurred local action, as the press, the public, and organizations—from the AFL, to the American Legion, to the American Eugenics Society—lined up to back the deportation of Mexicans.

In general, the repatriation programs that emerged during this period were highly decentralized, although they followed a definite pattern: Hoover's scapegoating of the undocumented workers for unemployment and the depression encouraged the popularization of nativist programs. At the national level, U.S. consuls restricted the number of visas issued and strictly enforced the terms of the Immigration Act of 1924, which excluded those "likely to become a public charge." Secretary of Labor William N. Doak stated, "My conviction is that by strict limitation and a wise selection of immigration, we can make America stronger in every way, hastening the day when our population shall be more homogeneous."[10]

On January 6, 1931, Doak requested that Congress appropriate funds for the deportation of illegals from the United States. He alleged that an investigation revealed that 400,000 aliens had evaded immigration laws and that at least a fourth of these illegals were readily deportable. "Doak's immigration agents raided both public and private places seeking aliens who were deportable, and they did so in a search which extended from New York to Los Angeles." The California Senate considered a bill to prohibit "illegal aliens from engaging in business or seeking employment, and making it a misdemeanor to have such an alien as a partner."[11] Antiforeign sentiment reached its zenith during this period of insecurity.

Local authorities throughout the Southwest and the Midwest emulated the actions of the chief executive; they went one step further and devised a program to encourage even documented immigrants to return to Mexico. They seized on Doak's statements, newspapers drummed the "take care of our own" theme, and they manufactured an enemy. Los Angeles papers ran articles with titles such as "U.S. and City Join in Drive on L.A. Aliens." They played up alleged Mexican crime, sensationalizing themes of shootings, fights, and rapes. They also applied the label "alien" to all Mexicans.[12]

On January 6, 1931, C. P. Visel, the Los Angeles local coordinator for unemployment relief, urgently requested guidance in a wire to Washington, D.C.:

> We note press notices this morning, figure four hundred thousand deportable aliens United States. Stop. Estimate five percent in this district. Stop. We can pick them all up through police and sheriff channels. Stop. United States Department of Emigration incapacitated to handle. Stop. You advise please as to method of getting rid. Stop. We need their jobs for needy citizens.[13]

Visel circulated leaflets in the Mexican community stating that deportations would include all Mexicans, legal or illegal. He admitted that he wanted to intimidate illegals and force them to abandon the Los Angeles areas.

Concerned over loss of Mexican labor, the Los Angeles Chamber of Commerce criticized Visel's actions and warned him that the Mexican community would misunderstand the "wholesale raids"; Visel did not moderate his attacks and issued press releases advertising arrests of Mexicans. He warned that "20,000 deportable aliens were in the Los Angeles area." So blatant were the raids that the normally apathetic Chicano business leaders protested the treatment of nationals to authorities both in Washington, D.C., and Mexico City.[14] The protests did not dissuade immigration authorities. On the 26th of February at 3 P.M., aided by a dozen police, they surrounded the Los Angeles *plaza,* detained over 400 people for over an hour, and arrested 11 Mexicans and 9 Chinese. They released 9 of the Mexicans the next day. In the next months authorities rounded up 3,000 to 4,000 Mexicans and held them without benefit of counsel.

Local officials continued to devise programs to encourage Mexicans to return home. In California charity organizations and the California Department of Unemployment cooperated. When a Mexican approached these agencies for assistance, a case worker called on the family and attempted to persuade them they would be happier in Mexico. If a Mexican agreed to return, fare and subsistence to the border were paid for the entire family. In many instances local authorities used the Mexican consul to help "persuade" the welfare recipient to return.

Generally, fathers wanted to leave, since they had never intended to stay permanently, but the children had friends here, were U.S. citizens, and desired to remain. Some teenage children bitterly resented being uprooted. The mother was caught between her husband and her children. When the client hesitated, the welfare or case worker became more persuasive. Just how persuasive officials were is open to conjecture, since local authorities always maintained that returns were voluntary. However, two leading authorities on the Chicano in the 1930s contradict local authorities' interpretation of "voluntary." Professor Norman D. Humphreys of Detroit wrote:

> Even the families of naturalized citizens were urged to repatriate, and the rights of American-born children to citizenship in their native lands were explicitly denied or not taken into account. The case workers themselves brought pressures to bear in the form of threats of deportation, stoppage of relief (wholly or in part, e.g., in matters of rent, or by means of trampling on customary procedures).[15]

Repatriation was severe in the Midwest. A disproportionate number of Mexicans were deported from Illinois, Michigan, Indiana, and Ohio. Newspapers there began a campaign to discredit the Mexicans, and by the mid-1930s job discrimination and exclusion from federal projects convinced many Mexicans to return to *la tierra del sol* (the land of the sun).

According to some experts, the repatriation program was allegedly a "money-saving device." Enthusiasm for the program lessened as local authorities learned that funds from the Reconstruction Finance Corporation (RFC) could no longer be used for the transportation of repatriates. For example, in the first three years of the Los Angeles program, 1931 to 1934, the county shipped 12,668 Chicanos back to Mexico at a cost of $181,228, whereas from 1935 to 1938 it shipped only 3,560 at a cost of $160,781.[16] Officials kept accounts to be sure their programs continued to yield a savings. Carey McWilliams underscored the dollars-and-cents approach: "It cost the County of Los Angeles $77,249.29 to repatriate one train load, but the savings in relief amounted to $347,468.41"—a net savings of $270,219.12.[17]

The facts, however, indicate that the repatriation was more than a "money-saving device," and popular support for the deportations suggests a nativist solution to the "Mexican problem." Mexican reaction to the repatriation was mixed. Officially, the Mexican government said that it welcomed back its prodigal children and assumed responsibility for transportation from the border, acting like Lazarillo's *hidalgo* (a nobleman), publicly sucking a toothpick while starving to death. Unofficially, the Mexican government did not have the resources to absorb such massive numbers. It knew, however, that repatriation would become deportation if it did not cooperate. Saving face, its consuls were helpful, at least, in making the process organized. The Mexican press was not as generous. The

Excelsior on May 11, 1931, called U.S. actions "shameful from the legal and humanitarian point of view."[18]

Deportation and Dislocation in Texas

The Texas Repatriation program differed from that in other states because it was largely rural. Antipathy toward Mexicans in Texas was not new, of course. The displacement of the Mexican population had begun immediately after the Anglo-American invasion of Texas. "In 1856 the entire Mexican population of Colorado County was arrested and ordered to leave the state." This pattern continued throughout the nineteenth century and into the twentieth. "Harassment of Texas Mexicans by vigilance groups [1915–1916] became so severe that an estimated 25,000 Valley residents were driven across the Río Grande into Mexico."[19] The post–World War I recessions, 1919–1923, also encouraged the repatriation of thousands of Mexicans.

The federal deportation campaign actually began some 18 months before the Great Depression, intensifying between 1929 and 1931. As in the case of urban repatriation, the threat of deportation drove many Texas Mexicans out of the country. Since unemployment was not widespread in 1928, and no effort was made to justify the deportation on economic grounds, the conclusion can be reached that racism was the primary factor. Gross violations of human rights took place: authorities often did not permit deportees to sell their property or collect wages; the healthy and the sick alike were shipped off and often families separated. Long-time U.S. residents were as vulnerable as transients; even U.S.-born children received no special protection. For example, in February 1931, Mrs. Angeles Hernández de Sánchez, who had lived in the United States for 14 years, returned from a long visit in Chihuahua. Authorities detained her for medical reasons and proof of residence. Although an examination proved that she did not have VD and she was able to verify her residence, the doctor stated that he suspected she had syphilis. The Department of Labor ordered Mrs. Hernández and her children deported. In Juárez Hernández worked as a servant. In 1938, when she applied for reentry, authorities denied her petition on the grounds that she had been deported. Hernández's fate as well as that of her two U.S.-born children is unknown.[20]

Mexicans who challenged the deportations were denied fair hearings. In July 1931, federal judge F. M. Kennerly heard the evidence in 83 cases, 70 of which violated immigration statutes, in *one* six-hour session. Kennerly found all of the immigration defendants guilty. The court deported 49 of them and jailed the rest. In Laredo, that same year, the same judge heard 98 cases in three hours and convicted all the defendants, deporting 72 and jailing 26.[21]

In rural Texas, transformations on the farms led to severe dislocations of Mexicans. In 1930, 35 percent of Mexicans worked as agricultural laborers, 15 percent as tenant farmers. Texas farmers, like other Euro-American farmers, did not fully participate in the golden 1920s. Texas agriculture had suffered financially since the end of World War I. Cotton production was especially affected, and, consequently, so were tenants and field workers. Competition from Egyptian, Brazilian, and Indian farmers cut their share of the world market. Increased surpluses and the sudden drop in prices further affected the industry. Between 1929 and 1940, moreover, Texas cotton acreage decreased by 60 percent; Mexicans farmed much of this marginalized land and, consequently, they were displaced.

The Texas Cotton Acreage Control Law of 1931 accelerated the reduction in the cotton harvest. It drove many tenant farmers and migrants off the land, with many moving to the cities while others went south. Although the law was declared unconstitutional, it devastated the tenant farmer, since landlords, anticipating that their allocations would be reduced, failed to renew their contracts with the tenants.

The Agricultural Ajustment Act (AAA) of 1933 had a similar affect. Texas farmers eagerly took part in the AAA's acreage reduction plan. Forty percent of all Texas cotton was destroyed. After 1933, Texas agriculture restructed itself to take full advantage of New Deal subsidies. Not only did the New Deal provide little help for the tenant and the agricultural laborer, but many farmers saved money when they called the immigration authorities to pick up their hired hands or sharecroppers before they paid them.

Natural disasters—droughts, hurricanes, and floods—devastated thousands of other tenants and farm workers. Many Anglo-Americans entered the farm labor market, often displacing Mexicans. Technological innovations also drove Mexicans off the land. Increased use of tractors and cotton sleds reduced the need for labor. From 1920 to 1938, the number of tractors operated in Texas went from 9,000 to 99,000; as a result, between 90,000 and 270,000 Texas farm families lost their livelihood. The price for picking seed cotton also dropped from $1.33 CWT (100 pound) in 1925 to 45¢ in 1933—a decline that spelled starvation for many Mexicans.[22]

The rapid deterioration of agriculture accelerated repatriation; so did the poorly organized relief effort. San Antonio did not have a Community Chest or United Way prior to the depression. The burden of relief fell on the federal government. In programs such as the Federal Emergency Relief Administration (FERA), the Civil Works Administration (CWA), and the Works Progress Administration (WPA), citizenship or first papers were required for employment. In Texas, it was widely publicized that undocumented workers were ineligible for work on these projects. Meanwhile, nativists demanded that federal jobs be limited to Euroamericans.

Mexicans thus had few alternatives. Caught between the inability to find employment and the deportation activities of the Bureau of Immigration, many sought the assistance of the Mexican consuls. In the fall of 1931, from Karnes County alone 2,700 persons returned to Mexico. "By January 1931, 60 percent of the Texas Mexican residents of the Austin area had reportedly returned to Mexico."[23] Most of the returnees were destitute; most had been tenant farmers or farm laborers going back to Mexico. Unlike their Californian or midwestern counterparts, they were not repatriated by welfare agencies but, instead, relied more on consular officials and Mexican and Mexican American organizations.

MEXICAN AMERICAN RURAL LABOR

During the 1930s a succession of catastrophes contributed to a crisis in agricultural which the Great Depression worsened. New Deal programs, intended to help agriculture, had a negative impact on Mexican workers. Along with technological advances, these programs hastened the demise of the small- and middle-sized farmers. Under crop reduction programs, for instance, the land farmed by tenants was the first taken out of production. The displacement of owners and sharecroppers contributed to the swelling of the ranks of rural labor. The lack of support for farm workers also widened the gap between the wages of urban and rural workers. Transformations such as these created a restlessness among workers, culminating in "a series of strikes of unprecedented scope and intensity throughout the country."[24] In the end, Mexican workers suffered greatly from the restructuring taking place in the Southwest in which production became concentrated in the hands of a few.

The Coming of Industrialization on the Farm

California farms were the most specialized and industrialized in the United States. According to Carey McWilliams, "farming [in California] has always resembled mining. . . . The soil is really mined, not farmed." Capital investment ownership was narrowly concentrated: 10 percent of California farms received 53.2 percent of the gross income; 9.4 percent of the farms spent 65 percent of the labor costs; and 7 percent employed 66 percent of all workers. Growers such as Joseph Di Giorgio owned 27 farm properties and leased 11 others; in addition, he purchased enormous quantities of fruit for distribution; he owned a major share of a company that produced 25 million feet of lumber annually; he also owned 37½ percent of Italian Swiss Colony Wine and the Baltimore Fruit Exchange.[25]

Large farming in California had escalated during the 1920s, with rapid expansion in labor-intensive crops like cotton, fruit, nuts, and vegetables, so that to the farmer a large supply of labor meant economic progress. Relations between employers and employees became more distant, resembling urban industrial relations. "The attitudes of seasonal wage laborers to their employers on large farms were no longer like those of the farm hand."[26] Industrialization of agriculture forged a class system resembling that in the urban areas with a definite stratification between growers at the top and migrant labor at the bottom.[27]

New techniques in production developed by federal and state extension services intensified farm industrialization—a process which benefited the farmer but not the farm workers. The California Farm Bureau controlled many activities which federal, state, and county agencies financed. Agriculture was big business. Growers saw themselves as equivalent to urban industrialists and regarded farm workers as equivalent to factory workers. The growers achieved economic rewards and social status equivalent to their industrial counterparts; the rural proletariat, however, was denied advantages of the urban proletariat.

In fact, the unstructured labor market that existed in California agriculture would have been envied by most urban capitalists. There were no unions to protect workers' rights such as seniority; the relationship between employer and employee was completely impersonal; the majority of productive employees were unskilled and available in large numbers; workers were paid by the piece not by the hour; and harvesting prior to 1920 was largely unmechanized.

The depression struck with terrifying force in agriculture. The volume of employed declined and the supply of labor mounted as the urban jobless sought work in the fields. The migrant pool in California expanded from 119,800 in 1920 to 190,000 in 1930 to nearly 350,000 in 1939. By the mid-1930s, Anglos outnumbered Mexicans in the California fields. At the same time, crop prices declined over 50 percent, while mortgage, electricity, water, fertilizer, and transportation expenses decreased little; surpluses piled up. The easiest solution for growers was to lower workers' wages by over 50 percent. This situation contributed to labor unrest throughout the 1930s.

The structure of agriculture in Texas differed from that in California. Up to the most recent times, Texas had housed the largest Mexican population in the United States. In 1930, Mexicans comprised 12 percent of the Texas population. As noted earlier, 50 percent of the Texas Mexican population worked in farming, 15 percent as sharecroppers. In 1930 the number of sharecroppers was 205,122; it declined to 76,468 in 1935 and reached a low of 39,821 in 1940. This process had been accelerated by state and federal acreage control laws that took cotton out of production.

After 1930, farmers also turned increasingly to mechanization, which lessened the demand for year-round labor. Industrialization was slow at first because the cost of machinery was often higher than the cost of employing Mexicans. Growers always threatened to use machines to depress wages. Moving produce sheds into the fields revolutionized harvesting of small vegetable crops and reduced labor costs in that sector. Machines, however, could not inspect, tie, and package vegetables or pick more sensitive varieties. Eventually, too, fruit and vegetable production would fill the labor vacuum left by the reduction in cotton acreage.

The Contract System

Labor contractors operated in agriculture and many other industries including the railroads, construction companies, and the garment trade. They were usually Mexicans who spoke English and thus could deal with both the growers and the labor supply. Mexican labor worked with the contractors because the contractors were familiar with their language and customs, gave them steady employment, and served as brokers to find jobs and arrange transportation to the farms. A sizeable number of the 66,100 Mexicans who left Texas annually worked through contractors. A majority of the some 3,000 to 4,000 who went each year to sugar beet fields in Minnesota, Kansas, and Missouri were recruited by contractors. Another 10,000 left for the sugar beet fields of Michigan and northern Ohio, where contractors handled 85 percent of recruiting and 57 percent of the workers were from Texas.

Labor contractors made substantial profits. They received 5¢ to 10¢ for every 100 pounds of cotton picked plus a daily allowance of $1.50 for transportation and $1.50 for supervising work and weighing. For example, Frank Cortez of San Antonio accumulated several stores, cafes, and a funeral parlor. He had contracts to ship 6,000 workers to Michigan at $1.00 a head. This fee was advanced to Cortez, but it was later taken out of the workers' pay. He did not have overhead cost and recruited right outside his funeral parlor. Cortez sent workers to the Midwest by railroad, truck, and passenger cars. Frequently 60 to 65 Mexicans were packed into a truck. Growers paid Cortez's agent $10 for each worker upon delivery. Passengers often stood all the way, stopping "a few times for bowel evacuation and eating" or for gas and oil.

Most labor contractors did not do the volume that Cortez did and traveled with their crews, acting as straw bosses. Some Mexican workers would work for as many as three employers a day. Employers and contractors charged workers for everything from cigarettes to transportation. Contractors were often paid directly by employers, and they, in turn, paid workers. In the beet industry contractors recruited workers, handled their wages, and ran camps. Pickers often received pay in tickets which could be redeemed at local stores for a discount. To employers, contractors were indispensable, since they delivered a crew on the day promised.

Proponents of the contract system claimed that it was not the cause of exploitation but merely a symptom; they claimed that child labor, substandard wages, and other abuses would have existed even without the system. However, even proponents admitted that contractors contributed to the injustice with excessive fees, overcharged for transportation, housing, and food, and frequently short-weighed pickers. Unscrupulous contractors often absconded with pay or worked in collusion with employers to depress wages. Employers were not liable for injuries and poor conditions and used contractors as insurance against unionization of workers. Understandably, contractors became the main grievance of workers.[28]

MEXICAN AMERICAN FARM WORKERS' REVOLT

Given the industrialization of agriculture, the exploitation of Mexican labor, and the abuses of the contract labor system, conflict would have occurred without the depression; the events of 1929 merely intensified the struggle. Farm industrialists determined to make up their losses. They fixed wages as low as possible. In California, wages plummeted from 35¢ to 50¢ an hour in 1931 to 15¢ to 16¢ an hour by mid-1933.[29]

Conditions forced Mexicans, whom growers had previously considered docile, to become angry strikers. An all-out war erupted in which growers relied on the Immigration Service to deport leaders, pressured state and federal agencies to deny Mexicans relief, used local and state authorities to terrorize workers, killed and imprisoned strikers, and made a sham of any semblance of human rights.

During these desperate times, workers, wanting to believe that their government was a friend, grabbed at straws. New Deal legislation such as the Agricultural Adjustment Act (AAA) and the National Industrial Recovery Act (NIRA), enacted to speed recovery, in fact excluded farm workers from the minimum wage provision. The AAA helped big farmers, paying them to balance supply against demand. The NIRA, for its part, gave the federal government powers to stabilize production and prices. Business people who promised to abide by NIRA standards received a blue eagle. The NIRA recommended maximum hours and minimum wages and prohibited the employment of children under 16. Because of pressure from organized labor, and in an effort to forestall labor legislation, Section 7(a), giving labor the right to organize, was included. It outlawed the "yellow dog" contract that required workers to join company unions. Section 7(a) was, however, not a panacea for labor, and unions interpreted it as antiunion, setting up a paternalistic structure in which government was the final arbiter. But even this legislation excluded farm workers. Nevertheless, farm laborers, believing that the laws applied to them, were encouraged to organize.

In 1930, *La Confederación de Uniones Obreros Mexicanas* (CUOM) was a skeleton of what it had been in 1928. CUOM's example was still fresh to many workers, though. The Mexican Mutual Aid Association of the Imperial Valley also operated. And displaced Mexican laborers in occupations such as mining now worked in the fields. By the 1930s, therefore, the core of politicized Mexicans in agriculture had widened considerably.

Early Attempts at Protest

In the decade of the depression, another current affecting farm labor militancy was Communist party. At the Sixth Congress of the Communist International, the party had given priority to the organization of farm laborers. The party abandoned its "boring from within" strategy and formed the Trade Union Unity League (TUUL) to set up militant trade union organizations. The effect of this action would be a double-edged sword. The party encouraged dual unionism,* an approach that often turned out to be disruptive and divisionist, however.

The party's first noteworthy involvement with Mexican workers was the Imperial Valley strike of 1930.[30] In January 1930, 5,000 Imperial Valley workers walked off the fields. They were led by the Mexican Mutual Aid Association, which had few resources and were vulnerable strikers because many members had no papers. The communists joined the strike, forming the Agricultural Workers Industrial League (AWIL). They accused the Mexican leadership of selling out and/or being reformist. Many members of the *mutualistas* admittedly represented the better-off elements of the community, merchants and tradespeople, and they felt threatened by radical solutions and pushy *gringos*. The tactics of inexperienced communist organizers—who had an antipathy toward Mexican nationalism, and believed that the fall of capitalism was imminent and that they would lead the workers to a Soviet America—created friction. The resulting confusion and lack of unity disillusioned many workers and contributed to the collapse of the strike.

---

*Dual unionism occurs when a second union is established that goes into competition with a legitimate workers' trade union. This competition has the effect of dividing the workers.

Imperial Valley farm workers struck again in February 1930. The strike, which involved native white packers and trimmers, was settled quickly. Workers looked to the spring cantaloupe harvest. The Mexican union was weakened by an internecine struggle between radicals and moderates, by the Mexican consul's conspiring with the Western Growers Protective Association and immigration authorities, and by a power struggle between the AWIL and the Mexican union. Nevertheless, that group provided resources not before available to the Mexican unionists. They had basic tools such as mimeograph machines, the International Labor Defense, and access to liberal organizations and press.[31] Also, to the AWIL's credit it attempted to break down racial barriers; to its discredit it encouraged interracial rivalry by incessantly emphasizing that they believed that the Filipinos were the most militant group. Finally, in April 1930, in an attempt to break the strike, Sheriff Charles L. Gillett conducted wholesale raids, making 103 arrests; eight union leaders were charged with criminal syndicalism; Braulio Orosco and Eduardo Herrera were among those convicted, and were sentenced to San Quentin from 2 to 28 years.

In California Mexicans participated in strikes throughout 1930, 1931, and 1932. In July 1931 the AWIL changed its name to the Cannery and Agricultural Workers Industrial Union (CAWIU). Failure of Mexican unions to gain concessions from employers opened the field for the communist union. In the first years the CAWIU generally joined the strikes after they had started; it was not until November 1932, at Vacaville, California, that it initiated strike activity. In 1933, 37 strikes took place, involving some 47,575 farm workers in California. The CAWIU participated in 25 of these strikes which involved 32,800 workers. Most of the strikes resulted in partial victory.[32]

The Pace Quickens: El Monte and San Joaquin

New Deal legislation passed in 1932 and 1933 helped urban workers, but no relief trickled down to farm laborers. In fact, conditions worsened and strike activities increased during 1933. The berry strike in El Monte and the cotton strike of the San Joaquin Valley stand out.

El Monte was an agricultural center. Although El Monte itself had only 4,000 inhabitants, it served a trade area for 12,000 local residents, 75 percent of whom were Anglos, 20 percent Mexicans, and 5 percent Japanese. The Chicano *barrio,* known as Hicks' Camp, was a shack village located across a dry river gulch from El Monte proper. Many of the 1,100 Mexicans were migratory workers, who constituted the bulk of the town's cheap labor force and earned an average 15¢ to 20¢ an hour.

In May 1933, Chicanos, Japanese, and Anglo workers demanded higher wages. When management refused, they formed a strike committee. The strike began on June 1. The CAWIU joined the strike, at first in cooperation with the Mexican union. Strikers, in an effort to compromise, lowered their initial demand. Growers acted quickly, since the berries were highly perishable, and made a counteroffer that was rejected. The sheriff at first left the strikers alone, but as the harvest season began, he increased pressure on them.

At the request of Armando Flores, the chair of the strike committee, the

Mexican consul, Alejandro Martínez, supported them. A power struggle between the leadership of the CAWIU and the Mexican consul developed. Martínez denounced the CAWIW organizers as "reds." At first the CAWIU gained control of the rank and file, but the Mexican farm labor union gained momentum when it affiliated with *La Confederación de Uniones de Campesinos y Obreros del Estado de California* (CUCOM), which had been recently formed by many of the leaders of the old CUOM."[33] The berry strike encouraged other strike activities; by the middle of June, strikes spread to the onion and celery fields of Venice, Culver City, and Santa Monica, that included 5,000–7,000 workers. On July 15, 1933, CUCOM held its organizing convention.

The Los Angeles Chamber of Commerce became concerned about the strike's duration. Ross H. Gast of the chamber, U.S. Labor Commissioner E. P. Marsh, and U.S. Department of Labor conciliator G. H. Fitzgerald urged the growers to compromise and to offer strikers a package of between 20¢ and 25¢ an hour for a 10-hour day. They pressured strikers to accept the offer, which they rejected. Mediators charged that outside agitators were involved and, in fact, red-baited even leaders such as Flores.

The Japanese consul worked behind the scenes with the Mexican consul to bring about a settlement. On July 6 an agreement was reached. Time favored the growers, since the peak of the harvest season had passed. As a consequence, terms of the agreement were lower than those previously rejected by the union. They called for $1.50 for a 9-hour day or, where the work was not steady, 20¢ an hour. The growers recognized the union whose members were to receive preferential hiring; and scabs were to be fired.

The El Monte strike failed miserably, gaining only in the creation of CUCOM. The CAWIU, a vanguard organization, ought to have been better prepared. Its failure to share control with the workers disillusioned many. Moreover, the CAWIU lost control of the bargaining process. It should have persuaded the workers to cut a deal instead of letting them react emotionally when they were not ready for the consequences. The CAWIU's criticism of Mexican leadership confused many less experienced rank and file members and frustrated the development of indigenous leadership.[34]

After the El Monte berry strike, militancy further intensified, with veterans of that strike exporting their fervor to other parts of California. In this charged climate the CAWIU became more attractive to the rank and file. The August 1933 strikes infused the "workers with a tremendous unifying spirit." The most important of the August strikes was that at the Taugus Ranch. CAWIU organizer Pat Chambers led the strike, which was directed primarily at the California Packing Corporation. The strike encompassed seven counties.[35] Deputies and ranch guards turned the strike into a war, arming themselves and conducting raids on union headquarters and conducting mass arrests and deportations. Growers demanded that the National Guard be sent in.

During the walkout, union organizers noticed the vulnerability of strikers who resided on company property and devised new strategies such as roving pickets. Union organizers, moreover, increasingly concentrated their struggle on the large orchards, attempting to win over the smaller farmers. Strikers got a

25¢ an hour settlement. This partial victory spread worker militancy, but left growers bitter and more resolute to break the worker movement.[36] These disputes set the stage for the San Joaquin cotton strike of October 1933.

In the spring of 1933 San Joaquin cotton growers signed contracts with ginning and banking companies, the Bank of America, the San Joaquin Ginning Company, and the local ginning operations of the Anderson Clayton Company, in return for cash advances for labor costs, seeds, electricity, and other expenses the farmers assigned their crops. Anderson Clayton ginned an estimated 35 percent of the total California and Arizona production, and the Bank of America held mortgages on many farms and leased land to smaller operators. In 1929 over 30 percent of the large-scale U.S. cotton farmers operated in California, with practically all of them producing in the San Joaquin Valley. These interests set wages through the San Joaquin Labor Bureau.

Chambers, an organizer for CAWIU, realized that the ginners and bankers determined wages and he knew that an industrywide contract would have to be negotiated. He therefore attempted to dissuade the workers from striking, but, according to Chambers, they would have walked out with or without the CAWIU. The San Joaquin growers set the price at 40¢ per hundred pounds. The strike committee demanded $1.00 per hundred, the abolition of the labor contract system, and the hiring of union members. Growers refused to negotiate, offering 60¢ CWT. The strike began on October 2. It involved 10,000 to 12,000 workers, 80 percent of whom were Mexican.[37]

Growers closed ranks. On October 10, 1933, in *The Visalia Times Delta,* the Farmers Protective Association of Tulare published a manifesto branding the strike communist. The association promised "armed aid" to ranchers. Local sheriffs dutifully deputized growers.

Growers mobilized for an all-out war. Business leaders, newspapers, chambers of commerce, farm bureaus, elected officials, and local city and county police authorities all supported growers. They arrested strikers, putting them in bullpens. Cotton growers pressured authorities to cut relief payments of Los Angeles residents to force them to work in the fields and even mobilized local schoolchildren. Federal authorities backed the growers and ordered the deportation of strikers L. S. Hill and Rubén Rodríguez. A local sheriff later testified:

> We protect our farmers here in Kern County. They are our best people. They are always with us. They keep the county going. They put us in here and they can always put us out again, so we serve them. But the Mexicans are trash. They have no standard of living. We herd them like pigs.[38]

The strikers had few resources. Many, veterans of other walkouts, earned just enough to get by between strikes. Others had arrived in the San Joaquin Valley with no surplus capital. Emotions reached frenzied levels. Racism and antipathy toward strikes were rampant. According to CAWIU organizer Caroline Decker, it was fortunate that whites had begun to enter the fields that year, since the strike could very easily have deteriorated into a race war.

As expected, on October 4, growers began evicting strikers, who had prepared for this contingency. Union organizers had rented five camp sites at Corcoran, McFarland, Porterville, Tulare, and Wasco. Strikers and their families moved into the camps. Each camp was given complete autonomy, and this self-control contributed to a spirit of unity and consciousness among Mexicans. Union organizers made it clear that if any one of the camp committees voted to break the strike, strike activities would be terminated. The success of the strike depended on the camps. Therefore, top security was maintained, and grower propaganda entering the camps was filtered.[39]

The Corcoran camp in retrospect symbolized the struggle and, according to Chambers, remains a tribute to the leadership and courage of the Mexican family. The Corcoran camp housed 3,780 strikers, who outnumbered the some 2,000 townspeople. An elected committee laid out streets, had toilet facilities dug, maintained sanitation and clean drinking water, settled disputes, and guarded the camp. Barbed wire enclosed the camp and guards were posted at the entrance and exit. There was a tent school for about 70 children and an assembly space for meetings, which were generally presided over by the mayor of the camp, Lino Sánchez. Strikers also held nightly performances that they dubbed an "Aztec Circus."

Chambers feared another Ludlow massacre, since he believed that the governor would yield to grower pressure to send the National Guard; in that eventuality Chambers was prepared to call off the strike. Even so, the number of fatalities that actually took place is not known for sure. At the Corcoran camp one woman died of pneumonia and two infants died of malnutrition.[40] The strikers were so desperate that many refused to sign the return-to-work forms in exchange for relief, or to accept milk for their children on condition that they sign waivers.[41]

Strike leaders devised guerrilla-style pickets—that is, roving caravans would stop at several big farms a day, picket for a while and drive off. The area covered by these guerrilla bands was extensive, over 100 miles of battle front.

Newspaper headlines inflamed growers, who formed the Agricultural Protective Association to hound labor organizers and strikers. Club-wielding growers broke up worker rallies. Finally, on October 11 the ranchers gunned down three strikers; two were murdered at a rally in Pixley and another on a picket line near Arvin. Most sources believed that these murders were planned; a small grower later testified that the violence against the strikers had been discussed at a growers' meeting four days before Pixley.

At Pixley, as unarmed strikers listened to Pat Chambers speak, a dozen cars surrounded the group. The strikers, wanting to avoid a confrontation, returned to the union hall. Farmers fired on them, killing 2 strikers and wounding 11. During the attack growers murdered Dolores Hernández, 52, and Delfino D'Avila, 55. Eight ranchers were tried for the murders, but they were acquitted. The California Highway Patrol (CHP) played a suspect role. B. H. Olivas of Madera stated that "ranchers told our patrolmen that beginning today they would beat to hell every striker who so much as laid a hand on the fences on their properties."[42] The CHP did nothing.

The killing at Arvin occurred almost at the same time. Tension had mounted that morning when the growers and picketers exchanged words—30 armed guards and about 200 picketers faced each other. At about three o'clock, fighting broke out. A prominent grower shot into the crowd, killing Pedro Subía, age 57, and wounding several strikers. Witnesses testified that all the shots came from the growers' side and that the strikers did not have guns. Eyewitnesses also identified the man who shot Subía. And although authorities knew the identity of the murderer, they tried seven picketers for Subía's murder. After the shooting, growers became even more aggressive.

The strike was settled through state intervention. The governor's fact-finding committee on October 23 recommended a compromise, raising the rate to 75¢ per hundred pounds. The committee found gross violations of human rights. Growers agreed to the terms but workers held out for 80¢. The governor then ordered a halt to relief payments, which the workers had just begun to draw to avoid starvation.[43]

The Role of CAWIU

As a result of the cotton strike, the CAWIU gained credibility among Mexican workers. The leadership moved to capitalize on this new popularity. In December the CAWIU again entered the Imperial Valley calling for more militant tactics. Many Mexicans joined the CAWIU but many retained their membership in the Mexican union. In January the CAWIU sent two well-known communist organizers, Dorothy Ray Healy and Stanley Hancock, to the valley. While the entrance of Healy and Hancock generated excitement, according to Pat Chambers, too much time was spent hiding them from police, time which could have been spent organizing.[44]

Police authorities in the Imperial Valley as usual supported the growers. On January 12, 1934, gun-wielding police attacked a union meeting, killing two, one of whom was a child. The CHP arrested 86 strikers in two weeks in August alone. Vigilantes attacked and tear-gassed the strikers at will, and on January 23, they kidnapped American Civil Liberties Union (ACLU) lawyer H. L. Wirin. On February 19, they literally crushed the strike by burning the workers' shacks and evicting 2,000. Meanwhile, even state authorities were shocked at the blatant disregard for the rights of the strikers and forced growers to arbitrate the pea strike in the northern end of the Imperial Valley.

Divisions among the workers widened. Mexican consul Joaquín Terrazas helped form *La Asociación Mexicana del Valle Imperial* (The Mexican Association of the Imperial Valley). The CAWIU immediately branded the *Asociación* a company union. Initially, the Mexican union seized leadership from the CAWIU during the cantaloupe strike of April, when its membership reached 1,806.[45] Although both groups won limited victories, the growers remained in control of the Imperial Valley.

On March 28, 1934, California growers led by the California Chamber of Commerce and the Farm Bureau formed the Associated Farmers of California. The Associated Farmers established an espionage service and employed the Pinkerton Detective Agency. Photos of labor agitators were sent to Frank J. Palomares of the San Joaquin Labor Bureau (SJLB), an organization supported by the industrialist interests in California including growers, sugar companies, oil companies, railroads, and utilities. Many small farmers refused to join the Associated Farmers because they did not identify with it and they were tired of the "bunch of big fellows who ran things." The Associated Farmers controlled local police, "influenced" the state legislature to pass laws that barred picketing, and, finally, secured the arrest and later conviction of labor leaders.[46]

On July 20, 1934, police raided Communist headquarters in Sacramento and confiscated numerous pamphlets and papers. Seventeen communists were indicted and 15 prosecuted on charges of criminal syndicalism. Eight of the 15 were convicted, among them Pat Chambers and Caroline Decker. They spent two years in jail before a higher court overturned the sentences. These arrests and convictions ended the four year career of the CAWIU.

In retrospect the CAWIU had excellent organizers such as Chambers. It had national contacts that called attention to the plight of the workers. Its flaunting of its communist affiliation, on the other hand, invited political repression. The CAWIU leadership, moreover, can be criticized for promoting unnecessary fights with Mexican unions, which they attempted to discredit by describing them as nationalist or reactionary—a tactic that, in this context, is in itself a form of red-baiting. Much too often CAWIU organizers did not understand the history of the people they were attempting to lead. Consequently, too much time and energy were spent fighting the Mexican- and Filipino-led unions.[47] In any event, workers were not dependent on the CAWIU.

Mexican Militancy: CUCOM and UCAPAWA

According to Jamieson, "The most effective agricultural-labor unions during 1935 and 1936 were those organized among Mexicans." The CUCOM continued to form and by 1934 had 10,000 members. Among the Mexican leaders Guillermo Velarde, José Espinosa, and Bernard Lucero stood out. CUCOM participated in the 1934 orange pickers strike in Riverside and San Bernardino. Velarde and Espinosa were active in strikes in 1935 at Chula Vista and 1936 in Compton. During this period, CUCOM's leadership often clashed with the *Comisión Honorífica,* which Mexican consuls controlled.

Factionalism within the CUCOM occurred between radical and moderate members. After the collapse of the CAWIU, Mexicans formed several independent unions. The Mexican Agricultural Workers Union in Santa Barbara led a vegetable workers strike in August 1934. It was a communist union, as was the American Mexican Union in San Joaquin County, which led a cherry strike near Lodi in June 1935. The Mexican Labor Union of the Santa María Valley (an independent) united with Filipinos to strike local growers.

With the demise of the CAWIU, left-wing organizers infiltrated CUCOM which assumed leadership in 6 of the 18 strikes called during 1935. Most of this activity centered in Orange and San Diego Counties. Also because of changing conditions the strikes were small in relation to the massive 1933 confrontations. A positive development was cooperation between CUCOM and Filipino unions.

In January 1936 the CUCOM cooperated in forming the Federation of Agricultural Workers of America which included 11 locals of Filipino, Japanese, and other nationalities. During the spring of 1936 in Los Angeles County, CUCOM led a walkout of 2,600 celery workers: The Los Angeles "red squads" tear-gassed parades and picket lines, beating and arresting union members.[48] A favorite grower tactic in breaking a strike was to withdraw relief. Growers had developed a statewide network and Los Angeles County housed their reserve labor pool.

For the remainder of 1936 CUCOM continued as the vanguard in the fields. In Orange County between 2,500 and 3,000 citrus-fruit pickers and packers went on strike on June 15. Workers averaged 22¢ an hour; they demanded an increase to 27.5¢, transportation, and union recognition. Led by the Associated Farmers, growers recruited 400 special guards. The California Highway Patrol harassed picketers along roads, and police authorities arrested some 200, herding them into stockades. Local newspapers described the situation as a civil war and blamed the communists.[49]

In 1935, the National Labor Relations Act (the Wagner Act), which guaranteed urban workers the right to organize, to engage in collective bargaining, and to strike, pointedly excluded farm workers. During 1937 and 1938, conditions in California verged on class warfare. In 1937 50,000 workers were needed to harvest crops; however, growers attracted 125,000 people and drove wages down to 75¢ to $1.25 a day, paying as low as $3.00 a week.[50]

By this time urban unions paid more attention to their rural counterparts, because they feared that conditions there might endanger their gains. At the same time, Mexican and Filipino unions realized that they were too small and isolated. The CUCOM during 1936 and 1937 negotiated with other ethnic labor unions to form alliances. In July 1937 they sent delegates to Denver and joined the newly formed United Cannery, Agricultural, Packing, and Allied Workers of America (UCAPAWA).

Although Mexican locals and independent unions continued to agitate throughout the 1930s, more and more growers used "Okies" and "Arkies" to break their strikes. Most veteran organizers realized that their only hope was to join UCAPUWA, which had charismatic Latino leaders such as Luisa Moreno. Moreno was the first Latina to serve on the executive committee of UCAPAWA. Born a wealthy Guatemalan, she gave up her inheritance. Working in New York's garment industry before joining UCAPAWA, she organized for the AFL.[51]

The farm struggle was similar in Arizona, where ownership and control of land was even more concentrated than in California. During the depression Arizona became a highway for Dust Bowl refugees en route to California, with 105,105 crossing the Arizona border in 1937 alone. During the 1920s and 1930s the AFL organized there, making early gains among cotton pickers. Organizational efforts met the same fate as in California and the independent unions there eventually consolidated into the UCAPAWA.[52]

Militancy Outside California

Strike activity outside California was also desperate. Conditions for sheep shearers in Texas were markedly worse than in other areas; they earned 5¢ to 6¢ a sheep versus 12¢ to 15¢ in Wyoming, Montana, and California. In 1934 in West Texas about 750 members of the Sheep Shearers Union (SSU) demanded 12¢ per head for sheep and 8¢ for goats (compared to 8¢ and 5¢ then currently paid). The Sheep and Goat Raisers Association refused to negotiate and workers struck in February. The employers pressured state officials to refuse shearers relief and discussed bringing in the Texas Rangers. The usual harassment followed; 42 SSU members were jailed as sheep and goat raisers organized vigilance committees. Ranchers hired white crews to break the Mexican strike; by March they met their goal. In October 1934 a Mexican crew leader by the name of Ramón attempted once more to organize sheepherders, but authorities in Sonora, Texas, arrested Ramón and his men for disturbing the peace.[53]

Many of the displaced strikers migrated permanently to urban centers, where many had lived and worked in the off-season. Until after World War II, this migrancy between the city and farm served as a safety-valve for Mexicans, who bounced between the two sectors, depending on the job market. This phenomenon was common until recent times.

In Texas 85 percent of the state's migrant labor force was Mexican. Although growers claimed a worker shortage, a farm labor surplus was the reality. The sheer size of the state formed an obstacle to farm union organizing and the hub of the migratory stream, the lower Río Grande Valley, was particularly difficult to organize because, first, it was not heavily industrialized and, second, it had a huge labor pool since it bordered Mexico. In the early 1930s, Texas farmers were smaller and more diversified than California growers; agriculture was in transition and the farm hand and sharecropper relationships that still existed were gradually being displaced.

In 1933, in Laredo, Texas, Mexicans fromed an independent union, *La Asociación de Jornaleros. Jornaleros* included hat makers, painters, carpenters, construction workers, miners, and farm laborers. During 1934 agent provocateurs disrupted union activity, but in the spring of 1935 the union led over 1,200 onion workers near Laredo on strike. The strike failed, partly because of the inexperience of the organizers and harassment by Texas Rangers who arrested 56 strikers. The union had refused to sign with individual growers and had held out for an industrywide contract, but were persuaded to return to work by a federal mediation agreement. Growers, however, broke the agreement as soon as the federal mediators left.

In the spring of 1936 workers exchanged delegates with the Farm Workers Union of Mexico and cooperated with communist-led unemployed councils of San Antonio. Relief was a major problem for farm workers throughout the depression. Federal relief agencies excluded migrants and state agencies often required a residency of one year before giving relief. When the *Asociación* attempted to organize workers on relief, local authorities, immigration officials, Texas Rangers, and the U.S. army harassed the *Jornaleros* and its sympathizers as well as members of relief organizations. The *Jornaleros* received a charter from the American Federation of Labor and became the Agriculture Workers Labor Union Local 20212.

In January 1937, the Texas Federation of Labor formed the Texas Agriculture Organizing Committee to organize Mexican farmworkers; it participated in a series of small strikes in late June and early July. However, growers and state authorities countered the TAOC's efforts by controlling the labor pool. The Texas State Employment Service, formed in 1935, recruited workers for the different crops and in 1939 alone placed 550,047 farm workers. The Texas labor pool was just too large to allow for effective organization. In the summer of 1937 the committee was absorbed by UCAPAWA, which eventually recruited 5,000 paid members.

Efforts increased to organize skilled Mexicans and Anglo packing-shed workers in the lower Río Grande Valley. Fruit and Vegetable Workers Local 20363, an AFL affiliate, claimed 500 to 600 members. In February 1938 it led a 50-car caravan across the lower Río Grande Valley protesting antiunion activity in the valley. Economic conditions worsened so that by 1938 all organizing efforts had disappeared.[54]

In Colorado Mexican beet laborers were denied admission to public places and segregated from the mainstream of society. When wages declined drastically in 1932, falling to $12.00 to $14.00 an acre, the Mountain States Beet Growers Association blamed conditions on the sugar-refining companies that preset rates for seasonal contracts between workers and growers. In turn, the refineries claimed that they were losing money. Meanwhile, communists formed the Agricultural Workers Industrial Union, establishing locals in Greeley, Fort Lupton, Fort Collins, and Denver. Mexican workers participated in these and other unions. Various factions in February 1932 formed the United Front Committee of Agricultural Workers Unions and it demanded $23.00 an acre and union recognition, and was active in Colorado, Nebraska, and Wyoming.

On May 10, 1932, it called a strike that was easily broken by the Great Western Sugar Company. Left-wing workers blamed their failure on "conservative" or "reformist organizations" such as the Spanish-American Citizens Association of Fort Collins, but, in fact, the strike was poorly planned. Refining companies had more than enough labor. Public agencies and law enforcement officials cooperated with growers to break the beet workers. Mass arrests and the deportation of militant Mexican members marked the end of the United Front. Mexican workers formed the Spanish-Speaking Workers League in Denver as a vehicle to hold more radical workers together after the 1932 strike.[55]

Nativism intensified in Colorado as the times worsened and Mexicans were laid off WPA projects on the basis of their surnames on the assumption that they were beet laborers. Beet companies, even though prices for sugar increased, kept wages depressed. The TUUL in Colorado formed "unemployed councils" of beet workers for the purpose of agitating for adequate relief; the groups merged with the Colorado State Federation of Labor (CFL). Membership in the council was free, but cards were forfeited when members found a job. The CFL reportedly had 25,000 unemployed members. A few of the councils struck work relief projects to improve conditions and took part in small agricultural strikes.

The Jones-Costigan Act of 1934 gave growers benefit payments averaging $17.15 per acre on the condition that they not use child labor. Stimulated by the ability of growers to pay higher wages, during the next two years labor organization increased. Active was the Beet Workers Association, which claimed 35,000 members in Colorado, Wyoming, Nebraska, and Montana. Based on Jones-Costigan, the workers demanded $23.00 an acre, but the United States Department of Agriculture in Colorado set a rate of $19.50 per acre in northern Colorado and $17.50 for the southern section. The previous year beet laborers had received $13.00 to $14.00 an acre. The Colorado State Federation of Labor in 1935 contributed to the expenses of Mexican organizers in the Beet Workers Association. In 1936 the latter held a convention in Denver attended by 50 delegates representing 39 local organizations in five states. Delegates condemned the practice of closing relief agencies to swell the size of the labor pool. Shortly afterward the CFL held its official convention and it ratified demands of the association and the wage demand of $23.00 per acre. As a result, the Colorado Federation of Agricultural Workers Unions was established; it included diverse groups, such as the *Comisión Honorífica Mexicana* (a protective association under the Mexican consul). Union leaders protested discrimination against Mexican beet workers on relief. The bargaining position of the union had been weakened the year before when the U.S. Supreme Court invalidated the Jones-Costigan Act and large numbers of children returned to the fields. The situation worsened as large numbers of workers were dropped from relief rolls and refineries threatened to import large numbers of workers from New Mexico.

The Sugar Act of 1937 subsidized farmers and empowered the secretary of agriculture to set a minimum wage for beet workers. It was the only piece of labor legislation that directly benefited Mexican farm labor. Discontent among workers with the AFL leadership, nevertheless, increased. Many complained that the AFL gave them insufficient financial and organizational support. And 14 federal unions surrendered their AFL charters and joined UCAPAWA. During 1937 and 1938 conditions worsened; growers were squeezed by refining companies. Surpluses shrank available acreage, and, while small strikes broke out, strategically a general strike was out of question. Migrating Dust Bowl refugees further weakened the union's position. Attempts to form alliances with small farmers against the sugar companies did not materialize, and little progress was made during the rest of the decade.[56]

In 1938, as a result of increased labor activity in the fields throughout the decade, Michigan sugar beet workers struck. In 1935, encouraged by the Jones-Costigan Act, Mexicans joined other nationalities to form the Agriculture Workers Union (AFL). Five hundred members struck that year near Blissfield and won a raise and union recognition. The next year, however, the U.S. Supreme Court declared the Jones-Costigan Act unconstitutional and the growers employed child labor, and imported WPA workers from the cities to break the union. Local authorities deputized over 400 vigilantes. UCAPAWA in 1938 attempted again to unionize workers, but growers broke the drive by importing huge pools of Mexicans.

MEXICAN AMERICAN URBAN LABOR

Los Angeles's mixed farm and industrial economy encouraged the movement of workers to the city. In the mid-1930s, 13,549 farms operated in the county, with

619,769 acres devoted to agriculture. Farming there represented a $76 million industry, surpassing the $23 million produced in the Imperial Valley. Thousands of Mexican workers either passed through Los Angeles or lived there during the off-season with their families. Farm labor strikes in the county spurred militancy among urban workers, and vice versa.[57]

Militancy Among Mexican Women Workers

By the 1930s Mexican women made up a major portion of the labor pool of the garment factories of the Southwest. Los Angeles had an estimated 150 dress factories, employing about 2,000 workers, 75 percent of whom were Mexicans (the rest were Italians, Russians, Jews, and Anglo-Americans). The depression made these poorly paid workers more vulnerable. In the summer of 1933, Los Angeles's garment industry began to revive its production, and the demand for workers increased. Employers, wanting to maximize their profits, hired Mexican women at substandard wages.

Although the NRA code stipulated a pay rate of $15 a week, employers paid 40 percent of the women less than $5 a week, with some earning as little as 50¢ a week. If the women protested, they lost their jobs, and, being Mexicans, public relief or support from local institutions for them was near impossible and subject to deportation. The mass repatriations of the times intimidated the women; if they persisted in protesting, the immigration authorities or local police were alerted. Rosa Pesotta, an organizer for the International Ladies Garment Workers Union (ILGWU), described the plight of the Mexican women:

> Poorly paid and hard driven, many of these agricultural workers, seeking to leave their thankless labors, naturally gravitated to the principal California cities, where compatriots had preceded them. Thus hundreds of Mexican women and girls, traditionally skillful with needle and eager to get away from family domination, had found their way into the garment industry in Los Angeles.[58]

Many of these women were the sole support of a family with an unemployed husband at home. For the most part, they lived in the outskirts of town "at the end of the car-lines, in rickety old shacks, unpainted, unheated, usually without baths and with outside toilets." When in 1933 the ILGWU began to recruit heavily among these Mexican women, they had everything to lose. Pesotta stated, "We get them . . . because we are the only *Americanos* who take them in as equals. They may well become the backbone of our union on the West Coast."

On October 12, 1933, the ILGWU closed down the Los Angeles dress industry, with much of its success attributed to Mexican strikers. When the local radio station was pressured to terminate broadcasting ILGWU news, "some of the Mexican girls solved our problem. At their suggestion, we bought time from another station, *El Eco de México*, in Tijuana, just across the border." Broadcasts at seven each morning transmitted progress of the strike to the Los Angeles Mexican community. The workers stood firm even when manufacturers closed the factories for two months. They responded to a court injunction against picketing by assembling a thousand people in front of the Paramount Dress

Company. Captain William Hynes and the "red squad" were powerless to disperse such a large force. They could only harass the picketers, make them march two abreast, and forbid them to holler "Scab!" Police arrested five strikers for disorderly conduct.

The NRA state board held hearings on October 13, 1933. The press distorted the testimony. Los Angeles employers put pressure on Washington, claiming their employees were "subnormal" and not entitled to minimum wages. The board found that "working conditions should be those established under Section 7(a) of the National Industrial Recovery Act" and, that employers should pay the wages provided in the Code for the dress industry. The workers did not get a contract, and without a signed agreement, they had to rely on the NRA to enforce the order, and from the past record of the NRA, union officials knew this was worthless. Union organizers, however, recommended that workers return and fight to enforce the order from within since they feared factionalism would confuse the workers. A struggle ensued, with the communist-led dual unionists issuing leaflets "Smash the Sellout!" and accusing the ILGWU of collaborating with the bosses. It urged the rank and file to join its dual union, the Needle Trades Workers Industrial Union (NTWIU). The tenure of the NTWIU was brief; it was soon disbanded and its members were ordered to join the ILGWU. Labor strife continued as owners avoided paying the minimum wage to workers. Manufacturers used the Bureau of County Welfare and the Los Angeles County Charities to intimidate workers, sending out ultimatum notices through these agencies' auspices to return to work. Employers did not break worker solidarity, however.

The union continued its activities. Local 96 of the ILGWU had charter members such as Anita Andrade, Jessie Carvantes, Emma Delmonte, Ramona Gonzales, Lola Patino, and Carmen and Marie Rodríguez. Throughout the 1930s Mexican women supported organizing efforts but demanded more independence. They resented that, while Mexicans comprised the majority of Local 96, they represented only 6 of the 19 board members of the union. By 1936, the ILGWU had signed contracts for 2,650 workers in 56 firms. The contacts were not without flaws, since women were paid $28 weekly while men earned $35. The next year, union membership rose to 3,000 and the local became part of the CIO.[59]

Mexican women in Los Angeles and California worked in other areas besides needles trades. They were employed as farm workers, domestics, restaurant help, and laundresses, and an elite few were secretaries. *Mexicanas* were, moreover, concentrated in food processing, with a large number employed in canneries and packing houses. Within these industries, *Mexicanas* were isolated not only by gender but by race. They performed the least skilled jobs. In spite of their vulnerability, they readily joined unions and participated in strikes.[60] Working outside the home encouraged independence not only within the family but also in the workplace.

San Antonio was another urban area with significant labor organizing. The city's Mexican population increased during the 1930s. Thousands of newcomers crowded into the West Side in search of year-round employment. "It [San Antonio] differed from other cities in that the Mexican American rather than blacks occupied the bottom of the economic ladder."[61] The new arrivals came from the fields with little or no urban experience. City agencies refused them relief, with only a few churches and a small number of middle- and upper-class Mexican organizations providing some help—handout food and clothing.

Our Lady of Guadalupe Church, where Father Carmelo Tranchese had worked since 1932, was one of the most active parishes. Throughout the 1930s, Fr. Carmelo stressed the need for better housing, employment, and treatment for Mexicans. San Antonio was the only major city in the United States refusing aid to starving citizens. Whatever welfare given was doled out by state and federal agencies. The WPA and other federal programs routinely excluded noncitizens. Consequently, San Antonio had a large labor pool of Mexicans who were willing to work for almost nothing.

Mexicans suffered disproportionately. In 1937, deaths attributed to tuberculosis among Mexicans ran five times higher than among whites and almost three times that of Blacks. Infant mortality rates were also much higher among Mexicans. Death and disease stalked the West Side. Often desperate people sought out desperate solutions. For example, in 1938, Mrs. Antonia Mena, 28, was found dead in the living room of an abortionist.[62]

Women were paid even less than men and, therefore, subsidized the San Antonio cottage industry. Mexican women were more apt to live at home when single; they often worked to keep their families from economically disintegrating. Older daughters took care of children while mothers worked; the burden was usually heaviest on the eldest daughter. Because of discrimination, lack of education, poor English, and a dozen other reasons, their choice of work was limited. Generally, Anglo women monopolized the white-collar clerical and sales occupations; 91 percent of the Black women worked as domestics or in service jobs; 79 percent of the Mexican women toiled in industrial occupations. "As industrial workers, Mexican-American women were more likely than other women to participate in strikes and other organized protests against Depression conditions."[63] During the 1930s, in fact, Chicanas struck more often than males against low wages and poor working conditions.

Tensions increased among Mexican women at the Finck Cigar Company during 1932. In August 1933 a hundred cigar rollers and tobacco strippers walked out of the Finck Company. The owner announced that the already low paid workers would be fined three good cigars for every one that was bad, a severe penalty for piece-good workers. Led by Mrs. W. H. Ernst, a Mexican woman, they organized an independent union.

Authorities cracked down, arresting Mrs. Ernst. The women strikers raised funds and set their goals, rejecting an offer of affiliation from the International Cigarmakers Union. Meanwhile, Finck signed an agreement with the NRA: strippers would earn 17.5¢ an hour, whereas rollers would receive 22.5¢. Significantly, even this rate was below the 30¢ minimum set by the NRA. Local authorities supported Finck.

Once the federal mediator left, Finck blatantly violated his agreement, firing all union leaders. Again, in early 1934, the *Mexicanas* walked out, this time affiliating with the San Antonio Trades Council. They stayed out until March. The NRA's Regional Board found working conditions at Finck's intolerable:

leaky pipes, unsanitary grounds, and inadequate toilet facilities. When the Regional Board ruled in favor of the workers, Finck appealed the findings, red-baiting the union and raising penalties for bad cigars to four to one.

Police Chief Owen Kilday harassed pickets and threatened women with deportation. Kilday helped break the strike, but in 1935 members walked out once again. Desperate, they attacked scabs by tearing off their clothes. Kilday arrested Mrs. Ernst. A week later, 25 women and 35 male supporters were arrested. Federal mediation again failed. Finck falsified reports to the government and lent money to workers at 8 percent a week interest. Friendly elected officials and the Chamber of Commerce secured exceptions for Finck, who, in any event, broke the strike by importing workers from Mexico.[64]

Like Los Angeles, San Antonio was a major garment manufacturing center. In the Texas city, some 550 garment workers worked 45 hours a week for $3.00 to $5.00 a week (6¢ to 11¢ an hour). In March 1934 the ILGWU chartered two locals in the city: the Infants and Childrens Wear Workers Union Local 180 and the Ladies Garment Workers Union Local 123. The ILGWU struck the A. B. Frank plant in 1936; this plant closed down when it was 100 percent organized. After six months of being picketed by Local 123, the Dorothy Frocks Company moved to Dallas, where a local continued the strike until the company signed a contract in November 1936.

Although the strike activity against Dorothy Frocks lasted only six months in San Antonio, it was bitter. During a car caravan through the city by President Franklin Delano Roosevelt, some 50 strikers publicly disrobed company scabs. Throughout these strikes Chief Kilday conducted mass arrests for unlawful assembly or obstructing the sidewalk. Still, city authorities even denied that a strike existed.

In the spring of 1937 Local 180 called a strike against the Shirlee Frock Company. Fifty pickets were arrested and picketing was limited to three persons by a local judge who also prohibited the use of banners. The strike was successful: the ILGWU was recognized, with workers receiving the minimum wage of 20¢ an hour. The union conducted several more strikes. Once again, Chicanas were at the forefront of organizing and strike activity; in 1939 of the 1,400 San Antonio women who belonged to the ILGWU 80 percent were Mexican.

The ILGWU also organized in other Texas cities with limited success. One of its main problems was that its national leadership never really seemed to make an effort to recruit Mexican organizers. For instance, the leaders hired Rebecca Taylor, an Anglo, as the educational director for the San Antonio office. Taylor, a schoolteacher, admittedly took the job because it paid more than teaching. Her sole qualifications were that she spoke Spanish and had a college degree. Taylor was born in Mexico in a middle-class Arkansas-Oklahoma-Texas religious colony established in the 1890s and later disbanded by revolutionaries. During her tenure with the union, she opposed anything involving radicals and militancy.[65] She opposed radical Chicano leadership during the pecan shellers' strike. In the 1950s, Taylor quit the union and went to work for Tex-Son, one of the ILGWU's principal adversaries.

La Pasionaria, the Pecan Shellers' Strike, and San Antonio

The pecan industry of San Antonio employed between 5,000 and 12,000 Mexicans. Gustave Duerler, a Swiss candy manufacturer, began the industry during the Civil War when he bought pecans from the native Americans and hired Mexicans to crack them open and extract the meat. By the 1880s Duerler shipped pecans east. In 1914 he mechanized the cracking phase of his operation, but still used Mexican women to extract meats by hand. Duerler remained the "Pecan King" until 1926, when the Southern Pecan Shelling Company, with an investment of $50,000, was formed. Ten years later the shelling company's gross business had climbed to $3 million. The company demechanized because it was cheaper to hire Chicanos than to maintain machines and factories.

The pecan industry used agribusiness employment practices. Contractors furnished crackers and pickers. Often contractors employed shellers to pick pecans in their own homes. They packed sweatshops with as many as 100 pickers in an unventilated room without toilets or running water.

The shellers averaged less than $2.00 per week in 1934. This rate increased only slightly by 1936, when they could earn from 5¢ to 6¢ a pound for pecan halves. A pecan workers' union claimed that the pay was even lower. Management rationalized its admittedly low wages: Chicanos ate pecans while working; shellers would not work the necessary hours if they were paid more—they would earn 75¢ and go home, whether it was 3:00 PM or 6:00 PM; Chicanos were satisfied; shellers had a nice warm place in which to work and could visit friends as they did so; if Mexicans earned more, they would just spend it "on tequila and on worthless trinkets in the dime stores."[66]

Conditions forced workers to organize. *El Nogal,* the largest of the pecan workers' unions, claimed 4,000 members between 1933 and 1936. Another group, the Pecan Shelling Workers Union of San Antonio, was a company union led by Mageleno Rodríguez. When management cut rates by 1¢ a pound, thousands of shellers walked off their jobs on February 1, 1938, at the peak of the pecan shelling season. Workers abandoned 130 plants throughout the West Side of San Antonio, affiliating with the CIO's UCAPAWA. Local law authorities backed management and arrested over 1,000 pickets on a variety of charges included blocking sidewalks, disturbing the peace, and unlawful assemblies. "Within the first two weeks tear gas was used at least a half-dozen times to disperse throngs that milled about the shelleries." City officials even enforced an obscure city ordinance aimed at sign-carrying picketers, which made it "unlawful for any person to carry . . . through any public street . . . any advertising" until a permit had been obtained from the city marshal (an office that no longer existed).[67] Since the picketers did not have the impossible permit, they were arrested and fined $10.

Immediately, Emma Tenayucca, in her early twenties, supported the strike. Tenayucca, popular among the workers, served as an organizer for the Workers Alliance, which had a membership of 3,800. Novelist Green Peyton in the mid-1940s wrote: "Of all the improbable spots you might have picked, San Antonio is the only city in the South where Communists once looked—for a while—like a going concern. San Antonio has virtually no [heavy] industry and only a smattering of negroes. But it has a tremendous bloc of ill-housed, ill-fed, and ill-understood Mexicans."[68]

The sensitive, intelligent, and committed Tenayucca understood these conditions and turned to communism for answers. Before finishing high school, she had walked the picket lines for the Finck strikers. After leaving high school, she worked as an elevator operator. In 1936, she met with Mrs. Ernst and discussed forming a Mexican American organization.

Tenayucca dedicated herself to building the Workers Alliance, organizing the unemployed. Over the years, Owen Kilday made her his favorite scapegoat; San Antonians called the fiery labor organizer *La Pasionaria* (after the communist passionflower, Dolores Ibarrui, of the Spanish Civil War). Tenayucca led demonstrations attracting 10,000 participants. To many pecan shellers, earning as little as $1.50 for a 54 hour week, she was a friend.

At the start of the strike, *La Prensa* supported Tenayucca. Unlike Rebecca Taylor, Tenayucca was an insider. However, almost immediately, a power struggle developed over control of the strike between Tenayucca and the UCAPAWA leaders. Tenayucca was apparently forced, on the second day of the strike, to resign her leadership role to remove charges of communist influence. Although removed from the leadership, out of respect, the workers voted her honorary strike leader.[69]

Tenayucca continued her activities. Along with her husband, Homer Brooks, she wrote one of the few works published by the party on the topic "The Mexican Question in the Southwest."[70] The article concluded that the Mexican struggle was tied to that of the Euroamerican working class. It outlined the needs of the Mexicans within the context of the workers' movement and the importance of Mexican participation in a changing society. The article itself exposed the lack of research by the Communist party on Chicanos, and, apparently, the lack of priority it assigned the "Mexican Question."

In August 1939, Emma Tenayucca planned a rally at the Municipal Auditorium. At 8 PM, 6,000 to 7,000 "ranchers, veterans, housewives, pig-tailed school-girls, skinny boys in high-heeled boots screamed at the small group of less than 100 people inside."[71] They yelled, "Kill the dirty reds!" breaking into the auditorium while the participants skirted out of the hall. After this point, Emma Tenayucca dropped out of political work. The reasons can only be speculated: nervous exhaustion, the contradictions within the party, the chauvinism of many of its white members, and, to a degree, her removal as head of the pecan shellers' struggle.

Owen Kilday used the communist issue in his fight with Maury Maverick for the control of San Antonio's political structure. Described as a "bushy-browed, hotheaded" Irishman, he made his reputation "among the conservative citizens by battling Tenayucca's Communists."[72] A Catholic in a predominately Catholic city, he and his brother Paul had the support of Vice President James Nance Garner when Paul beat Maverick for the 20th Congressional District. The Kildays had an excellent network on the West Side, having ties to many priests, the church hierarchy, and the rank and file white Catholics as well as many upper-middle-class Mexicans. When the pecan strike began, he said: "It is my duty to interfere with revolution, and Communism is revolution." The chief stated that if he did not act and if the strike were won, "25,000 workers on the West Side would fall into the Communist party." His definition of a communist was "a person who believes in living in a community on the government and tearing down all religion."[73]

The Mexican Chamber of Commerce and the League of United Latin American Citizens, as well as the Catholic church, refused to support the pecan strike. These groups rarely opposed the Kilday machine. The archbishop went so far as to congratulate the police for acting against "Communistic influences." The archbishop did urge pecan owners to pay higher wages, because in his view lower wages bred communism. Reverend John López, a Redemptorist priest from Our Lady of Perpetual Help, urged workers to return to the true friend of the working masses—the church. The San Antonio Ministers' Association called for a settlement and for a purge of "all Communistic, Fascist, or any un-American elements."

Federal and state officials disapproved of Kilday's methods. The National Labor Relations Board stated that "there has been a misuse of authority in handling the strike." The governor of Texas criticized Kilday's refusal to allow picketing. He censured the beatings and forcing Mexicans to become scabs under the threat of deportation. However, Chief Kilday was undaunted and even closed a soup kitchen, which provided free food to strikers, alleging a violation of city health ordinances.

After 37 days of Kilday, the parties submitted to arbitration. Pecan shellers had stopped production, calling national attention to conditions. The arbitration board recognized Local 172 as the sole bargaining agent and required owners to comply with the Fair Labor Standards Act which had been passed on June 25, 1938, and pay the minimum wage of 25¢ an hour. The victory was short lived; owners replaced workers with machinery. In 1938 the total annual income of 521 San Antonio pecan shellers' families, averaging 4.6 persons, was $251. This included all income, from relief work to the value of relief commodities.[74]

Throughout the country, after 1937, the plight of the noncitizens worsened as it became more difficult for them to get on relief or to work on public projects. For example, 1,800 jobs were set aside for the needy pecan shellers; however, only 700 qualified as citizens. Stiffer residency requirements were passed, qualifying fewer Mexicans for the Federal Emergency Relief Administration aid or the Civil Works Administration jobs.[75]

Labor Conditions in the Midwest: Chicago

In Chicago the impact of the depression fell hardest on the unskilled and semi-skilled; 83 percent of the Chicagoans on relief were unskilled workers in 1935. Generally, unemployment corresponded with skill and race. The Mexican population of Chicago was 66 percent unskilled in the 1930s versus 53 percent for Blacks, 35 percent for foreign-born white, and 33 percent for native whites. Mexicans had a lower median of education than other groups, 3.2 years versus a median of 4.7 for Blacks and 5.3 for European whites.

In 1935, 30 percent of Chicago's Mexican workers were unemployed. As elsewhere, employment and relief depended on citizenship. Employers and government authorities pressured Mexicans to prove legal residence or a willingness to become naturalized citizens. Government relief, in the form of work and aid, often required applicants to be citizens. Mexicans, however, were reluctant to become naturalized.[76]

By the mid-1930s conditions somewhat improved and a new wave of Chicanos from Texas and other sectors of the Midwest began arriving. During this period Mexicans actively joined a variety of labor clubs, unions, and workers' organizations for the employed and unemployed to counter the effects of the economic depression.

Mexicans in Chicago, influenced by *La Confederación de Trabajadores Mexicanos* (CTM), formed a Chicago chapter of *El Frente Popular Mexicano,* which sponsored "a series of meetings, discussions, and lectures regularly attended by more than 200 people." Refugio Martínez, a leading activist, was allegedly later deported during the McCarran-Walter witch-hunts of the 1950s. The *Frente,* housed in the University of Chicago Settlement House in Back of the Yards, actively defended Mexican workers; its interests extended beyond labor issues to protests against Franco's despotism. These stances alienated many Catholic organizations and the church began to publish *El Ideal Católico Mexicano* in 1935, specifically to counter the radical appeal of the *Frente* and to crusade against Marxist tendencies. It was supported by the *Sociedad de Obreros Católicos* (Society of Catholic Workers) that represented the conservative sector of the community. However, neither the *Frente* or the *Sociedad* had large followings. The most numerous of the Mexican workers' organizations remained the *mutualistas.*

Mexicans favored organizations predominately Mexican and local in character such as the *Sociedad de Obreros Libres Mexicanos de Sud Chicago* (Society of Free Mexican Workers of South Chicago), which was made up of steel and foundry workers. They also participated in the Illinois Workers Alliance, which had 72 locals throughout the state. It attracted a multiethnic membership of both employed and unemployed workers. Three locals operated in Mexican neighborhoods. As early as 1933 it advertised in Mexican newspapers for members. The alliance successfully pressured for more equitable relief and employment laws. Locals 32 and 36 each claimed 50 Mexican members.

Unions such as the Brotherhood of Railroad and Maintenance Workers discriminated against Mexicans. However, after the Wagner Act (1935), steel and meat packing industrial unions increasingly solicited Mexican membership. In four months during 1936, the Steel Workers Organizing Committee (SWOC) recruited between 150 and 200 Mexican workers. Mexican workers were particularly active in Local 65 at United States Steel South Works in Chicago. Alfredo Avila and his wife worked closely with the local's president, George Patterson. Manuel García along with Avila sponsored meetings in Spanish and prepared union literature. They enlisted the support of the Mexican consul and a priest at Our Lady of Guadalupe Church. By 1936, although they were only 5 percent of the South Works employees, Mexicans comprised 11 percent of the union; 54 percent of the general membership voted versus 88 percent of the Chicano membership. Following U.S. Steel's recognition of the union, workers elected Avila to the first executive board.

In East Chicago, Indiana, Juan Dávila, Basil Pacheco, who had led a worker walkout at the Youngstown Sheet and Tube plant in 1927, Max Luna, and Miguel Arredondo actively recruited Mexican steelworkers. On May 26, 1937, a strike was called against the "Little Steel" firms, Bethlehem, Republic, Inland, and Youngstown, when they refused to sign a contract. The Youngstown and Inland plants in East Chicago were completely shut down, with Mexicans playing a major role on the picket lines. At Inland, for example, Chicanos comprised 75 percent of the pickets.

When the union was unable to close down the Republic plant in South Chicago brothers and sisters from the other plants converged on Republic, holding meetings and demonstrations. During one of these demonstrations, on May 30, 1937, Chicago police fired at the strikers, killing 10 and injuring 68. Although the crowd had a wide racial mix, one of the police officers said it resembled the "Mexican army." In reality, Mexicans made up about 15 percent of the demonstrators. According to most sources, Max Guzmán, a Republic employee, was one of the two flag bearers. Mexicans such as Lupe Marshall, a Chicana social worker, marched at the front of the line; she played a leading role in caring for the wounded. At least 11 of the injured were Chicanos. Violence ended the strike and it was not until 1941 that the union was recognized. Chicanos remained active in union politics. Basil Pacheco, for example, chaired Labor's Non-Partisan League in East Chicago in 1938.[77] Mexicans increasingly joined urban unions, but, unlike in agriculture, Midwest Mexican workers more and more joined mixed ethnic and racial industrial unions.

Mexicans, the AFL, and the CIO

The growth of industry in Los Angeles augmented the ranks of the Mexican proletariat in the city. Even before World War II, heavy industry began to move to Los Angeles. Eastern corporations, enticed by cheap land, reduced fuel costs, and cheap labor looked west. Also, the corporations looked to the huge local markets for automobile-related products. Ford (1930), Willys-Overland (1929), Chrysler (1931), and General Motors (1936) all established plants in Los Angeles. Goodyear, Goodrich, Firestone, and U.S. Rubber soon followed. In 1936, Los Angeles ranked second only to Detroit in auto assembly and second only to Akron in tire and rubber manufacturing. The budding aircraft industry also centered itself in Los Angeles.

Just under 100,000 Mexicans lived in the city and 167,024 in the county in 1930. Mexicans, the largest minority, were followed by 46,000 Blacks and 35,000 Japanese. Mexicans, concentrated in limited industries, made up the majority of casual labor in construction, dominating the hod-carriers unions. The CIO's schism created increased competition between the two internationals—and suddenly Mexicans became attractive brothers. By 1940, the United Brick and Clay Workers Union (AFL) had 2,000 Mexican members. The CIO organized 15,000 Mexican workers in Los Angeles by the early 1940s.[78]

The International Longshoremens and Warehousemens Union (ILWU), founded on August 11, 1937, joined the CIO. Local 1-26 broke away from the AFL and affiliated with the ILWU. The local had about 600 members at that time. A year after the affiliation with the CIO, membership increased to 1,300 members. Bert Corona, William Trujillo, and other Chicanos worked as volunteer recruiters. Drives were conducted to enlist workers in the drug warehouse industry as well as milling, paper, and hardware. By 1939 Local 1-26 had about 1,500 members.

Between 1939 and 1941, organizers recruited warehouse laborers in the waste material industry, in which about 50 percent of the workers were Mexicans. The union successfully organized some 1,000 workers in that industry, half of whom were Mexicans. Charles "Chili" Duarte led ILWU organization drives in Los Angeles, engaging in bitter jurisdictional fights with the Teamsters. By the end of 1941 the local had 3,400 members in the drug, milling, paper, metal trades, and waste material industries. In 1941 Corona, elected president of Local 1-26, served in that capacity until he entered the U.S. army in 1943. The local continued organizing and by 1945 it held 60 contracts covering 73 shops. It had a multinational membership, one-third of whom were women. William Trujillo and Isidro Armenta held leadership positions. In 1950 Local 1-26 broke with the CIO when the CIO National Executive Board charged that the ILWU was dominated by communists. Chicanos remained in the ILWU and supported the break with the CIO.[79]

The Independent Furniture Workers Union (IFWU) Local 1, formed in 1933, had many Mexican workers. Two years later the IFWU had organized 14 factories, adding more Mexicans to its rank and file. The IFWU affiliated itself with the AFL (Local 1561), which complained about the militancy of the furniture workers, who continued to participate in strikes and boycotts throughout 1935 and 1936.

Local 1561, divided by the fight between craft and industrial unionism, struggled within the AFL under the umbrella of the Committee for Industrial Organization. In 1936, the AFL suspended ten industrial unions, among them the United Mine Workers, the United Rubber Workers, the United Auto Workers, and the ILGWU, which, in turn, formed the CIO or the Congress of Industrial Organization. In Los Angeles, this division produced a conflict within numerous unions.

The furniture workers, for a while, stayed inside the AFL. Suddenly, the AFL appeared more willing to organize mass-production workers. A split eventually occurred and the bulk of Local 1561 voted to join Local 576 (CIO) of the United Furniture Workers of America (UFWA), which had broken with the AFL in 1937. The leadership included Chicanos such as Armando Dávila, a business agent; Oscar Castro; who, in the mid-1940s, became a full-time organizer; and Ben Cruz, who rose to the presidency of the local. In 1946, Local 576 had 2,007 members, increasing in one year to 3,000. During the Cold War, the UFWA's executive board red-baited the local's leadership, chartering Local 1010 to compete with it. The Mexican rank and file were caught in the middle of this struggle between craft and industrial unionism.

In 1938, Upholsterers Local 15 was split by the industrial-craft debate. The membership, largely Mexican, voted to join the CIO's United Furniture Workers. The AFL leadership attempted to prevent a CIO takeover and barricaded themselves in the union hall. Two hundred members, led by Manuel García, their newly elected president, tore the front door down and occupied the auditorium. Mexican workers including women were fully integrated into the UFW.[80]

Competition between the AFL and CIO helped in the unionization of Chicanos in other cities and regions. Prior to 1937, the AFL cared little for unskilled minorities or women workers. It became less discriminative, however, given the successes of the CIO, whose industrial unionism was more attractive to Chicanos than the AFL's craft orientation.

THE MEXICAN AMERICAN MINERS' REVOLT

Professor Irving Bernstein writes that "the hard-rock metal miners had been virtually bereft of unionism since World War I. The tradition of the militant and romantic Western Federation of Miners, which became the Mine, Mill and Smelter Workers Union, AFL, in 1916, was little more than a nostalgic memory. In the copper, lead, zinc, and precious metals mining camps of the West on the eve of the New Deal there were neither viable unions nor collective bargaining."[81] In Arizona, the copper barons and other ruling elites of the metal mines had eliminated the trade union movement—its weapons had been subversion, slander and libel, and violence. In the 1930s these unions would rebuild themselves through militant worker struggle in which the Mexican played a leading role.

Token organizations existed in the early 1930s. The giants remained the same: Phelps Dodge, Anaconda, American Smelting and Refining, and Nevada Consolidated. They had tremendous power and did not hesitate to use it, proud of the legacies of Ludlow and Bisbee. In the 1930s Mexicans made up 50–60 percent of the Southwest's industrial mine labor. Segregated, they had substandard jobs and were locked into a two-tier pay structure. In places like Arizona, the mine owners controlled the state government and the company towns where workers lived.

In the middle of the decade, new life began to stir in the International Union of Mine, Mill and Smelter Workers. Encouraged by the short-lived National Industrial Recovery Act, workers and union representatives attempted to rebuild their locals. In the internecine struggles between craft and industrial unions, Mexicans generally supported the industrialists.[82] The process of union revitalization took until the mid-1930s, coinciding with the formation of the CIO.

The Struggle in New Mexico

Gallup, New Mexico, was one of the first mining districts of predominately Mexican workers to rebel. The depression had hit the area severely, and, by August 1933, 2,000 miners were reduced to a two- to three-day work week. The NIRA Code breathed new life into the miners, not so much by what it said as by what the workers hoped it said.

Gallup miners became involved in the struggle between John L. Lewis's United Mine Workers (UMW) and the National Miners Union (NMU). Rumblings had begun within the UMW ranks when Lewis centralized control in the early 1920s. A "Save the Union" movement lasted from 1926 to 1928. That year, the communists, who had been part of the opposition, bolted the UMW and formed a dual union, the NMU. It was about this time that the Communist party changed its strategy of "boring from within" to setting up dual unions. The NWU predated the Trade Union Unity League (see page 210), but federated with it when it was formed. The NWU, unsuccessful in strikes in Pennsylvania and Ohio as well as the bloody Harlan County, Kentucky, strikes of 1931 and 1932, found itself in Gallup in 1933.

The Gallup miners, mostly Mexican, did not know much about the NMU, but they were dissatisfied with the UMW. The NMU's stress on militant action and interracial solidarity appealed to the Mexican miners, whose grievances included wage cuts and insufficient pay for dead time. When the mine owners refused to bargain, workers picketed the five major mining companies. Threatened by striking workers, the governor mobilized the National Guard, putting McKinley County under martial law.

Authorities denied workers the right to assemble and the guard opened the coal fields. Management red-baited the NMU and made racial slurs against the Mexican workers and their families. In the fall, the strike was mediated in favor of the owners. At the same time, the Communist party established an unemployed council and a chapter of the International Labor Defense (ILD). And it helped organize *El Club Artístico de Obreros* (The Workers Drama Club).

Meanwhile, relations between the workers and the companies deteriorated. Company stores became more exploitive, housing even less adequate, and company agents constantly intimidated workers. Most promises made in the 1933 strike settlement were ignored. The governor had given his word that workers who were not immediately reemployed preferential hiring on public works programs. He lied, and the former strikers were blacklisted by both the mining companies and the state. The Unemployed Council led a protest against the Federal Emergency Relief Administration, forcing the agency to restore cuts.

By 1935, the Communist party abandoned its dual union strategy and formed popular fronts with other unions. In 1934, the CP dissolved the NMU; however, the Gallup local hung on for a year, because of bitter feelings toward the UMW among the rank and file who, at first, refused to merge with Lewis's union.

Other issues threatened the peace. Since 1917 Gallup American (GA) had rented land to Mexican workers, whom GA had originally imported as strikebreakers. These workers later became the rank and file of the NMU; they lived in a *colonia* known as *Chihuahuita,* where adobe houses and shacks dotted the hilly land. In the 1930s, mine owners had blacklisted many of the Mexican-born residents of *Chihuahuita,* while others were chronically unemployed. Gallup American, without notice, sold the property to State Senator Clarence F. Vogel, who gave the workers an ultimatum to purchase the land on his terms or to get out.

The first evictions began in April 1935. Authorities selected the residence of Victor Campos, putting his belongings outside the house. That night his neighbors returned his furnishings to the house. Police filed complaints against Campos, Exiquio Navarro, who owned the house, and Jeanie Lavato. They held Navarro without bail. Led by Juan Ochoa, the Unemployed Council immediately organized about 125 supporters who picketed the justice's office where Navarro was held. When deputies attempted to sneak Navarro out, an altercation erupted. Deputies fired a tear-gas bomb and shot at the demonstrators, causing the death of the sheriff and two miners. During the scuffle, Navarro took off, never to be heard from again.

Although many of the merchants and townspeople had at one time been miners themselves, they now resented the Mexicans, considering them outsiders. They felt that they were paying the Mexicans' relief bills. Led by the American Legion and the Veterans of Foreign Wars, vigilantes rounded up so-called radicals. They charged 14 miners and friends with first degree murder and 4 on lesser charges. Meanwhile, immigration officers cooperated with local authorities, harassing and deporting activists.

Officials targeted Juan Ochoa, a miner since age 16. Although blacklisted, Ochoa worked for the Unemployed Council. Before the trial, vigilantes kidnapped the two main defense attorneys. The state did nothing to prosecute the vigilantes and refused to guarantee the lawyers' safety. Afraid for their lives, the defense attorneys left New Mexico. The presiding judge then refused the new attorneys additional time to prepare their case.

Juan Ochoa, Manuel Avitia, and Leandro Velarde were found guilty of second degree murder. The judge delivered a speech on communism and Bolshevism before sentencing the defendants to 46 to 60 years. The court of appeals reversed the Velarde conviction; in 1939 the governor pardoned Ochoa and Avitia. Authorities had handed over five of the seven acquitted defendants to immigration authorities.[83]

Mexicans Gain a Foothold

Miners suffered similar travesties in other camps, and it was not until the CIO was formed that militant trade unionism became successful. The organizing effort was helped by a revival of mine production as owners geared up for war profits. Open pit mining required cheap labor, and in places like Clifton–Morenci the pit widened and eradicated the town of Metcalf. Worker militancy increased at Morenci, as it did at Bisbee, Arizona. Mexican miners at Silver City, New Mexico, resentful of social and economic conditions, began to organize. In Laredo, Texas, smelter workers built a union, led by Juan Peña, which evolved from UCAPAWA. It had the support of Mexican president Lázaro Cárdenas and *La Confederación de Trabajadores Mexicanos,* the influential Mexican labor federation. The depression also agitated worker militancy, in many cases popularizing protest. Prior to the depression, Mexicans could join few multiracial organizations. During the depression, Worker Alliances and other associations were open to impoverished Mexican workers.

Important trade union activity took place in El Paso that would affect the rest of the Southwest. The AFL had organized laborers at the American Smelting and Refining Company (ASARCO) smelter. Among the early cadre was the Nicaraguan Humberto Silex, who questioned the AFL's craft-union philosophy. Owners fired Silex and the president of the laborers local for their organizing activities. In 1937, when the U.S. Supreme Court upheld the constitutionality of the Wagner Act, the National Labor Relations Board (NLRB) began enforcing the act. The NLRB ruled that Silex and 40 members of the blacklisted Bisbee Miners Union had been discriminated against. Activists, returning to their jobs, began to agitate once more.

The International Union of Mine, Mill and Smelter Workers, headquartered in Denver, provided significant leadership. It had a full-time paid staff comprised of organizers such as Leo Ortiz and Arturo Mata; in addition, volunteers such as Silex, Ceferino Anchando, and Joe Chávez of El Paso, J. E. Vásquez of Douglas, Arizona, Juan Peña of Laredo, and Emilio Villegas of Morenci worked to build the union. "Many of them, radicalized in the Chicano labor market, favored a combined assault on the issues of membership, wages, and ethnic discrimination."[84] Veterans of other strikes, including some of their parents, had been union folk. Mata's father, a leader of the Morenci strike during World War I, had been deported with his family. When they returned, in the 1920s, Mata became active in farm and mine organizing as well as in civil rights.

Leo Ortiz helped revitalize the Clifton-Morenci movement, living by day in Safford, Arizona, and sneaking into the mining camps in the evening. Union building continued during World War II. Breaking the control of the craft unions over the mining industry proved to be of major importance to Mexican participation. During this time, the union won important victories in Silver City, as well as at the Phelps Dodge and ASARCO refineries in Douglas–Bisbee and Laredo. At Morenci, Mine-Mill represened 2,000 workers, most of them Mexican. By the war's end, Mine-Mill represented three-quarters of the copper production workers in the Southwest, with 3,000 members along the border alone. Mine-Mill was attractive to Mexicans because of its policy of ethnic and racial equality.[85]

In cities such as El Paso and Los Angeles, Chicanos worked in the foundries, where they comprised the majority of unskilled workers. In 1937, the Steel Workers Organizing Committee (SWOC) formed in Los Angeles; within two years the SWOC had begun to establish itself. At Utility Steel, workers elected a Chicano as lodge president while the committee made gains at Bethlehem Steel and Continental Can. During these drives, a clear division existed between skilled and nonskilled Mexican workers; the former were also difficult to organize. Mine-Mill, active in southern California, unionized in the foundries, smelters, and extraction plants, especially in the fabrication of construction components. As Chicanos trickled into these industries, white workers migrated to the war plants.[86]

In short, the unions that promoted policies of ethnic and racial equality attracted Mexicans. Because of their labor market skills and the prejudice of craft as well as many industrial unions, the Mexicans/Chicanos concentrated themselves in limitied industries. However, despite contradictions in its approach, the CIO was essential in the building of a strong Mexican American labor movement. Independent unions or associations simply did not have sufficient muscle against the giant corporations.

SURVIVAL IN A FAILED UTOPIA: CHICANOS IN THE CITY

The Mexicans' struggle for survival was not limited to immigration and/or labor. As mentioned earlier, the 1930s saw increased urbanization among Mexicans in the United States. Many new city dwellers shifted from the rural Southwest to places like San Antonio, Los Angeles, and Chicago where they formed *barrios* that reflected the personalities of those cities. The newcomers also arrived from the *ranchitos* (hamlets) of Jalisco, Guanajuato, Michoacán and so on, to the cities, either directly or via the migrant stream. There they joined long time Chicano residents, many of whom were in the process of assimilation, or were frozen into an underclass. Adjustments to the new environment were difficult and increased numbers generated tensions as new and old competed for space.

Ethnic identity, a common language, and the racism of the dominant society were some of the factors that created a sense of community among the various classes of Mexicans. New forms of organizations that concerned themselves with education, voter registration, political power through the electoral process, and human rights issues replaced the once popular *mutualistas*. Chicano trade union and community leaders attempted to form a national organization to bring all of the Mexicans/Latinos together under one umbrella—*el Congreso de los Pueblos de Habla Español,* the Congress of Spanish-speaking Peoples.

Also in the 1930s, the Council for Inter-Amerian Affairs was formed in the Southwest. The council sought to get the United States to live up to the terms of the Treaty of Guadalupe Hidalgo. This organization functioned into the 1940s, holding conferences and leadership training workshops.[87] LULAC continued as a force and expressed the aspirations of the Mexican American middle class, and, although it remained mainly a Texas affair, LULAC chapters were formed in other states. And even though much can be made of the growing division between middle-class interests of many LULAC members as opposed to the poor, many progressive strains emerged from the middle-class sector.

For instance, during the 1930s, it became even more popular for Anglo-American educators and social scientists to blame the Mexican for their failure to Americanize and progress in the utopia known as "America." Middle-class Mexican Americans rose to the occasion and countered the myths about the non-achieving Mexican. Drs. George I. Sánchez and H.T. Manuel answered the questions of why the Mexican remained at the bottom of the social structure. They re-examined the culturally biased I.Q. tests and how they rationalized the failure of the education system, and, consequently, the myth of equal opportunity in utopia. Sánchez and other Mexican American educators emphasized the role of environment on education. They raised the issue of identity—Mexican Americans were robbed of their historical heritage by Anglo scholars who dominated the analysis and interpretation of history.[88] These early pioneers also called for bilingual education and an end to de jure and de facto segregation.

The California Dream: In Search of a Community

In 1931 at Lemon Grove, California, near San Diego, the parents of 75 Chicano children refused to send their children to an all-Mexican school built for them by the school board. The parents accused the board members of wanting to segregate the Mexican students; the board members stated that they wanted to facilitate the learning of English. The parents organized a committee, visited the Mexican consul, and retained legal counsel. They sued the Lemon Grove Schools and won.[89] This was a landmark case that served as precedent for school desegregation cases that followed.

The Mexican community in Los Angeles, meanwhile, continued to grow. The *plaza* was no longer the center of activity, with its residential base reduced by the expansion of the Civic Center. Chicanos moved east to the Belvedere-Maravilla area as well as to other parts of the city and county. During the 1930s, the Mexican became more visible in the Boyle Heights area that was between downtown and Belvedere. Housing had improved little for Mexicans since the 1910s. Unplanned development scattered the uprooted without providing any replacement for the bulldozed structures. The house courtyards and makeshift shacks still sheltered the poor. During the decade, trade groups remained influential. The *plaza* shops still served the community, but the First Street merchants replaced them as the center for Chicano commerce. Apparently, few Chicano power brokers operated in Los Angeles as they did in San Antonio. Because of the lack of concentration—even in the East Side they were not yet the majority —the Los Angeles ruling elite did not have to depend on the Mexican vote. Moreover, the Mexican population was more recent than San Antonio's, and had not developed a middle-class community that spoke for the whole. In Los Angeles, political power under the leadership of Harry Chandler of the *Los Angeles Times* was much more centralized than in the Alamo City.

Outside Belvedere-Maravilla, the poor lived in segregated clusters, often surrounded by Anglo-Americans. Dr. Ernesto Galarza used to like to call them doughnut communities—the Mexican *barrio* was the hole and the Anglo neighborhoods were the dough. Rich Mexicans, who maintained little contact with the masses, often lived in such affluent districts as West Adams, Los Feliz, and San Marino where they sponsored social functions like the *Baile Blanco y Negro* (a white gown, black tie dance). The *ricos'* efforts to preserve Mexican culture were recorded in the social columns of *La Opinión*. Meanwhile, the Chicano middle class had begun to make tentative moves to the outskirts of the *barrios*.

Activities of the lower middle class and the poor differed from the upwardly mobile middle class. A few joined the Young Democrats; some participated in the Unemployed Councils and the Worker Alliance. In 1930, the Federation of Spanish-speaking Voters attempted to unite all Mexican societies. It was "perhaps the first political group to organize in Los Angeles." It ran candidates, but lost.[90] Protestant churches, and especially the Young Men's Christian Association

(YMCA) worked among Mexicans. The most powerful instituion, however, remained the Catholic Church, which reportedly turned out 40,000 to march in Los Angeles in honor of *Cristo Rey* (Christ the King) in 1934. The Catholic Church during this time was very conservative and in the late 1930s many priests were clearly partisan to Spain's fascist dictator, Francisco Franco.

The Catholic Church had become paranoid with the events of the Mexican Revolution. The *cristero* rebellion of the 1920s saw Mexican Catholics defy the Mexican government's enforcement of provisions of the Mexican Constitution of 1917 that separated church and state. As a consequence, bitter clashes between the Mexican government and the *cristeros* followed, with the church claiming that the government persecuted it. In the United States, the Mexican clergy was anti-Mexican government and anti-radical, and concentrated in forming male and female youth groups to propogate the faith. The church was also very much threatened by competition from Protestants, especially the YMCA. It formed the Catholic Youth Organization (CYO) and the Catholic settlement houses to attract youth.

On the other side, the communists were also active among Chicanos in Los Angeles. Reportedly 10 percent of their recruits locally were Mexican in 1936–1937. They formed *La Nueva Vida* Club and the *No Pasarán* branch of the Young Communist League (YCL). They publicized the issues at stake in the Spanish Civil War and discussed the need for improved conditions at home. The Workers Alliance, which included capable organizers such as Lupe Méndoza and Guillermo Taylor, reached out to WPA workers and people on relief. The Workers Alliance had close ties to UCAPAWA, through which Luisa Moreno and Frank López organized Chicanos.[91]

Independently, Chicano youth organized themselves. The Mexican American Movement (MAM) was an outgrowth of the YMCA's Older Boys' Conference held in San Pedro in 1934. Annual conferences held there were later renamed the Mexican Youth Congress. Through the years the functions of the Youth Conference broadened and it established a steering committee. In 1938 MAM published a newspaper, *The Mexican Voice*. In 1939 it established a leadership institute; in that same year it held its first regional conference at Santa Barbara, and by 1940 it sponsored a Mexican American Girls' Conference and a Mexican American Teachers' Association and had contacts with similar organizations in Arizona and Texas.

The philosophy of MAM was to create Chicano leadership in education, social work, business, and other professions. MAM struggled continuously toward its goal of "Progress Through Education"; it struggled for better school and better family relations as it fought against discrimination and juvenile delinquency. World War II curtailed some of its activities, but it survived until about 1949. *The Mexican Voice* became the *Forward* in 1945 and reported on its members' progress in the armed forces. Among those who participated were Félix Gutiérrez, Sr.; Richard Ibañez, a civil rights attorney and later a judge; Manuel Ceja; Mary Escudero of Claremont; and Mary Anne Chavolla of Placentia. Records of the organization indicate that many members were later absorbed into the Community Service Organization.[92]

MAM members participated with other organizations. In 1938 *El Congreso de los Pueblos de Habla Español* held the first national Conference of Spanish-Speaking Peoples. The principal organizer was Luisa Moreno, a national organizer and later vice president for UCAPAWA. Moreno traveled throughout the United States and generated considerable interest in the conference later held in Los Angeles. Representatives came from all over the United States: Spanish and Cuban cigar makers from Tampa, Florida; Puerto Ricans from Harlem; steelworkers from Pennsylvania, Illinois, and Indiana; meat packers, miners, and farm workers from many localities; and elected officials from New Mexico. The congress was broadly based—representatives included workers, politicians, youth, educators—and its stated purpose was "the economic and social and cultural betterment of the Mexican people, to have an understanding between Anglo-Americans and Mexicans, to promote organization of working people by aiding trade unions and to fight discrimination actively."

Newspapers and local elected officials labeled it a "subversive gathering." Delegates pushed through a radical and progressive platform. Workers were to be organized, and a newspaper and newsletter were to be published. Delegates set legislative priorities and took stands against oppressive laws, immigration officials, vigilantes, and police brutality. They demanded the right of farm workers to organize as well as the extension of the benefits of the National Labor Relations Act to farm workers.

The *Congreso* claimed over 6,000 members from 1938 to 1940.[93] However, it had committed a strategic blunder in setting too sectarian and too specific goals. Neither the *Congreso* nor the Chicano community had many friends in the media or in positions of power. Because of its radical stands, the *Congreso* exposed itself to intense red-baiting and the FBI harassed its members. After 1940 its effectiveness waned rapidly, even though it continued to function in the postwar period.

The *Congreso* was important because it provided a forum for activists like Luisa Moreno. On March 3, 1940, she addressed a Panel on Deportation and Right of Asylum of the Fourth Annual Conference of the American Committee for the Protection of the Foreign Born in Washington, D.C. She entitled her speech "Caravan of Sorrow":

> Long before the "Grapes of Wrath" had ripened in California's vineyards a people lived on highways, under trees or tents, in shacks or railroad sections, picking crops—cotton, fruits, vegetables, cultivating sugar beets, building railroads and dams, making barren land fertile for new crops and greater riches.

Moreno continued that they had been brought "by the fruit exchanges, railroad companies and cotton interests in great need of underpaid labor during the early post-war period." She condemned the repatriations and the sufferings caused by it, charging that "today the Latin Americans of the United States are alarmed by an 'antialien' drive." Citizenship became increasingly a requirement for continued employment and nativists conducted a drive to get federal legislation passed making it mandatory. Moreno explained that there were many reasons for not becoming a naturalized citizen: (1) lack of documentary proof because Mexicans were brought over *en masse* and many of the companies transporting Mexicans to the United States mishandled the paper work; (2) many did not learn English; and (3) many did not have money for the fee. Whatever the reason, Moreno added:

> These people are not aliens. They have contributed their endurance, sacrifices, youth and labor to the Southwest. Indirectly, they have paid more taxes than all the stockholders of California's industrialized agriculture, the sugar companies and the large cotton interests, that operate or have operated with the labor of Mexican workers.[94]

Moreno put *El Congreso de Los Pueblos de Habla Español* on record as opposing antialien legislation.

During the 1930s a few newspaper editors took stands again discrimination as well as against segregation in schools and public facilities. An exception was Ignacio López, editor of *El Espectador* and a graduate of the University of California at Berkeley, who held Master of Arts degrees in Spanish and history. In February 1939, in Upland, California, two Chicanos entered the movie theater, and looked for seats near the center. They were told that Mexicans sat only in the first 15 rows. The youths went to López who wrote a stinging editorial, calling for a mass meeting at which over a hundred community folk attended. They boycotted the theater which shortly afterward changed its policy.

In another incident that year, López exposed that Chaffey Junior College segregated its pool facilities during the summer. Chicanos could use the pool only on Mondays. Another boycott followed, with the college reversing its policy. Shortly afterward, with Reverend R. N. Nuñez of Guadalupe Parish in San Bernardino, suit was brought against the City of San Bernardino, and the courts enjoined the city from excluding Mexicans from its pools.[95]

The Texas Experience: Thinking Mexican American

The Texas Mexican experience differed from that in California only in degree. In Texas, Chicanos generally suffered more from segregation and racial barriers. Texas was a southern state with all the social, political, and intellectual limitations of the South. This isolation encouraged a cohesiveness among *Tejanos,* or Tex-Mexicans as they often called themselves. Therefore, it was not surprising that LULAC, which had chapters in California and throughout the Southwest, was in the last analysis a Texas affair. In Texas, the rise of LULAC during the 1930s created a network that included a sizable portion of the Chicano middle class that increasingly thought Mexican American.

LULAC symbolized the rise of the Mexican American middle class. As in the past, the organization did not really serve the interests of the poor, but, rather, reflected the philosophy of the middle class, who wanted assimilation. Their aim marked a departure from the upper-class leadership of the second decade of the century, which had promoted the virtues of Mexican culture. To achieve its goal, the middle-class leadership demanded constitutional and human rights for all

Mexicans. Thus LULAC and the Mexican American middle class looked north instead of south and began to deal with conditions in the United States.[96] Some of the organization's leaders, like Alonso Perales, were by no means revolutionary but worked within the tradition of U.S. civil rights activism. They demanded equality as North Americans; their major goals remained equal access to education and other public and private institutions, and the enactment of state laws to end discrimination against Mexicans.

San Antonio *ricos* differed from their Los Angeles counterparts, who moved out of the *barrio* and into affluent Anglo neighborhoods. In San Antonio, many lived in exclusive enclaves on the West Side. Discrimination in Texas was more rigid, and Anglos even looked down on old *Tejano* families. Author Green Peyton wrote, for instance, of his friend Marine Major Ralph Garza, a descendant of a founding family who lived on West Houston Street. "The Garzas are an anomaly in San Antonio. They do not belong, obviously, with the poor Mexican peons in the slums. Nor do they mingle with the cattlemen and rich oil operators." He also told of Dr. Aureliano Urrutia, an exiled *porfirista* cabinet minister, who maintained an extravagant home and ran the Urrutia Clinic on the West Side. Peyton remarked that Urrutia was rich when he arrived and got even richer running the clinic. The rich Mexicans associated with each other, preferring to socialize at the Club Casino than to join local organizations such as LULAC. Many of the *ricos* returned to Mexico in the late 1930s, when Cárdenas issued a general amnesty.[97]

Although the middle-class doctors, lawyers, educators, and merchants accumulated surpluses and improved their material circumstances, Euroamerican society did not accept them. But still they considered themselves *gente decente* (decent people) and flaunted their Americanism. It became their mission to uplift the poor Mexicans, to make them good Americans. By no means did the well-to-do consciously deny their Mexicanness. Their rationality was one that pretended to include both cultures. In public, the middle class made compromises, avoiding the term *Mexican* (since to some it compromised their Americanism), preferring not to insult their Euroamerican friends. When naming organizations, they often chose labels like Latin American, Spanish American, or *Hispano*. In 1936, the San Angelo, Texas, LULAC council sued the Social Security Administration regarding a regulation that required Mexicans to designate themselves as "Mexican" and not "white." The LULAC council successfully got the agency to reverse itself.

While LULAC and middle-class leaders sought, quite simply, equal access to U.S. institutions, members did not want to use LULAC as a political organization. The LULAC constitution stipulated that it was nonpolitical. Members, however, used fronts such as the *Club Democrático* and the League of Loyal Americans for their political activities. They felt they could achieve their goal—which was to become capitalists—in a dignified manner like "decent" people. Their method was to work within the system and not in the streets.

LULAC advocated uplifting the Mexican American through family, church, education, and voting. Members represented a new generation who wanted to do it in their own way. Throughout the 1930s they fought for more education and for equality. Consequently, LULAC, along with the Mexican

Chamber of Commerce and the Catholic Church, was disturbed and often out-raged by the militancy of the times, which challenged their leadership of the Chicano masses. Fundamentally, radicalism threatened their own interests.

This is not to suggest, however, that the Mexican American middle class was politically homogeneous. While many Catholic priests and LULAC leaders campaigned against Maury Maverick in his race for Congress in 1938 because he was liberal and pro-CIO, leaders such as Perales supported Maverick against Mayor Charles Quin's candidate, Paul Kilday (see p. 226). Maverick lost, but he immediately filed for mayor against Quin himself. Many LULAC members sup-ported Quin while Perales again backed Maverick; the Pecan Shellers also lined up with Maverick. The Mexican community turned out heavily for Maverick and he won. Two years later, Perales joined other LULAC leaders in opposing Maver-ick, because Maverick allegedly had not kept all of his campaign promises.[98]

New Mexico

Many New Mexicans held to the myth that they fared better than Mexicans elsewhere. The 1930s further exposed that contradiction between the myth and their reality. Even after World War II, out of 1,093 listings in *Who's Who in New Mexico,* only 57 were Mexican. In eastern New Mexico Chicanos were barred from "better" barber shops, cafes, hotels, and recreation centers. In Anglo towns such as Rosewell, Mexicans could not use the public pool. In the late 1930s, the illiteracy rate in Mexican counties, those in which they were the majority, was 16.6 percent versus 3.1 percent in Anglo counties. During the 1930s the public schools were widely segregated. It was obvious that Mexican schools were in-ferior. For instance, the percent of teachers in public schools in Anglo counties with degrees was 82.2 versus 46.6 percent in Mexican counties.

The 1930s saw the complete control of New Mexico by the Democratic party. In those years the Democrats controlled the presidency, the U.S. Congress, and the U.S. Supreme Court, and through the enormous patronage power it built a federal machine and a cadre of civil service and appointive office holders at the state level. In New Mexico 5,000 state jobs were available, which, when family members were counted, meant a bloc of 25,000 votes; add this to the federal bureaucracy and quite a bloc of votes existed. In a state without much industry and high unemployment, jobs were a powerful weapon. In January 1935 more than 135,000 people, or almost a third of the population, were on relief. The Democrats controlled relief groups. In New Mexico Chicanos traditionally turned out to vote in larger numbers than Anglos.

Bronson Cutting was considered the head of the machine and he based his power on the "Mexican vote" and the American Legion. In 1934 Congressman Dennis Chávez challenged Cutting for the U.S. Senate seat. Chávez ran as a Democrat; Cutting was a Republican, but he had vast resources at his disposal. Cutting had acquired chips from the Roosevelt administration for his support of New Deal legislation. Nevertheless, the administration supported Chávez, who lost 75,759 to 74,498—a difference of 1,261 votes.

Chávez charged fraud. Not getting satisfaction, Chávez petitioned the Senate to unseat Cutting. Before a decision could be made Cutting was killed in an air crash. The New Mexican governor, after pressure from the national Democratic machine, appointed Chávez senator, and a new *patrón* was born. Chávez championed the interest of the Chicano population, working for jobs and antidiscrimination legislation. Ironically Chávez was a Democrat and the majority of Chicanos were Republicans.[99]

By the end of the decade Anglos were reaching numerical superiority. The decline of the Republican party hurt their political influence. Deals at the top were more prevalent and more aggressive Mexicans migrated out of the state in larger numbers. At the same time, more Anglos migrated to New Mexico, where they later became a majority. The bulk of the Anglo migration came from Texas and Oklahoma. New Mexico became a one-party state, with the Democrats totally dominating state politics, and the New Mexican strategy of splitting the Anglo vote was no longer effective.

Aside from Chávez's rise to power, there were cases of individual contributions. The case of Jesús Pallares, 39, who came to the United States as a teenager, shows the abuse of immigration laws in suppressing legitimate protest. Pallares had worked as a miner in Gallup and Madrid, New Mexico. Fired and blacklisted for union activities, in 1934 he became an organizer for *La Liga Obrera de Habla Española* (The League of Spanish-Speaking Workers). A year later, the *Liga* had 8,000 members, who militantly defended the rights of the poor. Because Pallares led demonstrations, the state considered him dangerous. With the cooperation of the liberal U.S. secretary of Labor, Frances Perkins, state authorities had him deported.[100]

Isabel Malagram Gonzales worked in New Mexico and Colorado. In the late 1920s she led a strike of pea workers, and in 1930 she moved to Denver, where she worked for the Colorado Tuberculosis Society. In the 1940s she worked for *Challenge,* a progressive newspaper and was active in politics and ran for the city council. Gonzales later served as national president of the Friends of Wallace and was a delegate to the Independent Progressive party's national convention in Philadelphia. Later she was a founding member of *La Asociación Nacional Méx-ico-Americana.* In 1946 she was refused the right to testify before the War Food Administration. In the late 40s she worked as a political activist in northern New Mexico. On May 31, 1949 she died in Denver.[101]

Chicago

While in the 1920s the Chicago Mexican community had been composed largely of single males, in the 1930s the *barrios* were more balanced. The Chicano community in Chicago became more family-oriented. Fewer Chicano families shared apartments as in the previous decade, and the "boarding house" was disappearing. Official attitudes were slow to change and state relief agencies still counted Chicano as foreign-born. Chicanos concentrated in South Chicago, the Near West Side, and Back of the Yards, with each community evolving its individual character.

Interest in Mexico was still high, but the mere fact of having had to make a choice whether to return to Mexico or remain did cut ties. Many were, therefore, forced to accept the fight in Chicago, for there would be no escape and local needs had to be met. According to Dr. Kerr, the Chicano Chicagoans were "less concerned with politics than with jobs, relief, education, and accommodation to the urban environment." They joined a variety of clubs, unions, and workers' associations to meet these needs. Local Spanish-language newspapers such as *La Defensa del Ideal Católico Mexicano, La Voz de México,* and *La Alianza* delineated community issues and divisions.

The pool hall was no longer the center of activity. U.S. sports such as basketball became more accepted. Mexican club teams, such as *Los Aztecas, Los Mexicanos,* and *Los Reyes,* played in leagues. As in the case of other immigrant groups, Chicano youth gangs emerged. According to Dr. Kerr, "social workers felt that participation in youth gangs was a form of adaption to the local community," a form of assimilation "learned" by Mexican youths "from the Italians and Poles who preceded them." More Mexican-run small businesses came about and school attendance by Mexican youth increased. Adult English classes also became more popular.

Hull House in the Near West Side served the needs of Chicanos. However, as Hull House devoted more time to research, its advocacy role declined. During the late 1930s Frank Pax organized the Mexican youth party and the group met at Hull House. Some Mexicans preferred the smaller Mexican Social Center, established in the early 1930s. In South Chicago some Chicanos participated in the Byrd Memorial Center which was staffed by the Congregational church whose staff looked upon Mexicans as backward and undependable. Mexicans still were prohibited from attending many of the Catholic parishes.

Because the work of its long-time director, Mary McDowell, the University of Chicago Settlement House, located in Back of the Yards, had more personal involvement with Mexicans. She worked toward interethnic cooperation and actively trained women to take leadership roles under the auspices of the Mexican Mothers' Club. The groups encouraged by McDowell continued after her death; in 1937 the Mexican Mothers' Club sponsored a series of discussions on local Chicago issues and interethnic cooperation remained better in this area than in other sections of the city.[102]

SUMMARY

The depression intensified Euroamerican nativist assaults on Mexicans. During the 1930s, 500,000 to 600,000 Mexican workers and their families (many of whom were U.S.-born) were forcibly returned to Mexico. During the depression, Anglo-Americans took care of their own, pushing the Mexicans out of the labor market.

Worker militancy along with ethnic and working-class consciousness peaked during the Great Depression. This increased awareness had been evident throughout the Southwest in the 1920s. The urbanization of Mexicans in the United States spurred the networking of *mutualistas,* which, in turn, had led to the formation of trade unions in California. Texas experienced the transition from *mutualistas* to LULAC.

The Imperial Valley strike of 1928 was important in the transition to more permanent forms of trade union associations. Two years later the communist-led CAWIU entered another Imperial Valley strike called by Mexican workers. For the next four years, communists organized in the fields, often engaging in dual unionism, competing with Mexican unions. The most effective of the Mexican unions, CUCOM, was formed in 1933 as a result of the El Monte berry strike. By the mid-1930s, poor whites displaced Mexican workers in the California fields. In 1935, the Communist party, realizing the threat of world fascism, had entered its popular front period, which led to a time of comparative unity among farm-worker organizations.

By 1937, the AFL ejected 10 industrial unions which then formed the Congress of Industrial Organizations. Bringing in the unorganized became more popular. That year UCAPAWA was formed and it advanced the organization of farm workers regardless of race. Many rank and file Mexicans and Latinos became leaders in UCAPAWA. The CIO also had a huge impact on urban Mexicans.

During the early 1930s, Mexicans joined unions such as the ILGWU. In Los Angeles and Texas, rank and file Mexican women proved to be the most militant sector of the community. Differences arose between cities and states in the type of participation. In Chicago, Mexicans worked in the less desirable sectors of heavy industry. During this period, heavy industry moved into Los Angeles, resulting in limited openings for Mexicans. In San Antonio, Mexicans worked mostly in light industries.

Mexicans adjusted to the city and the depression. Upper- and middle-class Mexican organizations formed to ameliorate conditions among the poor. A new generation challenged the old leadership. Ideological differences became apparent, with Mexicans ranging from radical to conservative. Many Mexicans participated in the Workers Alliance and Spanish-Speaking People's Congress. Middle-class and professional groups such as LULAC and MAM became popular.

NOTES

1. Howard Zinn, *A People's History of the United States* (New York: Harper & Row, 1980), p. 383.
2. Leo Grebler, Joan W. Moore, and Ralph C. Guzmán, *The Mexican-American People: The Nation's Second Largest Majority* (New York: Free Press, 1970), p. 84; Elizabeth Broadbent, "The Distribution of Mexican Population in the U.S., (Ph.D. dissertation, University of Chicago, 1941), p. 33.
3. Richard O. Boyer and Herbert M. Morais, *Labor's Untold Story* 3rd. ed. (New York: United Electrical, Radio and Machine Workers of America, 1974), pp. 12, 177.
4. Job West Neal, "The Policy of the United States Toward Immigration from Mexico," (Master's thesis, University of Texas at Austin, 1941), p. 172.
5. U.S. Congress, House, Committee on Immigration and Naturalization, *Western Hemisphere Immigration, H.R. 8523, H.R. 8530, H.R. 8702,* 71st Cong., 2nd sess. (1930), p. 436.
6. Quoted in Cletus E. Daniel, *Bitter Harvest: A History of California Farmworkers, 1870–1941* (Berkeley, University of California Press, 1981), p. 105.
7. Neal, p. 194; James Hoffman Batten, "New Features of Mexican Immigration" (Address before the National Conference of Social Work, Boston, June 9, 1930), p. 960.
8. R. Reynolds McKay, "Texas Mexican Repatriation During The Great Depression," Ph.D. dissertation, University of Oklahoma, 1982, p. 556.

9. George C. Kiser and Martha Woody Kiser, eds., *Mexican Workers in the United States: Historical and Political Perspectives* (Albuquerque: University of New Mexico Press, 1979), p. 47.

10. Works that have been useful include Ronald W. López, *"Los Repatriados"* (Seminar paper, History Department, University of California at Los Angeles, 1968); Gregory Ochoa, "Some Aspects of the Repatriation of Mexican Aliens in Los Angeles County, 1931–1938" (Seminar paper, History Department, San Fernando Valley State College, 1966); the Clements Papers, Special Collections Library, University of California at Los Angeles; Abraham Hoffman, *Unwanted Mexican Americans in the Great Depression* (Tucson: University of Arizona Press, 1974); and Peter Neal Kirstein, "Anglo over Bracero: A History of the Mexican Worker in the United States from Roosevelt to Nixon" (Ph.D. dissertation, Saint Louis University, 1973).

11. Abraham Hoffman, "Stimulus to Repatriation: The 1931 Federal Deportation Drive and the Los Angeles Mexican Community," in Norris Hundley, ed., *The Chicano* (Santa Barbara, Calif.: Clio, 1975), p. 110; López, p. 63.

12. Quoted in Abraham Hoffman, *Unwanted Mexican Americans,* pp. 52, 55.

13. López, p. 55.

14. López, p. 58; Hoffman, "Stimulus to Repatriation," pp. 113, 116, 118.

15. López, p. 43; Emory S. Bogardus, "Repatriation and Readjustment," in Manuel P. Servín, ed., *The Mexican-Americans: An Awakening Minority* (Beverly Hills, Calif.: Glencoe Press, 1970), pp. 92–93; Norman D. Humphrey, "Mexican Repatriation from Michigan: Public Assistance in Historical Perspective," *Social Service Review* (September 1941):505.

16. Hoffman, *Unwanted Mexican Americans,* p. 120; Neil Betten and Raymond A. Mohl, "From Discrimination to Repatriation: Mexican Life in Gary, Indiana, During the Great Depression," in Hundley, pp. 125, 138, 139; George Kiser and David Silverman, "The Mexican Repatriation During the Great Depression," *Journal of Mexican American History* 3 (1973): 153; Ochoa, pp. 65–66.

17. Carey McWilliams, *North from Mexico* (New York: Greenwood Press, 1968), p. 193; Robert N. McLean, "Good-bye Vincente," *Survey* (May 1931), p. 195.

18. Kiser and Kiser, pp. 36–37.

19. McKay, pp. 17, 19.

20. McKay, pp. 98–100.

21. McKay, p. 131.

22. McKay, p. 201.

23. McKay, pp. 289–290.

24. Stuart Jamieson, *Labor Unionism in American Agriculture* (New York: Arno Press, 1976), p. 15.

25. Carey McWilliams, *California: The Great Exception* (Westport, Conn.: Grenwood Press, 1976), pp. 108, 101; Clark Chambers, *California Farm Organizations* (Berkeley: University of California Press, 1952), pp. 1–2; Carey McWilliams, *Ill Fares the Land: Migrants and Migratory Labor in the United States* (New York: Arno Press, 1976), pp. 16–17; Joan London and Henry Anderson, *So Shall Ye Reap* (New York: Crowell, 1971), p. 2. See Walter Goldschmidt, *As You Sow* (New York: Harcourt Brace Jovanovich, 1947), pp. 187, 262–263, for an excellent definition of an industrial farm. See also Lloyd Horace Fisher, *The Harvest Labor Market in California* (Cambridge: Harvard University Press, 1953), p. 113; Varden Fuller, "The Supply of Agricultural Labor as a Factor in the Evolution of Farm Organization in California," in Hearings Before a Subcommittee on Education and Labor, U.S. Senate, 76th Cong., part 54, (Washington, D.C.: Government Printing Office, 1940), p. 19782 (hereafter called *La Follette Hearings*); Margaret Greenfield, *Migratory Farm Labor Problems: Summary of Findings and Recommendations Made by Principal Investigative Committees, with Special Reference to California, 1915 to 1950* (Berkeley: University of California, Bureau of Administration, 1950), p. 326.

26. Jamieson, p. 7.

27. Ernesto Galarza, *Farmworkers and Agribusiness in California, 1947–1960* (Notre Dame: University of Notre Dame Press, 1977), p. 25; Ronald B. Taylor, *Chavez and the Farm Workers* (Boston: Beacon Press, 1975), p. 39; McWilliams, *California* p. 136; Ellen L. Halcomb, "Efforts to Organize the Migrant Workers by the Cannery and Agricultural Workers" (Master's thesis, Chico State College, pp. 1–2; Goldschmidt, p. 248; Dale Wright, *The Harvest of Despair: The Migrant Farm Worker* (Boston: Beacon Press, 1965), preface.

28. Fisher, pp. 22, 42; Hewes, pp. 55–56; McWilliams, *Ill Fares the Land,* pp. 141, 257, 259–260, 264–266; George O. Coalson, *The Development of the Migratory Farm Labor System in Texas: 1900–1954* (San Francisco: R & E Research Associates, 1977), p. 28; Moore, pp. 33–36; Montejano, p. 9; Mary G. Luck, "Labor Contractors," in Emily H. Huntington, ed., *Doors to Jobs* (Berkeley: University of California Press, 1942), pp. 314, 317, 338–341, 342; Tomasek, pp. 21–23.

29. Halcomb, p. 2.

30. Sam Kushner, *Long Road to Delano* (New York: International Publishers, 1975), p. 58; Jamieson, pp. 80–81.

31. Daniel, pp. 112–124.

32. Pat Chambers, interview, California State University at Northridge, April 14, 1978; Jamieson, pp. 83, 84–85; Kushner, pp. 28, 63; London and Anderson, pp. 28, 29. Debra Anne Weber, "The Organizing of Mexicano Agricultural Workers: Imperial Valley and Los Angeles, 1928–1934: An Oral History Approach," *Aztlán* 3, no. 2 (1972): 321, puts the number at nine. Also see "Syndicalism and 'Sedition' Laws in 35 States and in Philippine Islands Must Be Smashed!" in the Paul S. Taylor Collection of the Bancroft Library.

33. Charles B. Spaulding, "The Mexican Strike at El Monte, California," *Sociology and Social Research* (July–August 1934): 571–572; Jamieson, p. 90; Actually, the workers were in a no-win situation. In an interview on April 14, 1973, Pat Chambers, a CAWIU organizer, stated that it was a strike that should have never taken place; Ronald W. López, "The El Monte Berry Strike of 1933," *Aztlán* 1, no. 1 (Spring 1970): 105; Emory Bogardus, *The Mexican in the United States* (Los Angeles: University of Southern California Press, 1934), pp. 41–42; Weber, pp. 326, 328, 329.

34. Daniel, p. 153.

35. Halcomb, p. 9; Jamieson, p. 94.

36. Jamieson, pp. 95–96; Pat Chambers interview, April 13, 1978.

37. Clark Chambers, pp. 18, 66. *La Follette Hearings,* part 51, p. 18579; Mark Day, *Forty Acres: Cesar Chavez and the Farm Workers* (New York: Praeger, 1971), p. 27; Sharecropping was virtually nonexistent in California. See Paul S. Taylor and Clark Kerr, *San Joaquin Valley Strike, 1933. Violations of Free Speech and Rights of Labor,* Hearings Before a Subcommittee on Education and Labor, U.S. Senate, 77th Cong., pursuant to S. Res. 266, 74th Cong., part 54, *Agricultural Labor in California.* (Washington, D.C.: Government Printing Office, 1940), pp. 19947, 19949. Halcomb, p. 69, states that growers admitted that if they could break the power of finance companies, and the San Joaquin Light and Power Company in particular, they would have no problem paying the workers living wages. Goldschmidt, p. 36, summarizes the allocations for the different phases of cotton production. *The Bakersfield Californian,* on October 25, 1933, stated that the Southern California Edison Company registered a profit of $8,-498,703 in the first nine months of 1933. See also Porter Chaffee, *A History of the Cannery and Agricultural Workers Industrial Workers Union* (Unpublihed, Oakland, Calif.: Works Progress Administration, Federal Writers Project, 1938), p. 8. Pat Chambers, interview, April 13, 1978; Jamieson, p. 101. On p. 19947 Taylor and Kerr put the number of strikers at 15,000, 75 percent of whom were Mexican. In an interview given December 21, 1933, records of which are found in the Taylor Collection of the Bancroft Library, Sheriff Hill of Tulare County stated: "You know how the Mexicans are. You take off your hat and holler and they'll follow you any place. The strike was 95 percent Mexican with a few white leaders."

38. *Visalia Times Delta,* September 19, 1933; quotation from Taylor and Kerr, p. 19992.

39. John W. Webb, *Transient Unemployed,* Monograph III (Washington, D.C.: Works Progress Administration, Division of Social Research, 1935), pp. 1–5; Caroline Decker, interview, August 8, 1973; Halcomb, p. 5; Jamieson, pp. 102–104. On August 24, 1973, Pat Chambers stated that the Taugus Ranch strike had had the greatest influence on the San Joaquin cotton strike tactics; he emphasized the fact that the strikers were experienced. Issues of the Corcoran newspaper covering the strike dates are missing from the paper's back files. In an interview with Paul Taylor on December 20, 1933, Frank J. Palomares stated that the only reason that the strikers went on strike was for free food. The field notes for December 20–24, 1933, from the Taylor Collection of the Bancroft Library state that Mr. Morgan, a Corcoran farmer, rented some land to the

union. He ran camp facilities next to his gas station and installed a water tank and toilets. The strikers in the camp were armed, and many were veterans of the Mexican Revolution. They cleaned the camp and picked Morgan's cotton.

40. Taylor and Kerr, pp. 19958, 19975, 19976, 19981, 19984. Pat Chambers, interviews, August 24, 1973, October 4, 1973, November 6, 1973. Halcomb, pp. 75–76, reports 12 dead, 4 hurt, 113 jailed, and 9 children dead of malnutrition in the cotton camps.

41. According to "Report on Cotton Strikers, Kings County," in the Taylor Collection, relief did not start until October 14, 1933. See also Chaffee, "Organizational Efforts," pp. 35, 49.

42. *The Bakersfield Californian,* October 9, 1933; Taylor and Kerr, p. 19963; Chaffee, *"Cannery and Agricultural Workers,"* p. 49. O. W. Bryan, a local hardware store owner at the time of the strike, was interviewed on June 22, 1973; see Ronald Taylor, *Chavez and the Farm Workers* (Boston: Beacon Press, 1975), p. 54; Dr. Ira Cross to Raymond Cato, head of the CHP, February 20, 1934, Taylor Collection, Bancroft Library; *Pixley Enterprise,* January 12, 1934, February 2, 1934; *Visalia Times-Delta,* October 11, 1933.

43. In an interview with Paul Taylor on November 17, 1933, Kern County undersheriff Tom Carter stated that growers were well prepared for the strike. They had two machine guns and had bought $1,000 of tear gas (Taylor Collection, Bancroft Library); *The Bakersfield Californian,* October 11, 1933. Also see Pedro Subia, #4717, Coroner's Inquest, County of Kern, State of California, October 14, 1933; Taylor and Kerr, pp. 19949, 20000; Wofford B. Camp, *Cotton, Irrigation and the AAA: An Interview Conducted by Willa Lug Baum* (Berkeley, Calif.: Regional Oral History Office, University of California, Bancroft Library, 1971), p. 21; Chaffee, "Organizational Efforts," p. 16; Halcomb, pp. 72–74; Louis Block, California State Emergency Relief Administration, C-R, f.4, Taylor Collection, Bancroft Library, states that only $9,822.90 was paid in direct relief in Kern, Kings, and Tulare counties, with some $7,500 paid in December —after the strike had ended. These funds were spread over 1933. Local authorities called for the state to send 1,000 CHP officers to Corcoran. The local sheriffs disbanded the camps. Corcoran was the last camp to disband. The growers burned the camp after they left. *The Bakersfield Californian,* October 28, 1933, blared "Growers to Import 1000 L.A. Workers." For material on the effect of the AAA on workers, see the following: On July 20, 1932, the price of cotton was 5.8¢ a pound; a year later it rose to 10.5¢, an 81-percent increase (Taylor Collection, "Cotton Prices in California"). After government supports, the ginners made even higher profits. On January 13, 1934, *The Bakersfield Californian* reported "Cotton Men's Income Twice That of 1932." On February 6, it reported that the Agricultural Adjustment Agency paid Kern County growers $1,015,000 for plowing under 20 to 40 percent of their crop. According to the paper, the growers received 3.5¢ per pound for not harvesting the cotton. (See "Average Cost of Producing Cotton in the San Joaquin Valley," an unpublished manuscript in the Taylor Collection.) The February 20, 1934, issue of the *Agricultural Worker,* published by the CAWIU, analyzes the cotton strike and admits that preparations were inadequate.

44. Norman Lowenstein, "Strikes and Strike Tactics in California Agriculture: A History" (Master's thesis, University of California at Berkeley, 1940), p. 94; Jamieson, pp. 106–108; *La Follette Hearings,* part 55, pp. 20140, 20180; Weber, p. 321; Guillermo Martínez, interview, Los Angeles, June 23, 1978; Pat Chambers, interview, June 26, 1978. Halcomb, p. 79.

45. In February 1934, David Martínez, R. Salazar, and F. Bustamante were sentenced to eight months for disturbing the peace (Chaffee, "Cannery and Agricultural Workers," section entitled "Imperial Valley in 1934," p. 34). See also Jamieson, pp. 108–109, and Weber, p. 323. Halcomb, pp. 104–106, sets the date at January 24. See C. B. Hutchison, W. C. Jacobson, and John Phillips, *Imperial Valley Farm Situation,* Report of the Special Investigating Committee Appointed at the Request of the California State Board of Agriculture, the California Farm Bureau Federation and the Agricultural Department of the California State Chamber of Commerce, April 16, 1934, pp. 19, 24.

46. Among the other founders of the Associated Farmers of California were the Pacific Gas and Electric Company, the Southern Pacific Gas and Electric Company, the Southern Pacific Railroad, the Bank of America, the Canners League of California, the five largest banks in San Francisco, and Standard Oil. See Tomasek, p. 95; McWilliams, *California,* p. 162; Clark Chambers, pp. 33, 53, 69. The formation of the Associated Farmers was the result of the Contra Costa

county strike in the spring of 1934 (*La Follette Hearings,* part 67, p. 24459, exhibit 11327-A, Articles of Incorporation of Associated Farmers of California). Among the signers were S. Parker Frisselle of Fresno and Floyd W. Frick of Kern County. See Jamieson, p. 40; Auerbach, p. 186; Lowenstein, pp. 95, 120; Halcomb, p. 5; Richard S. Kirkendall, *Social Scientists and Farm Politics in the Age of Roosevelt* (Columbus: University of Missouri Press, 1966), pp. 118–119; London and Anderson, p. 4; Bryan Theodore Johns, "Field Workers in California Cotton," (Master's thesis, University of California at Berkeley, 1948), pp. 79–80; McWilliams, *Ill Fares the Land,* p. 16; *La Follette Hearings,* part 49, pp. 17911–17945; Block, p. 36.

47. Pat Chambers, interview, August 24, 1973; Clark Chambers, p. 108; Johns, p. 81; Chaffee, "Cannery and Agricultural Workers," section on "The Drive Against the Cannery and Agricultural Workers," pp. 6–7; Jamieson, pp. 114–115; Douglas Guy Monroy, "Mexicanos in Los Angeles, 1930–1941: An Ethnic Group in Relation to Class Forces (Ph.D. dissertation, University of California, Los Angeles, 1978), p. 165; London and Anderson, p. 3.

48. Jamieson, pp. 119, 122, 123, 124, 125, 128–134; Weber, pp. 330–331. Lowenstein, p. 29; Johns, pp. 86–92. Lucas Lucio was the leader of the *Comisión.* Most Mexican unions could not afford to affiliate with the AFL in this period.

49. Jamieson, pp. 126–127.

50. Ronald Taylor, *Sweatshops in the Sun: Child Labor on the Farms* (Boston: Beacon Press, 1973), pp. 6–7; Peter Mattiessen, *Sal Si Puedes: Cesar Chavez and the New American Revolution* (New York: Random House, 1969), p. 9; Auerbach, p. 177; Carey McWilliams, *Factories in the Fields: The Story of Migratory Labor in California* (Santa Barbara and Salt Lake City: Peregrine Publishers, 1971), p. 196.

51. Vicky Ruiz, "UCAPAWA, Chicanas, and the California Food Processing Industry, 1937–1950" (Ph.D. dissertation, Stanford University, 1982), p. 127; Jamieson, p. 191; Kushner, p. 92.

52. McWilliams, *Ill Fares the Land,* pp. 50, 71; Jamieson, pp. 193–199.

53. Jamieson, pp. 224–228.

54. According to Jamieson, pp. 57, 277, several union organizers thought that it was more difficult to organize Texas Mexicans than Mexican nationals because the former "were brought up in a situation of greater dependence, and less freedom of expression, because of their political impotence imposed by the State poll tax and their inferior social status." See Coalson, pp. 51, 58, 62, 63; Jamieson, pp. 270–273, 275–278; Nelson, pp. 248–250; Selden C. Menefee, *Mexican Migratory Workers of South Texas* (Washington, D.C.: Works Progress Administration, 1941), reprinted in Carlos E. Cortés, *Mexican Labor in the United States* (New York: Arno Press, 1974), p. 52.

55. Coalson, pp. 40–42, reviews labor conditions in Michigan, Ohio, and Wisconsin in the sugar beet industry. McWilliams, *Ill Fares the Land,* pp. 257–258, states that 66,100 Mexicans left Texas annually for seasonal work. Many went to the beet fields. See also Jamieson, pp. 233–235, 238–241.

56. Jamieson, pp. 242–255. Menefee, p. 24, states that an experienced man could work 10 acres per week, a woman 7 acres and children smaller amounts. See also Reisler, *By the Sweat of Their Brow,* pp. 248–249; McWilliams, *Ill Fares the Land,* p. 125; Kibbe, p. 201.

57. Monroy, p. 65; Selden C. Menefee and Orin C. Cassmore, *The Pecan Shellers of San Antonio: The Problem of Underpaid and Unemployed Mexican Labor* (Works Progress Administration), reprinted in Cortés, p. 24.

58. Rosa Pesotta, *Bread upon the Water* (New York: Dodd, Mead, 1944), pp. 19, 23, 27, 40; Manuel Gamio, *The Life Story of the Mexican Immigrant* (New York: Dover, 1971), pp. 249–251.

59. Pesotta, pp. 22, 28, 32, 40, 43, 50, 54–59; Pesotta, p. 75, states that Mary Gonzales and Beatrice López were union organizers in the sweatshops of San Francisco's Chinatown. See also Grebler, Moore, and Guzmán, p. 91; Monroy, pp. 114–115.

60. Vicki Lynn Ruiz, "UCAPWA, Chicanas, and the California Food Processing Industry, 1937–1950," (Dissertation, Stanford University, 1982), pp. 56–75.

61. Julia Kirk Blackwelder, *Women of the Depression: Caste and Culture in San Antonio, 1929–1939* (College Station: Texas A & M Press, 1984), p. 9. Black Welder, p. 9.

62. Blackwelder, pp. 31–32.

63. Blackwelder, pp. 76–77.

64. Blackwelder, pp. 131–135.
65. George N. Green, "The ILGWU in Texas, 1930–1970," *Journal of Mexican American History* 1, no. 2 (Spring 1971): 144–145, 154, 158; Nelson, pp. 254–256; Menefee and Cassmore, p. 16; Martha Cotera, *Profile of the Mexican American Woman* (Austin: National Educational Laboratory Publishers, 1976), pp. 86–87.
66. Harold Arthur Shapiro, "Workers of San Antonio, Texas, 1900–1940" (Ph.D. dissertation, University of Texas, 1952): 117, 119; Kenneth Walker, "The Pecan Shellers of San Antonio and Mechanization," *Southwestern Historical Quarterly* (July 1965).
67. Menefee and Cassmore, pp. 4–5; Shapiro, pp. 125, 126.
68. Green Peyton, *San Antonio: City in the Sun* (New York: McGraw-Hill, 1946), p. 169.
69. Blackfelder, pp. 145–153; also see Roberto Calderón and Emilio Zamora, "Manuela Solis and Emma Tenayucca: A Tribute," in *Chicana Voices. Interaction of Class, Race, and Gender* (Austin: CMAS Publications, 1986), pp. 30–41.
70. Emma Tenayucca and Homer Brooks, "The Mexican Question in the Southwest," *Communist* 18 (May 1939): 257–268.
71. Peyton, pp. 172–174.
72. Peyton, pp. 186–186.
73. Quote found in Shapiro, pp. 128–129; Shelton, p. 92; Larry Dickens, "The Political Role of Mexican Americans in San Antonio, Texas" (Ph.D. dissertation, Texas Tech University, 1969), pp. 47–48, says that the Kilday brothers controlled a large section of the Black and Chicano electorate; Hershel Bernard, an observer of San Antonio politics, is quoted as saying: "Sheriff Kilday could put fifty pistols on the west side on the election and fear did the rest. When you have a sheriff's deputy at every polling place wearing his pistol, Mexican-Americans vote 'right.' " Landolt, p. 232.
74. Landolt, p. 233; Shapiro, pp. 130–132; Menefee and Cassmore, p. 24.
75. Reisler, *By the Sweat of Their Brow* p. 246.
76. Louise Kerr, "The Chicano Experience in Chicago, 1920–1970" (Ph.D. dissertation, University of Illinois at Chicago Circle, 1976), pp. 69–70, 72–78. The Chicago Mexican population had fallen from 20,000 in 1930 to 14,000 in 1933 and to 12,500 in 1934. See also Francisco A. Rosales and Daniel T. Simon, "Chicano Steelworkers and Unionism in the Midwest, 1919–1945," *Aztlán* (Summer 1975): 267. By 1926 Chicago steel mills employed over 6,000 Mexicans, 14 percent of the total workforce.
77. Kerr, pp. 83–92; Rosales, pp. 267–272.
78. Luis Leobardo Arroyo, "Chicano Participation in Organized Labor: CIO in Los Angeles, 1938–1950: An Extended Research Note," *Aztlán* 6, no. 2 (Summer 1975): 277. Arroyo's article relied heavily on newspapers and oral interviews; Monroy, pp. 70, 99.
79. Arroyo, pp. 277–295.
80. Arroyo, pp. 284–290.
81. Bernstein, p. 106.
82. D. W. Dinwoodie, "The Rise of the Mine-Mill Union in Southwestern Copper," in James C. Foster, ed., *American Labor in the Southwest* (Tucson: University of Arizona Press, 1982), pp. 46–48.
83. Harry R. Rubenstein, "Political Regression in New Mexico: The Destruction of the National Miners' Union in Gallup," in Robert Kern, ed., *Labor in New Mexico: Unions, Strikers, and Social History Since 1881* (Albuquerque: University of New Mexico Press, 1983), pp. 93–95.
84. Dinwoodie, p. 51.
85. Dinwoodie, pp. 46–55.
86. Monroy, pp. 126–131.
87. Robin Fitzgerald Scott, "The Mexican-American in the Los Angeles Area, 1920–1950: From Acquiescence to Activity" (Ph.D. dissertation, University of Southern California, 1971), pp. 148–149.
88. Nick C. Vaca, "The Mexican-American in the Social Sciences, 1912–1970. Part II: 1936–1970," *El Grito* (Fall 1970): p. 18; Ralph C. Guzmán, *The Political Socialization of the Mexican-American People* (New York: Arno Press, 1976), p. 89.
89. Annie Reynolds, *The Education of Spanish-Speaking Children in Five Southwestern States,* U.S.

Department of Interior Bulletin No. 11 (Washington, D.C.:1933), in Carlos E. Cortés, ed., *Education and the Mexican-American* (New York: Arno Press, 1974), p. 13.

90. Scott, pp. 148–149.

91. Monroy, pp. 109, 195–196.

92. On March 6, 1979, Manuel Banda stated that Tom García, 33, the secretary of the YMCA, had had the idea for the MAM. For more data on the MAM, see "Mexican-American Movement: Its Origins and Personnel," in the Angel Cano papers at California State University, Northridge/Chicano Studies, July 12, 1944, pp. 3–4. (This collection is referred to hereafter as the Cano papers.) See also Albert R. Lozano, "Progress Through Education," Cano papers; *Forward,* October 28, 1945 and February 24, 1949; "Felix Gutierrez, Prominent Youth Worker, Dies at 37," *Lincoln Heights Bulletin-News,* December 1, 1955; *Forum News Bulletin,* August 7, 1949.

93. Miguel Tirado, "Mexican American Community Political Organization: The Key to Chicano Political Power," in F. Chris García, *La Causa Politica: A Chicano Politics Reader* (Notre Dame, Ind.: University of Notre-Dame Press, 1974): F. Chris García, "Manitos and Chicanos in New Mexico Politics," in García, *La Causa Politica.* Scott, pp. 147, 149.

94. Luisa Moreno, "Non-citizen Americans of the Southwest: Caravan of Sorrow," Cano papers, March 3, 1940.

95. Kaye Lyon Briegel, "*Alianza Hispano-Americana* and Some Mexican-American Civil Rights Cases in the 1950s," in Manuel P. Servín, ed., *An Awakening Minority: The Mexican-Americans,* 2nd ed. (Beverly Hills, Calif.: Glencoe Press, 1974), p. 176.

96. Richard García, "The Making of the Mexican-American Mind, San Antonio, Texas, 1929–1941: A Social and Intellectual History of An Ethnic Community" (Ph.D dissertation, University of California, Irvine, 1980), Chapter 6.

97. Peyton, pp. 156–159.

98. Arnoldo De León, *San Angelenos: Mexican Americans in San Angelo, Texas* (San Angelo: Fort Concho Museum, 1985), pp. 52–53; García, "Mexican-American Mind," pp. 628, 488–494.

99. E. R. Fincher, *Spanish Americans as a Political Factor in New Mexico, 1912–1950* (New York: Arno Press, 1974), pp. 49, 53, 68, 69, 77, 103–105, 107, 124, 142, 146, 149–153, 160, 177.

100. D. H. Dinwoodie, "Deportation: The Immigration Service and the Chicano Labor Movement in the 1930s," in Antonio Rios Bustamante, ed., *Immigration and Public Policy: Human Rights for Undocumented Workers and Their Families* (Los Angeles: Chicano Studies Center Publications, 1977), pp. 163–174; Philip Stevenson, "Deporting Jesus," *The Nation* 143 (July 18, 1936): 67–69.

101. Cotera, pp. 93–96.

102. Kerr, pp. 69–74, 76–80, 83, 95–96, 99, 101–104.

chapter *8*

World War II and the "Happy Days": Chicano Communities Under Siege

AN OVERVIEW

It is a historical truth that, while the United States fought World War II to free the world from fascism, neither that country nor western Europe planned to extend the benefits of democracy to people of color, at home or abroad. The Western world never intended to abolish colonialism. In Indochina, the victors armed the Japanese to continue French colonial rule. At home, Mexican Americans and other minorities returned to a racist society, separate and unequal.

It is unfortunate because, if the war had in fact been fought for democracy, millions of people would not later have died in India, Indochina, Algeria, the Middle East, and Africa. The United States would not have intervened in Korea or in Vietnam. Today Latin America would not be fighting to free itself from dictators. And, in the United States, there would be no need for marches, strikes, and urban rebellions.

Another historical truth is that the rich became richer because of World War II. New structural forms of accumulation emerged that were based not on the marketplace but on federal spending. Specifically, the national government selectively made a few capitalists overnight billionaires. In the first month of the war, for instance, the U.S. government approved $100 billion in contracts. In 1945, 45 percent of all defense contracts went to six corporations.

Meanwhile, the growth of the military-industrial complex dramatically transformed the Southwest's economy. The result was a strengthening of U.S. capitalism at home and abroad as additional billions were centralized in the hands of a narrower group of government contractors. During the war, contractors used tax- and almost rent-free war plants. And while government controlled wages and, in some cases, prevented workers from changing jobs, profits zoomed 250 percent above prewar levels. Moreover, war propaganda made labor protests unpatriotic.[1]

The period from 1945 to 1970 was one of unprecedented expansion. Immediately after the war, consumer spending, the baby boom, and easy credit helped create widespread prosperity. The Cold War, the Korean War, foreign aid, and mammoth missile and space programs primed the economy. Nationally, government gave billion-dollar concessions to the oil companies in the form of tidelands. As a result, gigantism in industry developed, with research and production growing beyond the ability of the smaller firms. By 1960, two-thirds of national production was in the hands of 500 corporations.

U.S. capitalists after the war moved to check the growth of organized labor, especially the industrial unions, just at a time when some of them had begun to provide access to Chicanos and other minorities. In 1947, Congress passed the Taft-Hartley Act. Taft-Hartley made the Wagner Act of 1935 and its National Labor Relations Board (NLRB) ineffective.[2] Under Taft-Hartley, states were granted the authority to pass right-to-work laws, giving anti-union forces more freedom to petition for another election; it empowered U.S. presidents to enjoin strikes, if they thought the walkouts imperiled national security; it gave the courts the power to fine strikers for alleged violations and the right to establish a 60-day cooling-off period; it prohibited the use of union dues for political contributions; and it required all labor leaders to take a loyalty oath swearing that they were not communists. If they refused to take the oath, the law denied their union the facilities of the NLRB. Taft-Hartley allowed employers to use its provisions as loopholes to frustrate the collective bargaining process.

During the "Happy Days" of the 1950s, real wages fell 5 percent and profits rose 69 percent. The power of labor declined as its leaders buckled under to rightist pressure to clean out the left. Some of the expelled members had been the strongest advocates for labor democracy. In the mid-1950s, the CIO again merged with the AFL, curtailing many of the CIO's community-oriented projects and slowing the admission of minorities.

Ultra-patriots used the Cold War as justification for the purging not only of the leftists but of minorities as well. The "Happy Days" legitimated Joe McCarthy and his followers; it produced fictional heroes like Mickey Spillane's Mike Hammer and Captain America, who saved the country from the "reds" through their direct action.[3] The McCarran-Walter Act of 1952 and Operation Wetback were products of this nativist/racist tradition of blaming the victim for inequality.

Government during the "Happy Days" allocated gigantic sums to the states to build highways. The poor paid the tab as bulldozers uprooted them. Highway building accelerated suburbanization, white flight, and the decay of the inner city. Low-interest loans and the freeways also encouraged the Mexican American middle class to abandon the ghettos for the suburbs where the "American Dream" home isolated them from public life and the problems of the inner city.

Central city business leaders, concerned about inner city decay and its effect on their investments, pressured the federal government to protect their property. The business community had accepted public housing as a temporary solution during the depression because substantial profits could be made from huge government outlays. By the 1950s, however, capitalism had sufficiently recovered to make it on its own.

In 1949, the federal government passed an urban renewal law whose scope broadened during the "Happy Days"; additional legislation gave local and state governments greater incentives to bulldoze inner cities. These measures changed the nation's land use policy, enlarging the power of eminent domain. State and local agencies could now condemn land, not only for public use but for the public good. Federal authorities handed out billions of dollars to cities to clear "blighted" areas; the land was then sold at bargain prices to private developers. The displaced had to fend for themselves, overcrowding and eventually blighting other areas.

The case of *Brown v. Board of Education* (1954) gave new hope to the civil rights movement. According to the U.S. Supreme Court ruling, the public schools could no longer segregate children based on race. By the end of the following year, Montgomery, Alabama, authorities arrested Mrs. Rosa Parks, a 43-year-old seamstress, for refusing to give her bus seat to a white man. Dr. Martin Luther King, Jr., 29, began his historic marches, setting the tone for the last of the "Happy Days."

The chapter deals with the way Mexican Americans coped with the dramatic changes that took place in the postwar years. Increasingly urbanized, Mexican Americans competed for space in the Southwest and Midwest. Exploiting the Chicanos' powerlessness in influencing government, developers disorganized and destroyed Mexican American communities. The Chicanos' organizational responses broadened during this period; older forms, such as *mutualistas,* ceased to be a force as community grass-roots projects, like the Community Service Organization (CSO), as well as the more radical *Asociación Nacional México-Americana* (ANMA), challenged groups like the League of United Latin American Citizens (LULAC). In the political arena, the rise of Henry B. González in San Antonio represented a break from LULAC's monopoly. Both González and Edward R. Roybal (Los Angeles) rose by building their own network of volunteers many of whom had never before been involved in politics.

During the "Happy Days," Mexicans replaced their rural isolation with an urban one. In 1940, some 60 percent of Mexicans had lived in cities; ten years later 70 percent did, while, by 1960, about 80 percent were urbanites.[4] As both the geographical location of their communities and the types of work available underwent significant changes, so did the Chicano experience.

WORLD WAR II AND THE CHICANO

Raúl Morín, in *Among the Valiant,* has documented the Chicanos' contribution to the war effort. Morín expressed the sense of betrayal that many Chicano soldiers experienced because of the racism at home. Morín wrote that 25 percent of the U.S. military personnel on the infamous Bataan "Death March" were Mexican Americans and that, in World War II, Mexicans earned more medals of honor than any other ethnic or racial group.

When the war began, about 2.69 million Chicanos lived in the United States, approximately one-third of whom were of draft age. According to Dr. Robin R. Scott, between 375,000 and 500,000 Chicanos served in the armed forces. In Los Angeles Mexicans comprised one-tenth of the population and one-fifth of the casualties.[5]

Throughout the war Mexicans were treated as second-class citizens. For example, Sergeant Macario García, from Sugarland, Texas, a recipient of the Congressional Medal of Honor, could not buy a cup of coffee in a restaurant in Richmond, California. "An Anglo-American chased him out with a baseball bat." The García incident was not isolated.[6]

The Sleepy Lagoon case (1942) and the zoot-suit riots (1943) insulted Mexicans throughout the United States. The events in Los Angeles generated sympathy and solidarity from as far away as Chicago. Angelenos as well as other North Americans had been conditioned for these events by the mass deportations of the 1930s. The war-like propaganda conducted during the repatriation reinforced in the minds of many Anglos the stereotype that Mexican Americans were aliens. The events of 1942 proved the extent of Anglo racism. Euroamericans herded Japanese-Americans into internment camps. When the Japanese left, Mexicans became the most natural scapegoats.

During the war, Los Angeles became a magnet for the rapid migration of all races to the area. The mass influx overtaxed the infrastructure's ability to serve the expanding population. The Mexican *barrios,* already overcrowded, were the most affected, as the city's economic growth drew many Mexicans from other regions. Whites took higher paying defense jobs, while Mexicans assumed their place in heavy industry.

Mexicans occupied the oldest housing stock; segregation was common; and many recreational facilities excluded Mexican Americans. For instance, they could not use swimming pools in East Los Angeles and in other Southland communities. Often Mexicans and Blacks could only swim on Wednesday—the day the county drained the water. In movie houses in places like San Fernando, Mexicans sat in the balcony.

In this environment, a minority of Chicano youth between the ages of 13 and 17 belonged to *barrio* clubs that carried the name of their neighborhoods— White Fence, Alpine Street, El Hoyo, Happy Valley. The fad among gang members, or *pachucos* as they were called, was to tattoo the left hand, between the thumb and index finger, with a small cross with three dots or dashes above it. Many *pachucos,* when they dressed up, wore the so-called zoot suit, popular among low-income youths at that time. *Pachucos* spoke Spanish, but also used *Chuco* among their companions. *Chuco* was the *barrio* language, a mixture of Spanish, English, old Spanish, and words adapted by the border Mexicans. Many experts indicate that the language originated around El Paso among Chicanos, who brought it to Los Angeles in the 1930s.

Although similar gangs existed among Anglo youth, Angelenos with little sense of history called gangs a Mexican problem, forgetting that the Euroamerican urban experience caused the gang phenomenon. The *Los Angeles Times,* not known for its analytic content, reinforced this stereotype and influenced the public with stories about "Mexican" hoodlums.

The Sleepy Lagoon case was the most notorious example of racism toward

Chicanos in this era. The name came from a popular melody played by band leader Harry James. Unable to go to the public pool, Chicanos romanticized a gravel pit they frequently used for recreational purposes. On the evening of August 1, 1942, members of the 38th Street Club were jumped by another gang. When they returned with their home boys, the rival gang was not there. Later they witnessed a party in progress at the Williams Ranch nearby. They crashed the party and a fight followed.

The next morning José Díaz, an invited guest at the party, was found dead on a dirt road near the house. Díaz had no wounds and could have been killed by a hit-and-run driver, but authorities suspected that some members of the 38th Street Club had beaten him, and the police immediately jailed the entire gang. Newspapers sensationalized the story. Police flagrantly violated the rights of the accused and authorities charged 22 of the 38th Street boys with criminal conspiracy. "According to the prosecution, every defendant, even if he had nothing whatsoever to do with the killing of Díaz, was chargeable with the death of Díaz, which according to the prosecution, occurred during the fight at the Williams Ranch."[7]

The press portrayed the Sleepy Lagoon defendants as Mexican hoodlums. A special committee of the grand jury, shortly after the death of José Díaz, accepted a report by Lt. Ed Durán Ayres, head of the Foreign Relations Bureau of the Los Angeles Sheriff's Department, which justified the gross violation of human rights suffered by the defendants. Although the report admitted that discrimination against Chicanos in employment, education, schooling, recreation, and labor unions was common, it concluded that Chicanos were inherently criminal and violent. Ayres stated that Chicanos were Indians, that Indians were Orientals, and that Orientals had an utter disregard for life. Therefore, because Chicanos had this inborn characteristic, they too were violent. The report further alleged that Chicanos were cruel, for they descended from the Aztecs who supposedly sacrificed 30,000 victims a day! Ayres wrote that Indians considered leniency a sign of weakness, pointing to the Mexican government's treatment of the Indians, which he maintained was quick and severe. He urged that all gang members be imprisoned and that all Chicano youths over the age of 18 be given the option of working or enlisting in the armed forces. Chicanos, according to Ayres, could not change their spots; they had an innate desire to use a knife and let blood, and this inborn cruelty was aggravated by liquor and jealousy.[8] The Ayres report, which represented official law enforcement views, goes a long way in explaining the events around Sleepy Lagoon.

The Honorable Charles W. Fricke permitted numerous irregularities in the courtroom during the trial. The defendants were not allowed to cut their hair or change their clothes for the duration of the proceedings. The prosecution failed to prove that the 38th Street Club was a gang, that any criminal agreement or conspiracy existed, or that the accused had killed Díaz. In fact, witnesses testified that considerable drinking had occurred at the party before the 38th Street people arrived. If the theory of conspiracy to commit a crime had been strictly pressed, logically the defendants would have received equal verdicts. However, on January 12, 1943, the court passed sentences ranging from assault to first-degree murder.

The Sleepy Lagoon Defense Committee had been organized to protect the defendants' rights. It was chaired by Carey McWilliams, a noted journalist and lawyer. McWilliams and other members were harassed and red-baited by the press and by government agencies. The California Committee on Un-American Activities, headed by State Senator Jack Tenney, investigated the committee, charging that it was a Communist-front organization and that Carey McWilliams had "Communist leanings" because he opposed segregation and favored miscegenation. Authorities, including the FBI, conducted heavy surveillance of the committee and support groups such as *El Congreso de los Pueblos de Habla Español* (the Spanish-Speaking Congress). The FBI viewed it as a Communist front, stating that it "opposed all types of discrimination against Mexicans."[9]

On October 4, 1944, the Second District Court of Appeals reversed the lower court in a unanimous decision stating that Judge Fricke had conducted a biased trial, that he had violated the constitutional rights of the defendants, and that no evidence existed that linked the Chicanos with the death of José Díaz.

After the Sleepy Lagoon arrests Los Angeles police and the sheriff's departments set up roadblocks and indiscriminately arrested large numbers of Chicanos on countless charges, most popular being suspicion of burglary. These arrests naturally made headlines, inflaming the public to the point that the Office of War Information became concerned over the media's sensationalism as well as its racism.

The tension did not end there. Large numbers of servicemen on furlough or on short-duration passes visited Los Angeles. Numerous training centers were located in the vicinity, and the glitter of Hollywood and its famous canteen attracted hordes of GIs. Sailors on shore leave from ships docked in San Pedro and San Diego went to Los Angeles looking for a good time. Most were young and anxious to prove their manhood. A visible "foe" was the "alien" Chicano, dressed in the outlandish zoot suit that everyone ridiculed. The sailors also looked for Mexican girls to pick up, associating the Chicanas with the prostitutes in Tijuana. The sailors behaved boisterously and rudely to the women in the Mexican community.

In the spring of 1943 several small altercations erupted in Los Angeles. In April marines and sailors in Oakland invaded the Chicano *barrio* and Black ghetto, assaulted the people, and "depantsed" zoot-suiters. On May 8 a fight between sailors and Chicanos, many of whom belonged to the Alpine, broke out at the Aragon Ballroom in Venice, California, when some high school students told the sailors that *pachucos* had stabbed a sailor. Joined by other servicemen, sailors indiscriminately attacked Mexican youths. The battle cry was; "Let's get 'em! Let's get the chili-eating bastards!" Twenty-five hundred spectators watched the assault on innocent Chicano youths; the police did virtually nothing to restrain the servicemen, arresting instead the victims, charging them with disturbing the peace. Although Judge Arthur Guerin dismissed the charges for want of sufficient evidence, he warned the youths "that their antics might get them into serious difficulties unless they changed their attitudes." The press continued to sensationalize the theme of "zoot-suit equals hoodlum."[10]

The "sailors riots" began on June 3, 1943. Allegedly, a group of sailors had been attacked by Chicanos when they attempted to pick up some Chicanas. The details are vague; the police supposedly did not attempt to get the Chicano side of the story, but instead took the sailors' report at face value. Fourteen off-duty police officers, led by a detective lieutenant, went looking for the "criminals." They found nothing, but made certain that the press covered the story.

That same night, sailors went on a rampage; they broke into the Carmen Theater, tore zoot-suits off Chicanos, and beat the youths. Police again arrested the victim. Word spread that *pachucos* were fair game and that they could be gang-banged without fear of arrest.

Sailors returned the next evening with some 200 allies. In 20 hired cabs they cruised Whittier Boulevard, in the heart of the East Los Angeles *barrio,* jumping out of the cars to gang up on neighborhood youths. Police and sheriff maintained that they could not establish contact with the sailors. They finally did arrest nine sailors, but released them immediately without filing charges. The press portrayed the sailors as heroes. Articles and headlines were designed to inflame racial hatred.

Sailors, encouraged by the press and "responsible" elements of Los Angeles, gathered on the night of June 5 and marched four abreast down the streets, warning Chicanos to shed their zoot suits or they would take them off for them. On that night and the next, servicemen broke into bars and other establishments and beat up Chicanos. Police continued to abet the lawlessness, arriving only after damage had been done and the servicemen had left. Even though sailors destroyed private property, law enforcement officials still refused to do their duty. When the Chicano community attempted to defend itself, police arrested them.

Events climaxed on the evening of June 7, when thousands of soldiers, sailors, and civilians surged down Main Street and Broadway in search of *pachucos.* The mob crashed into bars and broke the legs off stools using them as clubs. The press reported 500 "zoot suiters" ready for battle. By this time Filipinos and Blacks also became targets. Chicanos had their clothes ripped off, and the youths were left bleeding in the streets. The mob surged into movie theaters, where they turned on the lights, marched down the aisles, and pulled zoot-suit-clad youngsters out of their seats. Seventeen-year-old Enrico Herrera, after he was beaten and arrested, spent three hours at a police station, where he was found by his mother, still naked and bleeding. A 12-year-old boy's jaw was broken. Police arrested over 600 Chicano youths without cause and labeled the arrests "preventive" action. Angelenos cheered on the servicemen and their civilian allies.[11]

Panic gripped the Chicano community. At the height of the turmoil servicemen pulled a Black off a streetcar and gouged out his eye with a knife. Military authorities, realizing that the Los Angeles law enforcement agencies would not curtail the brutality, intervened and declared downtown Los Angeles off limits for military personnel. Classified naval documents prove that the navy believed it had a mutiny on its hands. Documents leave no doubt that military shore patrols quelled the riot, accomplishing what the Los Angeles police could or would not do.

For the next few days police ordered mass arrests, even raiding a Catholic welfare center to arrest some of its occupants. The press and city officials provoked the mob. An editorial by Manchester Boddy on June 9 in the *Los Angeles Daily News* (supposedly the city's liberal newspaper) stated:

> The time for temporizing is past. . . . The time has come to serve notice that the City of Los Angeles will no longer be terrorized by a relatively small handful of morons parading as zoot-suit hoodlums. To delay action now means to court disaster later on.[12]

Boddy's statement taken alone would not mean much; it could be considered to be just one man's opinion. But consider that before the naval invasion of East Los Angeles, the following headlines had appeared in the *Times:*

> November 2, 1942: "Ten Seized in Drive on Zoot-Suit Gangsters"
> February 23, 1943: "One Slain and Another Knifed in 'Zoot' Fracas"
> March 7, 1943: "Magistrate 'Unfrocks' Pair of Zoot-Suiters"
> May 25, 1943: "Four Zoot-Suit Gangs Beat Up Their Victims"
> June 1, 1943: "Attacks by Orange County Zoot-Suiters Injure Five"

During the assault servicemen were encouraged by headlines in the *Los Angeles Daily News,* such as "Zoot Suit Chiefs Girding for War on Navy," and in the *Los Angeles Times,* such as "Zoot Suiters Learn Lesson in Fight with Servicemen." Three other major newspapers ran similar headlines that generated an atmosphere of zoot-suit violence. The radio also contributed to the hysteria.

Rear Admiral D. W. Bagley, commanding officer of the naval district, took the public position that the sailors acted in "self-defense against the rowdy element." Privately Bagley directed his commanders to order their men to stop the raids and then conducted a low profile cover-up. Sailors were, however, not the only vandals. Army personnel often outnumbered sailors. According to Commander Fogg, on June 8, 1943, hundreds of servicemen were "prowling downtown Los Angeles mostly on foot—disorderly—apparently on the prowl for Mexicans." By June 11, 1943, in a restricted memo, the navy and army recognized that the rioting resulted from "mob action. It is obvious that many soldiers are not aware of the serious nature of riot charges, which could carry the death sentence or a long prison term."[13]

On June 16 the *Los Angeles Times* ran a story from Mexico City, headlined: "Mexican Government Expects Damages for Zoot Suit Riot Victims." The article stated that "the Mexican government took a mildly firm stand on the rights of its nationals, emphasizing its conviction that American justice would grant 'innocent victims' their proper retribution." Federal authorities expressed concern, and Mayor Fletcher Bowron assured Washington, D.C., that there was no racism involved. Soon afterward Bowron told the Los Angeles police to stop using "cream-puff techniques on the Mexican youths." At the same time he ordered the formation of a committee to "study the problem." City officials and the Los Angeles press became exceedingly touchy about charges of racism. When Eleanor

Roosevelt commented in her column that the riots had been caused by "long-standing discrimination against the Mexicans in the Southwest," on June 18 the *Los Angeles Times* reacted with the headline "Mrs. Roosevelt Blindly Stirs Race Discord." The article denied that racial discrimination had been a factor in the riots and charged that Mrs. Roosevelt's statement resembled propaganda used by the communists, stating that servicemen had looked for "costumes and not races." The article said that Angelenos were proud of their missions and of Olvera Street, "a bit of old Mexico," and concluded "We like Mexicans and think they like us."

Governor Earl Warren formed a committee to investigate the riots. Participating on the committee were Attorney General Robert W. Kenny; Catholic bishop Joseph T. McGucken, who served as chair; Walter A. Gordon, Berkeley attorney; Leo Carrillo, screen actor; and Karl Holton, director of the California Youth Authority.

The committee's report recommended punishment of all persons responsible for the riots—military and civilian alike. It took a left-handed slap at the press, recommending that newspapers minimize the use of names and photos of juveniles. Moreover, it called for a better-educated and trained police officers work with Spanish-speaking youth.[14]

Little was done to implement the recommendations of the report, and most of the same conditions exist today in Los Angeles city and county. "The kid gloves are off!" approach of Sheriff Eugene Biscailuz has, if anything, hardened since the 1940s.

THE SPY GAME

During World War II, police authorities sought to strengthen social control of the *barrios* and spied extensively on the Mexican community. Most available data on this phenomenon can be obtained through the federal Freedom of Information Act. Little is known about domestic spying at the local or state levels, since these government units are not required to provide copies of their reports to individuals or organizations.

Dr. José Angel Gutiérrez has done pioneer research in this area. Through the Freedom of Information Act, he received documents proving that the FBI spied even on patriotic groups such as LULAC and later the G.I. Forum. In 1941, the FBI's Denver Office reported on the LULAC chapter of Antonio, Colorado. Its officers included a county judge and a town marshal. The FBI also investigated respected leaders such as George I. Sánchez and Alonso Perales, reporting that the Mexican community distrusted Sánchez because he had converted to reformed Methodism.

In May 1946, the FBI infiltrated a Los Angeles meeting of LULAC. An informant asserted that participants had a long history of communist activity but made no effort to document the statement. Early in the 1950s, the FBI again investigated LULAC because it demanded racial integration. In Pecos, Texas, the FBI spied on the local LULAC council because a member wanted to be on the Selective Service Board.[15]

FBI files suggest that, in addition to the California Committee on Un-American Activities, the federal agency also conducted extensive surveillance of Los Angeles Mexican Americans during the Sleepy Lagoon case and the so-called zoot-suit riots. The bureau, highly critical of the Sleepy Lagoon Defense Committee, red-baited its members, singled out Eduardo Quevedo, chair of the Coordinating Council for Latin American Youth, and M. J. Avila, secretary of the Hollywood Bar Association. According to the FBI, local police authorities bent over backward to get along with Mexicans.[16]

The files also indicate that another FBI target was the "Hispanic Movement" within the Catholic Church. At the time, many pro-Franco Spanish priests began a program "to instill into the minds of all peoples of Spanish extraction the importance of preserving the Spanish empire and of considering Spain the mother country." Mexicans allegedly resented pro-Franco sermons and rejected the call for Hispanic identity.[17]

Despite its thoroughgoing scrutiny of Chicano activities in the 1940s and 1950s, FBI reports did not uncover any evidence of Mexican American disloyalty. And from the quality of the reports, it can only be surmised that the bureau wasted taxpayers' money.

MEXICAN AMERICAN WORKERS: THE WAR YEARS

World War II did not end job discrimination and few Mexicans were employed even in defense industries. Fewer rose to supervisory positions. Alonso S. Perales stated before the Senate Fair Employment Practices Act hearings in San Antonio in 1944 that at Kelley Field in Texas the federal government employed 10,000 people, and not one Mexican held a position above that of a laborer or mechanic's helper. According to testimony, there were 150 towns and cities in Texas which had public places that refused to serve Mexicans—many of whom were servicemen.

At the same hearings Frank Paz,* president of the Spanish-Speaking People's Council of Chicago, stated that 45,000 Chicanos worked in and around Chicago, mostly concentrated in railroads, steel mills, and packinghouses. The overwhelming majority worked as railroad section hands. The railroad companies refused to promote them, and in fact were importing 150 temporary workers from Mexico to do skilled work as electricians, pipe fitters, steam fitters, millwrights, and so forth. According to Paz, between 1943 and 1945 the railroads imported 15,000 *braceros*. The Railroad Brotherhood, meanwhile, refused membership to Mexicans or Blacks, and consequently Mexicans worked in track repair and maintenance, supervised by Anglo foremen.

Paz described the case of steelworker Ramón Martínez, a 20-year veteran, who was placed in charge of a section of workers because they spoke only Spanish. When he learned that he was paid $50.00 a month less than the other foremen, Martínez complained. The given reasons for the wage difference were that he was

---

*In the cited hearings, *Paz* is spelt with a "z." In Louise Kerr's work the name is with an "x": Pax.

not a citizen and he did not have a high school education. Martínez attended night school and received a diploma, but he was still refused foremen's wages.

Historian Dr. Carlos E. Castañeda testified that, in Arizona, Mexicans comprised 8,000 to 10,000 out of the 15,000 to 16,000 of the state's miners but that the copper barons restricted them to common labor categories. The war had not broken down racial barriers. According to Castañeda, Mexicans throughout the United States were paid less than Anglos for equal work. In California Mexicans numbered about 457,900 out of a total population of 6,907,387; 315,000 Chicanos lived in Los Angeles. As of the summer of 1942, only 5,000 Chicanos worked in the basic industries of that city. Further, Los Angeles County employed about 16,000 workers, 400 of whom were Chicanos.[18]

It is ironic that the best reports on the lack of Chicano participation in the defense economy came from the FBI. A confidential report of January 14, 1944, titled "Racial Conditions (Spanish-Mexican Activities in Los Angeles Field Division)" gave the following sampling of Mexican American workers in Los Angeles war-related industries:

Company	Numbers of employees	Numbers of Mexicans
Vultee Aircraft	7,700	275–300
Consolidated Steel	4,000	Below 50
Bethlehem Steel	7,450	300
California Ship Building	43,000	Below 1,200
Los Angeles Shipbuilding & Dry Dock	12,000	300
Western Pipe & Sheet	13,250	700

The same report concluded that the Los Angeles Police Department employed 22 Mexican American officers out of a force of 2,547; the Los Angeles Sheriff's Department had 30 Spanish-surnamed deputies out of a total of 821. The probation department employed three officers of Mexican extraction. Evidentally, Mexicans were better represented in combat troops, enlisted to fight in a war presumably to ensure human rights.

MANAGING THE FLOW OF LABOR

The Pharaohs Rent Their *Braceros*

World War II removed many Chicano workers from the fields and railroads and sent them to war. Others migrated to the cities for better-paying jobs. The farm labor shortage became more acute when federal authorities placed Japanese-Americans, who included small farmers as well as agricultural workers, in concentration camps. The U.S. government had two alternatives to meet the labor shortage: simply open the border and allow Mexican workers to come into the United States unencumbered, or enter into an agreement with Mexico for an agreed upon number of Mexican *braceros* (helping arms). Growers themselves preferred the first alternative, since they could hire the unencumbered Mexicans at the lowest possible wage. The Mexican government, however, would not permit this and insisted on a contract that protected the rights of its workers. Mexico was not enthusiastic about sending large numbers of workers to the United States, but U.S. authorities pressured that country to consent. The two governments entered into a preliminary agreement in 1942, called the Emergency Labor Program, under which both would supervise the recruitment of *braceros*. [19] It is important to note that "[the *bracero* program] sold to the nation as an emergency measure, neither nativist groups, nor organized labor, nor even the Communist party objected to the admission of seasonal agricultural laborers under the terms of an agreement worked out between the American and Mexican governments." [20]

The contract guaranteed the workers' rights. It assured that, among other things, Mexican workers would not displace domestic workers, they would be exempted from military service, and discrimination would not be tolerated. It also regulated transportation, housing, and wages of the *braceros*. Under this agreement about 220,000 *braceros* were imported into the United States from 1942 to 1947.

At first many farmers opposed the *bracero* agreement, preferring the World War I arrangement under which they recruited directly in Mexico with no government interference. Texas growers in particular wanted the government to open the border. Only a handful of U.S. growers participated during the first year. States like Texas had always had all the undocumented workers they needed, and wanted to continue to control their "free market." They did not want the federal government to regulate the Mexicans' wages and housing. Growers especially disliked the 30¢ an hour minimum wage, charging that this was the first step in federal farm-labor legislation. Texas growers thus boycotted the program in 1942 and moved to circumvent the agreement. [21]

The executive branch did not receive congressional approval for the *bracero* program until 1943, when Congress passed Public Law 45. This law began the "administered migration" of Mexicans into the United States. The initial contract placed the program under the Farm Security Administration. "The growers' primary concern was crops; the FSA was concerned about those who worked the crops." One year later, because of grower pressure, the *bracero* program was transferred to the War Food Administration.

As a result of lobbying by the powerful American Farm Bureau Federation, an escape clause had been written into the act. Under section 5(g), the commissioner of immigration could lift the statutory limitations of the act on the condition that such an action was vital to the war effort. Almost immediately farmers pressured the commissioner to use the escape clause; he acceded, and the border was unilaterally left open and unregulated (an amazing action considering that the United States was at total war).

Mexicans flooded into border areas where farmers freely employed them. The United States had breached its agreement, and the Mexican government objected. In Washington some officials bluntly advocated disregarding Mexico's complaints. In the face of pressure, Mexican authorities agreed to allow workers who had entered outside the contract agreement to remain for one year, but made it clear that they would not tolerate uncontrolled migration in the future and that if farmers wanted a steady supply of labor, they would have to adhere to the bilateral agreement.

In the summer of 1943, Texas growers finally asked for *braceros,* but the Mexican government refused to issue permits for Texas-bound temporary workers. They considered intolerable the Anglo-Texans' racism and brutal transgressions against Mexican workers. Governor Coke Stevenson, in an attempt to placate the Mexican government, induced the Texas legislature to pass the so-called Caucasian Race Resolution, which affirmed the rights of all Caucasians to equal treatment within Texas. Since most Texans did not consider Mexicans Caucasians, the law had no relevance. Governor Stevenson attempted to ameliorate tensions by publicly condemning racism. The Mexican government seemed on the verge of relenting when further racist incidents were reported from Texas. On September 4, 1943, Stevenson established the Good Neighbor Commission of Texas, financed by federal funds, supposedly to end discrimination toward Chicanos through better understanding. Because the Mexican government did not change its position, Texas growers were forced to finish the season without *braceros.* [22]

Not all *braceros* worked on farms; by August 1945, 67,704 *braceros* were working on U.S. railroads. The work was in general physically oppressive and often hazardous. There are several recorded cases of death resulting from accidents on the railroads, sunstroke, heat prostration, and the like. Abuses of the contract agreement were frequent. Many *braceros* were not paid, and many had to make involuntary payments from their wages to employers, as in the case of workers for the New York Central, who had to pay $1.50 per day for food whether they ate or not. *Braceros* had other complaints such as unsafe transportation, unsanitary toilets, substandard living quarters, and lack of heat in winter months. Some growers worked the *braceros* for 12 hours while paying them only for 8. *Braceros* did not take it lying down. For example, in December 1943 they struck the Southern Pacific at Live Oaks, California, over the dismissals of Anastacio B. Cortés and Manuel M. Rivas. [23]

From 1943 to 1947 the Mexican government refused Texas's requests, since there was no evidence of any decline in its racist actions. Nevertheless, Texas growers continued to press for *braceros.* In October 1947 the Mexican government finally agreed to issue permits to Texas.

During this period, federal authorities shipped 46,972 *braceros* to Washington, Oregon, and Idaho. Mexicans had trickled into the region since the late 1910s in search of sugar beet work. The war created a desperate need for labor, and northwestern growers rented their *braceros.* Mexican workers were ill-prepared for the cold winters of the Yakima Valley and the Northwest. Managers at prison-like camps did not speak Spanish. Frequent food poisoning epidemics broke out. Townspeople, overtly racist, posted "No Mexicans, White Trade Only" signs in beer parlors and pool halls. *Braceros* often revolted and, throughout the war, attempted to ameliorate these conditions. By 1945, the need for Mexican *braceros* decreased as Mexicans began infiltrating the Northwest from Texas. [24]

Although labor shortages ceased after the war, the *bracero* program continued. The U.S. government functioned as a labor contractor at taxpayers' expense, assuring nativists that workers would return to Mexico after they finished picking the crops. Growers did not have to worry about labor disputes. The *braceros* were used to glut the labor market to depress wages and were also used as strikebreakers. The U.S. government fully cooperated with growers, allocating insufficient funds to the border patrol, insuring a constant supply of undocumented laborers.

When negotiations to renew the contract began, Mexico did not have the leverage it had during the war, having become dependent on the money brought back by the workers. The United States, now in a stronger negotiating position, pressured Mexico to continue the program on U.S. terms. The 1947 agreement allowed U.S. growers to recruit their own workers and did not require direct U.S. government involvement. The Mexican government had wanted recruitment in the interior and more guarantees for its citizens, but it got few of its demands. Growers were permitted to hire undocumented workers and certify them on the spot.

In October 1948, Mexican officials finally took a hard line, refusing to sign *bracero* contracts if workers were not paid $3.00 per hundred pounds for picked cotton rather than the $2.00 offered by Anglo-Americans. The Mexican government was still concerned about racism in Texas and still wanted recruitment from the interior rather than at the border, as was then the case. Border recruitment created hardships on border towns, with workers frequently traveling thousands of miles only not to be selected. (Border towns have grown over 1000 percent since 1920 and unemployment remains extremely high; they serve as employment centers for Anglo-American industry.)

The Truman administration sided with the farmers. On a whistle-stop tour in October 1948, El Paso farm agents, sugar company officials, and immigration agents told Truman of their problem with Mexico. Shortly after he left, the INS allowed Mexicans to pour across the bridge into the United States with or without Mexico's approval. Farmers waited with trucks and the Great Western Sugar Company representative had a special train ready. "Though there were some exceptions, the 'wetbacks'* were employed mainly by small growers. It was from these United States farmers that President Truman received support in his upset election in 1948."[25]

Opening the border effectively destroyed Mexico's negotiating position. It could only accept official "regrets" and continue negotiations. A new agreement reaffirmed the growers' right to recruit *braceros* directly on either side of the border. The agreement failed to provide any substantial protection for the Mexicans. Between 1947 and 1949 alone 142,000 undocumented workers were certified, whereas only 74,600 *braceros* were hired by contract from Mexico.

Under the Republican administration of the 1950s farmers had increasingly more to say about the administration of programs, while the Mexican government

---

*"Wetback" is a pejorative name applied to undocumented workers; it refers to the act of swimming across the Río Grande to avoid the border patrol.

had fewer alternatives. In 1951 Public Law 78 renewed the *bracero* agreement putting the federal government back into the employment business. PL 78 went a long way in institutionalizing the *bracero* program.

In 1953, negotiations began for renewal of the *bracero* program. An impasse developed when U.S. bargainers refused to make any concession to Mexico's demands for better wages. To force Mexico's hand, the departments of State, Justice, and Labor agreed to open the border until Mexico agreed to their terms. They issued a press release on January 15, 1954, that as of the 18th the U.S. would act unilaterally.

From January 23 to February 5, the United States unilaterally opened the border. Short of shooting its own citizens, Mexico could not prevent the flood that followed. Mexico had no other choice but to sign a contract favorable to the United States.

An administration representative displayed an arrogance of power: "They [the Mexican government] want to set the wages. We [the U.S.] are going to set them. We'll give them the right of appeal if they think they are too low." This arrogance was underscored when Congress passed legislation authorizing unilateral recruitment at the border.

The gunboat-like diplomacy of Anglo-American authorities flagrantly violated international law and caused bitter resentment in Latin America at U.S. reliance on the "big stick" and Mexico's obvious humiliation. Opening the border ended the labor shortage, and thereby served notice to Mexico that it had better negotiate because the United States had the power to get all the workers from Mexico it wanted—agreement or no agreement. It was evident that the United States would act unilaterally and that it completely controlled the *bracero* program. In fact many members of Congress suggested that they abandon the *bracero* program and just open the border.[26]

The increased grower dependence on the *braceros* is substantiated in the following chart, which indicates how many were imported annually:

1942	4,203	1950	67,500	1958	432,857
1943	52,098	1951	192,000	1959	437,643
1944	62,170	1952	197,100	1960	315,846
1945	49,454	1953	201,388	1961	291,429
1946	32,043	1954	309,033	1962	194,978
1947	19,632	1955	398,650	1963	186,865
1948	35,345	1956	445,197	1964	177,736
1949	107,000	1957	436,049		

Source: Leo Grebler, Joan W. Moore, and Ralph C. Guzmán *The Mexican-American People: The Nation's Second Largest Minority* (New York: Free Press, 1970), p. 68.

The steady decline beginning in the 1960s marks a convergence of several factors working against the program: resentment of the Mexican government, grievances of the *braceros,* increased opposition by domestic labor, and, probably most important, changes in agricultural labor-saving techniques and in the U.S. economy.

The work of Dr. Ernesto Galarza vividly conveyed the humiliating treat-ment and exploitation of the *bracero*. Workers had many grievances; they espe-cially resented paying $1.75 (in 1955) for meals consisting of mainly beans and tortillas when they earned $3.00 for a 10-hour day. Growers recovered a good part of their wage outlay through the company store and in some camps by acting as pimps. According to a physician, the *bracero,* after he was used, was just dumped across the border to fend for himself.

Tremendous changes in agriculture took place in the 1950s. From 1949 to 1965 the total U.S. population increased some 45 million, while the farm popula-tion dropped almost 12 million; in 1949 the farm population was 16.3 percent of the total, but in 1963 it was down to 6.4 percent. The number of farms declined from 9,640,000 to 5,610,000. During the same period the number of migrants rose from 422,000 to 466,000.[27] This increase, however, did not occur in areas of agriculture heavily dependent on *braceros*. Mechanization lessened the demand for *braceros:*

> In 1950, approximately 8 percent of United States cotton was machine har-vested. By 1964, the final year of the bracero contracting, the figure had risen to 78 percent. In Arizona and California, two principal bracero-using states, 97 percent of the 1964 cotton crop was machine harvested.[28]

The principal justification for the *bracero* program was that farmers could not find sufficient domestic labor and that without the *braceros* their crops would rot. However, unemployment caused by the 1958 recession intensified domestic labor's opposition to the *bracero* program. Moreover, the election of a Demo-cratic president in 1960 moved the executive branch and Congress toward a prolabor position. The AFL-CIO also placed pressure on Democrats to end the *bracero* program. Congress and the administration, confronted with massive lobbying from not only labor but also Chicano organizations, allowed the *bracero* contract to lapse on December 31, 1964.[29]

The Militarization of the Immigration and Naturalization Service

Several factors, during the 1940s and 1950s, contributed to the mass migration of Mexicans north. Improved transportation in Mexico facilitated flow from the interior. In 1940 all-weather roads numbered 9,929 kilometers; by 1950 the figure increased to 23,925 kilometers. Moreover there were 23,672 kilometers of railroad lines. Mexico's population rose between 1940 and 1950 by 16.5 million or 30 percent. Cotton production on the Mexican side of the border, especially around Matamoros, provided employment for workers from the interior. Since, as in the United States, Mexican growers advertised for more workers than needed, many continued northward across the border to find work in the expanding cotton fields of the Río Grande Valley of Texas.[30]

Collusion between the Immigration and Naturalization Service (INS) and the growers was a fact. For instance, the INS rarely rounded up undocumented workers during harvest time, and, moreover, it instructed its agents to withhold searches and deportations until after the picking season. A rule of thumb was that when sufficient numbers of *braceros* or domestic labor worked cheaply enough, agents enforced the laws; when a labor shortage occurred, they opened the doors, regardless of international or moral law.

Mexican migration was reinvigorated during the war. The postwar period brought relatively good times that encouraged more Mexicans to enter the country. However, in 1949, an economic recession caused massive roundups of undocumented workers. When the Korean War broke the recession, good times returned. The availability of jobs renewed the flow of the undocumented northward. The *bracero* program also stimulated migration. The end of the Korean War brought another recession, 1953–1955, which served as an excuse for the brutal massive roundup of Mexicans.

Official U.S. policy excluded "illegals," but during the 1950s hundreds of thousands of Mexicans crossed the border in search of work. Newspapers reacted by calling for their exclusion, and arousing antialien sentiments: they portrayed undocumented workers as dangerous, malicious, and subversive.[31] It is ironic that while the press condemned the migration from Mexico, the *bracero* program magnetized the border and the border patrol looked the other way when growers asked.

Even liberal Democrats supported the border patrol, calling for fines on employers who hired undocumented workers. Hubert Humphrey, Paul Douglas, Herbert Lehman, and others supported the traditional trade union position. The Mexican government, as well as most Chicano organizations, called for fining U.S. employers who hired undocumented workers. These associations, however, were offended by the excesses that followed:

In 1953 Lieutenant General Joseph M. Swing, sometimes called a "professional, long-time Mexican hater," was appointed commissioner of the INS. Swing had been a classmate of President Dwight Eisenhower at West Point in 1911, and had been on General Pershing's punitive expedition against Pancho Villa in 1916. He conducted his operations in a military manner and regarded his objective to be to flush out Mexicans. He even requested $10 million to build a 150-mile-long fence to keep Mexicans out, and set a quota to be deported for each target area.

In the fiscal year 1953 the INS deported 875,000 Mexicans; 20,174 Mexicans were airlifted into the interior from Spokane, Chicago, Kansas City, St. Louis, and other cities. In 1954 it deported 1,035,282, in 1955 256,290, and in 1956 90,122. The accuracy of the figures is questionable since the INS added estimates of the number it assumed were scared out of the country to the number it actually apprehended and deported. Moreover, the INS stood to gain by inflating the figures, since success of the operation might be used as grounds for an increase in budget. And, in fact, in 1957 the border patrol budget doubled.

Local police actively supported the INS. Swing hired two other generals— Frank Partridge and Frank Howard. Operations reached extreme proportions with John P. Swanson, chief patrol inspector, even contracting with Native Americans north of Yuma, Arizona, to hunt down undocumented workers who crossed their reservation for a bounty of $2.50 to $3.00 per person.

During the raids U.S.-born citizens became entangled in the web. It was a victory for the INS, and a blow to the human rights of Mexicans. Every brown person was suspect. Homes were searched illegally and U.S. citizens were seized and detained illegally. To this day, immigration authorities periodically conduct similar roundups that spread terror in the *barrios.* (One such raid occurred in Los Angeles when the 1970 census was being conducted, compromising the legitimacy of the statistics regarding the Chicano population.)[32]

A sometimes forgotten aspect of "Operation Wetback" was the role of Attorney General Herbert Brownell. Professor Juan García at the University of Arizona illuminates this dark passage of history. Brownell had testified before the House Appropriations Committee, soon after the Senate confirmation in 1953, that he opposed additional appropriations for the border patrol. Four months later at the request of President Eisenhower he made a tour of the border, after which he suddenly called for increased appropriations for the patrol as well as tougher laws. It was on this tour that Brownell met Swing, who had commanded the Sixth Army. Brownell had wanted to use the army to stem the "tide" by sending soldiers to the border, but army brass was cool to the idea. When Swing retired from the army, Brownell offered him the job as commissioner. Brownell seems to have reached a state of near paranoia.

On October 15, 1953, Ralph Guzmán, a Chicano activist, wrote, "A few weeks ago Herbert Brownell, the U.S. Attorney General, wanted to shoot wet-backs crossing into the U.S., but farmers fearing the loss of a cheap labor market because of G.I. bullets, complained bitterly and Brownell changes [sic] his mind."[33] Guzmán's charge was not unfounded. In May 1954 William P. Allen, publisher of the *Laredo Times,* wrote Eisenhower that Brownell had asked for the support of labor leaders at a May 11 dinner if he shot the "wetbacks" down in cold blood.[34]

It is ironic that no public outcry occurred at least to censure Brownell. The Euroamericans, for their part, were in all probability too busy worrying about the Russians. The outcry from Chicanos was generally limited, with the exception of *La Asociación Nacional México-Americana* (ANMA), which closely affiliated with progressive trade unions such as the Mine, Mill and Smelter Workers and actively cooperated with the Independent Progressive Party and the National Committee for the Protection of the Foreign Born. ANMA continuously condemned the raids. Meanwhile, "Operation Wetback" spread fear and, for a time, supposedly ended the flow. Some Anglos believed that the migration of Mexican workers had been permanently halted. However, improvements in the U.S. economy accelerated the northern migration.

Concerned Euro- and Mexican Americans protested the blatant abuse of Mexicans' human rights. On April 17, 1959, they presented a petition to the United Nations, charging that, in violation of the Universal Declaration of Human Rights, adopted in 1948, the U.S. government had mistreated Mexican immigrants. In the preface to the petition, San Antonio Archbishop Robert E. Lucey stated: "And so the poor bracero, compelled by force and fear, will endure any kind of injustice and exploitation to gain a few dollars that he needs so desperately." The report recalled the military-like sweeps of the mid-1950s, which kept Mexicans in "a state of permanent insecurity," subjecting them to "raids, arrests, and deportation drives."[35]

KEEPING AMERICA PURE

Historically, Congress has passed immigration laws to control ideas and to protect the hegemony of the white race. The McCarran-Walter Act, which reflected this ideology, provided the mechanism for political control of naturalized citizens and laid the foundation for a police state.

Francis E. Walter, chairman of the House Un-American Activities Committee, and Senator Pat McCarran from Nevada sponsored the McCarran Act to tighten immigration laws to exclude subversive elements. By the late 1940s the problems of refugees and displaced persons created by World War II had encouraged many liberals to think about scrapping the system of immigration quotas based on national origins. However, McCarran, who thought of himself as the chief guardian of the nation's racial purity, saw the admission of any number of foreigners as a threat. "To forestall the impending breakdown in American culture, Senator McCarran had been busy since 1947 with hearings and drafting of legislation; his aim: the codification of all the scattered immigration and naturalization acts in the federal statute books." In 1951, McCarran testified: "The times, Mr. President, are too perilous for us to tinker blindly with our basic institutions. . . . If we scrap the national origin formula we will, in the course of a generation or so, change the ethnic and cultural composition of this nation."[36] Chicanos, along with many other immigrants, became victims of McCarran's crusade.

Title I of the 1950 McCarran Act established a Subversive Activities Control Board that would investigate subversion in the United States. Title II authorized construction of concentration camps to intern suspected subversives without a trial or hearing if either the president or Congress declared a national emergency. Two years later, the government built six camps. Largely through efforts of Japanese-American Citizens League, Title II was abolished in the 1970s. Briefly, the 1952 McCarran-Walter Act provided for (1) the codification of previous immigration acts, relating to national origins; (2) the abolition of racial bars to entry and citizenship; (3) the establishment of a complicated procedure for admitting Asians; (4) the inclusion of a long list of grounds on which aliens could be deported or excluded; (5) the inclusion of conditions whereby naturalized citizens could be denaturalized; and (6) the granting of power to the INS "to interrogate aliens suspected of being illegally in the country, to search boats, trains, cars, trucks, or planes, to enter and search private lands within 25 miles of the border, and to arrest so-called 'illegals' and also those committing felonies under immigration laws."

The McCarran-Walter Act passed in 1952 over President Harry S. Truman's veto. The president protested that it created a group of second-class citizens by distinguishing between native and naturalized citizens. The naturalized citizens' citizenship could be revoked and they could be deported for political reasons.

The President's Commission on Immigration and Naturalization, appointed by Truman in 1952, criticized denaturalization clauses of the act, charging that provisions were too vague and gave administrators too much latitude. Visits to the United States for political reasons could be banned. The commission complained that "a substantial proportion of deportations are based on technical violations of the laws." Additionally, while a statute of limitations under federal law protected criminals, the 1952 act eliminated protection for foreigners "and therefore, an alien now is subject to deportation at any time for even minor technical violations." In fact, it "retroactively rescinded the limited statute of limitations fixed by previous law." The commission stated it violated the *ex post facto* provisions of the Constitution, and concluded that "the new act actually restores the threat of cruel and inhuman punishment for offenses long since forgiven."[37] The commission criticized the shotgun approach, because it forbade entry or could denaturalize and deport members or affiliates of "subversive organizations." The law further did not spell out the term "affiliation" but left it to the arbitrary determination of the U.S. attorney general.

These two laws led to gross violations of human rights. The law intimidated many activists, who feared being placed in a concentration camp, being labeled a subversive, or being deported. The Los Angeles Committee for the Protection of the Foreign Born, an affiliate of the American Committee for the Protection of the Foreign Born, was placed on the subversive list by the Subversive Activities Control Board because it challenged the two acts. The committee, as well as many of its members, was cleared after extensive litigation.[38]

Union busting under the McCarran-Walter Act was common. A popular case was that of Humberto Silex, who had organized Local 509 of the Mine, Mill and Smelter Workers Union of El Paso (see Chapter 7). He had entered the United States legally in 1921, had served in the armed forces, and had two children. Silex, employed by American Smelting and Refining Company, helped organize the local and served as its president. In 1945 he got into a fist fight, was arrested and fined $35, and discharged from his job. Shortly afterward, his union called a strike; a warrant was issued for Silex's deportation on grounds of "moral turpitude," citing the fist fight. The union helped contest the case and eventually the order was set aside.

The 1950 and 1952 McCarran acts intimidated Mexican trade unionists. The Los Angeles Committee for the Protection of the Foreign Born reported in 1954 that of Chicanos defended by the committee on deportation charges, 7 had been in the country for over 7 years, 3 for more than 20 years, 3 for over 30 years, 17 had U.S.-born children and grandchildren, and 22 were trade unionists.

Justo S. Cruz, 66, had entered the United States at the age of 19. He had joined the Workers Alliance during the depression. Immigration authorities attempted to have Cruz fired, but his employer refused. The INS then issued an order for his deportation. Cruz was finally cleared. He had been supported by *La Asociación Nacional México-Americana.* María Cruz, 51, the widow of Jesús Cruz, who died after deportation to Mexico, had entered the United States legally at the age of 5 and was the mother of two U.S.-born children, one of whom was a war hero. When her purse was stolen, she applied for a new registration card.

Immigration authorities attempted to force her to inform on her husband's associates. When she refused, the government arrested Mrs. Cruz and charged her with illegal entry. Later the charge was altered to membership in the Communist party. She had once been a member of the CIO Cannery Workers Union.

Agapito Gómez, 46, legally in the United States since the age of 21, had a U.S.-born wife and two children. During the war he joined the United Steelworkers of America (CIO). After the passage of the McCarran Act of 1950, immigration agents demanded that he give them a list of fellow workers and union members. When he refused, the agents took away his alien card. He had joined a depression relief organization in the 1930s and had been a member of the CIO.

José Noriega, 67, came to the United States legally at the age of 25. He worked in the construction industry in Texas and became a longshoreman when he moved to California. He joined the International Longshoremens Association. He took part in the longshoremen's strike of 1923 and was arrested. Noriega was blacklisted and he moved to San Bernardino. He later returned to the docks and joined the International Longshoremens and Warehousemens Union, working in Wilmington, a port section of Los Angeles. In 1952 immigration agents called. They wanted information, names, dates, and places of organizational meetings and participants. When he refused to cooperate, deportation proceedings were initiated.

The INS's abuse of power was dramatized by Tobias Navarrette's deportation proceedings before the U.S. Board of Immigration Appeals on May 17, 1957. Navarrette, 55, entered the United States in 1927, was married, had eight U.S.-born children, and had served in the armed forces. From 1936 to 1938 he had been a member of the Workers Alliance. The INS alleged that he was also a member of the Communist party. In its case, the INS presented witnesses of questionable character. Hernández (no first name listed) had been deported in 1951 for membership in the Communist party. He admitted that he wanted to return and that he hoped his testimony would help him in this endeavor. The INS paid Hernández $25.00 a day and placed him on parole during the numerous trials at which he testified for the state. He alleged that he saw Navarrette at two Communist party meetings in 1938 and at a rally.

Another state witness, Gonzales (no first name), had been a member of the party from 1934 to 1942. He testified that Navarrette had been a member of the Belvedere chapter and had been active in the Spanish-Speaking People's Congress. He further stated that he had seen Navarrette pay dues. Gonzales like Hernández was a professional witness for the INS, who paid him $37.00 a day. He wanted to return to the United States and work against the communists. The testimony of the two state witnesses contained inconsistencies and contradictions. After a long struggle Navarrette won his case and continued to work in Boyle Heights as a jeweler and watch repairman, dying in April 1964.[39]

Bernardo Díaz, a U.S.-born Mexican, had a wife and six children. In 1945 at the age of 19 he had gone AWOL from Camp Roberts, was tried for desertion and convicted, and spent 18 months in Ft. Leavenworth. Díaz thought that he had paid his debt and was never again in trouble, working as a groundskeeper at the La Habra Golf Course. He made frequent visits to Mexico. In January 1955 he was not allowed to return to the United States and he was later declared an inadmissible alien.

Díaz was forced to work in Tijuana for $2.00 a day. His wife, Inez, kept the family together by picking strawberries at 90¢ an hour, refusing to apply for state aid because this required her to sign a statement that her husband had abandoned her and she did not want to prejudice his case.

Many of the victims of McCarran-Walter had to wait for years for final disposition of their cases. After seven years the U.S. Supreme Court freed José Gastelum of deportation charges, on a 5–4 decision. The Los Angeles Committee for the Protection of the Foreign Born defended Gastelum. Organizations such as the American Civil Liberties Union committed resources to fighting those violations of human rights and the Community Service Organization in Los Angeles extended free legal services to anyone whose human rights immigration policies violated.[40]

AGAINST ALL ODDS: CONTINUED LABOR STRUGGLES

The California Experience: Sabotage by Politicians

Carey McWilliams described California agriculture as "farm factories." The "green giants" of agriculture in many cases dwarfed their urban counterparts, more successfully lobbying government for subsidies and exemptions from regulations such as the immigration quota and land guarantees to workers under the National Labor Relations Act.

As late as 1968 John G. Boswell of Corcoran in the San Joaquin Valley netted $3,027,384 for not growing cotton and other designated crops. The Russell Giffen Corporation of Huron earned $2,275,274 in subsidies that year. South Lake Farms in Corcoran received $1,194,022, the Saylor Land Company $786,-459, and the Kern County Land Company $780,073. In the Valley the Southern Pacific owned about 201,852 acres, Kern County Land 348,460 acres, Standard Oil 218,485 acres, the Tejon Ranch (the Times-Mirror Corporation or, better still, the *Los Angeles Times*) 168,537, and the Boston Ranch Company 37,556 acres. The agricultural yield of the San Joaquin Valley ranked above 41 states in the union.[41]

Aside from these cash payments, farmers received indirect water subsidies. During the 1950s the water subsidy from the Central Valley Project amounted to $577 per acre annually or $92,320 for 160 acres. In California 1,090,394 acres were classified as excess acreage, in Arizona 25,490, in New Mexico 9,498, in Texas 62,128, and in Colorado 16,371. In the Imperial Valley of California farmers have received over $100 million in water subsidies.[42]

In spite of the awesome power of agribusiness and its use of the *bracero* to depress wages and to break strikes, Chicanos and other farm workers continued to organize. The strike against the Di Giorgio Fruit Corporation at Arvin, California, holds its place in the heroic struggle against agribusiness. On October 1, 1947, workers picketed the Di Giorgio farm. Local 218 of the National Farm Labor Union (NFLU) led the strike. It demanded a 10¢ an hour increase in wages, seniority rights, a grievance procedure, and recognition of the union as the sole bargaining agent. Joseph Di Giorgio, founder of the corporation, refused the union's demands. *Fortune* magazine dubbed him the "Kublai Khan of Kern County"; in 1946 he had sales of $18 million. When the demands were refused, efforts to stop production began.

The press and local authorities unconditionally supported Di Giorgio: He evicted strikers, his goons and the police attacked picketers, and vandalism of any kind was blamed on the strikers. Di Giorgio used undocumented workers at will. Faced with this power, the union failed to stop production, and when it attempted a boycott, the growers merely relabeled their products.

Joseph Di Giorgio manipulated the press and politicians effectively. Hugh M. Burns, California state senator and member of the Senate Committee on Un-American Activities, convened his committee to investigate charges against the union. Jack Tenney, co-chair of the committee, led the investigation, but did not uncover any evidence of communist involvement.

Di Giorgio then mobilized friends in Washington. Congressman Alfred J. Elliot, led the fight in the House of Representatives. On March 22, 1948, he read a document, allegedly signed by 1,160 Di Giorgio employees, stating that workers did not want Local 218 to represent them; Representative Elliot demanded a federal investigation.

In November 1949 a subcommittee of the House Committee on Education and Labor held hearings at Bakersfield, California. Representative Cleveland M. Bailey (West Virginia) presided and Representatives Richard M. Nixon (California) and Tom Steed (Oklahoma) joined him. The two other members of the subcommittee, Thurston B. Morton (Kentucky) and Leonard Irving (Missouri), did not attend the hearings. The proceedings took two days, hardly enough time to conduct an in-depth investigation. The hearings were nonetheless dramatic, for the Di Giorgio Corporation had filed a $2 million suit against the union and the Hollywood Film Council, claiming that *Poverty in the Land of Plenty,* produced in the spring of 1948, libeled the corporation. Di Giorgio wanted the subcommittee to substantiate this charge. In the Arvin strike case, the subcommittee found nothing, so Congressman Bailey made no move to file an official report on the strike. Nor did he mention the controversy between the union and Di Giorgio in the report that the subcommittee eventually made to the committee of the whole. (A partial explanation is that Bailey realized that the union had lost the strike.)

On March 9, 1949, Di Giorgio, still intent on an official condemnation of the union, commissioned Representative Thomas H. Werdel from Kern County to file a report, signed by Steed, Morton, and Nixon, in the appendix of the *Congressional Record.* The appendix serves no official function other than to provide members of Congress with a forum in which to publish material sent them by constituents.

The report, a deceptive piece of literature entitled "Agricultural Labor at Di Giorgio Farms, California," stated that *Poverty in the Land of Plenty* was libelous. The report, which included a favorable biography of Joseph Di Giorgio, claimed that the strike was "solely one for the purpose of organization" and that workers had no grievances, for "wages, hours, working conditions, and living conditions have never been a real issue in the Di Giorgio strike." The report further charged that taxpayers' money had been misused by holding hearings, since they publicized "the leadership of a labor organization which has no contracts, no grievances, no strike, no pickets, and only a handful of members." It concluded that it would be against the public interest to introduce new laws or to extend present laws to protect farm workers.

The report was a death blow to the NFLU. It panicked the California Federation of Labor leadership, who ordered Local 218 to settle the libel suit (the CFL would not pay defense costs) and demanded that the strike be ended. Big labor had been scared off by a phony report that purported to be an official record, one that had been published in the "wastebasket" of the *Congressional Record*. The misleading document had appeared on March 9 and by May the strike ended. The Di Giorgios agreed to settle the suit for $1 on the conditions that the NFLU plead guilty to the judgment, thus admitting libel; that they remove the film from circulation and recall all prints; that they reimburse the corporation for attorney fees; and that they call off the strike.

For the next 18 years Di Giorgio sued every time the film was shown or negative public commentary was made on his role in the strike. Slowly Ernesto Galarza gathered data which proved that the Werdel report had no official standing, that it had been in fact written by the Di Giorgio attorneys, and that the signers, according to them, did not know who drafted it or, for that matter, remembered signing it. Werdel, Steed, Morton, and Nixon all knew that the report had no official status and was, at best, an opinion. In other words, they knowingly deceived the public to break the strike. Agribusiness had enough power to induce four members of Congress to endorse a blank check in order to satisfy the whim of a very powerful and vindictive man. Farm workers did not have countervailing power.[43]

The story of the NFLU during the 1950s is one of frustration for farm workers in California. Every time workers were able to stop production, growers broke the movement by using *braceros* and undocumented workers. Growers used the departments of Labor, Agriculture, Justice, and State as their personal agents. The so-called liberal Democratic administrations favored growers. Little difference existed between Republican governor Goodwin Knight and Democratic governor Edmund G. Brown, Sr., both of whom served the growers.

Growers based their control on the labor contractor who furnished farmers with an abundance of domestic scabs and undocumented workers once a union called a strike. These contractors, usually of Mexican descent, were indispensable in keeping the exploitive system functioning. This reality forced the NFLU to change its response from conducting militant strikes to thoroughly documenting working conditions and the misuse of the *bracero* program and exposing them to the public. By the end of the decade the NFLU died an unnatural death; in June 1960 it surrendered its charter. The Agricultural Workers Organizing Committee (AWOC) took its place.

During the 1950s, numerous examples of individual heroism came to light: In 1950 Ignacio Guerrero, his wife, and 13 children lived in a makeshift home on the outskirts of Tracy, California. He read leaflets about the Di Giorgio and the potato strikes in Kern County. In Tracy 20 contractors, mostly Mexicans, managed several thousand tomato pickers. Conditions were miserable. Growers paid 18¢ a bag for first pickings, withholding 2¢ per box as a "bonus." The workers would lose the "bonus" if they left before the harvest ended. Guerrero took the initiative and held meetings in his home. Local 300 was chartered.

The Tomato Growers Association had substantial resources, while Local 300 had "no treasury, no strike fund, no regular staff, and only a token membership base." In spite of the handicaps, the workers stopped production for a time. However, the strike was doomed when Teamster officials directed their drivers to cross the tomato workers' picket and the growers imported massive numbers of *braceros*. The union won a limited victory; it signed some contracts and eliminated the bonus.

The next year the Federal Wage Stabilization Board wiped out whatever gains were made by fixing a ceiling of 20¢ for all pickings (second and third pickings had gone as high as 28¢). Many growers restored the bonus system. Workers again turned to Local 300. It was powerless; the NFLU had financial problems and the California Federation of Labor ignored appeals. Ignacio Guerrero had to move his family in search of work.

The Guerrero story was repeated in the Imperial Valley. The Imperial Valley Farmers Association, comprised of 480 members, controlled 90 percent of the acreage. The local labor force struggled to improve its working and living conditions, which had deteriorated because the heavy use of *braceros* allowed growers to introduce backbreaking methods such as the short-handled hoe. They also substituted piecework for hourly wages. In 1950 about 5,000 undocumented workers labored in the valley, earning between 40¢ and 50¢ an hour, and sometimes as low as 35¢ an hour. *Braceros* earned 70¢ an hour.

Workers of Local 280 attempted to convince the Mexican government to stop the flow of *braceros* into the valley. However, U.S. Ambassador William O'Dwyer, whose brother was a partner of the president of the Imperial Valley Farmers Association, represented the growers' interests in Mexico City. After three years of struggle, the results were the same as at Tracy; over 150 families moved north in search of work.

By 1953 the NFLU changed its tactics, and concentrated its efforts on informing the public about the abuses in the *bracero* program and treatment of workers. During the next seven years an attack was launched against the *bracero* program which exposed its contradictions. Galarza and NFLU leaders realized that unionization was futile while the *bracero* program remained. During the late 1950s it seemed as if the *bracero* program had become an institution. Edward R. Murrow's *Harvest of Shame* was shown on national television on Thanksgiving Day, 1960. This documentary rekindled interest in the plight of farm workers.[44]

The Texas Experience

During the period from 1941 to 1960, Texas-Mexicans moved in increasing numbers to the Midwest. Housing and medical care were primitive, and entire families, including children, worked. Michigan Field Crops, Inc., organized during World War II, in 1950 included 8,767 beet growers, 6,800 pickle growers, and an estimated 3,300 growers of miscellaneous crops as members. In 1950 they imported 5,300 Texas-Mexican farm workers. Before the war Mexicans had been taken north by contractors: now larger numbers went on their own. The war did little to improve opportunity for Texas-Mexicans in the Midwest, where many depended on seasonal work in cherries, cucumbers, tomatoes, and the familiar sugar beet.

Texas-Mexicans also migrated in larger numbers to the Pacific Northwest, where after the war they migrated to urban areas, only to be replenished by more Texas Mexicans. By the 1940s Chicanos formed communities in the Yakima Valley, and by the end of the decade this region supported a Spanish-language radio.

Displacement of Texas-Mexicans accelerated in the late 1940s, when Mexico removed Texas from the *bracero* "blacklist." That year California received 8 percent of the *bracero* contract labor and raised cotton wages 15 percent; Texas received 56 percent of all *bracero* contract labor and lowered cotton wages 11 percent. As conditions worsened in Texas, Chicano migration to the Midwest increased.[45]

In the early 1940s contractors hauled workers throughout Texas. They followed the migrant stream, picking cotton along the Texas coast throughout central Texas and into western Texas. Many migrants, whether they went north or remained in Texas, returned for the winter to their base town where many owned small shacks. They would work at casual jobs until the trek began again. These South Texas towns by the postwar era were interwoven by a network of contractors which furnished cheap labor to growers.

Many Mexican contractors amassed sizable equities. By the late 1940s many had bought farms or leased land. In the postwar period a trend back to tenancy and lease-operation emerged. The leasers were predominantly second and third generation South Texas Anglos, but this group also included a dozen or so Mexican farmers, most of whom had originally been *contratistas* and truckers. One *Mexicano* family became one of the world's largest watermelon shippers, leasing several thousand acres of land.

Chicano migrants became increasingly independent of the contractor and the local *patrones.* Although they still worked for exploitive wages as migrants, they no longer totally depended on the South Texas economy. They had options as to where they went and could find sources of wages on their own.

Texas-Mexicans became increasingly urbanized. They worked in industries outside agriculture, such as oil, where they did the low-paying, backbreaking work. In 1945 the Fair Employment Practices Commission (FEPC) ordered Shell Oil to upgrade Mexican labor at the Deer Park refinery. The local Anglo union staged a wildcat strike in protest. In 1946 Gulf Oil's coast refinery hired 20 Chicanos; they were paid 91¢ an hour, while their Anglo counterparts earned $1.06 an hour.

The war had opened some occupations to Mexicans. For instance, in the Fort Worth area they moved into service jobs such as bus boys, elevator operators, and the like. However, the better paying industries, such as Consolidated Fort Worth and North American Aircraft of Dallas, hired a limited number of

Chicano workers. Unionization of industries helped Chicano workers little since unions relied on the seniority system and few Mexicans held membership in trade unions. In short, Texas industries followed the practice of discriminating against Mexican workers in terms of employment, wage scales, and opportunities for promotion.

Mexicans earned low wages in Texas agriculture with cotton farmers in 1948 in the El Paso area paying pickers $1.50 per hundredweight of cotton picked. In 1950, farmers in the Río Grande Valley paid $1.25 per hundred pounds, with many farmers along the river paying as low as 50¢ to 75¢. The nationwide average was $2.45 per hundred pounds.

The heavy use of contract and undocumented labor in agriculture made it difficult to organize and encouraged migration to other states. Organized labor in Texas frantically attempted to stop the manipulation of the *bracero* and undocumented worker by grower interests.[46] The number of *braceros* contracted in Texas increased from 42,218 in 1949 to 158,704 five years later, while emigration out of Texas jumped from just over 5,000 in 1939, to 22,460 in 1945, to 71,353 in 1949.

Despite a growing antilabor climate, AFL-CIO unions in Texas increased their membership from roughly 200,000 in 1940 to 450,000 in 1970. In spite of the success of labor in general, industries which had a heavy concentration of Mexicans, such as agriculture, remained unorganized. As in the 1930s, Chicanos organized in the garment industry. The number of garment workers increased from about 6,500 in 1940 to about 25,000 in 1970, but ILGWU membership dropped from about 2,750 in 1940 to 1,375 in 1953 and 1,000 in 1956. In 1962 it fell to about 500 dues-paying members. Considering the wealth (assets of $174 million in 1969) and growth in membership (340,000 in 1940 to 450,000 in 1970) of the ILGWU, the situation in Texas has to be blamed on the national office's unwillingness to commit funds or effort toward building a cadre of Chicano organizers.

During the late 1940s and the early 1950s San Antonio had about 800 garment union members. Half of them worked for the Juvenile Manufacturing Company, represented by Local 347. When ILGWU lost the certification election at that plant, this local died. Meyer Perlstein retired in 1956 and another easterner, Sol Chaikin, who had little experience in the Southwest and less with Mexicans, replaced him. He chose a staff, none of whom spoke Spanish. Rebecca Taylor (see Chapter 6) and Elizabeth Kimmel were told that they would be transferred; however, to everyone's surprise Taylor took a managerial position with the Tex-Son Company, which manufactured boys' clothing.

In December 1958 Tex-Son laid off large numbers of workers, subcontracting more and more work to a factory in Mississippi. The union had to negotiate a good contract with Tex-Son or abandon its efforts in San Antonio. Tex-Son had the support of the Southern Garment Manufacturing Association and the other garment shops in the city. Local 180 did not even send a representative to the San Antonio Central Labor Council. When negotiations slowed down, René Sándoval gave an impassioned speech and the workers walked out on February 24, 1959.

The strike was one of the roughest in San Antonio history. The picketers threw eggs at owner Harold Franzel, and the police responded by beating the strikers. An unknown person shot into the homes of two strikebreakers. As the tensions increased, Sophie Gonzales and Georgia Montalbe emerged as strike leaders. The ILGWU collected over $10,000 and began paying strike benefits of $20 a week. The strikers picketed stores carrying Tex-Son goods, solicited the support of the churches, marched in a parade, and improved relations with other unions.

The strikers could not stop production, however; there were too many workers ready to take their jobs. In the fall of 1959 the Landrum-Griffin Act stripped the strikers of the right to carry banners and signs outside of stores; the strikers were limited to leafletting the stores. The strike died of attrition in the spring of 1962, after costing the ILGWU $500,000.[47] The failure of the Tex-Son strike and the trend in the 1960s of moving plants to Mexico, Taiwan, Hong Kong, and Korea put an end to any effective efforts to organize in the garment trades.

"The Salt of the Earth": Growing Militancy Among Women

The so-called Salt of the Earth strike is the best-known Chicano strike. It inspired a classic film that received worldwide acclaim but was banned in the United States. The film depicts the strike as well the role of women in stopping production. The actual work stoppage lasted 15 months, from October 1950 to January 1952, the longest strike in New Mexico's history. It pitted the 1400 members (90 percent Mexican) of Local 890, International Union of Mine, Mill and Smelter Workers, against Empire Zinc and Grant County. Although some of the leaders were admitted communists, the rank and file were more concerned with exploitative conditions than with ideology.

The hysteria of the McCarthy period intimidated organized labor. The CIO buckled under and asked its union officers to sign affidavits that they were not communists. Even when officers signed an affidavit, employers often did not accept their word, charging that the union officials were communists. The burden of proof was shifted to the signers, who were guilty of perjury until they proved otherwise. This practice would have implications for the "Salt of the Earth" miners.[48]

The Empire Zinc workers' grievances were substantial. They suffered indignities such as separate payroll lines, toilet facilities, and housing. Owners limited Mexicans to backbreaking mucking and underground mining jobs while they gave Anglos surface and craft jobs. Local 890 demanded payment for collar to collar work—that is, compensation for all the time the miner spent underground— holiday pay, and the elimination of the no-strike clause in their contract. The miners did not consider these demands out of line, and Empire Zinc surprised the local when it refused to negotiate. It soon became evident that management wanted to break the union.

The miners lived in a company town. Mexicans made up 50 percent of Grant County. As soon as the strike began, the county authorities demanded that the governor send the National Guard to the area. The strike itself developed into a typical management/labor dispute until a local judge issued an injunction that the workers stop picketing the mine. At this point, the women's auxiliary, formed in 1948, took over the lines because the women were not covered by the injunction. A dramatic confrontation took place between the women and the deputies. At one point, deputies jailed 45 women, 17 children, and a 6-month-old baby. This event caught the imagination of other unions, and women's groups who supported the auxiliary. Frequent clashes occurred between the women and scabs and the sheriff's deputies.

Meanwhile, the steelworkers' union red-baited Local 890 and attempted to subvert Mine-Mill. The steelworkers, however, made the mistake of attempting to minimize the race issue. This turned off Mexican miners, who had joined Mine-Mill precisely because it recognized the importance of the race question.

The governor intervened on the side of management and sent in the state troopers, who enforced the injunction and prohibited the blocking of the road leading to the mine. The action of the governor checked the use of women on the picket line, since the state penitentiary could house all the picketers. The strike ground to a halt with the workers winning minimal gains. Empire Zinc, eager to settle because of wartime profits, refused to drop charges against union leaders, many of whom eventually spent three months in jail and paid thousands of dollars in fines.

POLITICS OF THE G.I. GENERATION

New Mexico

Mexicans, nearly 97 percent of them U.S.-born, numbered about half the population of New Mexico. They lived in seven northern counties while Anglos controlled East and South New Mexico. Anglos in the eastern half, called Little Texas, discriminated against Mexicans, who could not frequent the "better" barbershops, restaurants, hotels, and amusement centers. They attended separate schools and churches. Mexican War veterans could not even join the local American Legion post.

Racism worsened after World War II when large numbers of white Texans arrived to work in the oil fields. In Grant County, where a dual wage system operated, Mexican miners did the manual labor. In company towns, the Mexican homes lacked elementary plumbing facilities. Even in Albuquerque and Santa Fe, Mexicans suffered discrimination, and could not purchase homes in new residential tracts. And in the more liberal environment of the University of New Mexico, fraternities and sororities excluded Mexicans as members.

U.S. Senator Dennis Chávez, Jr., in power because of a solid Mexican voting bloc, had a liberal voting record, supporting the New Deal and the Fair Deal, sponsoring civil rights legislation (he was in the forefront of the fight for a Fair Employment Practices Commission), and publicly condemning Senator Joseph McCarthy. Chávez had prepared the way, in the 1940s and 1950s, for the rise of LULAC (led by Daniel T. Váldez) and the G.I. Forum (led by Vicente Ximénez) in New Mexico. During the 1930s, Chávez had pushed to have Mexican children taught exclusively in English, so that, according to him, they could compete with Anglos. Classes in northern New Mexican schools were often taught exclusively in Spanish. Chávez believed, in fact, that the omission of English was intentional, to deprive students of a weapon to fight back with.[49]

Drought, depression, and World War II almost ended the New Mexican way of life. Speculators bought off land lost at tax sales. During and after the war, Mexicans subsisted on 5 to 15 acres, while Anglos held 50 to 200. Mexican Americans could not compete with the large operators who had the capital to lease government and Indian lands. From 1940 to 1960, government expended enormous sums of money, accelerating the industrialization of the state. Merchant houses and speculative capital were displaced by chain stores, national corporations, and large-scale finance institutions. Industrialization in turn attracted more Anglo wage earners, who invaded even northern New Mexico. Throughout the 1950s the rural population declined. In 1949, 1,362 farms operated in Taos; ten years later only 674 farms remained.

The Atomic Energy Commission became one of the prime sources of industrial capital in northern New Mexico (this area had 50 percent of the nation's uranium resources). Its presence, too, brought about modernization and development. From 1947 to 1957, New Mexico manufacturing employment grew from 9,000 to 20,800 workers, an increase of 131 percent.[50] Mexicans, ill-prepared to meet labor market demands for high-tech workers, were pushed even further down.

In 1947, the median per capita income in the seven northern counties was $452.26, versus $870.04 in seven Anglo counties. A year before, the U.S. median had been $1,141. Poverty caused health problems: infant mortality was six times higher among Mexicans than Anglos, and the incidence of tuberculosis was almost 2.5 times greater. Out of 402 medical doctors practicing in 1949, 10 were Mexican, and 8 of 143 dentists were Mexican. In fact, few Mexican professionals of any sort lived in the state (24 out of 272 lawyers were Mexican). Although it boasted it had more Mexican officeholders than any other state, New Mexico's poverty worsened.

New Mexicans lacked education, a key factor in the new labor market. Illiteracy was 16.6 percent for Mexicans, versus 3.1 for others. Teachers in Mexican counties had less adequate training; 46.2 percent held BAs, versus 82.2 percent in the Anglo counties. According to the 1950 census, the median education for Mexicans was 6.1 years, as against 11.8 for Anglos. Ten years later, the figures were 7.4 and 12.2 respectively. In 1965, New Mexico had the highest percentage of draftees failing the mental exam of any southwestern state—25.4 percent.[51] This was hardly a population prepared to compete in a technological society.

With more Anglo-Americans arriving in the state, reelection for Chávez became more difficult. In 1952, Chávez won by only 5,000 votes. A U.S. Senate committee investigating the election found errors and irregularities but no fraud. In general, the Republican party at this time was more successful. Chávez became increasingly isolated from the Democratic party as it catered more and more to East New Mexico, and, as a consequence, he supported New Mexican Republican candidates.

Chávez symbolized Mexican politics during the postwar period. The decline in his power saw the lessening in strictly ethnic politics in New Mexico. Later political figures were not as dedicated to championing the cause of Mexican Americans as was Chávez.

El Paso

During the 1940s and 1950s, El Paso experienced unprecedented expansion. Employment increased 55.7 percent from 1950 to 1962 as compared to just under 29 percent for the national average. Even so, the per capita income in El Paso steadily declined relative to the nation during this decade. Like San Antonio, El Paso depended heavily on military installations. Both cities, too, were affected by the rabid antiunionism of the state. El Paso also had a large pool of Mexican labor fronting the city in Juárez, Mexico.

In 1900, El Paso was one of the four cities that had a Mexican population of over 5,000 (its Mexican American population was double that figure). By the 1950s, Mexicans were no longer confined exclusively to *Chihuahuita,* the oldest Chicano *barrio* in the city, located next to the border. In 1941, with the use of federal funds, the city had built the Alamito housing projects, whose 349 units represented 2.3 percent of the Southside's housing. Although there were calls in the community for increased construction, additional public housing was not built for 33 years because landlords and real estate interests opposed public housing and blocked efforts to pass the stricter housing codes necessary to obtain federal grants.

During World War II, the military brass at Fort Bliss demanded that the city clean up the Southside because it endangered the health of its trainees. After the war, federal housing loans to veterans and other low-interest loans accelerated the movement to the suburbs. Federal funding increased for highway construction. The Paisano Drive highway (1947), intended to improve transportation to the central city business district, displaced 750 families, 6,000 residents of *el segundo barrio* (the Second Ward). The highway further isolated South El Paso, causing a "shanty" boom—with *jacales,* made of plywood, sheet metal and cardboard, replacing former homes.[52]

A 1948 survey of South El Paso reported it had a population of 23,000. A lack of decent housing remained a major problem. Only 5 percent of the families had showers; 3 percent had tubs. The average number of people per toilet was 71. The area housed 19.07 percent of the city's population; it was the setting of 88.2 percent of its juvenile crime, 51 percent of its adult crime, and two-thirds of its infant mortality. Not surprisingly, street crime increased because of the poverty. The El Paso press, as in Los Angeles, exploited the powerlessness of the Mexican residents of *el segundo,* depicting them as murderers, drug users, and rapists. Conditions got so bad that without the church agencies and local Mexican American organizations, the Second Ward would have blown up.

The 1960 census showed little improvement. Seventy percent of the Southside's housing remained deteriorated or dilapidated. Throughout this period, as in the 1940s, landlords and tenement owners successfully lobbied against a strong building code. City officials ignored federal pressures to enact housing codes that would clean up the situation. Although local authorities requested federal urban renewal funds, they wanted them "without federal intervention."[53]

In 1957, Raymond Telles, a retired air force lieutenant colonel during the Korean War, ran for mayor of El Paso. Although he had served as county clerk, the city elite opposed Telles, a conservative who took every opportunity to assure voters of his Americanism. Members of the El Paso business establishment openly stated that they did not believe that a Mexican was qualified to be mayor. They billed his Anglo opponent as the "candidate for all El Paso." Telles's victory shattered the myth that Mexicans would not turn out—90 percent of the eligible Mexicans voted.

After the election, the Democratic party leaders abolished the primary for mayor. The party would now name its candidate, allegedly saving the cost of running a primary. Telles who had been himself chosen in a primary, supported the change because, he incorrectly predicted, it would improve the Mexican community's chances of electing a mayor.[54]

San Antonio

San Antonio in the mid-1940s, controlled by the Kilday brothers, was reputed to be the "most open city in the United States." The Kildays based much of their power on a network of Catholic priests, Catholic agencies, the American Legion, and the Mexican vote.[55] On election day, Owen Kilday put 50 pistols at the West Side polls to ensure that Mexicans voted correctly. As for the Mexican community, many saw little value in paying $1.75 every several months for the alleged right to vote.

Many Mexicans lived in floorless shacks without plumbing, sewerage connections, or electric lights. Open shallow water wells, used for drinking and washing, could be found next to outside toilets. The unpaved streets and sidewalks and overcrowded housing worsened after the war with the return of thousands of Chicano veterans. San Antonio during the war had had the distinction of having the highest tuberculosis death rate of any large city in the country—a distinction that it undoubtedly maintained in the postwar era.

Rapid economic growth generated by World War II and government spending in San Antonio accelerated the movement of South Texans into the Alamo City. Highly segregated, Mexicans still lived in the West Side. (Blacks resided in the east, lower- and middle-class whites in the south, and middle- and upper-class whites in the north.) Movement out of the *barrio* was still infrequent. The lack of unionization and the size of the reserve labor pool further depressed conditions. By design, the city attracted only light industry in order to keep heavy industry and unions out of San Antonio. During the 1940s, civilian jobs at the military installations helped the city's total population grow from 253,854 to just under 410,000. As in other Euroamerican cities, some San Antonians moved to the suburbs; the building of highways inevitably displaced the poorest. In turn, new housing meant jobs, as did the freeways and airport expansion.[56]

The Mexican population climbed from 160,420 in 1950 to 243,627 (out of a total of 587,718) by the end of the decade. In 1959, San Antonio was second only to Los Angeles in the number of Mexicans. The first and second generations increased to 30,299 and 75,590 respectively. San Antonio Mexicans were overconcentrated in the blue-collar and service occupations. Over a quarter of the Mexican women worked. A large number of Mexicans found opportunity at the military bases. In 1963, the civilian payroll amounted to $168,266,933 (the combined civilian–military payroll was $303 million), while manufacturing amounted to $88 million. Mexican employment in the military installations trebled during World War II and, by the 1950s, a very small core of Mexicans had moved into supervisory and technical positions. Access had been difficult and was often brought about by intervention of Mexican American elected officials. Opportunity remained unequal, however, and by the early 1960s the median salary of Mexican Americans was $2200 less than that for Anglos, $6700 vs. $4500.[57]

The 1950 census showed that San Antonio Mexicans still suffered from a lack of education; about half had not gone beyond the fifth grade. Less than 10 percent finished high school and less than 1 percent completed college. Their limited education checked the Mexicans' upward mobility during a time of prosperity for the majority of Euroamericans. The state's right-to-work law also frustrated the Mexicans' advance in occupational status. When Mexicans joined unions, they were mostly in manual jobs—for instance, they comprised almost 100 percent of the hod carriers and 90 percent of the plasters. They made up only 6 percent of the electricians and just over 10 percent of the cement masons. San Antonio unions were weak, and, consequently, wages were lower than in California, for example.

The masses of Mexican Americans remained nationalistic. They called themselves Mexicans and kept up the Spanish language. For Mexican American organizations, dominated by the middle class, assimilation continued to be the main objective; in public, some of the middle class often referred to themselves as Spanish or Latin Americans. The trend among Mexican American organizations toward assimilation, in fact, had been popular since the 1920s. According to Edwin L. Dickens, "From 1948 through 1964 there was a clear trend away from Mexican nationalism toward American acculturation." Emphasis at the annual *Cinco de Mayo* (5th of May) celebrations shifted from patriotic Mexican affairs to raising money for scholarships for education.[58] LULAC and the GI Forum replaced many patriotic societies formerly in charge of these events.

Definitely, the San Antonio Mexican community was more politically active during the postwar period. Voter turnout increased from 55.7 percent in 1948 to 68.7 percent in 1956 and 87.1 percent in 1964. However, the poll tax continued to frustrate mass voter registration. Without a doubt, the leading politician was Henry B. González, whose parents were political refugees from Durango, where they owned a mine. Born in 1916, Henry B. graduated from St. Mary's Law School, working for a time as a juvenile officer. Involved in civic affairs, Henry B. ran unsuccessfully for state representative in 1950. A year later, he won a seat on the City Council. González, who did not belong to the LULAC clique, put together a grass-roots campaign.

González acquired a reputation as an independent who often clashed with the Good Government League (GGL), which ran the city. Like Edward Roybal in Los Angeles, González championed civil rights causes. In 1956, he ran for the state Senate and won by 282 votes. The campaign of Albert Peña, Jr., for county commissioner greatly helped González. The race issue resurfaced, with opponents also frequently accusing González of being a leftist. In the state Senate, González continued to champion liberal causes. In 1958, he unsuccessfully ran for governor.

In 1960, González supported John F. Kennedy for president. Mexicans gave Kennedy the margin of victory he needed in Texas. In November 1961, González ran in a special election for the U.S. Congress. The West Side turned out, and González won. During this period, González's victories were unique, since other Mexican American candidates did not fare as well. LULAC-backed candidates such as M. C. Gonzales lost consistently.

Los Angeles

California's Mexican population between 1940 and 1960 tripled, from 416,140 to 1,426,538. (It had been 760,453 in 1950.) Migration from other states accounted for most of the rise. Mexican migration to California steadily increased to the point that 60 percent of all Mexican American movement was to California. In contrast, during the 1950s, Texas's Mexican population jumped from 1,083,768 to 1,417,810. California Chicanos were also the most urbanized in the Southwest, 85.4 percent. Los Angeles experienced a rapid growth, numbering over 600,000 Mexican Americans in 1960.

Structurally Los Angeles differed from San Antonio. Los Angeles's East Side did not have a majority of Mexicans until the 1950s, whereas San Antonio's West Side was from the beginning exclusively Mexican. Moreover, Mexicans were more concentrated in San Antonio, comprising 41 percent of the city. Los Angeles's Mexican population was only about 10 percent.

The GI bill encouraged the suburbanization of the Chicano middle class. Like other Angelenos the freeways took them to new communities like Pico-Rivera, La Puente, and Covina. A large number of Mexicans remained in outlying localities such as Wilmington, San Pedro, Venice, San Fernando, and Pacoima. Many communities had been agricultural colonies. In general, in Los Angeles, Mexicans were not as isolated as in Texas. Mexican neighborhoods such as Boyle Heights were more polyglot ethnically and racially, with Japanese, Jews, Armenians, and others living in close proximity to Mexicans.

Racism was not as overt as in Texas; rather, Mexicans in Los Angeles suffered more from a stifling indifference. Individually, they could move out of the *barrio* and could be treated with polite indifference by Anglos. Intermarriage also increased dramatically after the war. This mobility of the middle-class Mexican Americans drained the *barrios* of leadership. In San Antonio, all classes of Mexicans lived in the West Side, forming a community with similar interests. In Los Angeles, Mexicans in 1950 had been at the point of developing a community. However, the encroachment of the bulldozer and other factors disrupted this process, weakening the Mexicans' organizational responses.

Politically, Los Angeles Mexican Americans had no voice whatsoever. They mostly voted Democrat. The party took them for granted and gerrymandered their districts, not so much to keep Mexicans powerless as to maintain its incumbents in office. Liberal incumbents benefited from this abuse. Unlike the San Antonio elite, Los Angeles's ruling class did not need a traditional political machine to stay in office. It did not need the Mexican vote; the ruling elite was too secure. Headed by the Chandlers, owners of the *Los Angeles Times,* and joined by insurance, real estate, and petroleum interests and old-line merchants, the establishment controlled the mayor, the police, and the "five little kings" (the county supervisors). It dominated the zoning and planning commissions, which controlled land use in Los Angeles. These elites, headquartered at the California Club, excluded Jews, minorities, and women.

This group made huge profits promoting the development of the Westside and the San Fernando Valley. From 1940 to 1960, the freeway system expanded dramatically, accelerating suburbanization in the process. In order to revive the downtown area, the power elite formed the Greater Los Angeles Plans, Inc., setting three goals—to build a convention center, a sports arena, and a music center. This decision had far-reaching consequences for minorities and the poor, since these projects encroached on their living space. The downtown elite until 1958 was entirely Republican—after this point, the group expanded and supported "responsible" Democrats. In the next years, the group narrowed to a Committee of 25 within the Chamber of Commerce, and informally planned Los Angeles's future. During this time, few of the elite even bothered to think about Mexicans.[59]

From 1949 to 1962 Edward R. Roybal dominated the political history of Los Angeles Chicanos. His rise is linked to the emergence of the Community Service Organization (CSO), California's most important Chicano association. CSO differed from LULAC, employing more strident tactics. The CSO used the strategies of the Industrial Areas Foundation (IAF) and its founder, Saul Alinsky. Many CSO leaders could be considered middle class, but, unlike LULAC professionals, they did not monopolize the leadership; many CSO leaders came out of the labor movement. The Los Angeles group made an effort to encourage grass-roots participation.

CSO's roots could be found in the small towns beyond East Los Angeles —in Chino, Ontario, and Pomona, where Ignacio López organized Civic Unity Leagues. During the war López headed the Spanish department in the Office of Foreign Languages, Division of War Information, in Washington, and was the Spanish-speaking director of the Office of Coordinator of Inter-American Affairs in Los Angeles. His job was to get ethnic groups to support the war effort. Later in the East he organized European minorities into groups called liberty leagues, and on his return to Los Angeles he organized civic leagues among the Chicanos. Fred Ross from the American Council on Race Relations joined him. The leagues focused on the problems of poor Chicanos and stressed ethnic unity. They did not promote radical revolution or confrontation politics, but appealed to the conscience and goodwill of the majority. They emphasized mass action, bloc voting, and neighborhood protests. Organizers held meetings in homes, churches, and public buildings.

The unity leagues differed from previous Chicano organizations in that they were not formed to meet the needs of the middle class, nor were they trade unionist in orientation. They were designed to stimulate political action among the grass-roots Chicanos. In Chino, California, for instance, the league elected Andrew Morales to the City Council. They conducted intensive voter registration drives. Their tactics were to wait for the establishment to make a mistake, allow this mistake to prescipitate a crisis, and then organize around the issue. They established unity leagues in San Bernardino and Riverside, California, where school discrimination became a prime issue.

The leagues in turn influenced the IAF of the Back of the Yards area in South Chicago in the late 1940s. The IAF planned to work with Mexicans in Los Angeles. A group known as the Community Political Organization (CPO) formed in East Los Angeles at about the same time. Not wanting to be confused with the Communist party (CP) or partisan politics, it changed its name in 1947 to the Community Service Organization. The CSO evolved from Chicano steelworkers and the volunteers in Roybal's unsuccessful bid for a Los Angeles City Council seat in 1947. The IAF moved to Los Angeles and merged efforts with the CSO.

These groups held open forums to discuss community problems, attracting many workers to their meetings. Fred Ross influenced the direction of the CSO, drawing on his experience with the civic unity leagues. Although the CSO was allegedly not political, it registered 12,000 new voters. This increase in registered Chicano voters helped elect Roybal to the Los Angeles City Council in 1949— the first person of Mexican descent to serve on that body since 1881.

After Roybal's victory the CSO did not support another candidate for office. It concentrated on fighting housing discrimination, police brutality, and school segregation. In 1950 the CSO fielded 112 volunteer deputy registrars and within three months registered 32,000 new Latino voters.[60]

Meanwhile, Roybal developed in a much more politically liberal environment than Henry B. González. Los Angeles had an active industrial trade union movement. Other liberal currents influenced Mexican Americans; in Boyle Heights, Mexicans lived in proximity to Jewish-Americans during an era when Jews were leading the fight against racism. In 1948, many in the Boyle Heights community actively campaigned for the Independent Progressive party (IPP), which supported Henry Wallace for president. The IPP recruited many Chicanos to its ranks.

As a member of the City Council, Roybal had an outstanding career, confronting Los Angeles's power elite in defense of principle. He fought for a strong FEPC ordinance, opposed the registration of communists, supported rent controls, and campaigned against urban renewal. Roybal criticized the police in brutality cases; he supported public housing.[61]

Roybal's popularity went beyond the Mexican American community. His own district had 16,000 Chicano registered voters out of 87,000. Roybal easily won reelection. In 1954, Roybal lost a campaign for lieutenant governor. Four years later, he ran for county supervisor, an election he won on the first ballot, but lost after three recounts. At one point, ballots were "misplaced" and then found again. Ernest Debs, the elite's puppet, won.

Many contemporary political observers still believe that the county's power structure stole the election from Roybal. Roybal proved especially threatening to the downtown power structure's interests in exposing the Chávez Ravine give-away to the Dodgers (see p. 296) and the forced removal of the Bunker Hill residents. That same year, Hank López also ran for lieutenant governor of California. And although the party swept the statewide elections, Lopéz lost. Many Democrats during the campaign had refused to appear on the same platform as López.

During this same period, the CSO lobbied for civic improvements, sponsored civil rights litigation, and conducted massive and successful voter registration drives. Despite their effectiveness, such efforts were cut back in the late 1950s when the IAF withdrew funding. Numerous coordinating councils, the G.I. Forum, LULAC, and the Council for Mexican American Affairs (CMAA) also emerged in Los Angeles. The CMAA, made up of select professionals, wanted to get the various groups together to coordinate Chicano activities. Mexican American groups expressed optimism, predicting the awakening of the Mexican American and the community's achievement of political power. Nevertheless, Mexicans had few victories. And they celebrated the appointment of Carlos Terán to the municipal court in 1958 with all the grandeur of a coronation.

Chicago

World War II revived Mexican migration to Chicago. The repatriation of the 1930s had reduced the official number of Mexicans from 20,000 to 16,000. From 1943 to 1945, the railroads imported some 15,000 *braceros.* With the number of Mexicans increasing, racism intensified. Assimilation of Mexicans became almost impossible, not only because of the migration's size but because of the newcomers' skin color. After the war, Texas-Mexicans arrived in large numbers, and by 1947, the migration of undocumented workers supplemented these figures.

During the 1940s, the official Mexican population grew from 16,000 to 20,000 in the city (and from 21,000 to 35,000 in the metropolitan area). Some authorities claimed that many more Mexicans lived in Chicago. For example, the INS director, frequently given to exaggeration, asserted in 1953 that 100,000 Mexicans lived in Chicago, of whom 15,000 were, according to him, "wetbacks." Another important trend, begun in the postwar years, was the influx of Puerto Ricans and other Central and South Americans. From then on, Mexicans coexisted with other Latino groups.

Chicago, divided into ethnic and racial wards, was the most-racially segregated city in the United States. The building of expressways and the construction of suburban housing tracts quickened white flight. Like most changes in this period, it was financed largely by federal funds. The transformation caused problems for city dwellers. The "Happy Days" saw a decline in Chicago municipal employment, from 600,000 to 510,000 jobs. Many factories also moved to the outskirts, making it more difficult for Mexicans to find work.

Social scientists and social workers debated on the best method to assimilate Mexicans. Most wanted to treat them like the European immigrants and Americanize them. The Chicago Area Project (CAP) offered another alternative and stated that the best way to eradicate poverty, illiteracy, and delinquency was through the training of grass-roots leaders. CAP began working with Mexicans in 1943 in the Near West Side. In 1944, the Immigrants Protective League (IPL) and the Pan-American Council (PAC) emphasized the need to combat job discrimination. The IPL and the PAC collected valuable data on the Chicago Mexican community.

Meanwhile, in 1943, CAP founded the Mexican Civic Committee, whose chair, Frank X. Pax, established a social center in the Near West Side. This committee later joined the Metropolitan Welfare Council, which formed a subcommittee on Mexican affairs. By 1949, 23 organizations attended a citywide conference on Mexicans in Chicago. The principal Mexican American communities included the Near West Side, the Back of the Yards, South Chicago, and Pilsen. Politicians had badly gerrymandered the Near West Side, and, by the 1950s, city planners literally wiped out the community. Construction of the Eisenhower Expressway and the Chicago Circle campus of the University of Illinois displaced thousands of Mexicans, many of whom moved to the Pilsen district.

The Back of the Yards, more integrated than the other *barrios,* saw cooperation between new and older ethnic groups, which united to resist the city's encroachments. From the 1930s to the mid-1950s, Mexicans living in the Back of the Yards belonged to the meat packers' unions, which helped them assimilate. Work in the stockyards was stable and wages were higher than in other industries. The Back of the Yards Neighborhood Council, organized in 1939 by Saul Alinsky, depended on a network of Catholic Church groups. Unlike California's CSO, the council was multiethnic. In the mid-1950s, the meat packing companies restructured; no longer tied to the rail lines, they moved, severely disrupting the community.

Located on the South Shore of Lake Michigan, South Chicago was untouched by urban renewal. As the number of Mexican steelworkers increased during the 1950s, they formed the Mexican Community Committee, which concerned itself with local issues. South Chicago Mexicans thrived economically in comparison to Mexican Americans in other sections of the city.

The newest and fastest growing *barrio* was Pilsen, formerly a Czech and Bohemian neighborhood. Small clusters of Mexicans moved there in the 1920s. By the 1950s, a Mexican commercial district developed in east Pilsen, on 18th Street. When the Pilsen Neighbors formed in 1953, few Mexicans belonged to this new Alinskian organization. By the late 1950s, however, Mexicans played an important role in the Neighbors. Beginning in the 1960s, the Mexican community spread west.

Chicago Mexicans suffered the same indignities as in other parts of the Midwest and Southwest. Police brutality and racism were common. Other ethnics protested the spread of Mexicans into their communities. During this period, white neighbors vandalized Pedro Romero's house in South Chicago because they did not want "his kind" in their neighborhood. The McCarthy era also encouraged the repression of activists such as Ramón Refugio Martínez, a meat packing worker, who in the 1940s was accused of being a subversive. In the 1950s, authorities allegedly deported Martínez under the McCarran-Walter Act. Operation Wetback also terrorized Mexicans in Chicago.[62]

POST-WORLD WAR II HUMAN RIGHTS STRUGGLES

The Struggle for Constitutional Rights

The struggle for civil and human rights was intense during this period. The de facto exclusion of Mexicans from public facilities, schools, trade unions, juries, and voting was common in many sections of the country. The First Regional Conference on Education of the Spanish-Speaking People in the Southwest took place at the University of Texas at Austin on December 13–15, 1945. George I. Sánchez of the University of Texas and A. L. Campa of the University of New Mexico took an active part in the proceedings, one of whose most important acts was the condemnation of segregation. On May 20, 1946, in response to pressure from a Chicano veteran's group, the Chamber of Commerce of Tempe, Arizona, voted to admit Chicanos to the city swimming pool.

In 1946 Judge Paul J. McCormick in the U.S. District Court in southern California heard the *Méndez* v. *Westminster School District* case and declared the segregation of Mexican children unconstitutional. On April 14, 1947, the U.S. Court of Appeals for the Ninth Circuit affirmed the decision, stating that Mexicans and other children were entitled to "the equal protection of the laws," and that neither language nor race could be used as a reason to segregate them. On June 15, 1948, in another segregation case, Judge Ben H. Rice, Jr., U.S. District Court, Western District of Texas, found in *Delgado* v. *Bastrop Independent School District* that the Mexican childrens' rights under the Fourteenth Amendment had been violated. These two cases set precedents for the historic *Brown* case in 1954.[63]

The American G.I. Forum was organized by Dr. Hector García in Corpus Christi, Texas in 1948. Chicano veterans often became frustrated by the Veterans Administration because they did not receive their benefits on time. Ignored by the American Legion and other veteran organizations, they moved to form their own G.I. association in order to more effectively lobby for their rights. The Forum received its big push when a local funeral parlor at Three Rivers, Texas, denied the use of the facilities to Félix Longoria, a Chicano war hero, and his body had to be taken outside his home state to Arlington Cemetery. Chicano veterans vowed that this would never happen again. By the end of 1949 over 100 American GI Forum chapters had been organized. Eventually, forums spread to 23 states and had a total membership of over 20,000. This nonpartisan organization promoted political and social reform. The key to the forums' success was the inclusion of the entire family through participation in ladies' auxiliaries and junior forums. The Forum throughout the 1950s was one of the leading Chicano associations pressing for constitutional reforms.

The Chicano population actually benefited little from the nascent civil rights movement of the 1950s. The *Brown* decision of 1954 had no effect on schooling for Mexican Americans. Not until the *Cisneros* case in 1970 did "a

Federal district court . . . [rule] that Mexican Americans constitute an identifiable ethnic minority with a past pattern of discrimination in Corpus Christi, Texas." Authorities, in fact, took a stiffer stance toward Mexicans, and it was not until the 1970s that the courts declared: "We see no reason to believe that ethnic segregation is no less detrimental than racial segregation." In the *Keyes* case of 1973 the U.S. Supreme Court held that "negroes and Hispanos in Denver suffer identical discrimination in treatment when compared with the treatment afforded Anglo students."[64]

The G.I. Forum and other Chicano organizations fought segregation, filing cases against several school districts in Texas. Victimized by separate and unequal schools, Chicanos in Texas applauded the *Brown* case and in larger numbers than Blacks or whites approved of integration. A 1954 poll showed:

Question	Negros	Latins	Others whites
Disobey the law	18%	11%	21%
Get around the law	10	8	31
Mix races gradually	22	30	31
Let all go to same schools now	40	47	11
No opinion	10	4	6

Source: "Mexican-Americans Favor Negro School Integration," *G.I. Forum News Bulletin,* September–October, 1955.

Seventy-seven percent of all Mexicans surveyed supported immediate or gradual integration of Blacks versus 62 percent of the Blacks themselves. The Chicanos' own struggle for equal education conditioned their opinion.

In April 1955, suits were filed against the schools of Carrizo Springs and Kingsville, Texas. In Kingsville, Austin Elementary had been segregated since 1914 and was known as the "Mexican Ward School" with a 100 percent Chicano school population. Of the 31 Chicano teachers all but four taught in a 100 percent Mexican school.[65]

Rounding Them Up: The Failed System of Justice

Aside from education, politics, and discrimination, police brutality cases were of major concern to Chicano organizations. In July 1946, a sheriff's deputy in Monterey Park, California, shot Eugene Montenegro in the back; allegedly the 13-year-old was seen coming out of a window and did not stop when the deputy ordered him to. He was 5'3", unarmed, and an honor student at St. Alphonse parochial school. The press portrayed the mother as irrational because she confronted the deputy who mortally wounded her son. In September 1947 Bruno Cano, a member of the United Furniture Workers of America Local 576, was brutally beaten by the police in East Los Angeles. Cano had attempted to stop police from assaulting three Mexican youths at a tavern. Local 576, the Civil Rights Congress, and the American Veterans Committee (Belvedere Chapter) protested Cano's beating. One of the officers, William Keyes, had a history of brutality; in 1947 he shot two Mexicans in the back. Nothing happened to Keyes in either those shootings or Cano's beating.

On March 10, 1948, Keyes struck again; the victim was 17-year-old Agustino Salcido. Salcido was at a local bar where Keyes and his partner, E. R. Sánchez, in plain clothes, were drinking. Salcido knew Sánchez. According to Keyes and Sánchez, Salcido offered to sell them stolen watches. The officers arrested Salcido, but instead of taking him to the police station or to their car, they escorted him to "an empty, locked building" where they shot him. Salcido had only one watch on him, which he had purchased that afternoon. At the coroner's inquest Keyes stated that the unarmed Salcido attempted to escape during interrogation. Witnesses contradicted Keyes, but the inquest exonerated him.[66]

After the inquest the Los Angeles police terrorized witnesses—jailing, beating, and running them out of town. On March 12 the Los Angeles CIO Council adopted a resolution calling for the prosecution of Keyes. On April 1 the CIO and community organizations held a "people's trial" attended by nearly 600 Chicanos.

Leo Gallagher, attorney for the Civil Rights Congress, Oscar Castro, business agent for Local 576, and Ben Rinaldo, American Veterans Committee, played leading roles. Keyes was found guilty. Several days later Guillermo Gallegos, who had witnessed the murder, signed a manslaughter complaint against Keyes. The district attorney had refused to prosecute Keyes. Judge Stanley Moffatt courageously accepted Gallegos's complaint. Police retaliated by arresting Gallegos for "possession of marijuana." Officer Marvin Jacobsen of the narcotics bureau at one point in the interrogation asked Gallegos, "Who's behind all this?" and told him to run. In terror, Gallegos responded, "For Christ's sake, don't shoot me through the back."

At the preliminary trial defense attorney Joseph Scott red-baited Judge Moffatt and the witnesses and attacked Leo Gallagher, who appeared as a friend of the court, as a radical. Moffat found sufficient evidence to try Keyes and asked for a grand jury investigation as to why Keyes had not been prosecuted. The next day the *Hollywood Citizen-News* red-baited Moffatt for running for Congress on the Henry Wallace ticket and for his role in the Keyes trial. The *Los Angeles Times* also denounced Moffat, asking for vigilante action against him. The Committee for Justice for Salcido was subjected to intense harassment. Meanwhile, the jury in the Gallegos trial ended deadlocked, seven for acquittal and five for conviction.

Judge C. C. McDonald presided at Keyes's trial. The facts did not matter, for Keyes had waived a jury trial and McDonald was known as a law and order man. Although Scott did not rebut the evidence, and the prosecution proved that Keyes and Sánchez pumped bullets into Salcido, McDonald acquitted Keyes on the grounds that no evidence had been presented, that the gun examined by the Police Scientific Investigation Bureau belonged to Keyes, and that Gallegos had seen him fire only the last shot, which the court presumed was not the fatal one. The prosecution, which had not wanted to prosecute in the first place, made mistakes as to the rules of evidence. Therefore Keyes was released on a technicality.[67]

In Texas, the G.I. Forum took a leading role in the prosecution of police brutality cases. In Mercedes, it brought enough pressure on June 20, 1953, to force the resignation of Darrill F. Holmes who intimidated George Saenz and his wife at their grocery store. As the result of police abuse Saenz had to be treated for a nervous condition. The Forum was also involved in the Jesse Ledesma case. On the afternoon of June 22, 1953, Austin police officer Bill Crow stopped Ledesma who suffered from insulin shock. Crow claimed Ledesma looked drunk and beat him up, inflicting a one-inch cut on the right side of his head and bruises on his legs, back and shoulders.

On September 16, 1953, in Fort Worth, Texas, Officer Vernon Johnson shot Ernest L. García in the chest while delivering a court order for custody of a child. Johnson threatened members of the García family when they asked him if he had a warrant; the officer pulled a gun and pressed it against García's chest. Johnson claimed that he shot because he was afraid that the García family would mob him. The Forum lawyers handled the case and Johnson was indicted for aggravated assault.

On May 3, 1954, the U.S. Supreme Court in a unanimous decision banned discrimination in juries. Peter Hernández had been found guilty of the murder of Joe Espinosa by an all-white jury in Edna, Texas. The jury sentenced him to life. This case was turned down by the Court of Criminal Appeals because, according to the court, Mexicans were white and therefore could not be treated as a class apart. Hernández appealed and the U.S. Supreme court found that for 25 years Mexicans had been treated as a class apart and that out of 6,000 citizens considered for jury duty a Mexican had never been selected. Peter Hernández was tried again; he pleaded guilty and the court sentenced him to 20 years.[68]

As in other civil rights cases, Gus García, a brilliant lawyer, led the legal team. Many of his contemporaries considered him too radical. Disillusioned, bitter, and cynical about the lack of Mexican American progress, García died alone in 1964, on a park bench.

In the 1950s Los Angeles police established a pattern of repression. For the most part, as in cases such as the Salcido murder, officials gave officers *carte blanche*. In the "Bloody Christmas" case eight Los Angeles police on December 24, 1951, took seven young Chicanos out of their cells at the Lincoln Heights jail and brutally beat them. Police mauled Danny Rodella, so badly that he had to be sent to Los Angeles County General Hospital. Public outcry from the white, Black, and brown communities forced the courts to act and some of the officers were indicted and jailed.

In February 1950 Los Angeles county sheriffs raided a baby shower at the home of Mrs. Natalia Gonzales. Sheriffs had given occupants three minutes to evacuate the premise. They arrested some 50 guests for charges ranging from disturbing the peace to resisting arrest. The Maravilla Chapter of *La Asociación Nacional México-Americana* (ANMA) (see next page) petitioned the county supervisors, but were denied this right. Lieutenant Fimbres of the foreign relations bureau of the sheriff's department whitewashed the sheriffs. Virginia Ruiz and ANMA formed the Maravilla Defense Committee.

On May 26, 1951, police raided a baptismal party at the home of Simon

Fuentes. Officers received a call that the record player was too loud. They broke into the house without a warrant and assaulted the guests. A woman, eight months pregnant, and a handicapped man were thrown to the floor. Police broke Frank Rodríguez's leg when he went to the aid of the handicapped man. ANMA played an active role in this case.[69]

On May 8, 1953, Los Angeles deputy sheriffs Lester Moll and Kenneth Stiler beat David Hidalgo, age 15, while other deputies looked on as Hidalgo pleaded for mercy. Hidalgo's stepfather, Manuel Domínguez, pressed a civil suit against the Los Angeles county sheriff's department. *La Alianza Hispano-Americana* sponsored the case against the officers. Domínguez received a judgment two years later against the two deputy sheriffs with an award for damages of $1,000.

The *Alianza* handled the appeals in the murder and conspiracy conviction of Manuel Mata, Robert Márquez, and Ricardo Venegas. The three men were convicted of murdering William D. Cluff in a fight at Seventh and Broadway in Los Angeles on December 6, 1953. Cluff had intervened in a fight involving the three defendants and a marine, John W. Moore. Cluff died. The defense introduced expert medical testimony that Cluff had died of an enlarged heart, advanced arteriosclerosis of cerebral blood vessels, and arterial heart disease, and not of injuries inflicted during the fight. Los Angeles newspapers had inflamed public opinion and the three were convicted. After a series of appeals the defendants got a new trial.[70]

The CSO, along with the American Civil Liberties Union, took the leadership in police brutality cases in East Los Angeles. Chicano activist Ralph Guzmán wrote in the *Eastside Sun* on September 24, 1953: "It is no secret that for years law and order in the Eastside of Los Angeles County has been maintained through fear and brutal treatment." Los Angeles newspapers whipped up hysteria against Mexicans. Ralph Guzmán, in the *Eastside Sun,* on January 7, 1954, wrote, "It is becoming more and more difficult to walk through the streets of Los Angeles—and look Mexican!" On January 14, 1954, he continued, "Basically, Eugene Biscailuz's idea to curb kid gangs is the evening roundup, a well known western drive." Guzmán then vehemently castigated the Los Angeles press for its irresponsibility.

La Asociación Nacional México-Americana

The *Asociación Nacional México-Americana* had been founded in May 1949 in Grant County, New Mexico, coming about as the result of a clash between Mexican miners and police in the village of Fierro. ANMA in its first year had a membership of 1,500. Because of its progressive constituency it developed strong ties with the Independent Progressive party.

Alfredo Montoya, a trade union organizer with the Mine, Mill and Smelter Workers union, was its driving force. ANMA aggressively advocated human rights and had CIO backing. It launched its national organization in Albuquerque on August 14, 1949 and from the beginning, it attracted more radical members of the community.

ANMA encouraged Mexicans to join unions. This national organization conducted drives outside the Southwest, in cities such as Chicago, Detroit, and other industrial centers. It sought links with the Puerto Rican colony. From the beginning the Catholic clergy labeled it communist and interfered with its campaigns.

Interlocking of membership and issues linked the IPP and ANMA. For instance, Virginia Ruiz, the national secretary of ANMA, became a delegate to the IPP convention in Chicago in 1950. The IPP supported Mexican candidates, such as Arthur O. Casas for assembly and Richard Ibañez for the superior court. Both ANMA and the IPP called for a cessation of hostilities in Korea. The two groups also shared the harassment of reactionary elements in government.

Through 1952 ANMA was heavily involved with trade unions, and in the summer of that year Alfredo Montoya moved the national headquarters to Denver. By 1954 it made the U.S. attorney general's subversive list and even Chicano organizations red-baited it. Intense harassment undermined the organization and it faded away. The IPP also wilted and its members reverted to the Democratic party.

Attempts to Form a National Spanish-Speaking Council

Middle-class Mexican American organizations remained active during this period. Most preferred to follow the path set by the civil rights tradition, and to work within the mainstream. On May 18–19, 1951, leaders of many of these associations met at El Paso for the founding convention of the American Council of Spanish-Speaking People. Dr. George I. Sánchez called the convention. The *Alianza Hispano-Americana,* CSO, LULAC, the Texan G.I. Forum, and the Community Service Club of Colorado comprised the core group. Chicano leaders such as Gus García, Tony Ríos, Ignacio López, José Estrada, and Senator Dennis Chávez, Jr., of New Mexico attended the convention.

Tibo J. Chávez, the lieutenant governor of New Mexico, was elected president of the council, and Dr. Sánchez served as its executive director. In 1952 the organization received a grant to be used to promote the civil rights of Chicanos from the Robert Marshall Foundation.

The council worked closely with the *Alianza* in desegregation cases. In 1952, for instance, challenges were made in Glendale, Douglas, Miami, and Winslow, Arizona. In the case against Glendale and the Arizona Board of Education, they challenged segregation. The Glendale board refused to go to court and be forced to integrate.[71]

The council remained active for the next years, but like many similar attempts it failed when continued funding did not materialize. At this juncture in history, the Mexican American middle class was not large or prosperous enough to support such an ambitious project, and Anglo-American foundations did not recognize the need. It was left to the older Mexican American associations to continue this struggle through their own legal aid programs. For instance, in 1954 the *Alianza* initiated a suit against Winslow, Arizona, to open its swimming pool to Mexicans. Winslow officials settled the suit out of court. In 1955 the *Alianza* established a civil rights department and named Ralph Guzmán its director. In a desegregation case in El Centro, California, it cooperated with the National Association for the Advancement of Colored People. Black teachers were assigned to the two elementary schools which were predominately Mexican and Black. El Centro had avoided desegregation by allowing white students to transfer to an adjoining district which was itself overcrowded. A federal judge ruled that the plaintiffs must exhaust state courts before a federal court could hear the case, but the Court of Appeals for the Ninth Circuit reversed this decision and decided that El Centro practiced segregation of students and staff. This cooperation between the *Alianza* and the NAACP was significant since the *Alianza* itself had excluded Blacks. It indicated a change within the most traditional and nationalistic of Chicano groups which now began to reach out to other oppressed groups. Also important is that the *Alianza* as well as other groups were involved in self-amelioration long before the 1960s.[72]

BULLDOZERS IN THE *BARRIOS*

During the 1950s, urban *removal* menaced *Mexicanos*. By 1963, 609,000 people nationally had been uprooted as a consequence of urban renewal, two-thirds of whom were minority group members. For Chicanos, Los Angeles was the prototype, but other cities mirrored its experiences. In Los Angeles the Eastside *barrio* came under attack by urban land grabbers engaged in freeway building, business enterprises, and urban renewal. Like poor people throughout the United States, Mexicans had settled in the older sections near the center of town. When plans for freeways were proposed, these sections were considered expendable. Government used the power of eminent domain to remove Chicanos so money interests could reap large profits.

By the fall of 1953 the Mexican area was scarred by the San Bernardino, Santa Ana, and Long Beach freeways, and Chicanos protested the projected building of still another freeway through East Los Angeles. Unlike the residents of Beverly Hills, Chicanos were not able to stop the bulldozers; the $32 million Golden State wiped out another sector of the Mexican area. In 1957 the Pomona Freeway displaced thousands of Chicanos in the Hollenbeck area. The history of freeways through Los Angeles is one of plunder, fraud, and utter disregard for the lives and welfare of people. Land developers knew just where the routes were planned; the property of powerful corporate interests, such as the large Sears, Roebuck store and the *Los Angeles Times* facilities, was conveniently missed. Developers and politicians made millions.

The rationality for this outrageous plunder is found in the contradictions of federal policy which pretends to benefit the poor by wiping out blight when in truth it responds to the demands of local elites for government to accelerate the process of capital accumulation. In 1949, Congress passed the Housing Act of that year. It allocated $10 billion to municipalities that would clear and redevelop their blighted inner cities, which had deteriorated since the end of the war. This erosion was accelerated by the abandonment of the inner city by the white middle class and their flight to the suburbs.

Several factors contributed to the white flight: 1) in the 1950s middle-class North Americans fled to the suburbs in search of their "American Dream"; a tract home that isolated them from the problems of the city. The accessibility of low interest, no down payment loans through the FHA and the Veterans Administration made the dream possible, and the policy of these agencies in not giving loans to integrated housing projects kept them segregated; 2) the massive allocations to the state to build highways encouraged the construction of freeways linking downtown to the suburbs.

The loss of the middle class among other things meant the erosion of the city's tax base. Thus to revive the tax base elites pressured the federal government for relief which they received in the form of the Federal Housing Act of 1949. Over the years, the scope of the act broadened: Under the public housing legislation of the New Deal, government could force a landowner to sell under the power of eminent domain if the condemned property was for public use; under urban renewal, land could be taken for private use and profit. Under the program, municipalities bought and cleared the land and then sold it to developers at a loss. The federal government paid two-thirds of the loss. Often developers bought the redeveloped property at 30 percent of cost.

Encouraged by this renewal process, Mexican communities were kept in a state of flux throughout the 1950s as they became the targets of developers. In October 1957 the city removed Mexican homeowners from Chávez Ravine, near the center of Los Angeles, and gave over 300 acres of private land to Walter O'Malley, owner of the Dodgers baseball team. The Dodgers deal angered many people; residents of Chávez Ravine resisted physically. In 1959 the county sheriff's department forcibly removed the Aréchiga family. Councilman Ed Roybal condemned the action: "The eviction is the kind of thing you might expect in Nazi Germany or during the Spanish Inquisition." Supporters of the Arechigas protested to the City Council. Victoria Augustian, a witness, pointed a finger at Council member Rosalind Wyman, who with Mayor Norris Poulson supported the giveaway. Poulson was a puppet of the Chandler family, who owned the *Los Angeles Times,* which backed the handover.

During these years the Chicano community in central Los Angeles was in effect under invasion. If the freeways and the giveaway were not enough, other business interests actively grabbed land. For instance, in 1958 a group under Dr. Leland J. Fuller proposed a $20 million medical and shopping area in the Boyle Heights district in East Los Angeles. He called Boyle Heights a blighted area and claimed that the renewal program would generate jobs, raise the standard of living, and provide better housing. Fuller headed a dummy group called the Boyle Heights Urban Renewal Committee, which released publicity showing the advantages of the medical complex, and sent out notices attempting to panic the people into selling. While Fuller disclaimed association with the White Memorial Medical Center, the list of associates of the center clearly linked him to it.

Joseph Eli Kovner, publisher and editor of the *Eastside Sun,* uncovered connections between the mayor's office, capitalist interests in Los Angeles, and urban renewal proposals in Watts, Pacoima, Canoga Park, Bunker Hill, and Boyle Heights. (Watts is a Black community and the other four are predominantly Mexican.) Kovner cited a memo from the Sears Corporation to its executives, instructing them to support urban renewal because the company had an economic interest in protecting its investment. The presence of too many minorities in an area depressed land values and discouraged the trade of white, middle-class customers. Urban renewal insured construction of business sites and higher rent apartments which inflated property values.[73]

Kovner, on July 24, 1958, in an *Eastside Sun* editorial, questioned the motives of Sears in sending out a survey letter to the public. He charged that it paved the way for urban renewal by scaring residents into selling and conditioning the results. Kovner asked why Sears had never complained about the liquor stores and bars in the Boyle Heights area. On July 31, 1958, the *Eastside Sun* exposed the Boyle Heights Urban Renewal Committee plot to remove 480 homes north of Brooklyn between McDonnell and Mednick and to disperse over 4,000 people.

Actions of the neo-robber barons became so outlandish that De Witt McCann, an aide to Mayor Poulson's Urban Renewal Committee, resigned, stating, "I don't want to be responsible for taking one man's private property through the use of eminent domain and giving it over to another private individual for his private gain." Poulson and his associates displaced thousands of poor white senior citizens and Mexicans in Bunker Hill and turned over prime land in the downtown section of the city to private developers. Citizens of Bunker Hill lost their battle, but progressives derailed the scheme which eventually would have handed all of Boyle Heights, City Terrace, and Belvedere to private developers. Mayor Norris Poulson, responded to the critics of urban renewal: "If you are not prepared to be part of this greatness, if you want Los Angeles to revert to pueblo status . . . then my best advice to you is to prepare to resettle elsewhere."[74]

City officials and especially the mayor were guilty of criminal negligence. The Los Angeles Community Redevelopment Administration's board of directors ordered Gilbert Morris, superintendent of building and safety, not to enforce safety regulations in the Bunker Hill area. Improvements would raise the value of property and the officials wanted to keep costs down. Poulson also instructed the commissioner of the Board of Building and Safety not to issue building permits. Consequently, buildings deteriorated. The inevitable occurred when a four-story apartment building collapsed; firefighters saved the 200 occupants. Councilman Ed Roybal accused Poulson of playing politics with human lives. Further destruction was prevented by citizen groups that fought removal programs throughout the 1950s and 1960s.[75]

The renewal process dispersed Mexicans throughout Detroit; many moved to the suburbs. As in other cities, a pattern of uprooting by speculators, industrialists, and land developers emerged, disturbing the phenomenon of community building. For instance, the Bagely Avenue Mexican business district was wiped out and moved to Vernor in the 1960s. The G.I. Forum in Detroit dealt with civil rights and lobbied to gain access for Mexicans to public institutions. Detroit

Mexicans, plagued by a reactionary Catholic hierarchy, refused to rebuild Nuestra Señora de Guadalupe Church; and discouraged the formation of Mexican Catholic groups.

As mentioned, freeways, the expansion of the university campus, and renewal programs wiped out the Near West Side *barrio* in Chicago. In 1947, the Chicago Land Commission was organized to supervise slum clearance and urban "removal." The flight of white families and industries to the suburbs had begun and was reflected in a loss of city jobs that greatly affected Chicanos. Urban renewal followed a similar pattern in most cities in which Chicanos lived.

The after shock of urban renewal would be felt in the 1960s. It caused a major disruption of the dominant social order. Accelerated in the 1960s, redevelopment transformed downtown and surrounding areas, contributing greatly to the centralization of commercial and political power. The most obvious disruption for the poor was the destruction of sound, affordable housing without adequate replacement. Conditions in the inner city worsened as housing and sevices were stressed. Unemployment and inflation resulted and poverty increased as did crime and neighborhood gangs. Urban renewal, for all intents and purposes, also killed public housing that was labeled socialistic.[76]

SUMMARY

World War II clarified many contradictions in Euroamerican society. While Chicanos earned an outstanding war record, they were deprived of equal opportunity at home. The Sleepy Lagoon case and the *pachuco* riots symbolized North American racism and the third-class status suffered by Chicanos. During the war, while working-class people sacrificed for the war effort, U.S. industry profited fantastically by freezing wages. Generous government contracts allowed a relatively few defense contractors to reap billions of dollars.

After World War II, major shifts from the farm to the city and from the East and the Midwest to the Southwest took place. Mexican migration accelerated in the form of the *bracero* program and U.S. policy that encouraged undocumented Mexicans to come to the United States. The *bracero* program frustrated the unionization of Chicanos, preventing stabilization of the labor market. The lack of unions allowed agribusiness to depress wages to the point where only undocumented workers could afford to take the jobs. Many Texas agricultural workers were forced to move to the Midwest, where wages were higher.

The recessions of 1949 and 1953–1955 revived nativist and organized labor demands for the exclusion of the undocumented worker. As nativism increased, so did appropriations to the Immigration and Naturalization Service. The INS conducted Operation Wetback, a massive roundup directed by retired generals who treated the Mexicans like war criminals.

Beginning in 1947, the Cold War encouraged the rise of Joseph McCarthy and the passage of the McCarran acts. As the Cold War along with the Korean War accelerated the arms race, cities such as Los Angeles, San Antonio, and other Sunbelt areas benefited greatly from the military buildup. At the same time, the

Taft-Hartley Act, another product of the Cold War, intensified the antiunion movement. Conditions worsened for labor, as witnessed in the classic "Salt of the Earth" and Tex-Son strikes of the 1950s.

As in the case of World War I, the returning Chicano veterans formed their own organizations. Participation widened as new veterans' groups, such as the American G.I. Formum, competed with LULAC for hegemony. The leading issues were the lack of Chicano access to educational and political institutions, as well as the need for immigration reform and voter registration. The postwar period saw greater contact between Chicano groups and mainstream Anglo associations. Chicano *politicos* such as Dennis Chávez, Edward R. Roybal, and Henry B. González represented exceptions within a system that excluded Mexicans from the governing process. Their victories raised hopes that the "Sleeping Giant" would awaken.

By the end of the 1950s, 80 percent of the Mexican population lived in urban centers like San Antonio, Los Angeles, El Paso, and Chicago. The move to the cities taxed the infrastructures of the urban centers. Suburbanization took place, with whites leaving the inner city to Mexican Americans and other minorities. Land use policies changed as the property values in the inner city fell. When the investments of the urban elites were threatened, the federal government provided huge subsidies to redevelop so-called blighted areas. In almost every city new highways and urban renewal programs uprooted the poor by taking the land from them and giving it to the rich. Urban renewal altered the concept of eminent domain, giving local governments the power to take land away from individuals for private use instead of limiting the confiscated property to public use.

NOTES

1. Robert L. Heilbroner and Aaron Singer, *The Economic Transformation of America: 1600 to the Present,* 2nd ed. (San Diego: Harcourt Brace Jovanovich, 1984), pp. 314–315; George Mowry and Blaine A. Brownell, *The Urban Nation 1920–1980,* rev. ed. (New York: Hill and Wang, 1981), p. 169; Carl Allsup, *The American G.I. Forum: Origins and Evolution* (Austin: Mexican American Center, University of Texas, 1982), p. 15; Richard O. Boyer and Herbert M. Morais, *Labor's Untold Story,* 3rd ed. (New York: United Electrical, Radio and Machine Workers of America, 1974), p. 329.

2. Heilbroner, p. 345; Mowry and Brownell, p. 19.

3. Howard Zinn, *A People's History of the United States* (New York: Harper Colophon Books, 1980), p. 428; Boyer and Morais, p. 340.

4. Leo Grebler, Joan W. Moore, and Ralph C. Guzmán, *The Mexican-American People: The Nation's Second Largest Minority* (New York: Free Press, 1970), pp. 206–218.

5. Raúl Morín, *Among the Valiant* (Alhambra, Calif.: Borden, 1966), p. 16; Robin Fitzgerald Scott, "The Mexican-American in the Los Angeles Area, 1920–1950: From Acquiescence to Activity" (Ph.D. dissertation, University of Southern California, 1971), pp. 156, 195, 256, 261; Mauricio Mazón, "Social Upheaval in World War II. Zoot-Suiters and Servicemen in Los Angeles, 1943" (Ph.D. dissertation, University of California at Los Angeles, 1976), pp. 91–92. Special thanks are due to Dr. Russell Bartley of the History Department at the University of

Wisconsin/Milwaukee, whose student had been provided access under the Freedom of Information Act, for allowing me to review the FBI files on the zoot-suit riots, from 1943–1945.

6. Alonso Perales, *Are We Good Neighbors?* (New York: Arno Press, 1974), p. 79.

7. Ismael Dieppa. "The Zoot-Suit Riots Revisited: The Role of Private Philanthropy in Youth Problems of Mexican-Americans" (DSW dissertation, University of Southern California, 1973), p. 14; See Carey McWilliams Papers at the Special Collections Library at the University of California at Los Angeles.

8. Carey McWilliams, *North from Mexico* (New York: Greenwood Press, 1968), pp. 233–235. Interestingly, Deputy Sheriff Ed Durán Ayres was also an amateur historian who wrote a series of articles for the *Civic Center Sun* on "The Background of the History of California." Some of these articles appeared in the April 18, April 25, May 16, May 30, and June 6, 1940 issues of the paper. Throughout these articles Ayres seemed proud of the Hispano-Mexican heritage and gave no indication of his later negative conclusions about Mexicans. On July 4, 1940, Ayres stated that Francisco López, the discoverer of gold in California in 1842, was a grand-uncle of "our own Sheriff, Eugene Biscailuz." On August 1, 1940, he wrote in glowing terms about the Aztecs, saying, "Now . . . there is nothing Spanish about the Aztec eagle representing Mexico. It is 100 percent American." He also described "Astlan [sic]" General José Figueroa, one of the governors of California, as very proud of "his Aztec blood." Why his attitude changed 180 degrees in his report used at the Sleepy Lagoon trial is a matter for speculation. There is some question whether Ayres even wrote the grand jury report. According to Guy Endore, the report was developed by the sheriffs, who signed Ayres's name. Also see Stephanie Dias, "The Zoot Suit Riots" (Pro-seminar paper, San Fernando Valley State College at Northridge, History Department, May 28, 1969), pp. 12–14.

9. Scott, p. 223, 225; Citizen's Committee for the Defense of Mexican-American Youth, *The Sleepy Lagoon Case,* Los Angeles, 1942, p. 21; McWilliams, pp. 228–233. Two of the defendants demanded a separate trial and, on the basis of the same evidence, were acquitted (Citizen's Committee, pp. 7–8). The report charged, on p. 44, that the Sleepy Lagoon Defense Committee "had attempted to create antagonism between the Spanish-Mexicans and local law enforcement"; the Los Angeles Police Department, according to the FBI, had done everything it could to improve relations.

10. Dieppa, p. 15, emphasizes the sex motive, stating that there were five servicemen to every girl. Mazón, pp. 149–150, quotes an incident reported by a black minister riding a streetcar, who observed two sailors from the South trying to get a Mexican girl's eye: "Boy, uh white man can git any gal he wants, can't he boy? Can't he get 'em if he wants 'em?" A great number of the servicemen were of southern extraction. See also McWilliams, p. 248. Mazón, p. 113, reports that on June 10, 1943, San Diego City Councilman Charles C. Dail wrote to Rear Admiral David W. Bagley, commandant of the 11th Naval District in San Diego, complaining about the conduct of servicemen, who "insulted and vilified civilians on public streets." Mazón, pp. 16–19, breaks with the traditional analysis of the *pachuco* confrontations, stating that it was not frustration over losing battles that added to the servicemen's nervousness, but a reluctance to go overseas and become a statistic when they knew that the U.S. had already won the war. The riots became a way of rebelling against the "old men" who controlled the government. The *pachuco* became a scapegoat. Soldiers were also conditioned to view anyone who did not fall into step as disloyal. As time went on they became increasingly paranoid, hunting draft dodgers, pacifists, and communists.

11. McWilliams, pp. 244–254; Dias, pp. 22–23; *Los Angeles Times,* June 7, 1943; *Time* magazine, June 21, 1943; *PM,* June 10, 1943; Dieppa, p. 9.

12. FBI report, January 14, 1944. The *Eastside Journal,* June 9, 1943, wrote an editorial defending the zoot-suiters; it pointed out that 112 had been hospitalized, 150 hurt, and 12 treated in the hospitals. See also McWilliams, pp. 250–251; Ed Robbins, *PM,* June 9, 1943.

13. Mazón, pp. 114–118.

14. *Los Angeles Times,* June 10, 1943 and July 10, 1943; McGucken Report, California Legislature, Report and Recommendations of Citizens Committee on Civil Disturbances in Los Angeles, June 12, 1943, p. 1. Mazón, pp. 189–195, states that the authorities tried to make Blacks the scapegoats for the riots. In a report to the commandant of the Eleventh Naval District on July 29, 1943, Commander Fogg, the senior patrol officer in Los Angeles, reported that "arrests [by the police] of members of the negro race had increased nearly 100 percent, compared with a year ago." In a memo written on October 16, 1943, Fogg described "an aggressive campaign sponsored by local, state and national representatives of the negro race . . . to promote unrest and dis-satisfaction [sic] among the local negro population."

15. José Angel Gutiérrez, "Under Surveillance," The *Texas Observer* (January 9, 1987): 8–13.

16. FBI Report, June 16, 1943.

17. FBI Report, "Racial Conditions (Spanish-Mexican Activities in Los Angeles Field Division)," January 14, 1944.

18. Alonso S. Perales, *Are We Good Neighbors?* (San Antonio: Artes Gráficas, 1948), pp. 93, 94, 112–113, 117, 121; Robert Garland Landolt, *The Mexican-American Workers of San Antonio, Texas* (New York: Arno Press, 1976), pp. 76–77, 88–117; Pauline R. Kibbe, *Latin Americans in Texas* (New York: Arno Press, 1974), pp. 161–162; Charles Loomis and Nellie Loomis, "Skilled Spanish-American War Industry Workers from New Mexico," *Applied Anthropology* (October, November, December 1942):33.

19. George O. Coalson, *The Development of the Migratory Farm Labor System in Texas: 1900–1954* (San Francisco: R & E Research Associates, 1977), p. 67, states that in March 1943 the Bureau of Agricultural Economics reported a loss of 2.8 million agricultural workers since 1939, 40 percent to the armed forces and 60 percent to war industries, and that between April 1940 and January 1942 an estimated 280,000 workers left the farms for the armed forces. See also Juan Ramón García, "Operation Wetback: 1954" (Ph.D. dissertation, University of Notre Dame, 1977), pp. 16–17; Gilbert Cardenas, "United States Immigration Policy Toward Mexico: A Historical Perspective," *Chicano Law Review* 2 (Summer 1975): 75.

20. Mark Reisler, *By the Sweat of Their Brow: Mexican Immigration to the United States, 1900–1940* (Westport, Conn.: Greenwood Press, 1976), p. 260.

21. Ernesto Galarza, *Merchants of Labor* (Santa Barbara, Calif.: McNally & Lottin, 1964), p. 47; García, p. 23; Richard B. Craig, *The Bracero Program* (Austin: University of Texas Press, 1971), p. 198; O. M. Scruggs, "Texas and the Bracero Program," *Pacific Historical Review* (August 1962): 251–252.

22. Gilbert Cárdenas and Estebán Flores, "Political Economy of International Labor Migration" (Prepared for the Joint Annual Meeting of the Latin American Studies Association and African Studies Association, Houston, Texas, November, 1977), p. 14; Peter Neal Kirstein, "Anglo Over Bracero: A History of the Mexican Workers in the United States from Roosevelt to Nixon" (Ph.D. dissertation, Saint Louis University, 1973), p. 39; Coalson, p. 94; Scruggs, pp. 253–254.

23. Kirstein, pp. 83–84, 90–91, 94–95; Henry P. Anderson, *The Bracero Program in California* (Berkeley: School of Public Health, University of California, July 1961), p. 146.

24. Although the Mexican population in the Northwest is still small in comparison to other regions, it is growing. Moreover, established communities in Oregon and Washington have survived and retained their identification. The best work on Chicanos in the Northwest is Erasmo Gamboa, "Under the Thumb of Agriculture: Bracero and Mexican American Workers in the Pacific Northwest" (Ph.D. dissertation, University of Washington, 1984), pp. 24–26.

25. Craig, pp. 54, 58–59; García, p. 92; Coalson, p. 82; J.B. Jones, "Mexican-American Labor Problems in Texas" (Ph.D. dissertation, University of Texas, 1965), p. 23; Hart Stillwell, "The Wetback Tide," *Common Ground* (Summer 1949): 3–4; Kirstein, p. 147; Truman quote in Nelson Gage Copp, "Wetbacks and Braceros: Mexican Migrant Laborers and American Immigration Policy, 1930–1960" (Ph.D. dissertation, Boston University, 1963), pp. 156–189. Mexico, during

the 1940s, asked for the protection of *braceros* since it vividly remembered the repatriation of the 1930s when the United States literally dumped and stranded thousands of Mexicans at the border.

26. Craig, pp. 36, 104, 107, 109, 112, 119; Howard Lloyd Campbell, "Bracero Migration and the Mexican Economy, 1951–1964" (Ph.D. dissertation, The American University, 1972), pp. 69–71; Patricia Morgan, *Shame of a Nation* (Los Angeles Committee for the Protection of Foreign Born, September 1954), p. 28; Ray Gilmore and Gladys W. Gilmore, "Braceros in California," *Pacific Historical Review* (August 1962): 272.

27. Copp, pp. 107, 109; Anderson, p. 39; Craig, p. 10.

28. Quoted in Craig, p. 11. Campbell, pp. 5–6, 101, is an interesting study of the decline of the dependence on the *bracero* in the 1960s as the result of mechanization, particularly in cotton.

29. Copp, p. 102. Ernesto Galarza, *Tragedy at Chualar: El Crucero de las Treinta y dos Cruces* (Santa Barbara, Calif.: McNally & Loftin, 1977). The book describes the death of 32 *braceros* while being transported in a hazardous bus on September 18, 1963. The American Committee for the Protection of the Foreign Born, *Our Badge of Infamy, A Petition to the United Nations on the Treatment of the Mexican Immigrant* (April 1959), reviews the excesses of the program. On page 24 it tells of the decapitation of a *bracero* driving a tractor by a low-flying airplane on May 28, 1958. The Justice Department investigation took 24 hours. Ralph Guzmán's editorial in the *Eastside Sun,* March 4, 1954, is a good review of the literature up to that time and the exploitation of braceros. Guzmán states that Truman's Committee on Migratory Labor confirmed the influence of agribusiness on the INS.

30. John Phillip Carney, "Postwar Mexican Migration: 1945–1955, with Particular Reference to the Policies and Practices of the United States Concerning Its Control" (Ph.D. dissertation, University of Southern California, 1957), p. 20. Carney, p. 48, states that in 1950 an estimated 86 percent of the working population in Mexico made less than 300 pesos ($35) per month. In 1947, farm workers in the interior of Mexico earned 38¢ a day; on the border they earned $1.10 a day. See also Lyle Saunders and Olen E. Leonard, *The Wetback in the Lower Rio Grande Valley of Texas,* reprinted in Carlos E. Cortés, ed., *Mexican Migration to the United States* (New York: Arno Press, 1976), p. 165; Art Liebson, "The Wetback Invasion," *Common Ground* 10 (Autumn 1949): 11–19.

31. E. Idar, Jr., and Andrew C. McLellan, *What Price Wetbacks* (American G.I. Forum of Texas, Texas State Federation of Labor [AFL], Austin, Texas), reprinted in Cortés, pp. 28–29; García, p. 194.

32. Morgan, p. 3; García, pp. 76, 213, 215, 216, 265–268, 275, 317; Lamar Babington Jones, "Mexican American Labor Problems in Texas" (Ph.D. dissertation, University of Texas, 1965), pp. 25–26; Carney, p. 127. See also the following works by Gilbert Cárdenas: "United States Immigration Policy Toward Mexico"; in note 19 "A Theoretical Approach to the Sociology of Mexican Labor Migration" (Ph.D. dissertation, University of Notre Dame, 1977); "Public Data on Mexican Immigration into the United States: A Critical Evaluation," in W. Boyd Littrell and Gideon Sjoberg, eds., *Current Issues in Social Policy Research* (New York: Sage, 1976); and, with Estabán Flores, "Political Economy of International Labor Migration."

33. García, pp. 189–190, 191–192, 209–210; Ralph Guzmán, "Ojinaga, Chihuahua and Wetbacks," *Eastside Sun,* October 15, 1953.

34. García, pp. 214–215.

35. *Our Badge of Infamy, A Petition to the United Nations on the Treatment of the Mexican Immigrant,* American Committee for the Protection of the Foreign Born, April 1959, pp. iii–v.

36. Morgan, p. 4, states that "the McCarran-Walter Law passed in the midst of the war in Korea and at the end of a five-year 'anti-alien' drive in which the U.S. Justice Department had suffered

numerous court set-backs in seeking to deprive noncitizens of their constitutional rights." See also Jethro K. Lieberman, *Are Americans Extinct?* (New York: Walter, 1968), 106, 109.

37. *Whom We Shall Welcome* (New York: Da Capo Press, 1970) includes an excellent analysis of the McCarran acts, published by the President's Commission on Immigration and Naturalization in January 1953; quotes are from pp. 196–198. See also Robert K. Murray, *Red Scare* (Minneapolis: University of Minnesota Press, 1955), p. 65; Grebler, Moore, and Guzmán, p. 519. Grebler et al. state that "although the job-certification procedure was authorized in the 1952 Immigration and Naturalization Act for broad classes of immigrants from any country, it was implemented against Mexicans only."

38. "Hope Mendoza Gets Immigration Job Appointment," *Eastside Sun,* June 4, 1953; Ralph Guzmán, "Front Line G.I. Faces Deportation," *Eastside Sun,* June 30, 1953.

39. *Our Badge of Infamy,* pp. 13–14; Morgan, pp. 39–47; "Nacional-Mexico Americano [sic] Fights Deportation Move," *Eastside Sun,* March 13, 1952; Joseph Eli Kovner, "The Tobias Navarrette Case," *Eastside Sun,* July 25, 1957; *Eastside Sun,* August 8, 1957; *Eastside Sun,* August 29, 1957; George Mount, "Tobias Navarrette, E.L.A. Humanitarian, Is Dead," *Eastside Sun,* September 6, 1964.

40. *Our Badge of Infamy,* pp. 36–38. One of the best studies is Ralph Guzmán, *Roots Without Rights* (Los Angeles: American Civil Liberties Union, Los Angeles Chapter, 1958). See also "Jose Gastelum Free of Mexico Deportation," *Eastside Sun,* June 20, 1963; "Deportation Is Meeting Topic," *Eastside Sun,* March 28, 1957; John F. Mendez, *Eastside Sun,* May 2, 1957.

41. Carey McWilliams, *California: The Great Exception* (New York: Current Books, 1949), p. 48; *La Causa: The California Grape Strike* (New York: Collier, 1970), p. 56; Ernesto Galarza, *Farm Workers and Agribusiness in California, 1947–1960* (Notre Dame, Ind.: University of Notre Dame Press, 1977), pp. 23, 98–99; Paul S. Taylor, "Water, Land and People in Great Valley," *American West* (March 1968): 27. The net income of the Kern County Land Company in 1956 from oil, cotton, cattle, and crops was $11,745,000. See also David Nesmith, *National Land for People* (November 2, 1977).

42. See Paul S. Taylor, "The Excess Land Law: Pressure vs. Principle," *California Law Review* 47, no. 3 (August 1959): 499–541; Joan London and Henry Anderson, *So Shall Ye Reap* (New York: Crowell, 1971), p. 4. Growers pay $3.50 per acre foot for water; it costs the government $14 an acre foot. Galarza, p. 26, states that as of December 1959 the projected cost was $2 billion. Growers also received interest-free loans; McWilliams, *California,* p. 306. The Imperial Valley was once a desert; it bloomed because of water made available by U.S. taxpayers. In the 1940s unirrigated land sold for $75 an acre; in 1978 irrigated land sold for an average of $1,000 an acre. For an excellent background on the question of government water projects, see David Nesmith, "Discover America," *National Land For People* (October 1977).

43. Ernesto Galarza, *Spiders in the House and Workers in the Field* (Notre Dame, Ind.: University of Notre Dame Press, 1970), pp. 23–27, 35, 40–48, 64–66, 88, 153, 231–247, 288–297; Carney, p. 157; Galarza, *Farm Workers,* pp. 100, 103, 99; National Advisory Committee on Farm Labor, *Farm Labor Organizing, 1905–1967: A Brief History* (New York: National Advisory Committee on Farm Labor, 1967), p. 37; Sam Kushner, *Long Road to Delano* (New York: International Publishers, 1975), p. 82.

44. Galarza, *Farm Workers,* pp. 137, 145–146, 148–149, 171, 174, 186, 204–205, 259–260, 289–297, 315; London and Anderson, pp. 46–47, 118–119.

45. Gregory W. Hill, *Texas-Mexican Migratory Agricultural Workers in Wisconsin,* Agricultural Experimental Station Stencil Bulletin 6 (Madison: University of Wisconsin, 1948), pp. 5–6, 15–16, 18–20; George O. Coalson, *The Development of the Migratory Farm Labor System in Texas: 1900–1954* (San Francisco: R & E Research Associates, 1977), p. 110; Kibbe, New York: pp.

199–200; Richard W. Slatta, "Chicanos in the Pacific Northwest: An Historical Overview of Chicanos," *Aztlán 6, no. 3 (Fall 1975): 327;* Erasmo Gamboa, "Chicanos in the Northwest: An Historical Perspective," *El Grito* 7, no. 4 (Summer 1973): 61–63; Everett Ross Clinchy, Jr., *Equality of Opportunity for Latin-Americans in Texas:* (New York: Arno Press, 1974), p. 87; Perales.

46. Douglas E. Foley, Clarice Mota, Donald E. Post, and Ignacio Lozano, *From Peones to Politicos: Ethnic Relations in a South Texas Town, 1900–1977* (Austin: University of Texas, Center for Mexican American Studies, 1977), pp. 75, 85–86, 89; Kibbe, pp. 153, 160–163, 169; Landolt, p. 117; Coalson, pp. 87–88, 100–102, 107.

47. George N. Green, "The ILGWU in Texas, 1930–1970," *Journal of Mexican American History* 1, no. 2 (Spring 1971): 144–156.

48. Jack Cargill, "Empire and Opposition: The 'Salt of the Earth' Strike," in Kern, pp. 179–240.

49. E. B. Fincher, *Spanish-Americans as a Factor in New Mexico* (New York: Arno Press, 1974), pp. 67–73, 94, 150–158.

50. W. Eugene Hollon, *The Southwest: Old and New* (Lincoln: University of Nebraska Press, 1961), p. 345.

51. Fincher, pp. 27–49; Grebler, Moore, and Guzmán, p. 150.

52. See Benjamin Márquez, "Power and Politics in a Chicano Barrio" (Ph.D dissertation, University of Wisconsin—Madison, 1983), pp. 45–110, an excellent work that captures what was happening in the Mexican community.

53. Márquez, pp. 120–132.

54. Márquez, pp. 55–57, 72.

55. Eugene Rodríguez, Jr., *Henry B. González: A Political Profile* (New York: Arno Press, 1976), p. 19; Edwin Larry Dickens, "The Political Role of Mexican-Americans in San Antonio" (Ph.D. dissertation, Texas Tech University, 1969), p. 47.

56. David R. Johnson, John A. Booth, and Richard J. Harris, eds., *The Politics of San Antonio: Community, Progress, and Power* (Lincoln: University of Nebraska Press, 1983), pp. 19–23.

57. Landolt, pp. 44, 87–93; Rodríguez, p. 9.

58. Landolt, pp. 191–192; Dickens, p. 140; Woods, pp. 31–36.

59. See Rodolfo F. Acuña, *A Community Under Siege: A Chronicle of Chicanos East of the Los Angeles River, 1945–1975* (Los Angeles: Chicano Studies Research Center Publications, UCLA, 1984), pp. 21–121.

60. Kay Lyon Briegel, *Alianza Hispano-Americana, 1894–1965: A Mexican Fraternal Insurance Society"* (Ph.D. dissertation, University of Southern California, 1974), p. 175; George Sánchez, "Concerning Segregation of Spanish-Speaking Children in the Public Schools," Inter-American Education Papers (Austin: University of Texas, 1951), reprinted in Carlos E. Cortés, ed., *Education and the Mexican-American* (New York: Arno Press, 1974), pp. 13–19; Scott, p. 293; Ralph C. Guzmán, *The Political Socialization of the Mexican American People* (New York: Arno, 1976), pp. 138–139, 140, 141, 142.

61. Acuña, chapter 2.

62. Louise Año Nuevo Kerr, "The Chicano Experience in Chicago: 1920–1970" (Ph.D. dissertation, University of Illinois at Chicago Circle, 1976), pp. 116–210.

63. Kibbe, pp. 212, 214–215; "First Regional Conference on the Education of Spanish-Speaking people in the Southwest—A Report" (March 1946); *Image,* (Federation of Employed Latin American Descendents, Vallejo, California) FELAD, May 1976; Sánchez, pp. 9–11.

64. Meyer Weinberg, *Minority Students: Research Appraisal* (Washington, D.C.: U.S. Department of Health, Education and Welfare, 1977), pp. 286–87; quoted in Weinberg, p. 287.

65 Patricia Rae Adler, "The 1943 Zoot-suit Riots: Brief Episode in a Long Conflict," in Manuel P. Servín, ed., *The Mexican-Americans: An Awakening Minority* (Beverly Hills, Calif.: Glencoe Press,

1970), p. 146; G.I. Forum News Bulletin, December 1953; "Edgar Taken to Federal Court on Segregation," *G.I. Forum News Bulletin,* April 1955; *G.I. Forum News Bulletin,* January 1955.

66 Tony Castro, *Chicano Power: The Emergence of Mexican-Americans* (New York: Saturday Review Press, 1974), p. 188; Miguel Tirado, "The Mexican-American Minority's Participation in Voluntary Political Associations" (Ph.D. dissertation, Claremont Graduate School and University Center, 1970), p. 65; Luis Arroyo, "Chicano Participation in Organized Labor: The CIO in Los Angeles, 1938–1950, An Extended Research Note," *Aztlán* 6, no. 2 (Summer 1975): 297; *Eastside Sun,* April 2, 1948. Keyes had shot four people in 18 months. See also Guy Endore, *Justice for Salcido* (Los Angeles: Civil Rights Congress of Los Angeles, 1948), pp. 5–9, 13. Salcido was hit four times—in the head from ear to ear, twice in the back of the head, and in the arm.

67. *Eastside Sun,* April 9, 1948; August 22, 1947. Mexican screen star Margo Albert, wife of actor Eddie Albert, was very active in setting up the people's trial. Also active was Jack Berman of the Progressive Citizens of America; *Eastside Sun,* April 9, 1948. The IPP link to most leftist events is obvious. The Progressive Citizens of America, along with Councilman P. Christensen of the 9th Councilmanic District and Ed Elliot of the 44th Assembly District, requested the suspension of Keyes; *Eastside Sun,* April 23, 1948. The American Jewish Congress protested the admitted shooting of an unarmed Mexican, "AJC Requests Action in Salcido Killing," *Eastside Sun,* July 23, 1948; See also Endore, pp. 17, 19–21, 24, 29–30; "Community Teachers Support Civil Rights Congress," an article in the *Eastside Sun,* April 30, 1948, criticized the *Times* editorial, stating that Mexicans historically suffered police brutality.

68. "Mercedes Policeman Who Menaced Family Resigns as Result of G.I. Forum Pressure," *G.I. Forum News Bulletin,* June 15, 1953; June 15, 1963; September 1953; December 1953; May 1954; February-March 1956.

69. Briegel, *"Alianza Hispano-Americana* and Some Mexican Civil Rights Cases," p. 184; *Armando Morales,* "A Study of Mexican-American Perceptions of Law Enforcement Policies and Practices in East Los Angeles" (DSW dissertation, University of Southern California, 1972), p. 77. In August 1949 a "Committee of 21" had been created in the Hollenbeck area to improve police-community relations. It held two meetings and then faded away (Morales, pp. 83–84). See also *Eastside Sun,* March 9, April 13, April 20, 1950; "El Sereno Defense Group to Give Dance," *Eastside Sun,* July 12, 1951.

70. Ralph Guzmán, *Eastside Sun,* December 29, 1953; Morales, p. 41; *Eastside Sun,* September 17, 1953; *G.I. Forum News Bulletin,* February-March, 1956; Briegel, *"Alianza Hispano-Americana* and Some Mexican Civil Rights Cases," pp. 183–184.

71. Fincher, pp. 95–97. *Eastside Sun,* February 16, April 20, July 20, 1950; June 26, August 7, September 4, 1952; "New Spanish Speaking Group Formed in Texas," *Eastside Sun,* May 31, 1951. See also *Eastside Sun,* August 11, November 29, 1951; September 11, 1952. Briegel, *"Alianza Hispano-Americana* and Some Mexican Civil Rights Cases," pp. 179–180.

72. Briegel, *"Alianza Hispano-Americana* and Some Mexican Civil Rights Cases," pp. 181–183; *Eastside Sun,* February 10, 1955.

73. Joseph Eli Kovner, "Route Would Slash Through Residential and Business Districts; Protests Mount," *Eastside Sun,* October 1, 1953. See also *Eastside Sun,* March 10, 1955; October 3, October 17, October 24, 1957; February 27, December 30, 1958, and Joseph Eli Kovner, "The Arechiga Family Bodily Evicted from Home in Chavez Ravine," *Eastside Sun,* May 14, 1959. And see the Joseph Eli Kovner articles in the *Eastside Sun,* April 10, April 17, April 24, May 1, May 8, May 15, June 6, June 12, June 26, July 3, July 17, July 24, and July 31, 1958.

74. Joseph Eli Kovner, "Aide Quits in Bunker Hill Row," *Eastside Sun,* October 9, 1958; *Eastside Sun,* December 4, December 30, 1958; Joseph Eli Kovner, "Resettle Elsewhere, Says Mayor, 'If You Don't Want Urban Renewal,' " *Eastside Sun,* January 8, 1959.

75. Joseph Eli Kovner, "Brazen Politics Endangers Lives to Lower Property Taxes," *Eastside Sun,* March 12, 1959. Bunker Hill cost the taxpayers $30 million to profit private individuals.

76. This section draws heavily from Dennis Nodin Valdes, *El Pueblo Mexicano en Detroit y Michigan: A Social History* (Detroit: Wayne State University 1982), an excellent study of the sprouting Mexican *colonias* throughout Michigan in response to labor market needs. It suggests many themes for further study in the area; Manuel Castells, *The Urban Question: A Marxist Approach* (Cambridge, Mass.: the MIT Press, 1979), pp. 393–395.

chapter 9

Goodbye America: The Chicano in the 1960s

AN OVERVIEW

The 1960s were a time of discovery, a decade when presidential candidates and the media suddenly discovered that poor folk lived in "America." This revelation affected Mexican Americans, who had largely been unknown outside the Southwest. Chicanos, for a time, hoped that awareness of their plight would lead to a reform of the political structure, resulting in the removal of the barriers to their full participation in society. No such changes occurred, and, by the end of the decade, the poor remained poor.

The U.S. position in the world market severely handicapped the North American working class. By the 1960s, Germany and Japan, for instance, were turning out better and cheaper products, such as steel, than the United States. U.S. industry had opted to pay high dividends and extravagant executive salaries, and preferred to invest profits in other forms of production rather than to modernize its own plants. The result was the loss of hundreds of thousands of jobs in heavy industry, which Mexicans and other minorities had just entered and where they could, because of unions, make a decent living. The corporations ensured their profits in the shrinking market by raising prices.[1] For the Chicano, these developments effectively blocked the upward mobility that had been available to other immigrant groups at the turn of the century.

By the 1960s, better paying jobs were requiring more education, and thus poorer Mexicans and other minorities grew more incompatible with the nation's labor market's needs. The gap between Mexican Americans and mainstream North Americans widened. The rise of the military–industrial complex had ac-

307

celerated the modernization of the Southwest, where high-tech production required well-educated workers. A persistent pattern of unemployment developed among unskilled workers in the early 1960s. At the same time, highly trained workers were required to work overtime.

In 1960, unemployment ran between 5 and 6 percent, while 7 percent of the work nationally was done on overtime. Automation and, later, runaway shops eliminated many low-skilled jobs. In spite of increased production, fewer workers were employed in manufacturing in 1960 than in 1945. Moreover, one-third of working age women were either employed or searching for a job; 28 percent of all married women worked, compounding the surplus of workers.[2] In spite of popular myths, married women did not enter the workplace to acquire luxuries; families simply needed two paychecks to survive. The new statistics represented a setback for Chicanos, since regionally they only had a median education of just over the eighth grade. And, because they lived marginally, more Mexican females were obliged to enter the labor market.

In January 1961, North Americans, unaware of changes in production, and how they would affect them and their children, looked to the future with high expectations. They had faith that John Fitzgerald Kennedy would "get the country moving again."[3] Unemployment did not seriously affect most North Americans, whereas its impact on minorities was disproportionate to their numbers. Michael Harrington, in *The Other America,* wrote that "American" society segregated poverty in the inner cities, moving the middle class to the suburbs. North American society, according to Harrington, hid poverty: "Clothes make the poor invisible too: America has the best-dressed poverty the world has ever known."[4] The works of Harrington and sociologist Oscar Lewis generalized the poor's culture of poverty, providing Euroamerican social scientists with a trapdoor through which society could escape by blaming the victim. Behind the concept of the culture of poverty was the pretense that poverty did not exist solely because the poor did not have money, but rooted itself in a subculture—a culture of poverty—that developed its own values. The poor believed in "getting by" and, unlike the middle class, did not know they were supposed to succeed. Accordingly social scientists viewed the civil rights movement positively, since it was essential in helping the poor break out of this hereditary-like syndrome. They distorted Harrington and Lewis's thesis and, in the end, the culture of poverty glorified the virtues of middle-class North Americans, whom the poor were supposed to imitate.[5]

The national debate over the culture of poverty evoked a wealth of Chicano research. *El Grito,* founded in 1967, became the leading Chicano voice in the debate. Dr. Octavio Romano, its founder, offered a critique of this theory as well as other assumptions social scientists made about Mexicans. Chicano social literature questioned, in fact, whether poverty could be stemmed through public policy.

Meanwhile, the rise in unemployment during the spring of 1962 pressured President Kennedy to act. Kennedy dealt with the lag in the economy by proposing a deficit budget in a time of relative prosperity, while cutting taxes by $13.5 billion in order to stimulate the economy. Deficit spending did spur the economy; it also gave business a generous handout by allocating larger contracts. In cutting taxes, the government further subsidized corporate profits. Government generated support for increased spending through a series of scares: the Soviet buildup, the false missile gap, and so on. The Berlin Wall, the Cuban missile crisis, the promotion of fallout shelters, and escalation of the Vietnam War produced what became a mania for defense. Most Anglo-Americans wanted to feel safe from the Russians, and they paid for it.[6]

Kennedy's New Frontier was more a statement of aspirations than a program.[7] Moved by huge demonstrations and urban and campus unrest, a reluctant Congress acted. The assassination of Kennedy, in November 1963, changed the public mood, and President Lyndon B. Johnson skillfully pushed major civil rights legislation through Congress and launched his Great Society (the so-called war on poverty). Like Kennedy and Franklin Roosevelt, Johnson relied heavily on eastern intellectuals to plan his national program.

Congress passed the 1964 Economic Opportunity Act, laying the framework for the planning and coordination of the war on poverty through the Office of Economic Opportunity (OEO). This program dramatically escalated job training programs initiated by the Manpower Development and Training Act (MDTA) of 1962. Boundless new programs—for instance, the Job Corps, Head Start, Upward Bound, VISTA, and so on—all fell under OEO. Congress allocated $1.6 billion annually to eliminate poverty—an amount which, considering that 30–40 million poor lived in the United States, did not go very far. Mexican/Chicanos had high hopes—but, in the end, they fared badly: planners knew little about Chicanos, fitting most programs to preconceived needs of Blacks.[8]

In the incessant search for funding, Chicanos quickly learned to manipulate statistics. Often they romanticized their own poverty in order to persuade bureaucrats of the need to spend funds in their communities. In the private sector, the Ford Foundation funded the Mexican American Study Project at the University of California at Los Angeles to analyze the 1960 census and establish the status of Mexicans in the United States. Throughout the 1960s, Chicano activists criticized the UCLA project because Dr. Leo Grebler, a non–Mexican American economist who had had no previous experience with Chicanos, directed it. Activists resented the foundation's determining who would become the Chicano experts. In spite of these legitimate concerns, the data went a long way in establishing a profile of the Mexican American community and its needs.

Mexican Americans and other minorities had a difficult time convincing people that they belonged to the civil rights movement. The United Civil Rights Committee, formed in Los Angeles in 1963, refused to admit Mexican Americans. The Chicano had to wait until the *Cisneros* case in 1970 for the courts to classify Mexican Americans as an "identifiable ethnic minority with a pattern of discrimination."[9]

The intensity of their struggle forced Washington to pay attention to the demands of Blacks. During the mid-1960s, the Black community exploded. Urban renewal in the 1950s had dislocated thousands of the poor, reducing the supply of low-rent housing. Northern cities became tinderboxes. In Los Angeles, the Black population, small before World War II, zoomed in the postwar years. Freeways isolated that community, hiding poverty behind concrete walls. In places like Watts, the infrastructure was totally inadequate to absorb the newcomers. Unemployment hovered at 30 percent. In August 1965, Blacks rebelled, causing $200 million in property damage and leaving 35 dead. Fourteen thousand members of the National Guard occupied Watts. Two years later, a rebellion hit Newark, New Jersey, leaving 26 dead. In 1969, 43 died in a rebellion in Detroit, where 8,000 guardsmen and 4,700 paratroopers occupied the battle zone. Because the disorder heightened middle-class fears, Congress passed legislation to control this political threat by keeping the rebellious minorities in tow.

Although economic and social conditions similar to those of the Black existed in Chicano *barrios* throughout the United States, the *barrios* did not explode with the same fervor as Black ghettos. In the mid-1960s, some Chicanos offered cultural explanations as to why Mexicans did not riot; they pictured Mexicans as more peaceful than Blacks. A partial reason for the different responses to oppression is that the institutions of social control were stronger in the Mexican *barrios* than in Watts. Mexicans had lived in *colonias* such as San Antonio for generations. In Los Angeles, Chicano communities, although continuously disorganized, were more rooted than the Black areas. The Mexican family remained much more intact than its counterpart in Watts. A common language and a similar cultural background maintained at least the facade of a Mexican American community. Homeowner occupancy was also higher in Mexican American areas than in Watts.

From the beginning, the war on poverty was in trouble; it lacked funds that were syphoned off for the Vietnam War. In simple terms, the country could not afford two wars. Space, missile, and armament programs took precedence over people. More important, North American society did not consider the ending of poverty a worthwhile goal. Euroamericans paid lip service to their commitment to end poverty and they now wanted the poor to go away. According to U.S. Senator Barry Goldwater, "The fact is that most people who have no skill have no education for the same reason—low intelligence or low ambition."[10] The solution of the "silent majority" was to rely on the free enterprise system, which, like God, helped those who helped themselves.

Bureaucratic conflict also weakened the war on poverty. The Department of Labor refused to cooperate with OEO; social workers perceived it as a threat to the welfare bureaucracy and their hegemony among the poor. Local politicians alleged that it "fostered class struggle."[11] Meanwhile, as government officials and others quickly gained control of the programs, the participation of the poor declined. By 1966, President Johnson began dismantling OEO, with Head Start going to Health, Education and Welfare and the Job Corps to the Department of Labor. He then substituted the Model Cities program for OEO. The election of Richard Nixon in 1968 put the proverbial nail in the coffin.

The impact of the war on poverty on Chicanos cannot be overestimated. First, it proved that developmentalism could not and would not work in capitalist North America. "Power to the people" was incompatible with both government and middle-class interests. Second, the war on poverty did raise awareness: a study of 60 OEO advisory boards in East Los Angeles–Boyle Heights–South Lincoln Heights, for instance, showed that 1,520 individuals, 71 percent of whom lived in these communities, served on the boards. Two-thirds were women.[12] Many Chicano activists of the 1960s developed a sense of consciousness as the result of poverty programs. Third, poverty programs advertised the demands and grievances of the poor. They created an ideology that legitimated protest. Many minorities learned the lesson that they had the right to work in government and to petition it. Legal aid programs and Head Start also proved invaluable to the poor. Fourth, the number of poor fell dramatically between 1965 and 1970 as Social Security, health, and welfare payments more than doubled. When the last of these programs were cut, in the 1980s, poverty escalated: "An invisible hand" did not and could not eradicate poverty in "America."[13]

Along with the discovery of the existence of poverty, the youth revolution greatly affected Chicanos. It was in the 1960s that the bulk of the baby boom generation matured. Most had been raised in an era of relative prosperity, not having to endure the depression or World War II. Although not a majority, a significant number of young people began to question the values of their parents. The baby boomers were influenced by the civil rights and antipoverty movements, and, especially, by the struggles to end the Vietnam War. The campus revolts touched Chicanos relatively less because colleges and universities excluded them until the late 1960s. The civil rights movement reached them via the media—and sometimes through special antipoverty programs such as the Neighborhood Youth Corps, youth conferences, rock and roll, and the music of protest, which all mingled to create the 1960s.

The civil rights era made heroes of people of color. By the mid-1960s, Chicanos had a bona fide hero in César Chávez and a cause in the farm-worker movement. Just like "Black is beautiful," brown also became beautiful. In California, because of the large number of Chicano youth who entered the movement and the lack of a tradition of involvement in Mexican American organizations, Chicanos often acted outside the mainstream of the more established groups. Often lacking a knowledge of history or any contact with Chicano associations, many Chicanos outside of Texas believed that they had begun the Chicano movement and that militancy had never existed before their generation.

A PROFILE: SAN ANTONIO CHICANOS, 1960–1965

The U.S. census in 1960 reported that 3,464,999 Spanish-surnamed persons resided in the Southwest. Their per capita income was $968, compared to $2,047 for Anglos and $1,044 for other nonwhites; 29.7 percent of the Spanish-surnamed population lived in deteriorated houses, versus 7.5 percent of the Anglos and 27.1 percent of the other nonwhites. The census further showed that the average size of the Spanish-surnamed family was 4.77, compared to 3.39 for Anglos and 4.54 for other nonwhites.[14] Unemployment was higher among Chicanos than among Anglos.

Chicanos occupied the bottom of the education scale. The median school grade for Spanish-surnamed persons over 14 years of age was 8.1, versus 12.0 for Anglos and 9.7 for other nonwhites. Significantly, the grade median for the Spanish-surnamed in Texas was 4.8. Although Chicanos were not as strictly segregated as Blacks, the majority lived apart from the Anglo community. Social segregation still existed, and in places like Texas and eastern Oregon, "No Mexicans Allowed" signs were common.[15]

San Antonio in 1960 was unquestionably the most important Texas city for Chicanos in terms both of history and of population. San Antonio had a Mexican population of 243,627, 17.2 percent of the 1,417,810 *Mexicanos* in the state. It had a permanent Mexican population; 30,299 were first generation, 75,950 second generation, and 137,738 third or later generations. As in the case of El Paso and Corpus Christi, a substantial number worked as migrants. The total unemployment in San Antonio for males of all races was 5.1 percent in 1960 versus 7.7 percent for Spanish-surnamed; the unemployment of Chicanas was 7.9 percent versus 4.7 percent for all other females.[16] These figures did not include migrant workers.

Their lack of education made it difficult for Chicanos to compete in the job market. The educational median for Chicanos over 25 was 5.7 years; only 13.2 percent had a high school education, and only 1.4 percent had a college degree. Over three-quarters of Chicano high school students were enrolled in vocational classes.[17]

Because of blatant discrimination in transportation, communications, and other public facilities, in San Antonio only 4.9 percent worked in these sectors. A dual wage structure operated, with Mexicans generally averaging some $2,000 a year less than whites. For example, the median income for a Spanish-surnamed family was $3,446 versus $5,828 for whites; 21,458 out of 50,579 (42 percent) Spanish-surnamed families earned under the poverty line of $3,000, versus 16.2 percent of the Anglo-American families. The difference was even more startling in terms of per capita income, since Mexican families were larger than those of Anglos. Mexicans earned 59 percent of what Anglo families earned; even at Kelly Air Force Base, which employed a great percentage of the better paid Chicanos, in 1962 the average wage for Anglo-Americans was $6,700 versus $4,500 for Chicanos. Mexicans comprised 23.5 percent of the base's employees.[18] In 1960, only Corpus Christi Mexicans had a lower annual median income than San Antonio—$2,974 and 4.5 years of education. The median income for El Paso Mexicans was $3,857, and their median education was 6.5 years. In Houston, they earned $4,339 with 6.4 school years.[19] In South Texas, Mexicans lived in even more depressing conditions.

Adding to the Chicanos' economic inequality in San Antonio was the fact that it was the least unionized Texas city. Less than 10 percent of the workforce belonged to unions, while only 25 percent of the building and construction trades workers had union contracts. As of 1963 few Mexicans had participated in the city's craft unions' apprenticeship programs. The pattern was clear; the higher paying and more prestigious trades like electricians had the lowest number of Mexicans (6 percent), whereas the backbreaking occupations such as cement finishers had the highest (62.5 percent). Chicanos fared even worse in union membership. A survey of membership in selected construction trades showed that only the hod carriers and cement workers were predominantly Chicano (85.4 percent and 90 percent, respectively). The hod carriers who were not Mexicans were Blacks. Chicanos made up 90 percent of the cement masons, but comprised only 10 percent of the higher paid plasterers.[20]

In the manufacturing and nonmanufacturing sectors, Mexicans did as badly. Eighteen manufacturing firms had no Chicano administrators and only three first-line supervisors. Belatedly by the mid-1960s changes occurred, and organized labor slowly began to look to Chicano and Black organizations for support against San Antonio's reactionary leaders.[21]

Robert Coles, a medical doctor, and Harry Huge, an attorney, in their article "Thorns on the Yellow Rose of Texas" reported that Mexicans comprised 41.7 percent of the 700,000 people of San Antonio, and that two San Antonios existed, one that was Anglo-American and the other that was Mexican. Coles and Huge painted a dismal picture of the city's West Side:

> . . . we saw: unpaved, undrained streets; homes without water; homes with outdoor privies; homes that are nothing but rural shacks packed together in an urban ghetto that comprises 8 percent of San Antonio's land area, but whose residents must put up with a far higher percentage of suffering—32.3 percent of the city's infant deaths; 44.6 percent of its tuberculosis; and well over half its mid-wife deliveries.

The city had 12 housing projects; Mexicans constituted 59.5 percent of the residents. Only 49.7 percent of the Mexican population had housing with plumbing, versus 94 percent for the whites.[22]

During the 1960s, the Good Government League controlled San Antonio politics, which was comprised of a downtown elite of bankers, developers, merchants, and real estate brokers. Although, as noted, Mexicans numbered just over 40 percent of the population, the GGL determined who served on the City Council; from 1957 to 1971, the machine selected only two Mexican Americans. The GGL also filled the San Antonio utility boards and planning and zoning commissions. As a matter of policy, they made few improvements on the West Side. Mayor W. W. McAllister, hostile to civic improvements in minority areas, promoted the Hemisfair, the South Texas Medical Center, the University of Texas at San Antonio, and new industry. Taxes were kept low by depriving minority communities of services.

LULAC and the G.I. Forum remained active in San Antonio and South Texas. The early 1960s, however, saw an increased interest in partisan politics in Texas. In 1962, Henry B. González got reelected to the U.S. Congress. Albert Peña, Jr., and the Teamsters supported the Mexican American takeover of the Crystal City Council for two years. In 1964, Mexican Americans elected Elizo (Kika) de la Garza to Congress. Electoral politics received a shot in the arm in 1966 when a constitutional amendment abolished the poll tax.[23]

In 1960, the *Víva* Kennedy clubs and the election of President John F. Kennedy, as elsewhere, stimulated political activity. González and County Commissioner Peña had their political organizations in San Antonio. Peña and his aide Albert Fuentes organized *Víva* Kennedy clubs throughout Texas. (Carlos McCormick of *La Alianza Hispano-Americana* headed the national organization.) The clubs played a key role in electing Kennedy; they also constituted a national network that led to the formation of the Political Association of Spanish-Speaking Organizations (PASSO) in 1961. Debate took place over the name. In Texas and New Mexico, the term *Mexican* was controversial. In the end, California kept the name MAPA. Because of many factors, PASSO did not take root in other states, and it soon became an exclusively Texas association.[24]

In Texas, PASSO split into liberal and conservative factions. Peña led the liberals; the G.I. Forum's Dr. Hector García, along with LULAC's Bonilla brothers, William and Tony, headed the conservatives. García and the Bonillas criticized PASSO's role in the Crystal City takeover, claiming that the Teamsters had gained control of PASSO.[25] Dr. García walked out of PASSO's 1963 convention, followed by LULAC. García, a staunch supporter of Lyndon B. Johnson and Texas Governor John Connally, feared Chicano involvement with more liberal Democrats. Shortly afterward, LULAC and the Forum entered the poverty program network.

LULAC and the Forum undermined PASSO. The Crystal City takeover ended after only two years. The Chicano City Council had done a very good job of administering the city's finances. However, personality conflicts and factionalism tore the coalition apart. Matters worsened when LULAC established a chapter in Crystal City.

Awareness of political oppression and renewed hope spurred political activity in South Texas. Mexican Americans increasingly ran for office. In Mathis, in San Patricio County near Corpus Christi, Mexicans formed the Action party in 1965, taking control of the municipal government. Their goal was to improve municipal services for Mexicans. In 1967, the Action party won reelection.

New actors entered the political arena. They not only competed against Anglos but frequently challenged the old guard in the Mexican community, who jealously protected their hegemony. LULAC and Forum leaders resented groups like PASSO and/or younger leaders like Peña and their more strident tactics. However, the times encouraged mass participation. The 1966 constitutional amendment abolishing the poll tax encouraged massive voter registration drives. Strike activity in Starr County also raised the hopes of younger Chicanos that the *gringo* monopoly could be broken.

NORTH FROM TEXAS

The migration of Chicanos to the Midwest continued in the 1960s where farm production was undergoing a transformation. In the 1960s the cost of automation decreased. Government research grants cut the cost of the machinery, and the cost of food production decreased while profits increased. Midwestern employers rushed to modernize operations. For example, by 1970 in Wisconsin three-quarters of the cucumber crop and over half of the cherry crop were machine harvested. Anglo-Americans who once shunned stoop labor were more willing to take jobs operating machines, with Chicanos benefiting little from mechanization. The situation in the Midwest reflected national trends. The agricultural workforce declined from 9 percent of the U.S. total in 1960 to 6 percent in 1965 to

5 percent in 1970.[26] As a consequence, migration to the Midwestern cities increased.

Neither distance nor the lack of sun diminished the Mexicans' nationalism and their ties to Texas or Mexico. The differences between Chicanos in the Midwest and the Southwest were obvious—but so were the contrasts between Mexican Americans from Texas and California. The similarities were stronger. Chicano farm workers in both regions benefited from the expiration of Public Law 78, the *bracero* program, on December 31, 1964 (see Chapter 8). The discovery of the migrant's plight in the early 1960s raised an awareness of their needs. And, finally, the César Chávez farm-worker struggle in California inspired militancy among midwestern Chicanos.

Mechanization decreased the demand for migrants during the 1950s and 1960s. Even so, in 1968, 90,000 migrants worked in Michigan alone. Chicano farm workers throughout the region, excluded and isolated from the rest of society, suffered from intense racism and poor work conditions. By the late 1960s, federally funded programs—such as the United Migrants for Opportunity, located at Mt. Pleasant, Michigan—offered information and referral services. Poverty agency employees, influenced by the civil rights movement, acted as ombudsmen for the migrant families.[27] Similar activity occurred in Chicano *barrios* throughout the Midwest—East Lansing and Adrian, Michigan; Toledo, Ohio; Indianapolis and Gary, Indiana; Milwaukee, Wisconsin; and St. Paul, Minnesota, to name a few.

Detroit

Detroit, like many large cities in the Midwest, housed the fallout from the migrant stream. In the main *barrio* near Vernor, Chicanos and Puerto Ricans shared space. In the early 1960s, the G.I. Forum represented the interests of many residents. The Detroit riots of 1967 encouraged activism among Chicanos. The private sector and the Catholic Church sponsored programs for Blacks, but totally ignored Latino demands and needs. Chicanos, bitter at this neglect, more militantly petitioned both the church and the government. By the end of the 1960s, they attracted federal funds, and agencies such as *La Sed* (Latin Americans for Social and Economic Development), SER—Jobs for Progress, and other poverty agencies became semipermanent fixtures. *Latinos en marcha* spearheaded the demand for recruitment and retention of Latino students to Wayne State University, where a coalition of Chicanos and Puerto Ricans negotiated a Chicano/Boricua (Puerto Rican) studies program.

Chicago

Economically, life in Chicago improved for both Texas-Mexicans and Mexican nationals. The U.S. census in 1960 reported that the Mexican population had grown to 45,000; ten years later it had increased to 108,000, making Chicago one of the largest urban centers of Mexicans in the United States. The 1970 census reported that 45,000 Chicanos had been born in Illinois, 19,000 outside the state and 14,000 had migrated to Illinois from Texas. Eighty-three percent of the U.S.-born Chicano population had lived in Chicago for five years or more. An undercount was clear, since large numbers of undocumented Mexicans had begun to arrive after 1965; at the same time, the Texas migration slowed.[28]

While Chicanos were still clustered in less desirable employment, some working in steel averaged $12,500 a year by the late 1960s; a few skilled workers earned as much as $25,000. In the early 1970s, William Kornblum wrote: "The South Chicago area often seems little more than a grimy stretch of neighborhoods crowded between steel mills. The streets and houses are frequently coated with a layer of red mill dust, and the gasses from furnaces and coke ovens make the air over the community among the most polluted in the nation." In these neighborhoods lived the elite of the Chicago Mexican community. They had moved to Millgate as early as World War II, later spreading to the Irondale area. By the end of the 1960s, although they still went to their own taverns and lived in segregated neighborhoods, they were relatively tolerated by Anglos.[29] They now began to run for union leadership posts.

In the early 1960s, Chicanos participated in the Mexican Community Committee (1959), organized by the Chicago Area Project. They worked on local problems such as juvenile delinquency; at this time, they got more politically involved. Second generation steelworkers in 1966 integrated into the Chicago political milieu and formed the Tenth Ward Spanish-Speaking Democratic Organization, which functioned within the Democratic machine. In the 1960s, ethnic consciousness increased among Mexicans.

John Chico, a leader in the steelworkers' union of South Chicago, ran for the state constitutional convention in a special election in 1969. He was the first Mexican to run in that city. The Tenth Ward Spanish-Speaking Democratic Organization, as well as the steelworkers' union, supported Chico, who openly identified with the Chicano movement. He and other Mexican unionists challenged the Tenth Ward leaders who belonged to the Daley machine. Chico lost the election and Daley retaliated and withheld patronage, gerrymandering the Tenth into two separate wards to dilute Mexican voting power.[30]

In spite of growing ethnic cohesion within the neighborhoods, political unity between the neighborhoods eluded Chicago Mexicans. The largest *barrio*, Pilsen, developed a strong identity, differing from South Chicago both economically and in terms of homeowner occupancy. Rivalry developed between the youth in both communities, and occasionally rumbles broke out. In 1968, tensions increased when a Chicano youth was killed, preventing the two areas from joining under the banner of the Chicano movement. However, both supported the farmworker grape boycott and other Chicano causes. In 1970, both communities had ties with the Midwest Committee for *La Raza* at Notre Dame University.[31]

Between 1960 and 1970, the Little Village community (26th Street) grew and became integrated into the Pilsen (18th Street). Little Village Mexicans/Latinos were on the average economically better off than the Pilsen residents. Both these communities suffered from the inability of older ethnics and their institutions to adjust to the change in a Mexican neighborhood. A lag occurred and the schools, the churches, and the Daley machine responded to the older ethnics rather than to the new majority. By the end of the 1960s, however, Mexican institutions and agencies emerged: *El Centro de La Causa,* BASTA (Brotherhood Against Slavery to Addiction), Chicano Mental Health, the Mexican American Council on Education, Brown Berets, and the Organization of Latin American Students. In response to this growing nationalism, Howell House changed its name to Casa Aztlán, the home of the Benito Juárez Health Clinic. Chicanos in Chicago readily adopted the nationalist symbols of their Southwestern counterparts.

Return to the Sunbelt

Urbanization of Texas Chicanos during the decade saw cities such as Houston grow dramatically. Houston based its prosperity on geography, technology, and government assistance. Massive building developments required unskilled labor, which Blacks and Chicanos could provide. The Black population by 1970 numbered 316,922; Chicanos were about half that number. Chicanos lived in older sections in the Eastside, clustered around the Ship Channel.[32] The invisible hand of the free market supposedly ran Houston, with developers raping the city.

El Paso continued to serve as a port of entry. Mexicans spread throughout the city, with older *colonias* such a Ysleta making up the core of the expanded *barrios.* The poorest of the poor still lived in *el segundo barrio.* The building industry slumped in the 1960s, and housing deteriorated. As in other cities, the older LULAC and Forum were the largest groups. Meanwhile, the *Chamizal* treaty in 1966 displaced 5,595 residents. (The *Chamizal* was a disputed section of land on the Mexican-Texas border. A shift in the river put the *Chamizal* on the U.S. side. The treaty gave the land back to Mexico.) The Second Ward lost one-third of its businesses and 1,155 housing units. Construction at the border also affected the Second Ward as federal installations replaced the housing stock. Because of the building slump, developers pressured the city to apply for federal programs.

The decade was a time of increased political consciousness among Mexicans. In 1967, Ismael, 8, Orlando, 7, and Leticia Rosales, 4, were burned to death. When angry El Pasoans protested, the city responded by appointing Abelardo Delgado and Salvador Ramírez to a commission to study the problem. Poverty projects, especially juvenile delinquency programs, brought youth together, and inspired the Mexican American Youth Association (MAYA), the most active Chicano organization during this period. Tenants also formed tenant unions to press for public housing. Militancy carried over to the University of Texas at El Paso, where Chicano students demanded the admission of more Chicanos and a Chicano studies program.[33]

California and the Sleeping Giant

The Sleeping Giant, so often referred to in California during the 1950s, had still not awakened in the 1960s. The success of the *Víva* Kennedy clubs raised expectations among Chicanos, with many calling the 1960s the "Decade of the Mexican

American." MAPA's founding in 1959 demonstrated discontent with the Democratic party and, at least, gave lip service to bipartisan politics. The CSO proved that Mexican Americans would in large numbers register to vote; MAPA moved to concretize these votes into political gains.

California prided itself in not having political machines. The liberal California Democratic Council (CDC), dominated by grass-roots Democrats, indeed fielded an army of precinct workers. Although the CDC identified with the civil rights movement and promoted representation for Blacks, it almost totally ignored Mexicans. Party leaders and volunteers paternalistically rationalized the gerrymandering of Mexican districts as good for that community, since it was essential to keep liberal Democratic incumbents in office. Few leaders noticed when the reapportionments of 1961, 1965, and 1967 totally excluded Mexican Americans from political office. Incumbents helped themselves—blatantly gerrymandering Mexican *barrios* throughout California. One of the worst examples was East Los Angeles, where the 40th, 45th, 48th, 50th, and 51st assembly districts cut into East Los Angeles to pick up 20–30 percent Mexican American districts. The 52nd, 53rd, 65th, and 66th took smaller bites.

Mexicans consequently did not fare well in the political arena. In 1962, John Moreno and Phil Soto were elected to the California Assembly. Moreno was defeated two years later and Soto in 1966. The election of Edward R. Roybal to the U.S. Congress in 1962 left a void in local politics. The Los Angeles City Council, in spite of community protests, appointed a Black, Gilbert Lindsay, to replace Roybal. Members cared little about Mexicans when they reapportioned councilmanic districts, allowing for the election of three Blacks but making it impossible for a Mexican American to win. Without local leadership, the Mexican community was vulnerable to the schemes of opportunistic politicians such as Councilwoman Rosalind Wyman, who proposed swapping Hazard Park for federally owned land in Westwood so that her rich constituents in Westwood could build tennis courts. Mayor Sam Yorty supported the Hazard Park swap as well as other schemes to take public land away from the Eastside.[34]

Los Angeles, because of its wealth and population, dominated California politics. Although its Mexican population, the largest in the United States, developed an awareness of ethnicity during the early 1960s, Mexican Americans did not achieve political power. Based on voter registration, it, in fact, appeared to decline: "In a study of 14 selected census tracts in Los Angeles County, [political scientist] Ralph Guzmán found that registration was 17,948 voters in 1958, 18,585 in 1960, 18,187 in 1962 and 13,989 in 1965."[35] What happened was that CSO, which after 1958 lost Industrial Area Foundation funding, limited voter registration maintenance. In 1960, the *Víva* Kennedy clubs put money into voter registration, and in 1962 Roybal's congressional candidacy kept it high. After that point, the Democratic party ignored the registration of Mexicans.

In terms of political appointments, too, Mexican Americans got short shrift. In 1963, Los Angeles Municipal Court judge Leopold Sánchez stated that out of 5,000 appointments made by Governor Edmund G. Brown, Sr., less than 30 were Chicanos. Brown responded by implying that no qualified Mexican Americans lived in California.[36]

By the 1960s Mexicans made up over 80 percent of the Boyle Heights–East Los Angeles area, a trend that was followed by the rest of the Eastside. In 1945, the Mexican American was not quite a majority in these areas. In the postwar years, a mass exodus of middle-class Jews and Anglos took place, followed by lower-middle-class Mexican Americans who moved out of the *barrio* core to new housing tracts generally east and north of the Eastside.

As the Eastside became poorer and more Mexican, municipal and county authorities increasingly ignored it. Local leaders along with the press dwelled on the rise in juvenile delinquency and crime in the area. The schools also deteriorated and teacher expectations of student achievement and potential declined. In the 1930s and 1940s, Roosevelt High had had a large Jewish student population, with its curriculum emphasizing academic subjects; however, as the school browned, authorities introduced more vocational programs.

During this period, a growing number of Mexican Americans became aware of the inferior education they received. Overcrowded classrooms, double sessions, a lack of Mexican American teachers, and a general neglect of their schools encouraged pushouts. In contrast, the San Fernando Valley, then a suburb where the white baby boomers went to school, received the bulk of the building funds. At the same time, racial segregation increased as the Eastside became more Mexican and poorer.

Los Angeles County's Mexican population mushroomed during the 1960s, from 576,716 to 1,228,593, an increase of 113 percent. The Anglo population decreased from 4,877,150 to 4,777,909, a 2 percent drop. In 1966, 76,619 Anglo babies were born in Los Angeles, compared to 24,533 Latinos and 17,461 Blacks. Eight years later 41,940 Anglo babies were born, 16,173 Black babies, and 45,113 Latino babies. By 1970, the San Francisco–Oakland area experienced a similar growth, increasing to 362,900 Latinos.[37] This population, however, differed from that of Los Angeles, and it included a majority of Central and South Americans as well as Puerto Ricans.

Unemployment and poverty among Mexican Americans remained high throughout the first half of the 1960s. In a 1964 survey among unemployed Chicanos in Los Angeles, 90 percent felt that the fair employment legislation had produced no results whatsoever.[38] This hopelessness carried over into the streets, where police–community relations deteriorated.

On January 27, 1960, Chief William Parker stated before the U.S. Civil Rights Commission: "Some of these people [Mexicans] were here before we were but some are not far removed from the wild tribes of the district of the inner mountains of Mexico."[39] Parker expressed the official attitude of the LAPD toward Mexicans. Parker claimed that 40 percent of the arrests in the city were Black and 28 percent Mexican. Frank X. Paz led demonstrations against Parker, with over 500 attending a meeting of the Mexican–American Citizens Committee.[40] Dr. R. J. Carreón, Jr., the token Chicano police commissioner, refused to attend the meeting, stating that he had heard Parker's story and that the community should drop the issue. The community renewed its efforts to create a police review board. The American Civil Liberties Union, the NAACP, and the Mexican-American Citizens Committee joined to form the Committee for a Los Angeles Police Review Board.[41] Local newspapers excused Parker. They even went so far as to censure Roybal for demanding an apology and/or Parker's resignation. On February 9, the *Los Angeles Times* accused Roybal of demagoguery.

In East Los Angeles confrontations between Chicanos and police increased as the LAPD attempted to clamp down to discourage a Mexican Watts. In 1966, the police called for a back-up crew when an angry crowd gathered as they attempted to make an arrest. Two warning shots were fired.[42] In July the Happy Valley Parents Association organized a surveillance of police. In September of that year the ACLU in cooperation with the CSO opened a center in East Los Angeles. From September 1966 to July 1968 it investigated 205 police abuse cases, with 152 filed by Chicanos.

In the summer of 1967 some 300 Chicanos attended a conference at Camp Hess Kramer on police–community relations. They asked for federal government intervention into the deteriorated relations between the police and the community in Los Angeles.[43] Federal intervention was not forthcoming and relations worsened.

By 1967, in Los Angeles political consciousness had increased. Added to the older activists of MAPA, CSO, LULAC, and the Forum, youth, professionals and poverty workers criticized the schools and government in their treatment of Mexican Americans. Numerous new organizations such as the Association of Mexican American Educators (AMEA) (1965) and the United Mexican American Students (UMAS) (1967) made known the community's frustrations. Mexican Americans, concerned about the lack of gains made by them in comparison with Blacks, insisted that more attention be paid to their needs. Cultural nationalism, expressing itself in a pride of identity and a rejection of assimilation as a goal, increased. Tensions rose as the Vietnam War handicapped Lyndon Johnson's "Great Society" programs. By 1966, the government's commitment to ending poverty slid backward as it spent $22 billion on the war in Southeast Asia versus about $1.5 billion on fighting poverty.

THE MEXICAN CONNECTION: UN PUEBLO, UNA LUCHA

After the mid-1960s, the migration of documented and undocumented Mexicans to the United States steadily increased. The migration itself had multiple effects on the Chicano. First, after World War II, a marked trend toward assimilation had occurred and many Mexican American parents refused to teach their children Spanish. This trend was reversed by the growth of cultural nationalism and the presence of larger numbers of Mexican nationals. Rather than a rejection of Mexican heritage, cultural nationalism created a renaissance in Mexican consciousness. This phenomenon was the most noticeable in California, where the trend toward *pochoization** was the most advanced. And, second, events in Mexico increased its importance to Mexican Americans. It became clear to many Chicanos that their own status would not improve until the growing subservience of the Mexican nation to the multinational corporations ended. The image of a

---

Pocho is a term used by Mexicans, applied to U.S.-born Mexicans who speak no Spanish or speak it poorly. In a broader sense, a *pocho* is neither Mexican nor North American.

weak Mexican nation reinforced stereotypes of weak, dirty, lazy Mexican Americans. These caricatures were used to justify the exploitation of Mexican Americans.

Mexican migration itself was a response to industrial conditions in the United States. Increased division of labor brought about the rapid expansion of low-skilled jobs in agriculture, the service sector, and light industry—jobs that most Anglo-Americans would not accept because the pay was below the minimum wage or they were socially undesirable. This in turn created a demand for cheap labor in the United States.

The population boom during the 1960s threw millions into the labor pool. In 1950 Mexico had a population of 25.8 million, jumping to 34.9 million ten years later, and rushing toward 50 million by the end of the 1960s. Mexico's annual population growth had dramatically increased from an average of 1.75 percent (1922–1939) to 2.25 percent (1939–1946) to 2.8 percent (1947–1953) to well over 3 percent after 1954.[44]

Although Mexico had the fastest growing gross national product (GNP) in Latin America, it could not absorb the population boom as the first wave entered the workforce in the 1960s. Mexico, like many Third World countries, had launched a program of development and modernization after World War II, expecting to cure its economic and social ills. Modernization, however, did not solve the problem of the poor but accelerated the deterioration of their status. The mechanization of agriculture worsened the plight of the peasant and helped bring about the elimination of many subsistence farmers while increasing the division of labor—further widening the gap between rich and poor.

Industrialization made Mexico more vulnerable to the world market and encouraged U.S. penetration of the Mexican economy. Mexico's dependence on the United States was proved by the abrupt end of the *bracero* program, which had administered migration to the United States for special interests. Instead of attempting to lessen its dependence on the United States, Mexico substituted another U.S. program for the *bracero,* allowing greater North American control over the Mexican economy.

After World War II, multinational corporations (those doing business in more than one country) moved to dominate the marketing of Mexican agricultural products. Del Monte alone by 1967 had offices in 20 Latin American countries and ranked as the world's largest canning corporation. By 1964 Mexico shipped 334 million pounds of vegetables north; 13 years later, the flow increased to 1,108 million pounds, supplying, at certain seasons, 60 percent of U.S. fresh vegetables.

Anderson-Clayton, extensively involved in Third World nations, monopolized the sale of cotton in Mexico through credit and marketing. It loaned more credit to Mexican growers than El Banco Nacional Ejidal. Anderson-Clayton manipulated prices and kept Mexico in line by either dumping or threatening to dump cotton on the world market at depressed prices.[45] The process of monopolization, like mechanization, accelerated the elimination of subsistence and small farmers and led to the production of crops for export rather than staples such as corn and beans.

U.S. economic penetration into Mexico during the 1960s totaled $1.1 billion; however, total profits of $1.8 billion in the form of payments abroad in interests, royalties, and patents were drained out of the economy annually. The United States's monopoly of technology forced Mexico to purchase machinery, transistors, wires, generators, and similar equipment from it to the exclusion of other industrial nations. This kept Mexico constantly in debt and dependent on the World Bank and the International Monetary Fund for new loans.

Contrary to popular myth, North American and other foreign investors did not create jobs. During the decade, over 60 percent of the new foreign investment went to purchase already existing corporations. Between 1963 and 1970, the workers employed by foreign corporations increased by 180,000; however, 105,000 of these jobs already existed.[46] In fact, foreign companies controlled 31 percent of the total value of Mexican industrial production and employed only 16 percent of the industrial workforce.

Changes in the world market since World War II also affected Mexico. Simply, after the war, the decolonization of the Third World produced a restructuring of the multinationals. Under colonialism, governments protected and regulated their national corporations doing business in countries under their flag or within their sphere of influence. With the end of colonialism, multinationals sought to maintain their control of markets and natural resources in their former colonies. They also expanded their own spheres of influence beyond former limits. As "a result of decolonization and the economic growth and technological explosion following the end of World War II," many multinationals became superpowers and, by the 1960s, were assuming the character of transnational corporations.[47] Their principal place of business was not in one country. As the transnationals grew in economic power, they became more ungovernable and often acted independently of the home country.

Immediately after World War II, the United States had no competitors on the world market. Government contracts accelerated the growth and power of U.S. multinationals. However, by the 1960s, competition from Japanese, German, and other European nations threatened North American hegemony. U.S. transnationals sought to cut their costs by relocating the production of many commodities to Asia and Latin America to increase their profits. Labor in those regions was just as much a commodity as natural resources. Buying labor cheaply meant higher margins.

By the mid-1960s, the phenomenon of the runaway shop was well advanced in the electro-electronic and garment industries. This restructuring was made possible through special privileges extended to North American multinationals by loopholes in the U.S. Customs Simplification Act of 1956. Section 806.30 allowed the processing abroad of metal goods that returned to the United States for finishing. Section 807, passed in 1963, laid the basis for apparel, toy, and similar "light" industries to relocate overseas. Understandably, U.S. labor opposed these loopholes, but it lacked sufficient power to stop the flow of jobs out of the United States.

Meanwhile, conditions in Mexico worsened with the termination of the *bracero* program. Mexico had become dependent on renting out its workers. The border areas became an object of special concern for the Mexican government because of the accumulation of people who responded to the pull north as the Mexican economy deteriorated. In the early 1960s, it initiated *La Nacional Financiera* (PONAF), a program intended to (1) substitute Mexican manufacturing for U.S. goods which Mexicans commonly bought, (2) promote the sale of Mexican goods abroad, and (3) upgrade the social environment along the border.[48] PONAF's success was mixed. As unemployment mounted, Mexico responded by accepting more overt U.S. penetration.

Mexico agreed to the Border Industrialization Program (BIP). The purpose of the BIP was to create jobs, to attract capital, to introduce modern methods of manufacturing in assembling, processing, and exporting, and to increase consumption of Mexican raw materials. The Mexican government waived duties and regulations on the import of raw materials and relaxed restrictions on foreign capital within 12.5 miles of the border (this area has continuously been expanded); 100 percent of the finished products were to be exported out of the country, with 90 percent of the labor force comprised of Mexicans. In 1966, 20 BIP plants operated along the border.[49] This number increased to 120 in 1970 and to 476 in 1976. The majority were electro-electronic and apparel plants.

In reality, although these *maquiladoras* (assembly plants) did create jobs (20,327 in 1970), they did not ameliorate the unemployment problem, since they hired mostly from a sector of Mexican labor that was not previously employed. The BIP workforce, over 70 percent women, was paid minimum Mexican wages. North American employers gave no job security and the *maquiladoras* could move at the owner's whim. The BIP failed miserably as a strategy for development. The Mexican government had hoped that the *maquiladoras* would purchase Mexican parts; this did not occur. The BIP left relatively little capital in Mexico. The program itself provided multinationals an alternative to Taiwan and Hong Kong, dramatically cutting down transportation costs. BIP projects grew rapidly during the decade that followed. Just like the *bracero* program, it increased Mexican dependence on the United States, making both Mexico and its rented slaves more vulnerable to multinational penetration.[50]

Exploitation of Mexican labor was not confined to the BIP program nor multinational activity. Both documented and undocumented workers flowed freely into the United States in order to ensure a surplus of cheap labor for growers and other domestic interests. The commuter program served farmers, small businesses, and corporations along the border. The McCarran-Walter Act removed the alien contract provision from the immigration code and introduced "a system of selective immigration giving special preference to skilled aliens urgently needed in this country." It authorized the secretary of labor to grant a limited number of permits (green cards) for temporary residence if the workers did not compete with domestic workers. U.S. immigration and labor authorities constantly abused the commuter program, even losing count of the number of permits issued. As in the case of the El Paso Payton Packing Company strike of 1960, growers also received special treatment; they did not have to bother to pay living wages to attract U.S. workers. They just had to petition the Department of Labor for temporary workers and allege that they could not find sufficient numbers of domestic workers and that an emergency existed.[51]

By the mid-1960s, Chicano militancy concerned growers and other employers. The purpose of immigration policy was to control not only Mexicans but Chicanos. After 1965, this policy became more restrictive, designed to regulate both the flow of workers and the wages paid. Essential to this strategy was the criminalization of Mexican labor, which devalued and degraded the work performed by Mexicans and Chicanos. Criminalization intensified the division of labor and resulted in Chicanos, to avoid discrimination, pecking down on the undocumented worker; it also justified increased use of police power against all Mexicans, whether documented or undocumented.

The first step in the criminalization process was the passage of restrictive legislation that directly affected the documented immigration of Mexicans. Liberals such as Senator Edward Kennedy sponsored legislation in 1965 designed to correct the past injustice of excluding Asians from legal entry. Nativists took the opportunity to broaden the legislation and, for the first time, placed Latin America and Canada on a quota system. The law specified that 170,000 immigrants annually could enter from the Eastern Hemisphere and 120,000 from the Western. Up to this time Mexico had been the principal source of Latin American immigration; the new law put a cap of 40,000 from any one nation. Unfortunately, few Chicanos or progressive organizations protested the law. And it was not until the 1970s that its full impact and was felt; at that time it became a popular cause for progressives.[52]

THE ROAD TO DELANO: CREATING A MOVEMENT

Many Chicanos have incorrectly labeled the second half of the 1960s as the birth of the Chicano movement. As witnessed in preceding chapters, Mexicans in the United States have responded to injustice and oppression since the U.S. wars of aggression that took Texas and the Southwest from Mexico. Middle-class organizations generally spoke for the community, since its members had the education, money, and stability to maintain more or less permanent associations. Established Anglo power brokers also recognized these organizations.

By the mid-1960s, traditional groups such as LULAC and the G.I. Forum, along with recently formed political groups such as MAPA and PASSO, were challenged. For better or worse, the established Mexican American associations had served as agents of social control, setting the norm for conduct. The rise of cultural nationalism challenged the acceptance of assimilation as a goal. Sectors of youth, women, and more militant activists were skeptical of traditional methods of struggle and advocated direct action. They also questioned the legitimacy of established leaders.

For the most part, LULAC and Forum leaders at first rejected "street politics"—marches, walkouts, confrontations, civil disobedience, and so on. Over the years their ties with the system tightened. At the same time, the civil rights, antinuclear, and anti-Vietnam movements, along with community action programs, legitimated an ideology of confrontation, creating a new awareness among Chicanos that resulted in a demand for self-determination by *los de abajo* (the underdogs) and youth. Also important was that sectors of the North American left, as well as government agencies, no longer dealt with established groups exclusively but recognized more militant Chicanos organizations. This, for a time, broke the monopoly of the Mexican American middle class. Moreover, rank and file members of LULAC and the Forum grew closer to the new Chicano agenda.

César Chávez and the United Farm Workers

César Chávez gave the Chicano movement a national leader. In all probability Chávez was the only Mexican American to be so recognized by the mainstream civil rights and antiwar movements. Chávez and his farm workers were also supported by the center Mexican American organizations along with the left.

On September 8, 1965, the Filipinos in the Agricultural Workers Organizing Committee (AWOC) struck the grape growers of the Delano area in the San Joaquin Valley. Filipino workers had been encouraged by a victory in the spring of 1965 in the Coachella Valley, where the U.S. Labor Department announced that *braceros* would be paid $1.40 an hour. The domestic pickers received 20¢ to 30¢ an hour less. Joined by Mexicans, the Filipinos walked out, and ten days later they received a guarantee of equivalent pay with *braceros.* When the Filipinos requested the same guarantee in the San Joaquin Valley, growers refused, and led by Larry Itlong, they voted to strike. The strike demands were simple: $1.40 an hour or 25¢ a box. The Di Giorgio Corporation became the major target. The rank and file of the National Farm Workers Association (NFWA) voted on September 16 to join the Filipinos. The termination at the end of 1964 of Public Law 78 significantly strengthened the union's position.[53]

Chávez emerged as the central figure in the strike. Born in Yuma, Arizona, in 1927, he spent his childhood as a migrant worker. His father had belonged to farm labor unions and Chávez himself had been a member of the National Farm Labor Union. In the 1940s he moved to San Jose, California, where he married Helen Fávila. In San Jose Chávez met Father Donald McDonnell, who tutored him in *Rerum Novarum,* Pope Leo XIII's encyclical which supported labor unions and social justice. Through Father McDonnell Chávez met Fred Ross of the Community Service Organization. He became an organizer for the CSO and learned grass-roots strategies. Chávez rose to the position of general director of the national CSO, but in 1962 he resigned, moving to Delano, where he began to organize his union. Chávez went door to door visiting farm workers. Delano was chosen because of its substantial all-year farm-worker population; in 1968, 32 percent of the 7,000 harvest workers lived and worked in the Delano area year round.

Chávez concentrated his efforts on the Mexican field hands, for he knew the importance of nationalism in solidifying an organization. He carefully selected a loyal cadre of proven organizers, such as Dolores Huerta and Gil Padilla, whom he had met in the CSO. By the middle of 1964 the NFWA was self-supporting.

A year later the NFWA had some 1,700 members. Volunteers, fresh from civil rights activities in the South, joined the NFWA at Delano. Protestant groups, inspired by the civil rights movement, championed the cause of the workers. A minority of Catholic priests, influenced by Vatican II, joined Chávez.

Anglo-American labor belatedly jumped on the bandwagon. In Chávez's favor was the growing number of Chicano workers living in the United States. Over 80 percent lived in cities, and many belonged to unions. Many, in fact, belonged to big labor such as the United Auto Workers (UAW).[54]

The times allowed Chávez to make his movement a crusade. The stabilization of a large part of the Mexican American workforce made the forging of an organization possible. And, finally, the end of the *bracero* program took a lethal weapon from the growers.

The most effective strategy was the boycott. Supporters were urged not to buy Schenley products or Di Giorgio grapes. The first breakthrough came when the Schenley Corporation signed a contract in 1966. The Teamsters unexpectedly refused to cross picket lines in San Francisco. Rumors of a bartenders' boycott reached 75-year-old Lewis Solon Rosenstiel, Schenley's president, who decided that a settlement was advisable. Soon afterward Gallo, Christian Brothers, Paul Masson, Almaden, Franzia Brothers, and Novitiate signed contracts.

The next opponent was the Di Giorgio Corporation, one of the largest grape growers in the central valley. In April 1966, Robert Di Giorgio unexpectedly announced he would allow his workers at Sierra Vista to vote on whether they wanted a union and who would represent them. Di Giorgio did not act in good faith and his agents set out to intimidate the workers.

With the support of Di Giorgio the Teamsters opposed the farm workers and bid to represent the workers. Di Giorgio, without consulting the NFWA, set the date for the election. The NFWA urged its followers not to vote, since it did not have time to campaign or to participate in establishing the ground rules. It needed enough time to return eligible voters to the Delano area. Out of 732 eligible voters only 385 voted; 281 voters specified that they wanted the Teamsters as their union agent. The NFWA immediately branded the election as fraudulent and pressured Governor Edmund G. Brown, Sr., a friend of Di Giorgio, to investigate the election. Brown needed the Chicano vote as well as that of the liberals who were committed to the farm workers. The governor's investigator recommended a new election, and the date was set for August 30, 1966.[55]

That summer an intense campaign took place between the Teamsters and the NFWA. A state Senate committee investigated charges of communist infiltration of the NFWA; the committee found nothing to substantiate charges. As the election neared, Chávez became more somber. He had to keep the eligible voters in Delano, and he had the responsibility of feeding them and their families as well as the army of strikers and volunteers. The Di Giorgio campaign drained the union's financial resources. Some weeks before the strike vote, Chávez reluctantly merged the NFWA and AWOC into the United Farm Workers Organizing Committee (UFWOC).

Teamsters red-baited the UFWOC and circulated free copies of Gary Allen's John Birch Society pamphlet. The UFWOC passed out excerpts from *The Enemy Within,* in which Robert Kennedy indicted James Hoffa and the Teamsters in scathing terms; association with the Kennedy name helped. Finally the vote was taken. The UFWOC won the election, 573 votes to the Teamsters' 425.

Field workers voted 530 to 331 in favor of the UFWOC. Soon afterward the Di Giorgio Corporation and the UFWOC signed a contract.

Other growers proved to be more difficult. In 1967 the Giumarra Vineyards Corporation, the largest producer of table grapes in the United States, was targeted. When Guimarra used other companies' labels to circumvent the boycott, in violation of the Food and Drug Administration rules, the union boycotted all California table grapes. Boycott activities spread into Canada and Europe. Grape sales decreased significantly. Some of the slack was taken up by the U.S. Defense Department. In 1966 U.S. troops in Vietnam were shipped 468,000 pounds of grapes; in 1967, 555,000 pounds; in 1968, 2 million pounds; and by 1969, more than 4 million pounds. Later the U.S. Defense Department spent taxpayers' money to buy large quantities of lettuce when the union boycotted this product.[56] In the summer of 1970 the strike approached its fifth year. In June 1970 a group of Coachella Valley growers agreed to sign contracts, as did a majority of growers. Victories in the San Joaquin Valley followed.

After this victory the union turned to the lettuce fields of the Salinas Valley, where growers were among the most powerful in the state. During July 1970 the Growers–Shippers Association and 29 of the largest growers in the valley entered into negotiations with the Teamsters. Agreements signed with the truckers' union in Salinas were worse than sweetheart contracts: they provided no job security, no seniority rights, no hiring hall, and no protection against pesticides.

Many growers, like the Bud Antle Company (a partner of Dow Chemical), had dealt with the Teamsters since the 1950s. In 1961, in return for a $1 million loan, Antle signed a contract with the truckers. By August 1970 many workers refused to abide by the Teamster contracts and 5,000 walked off the lettuce fields. The growers launched a campaign of violence. Jerry Cohen, a farm-worker lawyer, was beaten unconscious. On December 4, 1970, Judge Gordon Campbell of Monterey County jailed Chávez for refusing to obey an injunction and held him without bail. This arbitrary action gave the boycott needed publicity. Dignitaries visited Chávez in jail; he was released on Christmas Eve.

By the spring of 1971 Chávez and the Teamsters signed an agreement that gave the UFWOC sole jurisdiction in the lettuce fields and that allowed George Meany, president of the AFL, and Teamsters president, Frank Fitzsimmons to arbitrate the situation. Throughout the summer and into the fall, however, growers refused to disqualify Teamster contracts and gradually the situation became stalemated.

The fight with the Teamsters hurt the UFWOC since it turned its attention from servicing contracts. Chávez refused help from the AFL for professional administrators, believing that farm workers had to learn from their own mistakes. According to *Fresno Bee* reporter Ron Taylor, although Chávez was a patient teacher, he did not delegate authority and involved himself with too much detail. Farm workers had never had the opportunity to govern themselves and Chávez had to build "ranch committees" from the bottom up. This took time and the corporate ranchers who ran agribusiness had little tolerance for democracy.[57]

ECHOES OF DELANO

The Texas Farm Worker Movement

Texas remained a union organizer's nightmare. Its long border ensured growers access to a constant and abundant supply of cheap labor. Efforts to unionize farm workers had been literally stomped to death by the overt misuse of the Texas Rangers, the local courts, and the right-to-work laws. Texas farm workers courageously struggled to organize, but their road to Delano was littered with broken strikes. The Texas farm worker organizing effort has its roots in the 1966–1967 strikes, which, like Mexican farm worker struggles in the Midwest, were influenced by the Chávez movement in California.

The 1966–1967 drive to organize Mexican farm workers in the Río Grande Valley was brief, fiery, and tumultuous. Eugene Nelson, 36, who had been with Chávez in California but who did not have his approval to organize in Texas, joined with Margil Sánchez and Lucio Galván to found the Independent Workers Association (IWA) in May of 1966. The need for a union was evident. Workers' per capita income was $1,568; most earned less than $1.00 per hour. The IWA called a strike and demanded $1.75 an hour. Farm workers saw hope and they enthusiastically joined pickets and rallies, supporting the IWA's demands. The success of the strike depended on whether the union could persuade Mexican nationals not to strike break. And several attempts were made to block entrance of undocumented workers into Texas at the international bridge at Roma, Texas.

In June 1966, IWA members voted to affiliate with the NFWA and became Local 2. This move was not popular among all the Texans. Galván and Sánchez resented California's control and moved to take over the local. Although Sánchez and Galván may have had legitimate grievances, they resorted to red-baiting, citing an article in the *American Opinion,* a John Birch Society publication, as positive proof that the NFWA leaders in California were communists. On July 18 a new vote was taken and the members voted 101 to 3 to maintain NFWA affiliation. Sánchez and Galván bolted and they formed the Texas Independent Workers Association.

On August 16, Local 2 voted 99 to 0 to affiliate with the AFL–CIO and became the United Farm Workers Organizing Committee. In the last days of June strikers marched from Río Grande City to Austin. In their trek through the Río Grande Valley the marchers were greeted by LULAC, G.I. Forum, and PASSO. On July 7, Al Ramírez, the mayor of Edinburg, left his hospital bed to welcome the 120 marchers. The next day a thousand people gathered to hear mass at San Juan Catholic Shrine. Union people along the route warmly cheered the strikers. By July 30 they reached Corpus Christi. The small band wound its way along Highway 181, and in spite of heavy rain, over a thousand partisans waited for them in San Antonio, where a two-hour parade followed. Archbishop Lucey celebrated mass. The march to Austin continued.

Outside the capital Governor John Connally met the marchers. He was accompanied by Ben Barnes, the speaker of the state House, and Waggoner Carr,

Texas attorney general. They chatted with the leadership and left. The strikers attempted to pressure Connally to call a special session to pass a minimum wage bill, but he refused and told the marchers he would not be in Austin on Labor Day.

Ten thousand converged on the Texas state capitol. Chávez and U.S. Senator Ralph Yarborough participated. Reyes Alaniz, 62, who had marched all the way, was also there. After the rally Chávez visited Río Grande City with Bill Kircher, national organizing director of the AFL–CIO and attended a rally in that city.

Demonstrations continued, mainly in Starr and Hidalgo counties. On October 25 a group of strikers locked arms and lay down on the Mexican side of the Roma Bridge. Starr County sheriff Rene Solis crossed to the Mexican side, grabbed a demonstrator by the foot, and dragged him across the bridge into the United States. Mexican authorities then forced the demonstrators onto the U.S. side, where they were apprehended. On October 31, Mexican authorities arrested Marshall Méndez of the Bishop's Committee for the Spanish Speaking and Antonio Orendain, national treasurer for the UFWOC, for locking the gate at the center crossing. On November 16 a report issued by a Starr County grand jury called the strike "unlawful and un-American" and "abusive of the rights and freedom granted them as citizens." Texas Rangers made mass arrests and guarded the undocumented workers bussed to the fields by growers to break the strike. Meanwhile, Gil Padilla had assumed leadership of the strike.

An organizing rally was held in Río Grande City on June 10, 1967. Hidalgo County officials demanded a $250,000 bond to ensure a peaceful demonstration and would not accept anything but cash. César Chávez attended the rally and, although the event was successful, the union could not stop production. On September 30, 1967, a hurricane destroyed the citrus crop, depressing labor conditions and ending all hope of success.

A postscript to the strike was that in June 1972 a three-judge federal panel ruled that the Texas Rangers used selective enforcement of Texas laws during the 1966–1969 strikes in Starr County. The court criticized the Rangers for taking sides and declared that the anti-mass picketing statute, the law against secondary boycotts, and the statute on breach of peace were all illegal. As to the laws on abusive language and unlawful assembly, the court stated: "The police authorities were openly hostile to the strike and individual strikers, and used their law enforcement powers to suppress the farm workers strike."[58] A small victory for the farm workers, considering it *only* took five years to find out that they were right.

After 1967 Chávez pulled back, realizing that the strike was premature. He realized that his California base was far from secure and that in Texas he did not have the liberal support that he had in California. The right-to-work laws also retarded a strong trade union movement that could support him. Lastly, Texas growers were not as vulnerable to a secondary boycott. He left Antonio Orendain, 37, in charge of member and placement services.

The Struggle Spreads

Inspired by the *campesino* (farm worker) movement in California, farm-worker activism in the Midwest increased during the second half of the 1960s. Texas-Mexican cucumber workers in Wisconsin were led by Jesús Salas, 22, from Crystal City, Texas. Salas organized an independent farm workers union called *Obreros Unidos* (United Workers) of Wisconsin in January 1967 and it remained active throughout that year.[59]

Michigan used more migrant workers than any other northern state. In March 1967, migrants took part in a 70-mile "March for Migrants" from Saginaw to Lansing. They reached the state capitol on Easter Sunday. These marchers spoke for the thousands of workers who would arrive in Michigan starting in May.

That same year in Ohio Mexican farm workers demanded better wages and enforcement of health and housing codes. Some 18,000–20,000 Mexicans worked in Wallace County, Ohio, and throughout the tomato belt, which circled northwest Ohio, southern Michigan, and northern Indiana. Hunt, Campbell Soup, Libby, McNeil, Vlasic, and Heinz controlled production. Baldemar Velásquez, 21, and his father organized a march in 1968 from Leipsic to the Libby tomato plant and later a march to the Campbell Soup plant. They established a newspaper, *Nuestra Lucha,* and a weekly radio program.

In 1968, the Farm Labor Organizing Committee (FLOC) signed 22 contracts. FLOC soon realized that the food processors throughout northwest Ohio and Indiana determined wages because they controlled the prices and paid farmers for their crops. Signing contracts with individual farmers was good for morale, but it did not touch the source of power. Further, the small farmer could get around a contract by merely switching crops the following year.[60]

Chicanos struggled to organize in other regions. On February 15, 1969, at the Kitayam Brothers' flower farm outside Brighton, Colorado, five Chicanas chained themselves to the main gate of the farm. They belonged to the National Florist Workers Organization and wanted to prevent scabs from entering the farm. They had called a strike to force management to meet their demands for higher wages and for better working conditions. Chicanas lay on the frozen ground as county sheriff deputies moved in wearing gas masks and carrying acetylene torches. Mary Padilla, Martha Del Real, Lupe Biseño, president of the NFWO, Rachel Sándoval, and Mary Salas held out to the last.

THE LEGITIMATION OF PROTEST

The civil rights movement and the ghetto revolts of the mid-1960s greatly affected the direction of the Economic Opportunity Act of 1964 and the subsequent war on poverty. The act emphasized education and training programs: Job Corps, Neighborhood Youth Corps, work-study and community action programs. Spin-offs were loans to farmers and small businesses, as well as the formation of VISTA (Volunteers in Service to America). The war on poverty supposedly attacked the causes of poverty through community participation. To understand the program, the mentality of President Lyndon B. Johnson must be explored. Johnson, a machine politician from Texas, had been greatly influenced by Franklin D. Roosevelt and the New Deal. The purpose of the New Deal had been to preserve the capitalist system in the United States and build a coalition of labor and ethnic peoples to support the Democratic party. Johnson was also influenced by Kennedy and his New Frontier, which in many ways was a revival of idealism at home and abroad. Almost from the beginning, however, the war on poverty ran into difficulties; the city bosses looked at its community action programs, which purportedly organized the poor, as subversive and, in effect, promoting rebellion. These political elites responded by moving to control poverty programs and their budgets.

Groups like the G.I. Forum and LULAC openly threw their fortunes behind LBJ. They saw the war on poverty as a key to social awareness. In 1964 the Forum along with LULAC sponsored Operation Service, Employment, and Redevelopment (SER), which worked with the disadvantaged in selected areas of the Southwest.[61] As in other regions of the country, the administrators controlled huge budgets.

Government funding often encouraged the formation of special interest groups, and the participation of many Chicanos who, to this point, had not been involved. In some instances, grass-roots activists resented the inclusion in new programs of old-line Mexican American leaders and internal struggles followed. As a whole, Mexican Americans felt that their community was being bypassed in the funding process and that federal, state, and, often, local authorities were ignorant of their needs. The Watts rebellions taught activists an important lesson —that power, for the moment, was in the streets.

On March 28, 1966, the Equal Employment Opportunity Commission held a meeting in Albuquerque, New Mexico, to investigate the Chicanos' employment problems. Approximately 50 Chicanos walked out because, although the commission advocated equal employment, it did not have one Mexican on its staff. Although these actions remained within the civil rights framework, they shook the stereotype of the docile Mexican. As a result of the walkout in Albuquerque and growing ferment among Chicanos, the federal government pacified the community in June 1967 by appointing Vicente Ximenes to the Equal Employment Opportunity Commission. Shortly thereafter he was named head of the newly created Interagency Committee on Mexican-American Affairs. This office mollified middle-class activists, whose primary goal was affirmative action.

Johnson had promised that he would hold a White House conference for Chicano leaders, but he feared that Chicanos would walk out and embarrass him politically. He did not keep his promise. Instead, in October 1967 he held cabinet committee hearings at El Paso, Texas. Johnson did not bother to invite the leading activists—César Chávez, Reies López Tijerina, or Rodolfo "Corky" Gonzales— who represented those previously not participating in the Mexican American mainstream. At El Paso Johnson bused his Mexicans to the celebrations which returned the *Chamizal* to Mexico. Many Chicanos wondered if this had not been the main reason for the hearings, since little else was accomplished. Activists boycotted and picketed the cabinet conference. They called their group *La Raza*

Unida. Ernesto Galarza of San Jose, Corky Gonzales, and Reies López Tijerina played leading roles in this opposition. Representatives of 50 Chicano organizations met at San Antonio and pledged support to the concept of *La Raza Unida;* about 1,200 people attended.[62]

La Chicana

The participation of Chicanas as leaders prior to the 1960s was more common in more militant and/or local organizations. In the 1950s, for example, Chicanas took part in *La Asociación México-Americana* and the Mexican Civil Rights Congress (Los Angeles), whereas in larger middle-class Mexican American groups, the *father* association relegated them to auxiliaries. In MAPA and PASSO, Chicanas often assumed power roles in local chapters but few occupied statewide leadership positions.

The 1960s greatly politicized women of all colors. Activism created heightened awareness and involvement. As in the case of the movement as a whole, the 1960s combined *veteranos/veteranas* with recent converts. Level of participation and type of role greatly depended on class, age, and/or experience. In general, attitudes and selection of tactics varied according to the kind of group the women belonged to. Middle-class women in middle-class associations shared the ideology of their male counterparts. It is important to note, however, that the rank and file as well as the leadership of groups such as the Forum and LULAC was not homogeneous. Ideologically they differed, ranging from the right to the left. And their agenda often clashed with that of their leaders.

María Hernández of Lytle, Texas, had been active since 1924. Like most women activists of her generation, she participated in middle-class groups, and took the lead in pushing the movement to take on a more militant tone. In the 1930s, she organized against segregated schools. Throughout the 1960s, she spoke at rallies, identifying with youth. In the 1970s, she helped form *La Raza Unida* party.

Virginia Musquiz, involved in the 1963 Crystal City takeover, ran unsuccessfully the following year for state representative. A year afterward, she campaigned for the Crystal City Council. In 1969, Musquiz helped organize the Crystal City walkouts and the eventual takeover of city government.

In California, Dolores Huerta became vice president of the UFW, while East Los Angeles Chicana activists like Julia Luna Mount and her sister Celia Luna de Rodríguez, active since the 1930s, continued working for social change in the 1960s. Luna de Rodríguez, a key organizer in the Barrio Defense Committee, spoke out against police abuse. Luna Mount, active in the 40th assembly district chapter of MAPA, often criticized MAPA leadership. She unsuccessfully ran for the Los Angeles School Board in 1967, and was one of the leading voices against the Vietnam War and a founding member of the Peace and Freedom party.

In the mid-1960s, Linda Benítez became a member of the executive board of the Los Angeles Central Committee of the Democratic party. In that same period, Geraldine Ledesma chaired the Mexican American Ad Hoc Education

Committee, a forum in which Chicanos throughout Los Angeles County discussed Mexican American education issues. Irene Tovar was a leading force and later president of the Latin American Civic Association in the San Fernando Valley in California. Cecilia Suárez assisted in the founding of the Association of Mexican American Educators in 1965.

Also in Los Angeles, Francisca Flores, a veteran activist, along with Ramona Morín, of the women's auxiliary of the Forum, co-founded the California League of Mexican American Women. Flores published and edited *La Carta Editorial,* which reported on political activism. In the later 1960s, Flores published *Regeneración,* an activist magazine, focusing on women's issues. Flores founded the Chicana Service Action Center and played a leading role in the establishment of the *Comisión Femenil.* She was the intellectual leader of many of the first Chicana conferences.

In 1967, Vicky Castro, an East Los Angeles student, was president of the Young Citizens for Community Action (YCCA), the precursor of the Brown Berets; Castro, a leader in the 1968 school walkouts (to be discussed in this chapter) later became a teacher and president of AMEA. Foremost among the activists was Alicía Escalante, who in 1967 founded the East Los Angeles Welfare Rights Organization, which later became the Chicano National Welfare Rights Organization. She broke away from the national organization because it did not meet the needs of Chicanas/Chicanos. Escalante, a leader in militant activities during this decade, in 1969 participated in *Catolícos por la Raza* and served four months in jail for her part in the demonstrations.[63]

The New Chicanos

It is an error to characterize Chicano youth in the 1960s as rebellious or to attribute the Chicano movement to them. Their activities differed from state to state and between regions. Initially, youth were not separatists but expressed a desire to work within progressive community organizations. As in the case of the Chicana, any narrative of the youth movement necessarily excludes important contributions. A comprehensive national history of the Chicano student movement has yet to be written.

Prior to the 1960s, middle-class Chicano youth had been limited to the auxiliaries of either the Forum and LULAC or related organizations. What distinguishes the 1960s is the entrance of large numbers of lower-middle and lower-class youth, who focused more on community problems than on academic and/or professional achievement.

Texas, California, and Colorado were the models for the youth movement. Texas and California were especially important because of the size of their *barrios* and *colonias.* Texas and California were situated at the center of regional media coverage. While their interests and goals were similar, youths in the two states differed even within their own boundaries. For instance, the influence on Mexicans of other Latinos, such as Puerto Ricans in the Mission District of San Francisco and in Oakland, made them unique; in Los Angeles and Texas the *barrios* were overwhelmingly Mexican, with little non-Mexican influence.

In Texas, students organized the Mexican American Youth Organization (MAYO). Although the initiative for MAYO came from college students, it did not limit itself to the campuses. MAYO began in Kingsville at Texas A&I some three years before its formal founding. José Angel Gutiérrez, Ambriocio Meléndez, and Gabriel Tafoya, among others, formed the A&I student group. They focused on the usual issues of admissions, discrimination, segregated dorms, and housing. Unlike many of their imitators on other campuses, who emphasized forging a Chicano student community, the A&I Mexicans were concerned with the development of the Chicano community, the protection of the underdogs, and the gaining of political power. In 1964, the A&I Chicano students attended PASSO's state convention and made a bid to integrate into that group. They met Chicano students from Austin who had similar goals. At this event, they were successful in lowering the membership eligibility from 21 to 18, but PASSO leadership held them at arm's length.

PASSO offered the logical vehicle for student participation. It was the most progressive mainstream organization in Texas. Neither LULAC nor the Forum was attractive to youth. However, they spoke to leaders such as Dr. Hector García, who reportedly talked down to them. The A&I students even invited Representative Henry B. González to address the group, but he refused and, in fact, was hostile to them.

MAYO, formally organized at St. Mary's College in San Antonio, included José Angel Gutiérrez, Nacho Pérez, Mario Compean, and Willie Velásquez. Soon other university and high school students formed MAYO chapters. Statewide, MAYO became typed as militant. It was active in the community, successfully influencing federal programs such as VISTA.

In 1968, the Ford Foundation granted MAYO $8,000 for community development. Representative González attacked the Ford Foundation for funding radicals. Because of the turmoil, MAYO founded the Mexican American Unity Council, which became a redevelopment corporation. In 1969, many members left the universities and returned to their communities—for instance, Gutiérrez returned to Crystal City and Mario Compean unsuccessfully ran for mayor in San Antonio.[64]

California's Mexican American youth movement took a different form from the one in Texas. California Chicanos were the most urbanized in the Southwest and consequently had fewer institutional constraints and/or social controls. For instance, the parish church in rural areas of Texas, Arizona, and New Mexico had a different relationship with Chicanos than did parishes of Boyle Heights, where transiency was much higher. When California youth began to be active in the community, they did not have to deal with the large, *entrenched* organizations such as the Forum or LULAC. Texas Chicanos, on the other hand, had to respond more to existing social attitudes and compete with established policies and beliefs. One consequence was that, in California, youth could more easily play the role of agitators than organizers. Present research suggests, too, that the building of Chicano student groups began later in California than in Texas. In California, the children of middle-class Mexicans, for better or worse, did not have the sense of community that Texas-Mexicans did. And in spite of class differences in Texas, feelings of nationalism cut across class lines.

It should not be concluded that young California Mexican Americans had not been involved in community issues. A fringe group had always participated in the Young Democrats or other youth-oriented organizations. The Mexican American Movement (MAM) had promoted a youth agenda in the 1930s and 1940s. College students volunteered in Roybal's election to the Los Angeles City Council, walking precincts for CSO. However, in the first half of the 1960s California had no apparent involvement comparable to that at Texas A&I. Moreover, intermarriage was higher in California, and the offspring of mixed unions did not always identify with a Mexican American agenda. But by the mid-1960s, youth in California became more aware—partly because of the national youth revolution and partly because the movement itself pushed educational issues to the forefront.

The Los Angeles County Human Relations Commission, beginning in 1963, sponsored annual Chicano student conferences at Camp Hess Kramer. The commission also conducted seminars, with invited speakers, for potential student leaders from *barrio* junior and senior high schools. At these sessions, students could compare the grievances they had against their schools. Many participants later became leaders in the 1968 student walkouts.

Influential among the community youth was Father John Luce's Social Action Training Center at the Church of the Epiphany (Episcopal) in Lincoln Heights. Chicano students under Fr. Luce's guidance formed the Young Citizens for Community Action, which later became the Brown Berets.

By 1967, a larger number of Mexican students began filtering into the colleges. That year students at East Los Angeles Community College formed the Mexican American Student Association (MASA). The same phenomenon occurred at other colleges and universities.

On May 13, 1967, Chicano students met at Loyola University and founded the United Mexican-American Students (UMAS). Most Chicano students clearly identified with the United Farm Workers; its successes and tribulations became their own. On campus they joined with the Black student movement and the Students for a Democratic Society (SDS). By the fall of 1967, Chicano college student organizations spread throughout California. Priority issues included public education, access to universities, Mexican American studies programs, and the Vietnam War. Speakers such as Corky Gonzales and Reies López Tijerina added to the momentum. On December 16–17, 1967, the second general UMAS conference was held, at the University of Southern California campus.[65]

In northern California many Chicano groups called themselves the Mexican-American Student Confederation (MASC). In the south the size of the Chicano *barrios* tended to encourage students to focus on community issues, while the northern groups' greater involvement with politics on campus led to an emphasis on radical issues.

The first Mexican American studies program in California began at Los Angeles State College in the fall of 1968. The administration made many promises but gave minimal assistance and support. It allowed hostile faculties to badger inexperienced students in pseudo-democratic faculty committees, and instructors in the program were rarely granted tenure. From the beginning the majority of the programs were set up to fail. The frustration of dealing with petty and bullying administrators added to student disillusionment and increased their alienation from the system.

From 1968 to 1971 the campuses provided a sizable portion of the cadre at protests and marches during those years. However, considerable discontent fomented in the *barrios* themselves. Community newspapers such as *Inside Eastside* and *La Raza* (established in September 1967) carried articles directed at high school students to articulate their grievances. In December 1967 Raúl Ruiz, writing in *Inside Eastside,* entreated: "If you are a student at Lincoln you should be angry! You should demand! You should protest! You should organize for better education! This is your right! This is your life!" In January 1968 Lazaro Q. (Raúl Ruiz) wrote: "Picket, Brother, Picket." He criticized incompetent teachers and urged action: "Something is terribly wrong in Eastside schools and the young Chicano students are not to blame. . . . It is easy for students to organize walk-outs."[66]

Sal Castro, a teacher at Lincoln High School, had considerable credibility among students. As early as September 1967, Castro, a charismatic speaker, addressed students at the Piranya Coffee House, making them aware of issues such as quality education, textbooks, and their right to learn. Discussions on strategies such as blow-outs (walkouts) were held among students, whose energies were directed into positive channels. Clear goals were articulated. In March 1968 close to 10,000 Chicano students walked out of five Los Angeles high schools— Lincoln, Roosevelt, Garfield, Wilson, and Belmont. The schools were in East Los Angeles, with populations that were overwhelmingly Mexican. Chicanos' grievances and demands can be summarized as follows: Over 50 percent of the Chicano high school community was forced to drop out of school either through expulsion and transfers to other schools or simply because they had not been taught to read and thus failed their courses. Chicano schools were overcrowded and run down compared to Anglo and Black schools of the district. Many teachers openly discriminated against Chicanos and students wanted racist teachers removed. The curriculum was designed to obscure the Chicanos' culture and to condition students to be content with low-skilled jobs. Students demanded more Chicano teachers and administrators. The community formed the Educational Issues Coordinating Committee (EICC) to support the walkouts and follow up on the demands.[67]

When students walked out, sheriff's deputies and police reacted by treating the protest as an insurrection, beating students, and arresting those who did not move fast enough. Many activists were caught by surprise; however, in general, community organizations supported the walkout and condemned police brutality. Sal Castro, who had walked out with his students, stated that he could not in good conscience remain inside the school, since the demands of his students were legitimate. Along with others, Castro was indicted by a Los Angeles grand jury on several charges, among them conspiracy to commit misdemeanors. After two years of appeals, the courts found the charges unconstitutional. The California Department of Education attempted to revoke his credentials, and he was subject to frequent and arbitrary administrative transfers.

The Los Angeles walkouts called national attention to the Chicanos' plight in education and encouraged other walkouts throughout the Southwest and the Midwest. In March, 120 students walked out in Denver. In April some 700 students walked out of Lanier High School in San Antonio, and shortly afterward 600 walked out at Edgewood High School in the same city. Similar walkouts occurred in Santa Clara, California, Elsa and Abilene, Texas, and Phoenix, Arizona. Demands were for Mexican teachers, counselors, and courses and for better facilities. On May 5, 1970, Chicano students walked out of Delano Joint Union High. Protest centered on the denial of a Chicano speaker for an assembly. On the 7th, police encircled the school. The walkout lasted until the end of the year, when strikers were arrested as they attempted to enter graduation ceremonies. Police beat protesters and dragged them into paddywagons.[68]

Luis Váldez, of the *Teatro Campesino,* contributed to the spread of this new consciousness. The *Teatro* used one-act plays to publicize the struggle of the farm worker and Chicanos. They played *corridos* that popularized the Chicanos' struggle for liberation in the United States. Another milestone was the publication of *El Grito: A Journal of Contemporary Mexican-American Thought,* in the fall of 1967. The journal was organized by a group called *Quinto Sol* Publications, headed by Octavio Romano, a professor at the University of California at Berkeley. It published articles challenging Anglo-American scholarship and criticized its effect on Chicanos. It carried scholarly articles, poetry, and art. The development of an active Chicano arts movement heightened cultural awareness.

The counterpart of the Black Panthers and the Puerto Rican Young Lords was the Brown Berets. In 1967 the Young Citizens for Community Action formed in East Los Angeles. The group was sponsored by an interfaith church organization. In time, the organization evolved from a community service club to an "alert patrol" that set as its goal the "defense" of the *barrio.*

The Brown Berets aroused a fear in Anglo-Americans that a Chicano group would counter U.S. oppression with its own violence. Law enforcement authorities believed that the Brown Berets were capable of inspiring violent action in other groups. The Brown Berets panicked police officials and exposed their basic undemocratic attitudes toward Mexicans or groups attempting to achieve liberation. The police and sheriff's departments in Los Angeles abandoned reason in harassing, intimidating, and persecuting the Brown Berets in a way that few other Chicano organizations have experienced in recent times. Police and sheriff's deputies raided the Berets, infiltrated them, libeled and slandered them, and even encouraged countergroups to attack members. The objective was to destroy the Berets and to invalidate the membership in the eyes of the Anglo and Chicano communities.[69]

The Berets were thrown into the national limelight by the East Los Angeles school walkouts. Although there is little evidence that the Berets took a leadership role in planning the walkouts, the police and sheriff's departments made it a scapegoat, branding the Brown Berets as outside agitators, while playing down the legitimate grievances of Chicano students. A grand jury later indicted 13 Chicanos on conspiracy charges stemming from the walkouts, and 7 were Brown Berets. The defendants appealed and the case was declared unconstitutional, but only after years of legal harassment. As the police and sheriff's repression increased, the popularity of the group spread.

Law enforcement agencies inundated the Berets with informers and special agents to entrap the members by encouraging acts of violence. They purposely subverted the Berets, keeping them in a state of flux and preventing the organization from solidifying. Meanwhile, Berets evolved into a radical group. Imbued with the politics of liberation, they dealt with the immediate needs of the *barrio* —food, housing, unemployment, education. Their ideology was molded by the conflict and the street.

By 1967, the California Mexican American student movement changed, and communication among the various groups increased. Students were especially productive in manufacturing nationalist symbols which, for a time, united the activist community. Later they adopted the name *Chicano,* which had historically been a pejorative term applied to lower-class Mexicans. Working-class people themselves, however, had always used it playfully to refer to each other.

The Crusade for Justice played a key role in the self-identification process. In March 1969, it sponsored the First National Chicano Youth Liberation Conference, held in Denver. At the conference, youth drew up *El Plan Espiritual de Aztlán,* setting the goals of cultural nationalism and self-determination. Shortly afterward, college and university students, faculty, staff, and community activists met at the University of California at Santa Barbara and drew up a plan of action called *El Plan de Santa Bárbara.* At this conference, Mexican American student organizations changed their name to *El Movimiento Estudiantil Chicano de Aztlán* (MECHA) (The Chicano Student Movement of Aztlán). The militancy of students reinforced tendencies already expressed in the community. Their mass entrance into the movement electrified events.

THE DAY OF THE HEROES

The 1960s produced heroes at every level of protest, from Joan Baez, to Che Guevara, to Stokeley Carmichael, to Herbert Marcuse. With the growth of nationalism, it was natural for Mexican Americans to identify leaders who best expressed their frustrations. During the late 1960s, therefore, Chicanos, for a brief time, had heroes that were legitimated by them and not the state.

José Angel Gutiérrez

The first national hero was a founder of MAYO and a leader in the student movement.

José Angel Gutiérrez rose to national prominence when only 22. Gutiérrez's approach was to attack the *gringo* establishment personally in order to create awareness among Chicanos as well as to call attention to their exploitation in Texas. His "Kill the *gringo*" statement made at a press conference caused considerable reaction among Anglo-Americans, who took the speech literally. Instantly, Gutiérrez became a controversial figure and was attacked by establishment Chicano politicians such as Representative Henry B. González from San Antonio.

Activism in Texas hit a high note on March 30, 1969, at San Félipe Del Río (about 160 miles west of San Antonio) when some 2,000 Chicanos assembled to protest cancellation of a VISTA program by Governor Preston Smith at the request of three Val Verde county commissioners. VISTA workers had participated in a protest rally against the police beatings of Natividad Fuentes of Uvalde and his wife. At Del Río Gutiérrez and MAYO demanded reinstatement of the program and protested inequality, poverty, and police brutality throughout Texas. The G.I. Forum, LULAC, and other organizations supported the mass rally. Gutiérrez at the rally said, "We are fed up. We are going to move to do away with the injustices to the Chicano and if the 'gringo' doesn't get out of our way, we will stampede over him." Participants pledged a commitment to cultural identity and condemned the racist system. They called it the Del Río Manifesto.

On June 20, 1969, Gutiérrez, accompanied by his wife, Luz, and several young volunteers, returned to his hometown, Crystal City (population 8,500), to organize politically. Although Chicanos comprised over 85 percent of the Winter Garden area, an Anglo-American minority controlled its politics. Anglo-Americans owned 95 percent of the land. In Zavala County the median family income was $1,754 a year; the agribusiness income in Dummit, La Salle, and Zavala counties totaled about $31 million. The median years of education for Chicanos was 2.3. School authorities vigorously enforced a "no-Spanish rule." Over 70 percent of the Chicano students dropped out of Crystal City High School. Few Mexicans held offices or were professionals. Those who received an education moved away. Anglo-Americans considered themselves racially and culturally superior to Chicanos. The Texas Rangers patrolled the area, terrorizing Mexicans. Adding to the plight of the Chicano was the fact that a substantial number of them were migrants who had to follow the crops. They left the Winter Garden area in late spring and did not return until the fall. Small hamlets of the region became ghost towns.[70]

A school crisis at Crystal City in November 1969 gave young volunteers the issue they wanted to confront the *gringo*. While Chicanos represented the majority of the system's students, school policy excluded them from participating in many extracurricular activities. When students complained, the school board ignored them and refused to discuss the students' grievances. Left with no other alternatives, parents and students organized a school boycott in December. After several days 1,700 Chicano students walked out. They formed a citizens' organization and decided that they would take over the school board in the spring election of 1970.

La Raza Unida party (LRUP) emerged from the citizen group action. Intensive mobilization took place during the first quarter of 1970. In April 1970 LRUP won four of the seven seats on the Crystal City Board of Education, and all of the Chicano City Council candidates were elected in Carrizo Springs, Cotulla, and Crystal City. In Cotulla the first Chicano mayor was elected. The box score for Chicanos in the Winter Garden area was 15 elected with two new mayors, two school board majorities, and two city council majorities.[71] One *gringo* was elected.

Reies López Tijerina

Reies López Tijerina, or *El Tigre,* was the most charismatic of the Chicano leaders. Born in 1926, in farm fields close to Fall City, Texas, he lived a marginal existence. The young man soon learned to hate his oppressors, especially Texas Rangers.

Tijerina became a preacher. He wandered into northern New Mexico, witnessing the poverty of the people there. Tejerina became interested in the land-grant question. He studied the Treaty of Guadalupe Hidalgo and became convinced that the national forest in Tierra Amarilla belonged to the *Pueblo de San Joaquín de Chama.* This was *ejido* land (communal or village land) that, according to Hispano-Mexican law, could not be sold and was to be held in common by the people. Villagers had the right to graze their animals and cut and gather timber in these forest lands. According to Tijerina, the U.S. government participated in frauds that deprived the people of the *ejido* lands. He got involved with the *Albiquiu* Corporation, an organization committed to the return of land grants to the New Mexicans.

In 1963 he incorporated *La Alianza Federal de Mercedes* (The Federal Alliance of Land Grants). It appealed to poor New Mexicans and to their lost dreams. The *Alianza* led marches on the state capital. On October 15, 1966, Tijerina and 350 members occupied the national forest campgrounds known as the Echo Amphitheatre and asserted the revival of the *ejido* rights of the *Pueblo de San Joaquín de Chama,* whose 1,400 acres lay mainly within the confines of the Kit Carson National Forest. In less than a week state police, sheriff's deputies, and Rangers moved in. On October 22 *Alianza* members took two Rangers into custody and tried them for trespassing and being a public nuisance. The *Alianza* court fined them and sentenced them to 11 months and 22 days in jail, and then "mercifully" suspended the sentence.

On November 6, 1967, Tijerina stood trial for the Amphitheatre affair. Original charges included conspiracy, but the jury threw it out. It did convict him of two counts of assault and he was sentenced to two years in a state penitentiary, with five years' probation.

Meanwhile, as the sentence was being appealed, Tijerina's actions alienated the establishment under the leadership of U.S. Senator Joseph Montoya. His support dwindled in New Mexico. Many followers were frightened by his growing militancy. Tijerina now entered Tierra Amarilla with the intention of making a citizen's arrest of District Attorney Alfonso Sánchez. A running gun battle followed and Tijerina was arrested. While on bail, he appeared at numerous protest rallies. Tijerina's uncompromising tactics gained him the admiration of militants and activists throughout the United States. In May and June 1968, Tijerina participated in the Poor People's Campaign, threatening to pull the Chicano contingent out if Black organizers did not treat them as equals. In the fall he ran for governor of New Mexico on the People's Constitutional party ticket.

Tijerina stood trial in late 1968 for the Tierra Amarilla raid. A key witness for the prosecution had been murdered. Tijerina defended himself. Much of the trial centered on the right to make a citizen's arrest. Tijerina proved his points, and the jury entered a verdict of not guilty.

In mid-February 1969 the Court of Appeals for the Tenth Circuit upheld the Amphitheatre conviction; Tijerina's lawyer immediately appealed to the Supreme Court. On June 5, 1969, *El Tigre* again attempted to occupy the Kit Carson National Forest at the Coyote Campsite. His wife, Patsy, and some of the participants burned a few signs. Two days later the Rangers and police arrested several of the liberators. Tijerina allegedly pointed a carbine at one of the Rangers, when deputies threatened his wife. Authorities charged him with aiding and abetting the destruction of U.S. Forest Service signs and assaulting and threatening a federal agent. The court sentenced him to three years in the federal penitentiary. On October 13, Chief Justice Warren Burger refused to hear his appeal on the Amphitheatre case, and Tijerina went to prison. For seven months prison authorities isolated him from the other prisoners. Tijerina became a symbol, convicted of political crimes, rather than of crimes against "society."[72] Tijerina was released in the summer of 1971.

Rodolfo "Corky" Gonzales

Rodolfo "Corky" Gonzales was born in Denver on June 18, 1928, son of migrant sugar beet workers. He came up the hard way—with his fists. A Golden Gloves champion who turned pro, he was a featherweight contender from 1947 to 1955.

In 1957 Gonzales became the first Chicano district captain for the Democratic party. Two years later he entered the bail bonds business and opened an auto insurance agency. He kept active in the community, and in 1963 he organized *Los Voluntarios* (The Volunteers), which demonstrated against police brutality. In 1965 he became a director of Denver's war on poverty's youth programs. He was fired a year later for involvement in the Albuquerque EEOC walkout. Poverty officials viewed Corky as too zealous in defense of the Chicano community. In 1966 he founded the Crusade for Justice, a community-based organization that emphasized total family involvement. His epic poem *I Am Joaquín* was probably the most inspiring piece of movement literature written in the 1960s. Its impact was immeasurable, and Luis Váldez of the *Teatro Campesino* made it into a movie.

Gonzales represented the frustrations of the *bato* and the *barrio* youth, who were so intimidated by the public schools that they suffered from a mental block in speaking Spanish. Among the Chicanos of the Río Grande Valley, the identity problem did not exist; the Chicanos knew that they were Mexicans, and they learned Spanish. It was different for the *barrio* dwellers. Schools menaced them. Corky understood this, and he understood the loss of identity when the Anglo teacher changed one's name from Rodolfo to Rudolph and when one is punished for speaking Spanish. All this is expressed in his poem *I Am Joaquín*.

The Crusade for Justice included a school, a curio shop, a book store, and a social center. The school, *Tlatelolco, La Plaza de las Tres Culturas,* had about 200 students, from preschool to college. He worked to take community control of the public schools. He stated, "We intend to nationalize every school in our community." He published his own newspaper, *El Gallo: La Voz de la Justicia.*

On June 29, 1968, Corky headed a march on police headquarters to protest Police Officer Theodore Zavashlak's shooting and killing of 15-year-old Joseph Archuleta. In 1969 when students walked out of West Side High School, Corky marched with parents in support. Corky and a number of other Chicanos were arrested when an altercation broke out at the demonstrations during the walkout. At the trial, films proved that it was actually a "police riot," and defendants were acquitted. In 1969 he called the First Annual Chicano Youth Conference at Denver. Gonzales was instrumental in establishing *La Raza Unida* party in Colorado, which ran candidates for state and local offices on November 4, 1970.[73]

ON THE EVE OF THE STORM

In the second half of the 1960s, authorities at all levels of government tightened up on dissidents. They moved to control so-called "revolutionaries." As a consequence, everyone of color became suspect. A report by the United States Commission on Civil Rights, *Mexican-Americans and the Administration of Justice in the Southwest,* issued in March 1970, documents this process. The intensification of police activity set the stage for the police–community confrontations of 1970.

On September 1, 1968, Jess Domínguez, 41, of Los Angeles, searched for his teenage children in the early morning. He approached a police car and asked the officers for assistance. They answered: "We don't have any time for you Mexicans." Domínguez protested, whereupon officers beat him. At least 15 officers joined in the brutal beating of Domínguez. They charged him with assaulting an officer. Domínguez, badly bruised, could not move his jaw, and constantly vomited; subsequently, he underwent surgery. The FBI looked into the incident and, based on police reports, claimed the facts did not warrant an investigation or prosecution of officers.

On November 9, 1968, Salvador Barba, 13, was beaten by Los Angeles police and had 40 stitches in the head. Again an FBI investigation found that the facts of the case did not warrant the arrest of the officers involved. Agents based their findings largely on Los Angeles Police Department reports.

On May 5, 1969, Frank Gonzales, 14, Los Angeles, was skipping school when an officer called to him, and the boy ran away. Officer Thomas Parkham, suspended twice before—once for pointing a cocked pistol at a juvenile and another time for being drunk and disorderly while off duty—drew his gun. He claimed that he had fired a warning shot before he fired at the boy. Authorities allowed him to resign in lieu of disciplinary action. District Attorney Evelle Younger decided not to prosecute Parkham.

On September 8, 1968, in Fairfield, California, Sergeant David Huff shot José Alvarado, who left a wife and five children. The chief of police would not meet with the community nor would he suspend Huff. The police claimed that

Alvarado had attacked five police officers with a meat cleaver. An enraged community formed the United Mexicans for Justice and questioned why no inquest had been conducted, why so many police could not disarm one man, why they had shot to kill, and why there had not been an investigation of Huff, who had previously pistol-whipped a man.[74]

On September 2, 1969, Judge Gerald S. Chargin of Santa Clara County (California) Juvenile Court passed sentence on a 17-year-old Chicano, allegedly convicted of incest. Chargin stated:

> Mexican people, after 13 years of age, think he is perfectly all right to go out and act like an animal. We ought to send you out of the country—send you back to Mexico. You belong in prison for the rest of your life for doing things of this kind. You ought to commit suicide. That's what I think of people of this kind. You are lower than animals and haven't the right to live in organized society —just miserable, lousy, rotten people. Maybe Hitler was right. The animals in our society probably ought to be destroyed because they have no right to live among human beings.[75]

The defense attorney attempted to moderate Chargin's conduct, but the judge would not restrain himself. Congressman Ed Roybal and Senator Joseph Montoya called for an investigation, as well as for the dismissal of Chargin. But despite this, court authorities merely transferred Chargin to the civil division of the Superior Court.[76]

In 1970 Dr. Fred Logan, Jr., an osteopath, 31, was murdered by Sheriff Erick Bauch in Mathis, Texas. The doctor arrived in 1966 and made the mistake of socializing with Mexicans; the previous doctor had been run out of town. Chicanos often could not pay for medical services, which Logan often rendered free. In mid-1970 Anglo doctors refused a $167,000 grant from Health, Education, and Welfare for a clinic for the poor, but Dr. Logan accepted. One day while drinking with Mexican friends, they fired blanks into the air. Bauch showed up and arrested Logan. "Six minutes later, the deputy sheriff put in a call for an ambulance. Logan, with two bullets from Bauch's .357 Magnum in his chest, was dead when the ambulance arrived on the scene. The official report—self-defense and attempted escape."[77]

Chicanos also suffered from a lack of justice, generally unable to be judged by their peers. Chicanos were excluded from both trial juries and grand juries by being barred from the roll of prospective jurors. In the "redneck" areas of the Southwest, the elimination of Mexicans from juries was almost total. Generally, grand juries were selected by county judges. Judges in Los Angeles readily admitted that they submitted primarily names of prominent people and rarely if ever nominated Mexicans.

Mike Gonzales, an attorney in South Texas, said that in ten years of legal practice he had never seen a Chicano on a jury, even though the population in some areas was 85 percent Chicano. R. P. Sánchez, a lawyer from McAllen, Texas, affirmed that although Hidalgo County had a Mexican population of about 75 percent, only one or two Chicanos had served on juries. Similar data were collected in Phoenix and Tucson, Arizona. In Fort Summer, New Mexico, an area more than 60 percent Mexican American, local Mexican Americans stated that their peers just did not serve on juries. Public defender Richard S. Buckley of Los Angeles related, "I recall very few Mexican Americans on any juries I have tried in a period of 15 years." Pete Tijerina, an attorney from San Antonio, told of a case he attempted to try in Jourdantown, Texas, in March 1966. Tijerina recalled that the town was 65 percent Mexican. Only one juror out of 48 listed was Mexican. The case was postponed until July when the names of two Mexican Americans were placed on the jury list, but it was found that one of them was dead. The case was again postponed until December. Five Chicanos were now on the list, but all five were peremptorily challenged by the insurance company. Tijerina's client was a Chicano.

The same pattern was repeated with grand juries. In the county of Los Angeles, where the Chicano population numbered about 1 million, only four Mexicans served on a grand jury in 12 years. In adjacent Orange County, which had over 44,000 Mexicans, there had been only one Chicano in 12 years on this panel. No Chicano had served on the grand jury of Monterey County from 1938 through 1968.[78]

In the late 1960s the California Rural Legal Assistance (CRLA) was organized with federal grants. CRLA established a distinguished record in defending the rights of the poor. Although it did not handle criminal cases, it represented the poor in various other matters. In Kings County, for example, where growers received $10,179,917 *not* to produce crops and where the board of supervisors raised their annual salaries from $2,400 to $12,000, less than $6,000 was spent on food for the poor. The CRLA sued the county on behalf of the poor, charging that it was violating federal statutes. The poor could not have afforded to pay an attorney for such an action. As complaints mounted against the CRLA by reactionary elements such as the California growers, Governor Ronald Reagan became more incensed about the federal government's support of an agency that brought suits against private enterprise. In December 1970 Reagan vetoed the federal appropriation to CRLA. The matter was taken to Washington, and the CRLA was put on a year's probation, during which time their actions were to be reviewed. An investigation showed that the CRLA had done nothing improper.[79]

Where Is God?

The history of the Catholic Church vis-à-vis social justice for Spanish-speaking Americans has been uneven. Although individual parish priests had been concerned about the plight of migrants, such clerics had been in the minority. Archbishop Robert Lucey of San Antonio throughout the 1950s and 1960s championed trade unionization among Mexican Americans and greatly expanded social services to Mexicans in San Antonio. And while discrimination toward Mexicans existed within the Texas Catholic Church, its record was better than that of its counterpart in Los Angeles, where the Chancery Office hardly seemed aware of the city's Chicanos. James Francis Cardinal McIntyre singlehandedly attempted to hold back the reforms of Pope John XXIII and Vatican II. McIntyre associated with the diocese's Catholic elites and censured priests for civil rights activities; he put the Los Angeles archdiocese in the hands of Msgr. Benjamin G. Hawkes, who proved that the church was more interested in dollars than in souls. Hawkes engaged in wheeler-dealer machinations with real estate developers and contributors. A reporter wrote of him: "Hawkes wore expensive black suits and gold cuff links, belonged to the exclusive Jonathan Club and the Los Angeles Country Club, routinely associated with the rich and powerful of Los Angeles and was fond of telling his fellow priests: 'The rich have souls, too.' "[80] It is perhaps no wonder, then, that tensions between the Church and its critics were mounting.

In November 1969 opposition to the Catholic Church's neglect of Chicanos crystallized with the formation of *Católicos Por La Raza* (CPLR), led by Ricardo Cruz, a young law student from Loyola University. The organization's members were infuriated over the closing, allegedly because of lack of funds, of Our Lady Queen of Girls' High School, which was predominantly Mexican. Cardinal McIntyre had just spent $4 million to build St. Basil's in Los Angeles's exclusive Wilshire District. The members were incensed at the church's refusal to involve itself in promoting social justice for Mexicans.

Although 65 percent of the Catholics in the Southwest were Mexicans, Mexicans had little voice in this institution. In 1969 fewer than 180 priests were of Mexican extraction and there were no Chicano bishops in the United States. The Euroamerican church remained basically an Irish-German institution. In 1970 *La Raza* magazine researched the holdings of the church in Los Angeles County and estimated that it owned about $1 billion in real estate alone. Most of this property was tax-free, and in other cases the church was an absentee landlord to the poor.

On Christmas Eve of 1969 members of CPLR demonstrated in front of St. Basil's Church (recently constructed for an estimated $4 million). Picketing was peaceful and orderly. When the Mass began, demonstrators attempted to enter the church, but sheriff's deputies posing as ushers locked them out. When a few gained entrance, armed deputies expelled the demonstrators. Police units arrested 21, 20 of whom stood trial for disturbing the peace and assaults on police officers. Ricardo Cruz was convicted of a misdemeanor. On May 8, 1972, he began serving a 120-day sentence for his conviction.[81]

CHICANOS UNDER SIEGE

The Moratorium Demonstration and Police Domination

The war in Southeast Asia propelled militancy in the Chicano *barrios.* Although it was similar to movements of other ethnic and racial communities, its form differed. The Vietnam War united Mexicans and moved even the middle class and flag-waving groups like the Forum to the left. In Los Angeles, community–police relations polarized even before the moratorium on August 29, 1970, a major anti-Vietnam demonstration. A casualty was news reporter Rubén Salazar.

The reporter's problems began on July 16, 1970, when five Los Angeles detectives and two San Leandro police officers burst into the room of a hotel in downtown Los Angeles, shooting and killing two Mexican nationals, Guillermo, 22, and Beltrán, 23, now known as the Sánchez cousins. Police claimed it was a case of "mistaken identity." No warrant had been issued for the cousins. Police alleged that they shouted, "Police! Give up!" The Sánchezes spoke no English. Police shot one of the cousins in the bedroom, the other cousin while he was dangling from a window.

In the weeks to come Rubén Salazar exposed the inconsistencies of police reports. Law enforcement officials called on Salazar and ordered him to tone down his television coverage. They alleged that he was inciting the people. Salazar responded that he merely reported the facts. Police persisted that the Chicano community was not ready for this kind of analysis. Police authorities left, telling Salazar that they would get him if he continued his coverage. Salazar did not stop and at the time of his death was, in fact, working on a series of stories on the enforcement agencies in the Los Angeles area, entitled "What Progress in Thirty Years of Police Community Relations?" The answer to this question and its importance to Salazar would be answered shortly during the August 29th march.

A federal grand jury issued an indictment against the officers involved in the Sánchez shootings for violation of the civil rights of the two men. The city of Los Angeles paid for the defense of three of the police officers, which produced a storm of protest. The officers were acquitted by a federal court. An interesting sidelight is that the U.S. attorney who persisted in prosecuting the case resigned about a year later.[82] News media attributed this resignation to pressure and criticisms from Chief Ed Davis and Mayor Sam Yorty.

According to Ralph Guzmán, between January 1961 and February 1967, although the Chicano population officially numbered 10 to 12 percent of the total population of the Southwest, Chicanos comprised 19.4 percent of those from that area killed in Vietnam. From December 1967 to March 1969, Chicanos suffered 19 percent of all casualties from the Southwest. Chicanos from Texas sustained 25.2 percent of the casualties of that state.

Chicano activists organized protests against the war. Rosalio Muñoz, a former student-body president at the University of California at Los Angeles, Sal Baldenegro, of the University of Arizona, and Ernesto Vigil, of the Crusade for Justice in Denver, refused induction.

In 1969 the Brown Berets formed the National Chicano Moratorium Committee, which held its first demonstration on December 20, 1969, with 2,000 in attendance. Rosalio Muñoz joined as co-chairperson. On February 28, 1970, the group staged another protest, with 6,000 Chicanos marching through the pouring rain.

In March 1970, Chicanos from all over the United States flocked to Denver to the Second Annual Chicano Youth Conference. They planned hundreds of local Chicano moratoria, climaxing with a national moratorium in Los Angeles on August 29. Demonstrations throughout the Southwest ranged from a few hundred to several thousand participants. Police–community tension increased. On July 4, 1970, disturbances broke out at the East Los Angeles sheriff's substation during a demonstration protesting the deaths of six Mexican American inmates in the preceding five months. There were 22 arrests, and 250 deputies and members of the California Highway Patrol quelled the rebellion. One youth was shot and windows were broken along Whittier Boulevard. Meanwhile, the tension increased as August 29 neared.

On the morning of the 29th contingents from all over the United States arrived in East Los Angeles. By noon participants numbered between 20,000 and 30,000. *Conjuntos* (musical groups) blared out *corridos; Vívas* and yells filled the air; placards read: *"Raza sí, guerra no!" "Aztlán:* Love it or Leave it!" as sheriff's deputies lined the parade route. They stood helmeted, making no attempt to establish contact with marchers: no smiles, no small talk. The march ended peaceably and the parade turned into Laguna Park. Marchers settled down to enjoy the program; many had brought picnic lunches. Mexican music and Chicano children entertained those assembled.

A minor incident at a liquor store took place a block from Laguna Park when teenagers pilfered some soft drinks. The police, instead of isolating this incident, rushed squad cars to the park, and armed officers prepared to enter the park area. Deputies refused to communicate with parade monitors. Their demeanor caused a reaction, and a few marchers angrily threw objects at the police. Authorities saw that monitors had restrained the few protestors. The reasonable person could deduce that the presence of such a large number of police caused a reaction. It became evident that the police had found an excuse to break up the demonstration.[83]

Monitors begged police not to enter the park, explaining that many women and small children had assembled in the area. Deputies, in spite of this, rushed into the arena, trapping men, women, and children and causing considerable panic. They wielded their clubs, trampled spectators, and hit those who did not move fast enough. In the main section of the park, police surprised the crowd. Many did not know what had happened, for up to that time they had not heard a warning to disperse. Deputies fired tear-gas canisters. Participants admittedly hurled objects at the troops, some maintaining that they did this in self-defense and others claiming that they acted simply out of hatred for what the police represented. By this time deputies numbered over 500. They moved in military formation, sweeping the park. Wreckage could be seen everywhere: the stampede trampled baby strollers into the ground; four deputies beat a man in his sixties; tear gas filled the air.

According to Dr. James S. Koopman, a physician at the UCLA School of Medicine, Department of Pediatrics:

Everyone was assembled peacefully at Laguna Park. My wife and I sat on the grass amongst diverse people. Immediately around us were little children playing with a puppy, an older woman with a cane, a pregnant woman with a small baby and a family eating hamburgers and french fries. The program began and after two speeches a Puerto Rican rhythm group was providing entertainment. The first sign of any disturbance I saw was when some people in the distance began to stand up. The loudspeaker calmly assured us that nothing was happening and that we should sit down. Seconds later I saw a row of gold helmets marching across the park, forcing everyone toward the high fences. The exit was too small for everyone to leave quickly. I, along with everyone else, panicked. The terrible tragedies of human stampedes in the soccer stadiums of Peru and Argentina were uppermost in my mind.[84]

Eventually, 1200 officers occupied Laguna Park. Los Angeles police joined the sheriff's deputies, as did police units from surrounding communities, extending the area of confrontation to Whittier Boulevard. Mass arrests followed. Prisoners were kept chained in fours, in two buses at the East Los Angeles substation. Sheriff's deputies did not allow them to drink water or go to the bathroom for about four hours. Deputies maced the chained prisoners at least three times. A deputy manhandled a pregnant girl and the deputies repeatedly maced the chained occupants of the bus.[85]

Deputies at Laguna Park shot at a Chicano when he allegedly ran a blockade; his car hit a telephone pole which electrocuted him. A tear-gas canister exploded in a trash can, killing a 15-year-old boy. These events preceded the most controversial incident of the day. Late in the afternoon Rubén Salazar and two coworkers from KMEX-TV, the Spanish language television station, stopped at the Silver Dollar Bar for a beer. Soon afterward deputies surrounded the bar, allegedly looking for a man with a rifle. When some occupants of the Silver Dollar attempted to leave, police forced them back into the premises. Police claimed that they then broadcast warnings for all occupants to come out; witnesses testified that they heard no warning. The suspect with the gun had been apprehended elsewhere and since released, but officers continued their activities at the Silver Dollar. They shot a 10-inch tear-gas projectile into the bar. The missile could pierce 7-inch plywood at 100 yards, and it struck Salazar in the head. Another shot filled the bar with gas. Customers made their way out of the establishment. About 5:30 PM Salazar's two colleagues frantically informed deputies that their friend was still in the bar. Deputies refused to listen, and not until two hours later was Salazar's body discovered.

On September 10, 1970, a coroner's inquest probed the circumstances surrounding Rubén Salazar's death. In Los Angeles a coroner's inquest is generally informal, with seven jurors selected at random. A hearing officer without judicial standing is appointed. Because of general interest, local television stations cooperated in airing the entire proceedings. The hearing officer did not limit testimony to the death of Salazar and allowed the proceedings to begin with an edited movie taken by the film crews of the sheriff's department. Officers testified as to the Chicano community's riotous nature. The hearing officer made no attempt to restrain deputies from introducing immaterial facts.

Chicano photographers proved police overreaction. A series of photographs taken by *La Raza* reporters Joe Razo and Raúl Ruiz, eyewitnesses to the events at the Silver Dollar Bar, contradicted the testimony of the deputies. For example, deputies claimed that they did not force the customers of the Silver Dollar to return to the bar. Ruiz produced a photo that showed that they did. The hearing officer repeatedly attempted to limit Ruiz's testimony, and he questioned him at length. Shortly afterward *La Raza* published a special issue featuring the photos taken on August 29. The *Los Angeles Times* obtained permission from the *barrio* publication to reprint many of the photos.[86]

Four inquest jurors found "death at the hands of another"; the three remaining jurors decided on "death by accident." The *Los Angeles Times,* on October 8, 1970, interviewed the jurors. A majority juror, George W. Sherard, stated: "All seven jurors reached the rapid conclusion that the killing was unintended. Four of us felt . . . deputies expected they had a good chance of killing someone." Another juror, Betty J. Clements, added: "The main surprise to me was the deputies' lack of organization, their lack of consideration for innocent people. I like to go into cocktail lounges to have a drink. I'd certainly hate to think somebody was going to shoot tear-gas or anything else in there simply because somebody reported there was a man with a gun." This juror questioned why deputies left Salazar's body in the bar for two hours and wondered whether they would have acted in the same manner in Beverly Hills.

Chicanos as well as many Anglos believed that Deputy Thomas Wilson would be tried. When Los Angeles District Attorney Evelle J. Younger announced on October 14, 1970, that he would not prosecute, many Chicanos charged that Younger had made this decision because of political opportunism. A candidate for California state attorney general (he was elected), he knew that the law-and-order mentality of Californians demanded such a response. The *Los Angeles Times,* which usually supported Younger, criticized his actions in an editorial on October 16, 1970:

> So this is where the matter stands: an innocent man was killed by a weapon that should not have been used when it was used, but the public authorities assign no blame. One does not have to enter a legal argument over whether there was, or was not, sufficient evidence for prosecution of the deputy to observe that the decision not to prosecute leaves the public in the dark as to the facts it should know.

On September 16, 1970, a peaceful Mexican Independence parade ended in violence when police attacked the crowd as marchers reached the end of the parade route. Feelings ran high, with many marchers carrying banners blaming the police for the murder of Salazar. Police accounts stated that teenagers had started the altercation between them and the Chicano community when the youths pelted police with rocks. According to police, they ordered the crowd to disperse and when it failed to do so, they moved in to restore order. However, eyewitnesses state that officers broke into apartments, destroying furniture and beating up occupants. The press condemned the marchers. In fact, TV newscasters Baxter Ward and George Putnam were inflammatory. Both relied on police information; they had not been there.[87]

Before the January 9, 1971, demonstration in front of Parker Center in the city of Los Angeles, Chief Ed Davis openly baited activists. The demonstration began at Hollenbeck police station; leaders planned to picket the station protesting against police brutality. Monitors cooled tempers. The main body reached Parker Center, the Los Angeles Police Department headquarters, and began to picket it. Police incited a riot and attacked demonstrators. Three hours later, when the melee was finally quelled, police had arrested 32 people. Again news media condemned Chicanos, with few questioning the methods of police or asking if they would have used similar vindictiveness in the west side of the city. Chief Davis blamed "swimming pool Communists" and the Brown Berets for the riot.[88]

Numerous smaller incidents occurred; however, the last major confrontation on January 31, 1971. Contingents arrived at Belvedere Park in East Los Angeles from the four major *barrios* in the Los Angeles. The demonstration was peaceful, and, as the rally ended, Rosalio Muñoz told some 5,000 supporters to disperse. Some, however, marched to the sheriff's substation on Third Street and staged a rally.

The crowd, heavily infiltrated by police provocateurs, walked up Whittier Boulevard. A small minority broke a few windows along the way, and tore down street signs.[89] At about 3:45 PM gunshots were heard at Whittier Boulevard, and the police moved in, shooting tear gas at demonstrators. They fired shotguns into the crowd, and the protesters, in turn, hurled objects at police. The confrontation left one man dead, 19 wounded by buckshot, two with stab wounds, and numerous with broken bones. Property damage climbed over $200,000. On February 4, the *Eastside Sun* quoted Peter Pitchess, the Los Angeles Sheriff, "This time they can't blame the disturbance on the department . . . because deputies were not in the area until after the burning and looting had started." Chicano leaders countered that the trouble, in reality, had begun many months, if not years, before. At the crux of the problem was the question Rubén Salazar had posed: What progress in thirty years of police community relations?

THE PROVOCATEURS

In October 1971 Louis Tackwood, a Black informer, stunned the Los Angeles public by testifying that the Criminal Conspiracy Section (CCS) of the Los Angeles Police Department paid him to spy on militants. The LAPD assigned Tackwood to a group of officers who, in cooperation with the FBI, planned to provoke a disruption by militants of the 1972 Republican convention in San Diego; they planned to kill minor officials to force President Richard Nixon to use his powers to break the militant movement. Tackwood named Dan Mahoney (CCS) and Ed Birch (FBI) as the supervisors of the operation. In private conversations he has also described the police use of drug pushers as informers in return for protection from prosecution.

Officer Fernando Sumaya also worked as an undercover agent for the Los Angeles Police Department. In the fall semester of 1968 he attempted to infiltrate the United Mexican-American Student chapter at San Fernando Valley State College (now California State University at Northridge) during campus protests there. He was ousted from the group because he was unknown and because he came on too strong. Sumaya then moved to East Los Angeles, where he infiltrated the Brown Berets. In the spring of 1969 he was involved in the Biltmore Hotel affair, where Chicanos were accused of disrupting a speech by Governor Ronald Reagan at a Nuevas Vistas Education Conference, sponsored by the California

Department of Education. Thirteen Chicanos were arrested on the charge of disturbing the peace; 10 of the 13 were charged with conspiracy to commit arson. After two years of appeals the defendants were tried. The key witness for the prosecution was Sumaya. The defendants all denied any involvement with the fires. Some charged that Sumaya set the fires. The jury found the defendants not guilty. Meanwhile, Carlos Montes, a Brown Beret, had left the area and he was not tried. He remained at large until the mid-1970s. After he was caught police continued to hound Montes. The LAPD destroyed records documenting Sumaya's role in the Biltmore fires. In November 1979, a jury found Montes not guilty—evidently the jury questioned Sumaya's and the LAPD's suspect role.

In a press conference on January 31, 1972, Eustacio (Frank) Martínez, 23, revealed that since July 1969 he had infiltrated Chicano groups. A federal agent for the Alcohol, Tobacco, and Firearms Division (ATF) of the Internal Revenue Service recruited Martínez, who, in return for not being prosecuted for a federal firearms violation, agreed to work as an informant and agent provocateur. He infiltrated the Mexican American Youth Organization and the Brown Berets in Houston and Kingsville, Texas. He admitted that he committed acts of violence to provoke others. From September 1969 to October 1970 he participated in a protest march in Alice, Texas, and tried to provoke trouble "by jumping on a car and trying to cave its top in." He attempted to entice militants to buy guns and to provoke police. He was rebuked by the MAYO members.[90]

In October 1970 ATF agents sent Martínez to Los Angeles, where he worked for agents Fernando Ramos and Jim Riggs. Martínez began spreading rumors against Rosalio Muñoz, accusing him of being too soft, and in November 1970 Martínez ousted Muñoz and became chair of the Chicano Moratorium Committee. Martínez named officers Valencia, Armas, Savillos, and Domínguez of the CCS as contacts. In other words, when Martínez took part in the Los Angeles rebellions on January 9 and 31, 1971, the Los Angeles police knew of his involvement. He continued in this capacity until March 1971, when he returned to Texas. There Martínez became a member of the Brown Berets and went around, according to informants, waving a carbine and advocating violent tactics. Upon his return from Texas he was instructed by Ramos and Riggs to infiltrate *La Casa de Carnalismo* to establish links between *Carnalismo* and the Chicano Liberation Front (CLF), which had been involved in numerous bombings. Martínez reported that the main functions of the group were to eliminate narcotics, to sponsor English classes, and to dispense food to the needy. He could find no links with CLF. The officers told him that his "information was a bunch of bullshit." He was to find evidence by any means necessary. They then instructed him to use his influence to get a heroin addict by the name of "Nacho" to infiltrate *Carnalismo.* Martínez refused to take part in the frameup. He finally became disillusioned when, on the first anniversary of the Chicano National Moratorium, agents told him to plead guilty to charges of inciting a riot. He had been promised protection from prosecution.[91]

Although reporters did not question the reliability of Martínez's disclosures, they did not call for congressional investigations into the provocateur activities of federal and local agencies. Louis Tackwood and Frank Martínez were admitted provocateurs. The latter's role cast a shadow on the actions of the police in the Los Angeles Chicano rebellions. Local police authorities knew of Martínez's involvement with the moratorium.

Whatever their role was, it lies buried in the files of the secret police of the different branches of the federal and local police agencies. These are the aspects of history that remain closed to historians. The American Civil Liberties Union, in a suit settled in the early 1980s, uncovered extensive police spying on white progressive, Black, and Chicano communities (see Chapter 10).

AFTER THE SMOKE CLEARED

Although the status of Chicanos improved as a result of the move to the cities and economic growth during three major wars, their opportunities for upward mobility remain collectively restricted. Since the 1930s the occupational distribution of Chicanos in the professional classes has changed relatively little.

OCCUPATIONAL DISTRIBUTION OF MEXICAN AMERICAN MALES IN THE SOUTHWEST

Occupation	1930	1950	1960	1970
Professionals and Technical	0.9%	2.2%	4.1%	6.4%
Managers	2.8	4.4	4.6	5.2
Sales	2.4	6.5	3.6	3.9
Clerical	1.0		4.8	6.6
Crafts	6.8	13.1	16.7	20.8
Operative	9.1	19.0	24.1	25.4
Service	4.0	6.3	7.5	10.5
Laborer	28.2	18.7	15.2	12.1
Farmers	9.8	5.1	2.4	0.9
Farm labor	35.1	24.7	16.8	8.1

Source: Vernon M. Briggs, Jr., Walter Fogel, and Fred Schmidt, *The Chicano Worker* (Austin: University of Texas Press, 1977), p. 76.

Change in labor market needs during the 1960s restricted the Chicanos' upward mobility. Opportunities in the industrial sector shrank, as job openings in better paying categories were more and more restricted to those having advanced education skills. The contradiction was that the 1960s were supposedly a decade spurred by a thriving civil rights movement and a war on poverty which meant to create jobs for the so-called disadvantaged. In fact, the gap between Chicano and Anglo males in the Southwest and nationally remained wide, with the majority of white Americans employed in white-collar occupations (46.8 percent in 1960 and 53.3 percent in 1970) and the overwhelming majority of Chicanos remaining in blue-collar occupations (80.9 percent in 1960 and 78.4 percent in 1970).[92]

This differential, according to Professor Vernon Briggs, Jr., contributed to a "social caste" system accentuating class differences between Mexicans and Anglos.[93] By the 1970s a rise in automation, the decline in population among the majority society, growing internationalization of capital and labor, and spiraling inflation all contributed to shrinking opportunities for Chicanos and further restricted upward mobility.

By the mid-1970s nearly 40 percent of Chicanas 16 and over were members of the workforce; a trend that had been accelerated during the 1960s. A decline in real wages and purchasing power drove them and their Anglo and Black counterparts into the labor force in larger numbers. Chicanas trailed their white and Black counterparts in almost every category. There were fewer Chicanas in professional occupations (7.6 percent versus 18.4 percent for Anglo women and 11.6 Black women) and twice as many in the operative occupations (23.3 percent versus 7.6 percent Anglo and 12.2 percent Black). The median income of Spanish-surnamed females in the Southwest relative to all white females in 1969 was 76 percent. The poverty level in 1970 was $4,200; the median income for Latin women over the age of 16 nationally was $2,313. Chicanas, in short, earned three-quarters of what both Black and Anglo female workers earned.

Both male and female Chicanos consistently had higher unemployment than Anglos. In 1969, although the Vietnam War stimulated heavy employment, unemployment among Mexicans in the Southwest was high (6.2 percent among males and 8.7 percent among females). Professor Briggs pointed out that the percentage of unemployed would have been higher if it had not been for job training programs.[94]

By the 1970s a large segment of the Chicano labor pool was condemned to a life of unemployment or poverty program migrancy.[95] The government funded a labyrinth of federal programs to train a small number of Chicanos, but in the end they remained frozen in an underclass, with most too frustrated to meander through the labyrinth again. In the 1960s and throughout the next decade, Chicanas who entered the labor force in increasing numbers as heads of households faced a "Catch 22" situation. Programs such as the Aid to Families with Dependent Children (AFDC) institutionalized poverty. Seventy percent of the aid was to female household heads. In San Antonio the figure was 80 percent. Nationally 17 percent of the Chicano families were headed by women with 51 percent of these female headed households living in poverty. The overwhelming proportion of these women were young, with one or two children, locked out of improving themselves because of rigid and arbitrary AFDC regulations.

Supposedly to improve the options for women on AFDC, the work incentives (WIN) program was initiated in 1967 to encourage employers to hire poor women. The government paid from 50 to 100 percent of the WIN employee's salary. There was no guarantee that employment was permanent, and critics saw it as a further way to get cheap labor for employers rather than as a way to help the poor. In 1971 Congress unanimously approved the Talmadge Amendment which expanded the categories for welfare recipients required to register for work or training; it included mothers of school-age children. Even a woman with dependents who wanted to pursue a college education was discouraged. Many were forced to quit college in their senior year because their child reached the arbitrary age of six.[96]

In 1969 86 percent of all Chicanos in the Southwest lived in urban areas. As in 1959 their median income per family still lagged behind the majority society. The income level for Chicanos in the Midwest was generally higher than other regions—$9,300 in Illinois and $9,400 in Michigan.[97]

MEDIAN INCOME PER FAMILY, 1970

State	Median income	Spanish-surnamed percentage of Anglo	Spanish-surnamed percentage of Black
Arizona	$7,350	74	129
California	8,430	73	113
Colorado	6,930	69	97
New Mexico	5,890	67	113
Texas	5,600	58	105

Source: Adapted from Vernon M. Briggs, Jr., Walter Fogel, and Fred Schmidt, *The Chicano Worker* (Austin: University of Texas Press, 1977), p. 47.

The figures for family income do not take into account the size of the families, which ran larger among Mexicans than either Anglos or Blacks. If per capita income were considered, the gap between Chicano and Anglo would increase and the Chicano and Black incomes would become approximately equal. In 1970 the average Mexican family consisted of 4.5 persons, Black and Puerto Rican 4.1 persons, and Anglo 3.6 persons.

In 1969 the poverty line for a nonfarm family was $3,743, and 24 percent of all Spanish-surnamed families fell below this line. By the mid-1970s, 27 percent of the Latino families fell below the poverty line versus 9.7 percent of Anglos and 31.3 percent of Blacks. More significant, in the Southwest between 1959 and 1969 the income of Mexicans in relation to Anglos had not increased more than 1 percent. Chicano income was 65 percent of the Anglo in 1959, 66 percent in 1969. During this same period in California Chicano family earning power dropped from 79 percent to 73 percent. These statistics dampened any optimism "about the rapid attainment of equality of Mexican-American income with that of Anglos."[98] In fact, many predicted that due to a constricting economy and a white backlash, the inequality would widen during the 1970s.

SUMMARY

During the first half of the 1960s, a decade of rapid change, the struggle for civil rights led to public recognition of poverty and forced the Kennedy and Johnson administrations to sponsor programs intended to mollify the Black masses. The Black–white confrontation produced a whirlwind of events that caused Mexican Americans, Native Americans, and other minorities to escalate demands for similar human rights and political gains. Expectations of Mexican American activists were raised by the dramatic increase in the Mexican American population to just under 4 million in 1960; by its concentration in key states and cities, suggesting the potential for political power; by the fact that 80 percent lived in the cities, where they had more freedom to organize; and by the success of the *Víva* Kennedy clubs, which created the illusion that participation in the Democratic party would give Mexican Americans greater access to elected and appointed offices.

Leaders of the *Víva* Kennedy clubs formed PASSO in the hope of founding a national political organization. However, Mexican Americans faced many barriers—for instance, the divisions in Texas between the traditional middle-class organizations such as LULAC and the Forum and independents who challenged the old guard. Texas in many ways took the lead, since it had the most established Mexican American communities. Natural networks made unity simpler; racism also contributed to cohesion.

Economic, social, and political barriers prevented the full participation of Mexican Americans within Anglo-American society. Institutional racism justified the exploitation of Mexican Americans, and the lack of education excluded them from higher paying jobs created by increased government funding of so-called defense industries. The more refined data generated by the 1960 census revealed to Mexican American activists and educators the extent of the exploitation of their poor as well as the lack of access to public and private institutions. Competition for programs and funds intensified, as did the syphoning off of these limited resources to pay for the war in Southeast Asia.

During the 1960s Los Angeles, Chicago, and Houston underwent dramatic increases in their Mexican American populations. Although less dramatic, cities throughout the Southwest and Midwest witnessed a growth in the number of Mexicans. As mentioned, government contracts to war-related industries produced an upswing in highly skilled jobs; they also boosted the number of unskilled jobs in light industry, construction, and the service sector. Mexicans, usually relegated to the low paying urban positions, still worked in agriculture. California became the center for farm-worker activity. The repeal of the *bracero* program removed a major hurdle to unionization. And César Chávez emerged not only as a union and civil rights leader but as a symbol for the Chicano movement.

Toward the middle of the decade, government moved to control Mexican labor through the passage of an immigration act that served to inspire further nativist laws more directly limiting the number of Mexicans entering the United States. Political efforts to stem Mexican migration would, however, prove useless since political realities and the need for Mexican labor neutralized the political solutions. For example, the mid-1960s also stepped up the penetration of U.S. capital into Mexico. The BIP encouraged the building of *maquiladoras* at the border, further promoting northward migration from the interior. In the United States, the labeling of unskilled work as "Mexican" made Mexicans/Chicanos more vulnerable to exploitation. Although migration from Mexico took place throughout the 1960s, it did not become a major issue until the 1970s as the U.S. economy worsened.

Militancy increased among Mexican Americans after the mid-1960s. Multiple factors such as the growing intensity of the Black movement, with its transformation from civil rights to Black power, helped Chicano awareness. The U.S. invasion of Santo Domingo and the expansion of the war in Southeast Asia also raised Chicano political consciousness. The rise of the cult of Che Guevara, the anticolonial struggles, the anti–Vietnam War marches, and the continuing civil rights rallies legitimated street politics.

More important, the decade saw the involvement of more sectors of the Mexican American community in social and political activism than had heretofore been the case. The new participants included students and the young, as well as the grass-roots *barrio* residents. The rise of *los de abajo* raised the expectations of the excluded sectors.

Education or the lack of it was the number one issue confronting the Chicano movement during the second half of the 1960s. Numerous ad hoc education committees throughout the Southwest and Midwest protested the poor quality of education, the high dropout rate, the absence of relevant curricula, and the lack of Mexican American teachers and counselors.

By 1965, AMEA formed in Los Angeles. Two years later, Representative Roybal introduced the first successful federal bilingual education legislation; that same year, California Chicano students formed UMAS, while *Tejanos* organized MAYO. The primary issues for these groups were the lack of Mexican American access to education and an increased dedication to the community. In 1968, 10,000 to 12,000 students walked out of Los Angeles high schools. Their demands included those of earlier education activists. Chicano students throughout the Southwest repeated these walkout tactics—dramatizing their resolve to find a solution. After this point, militancy escalated in the Chicano *barrios*.

After 1967, new Chicano leaders emerged, who articulated the concerns not only of farm workers but of urban Chicanos. The year 1968 represented a worldwide revolt among youth—for the Chicano it became the year of the heroes. Each hero expressed the community's frustrations over inadequate education, police brutality, the Vietnam War, and dislocation from their land. Later on, the focus narrowed, with the Vietnam War setting the stage for the largest protest in Los Angeles's history—the moratorium of August 29, 1970. The demonstrations produced a martyr—news reporter Rubén Salazar. Chicanos staggered into the 1970s—literally clubbed into temporary submission. After the smoke cleared, in spite of real change for most North Americans, very little progress had been made by Chicanos. The importance of activist, youth, and grass-roots organizations declined after this point. The 1970s restored to the middle class its hegemony over the movement. The 1970s would witness the emergence of the business and professional classes in the Mexican American community and the return of the brokers.

NOTES

1. William L. O'Neil, *An Informal History of America in the 1960s: Coming Apart* (New York: Quadrangle, 1980), pp. 61–63.
2. George Mowry and Blaine A. Brownell, *The Urban Nation 1920–1980,* rev. ed. (New York: Hill and Wang, 1981), pp. 173–175.
3. Mowry and Brownell, pp. 211–212.

4. Michael Harrington, *The Other America: Poverty in the United States* (Baltimore: Penguin Books, 1971), p. 5.

5. James T. Patterson, *America's Struggle Against Poverty, 1900–1980* (Cambridge, Mass.: Harvard University Press, 1981), pp. 113–121.

6. Robert L. Heilbroner and Aaron Singer, *The Economic Transformation of America: 1600 to the Present* 2nd ed. (San Diego: Harcourt Brace Jovanovich, 1984), p. 327; Michael Parenti, *Democracy for the Few,* 3rd ed. (New York: St. Martin's Press, 1980), pp. 80–81; Howard Zinn, *A People's History of the United States* (New York: Harper Colophon Books, 1980), p. 429; O'Neil, pp. 43–44.

7. Mowry and Brownell, pp. 213–214.

8. Mowry and Brownell, pp. 221–222; O'Neil, pp. 130–131.

9. Meyer Weinberg, *A Chance to Learn: A History of Race and Education in the United States* (Cambridge, England: Cambridge University Press, 1977), p. 174.

10. Quoted in Patterson, p. 145.

11. Patterson, p. 146.

12. Rodolfo Acuña, *A Community Under Siege: A Chronicle of Chicanos East of the Los Angeles River, 1945–1975* (Los Angeles: Chicano Resource Center, UCLA, 1984), p. 145.

13. Patterson, p. 148.

14. Leo Grebler, Joan W. Moore, and Ralph C. Guzmán, *The Mexican-American People: The Nation's Second Largest Minority* (New York: Free Press, 1970), pp. 106, 126, 185, 251.

15. Grebler, Moore, and Guzmán, pp. 143, 150, 236; Richard W. Slatta, "Chicanos in the Pacific Northwest: An Historical Overview of Oregon's Chicanos," *Aztlán* (Fall 1975): 335.

16. Robert Garland Landolt, *The Mexican-American Workers of San Antonio, Texas* (New York: Arno Press, 1976), pp. 29, 44, 53; El Paso had 125,745 Mexicans; Houston, 63,372; Corpus Christi, 59,859; and Laredo, 49,819.

17. Landolt, p. 291.

18. Lamar Babington Jones, "Mexican American Labor Problems in Texas" (Ph.D. dissertation, University of Texas, Austin, 1965); see Jones, p. 56, for occupation charts comparing San Antonio, Dallas, El Paso, and Houston. Figures in text are from Landolt, pp. 56–57, 69, 71, 87, 89, 353.

19. Landolt, p. 294.

20. Landolt, pp. 111, 120, 124, 127, 130. In July 1963, 13 out of 55 carpenters' apprentices (23.6 percent) were Mexican; 6 of 71 electricians (8.4 percent); 6 of 39 plumbers (15.4 percent); and 2 of 25 sheet metal workers' apprentices (8 percent) were also Mexican.

21. Landolt, pp. 144, 219. Also see Sam Frank Parigi, *A Case Study of Latin American Unionization in Austin Texas* (New York: Arno Press, 1976).

22. Robert Coles and Harry Huge, "Thorns on the Yellow Rose of Texas," *New Republic* (April 19, 1969): 13–17. Landolt, pp. 320, 326.

23. "Revolt of the Masses," *Time* Magazine (April 12, 1963); Tony Castro, *Chicano Power: The Emergence of Mexican Americans* (New York: Saturday Review Press, 1974), p. 28; Edwin Larry Dickens, "The Political Role of Mexican-Americans in San Antonio" (Ph.D. dissertation, Texas Tech University, 1969), p. 169.

24. Charles Ray Chandler, "The Mexican-American Protest Movement in Texas" (Ph.D. dissertation, Tulane University, 1968), pp. 157–160.

25. Chandler, pp. 173–190.

26. Barbara Jane Macklin, *Structural Stability and Cultural Change in a Mexican American Community* (New York: Arno Press, 1976), pp. 13–15; Mark Edward Erenberg, "A Study of the Political Relocation of Texas-Mexican Migratory Farm Workers to Wisconsin" (Ph.D. dissertation, University of Wisconsin, 1969), pp. 39, 40.

27. Dennis Nodin Váldes, *El Pueblo Mexicano en Detroit y Michigan: A Social History* (Detroit: Wayne State University Press, 1982), pp. 79–95.

28. Louise Año Nuevo Kerr, "The Chicano Experience in Chicago: 1920–1970" (Chicago: University of Illinois at Chicago Circle, 1976), pp. 171–176.

29. William Kornblum, *Blue Collar Community* (Chicago: University of Chicago Press, 1974), pp. 9, 30; Kerr, p. 179.

30. Kerr, pp. 183–184; Kornblum, pp. 161–182.

31. Kerr, pp. 183–187.

32. Barry J. Kaplan, *"Houston: The Golden Buckle of the Sunbelt,"* in Richard M. Bernard and Bradley R. Rice, *Sunbelt Cities: Politics and Growth Since World War II* (Austin: University of Texas Press, 1983), pp. 196–212.

33. Benjamin Márquez, "Power and Politics in a Chicano Barrio" (Ph.D. dissertation, University of Wisconsin—Madison, 1983), chapters 4 and 5.

34. Acuña, pp. 84–228.

35. Acuña, p. 85.

36. *G.I. Forum News Bulletin,* March 1963, September 1964.

37. Regional Planning Commission, County of Los Angeles, California, 1972. A basic problem with the 1970 census was that there were no specific guidelines for counting Mexicans such as there were for counting Blacks. Chicano organizations fought for guidelines, since they realized that all funding was based on numbers. See *Los Angeles Times,* March 8, 1972; Edward Murguia, *Assimilation, Colonialism and the Mexican American People* (Austin: Center for Mexican American Studies, University of Texas, 1975), p. 43; Ray Hebert, "L.A. County Latin Population Grows 113 Percent," *Los Angeles Times,* August 18, 1972; *Forumeer,* February 1970; Frank Del Olmo, "Spanish-Origin Census Figure Revised by U.S., *"Los Angeles Times,* January 15, 1974; "Census Hikes Spanish Count," *Denver Post,* January 16, 1974; "State Gains 643,000 Latins," *San Francisco Chronicle,* May 11, 1974; Citizens of Spanish Origin Gain in U.S.," *San Antonio Express,* March 31, 1974; "Births, Los Angeles County, 1966–1974," Chicano Resource Center, Clippings, East Los Angeles County Library Branch; Regional Planning Commission. For a good rundown of the Texas count, see Nell Fenner Grover, "S.A.'s Spanish Speakers Highest Concentration in State," *San Antonio Express,* August 10, 1972. For a good rundown of the San Francisco count, see Ralph Crail, "What the 1970 Census Showed About Bay Area," *San Francisco Chronicle,* August 3, 1972.

38. Gary A. Greenfield and Don B. Kates, Jr., "Mexican Americans, Racial Discrimination, and the Civil Rights Act of 1866," 5 *Cal Journal* (1975): 667.

39. Christopher Rand, *Los Angeles: The Ultimate City* (New York: Oxford University Press, 1967), p. 131; Joan W. Moore, *Mexican Americans,* 2nd ed. (Englewood Cliffs, N.J.: Prentice-Hall, 1976), p. 93; *G.I. Forum News Bulletin,* March-April 1960; *Eastside Sun,* February 4, 1960.

40. *Eastside Sun,* February 4, February 11, 1960.

41. *Eastside Sun,* February 11, 1960; "Roybal Comments on Crime Reports of East Los Angeles," *Eastside Sun,* March 10, 1960; "Police Maltreatment Subject at Conference at Biltmore Hotel," *Eastside Sun,* June 16, 1960.

42. Armando Morales, "A Study of Mexican-American Perceptions of Law Enforcement Policies and Practices in East Los Angeles" (DSW dissertation, University of Southern California, 1972), p. 87.

43. Morales, pp. 89, 90; *New York Times,* October 25, 1971.

44. Morris Singer, *Growth, Equality and the Mexican Experience* (Austin: University of Texas Press, 1969), p. 31.

45. Nelson Gage Copp, " 'Wetbacks' and Braceros: Mexican Migrant Laborers and American Immigration Policy, 1430–1960" (Ph.D. dissertation, Boston University, 1963). Copp, p. 16, states that Mexico has 494 million acres of land, of which 58 million are arable. In 1956, 22 million were

actually harvested. See also "Del Monte: Bitter Fruits," NACLA's *Latin America and Empire Report* 4, no. 7 (September 1976): 3–9; Ed McCaughan and Peter Baird, "Harvest of Anger: Agro-Imperialism in Mexico's Northwest," NACLA's *Latin America and Empire Report* 10, no. 6 (July-August 1976): 10–11; Carey McWilliams, "The Borderlands Let Justice Make Us Friends," *Fronteras 1976: A View of the Border from Mexico,* Proceedings of a Conference on Border Studies, San Diego, May 7–8, 1976, p. 3; Raúl A. Fernández, *The United States-Mexico Border* (Notre Dame, Ind.: University of Notre Dame Press, 1977), pp. 102, 108.

46. Ed McCaughan and Peter Baird, "Immigration Plan for People or Profit," *Immigration: Facts and Fallacies* (New York: North American Congress on Latin America, 1977), pp. 12, 18; Ed McCaughan and Peter Baird, *Carter's Immigration Policy: Attack on Immigrant Labor* (New York: North American Congress on Latin America, 1978), pp. 3–4.

47. Marlene Dixon, "Dual Power: The Rise of the Transnational Corporation and the Nation-State: Conceptual Explanations to Meet Popular Demand," in Marlene Dixon and Susanne Jonas, eds., *The New Nomads: From Immigrant Labor to Transnational Working Class* (San Francisco: Synthesis, 1982), p. 132.

48. María Fernández-Kelly, *For We Are Sold, I and My People: Women and Industry in Mexico's Frontier* (Albany: State University of New York Press, 1983), p. 24.

49. Fernández-Kelly, pp. 132, 134; Victor Urquidi and Sofia Méndez Villareal, "Economic Importance of Mexico's Northern Border Region," in Stanley R. Ross, ed., *Views Across the Border* (Albuquerque: University of New Mexico Press, 1978), pp. 135, 147, 148.

50. See Fernández-Kelly for a clear explanation of the BIP.

51. Gilbert Cárdenas, "United States Immigration Policy Toward Mexico: A Historical Perspective," *Chicano Law Review* 2 (summer 1975): 81–82, quoted in Jones, p. 33. See also Jones, pp. 35–37; F. Ray Marshall, "Economic Factors Influencing the International Migration of Workers," in Ross, p. 169.

52. Kerr, p. 177.

53. Howard Lloyd Campbell, "Bracero Migration and the Mexican Economy, 1951–1964" (Ph.D. dissertation, American University, 1972), p. 101. Mechanization in California was the chief reason for the decreased use of *braceros* in the last five years of this program. It reduced the need for them up to 73 percent.

54. Peter Matthiessen, *Sal Si Puedes: César Chávez and the New American Revolution* (New York: Random House, 1969), pp. 41, 50–51; Joan London and Henry Anderson, *So Shall Ye Reap* (New York: Crowell, 1971), pp. 146–148, 149; Mark Day, *Forty Acres: César Chávez and the Farm Workers* (New York: Praeger, 1971), pp. 54, 55.

55. Samuel R. Berger, *Dollar Harvest: The Story of the Farm Bureau* (Lexington, Mass.: Heath, 1971), pp. 161–163; *Forumeer,* May 1966. Schenley had also been influenced by the march to Sacramento, which covered 300 miles and ultimately drew 8,000 marchers in that city. See also Gregory Dunne, *Delano* (New York: Farrar, Straus & Giroux, 1967), pp. 51, 144, 145, 147–148; Ronald B. Taylor, *Chávez and the Farm Workers* (Boston: Beacon Press, 1975), pp. 157, 287; Day, p. 42.

56. Day, p. 43; Dunne, pp. 156, 166; Matthiessen, p. 22; Paul Wallace Gates, "Corporate Farming in California," in Ray Allen Billington, ed., *People of the Plains and Mountains* (Westport, Conn.: n.d.), in the Taylor Collection of the Bancroft Library; Armando Rendon, *Chicano Manifesto* (New York: Collier, 1971), p. 149. The growers' most powerful friend at the federal level was Senator James Eastland, who received $146,000 in farm subsidies in 1969 and consistently vetoed a $55,000 ceiling on subsidies. The headline in the *California Farmer* on July 6, 1968, was "Boycott Jeopardizes Entire Grape Crop" (quoted in Matthiessen, p. 40).

57. Sam Kushner, *Long Road to Delano* (New York: International Publishers, 1975), p. 173; Taylor, pp. 251, 259, 261–169; Matthiessen, pp. 333–334; *Los Angeles Times,* December 5, 6, 24, 1970. Two years later, the Supreme Court struck down the law that had imprisoned Chávez.

58. Charles Winn Carr, "Mexican Americans in Texas Labor Movement" (Ph.D. dissertation, Texas Christian University, 1972), pp. 98–100, 101, 106–128, 132, 133, 139–140, 144; National Advisory Committee on Farm Labor, *Farm Labor Organizing, 1905–1967: A Brief History* (New York: National Advisory Committee on Farm Labor, 1967), pp. 53–56; "U.S. Judges Rap Ranger Acts in Valley," *San Antonio Express,* June 27, 1972.

59. Mark Erenberg, *"Obreros Unidos* in Wisconsin," U.S. Bureau of Labor Statistics, *Monthly Labor Review* 91 (June 1968): 20–23; National Advisory Committee on Farm Labor, p. 59.

60. National Advisory Committee on Farm Labor, p. 60; Macklin, p. vi.

61. For general background on war on poverty see Biliana María Ambrecht, "Politicization as a Legacy of the War on Poverty: A Study of Advisory Council Members in a Mexican American Community" (Ph.D. dissertation, University of California at Los Angeles, 1973), and V. Kurtz, "Politics, Ethnicity, Integration: Mexican Americans in the War on Poverty" (Ph.D. dissertation, University of California, Davis, 1970). This section draws specifically from Greg Coronado, "Spanish-Speaking Organizations in Utah," in Paul Morgan and Vince Mayer, *Working Papers Toward a History of the Spanish Speaking in Utah* (Salt Lake City: American West Center, Mexican-American Documentation Project, University of Utah, 1973), p. 121. Vernon M. Briggs, Jr., Walter Fogel, and Fred H. Schmidt, *The Chicano Worker* (Austin: University of Texas Press, 1977), p. 38; *Forumeer,* March 1967. states that the Forum almost dropped sponsorship of SER because LBJ was hedging on the White House conference.

62. Carcy McWilliams, *North from Mexico* (New York: Greenwood Press, 1968), p. 17. I had extensive conversations with Miguel Montes and Louis García, both residents of San Fernando, California, who participated in the conference. They felt that what they did was a radical act, as did most Chicano activists at that time. *Forumeer,* October 1967. The Forum supported the conference and said nothing about the demonstrations. See also John Hart Lane, Jr., "Voluntary Associations Among Mexican Americans in San Antonio, Texas: Organization and Leadership Characteristics" (Ph.D. dissertation, University of Texas, 1968), p. 2; Richard Gardner, *Grito! Reies Tijerina and the New Mexico Land Grant War of 1967* (New York: Bobbs-Merrill, 1970), pp. 231–232.

63. Acuña, pp. 230–270.

64. Interviews with José Angel Gutiérrez, November 3, 1985; Mario Compean, September 23, 1985.

65. Juan Gómez-Quiñones, *Mexican Students por La Raza: The Chicano Student Movement in Southern California, 1967–1977* (Santa Barbara, Calif.: Editorial La Causa, 1978), pp. 17–18, 22–23; Gerald Paul Rosen, "Political Ideology and the Chicano Movement: A Study of the Political Ideology of Activists in the Chicano Movement" (Ph.D. dissertation, University of California at Los Angeles, 1972), p. 248. Julian Nava was selected by a coalition of community organizations. This victory led to the later formation of the Congress of Mexican American Unity, in which youth played an active role. See "Community Endorsement of Board of Education," *Eastside Sun,* January 29, 1967; "Calderon 'People's Choice' for Senator at Confab," *Eastside Sun,* February 29, 1968; *Forumeer,* March 1966.

66. "Tragedy of Lincoln High," *Inside Eastside,* December 8–21, 1967; January 5–19, 1968.

67. Rosen, pp. 143, 144, 145.

68. Oscar Acosta, "The East L.A. 13 vs. the Superior Court," *El Grito* 3, no. 2 (Winter 1970): 14; London and Anderson, p. 25; William Parker Frisbie, "Militancy Among Mexican Americans: A Study of High School Students" (Ph.D. dissertation, University of North Carolina at Chapel Hill, 1972), pp. 4, 143; *Forumeer,* October, December 1968; Eugene Acosta Marín, "The Mexican American Community and Leadership of the Dominant Society in Arizona: A Study of Their Mutual Attitudes and Perspections" (Ph.D. dissertation, U.S. International University, 1973), p. 12.

69. David Sánchez, *Expedition Through Aztlán* (La Puente, Calif.: Perspectiva Press, 1978); Rona M. Fields and Charles J. Fox, "Viva La Raza: The Saga of the Brown Berets" (unpublished manuscript). See also Rosen.

70. *Forumeer,* February, May 1969; Castro, pp. 156–157; José Angel Gutiérrez, *"Aztlán:* Chicano Revolt in the Winter Garden," *La Raza* 1, no. 4 (1971): 34–35, 37; For a background study of Crystal City, see John Staples Shockley, *Chicano Revolt in a Texas Town* (Notre Dame, Ind.: University of Notre Dame Press, 1974).

71. Shockley, pp. 119, 120–121; Gutiérrez, pp. 39–40.

72. Gardner, pp. 66–84, 129–130, 208, 265–279 (Gardner presents a gripping account of the trial); Peter Nabokov, *Tijerina and the Courthouse Raid* (Albuquerque: University of New Mexico Press, 1969), pp. 19, 28, 30, 250–266; Clark Knowlton, "Guerillas of Rio Arriba: The New Mexico Land Wars," in F. Chris García, ed., *La Causa Politica: A Chicano Politics Reader* (Notre Dame, Inc.: University of Notre Dame Press, 1974), p. 333.

73. Stan Steiner, *La Raza: The Mexican Americans* (New York: Harper & Row, 1969), pp. 378–392; Christine Marín, *A Spokesman of the Mexican American Movement: Rodolfo "Corky" Gonzales and the Fight for Chicano Liberation, 1966–1972* (San Francisco: R & E Research Associates, 1977), pp. 1–3, 5; *Forumeer,* November 1965, June 1966; *The Militant,* December 4, 1970.

74. Morales, pp. 103–104, 105–107; U.S. Commission on Civil Rights, *Mexican Americans and the Administration of Justice in the Southwest* (Washington, D.C.: Government Printing Office, 1970), pp. 4–5; *La Raza* 1, no. 2 (1970): 18–19; *Forumeer,* October 1968.

75. Quoted in Morales, p. 43.

76. *Forumeer,* January 19, 1970, March 1970; "Roybal Demands Removal of San Jose Judge," *Belvedere Citizen,* October 16, 1969; "Judge's Intemperate Outburst Against Mexicans Investigated," *Eastside Sun,* October 9, 1969.

77. Castro, pp. 52–54.

78. U.S. Commission on Civil Rights, pp. 37–38, 40; *Ideal,* February 15–28, 1970.

79. *Los Angeles Times,* February 7, 1972; *Justicia O* 1, no. 3 (January 1971).

80. *Los Angeles Times,* September 23, 1985.

81. Interviews and conversations with Ricardo Cruz. Cruz passed the California bar, but had to fight to be certified because of his conviction. He is today practicing in East Los Angeles. See "Law Students Seek Signatures; Petition Protests Denial of Certification by Bar for Chicanos Active in Barrios," *Belvedere Citizen,* March 16, 1972.

82. *Los Angeles Times,* July 17, 1970; Gene Blake and Howard Hertel, "Court Won't Drop Case Against Officers in 'Mistake' Slayings," *Los Angeles Times,* April 27, 1971; Letter from Manuel Ruiz, a member of the U.S. Commission on Civil Rights, to Herman Sillas, chairperson of the California State Advisory Committee to the Commission, September 14, 1970, in "A Report of the California State Advisory Committee to the U.S. Commission on Civil Rights: Police-Community Relations in East Los Angeles, California" (October 1970); *New York Times,* December 18, 1971; *Los Angeles Times,* December 18, 1971.

83. Ralph Guzmán, "Mexican American Casualties in Vietnam," *La Raza* 1, no. 1: 12. Many Chicano organizations supported the war in 1967, but by 1969 most were having second thoughts. The high mortality rate among Chicanos even sobered the *G.I. Forum,* which had openly backed LBJ's war effort; see *Forumeer,* November 1969. In "Population Control—Weeding Out Chicanos in Vietnam War?" *Forumeer,* April 1970, David Sierra asked why the United States should care about Vietnam if Australia did not. In the Southwest, out of 2,189 casualties, 316 were Chicanos. The article gave a good state-by-state rundown on casualties. An antiwar resolution was passed by the Forum during its June 26–28, 1970 convention; *Forumeer,* July 1970. A major reason for the change in position was the role of Chicano youth. See Ralph Guzmán, "Mexican-Americans Have Highest Vietnam Death Rate," *Belvedere Citizen,* October 16, 1969. Information about the moratorium is also from *The Belvedere Citizen,* July 9, 1970; Armando Morales, *Ando Sangrando! I Am Bleeding* (Los Angeles: Congress of Mexican American Unity, 1971), p. 106.

84. Morales, *Ando Sangrando!* p. 105.

85. In the spring of 1970 special units of the sheriff's department had been used to put down student

demonstrations near Santa Barbara. A grand jury investigation condemned the units' excessive use of force.

86. *La Raza,* 3, Special Issue (1970) features a photo essay of the moratorium, documenting police repression.

87. Putnam's transcript on file.

88. Morales, *Ando Sangrando!* p. 117, "Police Chief Davis Claims Latin Youths Being Used by Reds," *Belvedere Citizen,* January 21, 1971.

89. *Eastside Sun,* February 4, 1971.

90. Tackwood's conversation is on a tape in the possession of a colleague who remains nameless for obvious reasons; *Los Angeles Times,* July 27, August 18, 1971; *Valley News,* Van Nuys, California, November 27, 1979; Frank Del Olmo, "Provoked Trouble for Lawmen, Chicano Informer Claims," *Los Angeles Times,* February 1, 1972; *Los Angeles Free Press* February 4–10, 1972.

91. *Los Angeles Free Press,* February 4–10, 1972. Throughout 1971 there was considerable unrest in East Los Angeles. A series of bombings took place, with a group calling itself the Chicano Liberation Front taking the credit. Banks, chain stores, government buildings, squad cars, and so on were targets. See "Chicano Liberation Front Group Claims Bombing Credit," *Belvedere Citizen,* August 19, 1971. "Officials Probe, Seek Links in East LA Bombings," *Belvedere Citizen,* May 6, 1971; "Roosevelt High Bombings Linked to Series of Explosions in Area," *Belvedere Citizen,* June 10, 1971.

92. Moore, p. 64; Briggs, Fogel, and Schmidt, p. 5.

93. Briggs, Fogel, and Schmidt, p. 74.

94. John Mills Thompson, "Mobility, Income and Utilization of Mexican American Manpower in Lubbock, Texas, 1960–1970" (Ph.D. dissertation, Texas Tech University, 1972), p. 292; Rosaura Sánchez, "The Chicana Labor Force," in Rosaura Sánchez and Rosa Martínez Cruz, eds., *Essays on La Mujer,* Anthology no. 1 (Los Angeles: Chicano Studies Center Publications, UCLA, 1977), p. 6; Briggs, Fogel, and Schmidt, p. 64; U.S. Bureau of the Census, *1970 Census of Population: Subject Reports, Persons of Spanish Origin* (Washington, D.C.: U.S. Department of Commerce, 1973), p. 67; Yolanda Nava, "The Chicana and Employment: Needs Analysis and Recommendation for Legislation," *Regeneración* 2, no. 3 (1973): 7; "Some Statistics; Chicanas and Non-Chicanas," MALDEF 6, no. 4 (Fall, 1977).

95. Briggs, Fogel, and Schmidt, pp. 34, 36–38, 68. Castro, pp. 210–211, stated that nationally Latinos comprised 7 percent of the population, but only 2.9 percent of federal employees.

96. Lupe Anguiano, "Employment and Welfare Issues as They Affect Low Income Women," *Southwest Regional Office for the Spanish Speaking,* February 19, 1976. Also see "Chicano Rights: A Major MALDEF Issue," MALDEF 6, no. 4 (Fall 1977): 5; "Some Statistics; Chicanas; Non-Chicanas," MALDEF 6, no. 4 (Fall 1977); Alexis M. Herman, "Hispanic Women in the Labor Market," *SER News* 7, no. 11 (Winter 1978). Francis Fox Piven and Richard A. Cloward, *Poor People's Movements: Why They Succeed, How They Fail* (New York: Vintage Books, 1979), p. 264. In 1960 only 745,000 families were on AFDC and they received less than $1 billion; by 1972 3 million families were on AFDC and payments reached $6 billion. AFDC was part of Social Security.

97. Briggs, Fogel, and Schmidt, pp. 47–48.

98. Briggs, Fogel, and Schmidt, pp. 44, 53–54, 59–60; Moore, p. 60; *Los Desarriagados* (Winter 1976–1977): 6.

chapter *10*

The Age of the Brokers: The New Hispanics

AN OVERVIEW: THE ARCHIE BUNKER GENERATION

On January 23, 1973, the Vietnam War ended. The United States lost 56,000 lives, suffered 300,000 wounded, and killed more than a million Vietnamese. As in all wars, Chicanos, other minorities, and the poor suffered disproportionately. In material terms, the U.S. taxpayer laid out over $140 billion to achieve "peace with honor" in a war that should have never happened. In large part, the war ended because of the moral outrage expressed by many students and others, and because of the threat of minority communities exploding. Few at the time could have predicted that, in less than a dozen years, the country would move from intolerance with injustice, to an acceptance of poverty in "America" and the possibility of another Vietnam War in Central America.

Symbolic of this change is the television character Archie Bunker, who prepared the way for the Rambo of the 1980s. *All in the Family* debuted in January 1971.[1] Norman Lear, a man of liberal credentials and intentions, produced the series, which began during the twilight of the Vietnam War protest. Archie Bunker, a lower-middle-class hardhat, hated Blacks, Latinos, and Jews, and had a strong antipathy toward social and political reform. Lear intended Archie's son-in-law, Mike, and his daughter, Gloria, to ridicule Archie's outlandish prejudices and to make the audience laugh at Archie. In retrospect, just the opposite happened, as Archie gave bigotry respectability.

Like Archie, most North Americans believed in "American" principles and did not want to be bothered by facts. As the war ground to a halt, a backlash took place. From the beginning, most North Americans had never been convinced that poverty was the responsibility of society. Presidential advisor Arthur Burns, in the summer of 1969, defined poverty as an "intellectual concept."[2] Soon afterward, Nixon appointed Burns to the Federal Reserve Board. The Supreme Court also altered its approach, with the new Burger Court less interested in improving access for minorities.[3]

In 1970, Nixon initiated a strategy of courting the Chicano middle class. Knowing that his politics did not appeal to the masses of Mexican Americans, he promoted programs benefiting the managerial, professional, and business sector. In 1968 Nixon received 10 percent of the Chicano vote; four years later he captured 36 percent. After reelection, Nixon launched his New Federalism with renewed vigor. (New Federalism simply meant decentralizing social programs, returning tax monies to the municipalities and the states, and relying on the city bosses' good faith to care for the poor.)

Nixon also dismantled the war on poverty. He gave block grants to municipalities to spend as they wished. In 1973, Congress passed the Comprehensive Employment and Training Act (CETA), which changed job training policy. Previous programs had targeted low-skilled, unemployed, nonwhite workers; CETA included a better-off, white male client. The effect of CETA and other government programs was to reduce services to the disadvantaged, giving more control to local politicians and to the private sector.[4]

This policy shift was devastating to Chicanos; poverty, inflation, and a sharp rise in the cost of living worsened their plight, with the number of legally poor and unemployed increasing throughout the 1970s and into the 1980s.[5] The cause was corporate greed rather than rising wages. During 1969–1977, profits rose 25 percent faster than wages.[6]

An attitude developed among policy makers during the 1970s that unrelieved unemployment among the poor was acceptable. Since the 1940s the United States had been unable to eliminate joblessness. And even through the boom years, 1941–1970, the rate ran 4–5 percent. When it rose to 7–10 percent (much higher among minorities), the North American public accepted Washington's explanation that unemployment was natural and necessary for improvement of the economy. Meanwhile, as the plight of the poor worsened, U.S. capitalists got stronger and reaped higher profits.

On the international scene, the Arab nations invaded Israel on October 6, 1973. The United States responded by airlifting massive amounts of arms and supplies to Israel. The Arabs called an embargo of oil to the United States, Japan, and Western Europe that lasted from October 1973 to March 1974. As gasoline prices zoomed, the Archie Bunkers blamed the Arabs, although oil company profits skyrocketed and prices rose close to 400 percent.[7]

David Rockefeller, of the Chase Manhattan Bank, organized the Trilateral Commission in 1973, recruiting top business leaders, politicians, academicians, and lawyers from the United States, Japan, and Western Europe. The commission, a response to the disorder of the 1960s and the international turmoil of the early 1970s, represented a trend toward transnational business enterprises and world planning. For example, in 1960, 8 U.S. banks had foreign branches; 14

years later 129 had overseas offices. In 1960, the banks had foreign assets of $3 billion—in 1974, the figure increased to $155 billion.[8] This change would greatly affect Mexicans in the United States and Mexico.

Domestically, Vice President Spiro Agnew resigned in return for not being prosecuted for corruption when he was governor of Maryland. Investigations began into the break-in at the Watergate, the Democratic party headquarters. Confidence in government sank to new lows in August 1974, when Nixon resigned and Gerald Ford took the oath of office.[9]

The white backlash grew more bitter with the decline of U.S. prestige and shrinking opportunity at home. North Americans blamed minorities and civil rights programs. The Burger Court reflected the new mood. Twenty years after the *Brown* case (1954), the Supreme Court rejected metropolitan school desegregation. In September 1974, Bostonians rioted when authorities attempted to integrate Blacks and whites. A white demonstrator summed up the mood of the Archie Bunkers when he yelled: "The real issue is nigger!"

Meanwhile, capitalists became more aggressive in obtaining tax breaks. The recessions of the 1970s and 1980s saw so-called taxpayer revolts. California's Proposition 13 in 1978 limited taxation to 1 percent of the full value of the property, giving tax advantages to property owners who purchased before passage of the initiative. Proposition 13 represented a windfall to commercial, industrial, and landlord interests; it cut services to the majority and shifted the property tax burden to renters and those buying homes after 1978.

The business of "America" was still business. In 1976, 182 millionaires paid no taxes.[10] The Federal Revenue Act of 1978 gave a break to the wealthiest 2 percent, who received three-quarters of the savings. In 1945, corporations paid 50 percent of the nation's taxes. Their share by 1979 represented only 14 percent.

In 1979, the federal government guaranteed a $1.5 million loan to Chrysler. At the same time, the poor were shut out of the "American Dream" to own a home. Inflation that year reached 13 percent, and the Federal Reserve raised its prime interest rate to 15 percent.

In 1976, North Americans had elected Jimmy Carter to the presidency. In Texas, the combined Mexican and Black vote carried the state's electoral votes for Carter. His bumbling style accelerated the disillusionment moderates felt toward liberal programs. The North American public had no sympathy for losers, and Carter seemed like a loser. He harped on morality at a time when society preferred lies.

In 1979, Iranians stormed the U.S. embassy and took employees and visitors hostage, demanding the return of the shah who had fled the country. At the urging of David Rockefeller and Henry Kissinger, Carter had allowed the deposed shah of Iran to enter the United States for a gall bladder operation. Iranians retaliated and insisted that the shah be returned to stand trial for crimes against his people. Carter was unable to secure the release of the hostages, which frustrated North Americans, ending Carter's chances for reelection.

That same year the Nicaraguan people overthrew Anastasio Somoza, whose family had ruled Nicaragua, as surrogates for the United States, since the 1930s.

Carter supported Somoza to the last and only dumped him when he became a liability. Somoza's fall encouraged the liberation struggles in El Salvador and Guatemala. Again, the North American people blamed Carter.

In 1979, the last "American" hero—John Wayne—died of cancer. In his long career, Wayne had never let the North American people down. The Duke represented the two-fisted direct action that made "America" great, and the American ideal that everything could be solved through force. The Defense Department, from 1977 through 1980, had bombarded the public with anti-Russian propaganda to the point that it legitimated what the Duke represented, and many called for the Duke's way of handling problems.

These national and world events had a serious impact on the Chicano lower and middle classes. First, the nation's policy shift toward the inevitability of poverty and the maintenance of an underclass became accepted by both the private and public sectors. Unemployment, hunger, and poverty no longer shocked the nation; rather, they were rationalized as necessary for progress. The answer, according to the new brokers, was for more Mexican Americans to become middle class, setting an example for the poor. Second, North American society moved to control groups like the Mexicans by strengthening their middle class and giving the illusion of opportunity for minorities by celebrating the success of the middle class. Third, the world recession and the economic crisis worsened by international competition accelerated a restructuring of U.S. industry. Capitalists took their factories to less developed countries, creating domestic unemployment as well as depressing wages. As the United States moved into high-tech production, Chicanos, with and without documents, became more vulnerable. Fourth, the Arab oil embargo and the fall of the shah and Somoza unnerved North Americans. Xenophobia increased the demand for defense spending at the expense of domestic programs. Fifth, Chicanos suffered from the shift of personnel on the Supreme Court and its abandonment of the principle of educational equity. Lastly, society became less tolerant of protest as a legitimate mode of achieving social change. The private and public sectors popularized the rationality that change could be brought about through influence brokers. This transformation strengthened the hand of moderates and weakened the influence of progressives.

IN SEARCH OF *AZTLÁN*

La Raza Unida Party

Nationalism unified Chicano *barrios* throughout the United States into a movement. The 1960s had encouraged mass participation at a level heretofore not experienced. And for the first time large sectors of the poor and the young spoke for themselves. The emotionalism and sense of intolerance of the status quo no doubt resulted from the large number of youth in the movement—and certainly the times also contributed. And for a brief time the Chicano movement translated itself into a counterhegemonic force.

Activists concretized Chicano nationalism by forming *La Raza Unida* party

(RUP). They set the goal of brown power, the taking back of *Aztlán* through the electoral process. Even before the Chicano Moratorium to protest the Vietnam War, Mexican Americans had discussed the possibility of a Chicano party (see Chapter 9). On March 30, 1970, Corky Gonzales announced the formation of the Colorado RUP.[11]

The Moratorium hastened the nationalist process by bringing thousands of Chicanos together and strengthening their solidarity. Because of the moral outrage resulting from the brutal police repression of Chicano protest, talk of a national party became more frequent throughout 1971. In California, activists registered 10,000 new RUP voters, and the party ran candidates statewide. In July California State University at Northridge professor Raúl Ruiz ran for the 48th assembly district, receiving 7.93 percent (2,778) of the vote. Ruiz played the role of the spoiler, denying Democratic party candidate Richard Alatorre the victory; the Republican margin of victory was 46.71 percent (16,346 votes) to 42.17 percent (14,759 votes).[12] The RUP's moral victory put the Democratic party on notice that *La Raza Unida* candidates could give Chicanos an alternative. Alatorre easily won the next election, in which the RUP did not field a candidate.

By 1972 the Texas RUP registered 22,388 voters. In Crystal City, the RUP took over the Board of Education and swept city and county elections. Attorney Ramsey Muñiz ran for governor on the RUP ticket, accumulating 214,118 votes (6.28 percent). Republicans won the governorship by 100,000 votes.[13]

In September 1972 the RUP held its national convention in El Paso. Every Chicano leader with the exception of César Chávez participated (Chávez endorsed George McGovern). Three thousand Chicanos attended. Many wanted to field an RUP presidential candidate; however, the majority preferred to stay out of national politics.[14] A split occurred when José Angel Gutiérrez defeated Gonzales for the national chair. Although a symbolic show of unity followed, two camps developed. Two years later the Colorado RUP bolted the national organization.

After the 1972 convention, personal and ideological differences within the RUP banished any hopes of a third party. In California, cultural nationalism initially motivated many young Chicanos. With time, many became frustrated and sought other solutions to the class oppression that most Chicanos suffered.

Historically, Marxism has been an attractive alternative to members of an underclass as well as to petit bourgeois sectors seeking facile solutions. Consequently, in the process of becoming politicized, many Chicanos turned to Marxism for intellectual guidance. However, disagreements within the international communist movement affected this intrusion into Chicano politics. Instead of joining one organization, these Chicanos splintered into different groups that were often as antagonistic toward each other as they were toward the system. By 1973, the radical core within the movement had broken off. Others remained in the RUP and sought nationalist solutions. Often bitter recriminations followed, with former friends joining separate camps. A period of infantile disorder ensued. The end of the Vietnam War, in 1973, and the postwar recession and inflation worsened conditions, discouraging activism and contributing to a decline in popular movements. In this environment, much of the left coalition became unglued.

Meanwhile, in 1974 the City Terrace chapter unsuccessfully led a drive to incorporate East Los Angeles into a city. Unincorporated East Los Angeles included an area of 105,033 residents—over 90 percent of whom were Mexican. As in the case of past attempts, real estate, industrial, business, and political leaders conspired against home rule. They contributed thousands of dollars to defeat incorporation, which lost 3,262 votes to 2,369.[15]

The New Mexico RUP found it impossible to organize because Chicanos themselves often controlled the local Democratic party machines. State officials branded RUP members un-American, radicals, and outsiders. In May 1976 Río Arriba deputies shot two RUP activists.[16] Between 1970 and 1974, the Texas RUP seemed on a roll, winning elections in Crystal City and other small towns. In 1974 Ramsey Muñiz again unsuccessfully ran for governor. After this point, the RUP throughout Texas began to splinter and, by the late 1970s, it faded. Police provocateurs and an active campaign by the Democratic party to destroy the RUP accelerated the process.

The RUP's demise, aided by personality conflicts and internal power struggles, must be put into historical perspective. Minority parties in North American politics may, for a time, raise important issues and bring about some realignments, but they have neither survived as third parties nor brought about structural changes. The RUP did force the Democratic party to run more Chicano candidates and prepared the way in Texas for the electoral successes of the 1980s. In the end, however, the RUP followed the path of other third parties and died a sudden death. By the mid-1970s, factionalism ended the Crystal City experiment. By the spring of 1978, when Professor Andrés Torres ran unsuccessfully for the San Fernando, California, City Council, the RUP, for all intents and purposes, was nonfunctional.

The Road to Delano: The Uphill Climb

In the 1970s, while a majority of Euroamericans worked in white-collar occupations, Mexican Americans were predominately employed in blue-collar jobs. And although many Chicanos by this decade belonged to trade unions, the overwhelming majority worked in a secondary labor market that was not organized. This condition was especially acute among Chicanos, concentrated in industries such as garment manufacturing.

By the 1970s, farm workers represented a small minority of the Chicano workforce. César Chávez and the United Farm Workers (UFW) continued organizing workers in the fields of California. Chávez, more than a labor organizer, was a human rights leader.

During 1971 and 1972, the Nixon administration, heavily indebted to the large growers, supported the California grape producers by sponsoring a bill that outlawed farm-worker secondary boycotts and required farm workers to give ten days notice before striking. The bill set a 30-day cooling-off period before binding arbitration could be initiated. In effect, the legislation would have ended the possibility of stopping production during the harvest season.[17] While Nixon failed, the American Farm Bureau Federation sponsored similar proposals in Arizona and Oregon, consuming energies that could have been spent on organizing.

California growers pushed Proposition 22 on the November 1972 ballot. The proposition specified that farm workers could not call a secondary boycott. Many religious organizations and other liberal groups supported the UFW, and the people of California defeated "22."

In the summer, the Schenley Corporation, owned by Butler Gas and Oil, refused to renegotiate with the UFW and harvested its crop with the help of 600 small farmers and their families. Schenley lost a million dollars in an attempt to break the UFW. During this bitter struggle, police arrested 269 strikers. Secretary of Agriculture Earl Butz openly sided with the growers, stating that "such actions [the strike] should be outlawed. It is not fair for a farmer to work all year to produce a crop and then be wiped out by a two-week strike."[18] Nixon also backed Schenley and got the NLRB to bring an action against the UFW boycott. Although a federal court enjoined the NLRB, in the end the UFW lost the Schenley contract.

The Nixon administration then persuaded the Teamsters and the growers to cooperate. The Western Conference of Teamsters formed the Agricultural Workers Organizing Committee, and, in the spring of 1973, the Teamsters declared war on the UFW in the Imperial Valley. Teamsters signed sweetheart contracts with the growers and paid goons to assault UFW picketers. The Seafarers Union offered to help Chávez clean up the thugs, but Chávez, committed to nonviolence, refused. Meanwhile, the Teamsters brutally escalated their war.

The UFW moved to the San Joaquin Valley, where authorities arrested some 3,500 men, women, and children. Gallo signed a contract with the Teamsters, and the UFW posted 2,000 pickets. On August 14, a deputy sheriff inflicted massive wounds on a striker. Two days later, at Arvin, growers shot Juan de la Cruz, 60, to death. Violence escalated and even the Teamsters apparently had second thoughts. Its president opened negotiations with the AFL–CIO leadership to work out an agreement. However, Charles Colson, acting for Nixon, persuaded the Teamsters to breach the agreement.

In January 1974, as a result of grower negligence, a bus carrying strikebreakers plunged into a drainage ditch and drowned 19 men. State authorities did little to stop grower violations of human rights. Meanwhile, UFW membership plummeted from 55,000 in 1972 to some 6,000 in 1975.[19]

Many Californians were disturbed by the increasing violence on the part of growers. Under Governor Ronald Reagan, agribusinesses declared open season on farm workers. However, Governor Edmund G. Brown, Jr., who, unlike Reagan, was sympathetic to human rights, sat growers and farm workers down and pounded out a compromise bill. In May 1975, the state legislature passed the California Agricultural Labor Relations Act, which established the Agricultural Labor Relations Board (ALRB) to supervise elections and resolve appeals. The union was allowed to call secondary boycotts only when employers refused to negotiate after the UFW won the strike.[20]

The ALRB gave the UFW new life. Although the growers blatantly broke the rules and sided with the Teamsters, the farm workers clearly supported the UFW. In the first months the Chávez union won 17 elections to the Teamsters' 11. By 1975, the UFW took 167 elections to the Teamsters' 95. Facing overwhelming defeats, the growers resorted to illegal activities, like burglarizing union offices, employing labor spies, and pressuring their elected representatives in the California legislature to cripple the ALRB by refusing to allocate funds.

Forced to fight for its survival, the UFW presented Proposition 14 to the voters—a measure that would have taken the funding of the ALRB out of the legislature's hands. Confronted with this threat, the legislature appropriated funds to the ALRB. Farm interests then launched a statewide campaign, at the cost of millions of dollars, alleging that the UFW initiative threatened the integrity of the legislature. Proposition 14 lost.[21]

Farm workers had less visibility in other parts of the country. Right-to-work laws in Arizona and Texas frustrated organization. In Ohio, the Farm Labor Organizing Committee (FLOC) not only organized Mexicans in the fields of Ohio and Indiana but sensitized midwesterners regarding Immigration and Naturalization Service abuses. In 1977 FLOC, with the Ohio Council of Churches, co-sponsored a conference on immigration.[22] The Catholic bishops supported FLOC, which called a nationwide boycott of Campbell Soup products. Also strengthening FLOC was its affiliation with the UFW in the 1980s. This boycott lasted until the spring of 1986, when FLOC signed a contract with Campbell.

The UFW had been unsuccessful among Texas farm workers in the 1960s. Although Chávez wanted to expand operations there, his inability to secure his California base prevented this move. For a time, the UFW left Antonio Orendian in the Lone Star State. Orendian left the UFW in 1975 to organize the Texas union. But as the times worsened and the continual recessions swelled the ranks of labor, the Texas Farm Workers (TFW) became less effective.[23]

The Farah Strike

On the urban scene, the unionization of Farah caught the imagination of most Chicanos and Chicanas, as well as white feminists. Like the farm workers, garment workers occupied the lowest half of the underclass.

Willie Farah had plants in Texas and New Mexico; at his largest facility and headquarters, located in El Paso, Farah employed some 9,500 workers, 85 percent of whom were female. The Amalgamated Clothing Workers Union of America (ACWUA) had organized in Farah's San Antonio plant since the late 1960s. In October 1970, in an NLRB-supervised election, the cutting department voted to affiliate with the union. Willie Farah refused to bargain in good faith.

Locally and nationally, the strike was endorsed by religious and progressive leaders. In July 1972, the union called its nationwide boycott of Farah, which lasted for two years. In 1974, Willie signed a contract with the union, but continued to harass union activists. Meanwhile, Farah's fortunes fell. Recession, bad publicity from the boycott, and poor management all hurt Farah. By 1976, he began to move his operations across the border. Meanwhile, Willie closed his San Antonio factory. Slowly the workers' support of the union eroded.[24]

Part of the problem was that the union failed to develop indigenous leaders and continue the political education of the workers. The high point of the strike had been the leadership of the Chicana workers, whom the International never fully appreciated nor encouraged.

SIN FRONTERAS (WITHOUT BORDERS)

Mexico's Growing Dependency

The 1973 global recession made Third World countries more vulnerable than ever and profoundly affected North American–Mexican relations on both sides of the border. Foreign capitalists consolidated their control of Mexican markets, natural resources, and labor power. Mexico's vulnerability to foreign and especially U.S. capital increased as transnational corporations became more powerful. Beginning in 1970, foreign capital in Mexico doubled every five years. Investors regularly took twice as much out of the country as they brought in.[25] For Mexico, the constant drain of capital meant that its economy could not develop sufficiently to furnish enough jobs for its citizens.

In this context, respect for Mexico declined during the decade. A general demeaning of Mexicans on both sides of the border facilitated the acceptance of the identification of Chicanos as "Hispanics." The Border Industrialization Program (BIP) reduced Mexico to a sweatshop equivalent of Hong Kong, Singapore, the Philippines, and Taiwan. By the end of the decade, Mexico would gain the reputation of paying even lower wages and having lower energy costs than the Far East.

BIP contributed to this drain of capital from Mexico. It failed to generate industrial development, since the *maquiladoras* imported 98 percent of the raw materials from the United States and Japan. In 1974, 476 *maquiladoras* operated in Mexico. During the recession of 1973–1975, the numbers of *maquiladoras* dramatically declined. Mexico's weak position was demonstrated when workers attempted to bargain for better conditions. Worker militancy and the threat of strikes unsettled the transnational managers who, through the American Chamber of Commerce in Mexico, warned Mexican President Luis Echeverría to intervene on the side of capital or lose the *maquiladoras*. Meanwhile, Mexico was almost bankrupt. The International Monetary Fund (IMF) and the World Bank refinanced Mexico's loans, forcing the country to agree to an austerity plan that reduced the number of public jobs, produced more oil, and devalued the *peso*. Devaluation cut wages in half and revived the *maquiladoras* by doubling profits.[26]

The Singaporization of Mexico had dramatic effects on Mexicans in the United States. The flight of North American industry caused a loss of U.S.-based jobs and depressed wages. Many Chicanos had, for instance, moved to the Midwest in order to work in heavy industry. By the mid-1970s, a reverse migration from cities such as Detroit was underway.[27] The loss of electrical and garment jobs drove salaries down to the point that U.S. citizens could not afford to take these deskilled jobs. Consequently, the demand for cheap, pliable labor in North America increased the pull of Mexican nationals.

Interregional migration of businesses also took place, with industries moving from states that were unionized to right-to-work states such as Texas, New Mexico, and Arizona. This also had the effect of concentrating Chicanos in low paying jobs and increasing their insecurity.

As a result of the recession of 1973–1974, unemployment worsened and politicians, the INS, and the media blamed the undocumented workers. According to these groups, unemployment existed because the flood of foreign workers drove salaries down to the point that citizens would not take the jobs. The employers countered back that Chicanos and other poor people would not take the back-breaking work. In reality, the undocumented worked in a secondary labor market represented among restaurants, hotels, garment industries, agriculture, and light manufacturing. This work was often monotonous and/or arduous and required very little education, with few opportunities for advancement. Undocumented workers did not supplement the North American workers, but rather played a structural role in the U.S. economy. Theirs was work that paid little and that most North Americans were conditioned to believe they were above.

The Return of the Mexican Bandit

By the mid-1970s, an anti-immigrant hysteria was in full swing. The country had come full circle since the nineteenth century when the Mexican was stereotyped as a bandit in order to justify the maintenance of military forts essential to capital accumulation. In the 1970s, Mexicans again became bandits, blamed for stealing jobs. They were made outlaws in order to criminalize them, to justify paying them less and hounding them like the bandits of old, while at the same time demonstrating the pseudo-need to appropriate more funds to the INS. Many poor and middle-class Chicanos "believed" that the undocumented worker had invaded their land and taken their jobs. In the face of this hysteria, Chicano leaders witnessed their finest hour.

North Americans, in general, oversimplified the problem of undocumented migration. To them, aliens came to the United States and illegally consumed their resources. They had to protect their borders. Those defending the rights of the undocumented repeatedly pointed out that migration between Third World countries and industrialized ones represented a global phenomenon. In the case of Mexico, the migration had been accelerated by U.S. and foreign investment leading to the mechanization of agriculture. This process destroyed subsistence farms, uprooting Mexicans to the cities where they searched for jobs. Because foreigners drained capital out of the country, Mexico could not industrialize quickly enough to provide jobs for its people. This situation was aggravated by an emphasis on capital-intensive rather than labor-intensive industry. In particular, the heavy use of pesticides and the growing of crops for export rather than local consumption had cost workers jobs while providing Mexican capitalists with superprofits.

Bert Corona, founder of the *Centro de Acción Autonoma–Hermandad General de Trabajadores* (CASA–HGT), more than any other person furthered the ideological struggle against the nativists. Corona popularized the protection of the undocumented as a civil and human rights issue. Corona, born in El Paso in 1918, had been active in trade unions and civic and political groups since the 1930s. Foreseeing the revival of "Operation Wetback," Corona, by the late 1960s, built a mass-based organization of undocumented workers to defend their rights.

Liberal support came slowly: labor historically scapegoated the immigrant worker, and the Vietnam War occupied political activist space. CASA spread, establishing chapters in San Diego, San Jose, San Antonio, Colorado, and Chicago, claiming a membership of 2,000 undocumented workers. Along with the charismatic Soledad "Chole" Alatorre, Corona developed sympathy for the undocumented's cause. In 1973, under the leadership of Antonio Rodríguez, a *barrio* lawyer, *Casa Carnalismo,* the Committee to Free *Los Tres,* and the *Comité Estudiantil del Pueblo* (CEP) joined CASA. Two years later CASA shifted from a mass-based organization to a vanguard group. Soon afterward, Corona left CASA.

With the change in CASA, its members devoted less energy to organizing workers while operating more in Chicano, North American, and Mexican radical communities. More time was spent on Marxist study and publishing a newspaper, *Sin Fronteras.* The editorial staff included Magdalena Mora, a committed Chicana who had participated in the labor and student movements since she was a teenager (she died of cancer in 1981 at age 29). Because of internal problems, CASA broke up in the late 1970s.[28]

As Corona predicted, the end of the Vietnam War, in 1973, brought an economic recession and with it nativist attacks. In 1971, the INS apprehended 348,178 undocumented workers, the next year 430,213, and in 1973, 609,573. News reporters and scholars attribute this stepped-up activity, in part, to the bureau's effort to divert attention from internal problems—including rapes, prostitution, bribery, and the running of concentration-like detention camps. To hide the improprieties uncovered by "Operation Clean Sweep," INS commissioner Leonard Chapman, Jr., manufactured statistics to support his myth of a Mexican invasion. To save "America," the North American public should forget minor lapses and support the INS.[29]

The INS never intended to stop the flow of Mexican labor entirely. Powerful interests depended on undocumented labor for superprofits. Throughout the trumped-up invasion, North American authorities negotiated with Mexico's foreign minister Emilio O. Rabasa for a program that would export 300,000 Mexican *braceros* to the United States annually. Before any agreement had been finalized, however, Dr. Jorge A. Bustamante convinced Mexican President Luis Echeverría to meet with Dr. Ernesto Galarza. After the talks, Echeverría broke off negotiations, stating, "We cannot compromise ourselves in order to have a quota of workers every year. . . . The problem must resolve itself in Mexico. . . . It is the lack of land and water that has created the problem of *braceros.* "[30]

Nativists launched a legislative assault. In 1971, California passed the Dixon-Arnett Act, fining employers who hired undocumented workers. (The state supreme court declared it unconstitutional because it infringed on federal powers.) The next year, U.S. Representative Peter Rodino (D.–N.J.) proposed a bill that made it a felony to knowingly employ undocumented workers and placed penalties which ranged from warnings to first-time offenders to fines and jail terms for repeated offenders. Senator Edward Kennedy introduced a similar bill that additionally granted amnesty to all aliens who had been in the country for at least three years. Chicanos opposed the Rodino and Kennedy bills. Senator James O. Eastland (D.–Miss.), chair of the Senate Judiciary Committee and a large grower, killed the Rodino bill in committee.

In 1976, Representative Joshua Eilberg (D.–Pa.) successfully sponsored a bill lowering the number of immigrants entering from any one country from 40,000 to 20,000. Eilberg's bill was a slap in the face to Mexico, since, at the time, it was the only Latin American country sending more than 40,000 immigrants. The law further granted preferences to professionals and scientists, encouraging a brain drain from Latin America. Lastly, the law made the parents of U.S.-born children ineligible for immigration. Children had the option of being deported and returning when they reached legal age, or becoming wards of the court.[31]

The media molded this anti-immigrant ideology, legitimating the myth of the "Mexican invasion" by uncritically reporting INS propaganda. The press and television promoted the idea that the undocumented workers caused poverty, that they were criminals, and that they took jobs away from North Americans.

On May 2, 1977, *Time* magazine ran two articles: "Getting Their Share of Paradise" and "On the Track of the Invader." The press uncritically quoted INS sources that the "invaders came by land, sea, and air" and that U.S. taxpayers spent $13 billion annually on social services for aliens, who sent another $13 billion out of the country annually.[32] As absurd as the INS propaganda was, North Americans believed it. Thus these stateless workers, isolated from the rest of society, could be denied their human rights by employers who could buy their labor power at ever-lower rates.

Scholars played an important role in reinforcing nativism. They served corporate capitalism by blaming the undocumented workers for the system's structural failures. Rarely did they expose the fact that U.S. corporations and U.S. policy caused the migration north.

Their research facilitated the control and exploitation of the undocumented. Public and private foundations subsidized these policy brokers. For example, the National Endowment for the Humanities funded a Mexican specialist, Arthur Corwin, to produce a definitive border study. Corwin had little to recommend him; he was a Mexicanist but was not well informed about the border or Chicanos. Nevertheless, he received hundreds of thousands of dollars, giving his anti-Mexican migrant biases an air of legitimacy.

Behind the cover of pure research, Corwin launched an attack on Chicano scholars for questioning the role of the INS. Corwin, however, went too far and, on July 16, 1975, he sent Henry Kissinger a letter demanding action and control of migration from Latin America. According to Corwin, the United States was becoming a "welfare reservation," and if the trend continued, the Southwest would become a Mexican "Quebec." Corwin recommended that the president mobilize the army and Congress appropriate $1 billion to the INS, so that the agency could hire 50,000 additional border officers. Corwin also advocated the construction of an electrified fence. Fortunately, the Corwin letter fell into the hands of the Mexican press, who discredited him.[33]

Scholars F. Ray Marshall, an economics professor at the University of Texas and secretary of labor under Jimmy Carter, and Vernon M. Briggs, Jr., favored restricting undocumented workers. They called for fining employers as a means of discouraging migration and expressed concern that undocumented workers took jobs from Chicanos. They did not, however, consider the possibility that if, hypothetically, Chicanos took the vacated jobs, their position in society would in fact *not* improve, since the majority of such jobs paid below the poverty level. They also conveniently forgot that racism was alive and well in the United States. Instead they recommended political repression as a means of solving the problem. Like most advocates of employer sanctions, they did not adequately study the role of U.S. capitalism in creating the phenomenon.

In contrast, Chicano scholars—such as Gilberto Cárdenas, University of Texas at Austin, Jorge Bustamante, *Colegio de México,* and Esteban Flores, Southern Methodist University, along with Norris Clements, San Diego State, and Wayne Cornelius of the University of California at La Jolla—produced counterhegemonic studies proving that the undocumented worker does not burden society. They, like other progressive scholars, revealed that undocumented workers benefited society, paying taxes—Social Security and income—more than they cost society in social services.[34]

While scholars played with statistics, the INS committed flagrant abuses of human rights: in October 1972, border patrolman Kenneth Cook raped Martha López, 26, threatening to harm her two children.[35] In the summer of 1976, George Hannigan, a Douglas, Arizona, rancher and Dairy Queen owner, and his two sons, Patrick, 22, and Thomas, 17, kidnapped three undocumented workers looking for work. They "stripped, stabbed, burned [them] with hot pokers and dragged [them] across the desert." The Hannigans held a mock hanging for one of the Mexicans and shot another with buckshot. Judge Anthony Deddens, a friend of the Hannigans, refused to issue arrest warrants. Finally, an all-white jury acquitted the Hannigans. Activists on both sides of the border protested the verdict and pressured U.S. Attorney General Griffin Bell to file a suit. The Hannigan case went to a federal grand jury, which in 1979 indicted the Hannigans for violating the Hobbs Act, involving interference in interstate commerce (apparently because the undocumented workers had no civil rights). Another all-white jury in the first trial of the Hannigans was deadlocked. At a second trial, in 1981, the jury found the Hannigan brothers guilty (the father had died).[36]

As the economic picture worsened, so did nativism. Local governments made the undocumented a scapegoat, requesting additional revenues from federal authorities because of the increased burden of undocumented workers who overloaded their agencies. Prior to the late 1970s, Los Angeles police chief Ed Davis had stated on numerous occasions that undocumented workers did not present a problem. In 1977, Davis reversed his position, stating that he needed more funds because the character of undocumented persons had changed. The LAPD thus needed more officers (and administrators) to deal with the menace. In May, when

Commander Rudy de León of the Hollenbeck Division was asked, on an NBC interview, whether the character of the undocumented had changed, he emphatically responded, "No!"[37]

In June 1977, when the federal government was pushing the idea that undocumented workers took jobs from North Americans, the Carter administration certified 809 undocumented Mexican workers to pick onions and cantaloupes near Presidio, Texas. A flood of Mexicans streamed across the border in anticipation of receiving papers. Growers had refused to pay competitive wages that would attract domestic labor.[38]

President Carter, who called for human rights for other nationals, moved slowly to stop abuses in the United States. On May 13, 1977, Carter named Leonel Castillo, 37, INS commissioner. Castillo, a respected Houston government bureaucrat, stepped into an almost impossible situation. Because of his Mexican American background, it was hoped that his appointment would mute Chicano criticism of the INS and Carter. However, an individual cannot reform a bureaucracy. The agency in the end structured Castillo, who ultimately played the role of policeman, requesting 11,000 additional INS officers and a larger budget. To his credit, Castillo clamped down on smugglers. In 1979, Castillo resigned as a result of considerable internal criticism of his moderate reforms. After his resignation, raids increased.[39]

In the summer of 1977, Carter unveiled his plan to control the border. The Carter plan expanded on the Kennedy and Rodino bills. It offered amnesty for the undocumented workers and their families entering the country before January 1970; those arriving after January 1970 would assume a temporary nondeportable workers' status; it fined employers for hiring undocumented workers, allocating more funds for border guards and foreign aid and loans to Mexico.[40]

Chicano and human rights organizations attacked the Carter plan. They pointed out the difficulty in proving continuous residence for eight years. Given the INS's past record, could it enforce the plan? How was the government going to prevent unscrupulous employers from discriminating against all brown people under the guise of complying with the law? What prevented employers from taking fines out of the workers' pay in advance? Critics strenuously objected to aid to Mexico on the grounds that it would increase dependency and accelerate U.S. capital penetration.

Meanwhile, the INS harassed groups and individuals, attempting to protect the rights of the undocumented. In the spring of 1976, INS authorities broke into the Tucson office of *Concilio Manzo,* an organization that offered free counseling and legal services to undocumented workers. The INS confiscated files and arrested Marge Cowan, Sister Gabriel Marcaisq, the director, Margarita Ramírez, and Cathy Montano. The *Manzo* workers were accused of not reporting "aliens" to the INS. The case was dismissed.[41]

Throughout the 1970s, Chicano activists mobilized their constituencies in defense of the undocumented. Support came from every sector of the Chicano community and crossed party and class lines. In October 1977, José Angel Gutiérrez and *La Raza Unida* party held a conference in San Antonio attended by 2,600 Chicano activists from all over the country. In San Diego, over a thousand activists, headed by Herman Baca, Rodolfo "Corky" Gonzales, and Bert Corona, marched against the Ku Klux Klan, which had threatened the safety of the undocumented workers. In December, Dr. Armando Navarro of the San Bernardino–Riverside area assembled 1,200 community folk for a conference on immigration.[42] At the same time, many civil rights agencies such as the ACLU took up the defense of the undocumented, a trend that continued into the 1980s.

THE CELEBRATION OF SUCCESS: THE LEGITIMATION OF A BROKER CLASS

A Change in Type of Leadership

Organizational and leadership changes occurred in the Chicano community by the mid-1970s. The legitimation process for brokers became further removed from the masses, with government and private foundations playing a more active role in recognizing Chicano leaders. Brokers as such are not new. Clearly LULAC and the American G. I. Forum had received heavy government funding since the 1960s. In 1964, LULAC and the Forum began administering the Service, Employment, and Redevelopment Agency (SER). By the end of the 1970s, SER supervised 184 projects in 104 cities with an annual budget of $50 million.[43] LULAC and the Forum obtained these grants because of their Washington connections. In part, the growth of the federal bureaucracy, which made possible the government penetration of groups such as the Forum and LULAC, was based not only on the Great Society programs, but was also linked to the post-World War II expansion of the "national security state," into both military and civilian dimensions, with jobs and programs to be brokered. The 1960s only expanded the process.

The legitimation of leaders changed markedly from the 1960s. The 1967 White House conference in El Paso was one of the few instances in which the Chicano community did not allow the establishment to name its leaders for it. In this situation, President Lyndon Johnson invited *his* Mexicans, the people whom he thought he could trust, and excluded Chicano leaders such as Corky Gonzales, César Chávez, and Reies López Tijerina. Dr. Ernesto Galarza also stayed outside. At this time, the White House could neither isolate nor delegitimate the outsiders. The mass nature of the Chicano movement and the times guaranteed them a forum. Gradually, however, the process of legitimation shifted, with public and private institutions determining minority advocates. By the mid-1970s, although the heroes of the Chicano movement still struggled with the same intensity as they had in the previous decade, they were not as visible in the printed or electronic media or in the networks that constituted the movement.

After 1973, the priorities of the "Me Decade" also contrasted with those of the 1960s. Increasingly the rules of how to petition institutions altered, and militancy and intolerance with injustice were branded as rude and old-fashioned.

Well-educated professionals believed that they could influence those in power by negotiating for change. Like the rest of society, the new Chicano brokers accommodated the Archie Bunkers.

The brokers, individually sincere, hard-working people, believed that they were dedicated to their community. Their jobs and upward mobility, however, depended on the system and not on the people. Ultimately, these brokers ended up serving corporate capitalism. In most instances, they worked within the Democratic and Republican parties because the parties controlled access to the system. In other cases, they did faceless research for government or corporations that manipulated and exploited the community or served to maintain its subordinate status. Sometimes Chicanos acted as the token Mexicans for corporations or politicians. This broker sector came almost exclusively from the Mexican American middle class, which, like the white middle class, was the natural conduit to distribute patronage.

The Legitimation or Toleration of Chicano Republicans

Since the 1930s, Chicanos were assumed to be Catholics and Democrats. Many homes displayed photos of the Virgin of Guadalupe and Franklin D. Roosevelt with candles lit to venerate each in turn. To become a Republican was to commit heresy. But in truth, Democrats did little to deserve such loyalty. The Democratic party, during the 1960s, had kept its incumbents in office by diluting the Mexicans' voting strength, believing that Chicanos had no other place to go. In the 1970s, in part because of nationalist movements such as the RUP and partly because a growing number of Chicanos entered the middle class, the Democrat's hegemony was challenged.

In 1968 Hubert Humphrey received 90 percent of the Mexican vote. Analysts concluded that if Nixon had received 5 percent more of the Chicano vote in Texas, he would have carried the Lone Star State. As a consequence of this experience, Nixon developed a Latino strategy: "Their plan was simple: to woo Brown middle America by providing high administration positions and more government jobs to Mexican Americans and by doling out a bigger share of federal dollars to programs aimed at Mexican-Americans."[44] Chicanos for Nixon thus worked toward the "Republicanization of the Mexican-American."

In 1969 Nixon replaced the Inter-Agency Committee on Mexican-American Affairs with the Cabinet Committee on Opportunities for the Spanish-Speaking People, broadening the target group from Chicanos to Hispanics. Nixon appointed Martín Castillo head of the Cabinet Committee. Castillo resigned in 1970 when Chicanos voted heavily Democratic in the California U.S. senatorial election. By 1972 Nixon had appointed 50 Chicanos to high federal posts. The president recruited Romana Bañuelos, a Los Angeles food manufacturer, to serve as treasurer of the United States (1971–1974). In 1970 Nixon also helped form the National Economic Development Association (NEDA), or NADA, nothing, as it was affectionately called. NEDA was a national organization funded by state and federal agencies.[45]

The "brown mafia" played a key role in the Committee to Re-Elect the

President (CREEP). Alex Arméndaris of South Bend, Indiana, was its leader. The "brown mafia" fully expected to get at least 20 percent of the Latino vote and made it clear that if this did not happen, the administration would cut federal appointments and stop federal funding to Chicanos. Nixon received 31 percent of the Mexican vote nationally. After the election the president dismantled the war on poverty—this was a logical step, since poor Chicanos had not voted for him.[46]

In 1973 Nixon further showed his cynicism by appointing Ann Armstrong, an Anglo-American, to the post of White House aide on domestic Latino affairs. According to Nixon, she qualified because "Mrs. Armstrong and her husband own a large ranch at Armstrong, Texas, an area populated extensively by Mexican-Americans."

Nevertheless, after this point, the Chicano Republicans gained more stature within the community's organizational network. The administrations of Gerald Ford, and, later, Ronald Reagan, accelerated this process, which itself was a natural consequence of the growth of the Chicano middle class and the Mexican American voter population. As proof of this, the Republican National Hispanic Assembly, from 1972 to 1980, raised $400,000 to register Republican voters.[47]

The Containment of the Chicano in an Innocuous Wrapper

Meanwhile, the beer companies jumped on the bandwagon, distributing calendars with photos of "Hispanics" whom they celebrated as models for the community. Most of the new heroes and heroines were not activists but business executives, politicans, and political appointees—both Democrat and Republican. Newly formed Chicano and Chicana groups followed this pattern—celebrating the success of those selected by the system.

By the mid-1970s, the media and the public and private sector bureaucracies looked exclusively to the middle-class Hispanics to represent the community. Many new professionals had been alienated by the fervor and apparent radicalism of the 1960s Chicano movement. The term "Hispanic" appealed to this new wave of middle-class Mexican Americans. It was much more in line with their class biases and aspirations. The new Hispanic, in search of appointments and markets, liked the term "Hispanic"* because it packaged the Mexican American, the Puerto Rican, Cuban, and other Latin Americans in one innocuous wrapper. Credit for the revival of the Pan-Hispanic movement goes to the Nixon administration, which successfully popularized the term.[48] A master of organization, Nixon created one post that dealt with all Latino groups, giving conservative Cubans considerable power within this pseudo-coalition.

The media eagerly accepted the term—it was cheaper for advertising and programming purposes. Through repetition, the press and TV made the term a household word. A lack of a sense of history among Chicanos and Anglo-Ameri-

---

*The term *Hispanic,* like the image of the Mexican bandit, represented a return to the nineteenth century when the ruling elites made exceptions out of *los ricos,* dealing through them to control the masses. In many instances, *los ricos* were the Europeans, and the poor, *los cholos.*

cans facilitated the acceptance of the misleading label. Moreover, many Mexican Americans had colonial mentalities—cursed by the *mestizo*'s obsession with identifying with the European instead of his or her Indian heritage. In contrast, although middle-class Mexican Americans accepted the term *Hispanic,* the poor resisted it. A July 25, 1983, *Los Angeles Times* poll showed that 25 percent of Chicanos preferred the designation *Mexican,* 23 percent *Mexican American,* 18 percent *Latino,* and 14 percent *Hispanic.* This was after a decade of persistent propaganda.[49]

In the 1960s and early 1970s, the more blatant abuses of the brokerage system would not have been tolerated. Gradually, through the 1970s, protest was discredited and opportunism accepted as part of "making it." These years laid the groundwork for the Coors deal of October 1984, when so-called Hispanic organizations called off a boycott initiated by the Chicano community in 1968.* Over the years, both the G.I. Forum and the League of United Latin American Citizens had negotiated with the beer company in an effort to end the boycott. In 1975, the Forum reached an agreement with Coors, but the Forum members rejected it because of a recently called AFL–CIO strike against Coors.

In October 1984, the American G.I. Forum, the Cuban National Planning Committee, the National Council of *La Raza,* the National Puerto Rican Coalition, and the U.S. Hispanic Chamber of Commerce signed a contract with Coors ending the boycott. Supposedly the agreement made Coors a "good corporate citizen." The pact pledged that Coors, from 1985 to 1990, would return $350 million to the community in the form of advertisements in Hispanic media, investments in Hispanic businesses, grants to selected community organizations, and some scholarships. How much Coors returned depended on how much beer the "Hispanic" community drank.

Since Chicanos were the largest sector of the pseudo-Hispanic community, they would, of course, be expected to drink the most beer. LULAC's leadership at first refused to ratify the agreement because it linked the amount of money received to beer consumption. Coors, according to LULAC, had not insisted on the beer-drinking clause when it gave the Heritage Foundation, an arch-reactionary think tank, its grant.[50] Meanwhile, activists and trade union organizations such as the UFW continued the Coors boycott. Unfortunately, after LULAC elected new officers, the association ratified the pact.

The Gatekeepers to Idealand

Most brokerage situations were more subtle than the Coors deal. Foundations such as Ford have always relied on brokers, creating organizations like the National Council of *La Raza* (originally the Southwest Council of *La Raza*) and then the Mexican American Legal Defense and Education Fund. Although these

---

*In 1968, Coors's hiring policies discriminated against Chicanos. Moreover, the Coors family was ultra-right wing and they contributed to reactionary groups as well as donated helicopters to the Denver police, who confronted Chicano activism.

groups did valuable work and had some dedicated members, they tended to aspire to become clearinghouses for foundations.

In the mid-1970s, Ford pursued a policy of working through selected Chicanos and organizations and then discarding them, creating new leaders. For example, the Ford Foundation assisted in the formation of the National Chicano Council on Higher Education (NCCHE), whose board included selected Chicano scholars. For a time, NCCHE received Ford monies for postdoctoral research grants it administered. Later Ford downplayed its association with NCCHE, using another set of brokers, who aspired to become the new gatekeepers.

At about the same time, the Institute for Social Research at the University of Michigan founded the National Chicano Research Network. *La Red,* as it was popularly known, also aspired to become a clearinghouse for Chicano research and a broker for Chicano scholars. To this end, it established close contacts with foundations including Ford. Afterward, NCCHE and *La Red* merged, moving to Austin, where it worked closely with the Education Testing Service (Princeton). *La Red*/NCCHE finally relocated to the Claremont Graduate Schools in California, founding the Tómas Rivera Center. Its new director, Arturo Madrid, had extensive contacts with Ford and other foundations. He procured over a million dollars from the Carnegie and the Times-Mirror Foundations.

The history of these groups presents a paradox. Chicanos associated with them wanted to have an impact on policy. During the late 1960s and early 1970s, Chicanos talked about an advocacy research that was pro-community and unabashedly partisan to the interests of the poor. They criticized the abuse of quantitative methodology by Anglo scholars. Their new research would by more critical and would challenge the epistemological determinism of North American social scientists. In other words, they would be imaginative and not imprisoned by methodology. However, with time, changes in attitudes developed toward the role of research. Many came to accept their research as pure—with its own end. In many instances, the sole purpose of the researchers' studies was to acquire funds and resources for themselves. Their link to the community weakened. As this tendency increased, it became popular to regard qualitative methods as soft. This contributed to the decline of Chicano studies, which many Chicano scholars in private dismissed as too polemical.

By the mid-1980s, Ford sponsored another Latino group—the Inter-University Program for Latino Research. The IUP's scope and leadership included Puerto Ricans and a consortium of four universities. The IUP sought to influence and facilitate policy research on Latinos. It received sizable funds from Ford and, in turn, it became the gatekeeper, brokering grants to scholars it considered meritorious.* It paid for conferences for the recipients and other select scholars. While it is too early to predict the IUP's success, the commitment of Ford toward Chicanos has been uneven. Ford, for instance, does not employ high

---

*The selection process is subjective and often limited to a clique. For instance, José Angel Gutiérrez applied for a grant and was rejected. While he was one of the leaders of the movement, he has been excluded from the new Chicano Academy.

ranking Chicano administrators. As noted, it has a history of making and breaking its Chicano brokers. A basic weakness in the IUP's structure is that it depends solely on the whim of Ford and other funding sources. A more basic flow, however, is the gatekeeping system itself and its control of the direction of research and who will do it.

The Growth of Middle-Class Chicano Organizations

Literally dozens of self-interest business and professional groups emerged in the 1970s and 1980s. The California Association of Minority Contractors, the National Association of Bilingual Education, the Coalition of Hispanic Federal Employee Organizations, the Latin Business Association, the Society of Hispanic Professional Engineers, the Hispanic Bankers Association, and the Mexican-American Grocers Association, to name a few, all lobbied for their specific interests. The growth of these organizations increased the membership bases of the Chicano middle class and it reinforced an assimilation trend within the community.

By far the most attractive of the new professional publications, *Hispanic Business,* began in 1979. The magazine celebrates Latinos who have made it. Little is printed about the poor. And it does not criticize the failure of government to serve this sector. Its articles cover such topics as "Winning Federal Contracts." The new heroes are the political and business brokers who have replaced the César Chávezes as the new "Hispanic" leaders.

Self-interest conditions the form and the tone of the Chicano organizations involved in brokering. For example, the rank and file of LULAC and the Forum are community members who participate in local functions and have a history of supporting social change. Many local leaders are very issue-oriented. However, the direction of these groups is determined by its leaders who, in turn, often support North American hegemony even when it is against the interests of the majority of their own community. Over the years these leaders have built credibility with the establishment. Their own self-interest binds them to the system. They perpetuate a mind-set that is difficult to break.

For example, in 1979 Texas attorney Rubén Bonilla wanted to make LULAC more responsive to youth and women. Bonilla stated: "LULAC has led the fight for improved opportunities in a very quiet and dignified way. That approach has attracted the conservative middle—but at the expense of youth and women." Although he temporarily moved LULAC to the left, by criticizing U.S. immigration policy and Washington's intervention in Central America, Bonilla failed. According to him, many of the leaders were unwilling to lose friends in the White House and Austin.[51]

During the 1970s, the poor got poorer. From 1972 to 1982, poverty for Latinos rose nationally from 21.5 percent to 29.6 percent.[52] Government schemes to help the community become self-sufficient were no more than fads; they were celebrated, implemented, and then disregarded. An example is the economic development corporations pushed by the Nixon administration which had limited success, often serving the interests of a small clique rather than the poor. For example, founded in 1968, the East Los Angeles Community Union (TELACU), had through the years received generous grants from the United Auto Workers, the Ford Foundation, poverty agencies, Model Cities, and the Department of Labor. In 1984, it ranked as the eighth largest "Hispanic" company, with almost $21 million in sales, employing 138 people.[53] In 1981, the Small Business Administration investigated TELACU's subsidiary, the TELACU Investment Company. The SBA found numerous violations—heavy investment outside the target area, sloppy management, unauthorized salary and executive payments, loans to board members, and the fact that a former employee had taken off with a Mercedes belonging to the company.[54] In 1985, TELACU Investment surrendered its license to the SBA as well as $3.2 million in assets. What TELACU's cost-benefit ratio to the community is remains open to discussion, since the corporation has also managed projects giving valuable services. How much social change has TELACU effected? And can developmentalism really trickle down to the poor?

Does Brokering Work in Corporate America?

It is true that more Mexican Americans serve today on the boards of corporate America than previous to the mid-1970s. A small sample follows:

Tómas Arciniega	Carnegie Corporation of New York
Herman E. Gallegos	Pacific Telephone
	Rockefeller Corporation
Ignacio E. Lozano, Jr.	Bank of America
	Walt Disney Productions
	Pacific Lighting
Luis G. Nogales	United Press International
	Levi Strauss
	Bank of America
Edward Zapanta, M.D.	Southern California Edison
Vilma Martínez	Anheuser-Busch
Josefina A. Salas-Porras	El Paso Electric
	Gannet Foundation

Source: Hispanic Business (September 1985): 50.

These board members are honest, committed professionals who were chosen because they are Mexican American. But how much does their sitting on corporate boards help the majority of Chicanos, who work in blue-collar and service occupations? Why should they be any more effective than LULAC or the G.I. Forum? Or will they make more of a difference than Blacks who have sat on similar corporate boards for a much longer period of time and in greater numbers?

Lastly, corporate America changes people. Being Mexican and successful does not give an individual the license to represent the poor. Class and position affect political perspectives, as do life experiences. Many middle-class Mexican Americans are committed to the *barrio* because they themselves were raised in poverty. However, their children will not have the same background; many have grown up in integrated neighborhoods, and some are of mixed parentage. Their perspective, commitment, interests, and acceptance by the majority of Mexicans will differ from their fathers' and mothers'.

A gap exists between the political attitudes of the rich and the poor Mexicans. A poll conducted by the Southwest Voter Registration Education Project (SVREP) in 1984 showed that 71 percent of all Mexicans earning more than $50,000 (representing 3 percent) voted for Ronald Reagan. In contrast, the less a Mexican American family earned, the more probable it was that family members voted for Walter Mondale. According to the SVREP, the majority of Latinos earning over $40,000 no longer voted Democrat.[55] Mexican Americans are not unique in this tendency to vote along class lines. However, Mexicans differ from Anglo-Americans or Jewish Americans because their middle class is small and does not reflect the interests of the majority. Therefore, the impact on Chicanos promises to be negative if the gap between the poor and the middle class widens to the point that the middle class represents its own concerns rather than advocates the needs of the poor. This can very easily happen in U.S. society, where ethnic communities are encouraged to develop historical amnesia, and the middle class to forget the poor.

Reshaping the Political Agenda

Many Chicanos hoped that electoral participation would *automatically* improve political access for the Mexican poor. Previous chapters tell of the struggle against the poll tax, gerrymandering, and Democratic party nonsupport of Mexican candidates. The record, at the beginning of the 1970s, was bad. In Los Angeles, Chicanos remained unrepresented on the City Council and Board of Supervisors.[56] The situation was similar throughout the Southwest.

State	Total Number of Elected Representatives	Number of Chicano Elected Representatives	Percent of Chicano Elected Representatives	Percent of Chicanos in Total Population
Arizona	90	11	11.1	18.8
California	118	5	4.2	15.5
Colorado	100	4	4.0	13.0
New Mexico	112	32	34.0	40.1
Texas	181	10	5.5	18.4

Source: F. Chris Garcia and Rudolph O. de la Garza, *The Chicano Political Experience: Three Perspectives* (North Scituate, Mass.: Duxbury Press, 1977), p. 107.

The quality of Chicano representation was often poor. For instance, in Kika de la Garza's congressional district in South Texas, 25,000 people lived without potable water, and de la Garza "appeared uninterested in alleviating the condition." The congressman helped channel 90 to 95 percent of federal funds to support Anglos, who made up 25 percent of the district. In 1974 both de la Garza and Henry B. González voted against extending the benefits of the Voting Rights Act to Chicanos. Arizona Governor Raúl Castro, elected in 1974, spent most of his time supporting the state's right-to-work law and placating Arizona's conservatives. In 1977 Castro resigned under a cloud and became U.S. ambassador to Argentina.[57]

At the federal level, *El Congreso,* in the mid-1970s, lobbied Congress and the federal bureaucracy on Chicano issues. In 1976 the organization functioned as a Latino clearinghouse for President-elect Jimmy Carter. By the late 1970s, *El Congreso* faded because of a lack of funds. In 1975, led by Representative Edward R. Roybal, Chicanos in public office formed the National Association of Latino Elected Officials (NALEO). Its goals were to lobby, coordinate voter registration, and get out the vote. By 1980, NALEO had 2,500 members, with a potential of 5,000.

In the mid-1970s, the 4 Latino members of Congress formed the so-called Hispanic Caucus; by 1984, it had 11 members. In spite of concerns already expressed, these organizations played an important role in pressuring the federal establishment on Chicano issues. Roybal, for instance, pushed through important health-care legislation. The Hispanic Caucus as a group, however, had neither the muscle nor the ideological clarity of the Black Caucus.[58]

In 1976, Carter received 81 percent of the Latino vote. Chicanos gave him a 205,800 vote plurality in Texas.[59] Consequently, the Carter White House appointed more Latinos than previous administrations. Although the Latin population's growing size influenced these appointments, the appointees themselves were accountable only to those who signed their paychecks. Their positions gave neither the community nor the appointees any real say. The poor had no more access to power than in the past. Some officers under Carter, such as the special assistant for Hispanic affairs, a post held at first by José Aragón and then Esteban Torres (both from Los Angeles), had limited power because they could screen who could or could not see the president.

The most symbolic appointment during the waning days of the Carter administration was that of Dr. Julian Nava as ambassador to Mexico. The ambassadorship carried with it pitfalls, since in the last analysis Nava represented the interests of the United States. Expectations that a Mexican American could be any more effective than a North American proved unreasonable. John Gavin, a grade B actor whose credentials included the fact that his mother was allegedly Mexican, followed Nava. Gavin played the role of the Reagan administration's hatchet man. The fact that Gavin spoke Spanish and was presumably half Chicano was supposed to soften the blows.

In 1980, Carter's Latino vote fell to 71 percent.[60] Ronald Reagan then appointed *his* Mexicans to offices. However, no longer were basically committed human beings such as Graciela Olivares, head of the Community Services Administration under Carter, appointed.[61] Reagan's Latinos were conservative and, for the most part, had few links to the community. Nevertheless, by the 1980s, Republicans raced for the Chicanos' hearts and minds. The party played heavily to the self-interest of the Mexican American middle class as well as to the emotions of the lower classes. It celebrated the success of Chicanos whom Reagan considered legitimate, creating the atmosphere of a large festival. Anyone who criticized the festivities spoiled the *pachanga* (the party).

Moreover, by the 1980s, talk of a political alternative for Chicanos had been relegated to the lost pages of history. The political agenda of the 1960s had been reshaped with the political game played, not to establish a Chicano agenda, but on how to win in terms of numbers.

EDUCATION: INVENTING AN AMERICAN TRADITION[62]

U.S. education began with the invention of the myth that it is equally open to all North Americans, a myth that is rooted in the Euroamerican belief that North America is the land of opportunity and that if someone fails to make it, the fault is his or her own. The notion of equality, however, is in fact a contradiction of reality. Education is not meant to be equal. It establishes and perpetuates a social order, promoting the ends of capitalist production.

Within the Euroamerican schools, class struggle is regulated; society is neatly stratified. Schools, essential in a "pluralistic" society such as the United States, invent common traditions where none exists. U.S. public education celebrates the successes of North Americans. And when convenient, Mexicans are allowed to join the honor roll. In Texas, for instance, Chicanos annually celebrate San Jacinto Day, carrying flowers to those who robbed them of their birthright. The schools make good "Americans" out of students, instilling a sense of nationalism, often setting the native-born against the foreign-born.

Status of U.S. Education

Chicanos have struggled for the right to maintain a bilingual–bicultural heritage. This demand has been supported by the growing importance of Latin America and the continuous waves of new immigrants from Mexico and Central America.

In 1968, Congress passed the Bilingual Education Act. Title VII set the framework for bilingual instruction. In *Lau v. Nichols* (1974), involving the San Francisco Chinese community, the U.S. Supreme Court unanimously ruled that in the case of children who had a limited grasp of English, the school district had the duty to meet the linguistic needs of those children. If the district did not, it deprived the children of equal protection under the Civil Rights Act of 1964.

Lau v. Nichols encouraged the expansion of bilingual classrooms. By the mid-1970s, Mexican Americans believed that bilingual education was the law of the land. Bilingual education, however, threatened many nativist teachers and other North Americans who felt that it challenged Anglo institutions. They believed in the supremacy of the English language and culture. Their basic argument was simple: Spanish-speaking students lived in the United States and they had the burden of learning English; teachers had no such duty to learn Spanish.

As usual the social scientists entered the debate. Black sociologist Orlando Patterson of Harvard stated that bilingual education had failed: "After nearly nine years and more than half a billion dollars in federal funds . . . the government has not demonstrated whether such instruction makes much difference in students' achievement, in acquisition of English, or in their attitudes toward school."[63]

Patterson's work isolated bilingual education from the structure and purpose of public education. Much of the criticisms made of bilingual education could be directed at public education. If, after billions of dollars have been spent, some 50 percent of Latino students drop out of school and over three-quarters of twelfth graders read in the bottom quartile, then traditional education has indeed failed. In fact, less than 3 percent of Mexican students in the Southwest had been affected by bilingual education, and less than 5.5 percent by programs in English as a second language.[64] In contrast to Patterson's conclusions, Professor William Jefferson Mathis found that exposure to courses other than the traditional political socialization classes in U.S. history and government weakened the social control process and made students more receptive to other cultures. In other words, bilingual education subverted the purpose of U.S. education, which is to indoctrinate.

Although bilingual education was originally funded as a compensatory project, it was never meant to bring about educational equity. Proponents never intended it to assume the burden nor solve the problems of North American education. Furthermore, Spanish was not seen as an alternative to English. Ideally both languages would be taught to all children.

Bilingual education also challenged the "no-Spanish rule" that historically victimized Mexicans. Although it was no longer a *de jure* requirement, the U.S. Civil Rights Commission found that in the early 1970s some school districts still enforced the "no Spanish rule." In California, 13.5 percent of elementary schools discouraged the use of any Spanish; in Texas the figure was 66.4 percent. At the same time, the commission report found that 40 percent of the Chicano students in mentally retarded (EMR) classes spoke no English.[65]

Abuses by school districts frustrated bilingual programs. School districts often did not make a good-faith effort to hire bilingual teachers or to certify their competence. Knowingly non-Spanish-speaking teachers conducted bilingual classes with, at best, a Spanish-speaking aide. Moreover, the broker system favored friends rather than competency. And authorities allowed a bilingual mafia to treat bilingual education as a business.

For instance, Dr. Ernesto Galarza, the foremost Chicano activist scholar, opened a bilingual institute. Galarza, however, did not play the consultant game, and, in June 1975, Dr. John Molina, the national director of bilingual education, funded a group of his favorites to the tune of $1 million, defunding Galarza's institute. Galarza continued in bilingual education, but in a scaled-down capacity. In February 1977, Galarza's students at the University of California at Santa Cruz conducted a study on the effectiveness of bilingual education in the San Jose schools. Olivia Martínez, director of the San Jose Bilingual Consortium, retaliated and wrote to Dr. Angus Taylor, university chancellor, and threatened that Santa Cruz's student teachers might not be accepted in San Jose schools if Galarza was not controlled.[66]

Resistance to bilingual education increased during the Ronald Reagan years. In the 1980s, federal appropriations reached $171 million; five years later they were cut by 38 percent, to $143 million. In marked contrast, community support remained solid. In San Antonio 65 percent of the Mexican population surveyed thought that the federal government and the local schools spent too little on bilingual education; only 6 percent believed that the schools overspent on bilingual education. In East Los Angeles, 55 percent said that the schools spent too little, and only 9 percent disagreed. The survey showed that 89 percent of the Chicano leaders favored spending more money, while 2 percent did not. In San Antonio, 93 percent of the Mexicans favored bilingual education, 87 percent in East Los Angeles, and 96 percent of the Chicano leaders.[67]

Bilingual education programs also provided a shot in the arm for the Chicano community in yet another way. Through the grants to school districts, economic self-interest for a time countered nativism. Schools of education modified their curriculum and school districts recruited a small number of Spanish-speaking teachers. National Chicano groups, such as the Association of Mexican American Educators (AMEA), grew while new ones such as the National Association of Bilingual Educators (NABE) and the California Association of Bilingual Educators (CABE) were founded. Within these organizations progressive Chicanos battled the opportunists to set agendas. By the mid-1980s, however, the times isolated progressives and strengthened accommodationists.

Educational Equity

The question of educational equity must be considered apart from bilingual education. Most Mexican Americans, of whatever political persuasion, consider educational equity the most important factor enabling Chicanos to achieve social equality. Historically, Chicano organizations have demanded equal access to schools—more Chicano teachers, counselors, and administrators, as well as more academic course offerings and equal funding for Chicano schools. Almost without exception, Mexican American groups, regardless of class, have supported these goals. In fact, it was part of the strategy of middle-class associations such as LULAC to uplift the Mexican poor and make them loyal "Americans."

In spite of years of struggle, however, Chicanos had not achieved educational equity by the mid-1970s. While schools in rural areas of the Southwest had been desegregated after intense litigation, in metropolitan regions such as Los Angeles, Chicanos were more segregated in 1975 than in 1950. For instance, in 1950 the graduating class of Roosevelt High in East Los Angeles was mixed. By 1975, the class was almost totally Latino.

While Mexicans made some gains during the period of 1968–1974, after this point they slipped backward. The dropout rate again climbed. In 1974–1975, the percentage of Chicanos who had dropped out of high school was 38.7 among 20- and 21-year-olds, rising to 44.1 percent by 1977–1978.[68]

Many Anglo-Americans and some Mexican Americans blamed this lack of achievement on the victims, maintaining that equal opportunity did exist in U.S. education. "If you want an education, you can get one!" was a typical response. However, scientific scrutiny shows that the lack of progress can be attributed both to increased poverty among Chicanos and to the lack of educational equity within the system.

While a number of factors contributed to the poor quality of education available to Mexican Americans, the most obvious inequity was that predominately Chicano schools were not funded at the same level as Anglo schools. In Texas, for instance, Mexican schools in the 1970s received about three-fifths the appropriations that Anglo schools did. The state tied funding to teacher and professional salaries—since teachers in Chicano districts had less education, they received less. "In Bexar County, a poor 'Chicano district,' with five times less property value than the Anglo district, received less state aid per pupil than its wealthier Anglo neighbor."[69]

Chicanos went to court in pursuit of educational equity. Without it, access to higher education was impossible. In the first case, *Serrano v. Priest,* initiated in 1968, John Serrano, Jr., sued the California state treasurer on the grounds that his son received an inferior education in East Los Angeles because local property taxes financed the schools. Serrano alleged that poor districts did not have as much funds as the wealthier ones, and, consequently, the children were given unequal treatment. In 1971, the California Supreme Court held that financing primarily through local property taxes failed to provide equal protection under the law. In short, money determined the quality of education. Therefore, if equal educational opportunity was a right, the rich and poor had to be funded equally. The U.S. Supreme Court (1976) upheld the California Supreme Court's ruling in *Serrano* but limited its decision to California, holding that the financing system violated the state Constitution's equal protection clause by denying equal access to education.

In *San Antonio School District v. Rodríguez,* begun in 1968, the Supreme Court found that the U.S. Constitution did not include equal education as a fundamental right. San Antonio had multiple school districts segregated along race and class lines. The poorest, Edgewood, was Chicano. The richest, Alamo Heights, was almost all white. In 1968, the building of public housing units in the West Side spurred residents to take action. Since residents in these units did not pay property taxes, the financial burden fell on the district. Edgewood parents sued under the equal protection clause of the Fourteenth Amendment.

During the 1970–1971 school year, the state allocated Alamo Heights $492 per child versus $356 to Edgewood. In Texas, in 1971, the 162 poorest districts paid higher taxes than the 203 richest districts. For example, the poor spent $130 a year in property taxes for education on a $20,000 home while the rich paid $46 on the same type of home. In 1973, the Burger Court overturned a court of appeals judgment that found in favor of the Edgewood parents, ruling that the Texas method of funding was imperfect but rational and refusing to consider the question of race discrimination.

If the *Rodríguez* case had been heard in 1968, the outcome would have been different. In 1973, the court split was 4 in favor and 5 against. In 1968, Earl Warren, Abe Fortas, Hugo Black, and John Marshall Harlan sat on the bench. Between 1969 and 1971, they all resigned and Warren Burger, Harry Blackmun, Lewis Powell, and William Rehnquist, all Nixon appointees, took their places. Justice Thurgood Marshall summed up the importance of the ruling: "The majority's holding can only be seen as a retreat from our historic commitment to equality of educational opportunity and unsupportable acquiescense in a system which deprives children in their earliest years of the chance to reach their full potential as citizens."[70]

Chicanos throughout the 1970s attempted to lessen the impact of the Edgewood case. Although the state legislature passed equalization laws, these measures represented compensatory solutions, and therefore Edgewood continued to have fewer counselors, fewer library books, and fewer course offerings.

Meanwhile, the *Serrano* case had little effect. In larger districts such as Los Angeles, the Latino population skyrocketed during the decade. In 1970–1971, Latinos comprised just over 20 percent of the student population of the Los Angeles Unified Schools; by the end of the decade, they approached a majority. *Serrano* had brought few changes, because the wealthier districts still had better facilities and more experienced and better-educated teachers. Latino and Black schools continued to be overcrowded, and year-round schools in the 1980s were almost exclusively in Latino areas. The Latino school buildings were older; they had more students per square foot and smaller recreational areas. Thirty years after the *Brown* case (1954), schools remained separate and unequal.

Skimming Off the Top: Chicanos in Higher Education

Higher education was one of the few avenues open to Chicanos for upward mobility. As imperfect as they were, the Educational Opportunities Programs (EOP) recruited and retained more Mexican American students into the universities and colleges than at any point in history. More important, they created a mood among Chicanos that it was their right to attend college and to be part of *academe.* As a consequence of the early idealism and the openness of some institutions, a surge of Chicanos were recruited between the years 1968 and 1973; as a result, between 1973 and 1977, more Chicanos than ever before entered graduate and professional schools. After this point, however, enrollment plateaued at all levels. And although the Mexican American student population has doubled, fewer Chicanos are being admitted from the lower classes. It is much more difficult, moreover, to keep an accounting, since other Latinos, including Europeans, are also counted as "Hispanics."[71]

Early demands included the recruitment and retention of faculty as well as Chicano studies programs (departments, centers, institutes). Between 1968 and 1973, more than 50 such programs were established in California alone. By 1973, university and college acceptance of Chicano studies declined; a financial squeeze had forced cutbacks, and the ethnic studies programs were the first to go.

A paradox developed. Although programs were cut, recruitment of Chicanos remained a priority, since Anglo-American enrollment tapered off and the universities and colleges feared that a loss in student population would mean reduced allocations. During this period, EOP kept minority enrollment high. By the end of the decade, Anglo-Americans returned to the universities in large numbers. Correspondingly, institutional commitment to minorities lessened. National policy toward minorities changed as fewer funds became available for so-called minority programs.

Jimmy Carter, in an effort to appeal to middle-class Anglo-Americans, made the financial requirements of parents for loans and other forms of aid more flexible. Under Carter the annual earning limits were raised to $40,000. The president's gesture, however, did not significantly raise the total pool of aid available. This affected minorities especially, since most programs allocated money on a first-come, first-served basis, often ignoring need.

Government policy had also made Vietnam refugees eligible for these funds. Again the allocations remained relatively the same. EOP had to serve more students with the same budget. Lastly, Chicano students suffered as a result of recessions and inflation after 1973. It became increasingly difficult to survive financially as aid was cut, and more students had to work full time in order to remain in school.

The student movement shifted course during this period. At first, it was highly nationalistic, militantly demanding improvements in higher education. Students participated in *La Raza Unida* party and other community activities. By 1973, the students changed as the Chicano movement itself became less strident; the ideology of Chicano students grew more individualistic and fewer wanted to rock the boat. Even many former activists labeled the 1960s as the "old way"; in many states, divisions occurred as some students turned to Marxism. (The Sino-Soviet split of the 1960s encouraged the formation of numerous organizations, creating competition for the hearts and minds of Chicano students. These groups often clashed among themselves and with the nationalists, who remained the most popular current within the student movement.)

Damaging to the student movement were the party building efforts (heavy recruitment of Chicanos into the party) of the Socialist Workers party (SWP) and the struggle between CASA and the August 29th Movement (ATM). CASA represented a pro-Soviet tendency, whereas ATM was Maoist. Although competition between these two groups was the most intense in California, it took place in other states as well. The result was that factionalism turned off less political students, and, as a consequence, Chicano student groups declined in membership at a time when unity was essential. By 1977, CASA itself splintered and soon afterward disbanded as an organization. ATM merged with other groups to form the League of Revolutionary Struggle (LRS) and is today actively party building among Chicanos.

While it is true that Marxist groups, passing through their period of infantile disorder, contributed to the splintering of the Chicano student movement, it is also true that they have, for the most part, espoused progressive issues. Generally they published newspapers and literature and reported on labor and other community struggles, moving discussions to the left. Leftists also developed a framework through which to understand questions of racism and gender in relation to class oppression. Finally, they forced nationalists to identify the meaning of liberation.

Part of the identification process was a growing consciousness of androcentricism. As awareness increased among Chicanos and Chicanas, women often challenged men for leadership and won. This change did not occur without division, since many males were unwilling to surrender their petty privileges.

Nevertheless, increasingly during the 1970s, it became common to see Chicanas in positions of leadership in MECHA and other Mexican student organizations.

A growing problem for Chicano students in general was that as they approached the 1980s, they moved away from the activism that enabled them to succeed, and they began to believe that through their own abilities they had overcome the racial barriers that had excluded their parents. They started taking minority programs for granted.

The natural link between the students and the past was the Chicano professors on campus. In most cases, however, a gap resulted between students and the few Chicano professors at the university. The reasons varied for this alienation: many young Chicano professors faced pressures such as publishing and meeting the criteria set by the university for tenure. Others had never participated in the Chicano movement and, consequently, did not identify with students. More important, many Chicano faculty members became professionalized and often found student demands and methods of communication difficult to handle. A small percentage believed that their research would stimulate the movement and influence government policy; thus they felt that time spent with students detracted from more valuable work. In other instances, Chicano professors isolated themselves, becoming ideologues instead of teachers. Whatever the cause, the general lack of involvement by Chicano faculty proved harmful to the maintenance of a student movement.

By 1978, the student movement had significantly declined. The career goals of Chicano students had changed. More Mexican Americans pursued engineering, business, and professional degrees, while Chicano or behavioral studies were considered inferior as their market value fell. Many new students, in fact, rejected the term "Chicano." On the other hand, neither MECHA's leadership nor the more committed Chicano faculty were able to appeal to these ambitious students, who formed such groups as the Society of Hispanic Professional Engineers, the Latino Business Association, Chicanos for Creative Medicine, Chicanos for Law, and so on. Often these associations functioned apart from MECHA.

By the end of the 1970s, universities had lessened their commitment to equal opportunity. In order to divert public attention away from their failures to attract poor Chicano students, universities creamed the top off the Latino community, using Cubans, South Americans, and middle-class Chicanos to fill their recruitment quotas. The target became Hispanics—with less attention paid to the Chicano poor.

Statistically, educators pointed out that Chicanos entered college at the same rate as during the early 1970s. However, Chicanos and other minorities tended to enroll in community colleges, which were qualitatively inferior to the four-year schools. Few attended prestigious private universities until the 1970s, when the Harvards and Yales accepted a handful of the most qualified applicants. Financial aid made it possible for a small number of poor students to attend these elite institutions. But as government's commitment withered, the poor's ability to take advantage of this opportunity dimmed.

Those not matriculating at private colleges attended public institutions of higher learning. The state systems were tiered, generally in a three-level hierarchy, to serve society's different sectors. For example, in California, the two-year colleges served the masses. Ideally, they admitted everyone. However, they received less funding than either the University of California or California State University and Colleges. The quality of education was uneven. Often 80 percent of their faculty were part-time, and most of the instructors did not hold doctorates. Their libraries were inferior, their facilities spartan, and they had more students per classroom. Community college students who received financial assistance got less than their four-year counterparts.

The California State University system admitted the top one-third of California students. The CSU schools received more money than the community colleges but less than the University of California system. Their professors taught more classes, the libraries had fewer books, and students had fewer facilities. They had less Chicanos than the community colleges but more than the University of California.

The University of California system admitted roughly the top 10 percent. It was a research institution and supposedly admitted the best-prepared students. Since it had more money, prestige, and facilities, the quality of education was better. The students attending the University of California system received more financial aid and were more likely to enter graduate and professional schools.

In spite of the hurdles, some Chicanos were finding their way into professional schools; law, medicine, and the MBA programs held the keys to success and, at least, the illusion of power. Without access to professional degrees, the majority of Chicanos were limited not only to an underclass but to a petty broker status. Affirmative action had in part opened up all levels of education to minorities. But, as noted, by the mid-1970s the commitment to equal opportunity faded.

The *Bakke* case (1976) furthered this change in policy. It popularized the absurd concept of "reverse racism." During 1973 and 1974, Alan Bakke, a 34-year-old engineer, applied to 13 medical schools, which rejected him because of his age. A white administrator at the University of California at Davis encouraged Bakke to sue, since allegedly "less qualified minorities" had been admitted. Bakke challenged the Davis special admission program, initiated in 1970, that set aside 16 out of 100 slots for disadvantaged students. Prior to this plan, three minority students had been admitted to the medical school. A lower court found for Bakke, as did the California Supreme Court.[72]

The need for minority doctors and other professionals speaks for itself. In California, in 1975, one Anglo lawyer practiced for every 530 Anglos; one Asian for 1,750 Asians; the ratio for Blacks was 1:3,441; for Latinos, 1:9,482; and for Native Americans, 1:50,000. In primary care medicine, one white doctor practiced for every 990 whites; the ratio for Blacks was 1:4,028; for Native Americans, 1:7,539; and for Latinos, 1:21,245.[73] Bakke supporters argued that an oversupply of professionals existed and that service did not depend on the professional's ethnic or racial background. Admittedly, there is little research in this area. However, Dr. Stephen Keith of the Charles Drew Post Graduate School in Los Angeles conducted a study suggesting that the probability that Blacks and Latinos would work with the poor and minority clients was much higher than among whites.[74]

On June 28, 1978, the U.S. Supreme Court, in a 5–4 decision, upheld Bakke. It based its decision on the 1964 Civil Rights Act. Justice Thurgood Marshall dissented, stating that the Court had come "full circle," returning to the post–Civil War era when the courts stopped congressional initiatives to give former slaves full citizenship.[75] Justice Marshall's dissent proved to be prophetic. The *Bakke* decision gave the excuse to racist faculties and administrators to exclude minorities. It was the law of the land.

A CHALLENGE TO MALE DOMINATION

Many Chicanas conceptualized that their oppression was triple, comprised of class, race, and gender. Chicanas state that theoretically these issues cannot be confronted separately but must be considered as a unit and that they are of equal importance. However, another progressive school looks at sexism and racism as symptoms of the structural imperfections of capitalism, subordinating both to the class question. Research supporting both these positions promises to produce significant future debate.[76]

The current dialogue over gender owes an intellectual debt to socialism and anarchism, which, from the beginning, dealt with the women's question. It also draws much of its definition from the Euroamerican feminist movement that emerged in the 1960s, resulting from the contradictions of sexism within the youth movement. During the 1970s, an increased awareness of sexism in the Chicano community developed. As mentioned, groups such as MECHA changed in leadership after years of internal struggle.

As in the case of the Mexican American community, the approaches of early feminists ranged from those who reacted emotionally and often individualistically, to those who pushed the gender question to the forefront within the group as a whole, to those who accepted male chauvinism as natural. Divisions occurred for numerous reasons: in a minority of cases, some feminists engaged in infantile disorder, but, more often, male resistance to social change brought about dissension and disagreement.

In this context, the following is a brief overview of the development of Chicana organizations during the 1970s. One of the first activities among Chicanas was in a women's caucus within the Mexican American Political Association. Women found it necessary to form a pressure group to change MAPA from within. In 1970, the Mexican-American National Issues Conference in Sacramento sponsored a workshop on women. Participants at the issues conference formed *La Comisión Femenil Mexicana,* a group that was important in generating Chicana community programs. This event brought together Chicana activists who were frustrated by the lack of political maturity of many Chicanos in recognizing the equal participation of women. That year, local forums became more frequent—for instance, at California State University at Los Angeles, a Chicana Forum honored María Cristina de Penichet, Mexico's first woman brain surgeon, and Celia Luna Rodríguez, leader in the Barrio Defense Committee.

In 1971, the Mexican American Opportunity Foundation organized a Mexican American Women's Testimonial Committee, which other Los Angeles–

based groups supported. In May, over 600 Chicanas from 23 states attended *La Conferencia de Mujeres por La Raza,* sponsored by the YWCA in Houston. Some 40 percent of the delegates walked out, charging that the YWCA was racist. In these events, Francisca Flores stood out as a leader. She had been active in women's issues since the early 1960s and her experience brought the discussions to a higher level. An organizer of *La Comisión Femenil Mexicana,* she became the founding director of the Chicana Service Action Center in Los Angeles, one of the first antipoverty agencies exclusively serving *barrio* women.[77]

Chicana groups focused on the special problems of Mexican women. In 1973, Chicanas spearheaded opposition to the Talmadge Amendment to the Social Security Act, which required mothers on public assistance with children over 6 years to register with the state employment office and to report every two weeks until they obtained work. Talmadge made no provision for child care; President Nixon had vetoed a comprehensive child care bill in 1971. Again Flores and Alicía Escalante, founder of the East Los Angeles Welfare Rights Organization, led the opposition to Talmadge.[78]

During the 1970s, Chicanas more aggressively asserted their rights to control their own bodies. Prior to this time rape had often been treated as a sick joke. Chicanas now began educating Chicanos that rape was not only a sex crime but a violent one as well. Inez García, a 32-year-old Puerto Rican/Cuban who was raped by two drug addicts, picked up a .22 rifle and shot one of her assailants, a 300-pound man. A judge and jury in 1975 convicted García of second degree murder. A court of appeals reversed the case on procedural grounds. A second trial acquitted García.[79]

During the 1970s, abortion was widely discussed. Generally, feminist Chicanas agreed that the option of having an abortion belonged to the individual woman. They realized that after the Supreme Court ruling in 1973 making abortion legal, the procedure was readily available to the middle class, and they pushed for state aid for poor women for abortions. Within the community some opposition developed to abortions based on religious grounds, while others claimed that planned parenthood was a conspiracy to limit the number of minority groups.

During this decade, sterilization was also at issue. U.S. agencies in the Third World had routinely funded sterilizations since the mid-1960s. One-third of the women of child-bearing age on the island of Puerto Rico had been sterilized, and, from 1973 to 1976, over 3,000 Native Americans were surgically sterilized. In the Los Angeles General Hospital, serving the largest Mexican population in the United States, doctors routinely performed involuntary sterilizations. According to Dr. Bernard Rosenfeld, doctors developed the attitude that by sterilizing the breeders, they saved the taxpayers millions of dollars in welfare payments.[80] Moreover, the USC/Los Angeles County Hospital, aka as the General Hospital, was in the business of training doctors. Often physicians persuaded teenagers to accept tubal ligations and hysterectomies: "I want to ask every one of these girls if they want their tubes tied. I don't care how old they are. . . . Remember everyone you get to get her tubes tied now means less work for some son of a bitch next time." Some doctors bragged that they waited to ask for permission to perform the operations as the anesthesia wore off. Often English language forms were given to patients who spoke only Spanish. Sterilization of poor minority women became a national issue when two Black girls, ages 12 and 14, were sterilized in Montgomery, Alabama.[81]

Chicanas increased their contact with other feminists. In the mid-1970s they participated in the International Women's Conference in Mexico City. In 1977, the National Women's Conference in Houston brought together many Chicanas and feminists throughout the country. By now, however, feminism had become, like society in general, more "tolerant," and included women of a broad ideological spectrum; fewer students or activists were present in Houston than in Mexico City. Increasingly, moreover, state and private institutions played a role in the celebration of the success of middle-class women who promoted capitalism. Dozens of new associations such as the Mexican American Business and Professional Women's Association (MANA), as well as professional and service groups, were formed.[82]

A good example of the new Hispanic professional is Dr. Sylvia Castillo of Stanford University's Center for Research on Women and Gender. Castillo founded the National Network of Hispanic Women and published a national newsletter called *Intercambios Femeniles,* which focused on Hispanic women and their success in academia and business. By the mid-1980s, the group celebrated the successes of Hispanic women. This organization, considered the legitimate voice on Hispanic issues relating to gender, received solid funding from private and public agencies.

Although, as in the case of the Chicano movement as a whole, the legitimacy of Chicana feminist groups more often depended on the system, nonestablishment and often counterhegemonic currents survived. On the university campuses, *Mujeres Activas en Letras y Cambio Social* (MALCS) was formed in the early 1980s to promote progressive research. As with other currents, however, this counterhegemonic organization lacked the legitimacy of more traditional and celebrated groups.

THE DIALECTICS OF SPACE: COMMUNITIES UNDER SIEGE

Basic to the Chicanos struggle for equality is the land question. Throughout U.S. history the territory assigned to a particular group has been an indication of its wealth and status, reflecting its power and quality of life. However, no matter how undesirable a location may be, residents set down roots, form communities, and introduce their indigenous institutions and traditions. A consciousness of place evolves, and the people develop a historical memory that helps them survive urban disorganization. The siege of communities consists of planned deterioration: inadequate funding of schools and other facilities, the fostering of criminal elements, and the neglect of the infrastructure promote the ideology that the space occupied by the poor must be taken from them in order that business can use it more productively.

During the war on poverty, governments sponsored programs supposedly to organize the poor to enable them to reconstruct communities. The programs failed because the groups depended for funding on the very institutions they confronted. By the 1970s, the raw political and financial power of big business asserted itself. Capitalists reacted to the "excessive democracy" of the 1960s. This offensive of business against the left immobilized the latter and accelerated a backlash against the idealism of the past. Increasingly North Americans became pro-business and anti-minorities and anti-government. Under siege, progressive Chicano groups retreated to a political ghetto, attempting to rebuild the mass demonstrations of the 1960s.

This section focuses on the more spontaneous forms of movements and the Chicanos' efforts to preserve their communities by retaining space. El Paso's *el segundo barrio* had over the years spread northward, checked by Interstate 10. The Second Ward was a depressed area; Chicano politicians had historically brokered the residents' votes without giving anything in return. Housing, the worst in the city, consisted of a large number of tenements and courts. Its location, however, made the property potentially valuable.[83] Fortunately or unfortunately, during the 1950s, developers could not persuade the city to make the necessary reforms to qualify El Paso for urban renewal funds. Absentee slumlords vetoed the city's application because El Paso would have to implement zoning and building codes. Throughout the 1960s, residents unsuccessfully pressured the city to force the slumlords to maintain decent housing. The return of the Chamizal to Mexico, the construction of Interstate 10, and the building of Armijo Park compounded overcrowding in *el segundo barrio.*

By the 1970s, conditions had worsened. Under pressure, the city applied for federal rehabilitation funds with limited success. The city leaders again refused to meet federal guidelines. Renters and squatters, meanwhile, occupied a section of the Six Hells and built a tent city there. Tensions increased in April 1973 when a gas leak in a poorly maintained building exploded, killing seven.

During this period, El Paso's mayor implemented a Tenement Eradication Program, displacing some 3,000 residents, benefiting a small number of developers and speculators. From 1968 to 1974, *el segundo*'s population declined from 20,000 to 13,000; many feared the elimination of the *barrio.* Through the control of the planning commission, elites had final say on the development programs. It was in this context that a group of 1960s Chicano youth activists formed *La Campaña pro Preservación del Barrio* and literally declared war on the city.

When A. A. de la Torre, a slumlord, attempted to evict residents in order to convert his tenement into a poultry farm, the *Campaña* called a rent strike and occupied the building for eight months. The *Campaña* had a core of 10 to 15 members, most of whom were former MAYA and MAYO members. The core could always mobilize between 50 to 250 followers.

In 1976, El Paso elected Ray Salazar, a 47-year-old certified public accountant, to be mayor; he stopped the eradication program by refusing to issue demolition permits. The *Campaña* meanwhile pushed rent control. Salazar and the *Campaña* clashed. Salazar did not want to discourage investors by enacting a rent control ordinance and, therefore, proceeded cautiously. The *Campaña* attacked the mayor personally and a chasm developed.

The next year, under the leadership of Juan Montes, Oscar Lozano, and

Carmén Féliz, the group led sit-ins and wrote to federal agencies denouncing the city. In 1978, police authorities arrested the leaders three times in one week. During this period, the city made plans to redevelop a section of *el segundo barrio* into a parking lot for the Hyatt Regency Hotel.

Meanwhile, the *Campaña* made friends outside El Paso. The National Council of *La Raza* and the American Friends Service Committee helped members from the Southside Low Income Housing Development Corporation, which successfully applied for funds to rehabilitate units, receiving an allocation during 1980–1981. Compliance was, however, frustrated by the group's inexperience and idealism as well as by outside interference.

Simultaneously, *La Campaña* supported the *Comité Cívico Democrático*'s (CCD) strike of a 21-unit tenement owned by a California absentee landlord. Police arrested Mario Chavarría, and supporters responded by occupying the basement of police headquarters. City authorities threatened the activists, promising more arrests. A confrontation was averted when, in February 1981, Bishop Raymond Peña intervened and, with a group of Chicano business leaders, purchased the tenement.

The Rambo years marked the freezing of the *Campaña*'s rehabilitation funds. Despite human errors, the *Campaña* made history. Without the militancy of the members, most of *el segundo barrio* would have been eradicated in bits and pieces. Admittedly, the group often polarized the community, but the only weapon that the *Campaña* had was its power to persuade through disruption. In the situation it found itself, its strength lay in its ability to channel moral outrage.

Similar struggles occurred in *barrios* throughout the country. In cities such as Houston, a pro-growth environment encouraged building and attracted industry and developers by keeping taxes low, furnishing few services to minority communities, and placing few restrictions on profit making. On behalf of capitalist interests, minority housing stock was often torn down to make room for "development." As 1980 approached, however, groups such as the *Campaña* became scarcer. The impact on the Chicano would be felt in the future as communities were destroyed and residents scattered.[84]

JUSTICE USA

Justice is a contradiction because its purpose is not to bring about equity but to establish and maintain a social order. The justice system resolves the social problems that the state cannot solve. As the 1960s and 1970s saw a tremendous rise in the Mexican American population, the economic crisis caused severe hardships within this group. This dislocation led to crime and general unrest. Among North Americans, fear of strangers and apprehension over the disorder of the 1960s intensified methods of social control, which included the domination and repression of groups such as the Chicano. During the 1970s, police brutality set a pattern.

On June 23, 1970, Los Angeles police arrested Santa Clara businessman Hank Coca, because of a defective credit card. Officers severely beat Coca. An officer baited him: "You Mexican son-of-a-bitch, I wish you'd start running! Then I could kill you or beat the shit out of you!" In 1972 in Blythe, California, off-duty officer Richard Krupp stopped Mario Barreras, 23, after a chase; at point-blank range Krupp shot Barreras. The following year, Denver police invaded the Crusade for Justice, killing Luis H. Martínez, 20. Chicanos charged that Denver police dynamited the apartment. That summer officer Darryl Cain, while questioning Santos Rodríguez, 12, and his 13-year-old brother, attempted to frighten the boys by playing Russian roulette. Cain pulled the trigger of the .357 magnum, blowing Santos's head off. Cain received a five-year sentence.[85]

On September 14, 1975, chief of police Frank Hayes took Ricardo Morales, 27, of Castroville, Texas, to an isolated field and murdered him. Hayes received a sentence of two to ten years for the cold-blooded murder. The Justice Department, after community pressure, tried Hayes for violating Morales's civil rights, the first time since the late 1950s that the U.S. attorney general had intervened once the state court had made its decision. A federal court sentenced Hayes to life imprisonment. In November, Lorenzo Verdugo, 25, was found hanged in the Huntington Park jail (Los Angeles County), dead of a ruptured trachea, which could not have been caused by hanging. His death was one in a series of suspected jail suicides.[86]

In 1976, San Jose, California, police killed unarmed Danny Treviño, 29. In Oakland, an officer killed José Barlow Benavídez. The next year, San Antonio police allegedly blackjacked Juan Zepeda, 42, to death. That same year conservative Los Angeles City Council member Pat Russell pressured LAPD for a report on police shootings over the past two years. In 1975 and 1976, the LAPD had shredded its files, allegedly covering up its pattern of violence. Meanwhile, five Houston police officers viciously beat José Campos Torres, 23, throwing him into a bayou to drown. The state tried the two officers and found them guilty of misdemeanor negligent homicide. Sentence—one year in jail and a $2,000 fine. The judge waived execution. A federal court tried the officers for violation of Torres's civil rights. Again, the officers received a one-year sentence; a riot broke out on May 5, 1978.[87]

In May 1977 Hudspeth, Texas, county sheriff Claymon McCutcheon beat Juan Véloz Zúñiga, 33, to death with a pool stick. Arrested for alleged drunk driving, the defendant had been crying in jail for his wife and children. McCutcheon wanted to shut him up. Véloz Zúñiga did not have a record of criminal activity. In 1977, the Moline, Illinois, chief of police ordered his officers to stop every Mexican-looking person. In October, South Tucson officer Christopher Dean shot and killed Joe H. Sinohui, Jr. The victim had been driving away from a disturbance. A jury found Dean not guilty of manslaughter; an all-white federal grand jury did not prosecute because, the panel said, Dean shot at the tires.[88]

Frustrations increased throughout the 1970s. In 1972, Ricardo Chávez Ortiz, 36, an immigrant father of eight children, skyjacketed a Frontier Airlines plane over New Mexico with an unloaded .22. His only demand was to talk to the media. *Los Angeles Times* reporter Frank Del Olmo wrote:

> No other hijacker has demanded and gotten what the 36-year-old Mexican national did—live broadcast time in which to voice the frustrations of a man who feared the world would not listen to his problems, and those of his people, under any circumstances.

Chávez Ortiz spoke for 35 minutes in Spanish over radio station KWKW and KMEX-TV. Chávez Ortiz received a life sentence. He remained in jail until 1978, when he apologized and left for Mexico. Chávez Ortiz served twice the time of a rapist or armed robber, three times the sentence of a Watergate conspirator, and more time than the murderer of Santos Rodríguez.[89]

Breakdowns in the justice system were often based on race and class. The case of Gordon Castillo Hall, 16, proved that the Sleepy Lagoon trial of 1942 was not just a thing of the past (see Chapter 8). In 1978, in Duarte, California, a gang member shot at postal officer Jesse Ortiz and his two stepbrothers, killing Ortiz. Los Angeles sheriff's deputies raided a party, arresting Gordon Castillo Hall, dragging him in front of a makeshift lineup with squad car lights shining in Castillo Hall's face. The Laras, Ortiz's half brothers, contradicted an earlier description of the murderer and identified Castillo Hall, who was much smaller than the suspect.

The trial proved a farce. The Pasadena attorney defending Castillo Hall did not conduct a proper pretrial investigation, nor did he call witnesses to prove that Castillo Hall had not been at the scene of the crime. The judge allowed expert testimony documenting the so-called violent nature of Mexican gang members toward Black and white gang members. The prosecution underscored that Castillo Hall, a Mexican, had belonged to a gang.

Bertha Castillo Hall, Gordon's mother, sold her home to pay for the trial attorney. Convinced of her son's innocence, she approached Chicano attorney Ricardo Cruz, who agreed to take the appeal. With no money for expenses, the Committee to free Gordon Castillo Hall raised over $60,000 for legal fees.

Many Duarte residents knew the murderer but had been afraid to testify in open court. The Laras now told authorities that they were sure that they had made a mistake in identifying Castillo Hall. The investigating deputies, in the light of the new evidence, urged that the case be reopened. However, the trial judge and District Attorney John Van DeKamp, running for state attorney general, refused.

Cruz filed a motion of habeas corpus. After several years, the state Supreme Court appointed a referee to investigate the case. The referee recommended a reopening of the case: he cited an overzealous district attorney, trial errors, and an incompetent defense. Castillo Hall was released. The D.A. did not refile. Castillo Hall, now 20, simply said, "They took my youth."[90]

The full impact of police surveillance and provocateuring on the movement has not been fully studied. Documents obtained under the Freedom of Information Act suggests the extent of federal activity. Almost no evidence is available on local police spying. The American Civil Liberties Union in 1978 filed one of the few cases involving local police, *CAPA* (Committee Against Police Abuse) *v. Los Angeles Police Department.* Some 141 plaintiffs, individuals, and groups went to court in an attempt to restrain police infiltration of political organizations.

During a lengthy suit, the ACLU discovered evidence of extensive police spying, ranging from a police officer living with a woman for seven years and having a child with her in the process of conducting surveillance of her friends, to officers enrolling in Chicano studies classes at California State University at Northridge. The target Chicano groups included *La Raza Unida* party, CASA, and the Cal State Northridge chapter of MECHA. Two identified undercover officers, Augie Moreno and José Ramírez, attended Chicano studies classes at CSUN, and at least two other officers and some six paid informants spied on MECHA Northridge and professors, from 1971 to 1978. During this period, campus police cooperated with the Los Angeles police; campus officers wiretapped a statewide MECHA conference at Northridge for the LAPD in the early 1970s.

Pretrial discovery found that Los Angeles Police Department detective Jay Paul, when ordered to destroy files, stored them in his garage, later giving them to the right-wing Western Goals Foundation, which logged them. The City of Los Angeles, after spending about $3 million, finally settled the LAPD case for $1.9 million.

The ACLU, in debt to the tune of almost a million dollars, was almost bankrupted by *CAPA v. LAPD.* Los Angeles City hired the high-powered firm of Gibson, Dunn & Crutcher, paying them $300,000 a month to defend the LAPD. A negotiated settlement included extensive guidelines that called for outside monitoring of the LAPD, and the court set up an audit committee to conduct the audit. For the first time, the court ordered the police department not to investigate private individuals or groups "without reasonable and articulated suspicion." The majority of the plaintiffs had felt that going to trial would not produce more constraints on police surveillance. While the plaintiffs agreed that responsibility for spying went all the way to Chief Darryl Gates, they realized that the system would protect him. A minority of the plaintiffs wanted to continue the case in order to discover more about the activities of the police. All acquiesced to settling the case, however, because of the ACLU's financial condition. Justice is not cheap in "America."[91]

The federal government through the Law Enforcement Assistance Administration (LEAA) distributed $4 billion from the late 1960s to 1979. The funds modernized local police units and coordinated data gathered from them. In many instances statistics were used not to prevent crime but to control critics. The publication of crime data, and the negative stereotypes played up in the media, often alarmed residents, increasing fear of minorities. LEAA funds also went to Chicano organizations such as the National Council of *La Raza*'s *Acción Local Anti-Crimén.*

Crime itself became a larger concern for *barrio* dwellers—for, as poverty increased, so did crime. A Southwest Voter Registration Education Project survey in 1982 showed that East Los Angeles residents considered crime the area's number one problem. Drugs were a major problem, with Chicano inmates two and one-half times more likely to be in jail for drugs than Blacks and three and one-half times more likely than whites. Little effort was spent on rehabilitation. Instead, drug victims were warehoused in the same prisons as those commiting violent crimes. Prison conditions worsened and tensions within the prisons often reached the crisis level. For example, the Santa Fe, New Mexico, prison riots of February 2 and 3, 1980, cost 33 lives.[92]

SUMMARY

The mood of the country changed rapidly in the 1970s, from one of intolerance of the establishment to a severe backlash against the poor and the minorities. The shift facilitated the dismantling of the civil rights gains of the 1960s. During the decade, government and industry created a pro-business attitude and moved toward greater control of "foreigners" at home and abroad.

Nixon initiated a policy of wooing the Mexican American middle class, sowing the seeds for a change from the designation *Chicano* to *Hispanic*. This middle sector widened considerably since World War II. Even prior to the 1960s, the establishment had recognized LULAC and the G.I. Forum as legitimate representatives of the community. In the 1970s, Anglo recognition broadened to include the professional and business groups, which sought to stifle the more strident voices of the 1960s.

The acceptance of the brokerage system did not come automatically; it was a slow process, resisted by progressive elements within even the most established groups. The mood change was not absolute, and Chicano activists of every ideological and class persuasion supported key issues such as bilingual education, educational equity, affirmative action, immigration, and the farm workers' struggle. Only the more opportunistic "Hispanics" opposed the Chicano agenda on these bread and butter issues. In general, the masses lagged behind the leadership on these questions.

The 1970s saw a grinding away of the Chicano middle class, which had been largely made up of industrial workers belonging to trade unions. Labor in general became more vulnerable during these times of economic crisis, as capitalists restructured and strengthened their hold. Transnational corporations became more common; North American companies moved their operations overseas in search of greater profits.

The world recession accelerated the northward migration to the United States. As the numbers of Mexicans increased, Anglo-American fears that these brown people would become permanent residents and change Euroamerican culture and national origins intensified. In response, nativists pressured government to initiate greater control over the "alien" population.

By the end of the decade, an all-out war had been declared against bilingual education and educational equity. During the late 1960s, in an effort to showcase educational equity, colleges and universities recruited large numbers of Mexican Americans. By the mid-1970s, surpluses occurred in the professions such as law, medicine, and teaching; this produced a backlash against affirmative action admission to professional schools. Suddenly, everyone was "American" and the pseudo-argument was made that society had too many doctors, lawyers, and teachers. The *Bakke* case (1976) marked the end of government policy to integrate the poor.

On the university and college campuses a marked decrease in interest in Chicano studies took place. For all their failings, Chicano studies had been a progressive force in mounting a counterhegemonic force and in keeping a Chicano agenda alive. The decline in the number and size of Chicano studies parallels the decline of student activism, which, among other reasons, decreased as left-wing party building contributed to student confusion, disillusionment, and factionalism. The times were also a factor in the change in student priorities. No longer were social issues as important as acquiring marketable skills.

Chicano awareness of the oppressive effects of sexism increased. Mexican women took leadership roles in most groups. Like mainstream Chicano groups, Chicana organizations were predominately middle class. In general, the counter-hegemonic forces within the movement became less strident as the 1980s approached. By the end of the decade, Chicanos were largely urban, concentrated mostly in the older sections of the cities. For the most part, they were renters, vulnerable to unscrupulous landlords. Justice remained a contradiction during the decade, with a pattern of police violence toward Chicanos repeating that of previous decades. A resurrection of the stereotype of the Mexican bandit justified repression of U.S.- and foreign-born Mexicans. Agencies such as local police and the INS justified larger budgets.

NOTES

1. For an excellent treatment of *All in the Family* and its impact, see Richard P. Adler, ed., *All in the Family: A Critical Appraisal* (New York: Praeger, 1979).
2. Michael Harrington, *The Other America: Poverty in the United States* (Baltimore: Penguin Books, 1963), p. x.
3. George Mowry and Blaine A. Brownell, *The Urban Nation 1920–1980,* Rev. ed. (New York: Hill and Wang, 1981), p. 311.
4. Grace A. Franklin and Randall B. Ripley, *C.E.T.A.: Politics and Policy, 1973–1982* (Knoxville: University of Tennessee Press, 1984), pp. 12, 67, 120.
5. Howard Zinn, *A People's History of the United States* (New York: Harper Colophon Books, 1980), p. 545.
6. Michael Parenti, *Democracy for the Few,* 3rd ed. (New York: St. Martin's Press, 1980), p. 15.
7. Zinn, p. 536.
8. Zinn, p. 549.
9. Zinn, pp. 536–537, 560.
10. Parenti, pp. 95–96.
11. Christine Marín, *A Spokesman of the Mexican American Movement: Rodolfo "Corky" Gonzales and the Fight for Chicano Liberation, 1966–1972* (San Francisco: R & E Research Associates, 1977), p. 17.
12. Richard Santillán, *La Raza Unida* (Los Angeles: Tlaquila, 1973), pp. 84–86.
13. Tony Castro, *Chicano Power: The Emergence of Mexican Americans* (New York: Saturday Review Press, 1974), pp. 21–33; John Staples Shockley, *Chicano Revolt in a Texas Town* (Notre Dame, Ind.: University of Notre Dame Press, 1974), pp. 202–203.
14. "Raza Unida Party Enters Presidential Politics," *Arizona Republic,* September 2, 1972; "Raza Unida Urges Bilingual Education, Stays Neutral on President," *Arizona Republic,* September 4, 1972; "Raza Unida Vows Fight for Self-determination," *Arizona Republic,* September 5, 1972; Marín, p. 29.
15. Jorge García, "Incorporation of East Los Angeles 1974, Part One," *La Raza Magazine* (Summer 1977): 29–33. See also Frank Del Olmo, "Early Returns Show East L.A. Incorporation Measure Failing," *Los Angeles Times,* November 6, 1974; "L.A.'s Huge Chicano Section Divided by Social Prejudice and Freeways," *Arizona Republic,* November 28, 1974; Frank Del Olmo, "Defeat of

East L.A. Plan Laid to Fear of High Property Tax," *Los Angeles Times,* November 7, 1974; another dimension is that some Chicano organizations such as TELACU supported home rule in an effort to control the development of ELA through a more sympathetic municipal government.

16. "Man Shot; 2 Arrested in La Raza Incident," *Albuquerque Journal,* May 22, 1976.

17. Ronald B. Taylor, *Chavez and the Farm Workers* (Boston: Beacon Press, 1975), p. 278.

18. Quoted in Taylor, p. 289.

19. Harry Bernstein and Frank Del Olmo, "Picketing Resumed at Vineyards as Harvest Speeds Up," *Los Angeles Times,* June 5, 1973, and "Teamsters Hit Use of Guards by Farm Workers," *Los Angeles Times,* June 12, 1973; Taylor, pp. 296–303; 314–315; *Los Angeles Times,* June 24, 1973; Frank Del Olmo, "30 Teamsters Arrested After Battle at Ranch, Four UFW Members Hospitalized," *Los Angeles Times,* June 24, 1973; Frank Del Olmo, "450 Arrested in Kern County Farm Dispute," *Los Angeles Times,* July 19, 1973, Frank Del Olmo and Tom Paegel, "Chavez Picket Shot to Death in Violence near Bakersfield," *Los Angeles Times,* August 17, 1973; Frank Del Olmo, "Farm Union Halt? Picketing; Rites Held for Striker," *Los Angeles Times,* August 18, 1973; Harry Bernstein, "Peace Talks Collapse in Grape Strike Dispute," *Los Angeles Times,* August 11, 1973. The following series of articles document a pattern of Teamster duplicity: Harry Bernstein, "Teamsters-Farm Union Partial Cease-Fire Seen," *Los Angeles Times,* August 9, 1973; Frank Del Olmo, "Teamsters Void Contracts with Delano Growers," *Los Angeles Times,* August 22, 1973; "Teamsters Allow Chavez Free Hand with Farm Labor," *Arizona Republic,* September 29, 1973; Harry Bernstein and Frank Del Olmo, "Chavez Union, Teamsters End Long Fight, Agree on Treaty," *Los Angeles Times,* September 28, 1973; "U.S. Threatens to Sue Teamsters, Truckers," *Los Angeles Times* October 31, 1973; Harry Bernstein, "Hoped for Teamsters-Chavez Union Peace Pact Hits Snag," *Los Angeles Times,* October 16, 1973; and Harry Bernstein, "Teamsters Break Chavez Peace Promise—Meany," *Los Angeles Times,* November 17, 1973. For material on the fatal bus accident, see Frank Del Olmo, "Pablo Torres: Farm Work Gave Him a Life—and Took It," *Los Angeles Times,* January 26, 1974; Paul Houston, "Flimsy Seats on Bus Blamed for High Death Toll," *Los Angeles Times,* February 8, 1974; César Chávez, "Chavez Blames Fatal Bus on Greed," *Los Angeles Times,* February 11, 1974; *Los Angeles Times,* March 9, 1974; *Time* (May 19, 1975).

20. "A Boost for Chavez," *Newsweek* (May 26, 1975); "California Compromise," *Time* (May 19, 1975).

21. For articles on ALRB elections, see "Chavez vs. the Teamsters: Farm Workers' Historic Vote," *U.S. News & World Report* (September 22, 1975): 82–83; *U.S. News & World Report* (September 22, 1975): 82. See César Chávez, "Why the Farm Labor Act Isn't Working," *Los Angeles Times,* November 17, 1975, for Chávez's side. See Lloyd Evenland, "Why the Farm Labor Act Isn't Working," *Los Angeles Times,* November 17, 1975, for the growers' side. "Strengthening the Farm Board," *Los Angeles Times,* January 18, 1976; Larry Liebert, "Farm Board Funds Refused by Senate," *San Francisco Chronicle,* January 28, 1976. For section on grower duplicity, see Rick Carroll, "Political Burglar Says Harmer Knew of the Chavez Break-ins," *San Francisco Chronicle,* January 15, 1976, Daryl Tembke, "Farmer Deputy Tells of Burglarizing UFW Office," *Los Angeles Times,* June 25, 1976. Finally, for articles on efforts to pass Proposition 14, see César Chávez, "Chavez, Farm Worker Initiative Is Needed to Guard Against Abuses," *Los Angeles Times,* April 18, 1976; Harry Bernstein, "Chavez Supporters Cap Drive: Farm Initiative Petitions Turned in Around State," *Los Angeles Times,* May 1, 1976; "Farm Bureau Giants to Battle Chavez," *Los Angeles Times,* June 27, 1976. Mervin D. Field, "Majority Swings to No on 14," *San Francisco Chronicle,* October 15, 1976; and Harry Bernstein, "State to Investigate 'No on 14' Charges," *San Francisco Chronicle,* October 24, 1976. Harry Bernstein, "Brown Assails Oil Firm on Farm Law: Charges Alliance with Growers & Sabotage State," *Los Angeles Times,* October 29, 1976; Harry Bernstein, "Prop. 14 Foes Attack Statements by Brown," *Los Angeles Times,* October 30, 1976.

22. American Friends Service Committee, "A Report of Research on the Wages of Migrant Farm Workers in Northwest Ohio," July, August 1976, pp. 1–9. For a background on the development of FLOC, the following material was relied upon: Baldemar Velásquez, interview, Toledo, Ohio, August 8, 1977; "Statement of Problem," *Farm Labor Organizing Committee Newsletter,* January 1977; "FLOC: Both a Union and a Movement," *Worker's Power,* May 9, 1977; Thomas Ruge, "Indiana Farm Workers, Legislative Coalition Fights H.B. 1306," *OLA,* April 1977; Jim Wasserman, "FLOC Goal Is Power Base for Migrants," *Fort Wayne Journal-Gazette,* September 14, 1976; "FLOC Hearing—Abuses of Undocumented Workers," *Los Desarriagados* (Winter 1976–1977).

23. *The Struggle of the Texas Farm Workers' Union* (Chicago: Vanguard Press, 1977), pp. 4, 14–15; Jacques Levy, *César Chávez: Autobiography of La Causa* (New York: Norton, 1975), pp. 227, 282; Ignacio M. García, "The Many Battles of Antonio Orendian," *Nuestro* (November 1979): 25–29.

24. The following bibliography on the Farah strike is based mostly on contemporary news articles: "Farah Workers on Strike—Do Not Buy Any Pants," *Texas Observer,* December 29, 1972, reprinted in *Regeneración* 2, no. 3 (1973): 10. Another work on the subject is Laurie Coyle, Gail Hershatter, and Emily Honig, *Women at Farah: An Unfinished Story* (El Paso: Reforma, 1979). Bill Finger, "Victoria Sobre Farah," *Southern Exposure* 4, no. 1–2 (1976): 5, 46, 47–49; Castro, pp. 19, 193, 194; "Farah Workers on Strike," p. 10; "Farah Has Troubled Times," *San Antonio Express,* November 24, 1972; "Clothing Workers Union Blasts Farah Vote Request as 'Gimmick,'" *El Paso Times,* August 10, 1973; Workers at Farah Protest Metzger's Union Support," *El Paso Times,* November 4, 1973; "Retaliatory Pickets 'Visit' Farah Home," *El Paso Times,* November 5, 1973. "Why the Union Lost the Strike Against Farah," *San Antonio Express,* August 8, 1973; "Farah Stance Rapped," *San Antonio Express,* December 31, 1973; Farah blamed the work cutbacks and the closing of the Victoria and Los Cruces plants on the union. See Nell Fenner Grover, "Union Tells of Farah Plants' Work Cutbacks," *San Antonio Express,* August 15, 1973; "Farah Closes Two Plants," *San Antonio Express,* November 2, 1973, and "Editorial: Union Boycott Costs 900 San Antonians Jobs," *San Antonio Express,* December 8, 1973. For Catholic Church support of the boycott, see Sylvia Thomas, "Fury Faces Farah Fury," *San Antonio Express* December 8, 1973. Nell Fenner Grover, "Fury Stands Pat on Farah," *San Antonio Express,* December 14, 1973, is a solid article that lays out reasons for the bishops' support of boycott. For profile of Farah, see Fritz Wirt, "Willie Farah More Than Just a President of Company," *El Paso Times,* March 26, 1974. "Farah Workers OK Three-Year Pact," *El Paso Times,* March 8, 1974, "Import of Foreign Textiles Hit by Farah Workers," *Chicano Times,* April 15–April 29, 1977; Sara Martínez, "Employees Were Not Told of the Plant Closing Until It Was All Over," *San Antonio Express,* April 1, 1977; Sara Martínez, "800 Lose Jobs as Farah Closes Down," *San Antonio Express,* April 6, 1977. Laura E. Arroyo, "Industrial and Occupational Distribution of Chicana Workers," *Aztlán 4,* no. 2 (1973): 358–359.

25. Jorge A. Bustamante and James D. Cockcroft, "Unequal Exchange in Binational Relationship: The Case of Immigrant Labor," in Carlos Vasquez and Manuel Garcia y Griego, *Mexican-U.S. Relations: Conflict and Convergence* (Los Angeles: UCLA Chicano Studies Research Center, 1983), pp. 309–310.

26. Peter Wiley and Robert Gottlieb, *Empires in the Sun* (Tucson: University of Arizona Press, 1982), pp. 257, 265.

27. Conversations with Dr. Dennis Valdes, University of Minnesota, have been important in understanding the personality of the Midwest.

28. For a fuller account see Rodolfo Acuña, *Occupied America: A History of Chicanos,* 2nd ed. (New York: Harper & Row, 1981), pp. 168–171.

29. For corruption in INS, see *Los Angeles Times,* September 13, 1974; Frank Del Olmo, "Rodino Reportedly Tied to Border Probe," *Los Angeles Times,* July 19, 1974; Robert L. Jackson, "Witness Says Border Agents Offered Him Girls," *Los Angeles Times,* August 14, 1974; Robert L. Jackson, "Clean Sweep Probe Criticized as 'Incompetent,'" *Los Angeles Times,* September 18,

1974. The following articles deal with abuses, *The Forumeer,* June 1972, reported a woman stripped and examined at the U.S.-Mexico border. See also John Mosqueda and Frank Del Olmo, "Roundup of Illegal Aliens Stirs Angry Charges," *Los Angeles Times,* June 27, 1973; "Kidnapped Boy, 4, Had Been Deported," *San Francisco Chronicle,* December 10, 1976; Frank Del Olmo, "Alien Detention Center at El Centro Stirs Up Criticism," *Los Angeles Times,* February 24, 1974; "Blast at U.S. Over Illegal Aliens Rights," *San Francisco Chronicle,* September 2, 1976; *Albuquerque Journal,* March 1, 1977.

30. "Mexico Seeking to Allow Farm Workers to Enter U.S. Legally," *El Paso Times,* August 30, 1974; Stanley Meisler, "Echeverría Expected to Press Ford Today on Bracero Issue," *Los Angeles Times,* October 21, 1974; Stanley Meisler, "Mexico Drops Goal of Migrant Pact with U.S.," *Los Angeles Times,* October 24, 1974.

31. Gilbert Cardenas, "The United States Immigration Policy Toward Mexico: An Historical Perspective," *Chicano Law Review* 2 (Summer 1975), p. 84; Vernon M. Briggs, "Labor Market Aspects of Mexican Migration to the United States," in Stanley R. Ross, ed., *Views Across the Border* (Albuquerque: University of New Mexico Press, 1979), pp. 21, 211, 221; Ronald Bonaparte, "The Rodino Bill: An Example of Prejudice Toward Mexican Immigration to the United States," *Chicano Law Review* (Summer 1975): 40; Frank Del Olmo, "Softer Penalties in Alien Cases Urged," *Los Angeles Times,* April 20, 1977.

32. *Time* (May 2, 1977): 26–30. See also *Washington Post,* February 2, 1975; *El Paso Times,* February 29, 1976; *San Antonio Express,* May 30, 1976; *Los Angeles Herald Examiner,* June 28, 1976; *New York Times,* August 8, 1977.

33. Arthur F. Corwin, Letter to Kissinger, July 16, 1975, pp. 2–3, 20, 21, 39.

34. For early studies concluding that the undocumented was not a burden, see David S. North and Marion Houston, "Illegal Aliens: Their Characteristics and Role in the U.S. Labor Market," study conducted for the U.S. Department of Labor by Linton and Co. (November 17, 1975); Vic Villalpando, "Abstract: A Study of the Impact of Illegal Aliens in the County of San Diego on Specific Socioeconomic Areas," in Antonio José Ríos-Bustamante, ed., *Immigration and Public Policy: Human Rights for Undocumented Workers and Their Families,* Chicano Studies Center Document no. 5 (Los Angeles: Chicano Studies Center Publications, UCLA, 1977), pp. 223–231; Also see Orange County Board of Supervisors (Task Force on Medical Care for Illegal Aliens), *The Economic Impact of Undocumented Immigrants on Public Health Services in Orange County,* March 1978; Jorge Bustamante, "The Impact of the Undocumented Immigration from Mexico on the U.S.-Mexican Economics: Preliminary Findings and Suggestions for Bilateral Cooperation," Forty-sixth Annual Meeting of the Southern Economic Association, Atlanta, Georgia, November 1976; Wayne A. Cornelius, "When the Door Is Closed to Illegal Aliens, Who Pays?" *New York Times,* June 1, 1977; Wayne A. Cornelius, "A Critique of the Carter Administration's Policy Proposals on Illegal Immigration," Presentation to the Carnegie Endowment for International Peace, "Face to Face" Seminar, Washington, D.C., August 10, 1977 in Ríos-Bustamante.

35. *American G.I. Forum Newsletter,* October 1972.

36. Tom Miller, *On the Border* (New York: Ace Books, 1981), pp. 158–179; *El Paso Times,* August 22, 1976; Patricia Bell Blawes, *People's World,* October 29, 1977; *Sin Fronteras,* October 1976; *Arizona Republic,* August 31, 1976; *People's World,* October 29, 1977; *Arizona Republic,* October 11, October 19, 1977.

37. De León interview with Frank Cruz, KNBC-TV, May 24, 1977: See also John Kendall, "L.A. May Have 1 Million Aliens By 1981: Police Study Calls Peaceful Image False," *Los Angeles Times,* January 30, 1977; Illegal Alien Committee, "The Illegal Alien Problem and Its Impact on Los Angeles Police Department Resources," Los Angeles Police Department report, January 1977; Illegal Alien Committee, pp. 5, 9, 10.

38. Tom Butler, *El Paso Times,* June 19, June 20, 1977. Neil Paulson, "Few Farmers, Rangers Favor Tightened Alien Jobs Plan," *Denver Post,* June 3, 1977; Guy Cook, in "Apple Growers May Seek

Alien Okay," *Denver Post,* October 6, 1977, wrote that the apple growers around Grand Junction, Colorado, sought an injunction preventing INS enforcement of laws against the use of illegal aliens.

39. James P. Sterba, "Tackling the Immigration Mess," *New York Times,* May 14, 1977. See also James Reston, "The Silent Invasion," *New York Times,* May 4, 1977; Marjorie Hunter, "Immigration Agency Engulfed in Trouble," *New York Times,* May 13, 1977; James P. Sterba, "100 Border Patrolmen Rushed to California," *New York Times,* May 24, 1977; "Why the Tide of Illegal Aliens Keeps Rising: Interview with Leonel J. Castillo, Commissioner INS," *U.S. News & World Report* (February 20, 1978): 33–35.

40. Jimmy Carter, "Undocumented Aliens: Message to Congress, August 4, 1977," in Ríos-Bustamante, pp. 52–57.

41. *Tucson Daily Citizen,* April 17, 1976; *Arizona Daily Star,* April 4 and 22, 1976; *Sin Fronteras,* December 1976. In the spring of 1977, due to a public outcry, charges were dropped.

42. The years 1976 and 1977 were especially active. While demonstrations were held in support of the undocumented workers, the court system was also used as an arena. For instance, from July 1, 1968, to December 31, 1976, the INS had arbitrarily admitted Cuban "refugees" under the 120,000 quota. The Illinois Migrant Legal Action program brought a class action suit in November 1976 for undocumented workers who had applied before January 11, 1977 and had been put on a waiting list for immigration to the United States. U.S. District Judge John F. Grady of Chicago found in favor of the undocumented workers and issued a restraining order prohibiting deportation of this class of undocumented workers until the issue was resolved by the courts. The protected undocumented workers received so-called Silva letters to prevent their deportation. These letters were revoked during the first administration of Ronald Reagan. See Ron Dusek, "Aliens Given Deportation Reprieve by Chicago Judge," *El Paso Times,* March 25, 1977; *Los Desarraigados,* Notre Dame University (Winter 1976–1977): 9; James P. Sterba, "Alien Ruling Snarls Migrant Job Inquiry," *New York Times,* August 14, 1977; Robert Kistler, "No Effort to Block KKK 'Patrol' of Border Planned," *Los Angeles Times,* October 10, 1977; and *CCR Newsletter* (San Diego), October 29, 1977.

43. Moises Sándoval, "The Struggle Within LULAC," *Nuestro* (September 1979): 30.

44. Castro, pp. 198–199.

45. Castro, pp. 103, 199–201; Santillán, pp. 80–81. On October 6, 1972, the INS raided the Bañuelos factory. Bañuelos was employing undocumented workers.

46. Frank Del Olmo, "Watergate Panel Calls 4 Mexican-Americans," *Los Angeles Times,* June 5, 1974; Report of the Senate Select Committee on Presidential Activities, *The Senate Watergate Reports* (New York: Dell, 1974), vol. 1, pp. 345–372; Castro, pp. 7–8, 202–203, 210. See also "La Raza Platform Prohibits Support of Non-Chicanos," *Los Angeles Times,* July 4, 1972; Cindy Parmenter, "La Raza Unida Plans Outlined," *Denver Post,* June 20, 1974; Jim Wood, "La Raza Sought Nixon Cash," *San Antonio Express,* November 18, 1973. Accusations circulated that RUP leaders took money not to endorse McGovern. This was highly unlikely, since most RUP leaders wanted to stay neutral. Specific charges against José Angel Gutiérrez were never proven and evidence suggests that they were exaggerated and, in fact, spread to cause division among Chicanos.

47. "Top Woman Aide Gets U.S. Latin Position," *Los Angeles Times,* March 8, 1977; "Spanish-Speaking Aide Hits Cutbacks," *Santa Fe New Mexican,* March 26, 1973; Julia Moran, "The GOP Wants Us," *Nuestro* (August 1980): 26.

48. David Reyes, "In Pursuit of the Latino American Dream," Orange County Section, *Los Angeles Times,* July 24, 1983.

49. "A Box Full of Ethnic Labels," *Los Angeles Times,* July 25, 1983. See Eric Hobsbawn and Terence Ranger, eds., *The Invention of Tradition* (Cambridge, England: Cambridge University Press, 1983), on the way false traditions can be invented.

50. *New York Times,* October 30, 1984; "Victory Claimed by Early Boycott Leaders," *La Luz* (July

1978): 16–17; Tom Díaz, "Coors Gets on Board Hispanic Trend," *Nuestro* (January–February 1985): 12–14.

51. Ron Ozio, "The Hell with Being Quiet and Dignified, Says Rubén Bonilla," *Nuestro* (September 1979): 31–32.

52. Donald J. Bogue, *The Population of the United States: Historical Trends and Future Projections* (New York: The Free Press, 1985), p. 570.

53. *Hispanic Business* (June 1985): 24.

54. Claire Spiegel, "TELACU to Surrender License, Assets," *Los Angeles Times,* August 8, 1985.

55. Southwest Voter Registration Education Project, Memo, November 11, 1984.

56. "3 Million Chicanos Voiceless in California," *Forumeer,* October 1971. In California in 1971 out of 15,650 elected and appointed officials, 310, or 1.98 percent, were Chicanos. None of the 46 state officials and none of the advisors to the governor were Mexican.

57. Castro, p. 106; Don Bolles, "Raul Castro Scoffs at Reports He'll Put Latinos in Top Offices," *Arizona Republic,* October 16, 1974; Ben Cole, "Castro Takes Oath as Ambassador to Buenos Aires," *Arizona Republic,* October 21, 1977.

58. Patricía C. Ramírez, "NALEO and the Caucus," *Agenda* (March/April 1979): 7.

59. Andrew Hernández, *The Latin Vote in the 1976 Presidential Election* (San Antonio, Tex.: Southwest Voter Registration Education Project, 1977), pp. i, 1–2, 9. Starting in 1975 the Southwest voter registration project registered over 160,000 Latinos. In 1976, 4,947,000 Latinos were eligible to register and vote. Approximately 2,735,700 were actually registered and 1,887,600 actually voted.

60. Choco González Meza, *The Latin Vote in the 1980 Presidential Election: Political Research Report,* Southwest Voter Registration Education Project, January 1, 1981, p. 13.

61. Larry Véloz, "Washington's Top Advocate for the Poor," *Nuestro* (June/July 1979): 33.

62. Hobsbawm and Ranger, in *The Invention of Tradition,* give an excellent discussion on the topic.

63. William Jefferson Mathis, "Political Socialization in a Mexican American High School" (Ph.D. dissertation, University of Texas, 1973), pp. 7, 35, 67–68, 112; Phillip Lee Paris, "The Mexican American Informal Policy and the Political Socialization of Brown Students: A Case Study in Ventura County" (Ph.D. dissertation, University of Southern California, 1973), p. vii. Paris's study shows that the poorer and more rural Mexicans are, the more apt they are to express ethnic awareness and political unity.

64. Keith J. Henderson, "Bilingual Education Programs Spawning Flood of Questions," *Albuquerque Journal,* June 11, 1978. See also Vernon M. Briggs, Jr., Walter Fogel, and Fred H. Schmidt, *The Chicano Worker* (Austin: University of Texas Press, 1977), p. 21; Myer Weinberg, *Minority Students: A Research Appraisal* (Washington, D.C.: U.S. Department of Health, Education and Welfare, 1977), p. 287. According to the U.S. Commission on Civil Rights, *The Excluded Student: Educational Practices Affecting Mexican Americans in the Southwest,* Mexican American Education Study, Report iii (Washington, D.C.: Government Printing Office, 1972), bilingual education reached only 2.7 percent of the entire Chicano population. Data tabulated on p. 34 of the report dramatically demonstrated the lack of Chicano/Mexican-heritage courses actually taught.

PERCENTAGE OF CHICANO SECONDARY-SCHOOL CHILDREN ENROLLED IN

	Chicano history courses	Mexican history courses
Arizona	1.4	1.1
California	0.7	0.5
Colorado	0.7	0.8
New Mexico	0.8	1.7
Texas	0.5	1.7
Southwest	0.7	0.9

65. U.S. Commission on Civil Rights, pp. 13–16, 19.
66. María Eugenia Matute-Bianchi, "Educational Equity and Chicanos: Beyond Bilingual Educa-tion," Unpublished paper, University of California, Santa Cruz, February 1986; Ernesto Galarza, Statement submitted to the Subcommittee on Elementary, Secondary, and Vocational Education of the House Committee on Education and Labor, Hearings on Title VII, Bilingual Education Program, Washington, D.C., San Jose, June 3, 1977; Olivia Martínez, director of the San Jose Bilingual Consortium, letter to Dr. Angus Taylor, chancellor of University of California at Santa Cruz, February 4, 1977; Galarza letter to Taylor, February 17, 1977; Galarza letter to Mrs. Terry Pockets, April 27, 1977.
67. Press release, Southwest Voter Registration Education Project, "Bilingual Education Programs Cut Nearly 40 Percent," November 7, 1984; Robert Brischetto, "How Mexican Americans View Issues," Southwest Voter Registration Education Project, January 1982, pp. 5, 7.
68. Alexander W. Astin, *Minorities in American Higher Education* (San Francisco: Jossey-Bass, 1982), p. 29. Also see Meyer Weinberg, *A Chance to Learn: A History of Race and Education in the United States* (Cambridge, England: Cambridge University Press, 1977), pp. 340–345.
69. Quoted in Weinberg, p. 164.
70. For material on the *Serrano* case, see Thomas P. Carter and Roberto D. Segura, *Mexican Americans in School* (New York: College Examination Board, 1979), pp. 233–235; for material on the *Rodriguez* case, see p. 235 in the same source; Richard A. Gambritta, Robert A. Milne, and Earl R. Davis, "The Politics of Unequal Educational Opportunity," in Johnson, eds, pp. 133–156; Marshall quote in Gambritta, Milne, and Davis, p. 151.
71. See Astin; Bogue gives an excellent synthesis of historical trends in Chicano education.
72. The Bakke decision is very important to minorities. The following is a partial list of contemporary works on Bakke, giving an insight to how minorities felt about the decision. Minority Admissions Summer Project, sponsored by the National Lawyers Guild and the National Congress of Black Lawyers, *Affirmative Action in Crisis: A Handbook for Activists* (Detroit, 1977) hereafter referred to as *Minority Admissions*. See also Marian Kromkowiki and Izetta Bright, "Affirmative Action History and Results," in *Minority Admissions*, p. 2. In 1910, 7 of the 155 medical schools in the United States were black. An AMA study by Abraham Flexner found that its members did not have the high incomes they "deserved." The study recommended that the AMA upgrade all the medical schools or close most of them; 124 of the 155 were closed, including 5 of the 7 black schools. See also William Trombley, "Court Rejects College Plans for Minorities," *Los Angeles Times*, September 17, 1976. For basic documents, including the California Supreme Court's transcripts, see Carlos Manuel Haro, ed., *The Bakke Decision: The Question of Chicano Access to Higher Education*, Chicano Studies Center Document No. 4 (Los Angeles: UCLA, 1976); Ronald D. Moskowitz, "The Man Behind the Storm," *San Francisco Chronicle*, June 29, 1978; Steven Schear, "Bakke: A Lesson in Minimal Adversity," in *Minority Admissions*, p. 49. See *Minority Admissions*, pp. 21–23, for an annotated chronology of events and dates surround-ing *Bakke;* Bonnie K. Solow, "Past Discrimination at the University of California," in *Minority Admissions*, pp. 55–65. Sharon Blackman, "Bakke Boogaloo," in *Minority Admissions*, pp. 27–28.
73. Celeste Durant, "California Bar Exam—Pain and Trauma Twice a Year," *Los Angeles Times*, August 27, 1978; Robert Montoya, "Minority Health Professional Development: An Issue of Freedom of Choice for Young Anglo Health Professionals," Paper presented at the Annual Convention of the American Medical Student Association, Atlanta, Ga., March 4, 1978, p. 4;
74. *New York Times*, September 20, 1983.
75. John Fogarty, "Race Can Still Be a Factor," *San Francisco Chronicle*, June 29, 1978.
76. The best overview of triple oppression theory is Denise A. Segura, "Chicanas and Triple Oppres-sion in the Labor Force," in National Association for Chicano Studies, *Chicana Voices: Intersec-tions of Class, Race, and Gender* (Austin: Center for Mexican American Studies, University of Texas, 1986), pp. 47–61.

77. Francisca Flores, "Mexican-American Women Ponder Future Role of the Chicana," *Eastside Sun,* July 1, 1971; "Chicanas Meet at Houston: La Confederación de Mujeres in Houston, May 28–30," *Forumeer,* July 1971; Martha Cotera, *Profile on the Mexican American Women* (Austin: National Educational Laboratory Publishers, 1976), p. 183. See also Rosaura Sánchez and Rosa Martínez, eds., *Essays on la Mujer* (Los Angeles: Chicano Studies Center, UCLA, 1977), esp. Judith Sweeney, "Chicanas' History: A Review of the Literature," and Cotera, 183; Sonia A. López, "The Role of the Chicana Within the Student Movement"; Arlene Stewart, *"Las Mujeres de Aztlán:* A Consultation with Elderly Mexican American Women in a Sociological Historical Perspective" (Ph.D. dissertation, California School of Professional Psychology, 1973), p. 77. See Cotera, pp. 184–188, for a list of resultant conferences. The *Comisión Femenil Mexicana* had been formed on October 11, 1970, and it played a leading role in calling the spring 1971 Chicana conference. See Dorinda Moreno, ed., *La Mujer en Pie de Lucha* (San Francisco, Espina Del Norte, 1973); Cotera, pp. 183–184. The early Chicana conferences of the 1970s owe a debt to Francisca Flores, who pioneered concern over women's issues. In the mid-1960s she established *La Carta Editorial,* the Mexican American Women's League, and later the magazine *Regeneración.* "Women's Club to Confer Achievement Awards," *Belvedere Citizen,* May 7, 1964; "Twelve Women Honored at Women's League," *Belvedere Citizen,* April 1, 1965; "Chicana Action Service Center Opens Fri., Sept. 8," *Belvedere Citizen,* August 31, 1972. The Chicana Action Service Center was first funded under a grant to the *Comisión Femenil Mexicana.*

78. Jim Wood, "Report on Bias Against Latinos in Welfare," *San Francisco Chronicle,* July 2, 1972; Cotera, pp. 108–109. Also see Rodolfo Acuña, *A Community Under Siege: A Chronicle of Chicanos East of the Los Angeles River, 1945–1975* (Los Angeles: Chicano Studies Resource Center, UCLA, 1984).

79. "Inez Garcia Gains Victory," *Sin Fronteras,* January 1976; "Justice," *La Gente,* March 1976; *San Francisco Chronicle,* January 4, 1976; "The Book Report: Inez Garcia, "A Tale of 2 Rapes," *Los Angeles Times,* April 2, 1976; "Acquitted in Her Second Trial," *San Francisco Chronicle,* March 5, 1977.

80. Norma Solis, "Do Doctors Abuse Low-Income Women?" *Chicano Times,* April 15–29, 1977; "Doctor Raps Sterilization of Indian Women," *Los Angeles Times,* May 22, 1977; "Puerto Rican Doctor Denounces Sterilization," *Sin Fronteras,* May 1976. Dr. Helen Rodrigues, head of pediatrics at Lincoln Hospital in San Francisco, said that by 1968 35 percent of the women in Puerto Rico had been sterilized. See also Bernard Rosenfeld, Sidney M. Wolfe, and Robert E. McGarrah, Jr., *A Health Research Group Study on Surgical Sterilization: Present Abuses and Proposed Regulation* (Washington, D.C.: Public Citizens, 1973), pp. 1, 7.

81. Quoted in Robert Kistler, "Women 'Pushed' into Sterilization, Doctor Charges," *Los Angeles Times,* December 2, 1974. See also Robert Kistler, "Many U.S. Rules on Sterilization Abuses Ignored Here," *Los Angeles Times,* December 3, 1974; Georgina Torres Rizk, "Sterilization Abuses Against Chicanos in Los Angeles," published by the Los Angeles Center for Law and Justice, December 2, 1976; Richard Siggins, "Coerced Sterilization: A National Civil Conspiracy to Commit Genocide upon the Poor?" (Loyola University School of Law, January 15, 1977), p. 12.

82. For a pattern, review articles in *La Luz, Nuestro, Hispanic Business,* and *Agenda.* Pilar Saavedra-Vela, "Hispanic Women in Double Jeopardy," *Agenda* (November/December 1977): 4.

83. Based on the excellent work of Benjamin Márquez, "Power and Politics in a Chicano Barrio" (Ph.D. dissertation, University of Wisconsin, Madison, 1983), pp. 188–353.

84. Barry J. Kaplan, "Houston: The Golden Buckle of the Sunbelt," in Richard M. Bernard and Bradley R. Rice, eds. *Sunbelt Cities* (Austin: University of Texas Press, 1983), pp. 196–202.

85. *Forumeer,* April 1971; "Shooting Death of Latin Sets Off Riot in Blythe," *Los Angeles Times,* May 20, 1972; *Forumeer,* July 1972; Castro, *Chicano Power,* pp. 55–57, 219; George Lane, "Police Actions; Condemned, Lauded," *Denver Post,* February 18, 1973; "4 Face D.A. Charges

in Gun Battle Case," *Denver Post,* March 27, 1973; *Los Angeles Times,* July 25, 1973; *Arizona Republic,* July 29, November 16, 1973; See also Shirley Achor, *Mexican American in a Dallas Barrio* (Tucson: University of Arizona Press, 1978), pp. 102–108; *San Antonio Express,* April 21, 1976, March 10, 1977.

86. Rick Scott, "Morales Killing Still Stirs Ire," *San Antonio Express,* October 30, 1976; *San Antonio Express,* February 2, February 24, 1977; *El Paso Times,* February 24, 1977; Bill Mintz, "Frank Hayes Indictment Dismissal Being Sought," *San Antonio Express,* March 24, 1977; *San Antonio Express,* February 18, 1978; *Sin Fronteras,* January, February 1976.

87. *Sin Fronteras,* February 1976; Rich Carroll, "Cops Cleared in Slaying of Chicano," *San Francisco Chronicle,* April 3, 1976; *Sin Fronteras,* July 1976; "U.S. Clears Oakland Cop in Killing," *San Francisco Chronicle,* May 25, 1978; "Probe into Mark Villanueva, Texas Jail Death," *San Antonio Express,* March 15, 1977; Gregory James and Tom Butler, "Beating Investigation Ordered," *El Paso Times,* April 6, April 8, 1977; Narda Zacchino, "Davis Flays Channel 7's Masked Officer Interview," *Los Angeles Times,* May 12, 1977; Gene Blake and Michael A. Levett, "Pines Acts to Avoid Conflict of Interest," *Los Angeles Times,* May 11, 1977; Gene Blake, "Ex Pines Aide Changes Story on Files," *Los Angeles Times,* May 31, 1977; Gene Blake, "File-Shredding Case Testimony Disrupted," *Los Angeles Times,* June 1, 1977; Gene Blake, "Judge in Shredding Case Charges Perjury in Perez," *Los Angeles Times,* June 3, 1977; Gene Blake, "Final 16 Cases Dismissed in File-Shredding Controversy," *Los Angeles Times,* June 14, 1977; Nicholas C. Chriss, "5 Houston Police Officers Suspended in Beating, Drowning of Mexican-American," *Los Angeles Times,* May 13, 1977; *Chicano Times,* May 20–June 3, 1977; *Los Angeles Times,* October 8, 1977; *El Paso Times,* October 8, October 11, 1977; *Los Angeles Times,* March 29, May 9, 1978.

88. Allen Pusey, "Sheriff Claims Prisoner Went Berserk," *El Paso Times,* May 20, 1977; *El Paso Times,* May 21, May 24, May 25, June 1, 1977; Allen Pusey, "Pathologist Doubts Hudspeth Jail Death Autopsy," *El Paso Times,* June 4, 1977; Allen Pusey, "Juan Véloz Zúñiga Was Just Wanting to Get to His Job," *El Paso Times,* June 5, 1977; Allen Pusey, "Ex-Hudspeth Prisoners Claim Seeing Beatings," *El Paso Times,* June 12, 1977. See also Howard S. Erlanger, in collaboration with Fred Persity, "Estrangement, Machismo, and Gang Violence" (Unpublished paper written for the National Institute of Mental Health, Madison, Wisc. 1977); "Cases Compiled by the Mexican American Legal Defense and Educational Fund," parts 1 and 2 of the Case Summaries (San Francisco: Mexican American Legal Defense and Education Fund, 1978) for an excellent summary of 56 police brutality cases in which Maldef has been involved; María Recio, "Hispanics and the Legal System: Unequal Access, Unequal Justice," *Agenda* (January/February 1977): 34; *New York Times,* October 9, 1980; *Nuestro* (April 1981): 47.

89. "Hijack Defense to Put Stress on Ills of South," *Los Angeles Times,* July 6, 1972; Joan Sweeney, "Latin Hijacks Jet in L.A., Surrenders After Radio Protest," *Los Angeles Times,* April 14, 1972; Frank Del Olmo, "Hijacking Trial Opens, Plane Crewmen Testify," *Los Angeles Times,* July 19, 1972; Frank Del Olmo, "Hijacked Jet to Save America and World, Chávez-Ortiz Says," *Los Angeles Times,* July 19, 1972; Frank Del Olmo, "Chávez-Ortiz Convicted of Air Piracy, Receives Life in Prison," *Los Angeles Times,* July 24, 1972; *Denver Post,* November 30, 1972; "Defend Ricardo Chávez Ortiz," *La Raza* (Summer 1977): 48.

90. The author participated in the Committee to Free Gordon Castillo Hall; "*Los Angeles Times,* July 3, 1981; Frank del Olmo, "The System Can Be Murder," *Los Angeles Times,* July 16, 1981; Henry Mendoza, "For Gordon Castillo Hall, First Steps Taken in Freedom Are Frightening," *Los Angeles Times,* July 15, 1981.

91. I was one of the plaintiffs; Paul Hoffman and Robert Newman, "Police Spying Settlement," *Los Angeles Lawyer* (May 1984): 17–25. On March 23, 1979, Roberto Rodríguez, a journalist and long-time Chicano activist, was severly beaten by members of the Selective Enforcement Bureau of the Los Angeles Sheriffs Department. He was hospitalized and charged with assault with a deadly weapon. Rodríguez had been photographing the deputies beating innocent people. His

seven-year ordeal in successfully suing the Sheriffs is told in R. Rodríguez, *Assault with a Deadly Weapon: About an Incident in E.L.A. and the Closing of Whittier Boulevard* (Los Angeles: Libería Latinoamericana, 1985).

92. Recio, p. 34; Jerry Mandel, "Hispanics in the Criminal Justice System—the 'Nonexistent' Problem," *Agenda* (May/June 1979): 16, 17–18; Brischetto, pp. 2–3; Jerry Mandel, "The Santa Fe Prison Riots": 'The Flower of the Dragon,' " *Agenda* (May/June 1980): 4.

chapter *11*

The Age of the Brokers: The Rambo Years

AN OVERVIEW

At the beginning of the 1980s, Raúl Izaguirre, director of the National Council of *La Raza,* wrote an article entitled "The Decade for the Hispanic." Izaguirre prophesized: "I firmly believe that the immediate future will be our 'Golden Age.' "[1] History has since proven Izaguirre wrong. For the poor, as well as for the industrial working class, the first half of the 1980s was a nightmare. Yet many middle-class Chicanos shared and still believe Izaguirre's illusion that prosperity is just around the corner.[2]

In 1980, North Americans resurrected John Wayne and elected Ronald Reagan, also an actor, president of the United States. Reagan talked the plain language that the Archies understood. The 1980s were important years, almost too important to entrust to a man with a faulty memory and nineteenth-century answers to the present. During this decade, the United States marched fully into the post-industrial age. In 1980, Japan, for the first time, produced more cars and trucks than the United States. That same year, Japan outproduced the United States in steel production, 123 million tons to 112 million. Despite U.S. industry's decline and the depressed status of workers, U.S. corporations made record-breaking profits. After taxes, for example, Exxon earned $5.7 billion in net profits, grossing some $113 billion.

North Americans blamed the decline in U.S. industrial power on the worker, who pseudo-economists said earned too much. However, in 1950, it took seven Japanese workers to do the job of one U.S. worker. Thirty years later

Japanese operatives outproduced their North American counterparts. The decline in worker productivity can be attributed to the fact that U.S. industry chose to earn higher profits rather than modernize its factories. While the Japanese invested 17 percent of the nation's GNP for modernization, U.S. capitalists spent only 10 percent annually. U.S. corporations spent less on research and on factories, machines, tools, and technology than their competitors. Instead, they purchased other companies, and paid higher dividends to stockholders and larger bonuses to managers. And while North American capitalists sung the praises of the Japanese workers, they refused to give their own workers the same lifetime employment guarantee. The choice of U.S. industry to deindustrialize affected Chicanos, whose highest paid workers were concentrated in heavy industry.

Other changes during the decade also affected Chicanos. "Just as America was unusually young in the 1960s, so it is becoming disproportionately middle-aged in the 1980s."[3] With the graying of "America" came an apparent growing conservatism, as middle-aged people, who made up a large bloc, became more reluctant to pay for education. Because of their vulnerability, they became more law-and-order minded as well.

The expanded use in the workplace of computers also spelled trouble for Chicanos. And, although high tech broadened opportunity for some, the median level of education for Chicanos at the beginning of the decade remained below the tenth grade, hardly enough to qualify them as technocrats.

By the 1980s, most of the social programs of the 1960s had been cut, and poverty once more climbed. Between 1972 and 1982, North Americans made no improvement in income, and, in fact, inflation reduced their buying power. Latinos suffered disproportionately from the recessions of 1973–1974 and 1980–1983. The nation seemed to return to Archie's "Good Old Days of Herbert Hoover Again" with trickle-down economics becoming respectable once more.[4]

Reagan also initiated a policy of Rambo diplomacy. During the 1980s, the United States landed marines in Lebanon; it invaded the small island of Grenada; and it bombed Libya. In Central America, Reagan propped up the Salvadorian government, ignoring that nation's death squads; he sponsored the military suppression of the Guatemalan people; and he waged war on the Nicaraguan people through his surrogates, the *contras,* former Somoza National Guards officers, who launched a counterrevolution from Honduras.

Reagan carefully cultivated the image of a man of God and action. On February 5, 1985, the *Los Angeles Times* reported that Reagan told a group of business and trade representatives that God supported his military buildup: "You might be interested to know that the Scriptures are on our side in this," citing Luke 14:31–32. The president told a gathering of religious broadcasters: "I don't think the Lord that blessed this country as no other country has ever been blessed intends for us to have to some day negotiate because of our weakness." Reagan wanted prayers in the schools and sided openly with the Moral Majority on issues such as abortion. Anyone who disagreed with Reagan was accused of supporting the Russians.

Reagan constantly celebrated "America." He trumpeted "American" superiority during the 1984 Olympics; two years later he celebrated the centennial of the Statue of Liberty, grossly distorting immigrant history. At the White House, too, the president enjoyed playing the role of a real-life television host: Reagan spotlighted hostages held on an airline for a day as heroes, as he did pilots returning from a single Libyan bombing mission; he rolled out the red carpet for selected minorities and sports stars. As the years progressed, Reagan himself seemed to be unable to distinguish fact from the movies. Once, after seeing the movie *Rambo,* Reagan said that he now knew what to do about the terrorists.

THE CELEBRATION OF SUCCESS, HISPANIC STYLE

By the 1980s, Chicanos began moving into government positions that dealt with the implementation of policy. Few questioned whether affirmative action of this sort did not in fact represent a double-edged sword. For instance, by 1982, more Latinos than Blacks were FBI agents, even though the Black community was larger; Latinos also worked as CIA operatives in Latin America.[5]

Out of the CIA's ranks came Nestor D. Sánchez, who retired from the agency in 1981. Sánchez became Reagan's principal architect of national security in Central America. *Nuestro* magazine described Sánchez, the deputy assistant secretary of defense for inter-American affairs, who was born in Magdalena, New Mexico, in 1927, as a "New Mexican descendant of the conquistadors [sic]." It quoted Sánchez as saying of the U.S. Salvadorian policy: "We have to confront this challenge to the democratic governments in the region." Sánchez did not criticize the death squads who brutally assassinated Archbishop Oscar Romero, the killings of 50,000 civilians since 1980, or the Salvadorian guardsmen's rape and murder of four North American churchwomen. He accused the Russians and Cubans of involvement in the region, stating, "We can afford to go eyeball to eyeball with the Soviets because we know they will blink."[6]

Another Reagan appointee, Linda Chávez, headed the staff of the U.S. Civil Rights Commission. Chávez had been on the president's staff and before that worked for the American Federation of Teachers journal. In 1983, she joined the commission, a 26-year-old bipartisan agency that had been relatively free of partisan politics. Chávez and a conservative Black commissioner acted as Reagan's hatchet wielders on the commission. Reagan, irritated by the documentation of the lack of access to U.S. institutions by Chicanos, other minorities, and women, wanted to destroy the agency because it exposed his failures as well as those of the system.

Chávez, who described herself as half Mexican, a quarter Irish, and a quarter English, characterized Mexican American organizations who disagreed with the president as "out of touch." She displayed antipathy toward the rights of the undocumented and branded LULAC's opposition to Reagan's Central American policy as leftist.[7] In 1986 Chávez won the Republican party primary nomination for the U.S. Senate; she lost the election to Democrat Barbara Mukulski.

A less offensive appointee, Cathi Villapando, served as special assistant to the president. From San Marcos, Texas, she became a Republican in the 1960s, and at a time when everyone else was concerned about social issues, Villapando attached herself to ultraconservative concerns. She rose through the bureaucracy and was recommended to the president by arch-conservative Texas Senator John Tower. Villapando, who did not have a history of involvement within the Mexican American community, became an instant expert on Chicano affairs. Her lack of experience badly compromiséd bilingual education. Like Chávez, she championed Simpson-Mazzoli because "*our* (italics the author's) surveys showed that the Hispanic community was in favor of the Simpson-Mazzoli bill"; but that support was distorted by Hispanic leaders. Villapando naively stated that she was not troubled by the idea of a mandatory national identity card because she had to wear a tag to work.[8] The 1982 version of Simpson-Mazzoli passed the Senate. It provided for employer sanctions, amnesty, a guest worker program, and more funds for the INS. Although Reagan lobbied for the bill, it did not pass the House. Villapando's and Chávez's support of Simpson-Mazzoli was unusual since even Hispanic Republicans opposed the bill.

Reagan made many more appointments of so-called Hispanics supporting his policies. It became evident by the mid-1980s that these appointees were integral to the legitimation of government policy. They were the role models that had been picked to be celebrated.

The Invisible Network

Organic links between the brokers and the Chicano masses also weakened at the local level. Many invisible networks developed whose operators the community knew little about. As in the case of organizations, a number of these brokers were progressive and did represent the interests of the community. However, an evaluation or even accountability became more difficult as time passed.

In cities across the country, an important source of power evolved from the growing cadre of Chicano lawyers who were, as a group, becoming more affluent and joining prestigious firms. For example, in Los Angeles, Vilma Martínez, past general counsel of the Mexican American Legal Defense and Education Fund (MALDEF), joined the firm of Munger, Tolles & Rickerhauser. Martínez sat on the Board of Regents of the University of California, and the political establishment recognized her as a spokesperson for Latinos. Her associate, Dan García, chair of the Los Angeles City Planning Commission and member of the California Democratic Central Committee, also wielded considerable power in political circles. Close to Mayor Tom Bradley, his firm did a considerable amount of business with the city. García in this capacity was rarely called to make public statements or give a public accounting to a constituency.

Bradley named a number of other Chicano attorneys to city commissions: Dominick Rubalcava served on the Fire Department Commission before joining the prestigious Harbor Commission. Stephen Yslas sat on the Police Commission.

Unlike many appointees and staff personnel, commissioners have real power in many cities—especially Los Angeles. In a real sense they are the invisible network, since their activities are rarely reported in the news media. They are not accountable to anyone but the person who appoints them, and they are free to use their connections to benefit themselves. Yet their selection can be celebrated as proof of concern for the "Hispanics."

Many Chicano political appointees did not have a history of public service. They often came from the ranks of campaign contributors and did not share the interests of the majority in the Chicano community. For example, Mayor Bradley named Angel Echevarría to the influential Water and Power Commission. Owner of a furniture company manufacturing Somma water beds, Echevarría employed 200 workers, most of whom did not have documents. When the International Ladies Garment Workers Union attempted to organize the plant, Echevarría fired 30 union sympathizers. The National Labor Relations Board in a rare prolabor ruling found that Echevarría had violated the NLRB code. Echevarría then tried to use his political influence in Washington to reverse the decision. The extent of Echevarría's commitment to the community was his contribution to Bradley's campaign and that of Los Angeles City Council member Richard Alatorre.[9]

Building a Political Base

Many Chicano gains in electoral politics can be attributed to the Southwest Voter Registration Education Project (SVREP). Established in 1974, the SVREP doubled Chicano registration from 488,000 in 1976 to over a million by 1985. The project publishes reports and analyses of Chicano voting potential and trends. Along with MALDEF and sympathetic lawyers, the SVREP has brought hundreds of suits challenging reapportionment and at-large voting practices that dilute Latino electoral strength. San Antonian Willie Velásquez, 40, its founder, has developed a network throughout the Southwest and Midwest. The SVREP concerns itself, however, with nuts and bolts issues and not the quality of representation. The organization's priorities are: How do you get more Chicanos registered and out to vote? How do you assure Mexican American candidates the best shot of getting elected?[10]

During the 1970s, the Latino population increased from 9 million to 14.6 million, of whom over 60 percent were Mexican. This represented a jump of 61 percent during the decade, versus 9 percent for non-Latinos. In 1980, Chicanos comprised almost 80 percent of California's 2,775,170 Latinos and just over 90 percent of Texas's 1,756,971 Latinos.[11]

Changes in the Voting Rights Act in 1975 and 1982 made it easier for the SVREP to *persuade* local municipalities to restructure their electoral units. Why the Reagan administration chose to enforce the Voting Rights Act is understandable, since the gerrymandering and manipulation of Chicanos more directly benefited Democrats. The Voting Rights Act therefore became the only piece of civil rights legislation that effectively helped Chicanos, who made gains in the *number* of elected representatives.

MEXICAN AMERICAN STATE REPRESENTATIVES, 1950–1983

State	1950	1960	1965	1974	1983
Arizona	0	4	6	11	12
California	0	0	0	8	7
Colorado	0	1	1	6	7
New Mexico	20	20	22	33	30
Texas .	0	7	6	15	19

Source: Joan Moore and Harry Pachon, *Hispanics in the United States* (Englewood Cliffs, N.J.: Prentice-Hall, 1985), p. 185.

In 1986, Texas led the nation in the number of Latino elected officials: 1,466, compared to 588 in New Mexico and 450 in California. It is important to point out, however, that although Mexican American representation increased, the Mexican American population quadrupled from 1950 to 1983. Also, while Texas has made gains, there are still problems: although Chicanos make up one-fifth of the population, only 5.6 percent of the Texas city council members are Chicanos. Fifty percent of its first graders are Chicano, but only 6.6 percent of Texas school board members are of Mexican extraction. Moreover, the question of quality of representation has not yet been addressed.

Democratic party dependence on the Mexican American vote is clearest in Texas. On November 2, 1982, Democrat Mark White won the governorship, although he received only 44.6 percent of the Anglo vote. Mexicans gave White 231,575 votes, 86.1 percent of their total. The potential strength of the Chicano vote had increased dramatically from 1978 to 1982. In 1978, Mexicans had voted heavily for the Democratic candidate for governor, John Hill, but Hill lost. The difference was that, by 1982, Mexicans had 145,411 new registered voters. In 1982 the Mexican vote also swept in Lloyd Bentsen to the U.S. Senate, giving him 89.4 percent of the total.[12]

The Mexican vote played a key role in the 1984 U.S. Senate primary, when ultra-conservative state representative Kent Hance (Lubbock) ran against liberal state senator Lloyd Dogget and former U.S. Representative Bob Krueger. During the campaign, Hance opposed amnesty for undocumented workers and made racist remarks. Hance received a plurality of the vote on May 5, with Dogget and Krueger splitting the Mexican vote. In the runoff, Hance received 54.8 percent of the non-Mexican vote; Dogget received 75.5 percent of the Mexican vote, with Chicanos turning out in greater numbers than whites. Dogget won the election by 509 votes.[13]

The Midwestern Voter Registration Project and the Labor Council for Latin American Advancement, like the SVREP, registered Latinos. In 1983, Mexicans, along with Puerto Ricans, Blacks, and progressive whites, elected Harold Washington, a Black, mayor of Chicago.

During the 1980s, Latinos made gains in Chicago; in 1986 that city had a Latino population of close to 540,000, 19 percent of the total Chicago population. About 60 percent of the Latino group were of Mexican extraction. Although the Pilsen district remained the principal port of entry, and the *barrio* with the greatest concentration of Mexicans, more of them lived in the northside. Chicanos, however, shared that space with Puerto Ricans and other Latino groups. The southside *barrios* of Pilsen, Little Village, and South Chicago had more Mexicans than other Latinos. And although a large number of the Mexican population was foreign-born, in the mid-1980s the Latino Institute found that 83 percent of the Latino youth had been born in the continental U.S.A.

In 1981, not a single Latino served on the Chicago City Council; that year the council members had blatantly gerrymandered the districts, making the future election of a Latino almost impossible. The following year, MALDEF sued the Chicago City Council under the 1965 Voters Rights Act as amended in 1982. The remapping of the district, according to MALDEF, diluted Latino voting strength. Four years later the court issued a judicial order that created four Latino wards—the 22nd, 25th, 26th, and 31st. The 22nd and 25th were predominantly Chicano. A special election took place in March in which Jesús García and Juan Solíz were elected to the 22nd and 25th respectively. The creation of the Latino wards was crucial to the growing power of Chicanos and Latinos in Chicago; they were actively sought by the progressive forces of Mayor Washington and by the Democratic machine led by Edward Vrdolyak, giving them, at least the illusion of power.[14]

Increasingly, in the 1980s, the voters elected Chicano mayors and governors. The best known were New Mexican Governor Toney Anaya, Denver Mayor Federico Peña, and San Antonio Mayor Henry Cisneros. In 1982, Mexican Americans turned out heavily to elect Anaya governor. The former state attorney general received 85 percent of the Mexican vote.[15] Anaya also received strong labor backing. As governor, Anaya took courageous stands such as forcefully speaking out against U.S. intervention in Nicaragua and the racist policies of the South African government. However, the press and Little Texas (Eastern New Mexican) racists constantly attacked Anaya. His populist style alienated him not only from Anglos but from many of the northern New Mexican bosses. They frustrated Anaya's attempts to get his agenda through the legislature. In the last days of his term in 1986, Anaya stirred additional controversy by granting executive clemency to prisoners on New Mexico's death row. (He was opposed to capital punishment.)

Federico Peña, 36, Denver's first Mexican American mayor, received his law degree from the University of Texas in 1971. He was born in Laredo in 1947; his father was a college graduate. Raised in Brownsville, he attended St. Joseph's Academy. After law school, on his way to California, he stopped in Denver to visit his brother and decided to stay. In 1978, voters elected him state representative; in the legislature he pushed for a liberal agenda. In December 1982, Denver voters elected Peña mayor, 79,200 votes to 74,700. Mexicans comprised only 18 percent of the city's population and 12 percent of its voters. However, the SVREP had recently registered 6,000 new Latin voters, and they gave Peña the margin he needed.

Peña, not in the mold of the Denver western image, preferred pinstripes and jogging shorts to jeans. He represented the young, upwardly mobile urban Chicano who had been migrating to Denver in recent years. Peña was close to the younger developers. He unsuccessfully pushed for a $138 million convention center to be built near the old railroad tracks, alienating downtown elites and older homeowners who feared higher taxes. Peña, however, had the support of the younger professionals, who were pro-growth. Denver depended on sales taxes for 50 percent of its revenues, and the pro-growth people wanted to attract tourism. Peña, meanwhile, maintained the support of unions and construction companies because he promoted the expansion of Denver's infrastructure, which to them meant jobs.

While Peña benefited from being Mexican American, attracting a national press, locally he played down his ethnicity. Unlike Anaya, Peña did not promote a Mexican agenda, stating, "I am not an Hispanic candidate. I just happen to be Hispanic."[16]

In comparison, Henry Cisneros came from a city that was heavily Mexican and where, without the Mexican vote, he could not have been elected. First elected to the San Antonio City Council in 1975, he ran citywide, endorsed by the Good Government League (GGL). Mexicans that year comprised 51.8 percent of the city but only 37 percent of the registered voters; Anglos made up 39 percent of the population and almost 56 percent of the registered voters. Two years later, when Chicanos and Blacks took over the City Council, Cisneros's role within that alliance was tenuous.

The 1977 election of five Mexicans and one Black resulted in part from the 1975 amendments to the Voting Rights Act that changed San Antonio City Council elections from citywide to district seats. Additionally, in 1976, the Justice Department halted San Antonio annexations, a gimmick used by the white elite to dilute minority voting power. Simply, in Texas it was easy for municipalities to annex surrounding land. The elites could continuously absorb white areas to offset the Mexican and Black increases. Another factor contributing to the City Council takeover was the rise of the Communities Organized for Public Service (COPS). COPS played an important role in politicizing and registering Mexican voters (see later in chapter). Lastly, an internal feud between the Northside developers and business community and the old guard of the GGL divided the forces of the white elite.[17]

In 1981, Cisneros became the first Mexican American mayor of San Antonio since the 1840s. An urban planner, born in San Antonio, Cisneros had attended Central Catholic High, and then graduated from Texas A&M. Cisneros received his doctorate from George Washington University, returning in 1974 to San Antonio, where he solicited the GGL sponsorship. On the City Council, conservative Lila Cockrell, the first female mayor of San Antonio, was his mentor.

Cisneros had deep roots in San Antonio. His father, a retired army reserve colonel, worked at Fort Sam Houston. His mother, Elvira Mungía Cisneros, came from an elite exile family who fled Mexico because of the radical turn of the revolution. His maternal grandfather, Henry Romulo Mungía, ran a print shop and had close ties with the other exile families, from which a surprising number of the present generation of San Antonio's Chicano leaders descended.

During the 1960s, Henry Cisneros wanted to become a career military officer. At Texas A&M, Cisneros joined the Reserve Officers Training Corps (ROTC) at a time when others were protesting its morality. Nothing in his early career suggests a commitment to a Mexican American agenda. The plight of the poor and/or the farm workers apparently did not interest him.

Back in San Antonio, Cisneros taught urban studies and labor economics. Ideologically more Republican than Democrat, Cisneros liked to quote the neo-conservative quarterly *The Public Interest.* Having worked as a White House Fellow for Republican Elliot Richardson, he had close friends in the Republican party. Cisneros stated as late as 1982, "There is no alternative to trickle-down economics."[18] As mayor his rhetoric emphasized economic growth, participation in the technological revolution, and the necessity of attracting high-tech business to San Antonio. What this would mean to the majority of San Antonio's Mexicans, undereducated by unequal schools, would be employment at minimum wages. However, for middle-class Mexican Americans with an education, it represented an opportunity. The leader of the San Antonio Chamber of Commerce praised Cisneros: "Perhaps the best thing that has happened to this city since it was founded."[19]

Cisneros continued as one of Reagan's favorite Democrats. His philosophy fitted in with the New Federalism. In 1983, Reagan appointed Cisneros to the National Bipartisan Commission on Central America (the so-called Kissinger Commission). Reagan carefully selected the commission members, whose findings had been predetermined. Among other things, the Kissinger Commission blamed the Soviets and Cubans for problems in the region, calling for massive aid to the *contras* and military and other aid to El Salvador. The report manufactured a justification for the invasion of Nicaragua.

Cisneros and the other Democrats proceeded more cautiously, forming the loyal opposition. Cisneros expressed fear of another Vietnam, called for negotiations through the Contadora nations (see page 445), and stated that Reagan was acting too hastily. When the ultraconservative president of Boston University, John Silber, criticized Cisneros for not being a team player, the San Antonian did not respond. Critics questioned Cisneros's role in the bipartisan commission, alleging that Cisnero's moves were calculated to advance his career without taking serious risks. During the Nicaraguan visit, Sandinista leader Daniel Ortega attempted to meet with Cisneros and North American labor leaders; Cisneros did not want to take a chance of offending Reagan and he refused. Once in the United States, seeking to avoid the impression that he was "soft on communism," Cisneros criticized the Sandinistas for being heavily influenced by Marxists.[20]

In San Antonio, few Chicanos faulted Cisneros. In 1983, the voters re-elected him, giving him 94 percent of the vote. Feelings can be summarized as follows: "He's sharp. Hangs around with the new rich developers." "He's a great leader." *"Déjalo que haga su cosa."* ("Let him do his thing.") "He has to be the way he is; he's dealing with powerful *gringos;* it takes money to move things." "Well, the Anglo has made it that way, why shouldn't a Chicano?" "It is better to have Cisneros than McAllister or Cockrell."

His critics, on the other hand, call Cisneros an opportunist. Former City Council member Bernardo Eureste states that Cisneros does not have an "Hispanic agenda" and that he does not identify with progressive issues. The mayor, according to Eureste, tailors his speeches to the audience. Cisneros also is all things to all men. For example, although backed by Northside developers, Cisneros played an elusive role in the Edwards Aquifer affair. The Northside, a white area with an air of exclusiveness, had the best prime land in the city, both topographically and demographically. Builders planned an 88,000-person housing development in the Northside. The only problem, the Edwards Aquifer was located over the city's underground water supply. Environmentalists opposed the project, as did politically powerful Congressman Henry B. González.[21] In the press, Henry Cisneros made progressive statements opposing the Edwards Aquifer development. However, behind the scenes, he promoted the Apple White Dam, which would eventually bring groundwater to San Antonio, cancelling out the need for the aquifer. Moreover, in 1977, according to Eureste, when the vote was taken on the Edwards Aquifer, Cisneros quietly abstained. Developers sued the City Council members voting against the project as well as the city. In effect, the developers won, when the courts ruled that the city either had to buy the land in question or allow the housing development. The city could, therefore, not stop the development since it lacked the financial resources to buy the land.[22]

Explanations for Cisneros's success go beyond his charisma or the national reputation he has gained as a celebrity. The causes are rooted in the same soil that made possible the Chicano's political takeover of the City Council and the accomplishments of COPS. Unlike Los Angeles and other cities, the Chicano West Side *barrio* has maintained itself as a community. Until recently, Chicanos of whatever social class lived there. Because racism in Texas was harsh and persistent, few people could move to other neighborhoods. In Los Angeles, in contrast, communities are always in a state of development but are never allowed to achieve any sort of stability.

San Antonio's community is both its strength and its weakness. It has allowed the residents to retain a strong sense of identity and keep intact the essential networks for organic growth. Cisneros has strong links with the Chicano middle class, who see him as a vehicle for their own upward mobility. Moreover, Chicano nationalism is strong, cutting across class lines. Although much of the West Side is poor, Chicanos identify with Cisneros because he gives them hope. Lastly, political indoctrination in San Antonio public schools pushes the theme of free enterprise, promoting "trickle-down economics." San Antonio is conservative, and it sets the limits for Chicano participation. Henry Cisneros to date has been the most successful Chicano to play the game there, and currently Mexican Americans vicariously identify with his attainments.

Texas has led the electoral revolution among Chicanos. By 1984, *Tejanos* had three members of Congress, four state senators, and 21 state representatives. In 1986, Texas also led in the number of Chicanas elected to public office. Irma Rangel of Kingsville and Lina Guerrero of Austin were reelected to the state house of representatives, and Judy Zaffirini of Laredo got elected to the state senate.

In contrast, Polly Baca Barragán was a casualty in 1986. She had been one of Colorado's most successful politicians, having served in the state house of representatives and senate. In this year she put it all on the line and ran for the

U.S. Congress. Baca Barragán, however, lost in the Democratic party primary; she had opted not to run for reelection to the senate.

In all probability, the best political appointment insofar as Chicanos were concerned was that of Cruz Reynoso to the California Supreme Court in 1982. Reynoso was on the court because he earned it: he had devoted his career to the poor and to the promotion of social change. Reynoso had also been a law professor at the University of New Mexico School of Law. However, he was unpopular with many California corporate leaders and special interests. In 1986, these interests joined to remove Supreme Court Justice Rose Bird and Associate Justices Reynoso and Joseph Grodin from the bench. The pretense was that they had not voted to uphold the death penalty. In reality, it was a conspiracy to pack the court with pro-business Deukmejian appointments. Throughout the campaign Reynoso's race was constantly under attack.

California in 1986 showed that a backlash against minorities was in full swing. Aside from the removal of Reynoso, voters passed Proposition 63, the "English is the Official Language" initiative. This proposition was sponsored by the same nativists who pushed for the exclusion of Mexican and other Latin immigration. Playing to the cultural panic of Californians, and to fears that California was going Latin, voters passed an initiative whereby citizens could sue if English was not given adequate attention. After its passage, legislators opened attacks on bilingual education, the Spanish language ballot, merit increments given to government workers for knowing a foreign language, and so on. Proposition 63, along with the removal of Reynoso and the anti-immigrant propaganda, encouraged ugly confrontations in California as other states prepared to follow California's lead.

A welcome relief to the setbacks in California was Gloria Molina who bucked the Chicano political brokers. In 1982 Molina ran against Richard Polanco in Democratic primary race for the Assembly. Chicano *politicos* told Molina not to run because a woman could not win in East Los Angeles, she was not tough enough to negotiate with the heavyweights, and she could not raise sufficient funds without their support. Molina stayed in the race and won. Molina, a product of the 1960s student movement, got involved in counseling dropouts. She was a field representative to Assemblyman Art Torres. A participant in the founding of the national *Comisión Femenil* as well as the East Los Angeles chapter, Molina has been strong on women's issues as well as on local gut issues like redlining (the practice of insurance companies in certain areas setting higher rates than those in other areas) and prison reform, and has continued her interest in education.

In 1986, Molina unsuccessfully bucked the Chicano political establishment by not endorsing its candidate for Richard Alatorre's vacated assembly seat (Alatorre had won election to the Los Angeles City Council). Because Assembly Speaker Willie Brown backed recently elected assemblyman Richard Polanco and had to spend large amounts of money for him to win, he was angry at Molina and attempted to discipline her by appointing Polanco to the Public Safety Committee, which was choosing the site of a state prison. Although Polanco had promised he would vote against a prison in downtown Los Angeles, he switched positions and voted for the bill, allowing it to go to the full assembly where that chamber approved the bill. The prison was in Molina's district and she strongly opposed it.

Molina, at first, was the only Chicano state legislator to oppose the downtown prison; she joined forces with Mothers of East Los Angeles, a lay Catholic group from Resurrection Parish, neighboring Boyle Heights, and mobilized grassroots opposition to the prison. They were soon joined by the Chambers of Commerce of Boyle Heights and Lincoln Heights as well as numerous professional and service organizations. Rallies held throughout the months of July and August attracted between 1,500 to 3,000 protestors. Soon every Chicano politician in Los Angeles made it a point to be seen at the rallies and State Senator Art Torres, who had at first voted for the prison, led the fight to locate it elsewhere. Prison opponents pointed out that East Los Angeles already had five prisons, and that another prison would negatively impact the community.

Governor George Deukmejian, meanwhile, lobbied hard for the prison, stating that it was a logical site since it was in downtown Los Angeles and was thus close to the inmates's homes. In reality, other sites had been recommended in the Lancaster and Saugus-Newhall areas, but the governor objected to them because these were heavily white Republican districts. East Los Angeles, in turn, housed a poor Latino community, and the governor believed the political repercussions would be minimal. By the late 1980s the trend seemed to be that Republicans gave less lip service to the poor, blatantly ignoring their interests, and catered only to those who voted for them.

The Chicano community's vehement opposition to the prison, however, gave some legislators second thoughts. President Pro-Tem of the Senate David Roberti joined the opposition to the downtown prison. Archbishop Roger Mahoney also publically supported efforts to "Stop the Prison in East Los Angeles." Through a series of maneuvers, Roberti and Torres stopped the prison bill in the state senate from leaving the committee stage. Infuriated, Deukmejian continued to lobby for the downtown jail. He was prepared to push it through when the new legislative session began in 1987. But the unexpected occurred, and the syndicate who owned the property sold it to private investors. The Chicano community was jubilant; the governor continued his fight to put the new prison in the East Side.

Meanwhile, the political stock of Gloria Molina grew, and in the fall of 1986, she announced her candidacy for the newly created 1st Councilmanic District. This decision put her in a collision course with City Councilman Richard Alatorre.

Although Los Angeles had more Mexicans than any other metropolitan area in the United States, Chicanos remained largely unrepresented. A breakthrough occurred when, in 1985, Arthur Snyder announced his resignation from the City Council. Richard Alatorre gave up a prestigious seat in the California Assembly to run for the 14th Councilmanic District. Alatorre spent $300,000 to get elected, beating Steve Rodríguez, an urban planner, and Antonio Rodríguez, a Chicano activist lawyer.

Alatorre's election was treated like a coronation. Federal, state, and local politicians celebrated his success. Even César Chávez attended the swearing-in ceremonies. Without a doubt Alatorre's victory had tremondous symbolic value; he was the first Chicano to be elected to the City Council in 23 years. Because of this, Alatorre became a national figure and was recognized as the political leader of the largest Mexican community in the United States.

While Alatorre's political skills as a broker had been respected in the Assembly, they became a liability in the City Council. There his political baggage was more visible to the voters. His access to Assembly Speaker Willie Brown, who made available large sums of money to Latino candidates whom Alatorre supported, proved a source of embarrassment during the downtown prison fight. Moreover, he was put in the middle of the political frying pan when the Council president appointed him to head the reapportionment committee. In 1982, the U.S. Justice Department had brought suit against the City Council, charging: "The Los Angeles City Council has demonstrated over the last two decades that it is unwilling to include the public interest of the city's Hispanic population in apportionment of Council Districts."[23] In mapping a Latino councilmatic district, Alatorre caused a stir by protecting the seats of incumbents, many of whom had taken part in the diluting of Latino voting strength, and forcing the only Asian Council member either to oppose the Latino candidate or to run in another district against an incumbent. The mayor vetoed the Alatorre plan; a stalemate was broken when a San Fernando Valley incumbent died and the Council was again remapped. It created a Latino 1st district.

Everyone expected Alatorre to name a crony; however, Molina's candidacy challenged his leadership of East Side *politicos*. The only Mexican American incumbent that supported her was Congressman Edward R. Roybal. Alatorre and his friends supported Los Angeles School Board Member Larry González. In a hotly contested race Molina in February 1987 won by a landslide.

Molina's challenge is important. She represents a strong populist strain and a departure from party politics dependent on the party leaders who are able to generate large sums of money for expensive campaigns. She is a maverick of sorts, who breaks with the pack on issues. Without her visibility in the downtown prison issue, for example, another jail may very well have been built next to the East Side. She is not Alatorre's crony and will break his monopoly on the Council. Many eastsiders hope that she will also move Alatorre to the left. While Alatorre's voting record has not been been conservative, the problem has been that he has pushed his own agenda rather than one that serves the entire community equally. His association with developers such as TELACU by no means enhances the quality of his representation. With Molina on the Council he will be forced to take a more even stand on progressive issues or he will be asked for an accounting.

SAL SI PUEDES ("GET OUT IF YOU CAN")

The expression *sal si puedes* refers to an attitude developed by Chicanos living in the poorest of the poor sections of Chicano *barrios*. This attitude defies Chicanos to improve themselves and get out of the neighborhood. César Chávez came from a *barrio* called *sal is puedes* in San Jose, California. Like other Chicanos in the 1960s, he used the expression *si se puede,* "it can be done." Although there was hope that change could be achieved, the 1970s destroyed this hope and the "Decade of the Hispanic" (the 1980s) brought despair as poverty and hunger became more visible in the U.S.

The recession of 1981–1982 hit the Mexican American hard—especially children. Census data showed that 42 percent of all Latino children under the age of 6 lived in poverty in 1984. President Reagan's Task Force on Food Assistance, however, chose to ignore these statistics, alleging that "there is no evidence that widespread undernourishment is a major health problem."[24]

Prior to the 1980s, most Chicanos believed that upward mobility depended solely on education. Improve the schools and change attitudes, and the Chicano could make it. Slowly, many Chicanos came to realize that it was not that simple. The parents' income is, in particular, much more important than the school that the child attends. The economic status of a child's family determines future success. For example, Donald J. Bogue, in his study of the 1980 census, *The Population of the United States: Historical Trends and Future Projections,* dismisses the role of culture in the Asian's school performance, concluding that income is more important than culture. Bogue generalizes, "The tendency to enroll one's children in preschool and for children not to drop out of high school is strongly correlated with income of the family in which the child is a member."[25] In other words, poverty affects educational equity.

In 1983, Latinos comprised 25 percent of the K–12 enrollment in California. Less than one in four Latino students worked at grade level. By the third grade, 80 percent of all Latino children, fluent in English, performed below level in reading, writing, and mathematics. Only 9 percent of the Latino twelfth graders attended schools evaluated in the top quartile by the California Assessment Program. All these factors contributed to the near 50 percent dropout rate for Mexican children, and made educational equity a sham. In Texas in 1987 the courts were still debating, Does the funding gap between rich and poor school districts violate the Texas Constitution? Texans still saw nothing wrong with a system that allocated $2,000 a year to some students and $12,000 to others. Chicanos again sued in *Edgewood* v. *Kirby*, claiming that they were denied fundamental rights, resulting in systematic discrimination.[26]

Nationwide, the median education of Mexican American students was 9.9 years, the lowest of the so-called Spanish-origin groups. That is, just over 50 percent of Mexican children had under a tenth grade education. Considering the high-tech revolution, the *possibility* of these students enjoying the benefits of technological change was minimal. After studying the 1980 census, Professor Bogue asked whether North American society had reached the saturation point in educational progress. And he concluded that perhaps the goal of 100 percent literacy could not be reached.[27]

The Rambo years worsened the despair of many poor Chicanos as Reagan wiped out the remaining gains of the 1960s. Instead of encouraging institutions of higher learning to implement affirmative action, the Reagan administration cut financial aid funds, making it clear to school administrators that minorities would no longer receive judicial relief. Without financial incentives, many educators lost interest in Mexican American students. And as funds for higher education became scarcer, academicians renewed a debate as to whether educational equity negatively affected the quality of higher education.

Meanwhile, the budget crunch hit California hard. Governor George Deukmejian cut the community colleges to the point that by 1986 they laid off tenured faculty. In order to survive, community colleges responded to pressures to end their open admissions policy. Since Mexican Americans and other minorities disproportionately attended community colleges, Deukmejian's policies severely affected their quest for educational equity.

The governor was much more generous to the next two tiers of higher education—the University of California and California State University and College Systems. Of the two systems, because of its size and mission, Cal State served more undergraduate Chicanos. Cal State Chancellor W. Ann Reynolds moved into the national debate, complaining that not enough minorities were graduating, blaming this failure on the lack of preparation of minority students. Her solution was to pile on required courses for admission to the CSUs in order to force the public schools to offer prescribed classes to students. In other words, she promoted "trickle-down education."

Reynolds railroaded her proposal through the CSU Board of Trustees, where Chicana trustee Celia Ballesteros supported her after expressing "concerns." Statewide the first organization to protest Reynold's assault was MECHA. Students launched a campaign to inform the public. They pointed out that in 1985 new and higher requirements had already been implemented; that Reynolds, without studying the effects of these requirements on minorities, pushed for additional courses for 1988; and that, in spite of their limitations, the educational equity programs had recruited and graduated Chicano students who never would have had the opportunity without it. MECHA accused Reynolds of blaming the victim. Students stated that the question of educational equity had to be faced in grades K–12 and that the CSU's exclusionary policies represented a reversal of hard-fought 1960 gains. They also charged that no evidence existed that the admission of minorities hurt the quality of higher education. They recommended that the CSU system should examine its own effectiveness, since the CSUs graduated about 70 percent of the state's teachers and thus perhaps contributed to the lack of student preparation.

The California debate is important because the state sets a national trend. Older North Americans in general are more reluctant to pay the price of education for other people's children. They support those institutions that promote their own self-interest. Once they have their education, middle-aged North Americans are unwilling to pay for the education of so many minorities.

Aside from MECHA, public protest was limited. Absent were the voices of professional, business, or civic organizations whose members had benefited from more open admission policies. In fact, support even from Chicano faculty and graduate students proved limited, reflecting the paralyzing tolerance that consumed middle-class "Hispanics." Many Chicanos appeared to accept the fallacy that quality could be evaluated only through quantitative methods. Tests and the number of courses taken became the standards for "objective" exclusion. *Sal is puedes* was increasingly the bitter reality for poor Chicanos.

THE URBAN NIGHTMARE

Nationally in 1980, 74 percent of all North Americans lived in cities, versus 87 percent of Latinos. Ninety-three percent of California Latinos and 86 percent of the *Tejanos* lived in urban areas. Close to 60 percent lived in the central city, a figure that was higher than for whites but lower than for Blacks. Many Mexicans still dwelled in former agricultural, track, or brickyard colonies.

The quality of life varied greatly, from a minority living comfortably, to those residing in overcrowded public housing projects, to those having no homes. In Los Angeles, an estimated 60,000 homeless roam the streets, approximately 30 percent of whom are Latino families. Rents are beyond the poor's ability to pay.[28]

Homeowner occupancy (h/o), an indicator for stability and assimilation, is uneven for Latinos. California's Mexican community, although statistically better off than those in other southwestern states, has the lowest h/o rate. Texas, which has the reputation as racist toward Chicanos, has the highest h/o.

TEN METROPOLITAN AREAS WITH THE HIGHEST HOMEOWNER OCCUPANCY

City	Percent H/O, 1980	Percent Below Poverty Line, 1979		Number of Latinos, 1985	
McAllen, TX	66.9	36.6	(1)*	319,477	(8)*
Pueblo, CO	65.1	18.6	(18)	40,777	(35)
Albuquerque, NM	63.9	16.8	(23)	171,097	(18)
Las Cruces, NM	63.8	27.6	(4)	61,642	(30)
Tucson, AZ	63.1	17.1	(22)	137,064	(22)
Laredo, TX	62.0	31.6	(3)	118,452	(24)
Brownsville, TX	61.7	33.7	(2)	214,979	(13)
San Antonio, TX	60.3	24.2	(7)	636,466	(2)
Corpus Christi, TX	59.4	23.6	(9)	211,706	(14)
Riverside/San Bernardino, CA	58.6	16.4	(26)	402,554	(3)

*Rank in category.
Source: *The Changing Profile of Mexican America: A Sourcebook for Policy Making* (Claremont, Calif.: Tomas Rivera Center, 1985), pp. 9, 41, 49.

In 1980 California Mexicans had the highest median income, $16,081, followed by Arizona, $15,468; New Mexico, $13,513; and Texas, $13,293. California had only one metropolitan area, Riverside/San Bernardino, that ranked in the top ten in h/o. Because of lower-cost housing, this area attracted a lot of new construction as well as middle-class Chicanos from both Los Angeles and Orange counties. Significantly, five of the top ten cities were Texan. All five Texas cities also ranked among the highest in Mexicans living under the poverty line. Therefore, income apparently was not a factor in h/o.

In all probability the main reason for higher h/o in Texas is that Mexicans there are more segregated and until recently fewer lived outside the *colonia*. Thus middle-class Mexicans and some lower-income Chicanos bought homes when prices were lower and have not moved out, as is the case in California and other parts of the Southwest. In California, Mexican American hegemony in East Los Angeles is a postwar phenomenon, and there has been more opportunity to buy outside the Eastside.

TEN METROPOLITAN AREAS WITH THE LOWEST HOMEOWNER OCCUPANCY

City	Percent H/O, 1980	Percent Below Poverty Line, 1979		Number of Latinos, 1985	
San Francisco/Oakland, CA	45.5	11.1	(37)*	429,214*	
Anaheim, CA	45.0	12.1	(35)	360,216	
Stockton, CA	44.7	20.8	(12)	90,960	(28)*
Fresno, CA	44.7	22.2	(11)	194,721	(16)
Houston, TX	43.2	14.6	(31)	566,194	(3)
San Diego, CA	42.9	18.1	(21)	359,919	
Santa Barbara, CA	40.8	12.8	(33)	70,064	(29)
Santa Cruz, CA	37.5	16.7	(24)	35,559	
Los Angeles, CA	36.7	18.2	(20)	2,543,329	(1)
Monterey, CA	35.7	16.2	(29)	97,235	

*Rank in category.
Source: *The Changing Profile of Mexican America: A Sourcebook for Policy Making* (Claremont, Calif.: Tomas Rivera Center, 1985), pp. 9, 41, 49.

Of the lowest ten h/o cities, nine are located in California. The only Texas city that ranked in the bottom ten was Houston, which, like most California cities, experienced dramatic growth after World War II. Santa Cruz, Santa Barbara, and Monterey can be considered exclusive retirement villages. Los Angeles, Houston, San Francisco/Oakland, Anaheim, and San Diego all have industrial bases with large high-tech centers. Fresno and Stockton are principally agricultural centers.

The lack of h/o in the large cities such as Los Angeles and Houston could spell future problems. Homeowner occupancy has proved a reliable method for social control since 1919, when Euroamerican capitalists promoted homeownership for workers as a method of giving them a stake in society, and stemming restlessness. Without this constraint, and with increased unemployment, the propensity toward urban riots will surely be greater in the coming years.

Aside from h/o, another indicator of the deteriorating status of poor urban Latinos is the lack of good rental housing. With the heavy migration of documented and undocumented Mexicans and Central Americans into cities such as Los Angeles and Chicago, in response to an increase in service sector jobs there, the competition for living space has become intense. Privately owned apartments are like tenements, with two or three families renting a one-bedroom apartment. In the San Fernando Valley, a suburb of Los Angeles, many older apartments have been converted into suburban ghettoes. Landlords take advantage of the large influx of Salvadorians and undocumented Mexican workers to charge higher rents, making few repairs and providing few services. Homeowners complain that these new ghettoes are blighted and have a high incidence of crime.

In 1985, the Bryant–Van Alden section of Northridge, California, housed

3,000 low-income Latinos in a large apartment house complex. Councilman Hal Bernson, in collusion with landlords, presented a plan to the City Council: evict the renters, give a one-time exemption to landowners who would fix the apartments, and then dramatically raise the rents, circumventing the city's rent control ordinance. Bernson proposed that Los Angeles extend low-interest loans to landlords to upgrade these properties. He concluded that the improved apartments would "attract a different kind of people."

In response, 100 tenants formed *Padres Unidos.* They enlisted the support of more established Chicano leaders and groups. Although the City Council tentatively approved the Bernson plan, Mayor Tom Bradley supported *Padres Unidos* and threatened to veto the legislation. After this rejection, police harassment increased and the slumlords continued to neglect Bryant–Van Alden.[29] Eventually the slumlords won out. Meanwhile, in nearby Santa Ana, 500 tenants in June 1985 mounted a rent strike against two landlords.[30]

The *Los Angeles Times* on June 5, 1986, reported: "Eight poor [Latino] families—fearful of sleeping at night because they are under constant attack by rats and cockroaches in their run-down apartment building near downtown Los Angeles—filed a $10 million law suit Wednesday against their landlords." By the 1980s, public interest lawyers began to fight back.

In Chicago's Southside, Chicano steelworkers, who had formerly lived relatively well, fell on bad times. Unemployment worsened as Wisconsin Steel and the surrounding mills closed: "The layoffs have left their mark. Once prosperous storefronts are now roughly boarded. Houses with broken windows and rotting porches wait for better times. The high school drop out rate is way up." Migration to Chicago continued during the Rambo years, mostly to the Pilsen/Little Village area, where unemployment, overcrowding, and juvenile crime increased. Migrants took service jobs. In 1980, 425,000 Latinos, probably an undercount, lived in Chicago, a 71 percent growth in the 1970s.[31]

The "American Dream" of owning a home became the impossible dream by the 1980s. Individual successes could be celebrated. For the majority, however, the quality of life deteriorated. The 1980s also saw the forces of urbanism destroying communities in many developing *barrios.* The ability of these communities to produce organic leaders and organizations suffered.

THE CATHOLIC CHURCH: A COUNTERHEGEMONIC FORCE?

The Catholic Church has historically acted as an agent of social control. It legitimated the state, rarely criticizing its injustices. Most of its hierarchy as well as its priests have been Irish and/or German, rarely identifying with minorities such as Mexicans and their social struggles. It has not played a vanguard role similar to the Black ministers, and then their offspring, who have historically been leaders in the civil rights struggles of the masses. More important, Mexicans have been robbed of a national church network that advocates for their rights. Only occasionally, as in the case of San Antonio's hierarchy, did progressive currents operate. Since the 1960s, however, many Catholic clergy have questioned their role within the church.

Unlike the Black churches, from whose ranks emerged local and national

Black leaders, the Catholic Church has sided more with the rich and the powerful. The church also failed to serve Latinos proportionately. In the late 1970s, an estimated 45 million Catholics lived in the United States, of whom just over 13 million were Latinos. Latinos made up only 7 of the 322 U.S. bishops; 585 of the 56,000 priests were Latinos (only 185 of them were U.S.-born). In 1970, 95 percent of Texas Chicanos were Catholic; 52 Chicano priests served this community. In contrast, Protestants were only 5 percent of the Texas Chicanos but were served by 554 Mexican American ministers. Although Latinos comprised 25 percent of all North American Catholics, they made up only 7.6 percent of the 3 million parochial-school children. San Antonio parochial schools in the late 1970s had only two bilingual programs.[32]

In the 1960s, a minority of the Roman Catholic clergy and hierarchy developed an awareness of Chicano problems and needs. In 1969, in response to the unrest of the 1960s, the U.S. bishops established the Campaign for Human Development (CHD), supported by a special annual collection. The CHD granted money to self-help projects with the goal of learning the causes of poverty, identifying structural injustices, and giving the poor the tools to bring about social change through education and community action.

The CHD funded some self-help Chicano groups. The organization itself, however, is representative of North American society and has little awareness of or commitment to Chicano groups specifically. While Latinos comprise over 25 percent of the nation's Catholics and between 60 and 70 percent of its poor, the CHD outlays do not reflect these statistics. The following table suggests a serious underfunding of Chicano/Latino groups. (The data are based on the categories white/Hispanic, Hispanic, and Black/Hispanic, and, therefore, Chicanos share much of the money with the other groups.)

CAMPAIGN FOR HUMAN DEVELOPMENT FUNDING, 1980–1984

Year	Number of Projects	Latino Share	Total Granted	Latino Share of Money*	Latino Percentage
1980	134	21	$5,429,900	$965,400	17.8
1981	153	28	5,511,630	1,031,000	18.7
1982	195	25	6,398,450	978,000	15.3
1983	220	31	7,530,000	1,246,500	16.5
1984	229	43	7,005,950	1,363,000	19.4

*Total share does not go entirely to Latino groups but includes mixed Black/Latino and white/Latino programs.

Source: Campaign for Human Development, *Annual Reports* (Washington, D.C., 1980–1984).

A partial explanation for its neglect of Chicanos is that the CHD is located in Washington and not in areas with large Latino populations. Another is that the lack of a Latino/Mexican presence in the church's hierarchy produces unequal access to the CHD.

In spite of structural flaws within the church, quantitative changes have taken place. For example, during the 1970s and 1980s the U.S. Catholic bishops became increasingly sensitive to the poor. This shift in attitude broke with the tradition of church businessmen such as the late Msgr. Benjamin Hawkes of the

Los Angeles archdiocese, who expressed his empathy for the rich by stating: "The rich have souls, too," forgetting that the poor are supposed to inherit the earth.[33]

In a 1984 pastoral letter on "Catholic Social Teaching and the U.S. Economy," the bishops condemned as a national disgrace the fact that 35 million North Americans lived below the poverty line. The bishops called for government to play a larger role in solving the nation's economic problems. The letter urged a national policy to cut unemployment to 3–4 percent. The bishops strongly criticized the growing militarization under Reagan, and stated that government should give priority to meeting basic human needs. This report, rooted in Vatican II and the teachings of Pope John XXIII, reflected a growing antihegemonic movement within the church itself.[34]

The U.S. bishops' letter further legitimated and sanctioned the poor's struggle. Recent church appointments also suggest a trend toward at least considering Latino Catholics. Previously, hierarchial appointments served the interests of the Irish/German minority who ran the church. In Los Angeles, conservative Timothy Manning replaced the arch-reactionary John Francis McIntyre. Upon the retirement of Manning, the Vatican named Roger Mahoney archbishop of Los Angeles. Mahoney, unlike his predecessors, had a history of supporting social causes.

Mahoney immediately showed his commitment to the poor. On October 23, 1985, in an article for the *Los Angeles Times,* "Democracy's Obligation to the Poor," the archbishop laid out his position on the state's responsibility to ameliorate poverty. Mahoney reversed Manning's decision to sell Cathedral High, an almost entirely Latino inner-city boys' school, to Hong Kong investors for about $10 million. Mahoney also took an uncompromising stance in defense of the rights of the undocumented. When Los Angeles County Supervisor Mike Antonovich ran commercials in his unsuccessful 1986 bid for the Republican nomination for the U.S. Senate, portraying the undocumented worker as a menace costing the taxpayers hundreds of millions in welfare, Mahoney demanded an apology to the Latino community. He was enraged by a remark made by Antonovich's aide that the situation was so bad he wished he had a Smith & Wesson (a revolver).[35]

Another important phenomenon taking place in Chicano communities during the 1970s and 1980s was the growth of Industrial Areas Foundation (IAF) groups. These organizations were made possible, in most instances, through seed money granted by the Campaign for Human Development.

Outsiders often confuse the IAF groups with Latin American Liberation Theology and the base communities. While some IAF activists are sympathetic with Liberation Theology, and base communities function in some IAF parishes, they are a different phenomenon. Liberation Theology is part of the Latin American historical experience; it is rooted in the post-World War II era, when many priests and laypersons became disillusioned with "developmentalism" and the dependence of their governments on the United States. Encouraged by Vatican II, the Latin American bishops met at Medillin, Colombia, in the late 1960s, and leaders such as Gustavo Gutiérrez argued for a theology that liberated the poor. Over the years, the literature affirmed class struggle and the church's duty to align itself with the masses. The base communities as religious bodies worked toward collective salvation.[36] Liberationists held that through an intense study of history and the Bible answers for the present could be found.

The difference between Liberation Theology and the IAF groups is situational. Conditions in the United States are not the same as in Latin America. The IAF appeals to the interests of North Americans, basing itself on the organizational tactics of the late Saul Alinsky. It is shaped by the political reality of the United States and what will work within that reality. Aside from Judeo-Christian principles, the IAF does not espouse a political ideology. In most instances organizers stay away from defining issues such as abortion or divorce since a consensus cannot be built on them.

Many IAF organizers are critical of the war on poverty and 1960s social programs because they depended on government funding. According to them, the IAF is building organizations, not movements. Movements, by definition, are single-issue phenomena, usually dependent on charismatic leaders. At a time when urbanism destroys communities, the IAF seeks to renovate them. The IAF method revolves around the following principles: (1) it trains organic leaders; (2) it organizes people around self-interest; (3) it organizes them around issues that they can win, using controlled "persuasive disruption" as a tool to politicize the rank and file; and (4) it makes the organization economically self-sufficient. In the case of the Mexican/Latino, Alinskian groups are based on a network of parishes that financially support its activities. A professional organizer, earning between $15,000 and $35,000 annually, trains the leaders and guides the group.

Chicano links with the IAF are not recent, reaching back to Chicago's Back of the Yards. In the 1940s and 1950s, the IAF also helped organize the Community Service Organization (CSO) throughout the state of California. The CSO, however, differed from the present-day groups since its base was not the churches but neighborhood organizations.

Today the IAF's success in the Southwest is the result of the work of San Antonio's Ernie Cortés, Jr. Cortés, a product of Central Catholic High and a graduate of Texas A&M, became committed to social causes during his college years, joining the farm-worker movement of the mid-1960s. Briefly, Cortés worked for the Mexican American Unity Council and for the political campaigns of progressives such as Albert Peña, Jr., and Pete Torres. In 1971, Cortés left for Chicago and trained at the IAF for two years before returning to San Antonio.[37]

Bishop Francis Furey gave Cortés permission to form the Community Organized for Public Service (COPS). Methodically, Cortés inventoried West Side parishes and leaders. Many COPS lay leaders worked for the civil service sector, for Kelly Air Force base and the four other military installations. Most were lower middle class, aware of the lack of public services offered by the city, the disproportionate taxes paid by them, their unequal education, and their lack of political representation. Cortés knew that this sector owned their homes and had a sense of the community.

In 1974 the torrential rains that threatened to flood the West Side gave COPS its issue. For years, open ditches and bad sewers overflowed during the rainy season. Small children often drowned. COPS turned out large numbers of West Siders to pressure City Hall to improve flood control. This issue politicized many members, who investigated how the city distributed services and how it allocated federal block grant monies.[38] COPS, for instance, objected to the use of $1.3 million in federal funds for the Pecan Valley Country Club and pressured the City Council to allocate more money to the West Side. To effect change, COPS got heavily involved in politics, and, in 1977, it played a pivotal role in electing a Chicano/Black Coalition majority in the council.[39]

In 1978 COPS initiated an unsuccessful campaign to persuade voters to approve a bond issue providing extensive improvements in the West Side. The Northside refused to support the bond issue. COPS also clashed with the city's private sector. In 1974, the elite founded the Economic Development Foundation (EDF) to diversify San Antonio's economic base. The EDF advertised San Antonio as a haven for cheap labor. In 1977, COPS demanded that the EDF change its policy and attempt to attract better paying jobs. The EDF refused and threatened a corporate boycott of San Antonio which would worsen the poor's economic plight. COPS, confronted by the possibility of economic stagnation, negotiated a compromise. Bringing higher paying industries to San Antonio would be a goal. COPS did not have an alternative because of the structure of capitalism. Citizens can gain control of the political process; however, the economy is still in the hands of capitalists. The compromise virtually locked a sizable portion of the Chicano community into a below-subsistence wage level.

While many predicted COPS' decline, it consolidated organizationally. Throughout the late 1970s and early 1980s, Cortés built what is today considered the IAF network, which cooperated closely with groups such as the Southwest Voter Registration and Education Project. Governor Mark White designated November 20, 1983, "COPS Day in Texas."[40]

In 1975, after visiting San Antonio, Los Angeles Auxiliary Bishop Juan Arzube helped found UNO (United Neighborhood Organization), sponsored by 22 parishes initially. Fr. Luis Olivares of *Nuestra Señora de Soledad* became one of UNO's first religious leaders and Gloria Chávez, its first president. As in the case of COPS, Cortés intensely trained its first religious and lay leaders. Again, the leadership came from among lower-middle-class homeowner occupants.

East Los Angeles, however, differed from San Antonio. Mexican Americans had not reached a majority in the East Los Angeles Mexican *barrio* until after World War II, whereas many of the San Antonio leaders had deep roots in the West Side, spanning more than three generations (some even longer). San Antonio Mexicans were also more concentrated. In the Alamo City, middle-class and lower-class Mexicans lived in proximity of each other, whereas the Los Angeles middle-class Mexicans lived outside the *barrio*. The poor of East Los Angeles were in large part made up of undocumented workers. It could be argued that San Antonio had a community and that Los Angeles's community was developing.

Unlike COPS, UNO did not get involved in electoral politics. It organized around issues such as redlining, the practice of charging certain districts more for auto and home insurance than others. UNO also organized around the deterioration of private facilities such as the Safeway store, which had poor service and low-quality merchandise. UNO's success in negotiating better conditions attracted considerable notoriety.

UNO wanted to take the lead in revitalizing the Eastside. To this end, members sat down with a subcommittee of the Los Angeles Chamber of Commerce, made up of Los Angeles's business elite who met periodically to plan the city's economic and political future. It was UNO's aim to establish itself as the Eastside's legitimate voice and to persuade the ruling elite to include East Los Angeles in its plans for future growth.[41]

Generally, UNO has been more successful with the public sector than the private. For example, in the neighboring city of Monterey Park, it negotiated with the owners of a gigantic corporate center for jobs and job training programs. The weakness in the approach was that the center had mostly high-tech jobs that the East Los Angeles poor did not have the education nor skills to fill. The few construction jobs that were generated went to unionized workers, hardly offsetting the pollution created by the building process.[42]

UNO was caught in a Catch-22 situation. What it needed was well paying industrial employment to meet eastsiders' present level of education and skills. This was at a time when heavy industry was leaving Los Angeles. The ideal solution would have been an industrial park, not a corporate center.

UNO found itself in other dilemmas. It lobbied for the extension of Metrorail (an 18-mile subway under Wilshire Boulevard that would end in the San Fernando Valley) into East Los Angeles. The extension would not be a subway but a light rail. There is no question that a light rail would improve transportation options for eastsiders, especially since present service would be cut back to pay for the light rail. However, there is a high probability, according to experts, that the rails would intensify pressure on land use, changing the Eastside from a single-family residential area to condos and apartments. No doubt landowners would benefit from increased land values; the losers, of course, would be the renter class.

In October 1979, 5,000 members participated in UNO's annual convention. In July 1985, with its sister organization, the South Central Organizing Committee (SCOC),* 10,000 attended a meeting at Mount St. Mary's downtown campus.[43] Their ability to turn out the troops makes UNO and the SCOC potentially strong mass organizations.

The Texas IAF has been especially successful. In San Antonio, the IAF formed another group called the East Side Alliance, which is primarily Black. It has also set up groups in Austin, Forth Worth, Houston, El Paso, and Valley Interfaith in the lower Río Grande Valley.

EPISO (El Paso Interreligious Sponsoring Organization) was established in late 1980. Unlike other IAF–Cortés organizations, it mixes churches and civic groups. EPISO's base is in El Paso's Tigua area, a lower-middle-class and lower-income region. It was also active in the second ward. At first, EPISO ran into some problems because it ignored local leadership and groups. However, it has gradually developed effectiveness doing solid work on such issues as reapportionment and gerrymandering of Chicano districts.[44]

Valley Interfaith began in 1983 and includes 33 Catholic and one Methodist

*The SCOC, in South Cental Los Angeles, is comprised of Blacks and Latinos.

parish. Working in the Southwest's poorest region, where unemployment fluctuates from 18 to 37 percent, Valley Interfaith has had dramatic success. It has turned out thousands of poor Mexican Americans to pressure for better public services and jobs.

The event that catapulted Valley Interfaith happened in November 1983 when the Environmental Protection Agency (EPA) wanted to issue a permit that would have allowed the burning of toxic waste on ships in the Gulf of Mexico. Valley Interfaith mobilized over 2,000 Latinos, packing the EPA hearings and forcing the agency to back down.[45] Valley Interfaith also successfully pushed for a Task Force on Border Economic Development and gave priority to water, sewerage, jobs, and education as issues. On December 8, 1985, it held its first convention, with 5,000 members attending. The organization called for the rebuilding of the region's infrastructure to create public jobs.[46]

Meanwhile, the IAF developed an impressive network, which will eventually operate in key Chicano congressional districts throughout the Southwest. The Texas IAF network influenced Governor Mark White, who knew that, although the IAF groups are tax-exempt and cannot participate in politics, they have considerable clout among constituents. Because of this power, the IAF by the mid-1980s successfully pressured an unfriendly legislature, with the governor's support, to pass a health care program for indigents, an equalization bill for poor schools, and workers' compensation for farm workers.

The IAF network's main contribution is that, in a time when activism is unpopular, it has been able to involve the poor; it has not been intimidated to abandon confrontational politics. The IAF recognizes struggle as a key to gaining political power. And while many on the left criticize the IAF as a populist organization that diverts attention from more progressive alternatives, without groups such as COPS and UNO many middle-class and poor Latinos would not be involved in social change programs. The fact is that the North American left has been unable to sustain mass movements and rarely has it reached poor Latinos. Dialectically, the IAF's emergence is a response to the disorder of the 1960s, which did not produce politicized the masses.[47]

The IAF's limitations are those of the system. First, while it is possible to influence the public sector, business remains in capitalism's hands. The Chicanos' main attraction is cheap labor. Self-interest means keeping wages down. In the present economic climate the most Chicanos can hope for is public works jobs. This is, however, improbable in today's political climate. Programs like Franklin Roosevelt's New Deal would be implemented only if the majority of white Americans were to be impoverished. Second, this society has a tremendous potential for socializing people. The fact that so much of the IAF network's leadership comes from the middle class has the potential of developing a gap between homeowner and renter. Third, what role will the church and/or the IAF itself play if the network radicalizes? Fourth, the 1960s civil rights movement proved that social change through legislation has its limitations. Setbacks cannot be attributed solely to the lack of organization. Although the Black community has a solid network of national associations and local churches, it failed to stem the backlash of the Archie Bunker years, and was impotent during the Rambo years. Lastly, the IAF's growth has been natural to

Texas. The highly urbanized environment of Los Angeles is another matter. In Texas, communities have remained intact, whereas in California urbanization has continuously destroyed or muted their development. With the destruction of neighborhoods comes a loss of historical consciousness and the ability to sustain an organization.[48]

FINAL PORTRAIT: THE RAMBO YEARS

This section presents a kaleidoscope of events and changes happening within the Mexican American communities. And although very little improvement occurred in the economic groups' status, changes in attitudes did take place. As often is the case, the shifts were not enough, but they have to be assessed in order to build on them.

For instance, a 1983 *Los Angeles Times* survey on "Views on the Status of Women" showed that 65 percent of the Latino males favored most efforts to strengthen the status of women, versus 61 percent of Black males and some 70 percent of white males. Seventy percent of the Chicanas favored these changes, versus 61 percent among both Black females and white females. Attitudes toward women's issues among Chicanos generally followed party lines. A 1984 SVREP survey showed that almost three-quarters of the Latino population favored the Equal Rights Amendment (ERA). Among delegates to national presidential conventions, 89 percent of the Democratic Latino delegates favored ERA while only 33 percent of the Republican Latinos did.[49]

Progressively, more Chicanas/Latinas joined the workforce—44.6 percent in 1976 to 49.9 percent in 1983. Contrary to popular myth, their salaries went not for luxury items but for food and shelter. At the turn of the decade, 51 percent of Latinas were either unemployed or underemployed; they earned 49¢ to every dollar made by white males, versus 58¢ for white females and 54¢ for Black women. Half had under 8.8 years of education. Some 67 percent who headed households had children under 18 and lived under the poverty line; Latinas headed some 29 percent of Chicano households.[50]

OCCUPATIONAL DISTRIBUTION OF FULL-TIME WORKERS 15 YEARS AND OVER BY SEX AND SPANISH ORIGIN IN THE U.S., 1981

	White		Spanish Origin	
	Male	Female	Male	Female
Professional, technical, and kindred workers	16.2%	13.7%	6.8%	8.1%
Managers and administrators	18.6	11.0	7.3	5.5
Sales workers	8.1	6.1	3.3	4.0
Clerical and kindred workers	5.8	4.3	6.5	34.7
Craft and kindred workers	24.0	2.7	21.8	3.0
Operatives (including transport)	17.2	12.6	30.0	25.4
Laborers	4.4	1.2	7.3	1.3
Service workers	3.9	11.0	11.6	17.5
Agricultural workers	1.7	—	5.4	—

Source: 1980 census, in Denise A. Segura, "Chicanas and Triple Oppression in the Labor Force," in National Association for Chicano Studies, *Chicana Voices: Intersections of Class, Race, and Gender* (Austin: in Center for Mexican American Studies, University of Texas, 1986), p. 55.

As indicated in the table, the Chicanas' numbers in the upper paying professions were small. Percentages were based on their numbers in the workforce and, therefore, are not suggestive of all Chicanas. Clearly, the poorer Mexican females were the most victimized, and basic necessities such as child care denied to them.

Just as did their male counterparts, Chicana activists became increasingly isolated during the 1980s. Most professional and middle-class Mexican American women's groups represented the interests of their class and followed mainstream trends. Topics such as abortion or birth control, popular during the Archie years, became less popular in the Rambo days. By the mid-1980s, even Chicana Republicans claimed to be part of the "Hispanic women's movement."

DEFENDING THE AMERICAN WAY

In 1985, Reagan cut the funds of the Bureau of Labor Statistics (BLS). The president, disturbed by a study on plant closures conducted by the BLS, moved to destroy the bureau and its respected journal, *The Monthly Labor Review.* Important sources of data on the economy both were used in spotting major economic and social trends. The *MLR* had been published for 70 years without partisan interference before Reagan moved to control it. Congress defended the BLS and made it more independent of the president. The absence of statistics would have allowed government to ignore its role in defining problems and solutions and would have encouraged its policy of blatant favoritism toward big business. "Some critics of the proposed cuts charge the Administration wants a less active BLS because the less the nation knows about the problem, the easier it is for government to avoid dealing with it."[51]

Farm Workers

The farm workers' fortunes worsened during the 1980s. In Texas and Arizona organizational efforts in the fields lessened. Bad times in Mexico and in Central America accelerated migration from those areas. The labor surplus depressed farm wages; non union workers earned $3.35 an hour while union workers earned $5.10 for about 23 weeks. The average annual income in 1985 for farm workers was $8,800—well below the poverty line. Ninety percent dropped out before finishing high school; 50 percent left school before finishing the ninth grade. Bombarded with pesticides and insecticides, farm workers were 26 times more likely to contract parasitic diseases.[52]

The United Farm Workers continued as the symbol of farm-worker struggle. How many belonged to the UFW is in doubt. Chávez claimed to represent over 100,000 dues-paying members, whereas many observers state that the existence of large labor surpluses and the bad economy had reduced UFW membership to a much lower level. The UFW, no matter what its numbers, kept up with technology and effectively used high-tech methods to maintain a support network. It had a modern print shop at its La Paz, California, headquarters along with computers that could print out specialized mailings to millions of potential supporters. By 1987 Chávez conducted his grape boycott largely through computers, bolstered by selective picketing of supermarkets. A major issue had become the indiscriminate use of pesticides which Chávez wanted controlled.

Chávez continued to live as he did in the 1960s, sleeping four hours, meditating, and attending daily mass. In February 1985, he remained popular with Californians. A poll revealed that 53 percent still favored Chávez, with only 21 percent opposed to him. His problems, related to the length and intensity of the struggle, caused personality clashes and dissatisfaction with the UFW's direction. Provocateurs no doubt deepened these differences. And, no doubt, Chávez himself in part contributed to rifts.

By the 1980s, Chávez's organizational problems grew: Jerry Cohen, a labor attorney, left the UFW; Marshall Ganz and Gil Padilla also left. Many alleged that Chávez could not delegate authority. Others maintain that he became paranoid about communist infiltration. In the end, the union survived in spite of insurmountable odds.

Compounding the UFW's problems, Governor George Deukmejian, heavily indebted to agricultural interests, set out to destroy the UFW; his main strategy was to torpedo the Agricultural Labor Relations Board by appointing David Stirling, a grower hatchet man, general counsel to the board. Under Stirling only 10 percent of the cases reached the ALRB, compared with 35 percent under Governor Edmund G. Brown, Jr. Deukmejian cut the ALRB's budget by one-third, and by 1986 the board became inoperative, when the ALRB, because of the governor's appointments, was totally under the control of the growers. Government continued to conspire against the UFW. In a case of "rural justice," Imperial County Superior Court Judge William Lehnhardt imposed a $1.7 million judgment against the union on January 8, 1987, for losses suffered by Maggio Inc. during a strike. Although Maggio only suffered $3,000 in property damages, the company claimed it suffered crop losses due to the strike. Four thousand workers had walked out on Maggio and the other vegetable farmers. Local businessmen, housewives, and children worked as strikebreakers to help their friends. Confrontations followed, with the growers employing armed guards and attack dogs. Many strikers were injured and Isauro López was permanently crippled when struck by a grower's car. Rufino Contreras was shot through the head and killed. Lehnhardt ruled that the union was responsible for the violence and crop loss and refused to prosecute grower employees for murder. Lehnhardt refused to disqualify himself from the case, although his wife had worked as a strikebreaker. Meanwhile, the union had to put up $3.3 million in order to appeal this perversion of justice, waiting for years to get its day in court.[53]

The UFW's troubles went beyond California. Reagan appointed John R. Norton, head of J. R. Norton Company, one of the world's largest lettuce producers, U.S. deputy secretary of agriculture. The ALRB had found Norton guilty of dealing in bad faith with workers. At the time of his appointment, Norton was appealing these cases, involving millions of dollars. Stirling, claiming impartiality, allowed Norton's lawyers to read the ALRB's confidential files, until the state Supreme Court finally prohibited Stirling from giving Norton file copies. Meanwhile, in Washington, Norton lobbied for a guest worker program, alleging that without the guest workers California crops would rot.

Undocumented Workers

Increased migration of workers and their families continued in the 1980s. In the Southwest and Midwest, the nature of this migration changed as Salvadorian and Guatemalan political refugees began to enter in large numbers because of political repression by the two Central American governments. U.S. intervention dramatically worsened conditions, stepping up the migration north.

The entrance of large numbers of Latinos intensified North American nativism. Ex-CIA director William Colby had stated in 1978 that Mexican migration represented a greater threat to the United States than the Soviet Union. The hysteria reached absurd levels when, in 1985, the Filmore, California, City Council passed an ordinance declaring English the official language. That same year Dallas Mayor Pro Tem Jim Hart warned voters that aliens had "no moral values" and were destroying Dallas neighborhoods and threatening the security of the city. According to Hart, Dallas women could be "robbed, raped or killed."[54] In the fall of 1986, as mentioned, California passed its "English Is the Official Language" proposition.

In this context, the Rodino-Simpson bill became law in the fall of 1986. Fueled by paranoia, it pretended to bring about a massive overhaul of the nation's immigration code. It had all of the features of previous bills: employer sanctions, an amnesty proviso for undocumented workers arriving before January 1982, a guest workers program, and additional funding for the INS. In addition, it also gave farmers special privileges by granting anyone who had worked in agriculture for 90 days in the past year special status. In the end, the act represented a compromise between liberal Congressman Howard Berman and grower interests. It also proved that the issue was racism and not that Latinos were taking jobs away from North Americans.

Critics charge that Simpson-Rodino was a major victory for North American nativists. They point to the fact that research study after study verified that the bill would not stem immigration from Mexico and that, in fact, the undocumented worker was an asset to the economy. For instance, in 1984 the Urban Institute of Washington reported that 645,000 jobs had been created in Los Angeles County since 1970. Mexican immigrants took about one-third of the jobs. However, the study indicated that, although one-half of the jobs Mexicans took were in manufacturing, they did not contribute to unemployment. In fact, without Mexican immigrants the factories employing them would have left the Los Angeles area. The undocumented, by working cheap, subsidized industry and because of them capital remained in California rather than going overseas.[55]

A 1985 Rand Corporation study, conducted for the California Roundtable, a group of 90 of the state's largest companies, found that undocumented workers did not burden society, and, in fact, contributed to economic growth. The report found that less than 5 percent of all Mexican immigrants received any form of public assistance. Rand concluded that Simpson-Mazzoli (then being proposed) would not stop immigration.[56]

Even after these and other similar studies, most North Americans believed that an "immigration crisis" existed and had to be controlled. Simpson-Rodino was the politicians answer to this manufactured panic. And in an election year, it was important for North Americans to feel secure.

The Pecking Order

An unfortunate side effect of years of INS overestimation of the undocumented population and of the false notion that undocumented workers are taking the jobs of Chicanos, is that many U.S. born Mexicans have blamed the foreign-born for their lack of mobility. (The INS uses a "got-away" ratio—for every undocumented worker that is caught, it estimates that 3 to 4 "get-away." Therefore, if 1.7 million arrests are made it multiplies that number by a factor of 3 or 4.) Tensions increased as the nation's labor market restructured, with blue-collar jobs becoming less plentiful. Many believed the myths despite the facts: 60–70 percent of the children of the foreign-born did not complete high school and they were consequently in no position to compete for the jobs Chicanos needed to advance socially or economically.

According to UCLA Law Professor José L. Bracamonte, social scientists distorted the nature of the work undocumented workers perform: "Once their access to the U.S. labor market is restricted or eliminated through employer sanctions, the argument goes, employers need only upgrade their wages and working conditions to attract the displaced U.S. workers." According to Bracamonte, current studies defy this view and indicate that undocumented workers do not play a supplemental role in the U.S. economy. They play a structural role and as such they are needed to sustain and enhance growth. They are part of a secondary labor market that creates jobs that many Chicanos now hold and that they may lose if sectors of this market go out of business or move to Mexico or Singapore or whatever. In any event, the remaining jobs in this secondary market will not be upgraded, and if they are, the probability is that they will be automated.

Bracamonte admits that this secondary labor market is exploitive and should not be permanently tolerated; however, Simpson-Rodino only promises to worsen the plight of the workers. Exploitation will not be eliminated by employer sanctions which will drive the undocumented underground, creating a lower tier in this sector. Unscrupulous employers will merely shift the risk to the undocumented by using gimmicks like subcontractors who will further depress wages below the present minimum.

Critics further charge that Simpson-Rodino is unenforceable. Lawmakers never meant to control immigration. With 85 percent of its personnel at the border, how will 15 percent be able to police employers who "knowingly" hire undocumented workers? How will they prove that they "knowingly" hired an undocumented worker? And is the law enforceable against the rich and powerful with their team of lawyers? Critics point to the agricultural compromise as evidence that they did not want to protect jobs. Farmers have created a revolving door that perpetuates a captive class that can only escape by leaving the farm. According to Bracamonte, "The ill-conceived Simpson-Rodino immigration bill will no doubt result in economic dislocation and a civil-rights nightmare for the Latino community."[57] Lastly, the amnesty provision is already creating a bureaucratic nightmare. The INS is reluctantly setting up guidelines. And aside from the problem of accumulating the necessary documentation that they were in the United States before January 1982, undocumented workers are finding that they may be subject to prosecution if they have not paid taxes or that if they do not have permanent employment, they may be ineligible to become residents. Moreover, most are reluctant to trust the INS.

The insecurity caused by Simpson-Rodino promises to depress conditions for those working in the secondary labor market. And the probability of Chicanos at any generational level getting an education preparing them for high-tech employment is minimal. Bad times since 1973 made it more difficult for Chicanos to accumulate the surplus to send their children to college. Census data showed that the Spanish-origin population, age 14–24, was much less educated than whites or Blacks and that the Mexican population was the lowest of any of the Spanish-origin population. Thirty percent never even entered high school. This trend is not new but existed long before the influx of undocumented workers. A hard fact is that Chicanos are more likely to be employed as blue-collar workers than non-Mexicans, and industrial jobs are on the decline. Changes in social policy, slow growth in production output, employment restructuring, and high interest rates have all aggravated the condition of U.S.-born Mexicans. Programs helping minorities have also shrunk. The demand of the business community for modernization, tax breaks, and increased defense spending have all collided with the poor's demands for more social programs.[58] And Simpson–Rodino offers no relief; it will only encourage discrimination against all Latinos—regardless of their status.

Singapore, Mexico

Simpson-Rodino completely fails to address the root cause of Mexican migration to the United States, which is Mexico's inability to produce enough permanent jobs that promise an economic future to its citizens. Relief for the Mexican worker, given the increased role of the United States in its economy, is not possible in the near future. Mexico in the last 20 years has become a haven for U.S. corporations that make super profits by paying low wages, low energy costs and operate with minimal environmental controls. They can operate in Mexico under conditions that U.S. citizens would not tolerate.

In the 1980s, North American capital continued to penetrate Mexico. By 1981, 600 *maquiladoras* operated south of the border, 90 percent of them along the border, employing 130,000 workers. Depending on the study, 75–90 percent were women, 70 percent of whom were single. In 1978, the minimum wage in Ciudad Juárez was 125 pesos a day, $5.30. Devaluations drastically cut this rate.[59]

By 1986, Ciudad Juárez had become a *maquiladora* boomtown; Mexican labor rates were lower than in Southeast Asia, South Korea, Taiwan, or Singapore. The system supported 80,000 workers in Juárez alone and another 5,000 white-collar jobs in El Paso. The number of assembly factories had doubled since 1982. Corporations such as General Motors, which sent wire harnesses to be assembled there, maintained large operations. Throughout the border, the transnationals spent $10 billion annually, and they were Mexico's second largest source of foreign exchange.

The *maquiladoras* produced a division of labor that saw the extreme exploitation of Mexican women. Euroamerican capitalists built their organizational control on the traditional Mexican patriarchy, setting up a network of male supervisors intended to dominate and subordinate the assemblers. Women lead workers were also used to manage the rank and file. The women were extremely vulnerable since their jobs were deskilled.[60] The future held very little for these workers, for the goals of upward mobility and improvement of their social status were improbable.

In 1982, an international crisis consumed Mexico, with outgoing President José López Portillo dramatically devaluing the *peso,* which, in the next three years, fell to over 700 pesos to the dollar. The reason for the devaluation supposedly was to stop the flight of dollars from Mexico. Mexico's external debt, both private and public, had climbed to $85 billion. Mexico needed the dollars to pay its debt (which approached $100 billion by 1986). López Portillo took this step at the end of his six-year spending spree. The calamity had been encouraged by U.S. or foreign bankers who extended easy credit to Mexican Americans and to the government. Flushed with large deposits of Arab money, drawn to the United States by high interest rates, North American banks literally dumped their surplus dollars on Third World countries for higher interest returns than could be earned at home. Often the banks gave little consideration to the fact that corrupt politicians would squander the money.

By 1986, Mexico was at the point that it either had to default on the loans or declare a repayment moratorium. Mexico's internal situation worsened and it could no longer knuckle under to the International Monetary Fund (IMF) and cut government spending without drastic internal consequences. The situation had been made almost impossible by the nearly 50 percent plunge in the price of oil, which furnished 70 percent of Mexico's export exchange and 50 percent of its government revenues.[61]

In spite of severe restraints on the movement of capital, rich Mexicans continued to shift their money to the United States. Many bought shopping centers and apartment complexes or invested in companies doing business with Latino populations in the United States. Mexican capitalists, in fact, controlled many of the top 500 so-called Hispanic businesses. Meanwhile, the poor paid Mexico's foreign debt through austerity programs which cost them jobs, hiked the cost of public services and food, and contributed to a runaway inflation. As conditions worsened in that country, migration accelerated. U.S.–Mexican relations were also affected by the debt, with Mexico's dependence increasing, and an erosion of the once independent Mexican foreign policy that became more and more compromised.

CENTRAL AMERICA: ANOTHER VIETNAM

In 1970, the overwhelming majority of Los Angeles Latinos were of Mexican extraction. Changes, however, occurred since 1980 when a mass migration of Salvadorians and Guatemalans arrived in the United States. By the mid-1980s, about 300,000 Salvadorians and 50,000 Guatemalans lived in Los Angeles alone.[62]

This migration of Central American political refugees is the result of U.S.–Latin American policy since the early nineteenth century. For instance, the Somozas ruled Nicaragua for almost a half a century. The family, educated in the United States, spoke perfect English, and they protected U.S. business interests. The family owned over half the nation's resources, and is even reported to have profited from the earthquake that devastated Nicaragua by appropriating humanitarian supplies sent to the country. Anastasio Somoza, Jr., had one of the region's best equipped armies and controlled unrest through terror. In 1979, the Sandinista army overthrew Somoza, whom Carter supported almost to the last moment.

After this point, North American involvement became more blatant. History literally repeated itself. From 1910 to 1940, the United States attempted to overthrow the Mexican government. U.S. politicians and business leaders, enamored of the dictator Porfirio Díaz (in power 1876–1911), wanted to bring back the good old days when North American investors enjoyed carte blanche. Anglos invaded the country, sent arms to counterrevolutionary forces, and declared an economic boycott.

In 1954, the United States masterminded the overthrow of Guatemalan President Jacobo Arbenz. In the 1960s, unable to control Fidel Castro's Cuban government, it conspired to overthrow and/or assassinate him. As recently as 1965, President Lyndon B. Johnson sent U.S. marines to Santo Domingo to prevent constitutionally elected President Juan Bosch from taking office.

The fall of Somoza weakened North American hegemony. Carter moved to bolster the ruling elites in El Salvador, where 14 families controlled the country. Unrest had existed in El Salvador since the 1920s; peasants wanted land and were tired of *latifundista* exploitation. Farabundo Martí, aided by the Communist party, led a revolt which was viciously suppressed in 1932. Over 12,000 peasants (mostly Indians) died, and Martí was murdered. The Carter administration pressured the ruling elites to initiate land reform programs to limit peasant unrest. However, the government subverted the reforms. The military believed that it could impose its own solution without relinquishing any power.

The situation in El Salvador polarized in 1977. In the early 1970s, the ruling elite subverted elections. Meanwhile, Robert D'Aubisson, a neo-Nazi, headed the death squads that conducted a campaign to rid the country of leftists. In 1977, D'Aubisson's so-called White Warriors machine gunned down Jesuit Father Rutilio Grande. The death squads then ordered all Jesuits out of the country. These events radicalized the church, and Archbishop Oscar Romero began to talk out against injustice. In 1980, rightist assassins murdered Romero as he celebrated mass. That year, the National Guard tortured, raped, and killed four North American churchwomen.

In 1980, a coalition of Christian Democrats, Social Democrats, minor parties, trade unions, students, and others formed the *Frente Democrático Revolucionario* (FDR), which represented the political arm of the revolution. The FDR joined the *Farabundo Martí Liberación Nacional* (FMLN), which included the military sector heading the armed struggle. At the same time, to give the government an air of legitimacy, a centrist party assumed the national presidency. However, the right controlled the legislature through use of the death squads. The United States financed military operations against the FMLN, contributing to the death of some 50,000 Salvadorians—most of whom were civilians. Unable to find peace at home, thousands of Salvadorians fled north.

Meanwhile, the United States did not give Nicaragua the opportunity to stabilize, initiating a policy of economic and political isolation. It pressured Mexico, Costa Rica, and other governments to boycott Nicaragua. Under the pretext that Nicaragua was supplying arms to El Salvador's insurgents, human rights advocate Carter suspended food and medical supply shipments to Nicaragua for 30 days. Reagan, in turn, launched an undeclared war against this nation of 3 million people. He stationed 2,000 troops in Honduras, where, along with the CIA, he financed and supported the *contras.*

From this base, the *contras,* with the help of U.S. advisors, regularly attacked Nicaraguan villages, killing thousands of innocent civilians. In Honduras, the CIA openly violated the Boland Amendment, which prohibited the use of U.S. funds to overthrow a foreign government.

Reagan insisted that Soviet and Cuban influence had grown in Nicaragua and that this tiny nation threatened U.S. security. To bring about a negotiated solution, neighboring Latin American countries—Mexico, Venezuela, Colombia, and Panama—met on the island of Contadora in 1982. The Contadora nations worked out a treaty that they believed all sides could live with. At first, Reagan approved of the process; however, when these Latin nations produced a treaty that the Sandinistas immediately accepted, Reagan rejected it. Reagan also refused to accept the World Court's jurisdiction and its ruling that the U.S. violated international law in its interference with Nicaragua.

U.S. national security documents prove that Reagan did not want a solution. An April 1983 National Security Council directive stated the U.S. intention "to coopt [the] negotiations to avoid congressionally mandated negotiations."[63] The central problem for the Contadora nations was that if a settlement guaranteed the elimination of Soviet and Cuban influence, it logically must also guarantee that the United States would not interfere in the region. What the Nicaraguans wanted was the opportunity to live without interference from any country—and this Reagan would not concede.

Faced with starvation and the threat of the U.S.-supplied *contras,* Nicaragua negotiated trade agreements with the Soviets. Reagan offered this as proof of Soviet domination. Sandinistas countered that they would gladly have bought the supplies from the United States. Reagan alleged that the Sandinistas were undemocratic because they did not hold elections immediately after Somoza's overthrow. In 1984, the Sandinistas held elections, which Western European and Latin American nations praised. Reagan said that they were a sham. Slowly, critics of Reagan's policies, in Congress and the media, toned down their opposition and conditionally supported him. They ignored Reagan's methodical isolation of Nicaragua and his obvious search for an excuse to invade that country.

In Guatemala, violence continued as U.S. investment in the nation remained heavy. Guatemalans had never forgiven the United States for overthrowing their constitutionally elected president in 1954. In the 1960s, a revolution broke out that lingered into the early 1970s, when government troops, using U.S. equipment, crushed it. When guerrilla activity increased in the 1980s, the government, knowing that the revolutionaries had peasant support, began burning Indian villages and forcing the Indians into key cities. Since 1954, the government has killed over 100,000 of its people; another 35,000 have disappeared. Today, some 50,000 Guatemalans live without documents in the Los Angeles area alone.

The Salvadorian and Guatemalan communities in the United States are working toward common goals. They have political and refugee organizations, and have integrated well into the Protestant and Catholic refugee relief network. North American groups such as the Committee in Solidarity with the People of El Salvador (CISPES), whose national director, Angela Sanbrano, is a Chicana, work full-time to counter Reagan's propaganda. Such groups seek support for a democratic solution. The Office of the Americas, directed by Blase Bonpane, in Santa Monica, California, serves as a clearinghouse for information on the region.

The sanctuary movement, founded on Judeo-Christian tradition, is also important. Religious groups throughout the United States have offered Salvadorian and Guatemalan political refugees sanctuary in their houses of worship. Many universities and cities have extended sanctuary. Former New Mexican governor Toney Anaya even declared the state a sanctuary. The Reagan government, disturbed by this movement, has initiated prosecutions of sanctuary movement leaders through the INS and the Justice Department. In Tucson, several church people have been convicted for violating U.S. immigration law.

Passage of Simpson-Rodino promises increased repression of Salvadorians and Guatemalans in the United States. Most in these groups arrived after 1982. Their presence is a reminder to North Americans of what their policy in the region has produced.

THE DECLINE OF THE BLUE-COLLAR SECTOR AND ITS IMPACT ON CHICANOS

Once upon a time auto and steelworkers represented the elite among Chicano labor. Since the late 1910s, many Mexicans have participated in the struggles to build a strong trade union movement. In the 1930s, when many industries relocated to the Southwest or built branches there, few Chicanos worked in these plants. With time their number grew, and the postwar period saw more Chicanos enter heavy industry. These union jobs paid relatively high salaries, and many Chicano workers owned their own homes. Other Chicanos also joined unions—retail clerks, meat cutters, warehouse workers, and so on. With heavy industry's decline, however, a sizable portion of the Chicano middle sector has been wiped out.

During the Rambo years, government policy encouraged union busting. The Reagan administration told "corporate America" that government would not intervene. Reagan's appointees to the courts reflected a corporate bias. In June 1985, the U.S. Supreme Court, in a 5–4 decision, ruled that a union could not fine or discipline members who had participated in a democratic election and then resigned and scabbed. The decision upset the balance of power between labor and management, allowing management to subvert union organizing efforts. If the ruling were carried to its logical conclusion, a minority of dissidents could undermine union discipline. The court majority, creating new fictions, called the practice "voluntary unionism." This decision gave the National Labor Relations Board the right to interfere in union business and veto the union's guidelines.[64]

A favorite strategy used by management to divide labor was the two-tier wage system. Management would give union workers the option of keeping their jobs and their present salary scale and benefits if they would allow future hires to be paid wages that sometimes were only half their own. This tactic, which can undercut the union's bargaining power, encourage management to fire older workers, and split the rank and file, was successfully promoted by the National Right to Work Committee.

By 1985 unions represented only 19 percent of the nation's workforce. An example of the decline in union shops occurred in California. In 1982, that state had only one union auto plant, the Van Nuys General Motors facility (the Fremont plant was a joint Toyota–GM experiment). Late in the 1970s, the Big Three (GM, Ford, and Chrysler) decided to centralize all their operations in the Midwest and to leave the subcompacts to Mitsubishi and Isuzu. Ford closed its Pico Rivera and San Jose plants, Mack Truck shut down in Haywood, and General Motors eliminated its Fremont and South Gate plants. Only Van Nuys remained, employing 4200 workers, over 50 percent of whom were Mexican/Latinos. United Auto Workers Local 645, led by its president, Pete Beltrán, was the only link between the International and the West Coast Mexican community. Local 645 was a progressive force, organizing undocumented workers at factories, such as Superior Industries, that supplied the GM–Van Nuys plant.

General Motors threatened in, 1982, to shut down the plant and move its operations to the Midwest. It demanded that the workers save GM $330 a unit before the company would even consider keeping the assembly line running. The issue was not that Van Nuys was not making a profit—it was—but that GM wanted higher profits. General Motors had some 45 percent of the national market and 30 percent of the California market. Extracting $3 billion in contract concessions from workers in the early 1980s, GM had purchased 40 percent of the Isuzu Motor Company. Making windfall profits from voluntary quotas on Japanese cars, instead of modernizing its plants, GM gave huge bonuses to its managers.[65] By the mid-1980s, the firm had bought the Hughes Tool Company and was the world's largest transnational.

A plant closure greatly affects entire communities. South Gate, California, became a ghost town after the plant shut down. In 1979, automakers employed 20,000 people in California; in 1982, less than 5,000 worked in these plants. "Unemployed auto workers may be able to get other jobs, but what will they earn?"[66] Former South Gate workers, now employed at Van Nuys, saw the handwriting on the wall when management began doing what it had done at South Gate before the closing there. Led by union members such as Eric Mann, Mike Gómez, Pete Beltrán, and others, workers set up the Campaign to Keep GM–Van Nuys Open. By 1983 the committee was organizing worker rallies.

That year, the community coalition to Save Van Nuys GM was formed.[67] The committee included a multiracial coalition of Blacks, Asians, Latinos, and whites. Ed Asner, Bishop Juan Arzube, Fr. Luis Olivares, and Black Baptist ministers called for a meeting with GM's general manager, Roger Smith. They met with GM president James McDonald in January 1984. The committee told McDonald that if the plant closed, the members would organize a boycott of GM vehicles.

Local 645 was at the crossroads in 1986. Management started a media campaign that magnified splits; it stepped up a quality of life program, under which the company sent groups of 30 workers each week for a three-day seminar indoctrinating them on the necessity of cooperating with management. In the plant it repeated the theme that if the workers did not cooperate, they would lose their jobs. The International, meanwhile, sold the locals out by allowing them to make separate contract concessions, thus encouraging a bidding war among the locals as to who would work more cheaply. In the fall of 1986, GM closed another 11 plants. Van Nuys was not among them. Management had squeezed concessions out of the workers to the point that it was *more* profitable. More important, GM knew that closing the plant would trigger a boycott, which would cause problems. For the time, the Van Nuys plant was safe.

In other industries, too, widespread layoffs took place. From 1980 to 1983, California lost 94,000 manufacturing jobs, suffering 562 plant closings. During the early 1980s, the loss, nationally, of 70,000 mining jobs had a serious impact on the Chicano community. In July 1983, 13 unions, led by steelworker Local 616, at Clifton–Morenci, struck Phelps-Dodge. PD imported large numbers of scabs. The NLRB, siding with management, conducted an election in which it allowed only the scabs to vote, thus decertifying the union. The mine workers attempted to gain support outside the area. A ladies auxiliary, led by activists such as Jessie Téllez, toured the Southwest, talking to Chicano and labor groups. In spite of insurmountable odds, the miners continued to strike, facing eviction and harassment. However, by 1987, still led by its president, Angel Rodríguez, the Morenci strike was all but dead. Many who had second guessed the leadership were gone. Only the diehards remained, learning from their mistakes and rebuilding their union.

TRENDS

The Day of the Heroes of the late 1960s by the second half of the 1980s was part of the nostalgic past, not so much because of the heroes themselves, but because of a change in the mind-set of society and of Chicanos themselves who did not react to the leaders of the 1960s in the same manner as they had then. Rodolfo "Corky" Gonzales, Reies López Tijerina, José Angel Gutiérrez, and Bert Corona, along with student organizations such as MECHA, were still active; the scope of their activity was nevertheless more restricted. The Day of the Heroes had given way to the new professionals, who joined the former baby-boom radicals in the mainstream of North American society. Unlike the "heroes" they did not aspire to lead the masses or to remake society.

By 1985, "The Decade of the Hispanic" had fulfilled few of the promises set forth by Latino leaders in 1979. Government policy worsened life for the poor. The rhetoric of the annointed Chicano leaders changed, from that of social reform to mainstreaming the community. Political leaders such as San Antonio Mayor Henry Cisneros stated that the solution to economic deprivation among Hispanics was for them to become middle class. Cisneros favored "Free Enterprise Zones," an approach that amounted to giving incentives to business—for instance, government would pay 50 percent of the workers' salaries, provide tax breaks, and so on—in return for the relocation of industry to designated areas of high unemployment. To most critics, enterprise zones amounted to the Singaporization of the *barrios*.

While in the early 1970s, even the establishment media identified people such as César Chávez, José Angel Gutiérrez, Corky Gonzales, and Bert Corona as leaders in the Mexican American community. In the 1980s, *Hispanic Business* assumed the role of naming the influentials. In 1985, when it named 100 important Hispanics, it did not list one activist; 21 were business people, 15 were doctors or lawyers, 10 were bankers, and 2 were academicians.

North American society was no longer interested in equal opportunity for minorities. A national survey of chief personnel officers revealed that affirmative action had fallen from sixth to thirteenth in order of importance (out of 13 key issues).[68] The priorities of Hispanic influentials also changed from the 1960s or even the 1970s; instead of help for the poor they wanted economic development, which in most cases constituted a return to "trickle-down" economics.

The Rambo years entrenched an antipoor ideology. Reagan himself firmly believed that in Euroamerica hunger and poverty did not exist. The president blamed hunger on a "lack of knowledge." If North Americans wanted to eat, food was available. Reagan's beliefs paralleled those of his second attorney general, Edwin Meese III, who in 1983, while working on the White House staff, stated that there was no authoritative evidence that hunger existed in "America." Meese added that people went to soup kitchens because they wanted a free meal. Government, according to Reagan, should take care of only the "truly needy," and the private sector should take care of the rest.[69]

Divisions between North Americans and Chicanos increased in more ways than one during the 1980s. Aside from the obvious class differences, the gap in ages of the two communities rose. In 1980 in California, the median age of Mexican Americans was under 22; by the year 2000, the median age would be about 26. The majority of white North Americans were over 30 years in 1980, and, by the turn of the century, the majority would be over 35.[70] The graying of "America" in all probability will result in a greater reluctance on the part of society to pay for education, a policy change that would greatly affect Chicanos.

The Mexican American population will continue to grow dramatically.

This factor alone will not automatically bring about either services or political power. Power, acceptance, and prosperity are not won in the bedroom. In fact, as the Latino population grows, so will Euroamerican "cultural panic." The failure of Simpson-Rodino promises to drive this panic to hysterical proportions as North Americans continue to blame the undocumented for structural defects in the economy. Simpson-Rodino has the probability of creating a political and economic nightmare for all Latinos.

The future, in fact, promises an intensification of methods of social control. Government strategy will be to split the community. The socialization process will increase, and, through the schools and media, patriotic symbols will be pushed by the state. For example, in 1992, the fifth centennial of Chiristopher Columbus's so-called discovery, Chicano organizations and individuals will be encouraged to join the celebration of the Hispanic triumph. The private sector will play a greater role in celebrating Hispanic successes.[71] Meanwhile, the English only movement, spurred by its success in California, will spread. North American nativist groups will become more strident and they will push for Americanization programs such as those sponsored by the American Legion after World War I.

Political gains in the future will be slower outside of Texas. In large urban centers such as Los Angeles, it will be more difficult to develop organic leaders. Middle-class Mexican Americans, both men and women, will play a larger role in speaking for the poor. The nature of urbanism, to exploit property to the maximum, will affect the poor Chicanos whose land is close to the center core. Population density as well as the dialectic of space and time will make this land more valuable, increasing the tendency to destroy *barrio* communities. The result will undoubtedly be further disorganization and fragmentation of the Chicano community.

Trends also suggest that many conveniences that U.S. residents have taken for granted will be eliminated. Public services will be cut and those remaining will be put on a pay-as-you-go basis. Owning and driving a car will become luxuries. The insurance companies have manufactured the myth that they are losing money and, therefore, have skyrocketed their premiums. Today in California the premiums often are higher than the worth of the car, running. Auto insurance runs between $1,200 and $2,400 a year, and costs are rising at a rate of 25 percent a year. Because of the insurance companies' political power, they have reaped billions if not trillions of dollars in tax breaks; even progressive legislators are reluctant to criticize the pillage. Owning a car has always been a form of social control; what will happen when this dream is removed remains to be seen.

It would be a disservice to portray the future in idealistic terms. Hope is important, but the falsification of reality can immobilize a community. The future's challenge is to preserve Chicano communities, to prevent the defection of the middle class, since it is vital in advocating community interests, to widen progressive, counterhegemonic ideology within the community, and to plan the class struggle that is inevitable, given the present restructuring of U.S. society where the majority of Chicanos/Mexicans are being forced into a secondary labor market, and where most North Americans are becoming a permanent class of tenants. Let us hope that it will not take another Vietnam in Central America to stir the masses.

NOTES

1. Raúl Izaguirre, "The Decade for the Hispanic," *Agenda* (January/February 1980): 2.
2. Robert D. Hershey, Jr., "U.S. Due to Report 10 Million New Jobs," *New York Times,* December 6, 1985.
3. Edmund Fawcett and Tony Thomas, *The American Condition* (New York: Harper & Row, 1982), p. 5.
4. Robert L. Heilbroner and Aaron Singer, *The Economic Transformation of America: 1600 to the Present,* 2nd ed. (San Diego: Harcourt Brace Jovanovich, 1984), p. 328; Donald J. Bogue, *The Population of the United States: Historical Trends and Future Projections* (New York: Free Press, 1985), pp. 564–565, 604.
5. Steve Padilla, "Working for the FBI," *Nuestro* (October 1982): 15.
6. Tom Díaz, "Eye Ball to Eye Ball with the Soviets," *Nuestro* (September 1985): 40–43.
7. *New York Times,* August 17, October 26, 1983; *San Antonio Express,* December 13, 1984; "Leadership Role Debated," *Nuestro* (January/February 1985): 9.
8. Stephen Goode, "Cathi Villapando, Special Assistant to the President," *Nuestro* (January/February 1985): 16–18.
9. Robert Montemayor, "Attorneys: Developing the Power Base," *Hispanic Business* (May 1985): 24–35; Harry Bernstein, "Illegal Issue Raise in East L.A. Dispute," *Los Angeles Times,* September 18, 1985.
10. *Dallas Morning News,* October 19, 1984; Juan Vásquez, "Watch Out for Willie Velásquez," *Nuestro* (March 1979): 20.
11. Robert R. Brishetto, "Latin Political Participation: 1972–1984," presented to the League of Women Voters Education Fund, Conference on Electoral Participation, Washington, D.C., July 18, 1985, pp. 1–2.
12. Mary Lenz, "The Emerging Hispanic Vote," *The Texas Observer* (February 20, 1987): 11. The Chicano voter turnout in 1982 had been 32 percent of the registered voters. In 1986, it fell to 29 percent in the governor's race. This lower turnout contributed to the victory of Republican Bill Clements over Mark White. See *The Texas Observer,* December 5, 1986, p. 14. See also *The Texas Observer,* November 14, 1983; *San Antonio Express News,* July 17, 1983; *Hispanic Business* (March 1983): 29.
13. *San Antonio Light,* June 7, 1984; *San Antonio Express News,* June 7, 1984; *Hispanic Monitor,* July 1984.
14. Andrew Mollison, "Hispanics Prepare to Register 1 Million Voters," *Arizona Daily Star,* August 3, 1983; Robert Reinhold, "Hispanic Leaders Open Vote Drive," *New York Times,* August 4, 1983; Raúl García, "City Council Upla," *Hispanic Business* (May 1986): 34, 44; Latino Institute, *Al Filo/At the Cutting Edge: The Empowerment of Chicago's Latino Electorate* (Chicago: Latino Institute, 1986), pp. 1–6, 11, 14–15, 18–19, 24–26.
15. "New Mexico Offers a Preview of Mobilization," *New York Times,* September 11, 1983; interview with nine academicians within the state.
16. Chip Martínez, "Federico Peña: Denver's First Hispanic Mayor," *Nuestro* (August 1983): 14–17; Steve Padilla, "In Search of Hispanic Voters," *Nuestro* (August 1983): 20; Richard Martínez, Memo to Executive Board, Southwest Voter Registration Education Project, August 3, 1984; *Denver Post,* March 1, 1983; *Rocky Mountain News,* January 10, 1983; *Arizona Republic,* July 8, 1983; *New York Times,* October 15, 1985.
17. Tucker Gibson, "Mayorality Politics in San Antonio, 1955–1979," in David R. Johnson et al.,

eds., *The Politics of San Antonio* (Lincoln: University of Nebraska Press, 1983), pp. 116–126; Robert R. Brischetto and Rudolpho de la Garza, *The Mexican American Electorate Political Opinions and Behavior Across Cultures in San Antonio* (San Antonio: SVREP Project, 1985), p. 2; Robert Brishetto, Charles L. Cotrell, and R. Michael Stevens, "Conflict and Change in the Political Culture of San Antonio in the 1970s," in Johnson et al., pp. 76–85.

18. *Washington Post,* December 18, 1982; *Christian Science Monitor,* April 6, 1981.

19. Marshall Ingwersol, "San Antonio's Mayor Is Simply 'Henry' to Everyone," *Christian Science Monitor,* March 24, 1984; *Christian Science Monitor,* January 12, 1984.

20. *Washington Post,* August 10, 1983; *Christian Science Monitor,* January 12, 1984.

21. Sidney Plotkin, "Democratic Change in Urban Political Economy: San Antonio's Edwards Aquifer Controversy," in Johnson et al., pp. 157–163. Telephone interview with Bernardo Eureste, December 12, 1985; others interviewed did not want to be identified.

22. Good biographies of Cisneros are in *New York Times,* April 6, 1981; Michael Barone, "Unequivocally American," *Washington Post,* July 23, 1985.

23. *Hispanic Business* (November 1985): 16–18; *Los Angeles Times,* December 8, 1985; quote in *Los Angeles Times,* December 7, 1985.

24. "Rise in Poverty, Level Highest Among Children of Hispanics," *San Antonio Light,* October 15, 1984; "Best of Times. Cloaks Plight of Impoverished," *San Antonio Express,* November 25, 1984.

25. Bogue, pp. 405, 611.

26. See Robert Montemayor, "Latino Students Advance, Only to Fail," *Los Angeles Times,* August 1, 1983; Mary Lenz, "The Shame Of The Schools," *Texas Observer* (January 23, 1987): 1, 7–9.

27. Bogue, p. 383.

28. *Nuestro* (April 1978): 18.

29. *Los Angeles Times,* Valley Section, October 16, 1985.

30. *Los Angeles Times,* June 2, 1985.

31. Patrick Barry, "Trouble in the Bush," *Nuestro* (April 1982): 21; Shirley Cayer, "Chicago's New Hispanic Alliance," *Nuestro* (June/July 1983): 45; Antonio Zavala, "Are Four Candidates Always Better Than One?" *Nuestro* (January/February 1983): 21.

32. Toni Breiter, "Hispanics and the Roman Catholic Church," *Agenda* (January/February 1977): 4–5; Lucy Norman de Sánchez and Pablo Sánchez, "Latinos in Parochial Schools: Divine Neglect?" *Nuestro* (September 1979): 42.

33. *Los Angeles Times,* September 23, 1985.

34. "Catholic Bishops Ask Vast Changes in Economy of U.S.," *New York Times,* November 12, 1984; Stephen Goode, "The Church and the Poor," *Nuestro* (April 1985): 11.

35. *Los Angeles Herald-Examiner,* December 4, 1985; *Los Angeles Times,* May 24, 1986; *Los Angeles Times,* June 2, 1986. Mahoney has come under fire for his opposition to sex education in the public schools and for pulling the church out of an AIDS education program because it advocated the use of condoms. See Rudy F. Acuña, "Keep Mahoney's AIDS Decision in Perspective," *Los Angeles Herald Examiner,* December 19, 1986.

36. Orbis Books, the Maryknoll Press, has the most complete offerings of works on Liberation Theology. Also see Stephen Goode, "The Church and the Poor."

37. Peter Skerry, "The Resurrection of Saul Alinsky: Neighborhood COPS," *The New Republic* (February 2, 1984): 23; Frank del Olmo, "2 Latin Activists Travel Separate Paths," *Los Angeles Times,* July 29, 1983; Chelo Avila, "COPs—Communities Organized for Public Service," *Agenda* (September 10, 1980).

38. Avila, pp. 12–13; Joseph D. Sekull, "Communities Organized for Public Service: Citizen Power and Public Policy in San Antonio," in Johnson et al., pp. 175–176; Thomas A. Baylis, "Leadership Change in Contemporary San Antonio," in Johnson et al., pp. 97, 111; Moises Sándoval, "The Latinization of the Catholic Church," *Agenda* (November/December 1978): 5–7.

39. Ignacio García, "COPS: San Antonio Policing the System," *Nuestro* (August 1980): 22; David

Hendricks, "Flores Leaves City He 'Loves,' " *San Antonio Express,* April 5, 1978; Calvin Trillin, "U.S. Journal: San Antonio. Some Elements of Power," *New Yorker* (May 2, 1977): 94–95, 97; Vickie Davidson, "5000 Mass for Third S.A. COPS Convention, *San Antonio Express,* November 22, 1976; *San Antonio Express,* October 16, October 26, 1976; James McCory, "COPS Hit as Raiders of Union," *San Antonio Express,* December 29, 1976; Sara Martínez and David McLemore, "COPS, Sutton Like 10-1 Plan," *San Antonio Express,* January 9, 1977; Roddy Stinson, " 'Get COPS Month' Should Be Discontinued," *San Antonio Express,* July 12, 1977.

40. John A. Booth, "Political Change in San Antonio, 1970s—Toward Decay or Democracy," in Johnson et al., pp. 193–206.

41. Adriana María Arzac, "The Developing of Community Competence Through a Neighborhood Organization" (Ph.D. dissertation in Public Health, University of Texas, Houston, 1982); Lee Haris, "2000 Protest High Auto Insurance Rates," *Los Angeles Times,* May 7, 1977; Frank del Olmo, "Community Coalition Mobilizing East Los Angeles," *Los Angeles Times,* December 16, 1977; Peter Wiley and Robert Gottlieb, *Empires in the Sun* (Tucson: University of Arizona Press, 1982), pp. 106–197.

42. Guadalupe Compean, "The Los Angeles Corporate Center: Its Probable Impact on North East Los Angeles," Client Project, School of Architecture and Urban Planning, University of California, Los Angeles, June 6, 1983. The study among other things proves considerable land speculation and land use change as the result of the corporate center.

43. *Los Angeles Times,* July 15, 1985.

44. Telephone interviews with Margarita Sánchez of EPISO and various activists who did not want to be identified.

45. *Wall Street Journal,* July 25, 1984.

46. Telephone interview with Elvira Aguayo of Valley Interfaith and Valley residents.

47. *Washington Post,* May 22, 1985; Ray Hunt, "The 20 Most Powerful Texans, Plus 12 on Standby," *Texas Business* (February 1986): 24, 59; *Austin American Statesman,* May 30, 1985; Kay Northcott, "To Agitate the Dispossessed," *Southern Exposure* (July–August 1985): 11–16; *Sam Kinch's Texas Weekly,* June 3, 1985.

48. See Harry C. Boyte, *The Backyard Revolution: Understanding the New Citizens' Movement* (Philadelphia: Temple University Press, 1980); Frances Fox Piven and Richard A. Cloward, *Poor People's Movements* (New York: Vintage Books, 1979).

49. Virginia Escalante et al., "Inside the World of Latinas," *Los Angeles Times,* August 7, 1983; Willie C. Velasquez to Board of Directors, Southwest Voter Registration and Education Project, December 1, 1984; *San Antonio Express,* August 24, 1984.

50. Escalante et al.

51. "Labor," *Los Angeles Times,* October 2, 1985.

52. Harry Bernstein, "Farm Workers Still Mired in Poverty," *Los Angeles Times,* July 25, 1985.

53. Judith Gaines, "César Chávez and the United Farm Workers," *Nuestro* (November 1985): 45–48; Harry Bernstein, "The Boycott: Chávez Gets a Slow Start," *Los Angeles Times,* July 25, 1985; Harry Bernstein, "Growers Still Addicted to Foreign Workers," *Los Angeles Times,* October 2, 1985; Harry Bernstein, "Ruling May Devastate Chavez's Union," *Los Angeles Times*, February 25, 1987.

54. James Cockcroft, "Mexican Migration, Economic Crisis, and the International Labor Struggle," in Marlene Dixon and Susanne Jonas, *The New Nomads* (San Francisco: Synthesis, 1985), p. 58; *Los Angeles Times,* May 7, 1985; Terry Maxon, "Hart Angers Hispanics With Letter on Aliens," *Dallas Morning News,* February 5, 1985.

55. John Guedella, "The Fourth Wave," *Hispanic Business* (May 1985): 18–19; Thomas Muller, *California's Newest Immigrants: A Summary* (Washington D.C.: Urban Institute Press, 1984), pp. ix–x, 7, 13, 28.

56. Laurie Becklund, "Immigrants May Slow Latino Achievement, Study Says," *Los Angeles Times,* December 10, 1985.

57. Jose A. Bracamonte, "Immigration Reform in Name Only," *Los Angeles Herald Examiner,* October 26, 1986.

58. *Hispanics and Jobs: Barriers to Progress,* National Commission for Employment Policy, Report No. 14, Washington, D.C., September 1982; Bernard Anderson, *Daedalus* (September 1981): 357–358; David Treadwell and Tom Redburn, "Workplace: Site of Latest Revolution," *Los Angeles Times,* April 24, 1983.

59. María Patricia Fernández-Kelly, *For We Are Sold. I and My People: Women and Industry in Mexico's Frontier* (Albany: State University of New York Press, 1983), pp. 45–84.

60. Devon Peña, "Between the Lines: A New Perspective on the Industrial Sociology of Women Workers in Transnational Labor Process," in National Association for Chicano Studies, *Chicana Voices: Intersections of Class, Race, and Gender* (Austin: Center for Mexican American Studies, University of Texas, 1986), pp. 77–95; *Los Angeles Times,* May 6, 1986.

61. For more extensive reading, see Marlene Dixon and Susanne Jonas, eds., *Revolution and Intervention in Central America* (San Francisco: Synthesis, 1983); Ignacio García, "El Salvador: A Profile of a Nation at War," *Nuestro* (October 1983): 26; Eldon Kenworthy, "United States Policy in Central America," *Current History* (March 1985): 98–99; *Time* (June 13, 1983): 22; entire issue of *Current History* (March 1985).

62. *Los Angeles Times,* May 12, 1986.

63. Kenworthy, p. 98.

64. Eric Mann, "A High Court Boost for Corporate Union Busting," *Los Angeles Times,* July 7, 1985.

65. Heilbroner and Singer, p. 343; *Los Angeles Times,* April 17, 1983.

66. Treadwell and Redburn.

67. Eric Mann, "Workers and Community Take On G.M.," *Nation* (February 11, 1984): 100; *Los Angeles Times,* May 15, 1983.

68. Herman Gallegos, "Hispanics Need a Strategy for the 90s," *Hispanic Business* (February 1985): 10; "100 Influentials and Their Assessment of the Critical Hispanic Issues," *Hispanic Business* (September 1985): 18, 33.

69. *Los Angeles Times,* May 22, 1986.

70. *Projections of Hispanic Population for the United States: 1990 and 2000,* Center for Continuing Study of the California Economy, Palo Alto, California, 1982; *Los Angeles Times,* December 12, 1985; Nancy Rivera, "Latinos Find Job Choices Are Both Limited, Limiting," *Los Angeles Times,* August 7, 1983.

71. Sánchez Jankowski, pp. 80–110.

INDEX

Abortion, 395
Adams, John Quincy, 7, 9
Adams-Onis (Transcontinental) Treaty
  of 1819, 6
Affirmative action, 393
Agnew, Spiro, 365
Agricultural Adjustment Act (AAA) of
  1933, 206, 210
Agricultural Labor Relations Board
  (ALRB), 369–370, 439
Agricultural Workers Industrial League
  (AWIL), 210, 211
Agricultural Workers Organizing
  Committee (AWOC), 274, 325, 326
Agriculture
  in Arizona, 83, 92, 94, 166
  braceros and, 261–268, 275, 315,
    321, 326
  in California, 111, 142, 154,
    178–179, 182–184, 198, 207, 208,
    210–217, 272–275, 368–370
  depression and, 208
  farm population, 266
  in Mexico, 147
  New Deal and, 206, 207
  in New Mexico, 54, 55, 61–62, 76
  strikes, 209–216, 219, 220,
    272–275, 328–329, 368–370, 439
  technology and, 136, 144, 154, 179,
    206, 207, 266, 314–315
  in Texas, 31, 152–153, 180, 198,
    199, 205–206, 208, 276
  unions, 210–220, 272, 325–327,
    438–439
  wages in, 143, 179, 180, 184, 209,
    211, 217, 219, 220, 275, 277
Aid to Families with Dependent
  Children (AFDC), 353

Alamo, the, 10–11
Alaniz, Reyes, 329
Alatorre, Richard, 367, 417, 423–425
Alba, Victor, 147
Alemán, Elisa, 151
Alianza Hispano-Americana, La, 96–97,
  293–295
Alinsky, Saul, 285
Allen, William P., 268
All in the Family, 363
Alvárez, Manuel, 57
Amalgamated Clothing Workers Union
  of America (ACWUA), 370–371
American Civil Liberties Union
  (ACLU), 293, 319, 320, 352, 377, 400
American Council of Spanish-Speaking
  People, 294–295
American Farm Bureau Federation
  (AFBF), 183, 199, 262, 369
American Federation of Labor (AFL),
  99, 100, 143, 154, 164, 166, 170, 181,
  182, 199, 218, 220, 229–231
American Federation of
  Labor–Congress of Industrial
  Organizations (AFL–CIO), 252, 266,
  277
American Protective Association, 96
American Southwest, The (Perrigo), 19
Anaya, Toney, 419, 446
Anchando, Ceferino, 234
Anders, Evan, 35
Androcentrism, 391–392
Antiwar protests, 345–350
Antonovich, Mike, 432
Apache Indians, 86–90, 92
Aragón, José, 385
Arbenz, Jacobo, 444
Archuleta, Diego, 59

Arizona, 19. *See also* names of cities
agriculture in, 83, 92, 94, 166
education in, 102
homeowner occupancy, 428
income in, 90–91, 98, 180, 428
industrialization in, 83, 96–101
intermarriage in, 83, 89
justice in, 95
land issue in, 95
military contracts in, 92
mining in, 83–87, 92–102, 261
occupation of, 82–103
politics in, 83, 91, 418
population of, 91–92, 93
racism in, 83, 87, 89, 93, 96, 185
railroads in, 83, 92, 96
social class in, 83, 88–89, 91
strikes in, 97–102
unions in, 97–102, 166, 179–180,
217, 231
women in, 89, 96
Arizona Cotton Growers Association
(ACGA), 179–180
Arizona Federation of Labor, 99, 100,
179, 180
Arizona Rangers, 98
Arkansas, 180
Armed forces, Mexican Americans in,
253–254
Armijo, Manuel, 57, 58
Armstrong, Ann, 379
Arredondo, Miguel, 229
Arvin strike, 272–274
Arzube, Juan, 434, 448
Asian immigration, 126–127, 142, 185,
218
Asner, Ed, 448
*Asociación Nacional México-Americana,
La* (ANMA), 253, 268, 270, 292–294
Associated Farmers of America, 199
Associated Farmers of California,
215–217
Association of Mexican American
Educators (AMAE), 320, 388
Atomic Energy Commission (AEC),
280
Augustian, Victoria, 296
August 29th Movement (ATM),
345–350, 367, 391
Austin, Moses, 6

Austin, Stephen, 7–10
Automobile
impact of, 182
insurance, 450
Avila, Alfredo, 228
Avila, M. J., 260
Avitia, Manuel, 233
Axtell, Samuel B., 68
Ayres, Ed Durán, 255

Baca, Herman, 377
Baca Barragán, Polly, 422–423
Bacon, Robert L., 187
Bagley, D. W., 258
Bailey, Cleveland M., 273
Bakke case (1976), 393–394
Bakunin, Mikhail, 146
Baldenegro, Sal, 346
Ballesteros, Celia, 427
Bancroft, Hubert Howe, 57–58, 84,
95–96
Banditry, 43–44, 108, 114, 124–125
Bañuelos, Romana, 378
Barker, Eugene C., 9–10
Barnes, Ben, 328
Barrios, 173, 174, 288, 310, 397–398
Barry, R. C., 119
Barton, James, 123
Bauch, Erick, 343
Bear Flag invasion, 110–111
Beaubien, Carlos, 58
Beaubien, Charles, 63
Beer companies, 379, 380
Beers, George A., 125
Beet Workers Association, 219–220
Belden, Sam, 27–28
Bell, Griffin, 375
Bell, Horace, 116, 117
Beltrán, Pete, 448
Benitez, Linda, 332
Bent, Charles, 56–59
Bentsen, Lloyd, 418
Berber, Laureano Calvo, 86
Berman, Howard, 440
Bernson, Hal, 430
Bernstein, Irving, 168, 231
Berreyesa family, 110, 121
Bilingual education, 386–388, 416
Bilingual Education Act of 1968, 386
Birch, Ed, 350

Bird, Rose, 423
Biscailuz, Eugene, 259
Biseño, Lupe, 330
Black, Hugo, 389
Black churches, 430–431
Blackmun, Harry, 389
Blacks
    Mexicans and, 180
    population, 309
    riots, 310
    slavery and, 7, 8, 25, 26–27, 31
    in zoot-suit riots, 257
Boddy, Manchester, 258
Bogue, Donald J., 426
Boland Amendment, 445
Bonilla, Rubén, 382
Bonilla, Tony, 314
Bonilla, William, 314
Bonpane, Blase, 446
Borajo, Antonio, 47–48
Border Industrialization Program (BIP), 323, 371
Border patrol, 200, 267, 268
Bosch, Juan, 444
Boswell, John G., 272
Bowie, James, 10
Bowron, Fletcher, 258
Box, John O., 186–188, 201
Bracamonte, José L., 441–442
Braceros, 261–268, 275, 315, 321, 326
Brack, Gene M., 15
Bradley, Tom, 416, 417, 430
Brahan, R. W., Jr., 32
Brent, Joseph Lancaster, 119, 120
Bressette, Linna E., 177
Briegel, Kay, 89
Briggs, Vernon, Jr., 352, 353, 375
Broker class, legitimation of, 377–386
Brooks, Homer, 226
Brotherhood of Railroad and Maintenance Workers, 228
Brown, Edmund G., Jr., 369, 439
Brown, Edmund G., Sr., 274, 318, 326
Brown, Willie, 423, 425
Brown Berets, 335, 337–338, 346, 350, 351
Brownell, Herbert, 268
"Brown mafia," 378–379
Brown scare, 160–161
Brownsville, Texas, 27–29, 45

Brown v. Board of Education (1954), 253, 289, 290, 365
Buchanan, James, 18, 87, 88
Buchanan, Joseph P., 71
Bureau of Labor Statistics, 438
Burger, Warren, 341, 389
Burns, Arthur, 364
Burns, Hugh M., 273
Bursum, Holm, 187
Bustamante, Jorge A., 373, 375
Butler, Anthony, 8
Butz, Earl, 369

Cabajal, José María, 44
Cabeza de Baca, Ezequiel, 77
Cabrera, Tomás, 45
Cahuenga, Treaty of, 111
Calhoun, James S., 60
California, 19, 107–130. *See also* names of cities
    agriculture in, 111, 142, 154, 178–179, 182–184, 198, 207, 208, 210–217, 272–275, 368–370
    banditry in, 108, 114, 124–125
    banking in, 112–113
    Catholic Church in, 108, 126, 345
    conquest of, 108–111
    education in, 236, 289, 290, 295, 336–338, 386–388, 393
    gold in, 108, 109, 111–114
    homeowner occupancy, 428–429
    income in, 179, 180, 184, 428
    intermarriage in, 109, 116–117, 284, 335
    land issue in, 114–117
    lynching in, 118–119, 121, 122, 124, 126, 128–129
    Mexico and, 108–111
    mining in, 112–114, 128
    mutualistas in, 174, 183–184
    occupation of, 111–112
    plant closings in, 447–448
    politics in, 117–118, 284–287, 317–320, 367–368, 423–425
    population of, 111, 127, 261, 284, 417
    racism in, 108, 117, 127–129, 159, 173, 174, 236, 239
    railroads in, 108, 127, 128
    resistance in, 121–126

California (*continued*)
  strikes in, 155, 159, 164–166, 184,
    209–217, 368–370
  trade in, 107, 109
  unions in, 155, 164, 182–184,
    229–231, 272, 325–327, 368–370.
    See also Strikes
  youth movement, 333–338
California Association of Bilingual
  Educators (CABE), 388
California Federation of Labor (CFL),
  274
California Rural Legal Assistance
  (CRLA), 344
Californios, 111, 115, 117, 120, 122,
  123
Callagan, Bryan, II, 33–34
Calvillo, Ignacio, 96
Campa, Arthur L., 55, 289
Campaign for Human Development
  (CHD), 431
*Campaña pro Preservación del Barrio,
  La,* 397–398
Campbell, Thomas E., 102, 179, 180
Campesinos, 146, 148
Canales, J. T., 35
Cananea strike, 98, 149
Cannery and Agricultural Workers
  Industrial Union (CAWIU), 211, 212,
  213, 215–216
Cannon, Fred, 118–119
Cárdenas, Gilberto, 375
Cárdenas, Juan, 34
Cárdenas, Lázaro, 233
Carr, Waggoner, 328
Carrancistas, 162
Carreón, R. J., Jr., 319
Carrillo, José A., 111
Carrillo, Leo, 259
Carson, Kit, 110
Carter, Jimmy, 365, 366, 376, 379, 385,
  391, 444, 445
Casas, Arthur O., 294
Cash, James, 100
Castañeda, Carlos, 8, 9, 11, 261
Castellón, Aureliano, 38
Castillo, Leonel, 376
Castillo, Martín, 378
Castillo, Pedro, 172
Castillo, Sylvia, 396

Castillo Hall, Gordon, 400
Castro, Fidel, 444
Castro, José, 109, 110
Castro, Oscar, 230, 291
Castro, Raúl, 384–385
Castro, Sal, 336–337
Castro, Vicky, 333
Catholic Church, 2, 344–345, 430–433
  in California, 108, 126, 345
  in Chicago, 177
  Hispanic Movement, 260
  in Los Angeles, 237, 432
  Mexican labor and, 157–158
  in New Mexico, 68–70
  in Texas, 344
Catholic Youth Organization (CYO),
  237
Católicos Por La Raza (CPLR), 345
Cattle, 30, 31, 65–66, 68, 116, 152
Catron, Thomas B., 62, 63, 67, 68
Caucasian Race Resolution, 263
Cavazos family, 28
Ceja, Manuel, 237
Central Intelligence Agency (CIA), 415,
  445
*Centro de Acción Autonoma-Hermandad
  General de Trabajadores*
  (CASA-HGT), 373, 391
Cerda family, 42
Chaikin, Sol, 277
Chamberlain, Samuel E., 17–18
Chambers, Pat, 212–216
Chandler, Harry, 236
Channing, William Ellery, 9
Chapman, Leonard, Jr., 373
Chargin, Gerald S., 343
Chávez, César, 311, 325–329, 331, 367,
  368, 370, 377, 425–426, 438–439, 449
Chávez, Dennis, 241–242, 279–281, 294
Chávez, Gloria, 434
Chávez, Joe, 234
Chávez, Linda, 415
Chávez, Tibo J., 294
Chávez Ortiz, Ricardo, 399–400
Chavolla, Mary Anne, 237
Chicago, Illinois, 243
  Catholic Church in, 177
  housing in, 242, 287, 288
  Mexican labor in, 174–177, 185
  mutualistas in, 175–177

politics in, 316–317, 418–419
population of, 175, 177, 227, 287, 315–316, 418
racism in, 287, 288
steel industry in, 430
unions in, 228–229
urban renewal in, 298
Chicago Area Project (CAP), 287, 288
Chicano, adoption of name, 338
Chicano Moratorium, 345–350, 367, 391
Chicano movement, birth of, 324–327
Chico, John, 316
Chihuahua trade, 54, 56
Chinese Exclusion Act of 1882, 127, 128
Chinese immigrants, 126–127, 128, 142
Chisum, John H., 66, 67
Chuco, 254
Churubusco, 16, 18
Cisneros, Henry, 419, 420–422, 449
Cisneros case (1970), 289, 309
City commissions, 416–417
Civil Practice Act of 1850, 117
Civil rights movement, 289–295, 311
Civil Works Administration (CWA), 206
Clamor Público, El, 121, 123
Clark, Victor, 150, 158
Class. *See* Social class
Clay, Henry, 27
Claypool-Kinney bill, 101
Clayton, Anderson, 213
Clements, Betty J., 349
Clements, Norris, 375
Clifton, Henry, 94
Clifton-Morenci strike, 98–99, 149
Coahuila, 6–8
Cockcroft, James, 145
Cockrell, Lila, 420
Coerver, Don M., 162
Cohen, Jerry, 439
Colby, William, 440
Cold War, 252
Coles, Robert, 313
Colombo, Frank, 98
Colonial America, 2
Colorado, 19, 181, 341–342
     education in, 337
     politics in, 418–423

population of, 178
racism in, 185
strikes in, 165, 219, 220
unions in, 181
walkouts, 337
Colorado State Federation of Labor (CFL), 219–220
Colson, Charles, 369
Committee to Re-Elect the President (CREEP), 379
Communist party, 199, 210, 215, 226–227, 232, 237, 271
Communities Organized for Public Service (COPS), 420, 434, 436
Community action programs, 330, 331
Community Political Organization (CPO), 286
Community Service Organization (CSO), 253, 285, 287, 293, 294, 318, 320
Commuter program, 323
Compean, Mario, 334
Comprehensive Employment and Training Act (CETA), 364
Comstock Strike of 1859, 113
Confederación de Uniónes de Campesinos y Obreros del Estado de California (CUCOM), 212, 216–217
Confederación de Uniónes Obreras Mexicanas (CUOM), 183, 210, 212
Confederación Regional Obrera Mexicana, La (CROM), 167
Congreso de los Pueblos de Habla Español, El, 235, 238–239
Congress of Industrial Organizations (CIO), 199, 200, 229–231, 234
Connally, John, 314, 328–329
Connor, Seymour, 49
Contadora nations, 445
Contract system, 208–209, 276
Coors beer, 380
Copeland, John, 66–67
Copper, 93, 94, 97–101
Corbet, Sam, 67–68
Corella, Joaquín, 86
Cornelius, Wayne, 375
Corona, Bert, 230, 373, 377, 448, 449
Coronel, Antonio, 118
Corporate boards, 383
Corridos, 40–41, 43

Cortés, Manuel, 60
Cortez, Gregorio, 43
Cortina, Juan, 26, 36–37, 40–41, 43–47
Corwin, Arthur, 374–375
Cota Robles, Amado, 102
Cottage industry, 223
Cotton, 142, 152, 153, 166, 181, 206,
    209, 213–215
Council for Inter-American Affairs, 235
Council for Mexican-American Affairs
    (CMAA), 287
Cowboys, 95
Crabb, Henry, 87
Crime, 401
Cristeros, 177, 237
Crockett, Davy, 10, 11
Crusade for Justice, 341–342
Cruz, A. C., 98
Cruz, Ben, 230
Cruz, Justo S., 270
Cruz, Maria, 270–271
Cruz, Natividad, 151
Cruz, Ricardo, 345, 400
Cultural nationalism, 320, 324, 367
Cutting, Bronson, 241–242

Daley, Richard, 316
Daniel, Pancho, 123, 124
D'Aubisson, Robert, 444
Dávila, Armando, 230
Dávila, Juan, 229
Davis, Ed, 346, 349, 350, 375
Davis, James L., 186
Debs, Ernest, 286
Decker, Caroline, 213, 216
Defense contracts, 251
De León, Arnoldo, 32, 34, 38
Del Real, Martha, 330
Del Río Manifesto, 339
Democratic party, 241–242, 378, 384,
    417, 418
Dent, Julia, 16
Deportations, 202–206, 267, 271–272
Depressions, 144, 185
Desegregation, 236, 295, 365
Detroit, Michigan, 177, 297–298, 315
Deukmejian, George, 423, 424, 427, 439
Díaz, Bernardo, 271–272
Díaz, José, 255
Díaz, María, 148

Díaz, Porfirio, 36, 37, 47, 98, 136, 145,
    147–150, 159, 444
Díaz de Pensamiento, Isabel, 149
Dickens, Edwin L., 283
Di Giorgio, Joseph, 273–274
Di Giorgio, Robert, 326
Di Giorgio Corporation, 326, 327
Dingley Tariff of 1897, 142, 153
Discrimination. *See* Racism
Dixon-Arnett Act of 1971, 373
Doak, William N., 202–203
Doane, Lester, 180
Dodge, Cleveland, 101
Dogget, Lloyd, 418
Doheny, Edward L., 147
Domínguez, Frank, 174
Domínguez, Manuel, 117
Doniphan, Alexander W., 59
Douglas, Paul, 267
Douglas, Walter, 100, 101
Duarte, Charles "Chili," 230
Duerler, Gustave, 225
Durst, Ralph, 165
Dysart, Jane, 32

Eastland, James O., 374
East Los Angeles Community Union
    (TELACU), 383
Echevarría, Angel, 417
Economic Opportunity Act of 1964,
    309, 330
Education, 414
    in Arizona, 102
    bilingual, 386–388, 416
    in California, 236, 289, 290, 295,
        336–338, 386–388, 393, 426, 427
    in Colorado, 337
    desegregation, 236, 295, 365
    equity in, 388–390
    higher, 390–394
    in Los Angeles, 319, 388–390
    in New Mexico, 75, 241, 279–280
    in San Antonio, 283, 312, 387–389
    in Texas, 157–158, 171–172, 311,
        339–340, 389–390, 426
    walkouts, 336–338
Educational Opportunities Programs
    (EOP), 390
Edwards, Hayden, 7
Ehrenberg, Herman, 84, 87

Eilberg, Joshua, 374
Eisenhower, Dwight D., 268
Elías, Eulalia, 89
Elkins, John T., 65
Elkins, Stephen B., 62, 63, 67, 68
Elliott, Alfred J., 273
El Monte berry strike, 211–212
El Monte gang, 120, 123
El Paso, Texas, 317
    housing, 281, 397–398
    politics in, 282
    population of, 281
El Paso Interreligious Sponsoring
    Organization (EPISO), 435
El Paso Salt War of 1877, 47–49
El Salvador, 366, 414, 415, 421,
    444–445
Emergency Labor Program, 262
Equal Employment Opportunity
    Commission, 331
Equal Rights Amendment (ERA), 437
Ernst, Mrs. W. H., 223, 224, 226
Escalante, Alicía, 333, 395
Escheverría, Luis, 371, 373
Escudero, Mary, 237
Espinosa, Ignacio, 101
Espinosa, José, 216
Estrada, José, 294
Estrada, Rafael, 179
Eureste, Bernardo, 421
European immigration, 185–186
Ewell, R. S., 86, 88

Fair Labor Standards Act, 227
Farah, Willie, 370–371
Farm Labor Organizing Committee
    (FLOC), 330
Farm Security Administration, 262
Farm Workers Union of Mexico, 218
Federal Bureau of Investigation (FBI),
    259–261, 342
Federal Emergency Relief
    Administration (FERA), 206, 232
Federal Revenue Act of 1978, 365
Federal Ring, 91
Federation of Mexican Workers Unions,
    184
Fehrenbach, T. R., 41
Féliz, Carmén, 398
Female-headed households, 353

Feminism, 169–170, 394–396
Filipinos, 216, 217, 257, 325
Fitzgerald, G. H., 212
Fitzsimmons, Frank, 327
Flores, Armando, 211
Flores, E. M., 179
Flores, Estebán, 375
Flores, Feliciano G., 171
Flores, Francisca, 333, 395
Flores, José María, 110, 111
Flores, Juan, 120, 123, 124
Ford, Gerald, 365, 379
Ford, "Rip," 28, 41, 45, 46
Ford Foundation, 309, 334, 380–382
Foreign investment in Mexico, 147–148,
    149, 321–322, 371
Fortas, Abe, 389
Franco, Francisco, 237, 260
Franklin, Benjamin, 6
Franzel, Harold, 277
Fredonia, Republic of, 7
Freedom of Information Act, 259,
    400
Frémont, John C., 108–111
Fricke, Charles W., 255, 256
Friend, Llerena B., 39
Frieselle, S. Parker, 187
Frontier Protection Act of 1874, 46
Frost, Max, 62–63
Fuentes, Albert, 313
Fuller, Elizabeth, 173
Fuller, Leland J., 296
Fulton, Maurice, 67

Gadsden, James, 85
Gadsden Purchase, 82, 84–86, 95
Gaines, Edmund P., 12
Galarza, Ernesto, 266, 274, 275, 332,
    373, 377, 387
Gallagher, Leo, 291
Gallegos, Guillermo, 291
Galván, Jeremiah, 27
Galván, Lucio, 328
Galveston, Texas, 29
Galveston Bay and Texas Land
    Company, 8
Gamboa, Don Francisco de, 84
Ganz, Marshall, 439
Garber, James Neff, 85
García, Dan, 416

García, Gus, 294
García, Hector, 168, 289, 314, 334
García, Jesús, 419
García, Juan, 268
García, Macario, 254
García, Manuel, 228, 231
Garcilazo, Jeffrey, 167
Garis, Roy L., 201
Garment industry, 221–222, 224, 277–278, 370–371
Garner, John Nance, 187
Gary, Indiana, 177
Garza, Ben, 171
Garza, Catarino, 36
Garza, Elizo (Kika) de la, 313, 384
Garza, Marcelo, Sr., 42
Garza, Ralph, 240
Gast, Ross H., 212
Gastelum, José, 272
Gates, Darryl, 401
Gavin, John, 385
General Motors Corporation, 447–448
Germans, 159, 162, 163
Gerrymandering, 417, 419
G.I. Forum, 279, 283, 287, 289, 292, 294, 313–315, 317, 320, 324, 325, 328, 331, 332, 334, 377, 380, 382
Gillespie, Archibald, 110
Gillett, Charles L., 184, 211
Giumarra Vineyards Corporation, 327
Glavecke, Adolphus, 44
Gold, 84, 93, 108, 109, 111–114
Goldman, Emma, 151
Goldsmith, Raquel Rubio, 92
Goldwater, Barry, 310
Goliad, 11
Gómez, Agapito, 271
Gómez, Mike, 448
Gompers, Samuel, 155, 166, 174, 186
Gonzales, Isabel Malagram, 242
Gonzales, Lucy Eldine, 151–152
Gonzales, M. C., 284
Gonzales, Rodolfo "Corky," 331, 332, 335, 341–342, 367, 377, 448, 449
González, Henry B., 253, 283–284, 286, 313, 334, 339, 384, 422
González, Larry, 425
González, Nancie, 55
Good Government League, 313

Good Neighbor Commission of Texas, 263
Gordon, Walter A., 259
Gorostiza, Manuel Eduardo, 12
Gorras Blancos, Las. See White Caps
Gotari, Rosaura, 151
Government positions, 415–418
Governors, 419
Gran Círculo de Obreros de México, El, 146, 148
Grant, Ulysses S., 13, 16
Grape Pickers Union, 182
Grape producers, 326–327, 368–369
Great Society programs, 309, 320
Grebler, Leo, 309
Green, Thomas Jefferson, 114
Greene, William C., 149
Grenada, 414
Grito, El, 30
Grodin, Joseph, 423
Gross national product (GNP), Mexican, 321
Guadalupe Hidalgo, Treaty of, 6, 19–20, 54, 61, 108, 113, 115, 235
Guatemala, 366, 414, 444, 446
Guaymas, 83, 85
Guerin, Arthur, 256
Guerra, Deodora, 35
Guerra, José Alejandro, 35
Guerra, Manuel, 35
Guerra, Ramón, 28
Guerrero, Lina, 422
Guerrero, Práxedis G., 151
Guilds, 145
Gutiérrez, Félix, Sr., 237
Gutiérrez, José Angel, 259, 334, 338–339, 367, 376, 381*n,* 448, 449
Gutiérrez de Lara, Lazaro, 151, 164
Guzmán, Max, 229
Guzmán, Ralph, 268, 293, 295, 346
Gwinn, William, 115

Hall, Linda B., 162
Hance, Kent, 418
Hancock, Stanley, 215
Harding, Warren G., 183
Harlan, John Marshall, 389
Harrington, Michael, 308
Harris bill, 201
Hart, Jim, 440

Hawkes, Benjamin G., 345, 431–432
Hayes, Rutherford B., 68
Head Start, 309–311
Healy, Dorothy Ray, 215
Heras, Juan de, 174
Hernández, J. A., 164
Hernández, María, 332
Herrera, Eduardo, 211
Herrera, Juan José, 70–74
Herrera, Nicanor, 71, 74
Herrera, Pablo, 71–73
Hidalgo, Miguel, 1
Higher education, 390–394
Hijos movement, 171
Hill, John, 418
Hinojosa, Federico Allen, 170
Hispanic, defined, 379
Hispanic Caucus, 385
Hispanic Movement, 260
Hispanos, 55–56
Hobsbawm, E. J., 43, 44
Holton, Karl, 259
Homeless, 428
Homeowner occupancy, 428–429
Homestead Act of 1862, 92
Hoover, Herbert, 200, 201
Housing, 136
    in Chicago, 242, 287, 288
    in El Paso, 281, 397–398
    in Los Angeles, 173, 236, 254,
        429–430
    in San Antonio, 282, 313
Houston, Sam, 7, 8, 11, 46, 87
Houston, Texas, 29, 317
Howard, Charles, 48
Howard, Frank, 267
Hubbard, Richard B., 48
Huerta, Adolfo de la, 179
Huerta, Carmen, 146
Huerta, Dolores, 325, 332
Huerta, Victoriano, 159, 162
Huge, Harry, 313
Hull House, Chicago, 243
Humphrey, Hubert, 267, 378
Humphreys, Norman D., 204
Hunt, Charles, 64
Hunt, George W. P., 100
Huntington, Collis P., 113
Huntington, Henry E., 155
Hynes, William, 222

Ibañez, Richard, 237, 294
Idaho, 178, 181
Idar, C. N., 180–182
Illinois, 181. *See also* Chicago, Illinois
Immigrants Protective League (IPL),
    288
Immigration
    Asian, 126–127, 128, 142, 185
    braceros, 261–268, 275, 315, 321,
        326
    European, 185–186
    legislation, 163–164, 168, 373–374,
        440–442
    Operation Wetback, 252, 266–268,
        289
Immigration Act of 1921, 185
Immigration Act of 1924, 186
Immigration and Naturalization Service
    (INS), 266–268, 372–374, 376, 441,
    442
Imperial Valley Farmers Association,
    275
Income and wages, 353, 354
    in agriculture, 143, 179, 180, 184,
        209, 211, 217, 219, 220, 275, 277
    in Arizona, 90–91, 98, 180, 428
    braceros and, 264
    in California, 179, 180, 184, 428
    in garment industry, 221, 224
    in Mexico, 147, 442
    in military installations, 283
    in New Mexico, 428
    in pecan industry, 225, 227
    in steel industry, 260–261, 316
    in sugar beet industry, 181
    in Texas, 156, 180, 312, 328, 428
    of women, 168, 221, 222, 353, 437
Independent Furniture Workers Union
    (IFWU), 230
Independent Progressive party, 293,
    294
Independent Workers Association
    (IWA), 328
Indiana, 181
Industrial Areas Foundation (IAF),
    285, 286, 432, 435, 436
Industrialization
    in Arizona, 83, 96–101
    in Mexico, 144–145, 147
    in New Mexico, 75–76

Industrial Workers of the World
(IWW), 100, 163–165, 170, 181–183
Infant mortality, 161, 174, 223
Intermarriage
in Arizona, 83, 89
in California, 109, 116–117, 284,
335
in Texas, 31–33
International Labor Defense (ILD),
199–200, 232
International Ladies Garment Workers
Union (ILGWU), 200, 221, 222, 224,
277, 278
International Longshoremen's and
Warehousemen's Union (ILWU),
229–230
International Monetary Fund (IMF),
322, 371, 443
International Union of Mine, Mill and
Smelter Workers, 231, 234, 278, 279
Inter-University Program for Latino
Research, 381–382
Iowa, 181
Iranian hostage crisis, 365
Irving, Leonard, 273
Isla, Jesús, 122
Itlong, Larry, 325
Izábal, Rafael, 149
Izaguirre, Raúl, 413

Jackson, Andrew, 5, 7, 109
Jamieson, Stuart, 164
Japanese-Americans, 211, 212, 254, 261
Japanese industry, 413–414
Japanese-Mexican Labor Association,
155
Jenkins, William W., 121
Job Corps, 309, 310, 330
Johnson, Albert, 186
Johnson, Hiram, 165
Johnson, Lyndon B., 309, 310, 320,
331, 377
Jones, John B., 48
Jones, Thomas, 109
Jones-Costigan Act of 1934, 219, 220
Jornaleros, 218
Josefa, 118–119
Juárez, Benito, 144
Junta Colonizadora de Sonora, 122
Juries, 343–344

Justice, 95, 398–401. *See also* Lynching;
Police brutality

Kansas, 181
Kearny, Stephen Watts, 58, 59, 110,
111
Keith, Stephen, 393
Kenedy, Mifflin, 27, 30, 31, 46
Kennedy, Edward M., 324, 374, 376
Kennedy, John F., 284, 308–309,
313–314, 331
Kennerly, F. M., 205
Kenny, Robert W., 259
Kerble, Fred, 34
Keyes, William, 290–291
Keyes case (1973), 290
Kilday, Owen, 224, 226, 227, 282
Kilday, Paul, 226, 241, 282
Kimmel, Elizabeth, 277
King, Martin Luther, Jr., 253
King, Richard, 27, 30–31, 46
Kinney, John, 48
Kircher, Bill, 329
Kissinger, Henry, 365, 374
Kissinger Commission, 421
Knight, Goodwin, 274
Knights of Columbus, 181
Knights of Labor, 71–73
Koopman, James S., 347
Korean War, 267
Kornblum, William, 316
Kovner, Joseph Eli, 296, 297
Krueger, Bob, 418
Ku Klux Klan, 171, 178, 377

Labor. *See* Mexican labor; Strikes;
Unions
Labor unions. *See* Unions
Lamar, Howard, 84, 85
Lamar, Mirabeau B., 26
Lamy, J. B., 69–70
Land Act of 1851, 108, 115
Land issue
in Arizona, 95
in California, 114–117
in New Mexico, 54–55, 60–62, 76,
340
Laredo, Texas, 38
Larkin, Thomas Oliver, 109
Larrazolo, Octaviano A., 77

Las Vegas Grant, 71–72
Latifundistas, 2
Laustenau, W. H., 98
Lau v. *Nichols* (1974), 386
Law Enforcement Assistance
  Administration (LEAA), 401
Lawyers, 416
Lea, Tom, 30
League of Revolutionary Struggle
  (LRS), 391
League of United Latin American
  Citizens (LULAC), 144, 171, 200,
  235, 239–241, 253, 259, 279, 283,
  285, 287, 294, 313, 314, 317, 320,
  324, 325, 328, 331, 332, 334, 377,
  380, 382
Lear, Norman, 363
Lebanon, 414
Ledesma, Geraldine, 332
Lee, Robert E., 46
Lehman, Herbert, 267
Lehnhardt, William, 439
Lesinsky, Henry, 94
Lettuce, 327
Lewis, Gideon K., 30
Lewis, John R., 232
Lewis, Oscar, 308
Liberation Theology, 432
Liberty leagues, 285
Libya, 414
Liga Protectora Latina, La, 101–102
Lincoln County War, 65–68
Lindsay, Gilbert, 318
Literacy Act of 1917, 142
Literacy requirement, 164
Livermore, Abiel Abbott, 15
Logan, Fred, Jr., 343
Loma, Pedro G. de la, 101
Long, James, 6
López, Fernando, 30
López, Francisco (Frank), 109, 237
López, Hank, 287
López, Ignacio, 239, 285, 294
López, Lorenzo, 72, 74
López Portillo, José, 443
Lord, Walter, 10
Los Angeles, 110, 111. *See also*
  California
    brown scare in, 160
    Catholic Church in, 237, 432

Central American refugees in, 444,
  446
community-police relations,
  345–350, 398–400
deportations from, 203, 204
education in, 319, 388–390
growth of, 127, 128, 143
housing in, 173, 236, 254, 429–430
juries in, 344
mutualistas in, 174
politics in, 284–287, 318–320
population of, 112, 127, 143, 161,
  172, 229, 284, 318, 319
racism in, 159, 173, 174
Sleepy Lagoon case, 254–256, 260,
  400
suburbanization and, 284–285
United Neighborhood Organization
  in, 434–435
urban renewal in, 295–297, 309
Watts riots in, 310
in World War II, 254
zoot-suit riots in, 254, 256–259
Louisiana, 180
Louisiana Purchase, 6, 56
Lozano, Oscar, 397
Luce, John, 335
Lucero, Bernard, 216
Lucey, Robert E., 268, 344
Ludlow massacre, 100
Lugo brothers, 119–120
Luna, Max, 229
Luna de Rodríguez, Celia, 332
Luna Mount, Julia, 332
Lundy, Benjamin, 9
Lynching
    in California, 118–119, 121, 122,
      124, 126, 128–129
    in New Mexico, 64
    in Texas, 28, 34, 38

McAllister, W. W., 313
McCarran, Pat, 269
McCarran-Walter Act of 1952, 252,
  269–272, 323
McCarthy, Joe, 252, 279
McClosky, J. J., 118
McCormick, Carlos, 313
McCormick, Paul J., 289
McCormick, Richard, 92

McDonald, C. C., 291
McDonald, James, 448
MacDonald, William C., 77
McDonnell, Donald, 325
McDowell, Mary, 243
McEuen, William Wilson, 173
McGovern, George, 367
McGucken, Joseph T., 259
Machine politics. *See* Politics
McIntyre, James Francis, 344–345
McLeod, Hugh, 57
McMurty, Larry, 39, 40
McNeely, L. H., 31, 39–40
McSween, Alexander, 67
McWilliams, Carey, 55, 62, 204, 207,
    256, 272
Madden, Martin, 186
Madero, Francisco, 150
Madrid, Arturo, 381
Magoffin, James W., 58
Magón, Ricardo Flores, 150–151, 162
Magonistas, 159, 164
Mahoney, Dan, 350
Mahoney, Roger, 424, 432
Mancillas, Julio, 164
Maney, Mitch, 68
Manifest Destiny, 13
Mann, Eric, 448
Manpower Development and Training
    Act (MDTA) of 1962, 309
Manuel, H. T., 235
MAPA, 314, 318, 320, 324, 332, 394
Maquiladoras, 323, 371, 442, 443
Marsh, E. P., 212
Marshall, F. Ray, 375
Marshall, James Wilson, 111
Marshall, Lupe, 229
Marshall, Thurgood, 389–390, 394
Martínez, Alejandro, 212
Martínez, Antonio José, 58, 59, 69–70
Martínez, Eustacio (Frank), 351–352
Martínez, Félix, 73, 74
Martínez, Fray, 63
Martínez, Juan Ramón, 178
Martínez, Margarita, 149
Martínez, Olivia, 387
Martínez, Ramón, 260–261, 288–289
Martínez, Refugio, 228
Martínez, Vilma, 416
Marvin, George, 163

Marxism, 367
Mata, Arturo, 234
Matamoros, 15–16, 28
Mathis, William Jefferson, 387
Maverick, Maury, 226, 241
Maverick, Sam, 47
Maxwell, Lucien, 63, 64
Maxwell Land Grant, 54, 63–65,
    75
Mayors, 419–422
Meade, George Gordon, 16, 17
Meany, George, 327
MECHA, 392, 394, 401, 427, 449
Meese, Edwin, III, 449
Meléndez, Ambriocio, 334
Meléndez, Jesús, 101
Mendiola, Enrique, 40
Méndoza, Lupe, 237
Mesilla Treaty, 82, 84–86, 95
Mestizos, 1, 112
Mexican-American Legal Defense and
    Education Fund (MALDEF), 416,
    417, 419
Mexican-American Movement (MAM),
    200, 237–238, 335
Mexican-American Student Association
    (MASA), 335
Mexican-American Student
    Confederation (MASC), 335
Mexican-American Study Project,
    University of California, 309
Mexican-American War, 5, 6, 13–20
Mexican-American Youth Organization
    (MAYO), 334, 338, 339
Mexican labor, 141–190. *See also*
    Agriculture; California; New Mexico;
    Texas
    automobile and, 182
    Blacks and, 180
    Catholic Church and, 157–158
    in Chicago, 174–177, 185
    deportations and, 202–206, 267,
        271–272
    depressions and recessions and,
        144, 185, 267
    discrimination against. *See* Racism
    in Los Angeles, 172–174
    migration north, 144, 150
    in mining, 143, 152, 154, 156,
        165–166

nativist reactions to, 136, 158–163, 185–188, 198, 200–206, 372–377, 440–441, 450
radicalism (early), 150–152
railroads and, 154
in steel industry, 167
strikes and. *See* Strikes
unemployment and, 185
unions and, 143–144, 151, 154–156, 159, 164–168, 179–182. *See also* Strikes
World War I and, 159–160
World War II and, 260–263
Mexico
agriculture in, 147
Border Industrialization Program (BIP), 323
border issue, 12–13, 26
early workers groups in, 145–146, 148–149
foreign debt of, 443
foreign investment in, 147–148, 149, 321–322, 371
independence of, 2
industrialization of, 144–145, 147
population of, 1, 12, 144, 146–147, 158, 266, 321
railroads in, 147, 148
Spanish conquest and colonization of, 1, 2
strikes in, 146, 148–149
Texas War, 5–12
transportation in, 266
wages in, 147, 442
Mexico City, fall of, 18
Michigan, 181
Middle-class Chicano organizations, growth of, 382–383
Military bases, Mexican labor at, 283
Military contracts, 92
Military-industrial complex, 251–252, 307
Miller, Henry, 115–116
Mills, W. W., 47
Mining, 136
in Arizona, 83–87, 92–102, 261
in California, 112–114, 128
Mexican labor in, 143, 152, 154, 156, 165–166

in New Mexico, 61, 76, 165–166, 231–233
strikes in, 156, 165, 278–279
unions, 97–102, 231–234, 278–279
Minnesota, 181
Miranda, Guadalupe, 63
Missions, 107–109
Mississippi, 180
Model Cities program, 310
Moffatt, Stanley, 291
Molina, Gloria, 423–425
Molina, John, 387
Mondale, Walter, 384
Monroe Doctrine, 14
Montalvo, A. L., 37
Montana, 181
Montes, Carlos, 351
Montes, Juan, 397
Montoya, Alfredo, 293, 294
Montoya, Joseph, 340, 343
Montoya, Nestor, 73
Montoya, Pablo, 59
Mora, Magdalena, 373
Morales, Andrew, 286
Moreno, Augie, 401
Moreno, John, 318
Moreno, Luisa, 217, 237–239
Morín, Ramona, 333
Morín, Raúl, 253
Morris, George, 45
Morris, Gilbert, 297
Morton, Thurston B., 273, 274
Mowry, Sylvester, 84, 86–87, 90
Moyer, Charles, 100
Mukulski, Barbara, 415
Mulattoes, 112
Mullin, Robert N., 65–66
Multinational corporations, 320, 321
Muñiz, Ramsey, 367
Muñoz, Rosalio, 346, 350, 351
Murietta, Joaquín, 123
Murphy, Laurance Gustave, 66, 67
Murrow, Edward R., 275
Musquiz, Virginia, 332
Mutualistas, 36, 76, 98, 142, 143, 145–146, 148, 157, 163, 169, 170
in California, 174, 183–184
in Chicago, 175–177
in San Antonio, 169–171
sugar beet workers and, 181

Nacional Financiera, La (PONAF), 323

Nafarrate, Emiliano P., 162

National Association for the Advancement of Colored People (NAACP), 295, 319

National Association of Bilingual Educators (NABE), 388

National Chicano Council on Higher Education (NCCHE), 381

National Chicano Research Network (*La Red*), 381

National Economic Development Association (NEDA), 378

National Farm Labor Union (NFLU), 272–275

National Farm Workers Association (NFWA), 325, 326, 328

National Industrial Recovery Act (NIRA), 210, 222, 231

National Labor Relations Act of 1935 (Wagner Act), 199, 217, 228, 234, 252, 272

National Labor Relations Board (NLRB), 234, 252, 369, 417, 447, 448

National Miners Union (NMU), 232

Nativism, 136, 158–163, 185–188, 198, 200–206, 372–377, 440–441, 450

Nava, Julian, 385

Navarrette, Tobias, 271

Navarro, Antonio, 33

Navarro, Armando, 377

Navarro, Diego, 120

Neal, William P., 45

Nebraska, 181

Needle Trades Workers Industrial Union (NTWIU), 222

Neeley, Matthew M., 187

Neighborhood Youth Corps, 330

Nelson, Eugene, 328

Nevada, 19

Newark, New Jersey, 310

New Deal, 199, 206, 207, 331

New Federalism, 364

New Frontier, 309, 331

Newlands Reclamation Act of 1902, 153

New Mexico, 19
    agriculture in, 54, 55, 61–62, 76
    Catholic Church in, 68–70

colonization of, 54–78
    Democratic party in, 241–242
    education in, 75, 241, 279–280
    homeowner occupancy, 428
    income in, 428
    industrialization in, 75–76
    land issue in, 54–55, .60–62, 76, 340
    Lincoln County War, 65–68
    lynching in, 64
    mining in, 61, 76, 165–166, 231–233
    myths about, 55–60
    politics in, 54, 55, 60–65, 74, 77, 241, 279–281, 368, 418, 419
    population of, 54, 74–75
    racism in, 54, 241, 279
    railroads in, 54, 70, 71, 74
    social class in, 55, 57
    strikes in, 278–279
    Texas and, 57–58
    trade in, 54, 56–57
    unions in, 71–73, 76
    White Caps in, 70–74

Nicaragua, 365–366, 414, 421, 444–446

Nieto, A. N., 155

Niños Héroes, Los, 18

Nixon, Richard M., 273, 274, 310, 350, 364, 365, 369, 378–379, 395

Noriega, José, 271

Norton, John R., 439

NRA, 221–223

Nueces River, 12, 26, 28

Obregón, Alvaro, 174, 185

Occupational distribution, 352–353

Ochoa, Juan, 233

O'Donnell, James, 27

O'Dwyer, William, 275

Office of Economic Opportunity (OEO), 309, 310

Ohio, 181, 370

Oil industry, 276, 281, 364

Olivares, Graciela, 385

Olivares, Luis, 434, 448

Operation Clean Sweep, 373

Operation Wetback, 252, 266–268, 289

Oregon, 178

Orendain, Antonio, 329, 370

Origins of the War with Mexico: The Polk Stockton Intrigue (Price), 13
Orosco, Braulio, 211
Ortega, Daniel, 421
Ortega, Margarita, 151
Ortiz, Juan Félipe, 59
Ortiz, Leo, 234
Ortiz, Rosa, 89
Ortiz, Roxanne Dunbar, 57
Ortiz, Tomás, 59
Ortiz Esquivel, José, 175
Otero, Miguel A., 64, 70, 72, 77
Other America, The (Harrington), 308

Pacheco, Basil, 229
Pachucos, 254, 256–257
Padilla, Gil, 325, 329, 439
Padilla, Mary, 330
Pallares, Jesús, 242
Pan-American Council (PAC), 288
Pan-Americanism, 187
Pan-Hispanic movement, 379
Papago Indians, 83, 92
Paredes, Américo, 39, 41–42
Paredes, Mairano, 13
Parker, William, 319–320
Parks, Rosa, 253
Parsons, Albert, 151
Partido Liberal Mexicano (PLM), 99, 151
Partridge, Frank, 267
Patterson, George, 228
Patterson, Orlando, 386–387
Patrón, Juan, 66–68
Paul, Jay, 401
Paz, Frank X., 243, 260, 288, 319
Pecan industry, 225–227
Pels, M. P., 64
Peña, Albert, Jr., 284, 313, 314
Peña, Federico, 419–420
Peña, Juan, 166, 233
Peña, Manuel de la, 18
Peninsulares, 1
Pennsylvania, 177
Peonage, 90
People's party (*partido*), 73–74, 75
Perales, Alonso, 171, 240, 241, 259, 260
Pérez, Nacho, 334
Perkins, Frances, 242

Perlstein, Meyer, 277
Perrigo, Lynn I., 19
Pesotta, Rosa, 221
Pesqueira, Ignacio, 87–88, 95
Peyton, Green, 225–226, 240
Phoenix, Arizona, 92
Pico, Andrés, 110, 111, 123–124
Pima Indians, 83, 92
Pitchess, Peter, 350
Pitt, Leonard, 110, 123
Pizaña, Ancieta, 162
Plan of San Diego, 161–162, 164
Pochoization, 320
Polanco, Richard, 423
Police brutality, 290–291, 342–343, 398–400
Police spying, 350–352, 400–401
Political Association of Spanish-Speaking Organizations (PASSO), 314, 324, 328, 332, 334
Politics
    in Arizona, 83, 91, 418
    in California, 117–118, 284–287, 317–320, 367–368, 423–425
    in Chicago, 316–317, 418–419
    Chicano gains in, 417–425
    in El Paso, 282
    Hispanic Caucus, 385
    in New Mexico, 54, 55, 60–65, 74, 77, 241, 279–281, 368, 418, 419
    in San Antonio, 282, 283–284, 313–314, 420–422, 434
    in Texas, 33–37, 313–314, 367, 418, 422
    voting patterns, 384
Polk, James K., 12–14, 18, 19, 109
Poll tax, 314
Pompa, Aurelio, 174
Population
    of Arizona, 91–92, 93
    of California, 111, 127, 261, 284, 417
    of Chicago, 175, 177, 227, 287, 315–316, 418
    of Colorado, 178
    of El Paso, 281
    farm, 266
    of Los Angeles, 112, 127, 143, 161, 172, 229, 284, 318, 319

Population (*continued*)
of Mexico, 1, 12, 144, 146–147,
158, 266, 321
of New Mexico, 54, 74–75
of San Antonio, 143, 169, 222,
282–283, 312
of Texas, 31, 37, 38, 417
Populist party, 37
Porter, William, 88
Poston, Charles, 84, 86, 87
Poulson, Norris, 296, 297
Poverty
culture of, 308
inevitability of, 366
as "intellectual concept," 364
line, 354
Powderly, Terence, 71–73
Powell, Lewis, 389
Powers, Stephen, 34
President's Commission on Immigration
and Naturalization, 270
Price, Glenn W., 13
Price, Sterling, 59, 60
*Primer Congreso Campesino de la
Ciudad de México,* 146
Prince, Le Baron Bradford, 62, 63, 72
Prison conditions, 401
Prisoners of war, 26
Professional groups, 382
Proposition 13, 365
Proposition 14, 370
Proposition 22, 369
Proposition 63, 423
Proudhon, Joseph, 146
Pueblo Indians, 55, 57, 59, 60
Puerto Ricans, 287, 315
Putnam, George, 349

Quevedo, Eduardo, 260
Quota provisions, 185–188

Rabasa, Emilio O., 373
Racism, 136, 154, 157–158, 160
in Arizona, 83, 87, 89, 93, 96, 185
in California, 108, 117, 127–129,
159, 173, 174, 236, 239
in Chicago, 287, 288
in Colorado, 185
in New Mexico, 54, 241, 279
in Texas, 31–33, 37–38, 185

Railroads, 135
in Arizona, 83, 92, 96
braceros and, 260, 263
in California, 108, 127, 128
in Mexico, 147, 148
in New Mexico, 54, 70, 71, 74
strikes and, 155–156
in Texas, 33
Raker, John E., 186
Rambo, 415
Ramírez, Al, 328
Ramírez, Francisco, 121–122, 124
Ramírez, José, 401
Ramírez, Juan, 159, 164
Ramírez, Sara Estela, 151
Ramos, Basilio, 162
Ramos, Fernando, 351
Rancho system, 107–109, 111, 112,
115–116
Rangel, Irma, 422
Rape, 395
Raza Unida party, *La* (LRUP), 332,
339, 342, 366–368, 376, 391
Razo, Joe, 348
Reagan, Ronald, 344, 350, 369, 384,
385, 413–416, 421, 426, 445–446
Recessions, 144, 267, 372, 414, 426
Reclamation Act of 1902, 142
Regeneración, 150
Rehnquist, William, 389
Rejón, Manuel Crescion, 20
Religion. *See* Catholic Church
Repatriation program, 202–206
Republican party, 378–379, 385
Reverse racism, 393–394
Revolt of 1837, 57
Reynolds, W. Ann, 427
Reynoso, Cruz, 423
Rhodakanaty, Plotino C., 146
Rhodes, Thadeus, 30
Richardson, F. W., 174
Riggs, Jim, 351
Riley, John, 66–67
Rinaldo, Ben, 291
Río Grande, 6, 7, 12, 13, 19, 26, 27, 57,
62
Ríos, Tony, 294
Riots, 310
Rivera, Librado, 151
Roberti, David, 424

Robinson, George W., 120
Robinson, Juan A., 84
Rockefeller, David, 364, 365
Rodino, Peter, 374, 376
Rodino-Simpson bill, 440–442, 446, 450
Rodríguez, Antonio, 373
Rodríguez, Chipita, 33
Rodríguez, Mageleno, 225
Rodríguez, Ricardo, 38
Roman Catholic Church. *See* Catholic
  Church
Romano, Octavio, 308, 337
Romero, Oscar, 415, 444
Romero, Tomasito, 59
Romo, Ricardo, 160, 174
Roosevelt, Eleanor, 258–269
Roosevelt, Franklin D., 199, 224, 331
Rosa, Luis de la, 162
Rose, Louis, 11
Rosenbaum, Robert J., 43
Rosenfeld, Bernard, 395
Ross, Edmund, 63
Ross, Fred, 285, 325
Roybal, Edward R., 253, 283, 285–287,
  296, 297, 318, 320, 335, 343, 385,
  425
Rubalcava, Dominick, 416
Ruis, Virginia, 294
Ruiz, Antonio, 121, 123
Ruiz, Raúl, 336, 348, 367
Runaway shop, 322

Sáenz, J. Luz, 171
Safford, A. P. K., 95
St. Paul, Minnesota, 177–178
Salas, Jesús, 330
Salas, Mary, 330
Salazar, Ray, 397
Salazar, Rubén, 345–346, 348–349, 350
Salcido, Abraham, 98, 99
Salcido, Agustino, 291
Salt of the Earth strike, 278–279
San Antonio, Texas, 29, 32–33
  cottage industry in, 223
  education in, 283, 312, 387–389
  garment industry in, 224
  Hijos movement in, 171
  housing in, 282, 313
  mutualistas in, 169–171
  pecan industry in, 225–227

politics in, 282, 283–284, 313–314,
  420–422, 434
population of, 143, 169, 222,
  282–283, 312
social class in, 240
unemployment in, 312
San Antonio School District v.
  Rodríguez (1968), 389
Sanbrano, Angela, 446
Sánchez, George I., 55, 235, 259, 289,
  294
Sánchez, Leopold, 318
Sánchez, Margil, 328
Sánchez, Nestor D., 415
Sánchez, R. M., 179, 180
Sánchez, Tomás, 118, 123–124
Sánchez cousins, 346
Sanctuary movement, 446
Sándoval, Rachel, 330
San Félipe de Austin, 7, 8
San Jacinto, battle of, 11
San Joaquin cotton strike, 211, 213–215
San Patricio Corps, 16
San Román, José, 27
Santa Anna, Antonio López, 9–11, 18,
  58
Santa Fe Expedition, 26
Santa Fe Ring, 54, 61–65, 74, 75
Santa Fe trade, 54, 56
Santistevan, Jacinto, 64–65
Santistevan, Julian, 64
Schenley Corporation, 326, 369
Schmitz, Eugene, 155
Scott, Joseph, 291
Scott, Robin R., 254
Scott, Winfield, 18, 19
Sebree, Victor, 36
Seguín, Josefa Becerra, 32
Seguín, Juan, 25
Self-interest groups, 382
Selman, John, 67
Serrano, John, Jr., 389
Serrano v. *Priest* (1968), 389, 390
Seward, William, 27
Sexism, 394
Sharecropping, 152
Sheep raising, 65–66, 68
Sheep shearers, 217–218
Shelby, W. W., 35
Sherard, George W., 349

Silber, John, 421
Silex, Humberto, 234, 270
Silver, 84
Simpson-Mazzoli bill, 416, 441
Slavery, in Texas, 7, 8, 25, 26–27,
  31
Sleepy Lagoon case (1942), 254–256,
  260, 400
Slidell, John, 12–13
Sloat, John Drake, 110
Smith, Henry, 8
Smith, Justin H., 14–15
Smith, Persifor F., 113
Smith, Roger, 448
Snively, Jacob, 58
Snyder, Arthur, 424
Social, La, 146
Social class, 200
    in Arizona, 83, 88–89, 91
    in New Mexico, 55, 57
    in Texas, 27, 31–32, 39, 239–241
Socialist Workers party, 391
Solis, Rene, 328
Solíz, Juan, 419
Somoza, Anastasio, 365–366, 444
Sonora, 82–90, 95, 96
Sonoratown, 172, 173
Soto, Phil, 318
Southwest Voter Registration Education
  Project (SVREP), 417
Spanish-Americans, 55–56
Spanish-American War, 38
Spears, Bob, 44
Sports, 243
Spying, police, 259–260, 350–352,
  400–401
Stafford, Anson, 89
Statement of Protocol (1848), 19–20,
  115
Steed, Tom, 273, 274
Steel industry, 135, 167, 181, 228–229,
  234, 260–261, 430
Steel Workers Organizing Committee
  (SWOC), 234
Sterilization, 395–396
Stevenson, Coke, 263
Stillman, Charles, 27–28, 30
Stiringo, Charles A., 74
Stirling, David, 439

Stockton, Robert F., 110
Stone, Charles P., 87–88
Streck, Michael, 86
Strikes
    in agriculture, 209–216, 219, 220,
      272–275, 368–370, 439
    in Arizona, 97–102
    Arvin, 272–274
    braceros and, 263
    in California, 155, 159, 164–166,
      184, 209–217, 368–370
    in Colorado, 165, 219, 220
    cotton, 211, 213–215
    Farah, 370–371
    garment industry, 221–222, 224,
      277–278
    in Mexico, 146, 148–149
    mining, 156, 165, 278–279
    in New Mexico, 278–279
    pecan industry, 225, 226
    railroad, 155–156
    Salt of the Earth, 278–279
    steel industry, 167, 229
    in Texas, 155, 156, 217–218,
      277–278, 328–329, 370–371
Student movement, 333–338, 391–392
Suárez, Cecilia, 333
Subversive Activities Control Board,
  269, 270
Sugar Act of 1937, 220
Sugar beet industry, 153, 167, 175, 178,
  181–182, 209, 219–220
Sumaya, Fernando, 350–351
Suter, Jennie, 158
Sutter, John, 111
Swanson, John P., 267
Swing, Joseph M., 267, 268

Tackwood, Louis, 350, 351
Tafolla, Santiago, 171
Tafoya, Gabriel, 334
Taft-Hartley Act of 1947, 252
Talmadge Amendment, 353, 395
Taylor, Angus, 387
Taylor, Guillermo, 237
Taylor, Paul S., 175
Taylor, Rebecca, 224, 226, 277
Taylor, Robert, 46
Taylor, Ron, 327

Taylor, Zachary, 12, 13, 15, 16, 18, 26, 58
Teamsters, 326, 327, 369, 370
Teatro Campesino, 337, 341
Technology, agriculture and, 136, 144, 154, 179, 206, 207, 266, 314–315
Telles, Raymond, 282
Téllez, Jessie, 448
Tenant farming, 152
Tenayucca, Emma, 225–226
Tenney, Jack, 256, 273
Terán, Carlos, 287
Texas. *See also* names of cities
    agriculture in, 31, 152–153, 180, 198, 199, 205–206, 208, 276
    annexation of, 5
    banditry in, 43
    Blacks in, 25, 26–27, 31, 37
    boundary issue, 12–13, 26, 57
    braceros in, 262, 263
    brown scare in, 161
    Catholic Church in, 344
    colonization of, 25–50
    contract system, 276
    Cortina's rebellion, 44–47
    debt peonage in, 182
    education in, 157–158, 171–172, 311, 339–340, 389–390, 426
    El Paso Salt War, 47–49
    garment industry in, 277, 370–371
    homeowner occupancy, 428–429
    income in, 156, 180, 312, 328, 428
    Industrial Areas Foundation in, 432, 435, 436
    intermarriage in, 31–33
    invasion of, 9–12
    lynching in, 28, 34, 38
    New Mexico and, 57–58
    oil industry in, 276
    Plan of San Diego, 161–162
    police brutality in, 399
    politics in, 33–37, 313–314, 367, 418, 422
    population of, 31, 37, 38, 417
    racism in, 31–33, 37–38, 185
    railroads in, 33
    robber barons in, 30
    slavery in, 7, 8, 25, 26–27, 31
    social class in, 27, 31–32, 39, 239–241
    strikes in, 155, 156, 217–218, 277–278, 328–329, 370–371
    trade in, 27–29
    trusteeship, 5
    unions in, 154, 156, 164, 276–278, 312, 328–329, 370. *See also* Strikes
    walkouts, 337
    White Caps in, 38
    youth movement in, 333–335
Texas Agricultural Organizing Committee (TAOC), 218–219
Texas Cotton Acreage Control Law of 1931, 206
Texas Independent Workers Association, 328
Texas Rangers, 17–18, 25, 31, 34, 36, 39–43, 45, 46, 48, 162, 163, 171, 218, 329, 339–341
Texas War, 5–12
Textile industry, Mexican, 145
Thompson, William Hall, 185
Tijerina, Patsy, 341
Tijerina, Reies López, 331, 332, 335, 340–341, 377, 448
Tingley, G. B., 113–114
Tolby, T. J., 64
Toledo, Ohio, 177
Torres, Andrés, 368
Torres, Art, 423, 424
Torres, Esteban, 385
Torres, Francisco, 128–129
Torres, Luis, 149
Tovar, Irene, 333
Tower, John, 416
Trabajadores Unidos, 167
Trade
    California and, 107, 109
    New Mexico and, 54, 56–57
    Texas and, 27–29
Trade unions. *See* Unions
Trade Union Unity League (TUUL), 210, 232
Tranchese, Carmelo, 223
Travis, William Barret, 10, 11
Trist, Nicholas, 18–19
Trujillo, William, 230

Truman, Harry S, 264, 269
Tucson, Arizona, 91–93
Tunstall, John H., 67, 68
Tyler, John, 12

Undocumented migration, 372–377,
440–442. *See also* Mexican labor
Unemployed Councils, 199–200
Unemployment, 185, 227–228, 308, 311,
312, 319, 353, 364
Unión Federal Mexicana, La, 155
Unión Liberal Humanidad, La,
149
Unions
agricultural, 210–220, 272,
325–327, 438–439
in Arizona, 97–102, 166, 179–180,
217, 231
in California, 155, 164, 182–184,
229–231, 272, 325–327, 368–370.
See also Strikes
in Chicago, 228–229
in Colorado, 181
decline of, 447
garment workers, 221–222, 224,
370–371
McCarran-Walter Act and, 270
Mexican labor and, 143–144, 151,
154–156, 159, 164–168, 179–182.
See also Strikes
mining, 97–102, 231–234, 278–279
New Deal legislation and, 210
in New Mexico, 71–73, 76
pecan workers, 225–227
steel workers, 228–229
sugar beet workers, 181–182
Taft-Hartley Act and, 252
in Texas, 154, 156, 164, 276–278,
312, 328–329, 370. *See also*
Strikes
women in, 200, 217, 221–223, 229,
231
United Auto Workers (UAW), 230, 326
United Cannery, Agricultural, Packing,
and Allied Workers of America
(UCAPAWA), 200, 217, 219, 220,
226, 233, 237
United Civil Rights Committee, 309
United Farm Workers (UFW),
368–370, 438–439

United Farm Workers Organizing
Committee (UFWOC), 326–327
United Furniture Workers of America
(UFWA), 230, 231
United Mexican American Students
(UMAS), 320, 335
United Mine Workers (UMW), 76, 156,
165, 230, 232
United Neighborhood Organization
(UNO), 434–435, 436
United Rubber Workers, 230
U.S. Customs Simplification Act of
1956, 322
Universal Declaration of Human
Rights, 268
Upward Bound, 309
Urban renewal, 252, 295–298, 309
Urrea, Teresa de, 99
Urrutia, Aureliano, 240
Utah, 19, 178

Váldez, Daniel T., 279
Váldez, Luis, 337, 341
Vallejo, Mariano, 110, 117
Valley Interfaith, 435–436
Vaqueros, 112, 120, 152
Vásquez, J. E., 234
Vásquez, Tiburcio, 124–125
Vásquez, Tomás, 30
Vega, Cruz, 64
Vela, Ed, 34
Vela de Vidal, Petra, 31
Velarde, Amelio B., 164
Velarde, Francisco B., 164
Velarde, Guillermo, 216
Velarde, Leandro, 233
Velásquez, Baldemar, 330
Velásquez, Willie, 334
Vera Cruz, bombardment of, 159
Veterans, 289
Vietnam War, 310, 320, 345–346, 363
Vigil, Ernesto, 346
Villa, Pancho, 100, 159
Villanueva, Santiago, 146
Villapando, Cathi, 416
Villavicencio, Hermengildo, 146
Villegas, Emilio, 234
Visel, C. P., 203
VISTA (Volunteers in Service to
America), 309, 330, 334, 339

Viva Kennedy clubs, 313–314, 317
Vogel, Clarence F., 232
Voting Rights Act, 417, 419
Vrdolyak, Edward, 419

Wages. *See* Income and wages
Wagner Act, 199, 217, 228, 234, 252,
    272
Walker, William, 122
Wallace, Henry, 286
Wallace, Lew, 68
Walter, Francis E., 269
Ward, Baxter, 349
Warfield, A., 58
War Food Administration, 262
War of 1812, 6
War on poverty, 309–311, 320,
    330–331, 364
Warren, Earl, 259, 389
War with Mexico, The (Smith), 14–15
War with Mexico Reviewed, The
    (Livermore), 15
Washington, Harold, 418, 419
Washington state, 178
Watergate, 365
Water subsidies, 272
Watts riots, 310
Wayne, John, 366, 413
Webb, Walter Prescott, 39–42, 163
Welfare, 353, 395
Weller, John B., 119
Wells, Jim, 34, 36
Werdel, Thomas H., 273, 274
Western Federation of Miners (WFM),
    76, 97–100, 143, 231
Wetbacks, 264, 287
Wheatland Riot of 1913, 165
White, Mark, 418, 434, 436
White Caps
    in New Mexico, 70–74
    in Texas, 38
White flight, 296
Willis, Frank B., 186–187
Wilson, Thomas, 349

Wilson, Woodrow, 101, 162
Wirin, H. L., 215
Wisconsin, 181
Women, 168
    activists, 332–333, 438
    in Arizona, 90, 96
    in Chicago, 176
    feminism and, 394–396
    income, 168, 221, 222, 353, 437
    in Mexico, 443
    in *mutualistas,* 170
    in politics, 422–425
    radicals, 151–152
    Salt of the Earth strike, 278–279
    in student organizations, 391–392
    in Texas, 32
    in unions, 200, 217, 221–223, 229,
        231
Woodman, Lyman, 44
Workers Alliance, 200, 237
Work incentives (WIN) program, 353
Works Progress Administration (WPA),
    206
World Bank, 322, 371
World War I, 159–160
World War II, 251–254, 260–263
Wyman, Rosalind, 296, 318
Wyoming, 181

Ximénez, Vicente, 279, 331

Yarborough, Ralph, 329
Yellow dog contracts, 210
Yorty, Sam, 318, 346
Young Communist League (YCL), 237
Younger, Evelle J., 349
Youth movement, 311, 333–338
Yslas, Stephen, 416
Ytúrria, Francisco, 27
Yucatán, 26

Zaffirini, Judy, 422
Zalacosta, Francisco, 146
Zoot-suit riots, 254, 256–260